A REPORT

ON THE

EXPEDITION TO WESTERN YUNAN

viâ

BHAMÔ.

BY

JOHN ANDERSON, M.D.,
Medical Officer and Naturalist to the Expedition.

Calcutta:
OFFICE OF THE SUPERINTENDENT OF GOVERNMENT PRINTING.
1871.

PRINTED AT THE OFFICE OF SUPERINTENDENT OF GOVERNMENT PRINTING, CALCUTTA.

PREFACE.

THE publication of this Report so long after the accomplishment of the Expedition to Bhamô and Western Yunan requires a few words of explanation.

On my return to Calcutta, I had at once to resume my usual official duties to which others were shortly afterwards superadded, so that, I was left without any leisure to take up the work, except at furtive intervals, during my byehours, and have never had any opportunity to give it consecutive thought. The portion now published embraces only the first section of my Report; the remainder more properly belonging to the appointment I held as Naturalist to the Expedition, and which I hope will shortly follow, has also been prepared under the disadvantage of not having been continuously worked out, and had it not been that the Natural History collections were to become the property of the Indian Museum, I could not have felt it my duty to have attempted the work.

In the present section, I have given some chapters relating to the early history of the still little known country we traversed; and of its contests with China, largely drawn as it will be observed from the valuable researches of Colonel Burney, with the object of bringing into view the important part Upper Burmah has played in the political relations of the Chinese and Burmese Empires in byegone years, and thus indirectly to show for how many centuries Bhamô has been recognized as a gateway into China. I have likewise indicated the extent of European intercourse with Bhamô and Yunan from early times, and described the physical features of the country, its inhabitants, and their customs and arts.

The chapter on Trade routes may be of interest to commercial men, for I have honestly endeavoured to lay down side by side the difficulties along with the facilities offered for trade. The gradients and other measurements I give with some diffidence, because the instruments supplied to me at Rangoon were most untrustworthy, and many a time Major Sladen and I regretted that we had not the means to make good use of the opportunities our detentions, at leading points in the route, afforded us for observations.

In accordance with my letter of instructions, I have stated all the information I could possibly gather relating to the probable sources of the Irawady. But considering the distance that Bhamô is below the point reached by Wilcox, it was not to be expected that much information could be obtained there, when he, at a higher latitude, and while investigating its north-western branch, failed to throw much light upon the sources of the great river of Burmah.

I have allotted a considerable portion of the following pages to a general narrative of the daily occurrences of the Expedition from the time of its departure from Mandalay until its return to Bhamô.

In the appendices, I give some routes, and thermometrical and other observations, as well as examples of the dialects of the hill tribes, and I also subjoin a short paper on the stone and bronze implements of Yunan collected on the Expedition.

The map of the country has been specially executed for this Report, and it is to be hoped that it may be approximately accurate, considering the instruments that were available for the observations which were made by Captain Bowers, and kindly supplied by him to me for the preparation of the map.

It will be observed that the British Government for nearly a period of two centuries has been striving to obtain a commercial footing at Bhamô or in its immediate neighbourhood, but that the attempts, although apparently at first attended by a measure of success, were ultimately frustrated. Now that the recent Expedition has resulted in the Burmese Government sanctioning the residence of a British representative at Bhamô for the protection of our commercial interests, it is extremely desirable that every judicious effort should be made to open to British commerce the great highway to China, by the valley of the Tapeng.

CONTENTS.

CHAPTER I.

KINGDOM OF PONG.

Antiquity—Pemberton's Report—extent—a powerful Shan kingdom—Du Halde's description—country of Tay-yays or Great Shans—Koshanpyi (Shan States) once included in Pong—Cis and Trans-Irawadian Shans one kingdom—Western Shans adopted customs of Burmese conquerors, 1596 A. D.—Eastern limits conterminous with China—interview of kings of Pong and China at Muangsee (Yunan city)—southern limits—at war with China and Burmah, 1333 A. D.—Chinese conquer Muangmo—new capital Muaukung on right bank of Irawady—loss of Trans-Irawadian Pong States—Discrepancy between Shan and Chinese chronicles—Marco Polo's Kardandan—Koshanpyi, tributary to China—Pong destroys Tsagain, 1364 A. D.—Settlement of boundaries with Munipore, 1475—first Burmese invasion of Pong, 1513—Pong over-runs Ava, 1526—Pong kings reign at Ava—invasion of Siam, 1568—attempted invasion of Burmah, 1587—Bhamô Tsawbwa declares independence, 1600—Pong becomes a Burmese province, 1752—last struggle for independence—conquest by Aloompra and annexation to Burmah ... ... pp. 1 to 11

CHAPTER II.

WARS BETWEEN BURMAH AND CHINA.

Tagoung, first capital of Burmah, destroyed by Tartars and Chinese, B. C.—Old Pagan founded about 107 A. D.—deserted for new Pagan, towards the close of 8th century—11th century wars, king of Pagan covets a tooth of Guadama in a Chinese shrine—China invades Burmah to enforce tribute—Burmese claim to Shan States of Muangmo, Hotha, and Latha—Pagan destroyed by Tartar-Chinese—Tsagain founded, 1332—destroyed, 1364—Angwa (Ava) rises on left bank of Irawady, almost opposite to Tsagain—Theinneo subject to Burmah—Chinese mission to Ava demanding tribute, 1442—China attacks Cis-Irawadian provinces of Pong, 1449—army of Pegu marches through Ava and erects a pillar on the borders of China, 1447—Pegu conquers Ava and all its dependencies, 1552—Buddhism introduced into Hotha and Latha—fall of Peguan empire, 1601—Tsawbwa of Bhamô asserts independence—Ava annexes Bhamô—Burmo-Chinese wars, 1644 to 1662—Colonel Burney's account—D'Orlean's—Du Halde's—Yunan's relation to Pekin about 1615—king of Yunan province—surrender of Yunlie—a century of peace—highways between China and Bhamô, frequented by traders and travellers—wars from misunderstandings between Chinese traders and Burmese officials, 1765-68—Gutzlaff's account—routes of armies—Chinese generals propose peace—their letter—representatives meet at Kaungtoung, December 1769—Peace concluded, known as that of Bhamô—trade restored—interchange of embassies and presents—embassy routes—Burmese mission to China, *viâ* Bhamô, 1823—elephants sent—Chinese mission to Burmah, 1833—comparison of Bhamô and Theinnee routes—importance of Bhamô ... ... pp. 12 to 35

CHAPTER III.
EUROPEAN INTERCOURSE WITH BHAMÔ.

Marco Polo, first European visitor—his account of *Kardandan*—its customs—use of tallies—consulting of persons supposed to be possessed—similar ceremonies of Kakhyens—sacrifice of buffaloes to Nâts, at Bhamô—Shans, Buddhists—peculiarities in value of precious metals in Polo's time and now—distribution of silver in Shan States—silver and gold exchanged for salt—custom of covering teeth with gold in Polo's time—present custom of blackening teeth—his account of climate—Marco Polo's *Kananzan* probably corresponds to district north-east of Kananzan mountains—custom of tying up ponies' tails—armour of inhabitants—Polo's description of country between Kardandan and Burmah—similarity to country between Sanda valley and Bhamô—Marco Polo's mart in Bhamô district probably near site of old Bhamô—rise of Kaungtoung, probable cause of desertion of old Bhamô—English and Dutch factories, beginning of 17th century—Dalrymple—Valentyn—revival of trade after peace of 1662—thriving traffic till 1765—unsuccessful attempt of authorities at Fort St. George (Madras) to gain footing at Bhamô, 1680—Du Chatz entered Burmah near Bhamô from Yunan, in end of 17th century—Jesuit missionaries, Fridelli, Bonjour, and Regis, survey China, and reach confines of Ava, beginning of 18th century—Dr. Hamilton Buchanan's contributions to the geography of Upper Burmah—Colonel Syme's account of trade in Upper Burmah—Wilcox's reference to Bhamô and country eastward—Crawford's account of the Irawady and trade—Sir J. F. Davis, on a map of some Jesuit missionaries—L'Amiot, on the climate of Western Yunan—on war of 1767—Colonel Burney's contributions to the history, geography and resources of Upper Burmah—Pemberton's proposal to open up trade between Yunan and Assam—Captain Hannay's visit to Bhamô and Mogoung in 1835—Griffith reaches Bhamô from Assam—Dr. Bayfield's mission from Ava to Mogoung, 1837—Hannay, Griffith and Bayfield's accounts of Bhamô—Kincaid at Bhamô, 1837—Baron Otto des Granges on trade between Bhamô and Munipore—Bishop Bigandet at Bhamô, 1857—Sir Arthur Phayre's mission to Mandalay—Dr. William's at Bhamô, 1863—General Fytche's proposal of an Expedition to explore Bhamô route to Yunan ... ... pp. 36 to 58

CHAPTER IV.
PHYSICAL FEATURES, GEOLOGY, &c.

Valley and plain of the Irawady defined—aspect described—low hill-ranges—their composition—limestone cliff at Bhamô—coal—position of Bhamô—proximity to Kakhyen hills—its situation between 1st and 2nd defiles of Irawady—populations around it—neighbouring towns and villages—Sawaddy—Kaungtoung—old Bhamô—Tsenbo—Mogoung—Kakhyo—Wainmô—Irawady navigable for 150 miles above Bhamô—survey of first defile by Captain Bowers, 1870—regular floods of Irawady—the Shuaylee—

the Tapeng—the Molay—the Mogoung—description communicated of country above 1st defile—soil around Bhamô—crops—animals—fish—climate—natural products—amber mines—jade mines—gold—silver and iron mines in Muanglan country—salt in Hukong valley—nature of country between Bhamô and Kakhyen hills—description of Kakhyen range—height and direction—constituent rocks—silver mines—Oldham's assays of galena ore—other silver mines—character of Tapeng valley—vegetable products of Kakhyen hills—opium—its introduction—extent of its cultivation—analysis—comparison with Indian drug—comparative table of Benares, Behar, and Yunan opium—Domestic animals of Kakhyens—climatic observations—cultivation of tea—Poloung tea—its characters—cakes of Chinese tea—country between Kakhyen hills and the Cambodia—Kakhyen hills in Tapeng and Hotha valleys—their primary and secondary ranges—direction of valleys and water-courses—intervals between water-sheds—parallel ranges to the east of Momien—Kananzan range—position of rivers from Burmese itineraries—distances between Irawady, Shuaylee, Salween, and Cambodia—the Hokyan—courses of Tapeng, Shuaylee, and Cambodia—general elevation of the country—Sanda valley—length, breadth and general appearance—almost divided into three basins, corresponding to the three states, Manwyne, Sanda, and Muangla—constitution of surrounding hills—Superficial deposits—Elephant's molar—hot springs—analysis of water—temperature—valley of Hotha—its rocks—soil—river Namsa—crops—Superior tobacco grown by Shans—Wild indigo—pasture—live-stock—climate—population of Sanda and Hotha valleys—the Mawphoo gorge—valley of Nantin—its river-terraces—geological structure—denuding action of Tahô—change in character of hills—hot springs of Nantin—temperature and analysis—soil—insecurity of life and property—scant population—little cultivation—Sawaddy, Hostene, and Sanda routes converge—high road to Momien from Bhamô—Extinct volcano of Hawshuenshan—its height and appearance—centre of earth-quakes—valley of Hawshuenshan—valley of Momien—its physical features and geological composition—Kananzan mountains—height, direction and richness in minerals—Khyto silver-mines—analysis of the ore—gold—pine forests—rice—potatoes—opium—Momien cattle, sheep, dogs, &c.—population of Momien, Nantin and Hawshuenshan valleys—climate—temperatures of June and July—snow in winter—its conditions for healthiness... ... ... pp. 59 to 95

CHAPTER V.

SHANS AND KAKHYENS AND OTHER RACES TO THE EAST OF BHAMÔ.

Shans.—Distribution in Upper Burmah and neighbouring countries—modifying influence of Burmese—probable ancient distribution—States of Western Yunan annexed to China, 1285—Western Yunan probably country of the Great Tais and kingdom of Pong—introduction of Buddhism into Burmah, 241 B. C.—into Shan valleys—present distribution of Shans in Western Yunan—two tribes, Shans proper and Poloungs—enigmatical character of Shan-Chinese or Chinese-Shans—physical characters of Shans proper and of Poloungs—physical characters of Chinese-Shans—dress of Shan women—costume of male peasantry—dress of Chinese-Shan women—ordinary ornaments of Shan women—ear-rings of Shans, Poloungs and Shan-Chinese—neck-rings or torques—similarity to ancient forms of Europe—penannular torques—finger-rings—bracelets—scent-bottles and chatelaines—dâhs—tobacco pipes—match-locks—powder-flasks—dress of Phoongyees in Sanda valley—in Hotha valley—diet of

Shans—towns—agriculture—blacksmiths—silversmiths—workers in straw—weaving and dyeing—feather ornaments—embroidered fabrics—character of Shan art—love for music—musical instruments—marriage—diseases—bury their dead—Shans, Buddhists—low state of Buddhism in Shan valleys—Nuns or Rahances—children educated by priests—horse-worship—snake-worship—morality of Shans—tribute to Mussulmans—land-tenure—present poverty of chiefs—its cause—*Kakhyens* or *Chingpaws*—their distribution—tribes—false reports of them by Burmese—their character—hospitality—physical appearance—dress of men—dress of women—construction of houses—division of property—morality—estimate of women—duties of women—language—religion—nât-worship—Lamshan or village-altar—belief in ghosts—in witches—two priestly orders—marriage ceremonials—widowhood—birth-ceremonies—death and burial rites—Tsawbwaships—Pawmines—slavery—periods of time—manufactures—tobacco and opium smoking—weapons—state of art—amusements—food—enumeration of chiefs—*Leesaws*—their distribution, physical characters and dress—affinity of language to Burmese—*Chinese* in Sanda valley—borders of China—dialect peculiar to Yunan—languages of various tribes ... ... pp. 96 to 137

CHAPTER VI.

MAHOMMEDANS IN YUNAN.

Earliest authentic notice of Arabs in China, 757—Abu Zaid's account—Massacre in China of Mahommedans, &c., A. D. 878—Mahommedanism among the Tartars—Onigours and Toonganees—Marco Polo's residence in China, 1271-1295, and account of Mahommedans—Ibn Buttata next authority—Jesuit fathers, 1680—Tartar oppression of Mahommedans and their rebellion, 1767—Abbé Grosier's account—revolts in Yunan, 1817-34—Pekin Gazettes—Gutzlaff—increase of Mahommedans in present century in Yunan—Major General Fytche's report—Du Halde's claim to Arab descent—sympathy between Mahommedans of Yunan and those of Kansi and Shensi—term 'Panthay'—devastations caused by rebellions—sympathies of Shans and Kakhyens with Chinese—now pay tribute to Panthays—capture of Yunan city, 1869—position of affairs at Momien, whilst Expedition was there—extent of devastation and bloodshed in Yunan and neighbouring provinces—Panthay king at Talifoo—his government and council—governorship of Momien—Panthay population almost exclusively military—physical aspect and dress—Governor of Momien's appearance and habits—general abstinence of Panthays—the Tahzyungyee's feast—mosque—Koran in Chinese—Panthay character—honesty—consideration for traders ... pp. 138 to 152

CHAPTER VII.

TRADE ROUTES OF UPPER BURMAH.

Three from Bhamô to Momien—more or less hill-paths—*Ponline route*—cross Tapeng—ascent to Ponline—descent to Nampung stream—ascent to Ponsee—descent to foot of Sanda valley—from Manwyne 46 miles of rise up valley—spur of Mawphoo hill—descent to Nantin valley—bridge over Tapeng—junction of routes at Nantin valley—steep ascent—slight descent to Hawshuenshan valley—rapid acclivity to Momien—practicability of level road between Nantin and Momien—*Louyloae route*—at Sit-nga cross the Tapeng—level 3 miles—over low hills to the Namthabet—skirts left bank of Tapeng—ascent to Hoetone—ascent to Loaylone—ordinary or embassy route into Muangwan valley—by it 3 marches to Nantin—*route viâ* Lassa and Hotha to Muangkah valley—over Muangkah ridge—two streams—steep ascent to Ashan—sudden descent to Namboke—to Hotha—to Nantin—5 days' march from Loaylone—*Sawaddy route*—assistant surveyor's report—to Muangwan *viâ* Loaylone—contrast of these 3 routes to Momien—*Routes beyond Momien*—to Yungchan—to Talifoo—to Yunan city—Yungchan to Shuenli—joins route from Mandalay by Thiennee and Kaingma—comparison of distances between Yunan and Mandalay *viâ* Thiennee and *viâ* Bhamô—Shuaylee route—Trade between Momien, Sanda valley, and Mogoung—route by Molay river—*Routes from Upper Assam to Yunan*—Dr. Griffith's mission—Captain Burnett's route—Mr. Jenkin's route—Patkoi range—Wilcox's Noa Dehing, 1825—capabilities for improvement of routes *viâ* Tapeng valley—advantages of Bhamô as a starting-point—practicability of a railway considered—gradients—engineering difficulties of Kakhyen hills—smallness of traffic—railway proposed through Pegu less justifiable—three water high-ways from Central and Western China to the sea—doubtfulness of survey being permitted in China—proposal of a tramway from the Cambodia to British territory considered—probable character of trade that might be developed between Bhamô and Yunan—opposition to be expected from merchants at Shanghai—Irawady cannot compete with the Yang-tse-Kiang for trade of Central China—much less the Brahmaputra with the Irawady—obstructions on our north-east frontier—little known of the Dihong—Hamilton Buchanan's route between Assam and Tibet—Pemberton—Turner—importance to Assam of a route by Brahmaputra ... ... pp. 153 to 177

CHAPTER VIII.
THE IRAWADY AND ITS SOURCES.

Upper waters unexplored—Klaproth's hypothesis of Sanpo being the Irawady doubted—Lieutenant Burlton's opinion of its rise in the Brahmakund—confirmed by Lieutenant Neufville—Captain Wilcox rejects Klaproth's theory, but fixes on an insufficiently small river for the true Irawady—he established, however, the existence of an eastern branch, the Sûhmaïkha—his views of the magnitude of Irawady—Colonel Hannay's description of the Irawady at 1st defile—Bayfield and Griffith's ascent of river above Bhamô—Griffith adopts the Sûhmaïkha as source of Irawady—Dr. William's impressions—the author's own visit to the 1st defile—two defiles below Bhamô—A Kampti Shan's account of the river—criticism of map of North-East frontier of Burmah and West China, Calcutta 1862—Wilcox's branch identical with the Shuaymai—eastern continuation of Irawady said to be the Kewboan—rivers in Western Yunan—easterly branch of Tapeng—the Shuaylee—the Salween—accuracy of the Jesuits' map—shows Tibetan rivers to be distinct from Shuaylee, Salween, or Cambodia—examination of Wilcox's claim to have discovered the sources of the Irawady—D'Anville connects Tibetan rivers with Cambodia and Salween—mistake perpetuated in the maps of Klaproth, Dalrymple, and Berghaus—Mr. Cooper's conjectures ... ... pp. 178 to 193

NARRATIVE OF THE JOURNEY.
CHAPTER IX.
MANDALAY TO BHAMÔ.

Departure of Expediton from Mandalay up the Irawady, by steamer—police-guard—Burmese court-official—Chinese interpreter—crew—Kala-woon *Mengoon*—scenery from heights above—*Shienpagah*—trade—salt—fish—firewood—island of Alékyoung—Kothung—Htseezeh—Nattoung hills—Makouk—Tsingu—Tsingu-myo—contraction of river—Tscittha—leopards and monkeys—*Coal-mines of Lek-ope-bin and Ket-zu-bin*—sand washed for gold—joviality of Burmese—*Bass' Beer*—Pon-nah creek—*island of Thechadaw*—stone pagoda—tame fish—*Thingadaw*—a coal depôt—curious appearance of surface soil—end of defile—Malé—a custom port—considerable trade—Burmese treatment of the provost—river above Malé—roundheaded dolphins—Kyan-Nhyat—breadth of river—Tsinuhat—walk to Tagoung—*ruins of Old Tagoung and of Old Pagan*—Burmese traditions of cities—metallic images and bas-reliefs of Buddha—supposed history of brick impressions—modern village of Tagoung—ngapé—range of Tagoungtoung-daw—Shuay-mein-toung hills—dangerous navigation—dolphins—serpentine course of river—island of Chowkyoung—Thigyain—*Myadoung* murder of Bhamô Woon at Momeit—*Katha*—Yunanese-Chinese merchants—entertained by the Woon—magnetic battery—character of river—dolphins—Shuay-goo-myo—immense flocks of birds—prejudice against fire-arms—villagers' dread of Kakhyens—Sladen and Williams' interview with Kakhyens—a kidnapped boy—island of *Shuaybaw*—its 1,000 pagodas—annual festival—colony of red-faced monkeys—description of 2nd defile—estimated breadth—character of rocks—*old mart of Kaungtoung*—encampment of traders—*Bhamô*—sensation at arrival of the first steamer,...   ... pp. 194 to 215

CHAPTER X.
RESIDENCE AT BHAMÔ.

Description of Bhamô—bamboo palisade—gates—population—Chinese—Shans—trade—Chinese temple—importance of head China-man—tactics of Chinese with reference to Expedition—the Woon's residence—cause of decay of public buildings—habits of Shan-Burmese—industry of women and girls—process of silver-smelting—colony of Shan-Chinese—brick and dâh manufactures—language—dress—Kakhyens—their habits—kidnapping—meditated attack on Bhamô—Hindoostanee slave—his history—country behind Bhamô—Assamese settlement—old town of Tsampenago—pagodas of Shuaykeenah—ceremonies at laying the foundation of a pagoda—fortune-telling—the Tapeng—its breadth at Bhamô—crowds visit the steamer—medical practice—diseases treated—our bamboo house—visit of Tsikkays on board the steamer—arguments of Tsikkays against advance of Expedition—difficulty of obtaining information regarding routes—persecution of a poor woman for acting as our interpreter to the Kakhyens—exaggerated reports of Kakhyens—intrigues of Chinese residents with the imperialist Leesetai—Major Sladen's course of action—the Tsawbwa of Ponline—his visit to the steamer—dress of himself and staff—his appearance—his promise of assistance—arrival of new governor of Bhamô—keeps his boat for three days—his landing—costume—proclamation—guns fired to call in Tsawbwas—arrangements for departure—despatch of baggage—difficulties—no interpreter nor change of coin—return of Mr. Burn—two incidents at Bhamô ...   . pp. 216 to 236

CHAPTER XI.
BHAMÔ TO PONSEE.

Start from Bhamô—head-jailor persuaded to show us the road—crossed the Tapeng—halt at *Tahmeglon*—put up in a monastery—birds—Manloung river—2nd town of Tsampenago—Mrs. Jemadar's travelling costume—*Tsitkaw*—Collector of Customs—Tapeng at Tsitkaw—inquisitiveness of Shans and Kakhyens—arrival of Tsawbwas and Pawmines—superstition—Manloung lake—village of Manloung—flourishing monastery—birds on the lake—trials from mule-men and drunken Tsawbwas—advance of mule-hire demanded—jealousy of chiefs—the phoongyee—departure from Tsitkaw—left the river at Hentha—Old Bhamô—Teihet—attraction of Tsawbwas to cash-chest—ascent of hills—an alarm—Talone—Kakhyen etiquette—*Ponline*—the Tsawbwa's house—his wife—her hospitality—rice-pounding by moonlight—non-appearance of cash-chest and reported loss of eight mules—ceremonious visit from the Tsawbwa's wife—her dress and ornaments—arrival of guard—cash-box and mules kept by the Talone Tsawbwa—death of a sepoy—dance at a Kakhyen death-ceremony—arrival of cash-box and mules—boxes looted—description of Ponline village and neighbourhood—Sladen distributes presents to chiefs and Pawmines—ceremony to determine whether the nâts favour our enterprise—more money demanded—cash-chest a mistake—descent to the Nampung—formerly western boundary of Yunan—old Chinese fort—ford the Nampung—precipitous ascent to Lakong—encampment—advice of Ponline Tsawbwa—arrival at Ponsee ... ... pp. 237 to 252

CHAPTER XII.
RESIDENCE AT PONSEE.

Violent thunder-storm—night in a Kakhyen tomb—character of Kakhyen burial-places—mule-men decamp with their mules—Ponline's intimidations—visit from Tsawbwas of Nyungen, Wacheoan, and Ponwah—costume of the latter—a night of wind and rain—recall of Ponsee Tsawbwa to Bhamô—desertion of Moungshnah-Yah—his history and character—compensation asked for a village burned near our Lakong encampment—women bring presents—experiment with a scent-bottle—view from hill behind our camp—Hoolocks—demand of money for the burned village and mule-hire—bamboo-rat, article of diet—arrival of letters from the Panthays—our messengers disguised as Panthays—letters in Arabic and Chinese—assurance of welcome at Momien—a Panthay officer—Sala and Kakhyens disappear—difficulty of pursuing investigations among Kakhyens—sparseness of land-mollusca—profusion of Rubiaceæ—large flocks of Sarus—terms arranged for the burned village—presents for the chiefs—Sladen secures a Kakhyen interpreter—difficulties of shooting—birds about our camp—a new partridge—burned village again—threats of Ponline—a bathing experience—alarm for my safety—arrival of the Seray Tsawbwa—proposals to take us by his road—the Manhleo Poogain—his dreaded character—threatened attack—friendly letters—supposed new monkey—village fire again discussed—Ponline demands more money—conference of Tsawbwas—mule-hire—Kakhyen tallies—Sladen exposes Ponline—Seray's demands—Kakhyens fire on the camp—Sala and Ponsee quarrel—Ponline carries off our interpreter—predicament of Sanda people—attempted ascent of mountain above camp frustrated—visit to Kakhyen burial-ground—explore the Tapeng—our cause prospers viii

beyond—a letter from the Governor of Momien—Kakhyen incident—a sick woman—Seray, intelligent and friendly—Ponsee asks for presents—present from a Tsawbwa's widow—opium—cure of a Kakhyen—visit of Shan traders—arrival of Burmese—dispersion of our bazaar-suppliers—sacrifice to the nâts who are consulted regarding our fate—visit to the Ponsee silver-mines—a Kakhyen raft—curious present from a Tsawbwa's widow—Ponline demands 8 maunds silver—value of empty beer-bottles—Death's head Pawmine—arrival of official letters in Chinese—news of Leesetai's defeat—Momien messenger—an impostor—breach between the Tsawbwa and his Pawmines—Seray's Pawmines bring mules—animal life in the neighbourhood—prepare for a start—characters of the Ponsee Pawmines—carriage insufficient—departure postponed—failure to get letters forwarded to Mandalay—letter from Moungshuay-Yah—a Shan interprets the Momien letters—their advice and encouragement—remarkable hail-shower—thunderstorms—arrival of 30 mules—start resolved for to-morrow—more messengers arrive—object of our mission suspected—its nature explained—no signs of a start—visit of women to our camp—their anxiety to get beads and anna-pieces—red cloth highly prized—further demand for money—reports from Manwyne and Sanda—visit of Pawmines for money—a *Macacus*—more presents—visits from sick and blind—more money asked for—defeat of Leesetai confirmed—insincerity of Tsawbwa—circular letter of Panthays to Tsawbwas—Oak-trees—weaving—phosphorescent wood—arrival of Burmese for silver-mines—sick people—the Tsawbwa a patient—ascent of hill behind Ponsee—road to the summit—reported route of Chinese army—Lawloo brings more Chinese letters—the Tsawbwa called to Manwyne—a letter in Arabic—Kakhyen game-trap—more visits from women—Sladen's circular to the members of the Expedition—Williams and Stewart resolve to return—their departure for Bhamô—accompanied by Moungmo—Panthays at Sanda waiting for us—prevalence of Tænia solium—Syme's bistoury—Kakhyen boys sent to Williams—camp incident—letter from Moungshuay-Yah—Moungmo's arrest at Bhamô—his liberation—rocks at Ponsee—irrigation—cultivation—another letter from Panthays—Moungmo's wife put in the stocks—Sladen writes to the Woon requesting her release—despatch of messengers for mules—their return, accompanied by representatives of the Shan towns—make a favourable impression—men despatched for mules—character of Ponline—a friendly Pawmine—Deen Mahomed claimed as a Kakhyen slave... ... pp. 253 to 286

CHAPTER XIII.
PONSEE TO MOMIEN.

Scene with Death's-head—leave Ponsee—abandon our tents—Kingdoung—encounter with the Tsawbwa-gadaw of Muang-gan—hear of missing property—the Tepeng valley—its fertility—numerous villages—curiosity to see us—greeting of Manwyne officials—*Manwyne*—a sand-bank allotted for our encampment—an inquisitive crowd—picturesque costumes—accommodated in the Khyoung—situation of Manwyne—description of Khyoung—the bazaar—its traffic—neatness of Shan quarters—suburban villages—women's tobacco—crowds of visitors—shooting exasperating to the great nât—morning worship in the Khyoung—the priests' pittance—Sladen distributes presents—visit to the Tsawbwa-gadaw—her house—dress—ornaments—pipe—appearance—the nuns—numerous patients—excitement at our departure—attack on the road—Shan guards—welcome from villagers—Karolokah—market-day—rice-fields—tobacco—red soil—

Sanda—put up in Khyoung—description of the Phoongyees—of the Khyoung—position of Sanda—the bazaar—Chinese Joss-house—shops and stalls—Leesaws—visit to the Tsawbwa—his house-dress—appearance and manner—friendliness—his grandson—presents—birds about Sanda—return visit from Tsawbwa—his presents—salute of guns on our departure—cross the Sanda stream—enter Muangla division of valley—hot-springs—magpies and minas—aspect of country—ford the Tapeng at Namon—junction of Tahô with Tapeng—bamboo pavilion on banks of Tahô—*Muangla*—conducted to a ruined Chinese Khyoung—a school—description of Muangla—surrounded by villages and Khyoungs—account of two Khyoungs—the Tsawbwa-ship—a regency—annual tribute to Panthays—burial-ground of Tsawbwas—their tombs—high mountain at Muangla—Poloung and Kakhyen villages—aqueduct for irrigation—a gorge—picturesque ferry—Moungshuay-Yah arrives with Panthay officials from Momien—Muangla officials consign us to the care of the Panthays—escort of the Hotha Tsawbwa—a large trader—the nuns of Manwyne—leave Muangla—Nahlow—a false rumour—Kampton—repetition of rumour—scouts sent forward—pass a robbed and wounded trader—ascend a spur of the Mawphoo mountain—a splendid view—Shuemuelong mountain—halt at Mawphoo village—its ruined state—proceed under a strong Panthay guard—arched stone-bridges and remains of paved roads—heights manned by Panthays and Kakhyen guards—emerge on the treeless Nantin valley—iron-chain suspension bridge over the Tahô—reach Shan town of Moangtee—received by a guard—crowds of women and children—*Nantin*—a walled town—delapidated and filthy—visit from the Governor and a hadji—the Tu-tu-du brings visitors—desire to search our luggage—evil reports about it—appeal to Momien—a new genus of *newt*—official visit to the Tu-tu-du—pass through the bazaar—his house—a salute—our host dressed as a Mandarin—ailments of villagers—orders from Momien to proceed—the governor, Chinese chief and Panthay garrison turn out to bid us farewell—music on the gongs—hot-springs—bathe in them—attack of dacoits—two officers and a man killed—8 mules carried off—loads looted—another attack dreaded—appearance of Hawshuenshan volcano—paved path-way—stone bridge—circular valley—*Momien*—meeting with the Governor—conducted to a Chinese Khyoung—loss of note-books and sketches—presents for Tasakone—our procession to his residence—his appearance and dress—cordial reception—the Governor gives the king's assurance of satisfaction with our mission—our advance to Tali discouraged—return visit of Tasakone—appearance of Momien valley—presents from Tasakone—another visit of Tasakone—a feast and theatricals—the magnetic battery—description of the governor's house—oppressive hospitality—water-fall on the Tahô—bridge—summary justice on thieves—visit to Governor—the bazaar—visit to the Chinese merchant—Hotha Tsawbwa, his guest—warned to go no distance beyond town walls—construction of walls—Tahô raised by water-wheel for irrigation—Small-pox in camp—visit to the pagoda hill—*Phasianus sladeni*—splendid view—potatoes—celery—Hotha and Tasakone urge our proceeding to Hotha by Muangla—spectators at breakfast—Bower's generosity—Tasakone rivals it—visit to the chief military officer's garden—tree-frogs—old quarry—mosquitoes—visit from the Tsawbwa-gadaw of Nantin—her costume and jewels—birds—Chinese medicines and styptics—overtures from Lowquanfang—rejected—Sladen declines to play two parts—prohibition of animal food removed—rain—effects of climate—wish to change our quarters—not allowed—Tasakone's anxiety for our safety—a present from the governor—death of a collector and of a Kakhyen chief—beggars—squalour and dirt—dress and appearance of inhabitants—prevalance of goitre—dress of peasantry—another present from Tasakone—flirtation with a Shan young lady—visit to waterfali—Lawloo's arrival—news of Ponline's defeat by a Tsawbwa-gadaw—her distinguishing feature—visit to bazaar—manufacture of copper discs—of jade ornaments—their value—mineral wealth of the province—news of the capture and fall of Yunan city—visit to Hawshuenshan valley—Shuayduay—a fine temple—its deities—town of Hawshuenshan—bridge—paved roadway—dine with the chief military officer—a Mahomedan—his house—the feast—domestic establishment—visit ruins of a large Khyoung—the Musjid—car vouchers—departure of the Hotha-Tsawbwa and the Tsawbwa of Muangtee—festival to the goddess of agriculture—Chinese attack Khyto—silver and copper—exchange of presents with military officer—review of his troops by Tasakone—his departure—seizure of mules by Chinese—description of ruined Khyoungs—school conducted by a priest—Sladen visits Tasakone—despatch read about the fall of Yunan—its size—Tasakone's estimate of the Cambodia route—our detention by the governor—an hour in the Khyoung school—ages and tasks of scholars—visit of Tasakone—arranges for our start—presents from Tali stopped at Sheedin—Tasakone promises to forward the presents to Rangoon—theft of mules—dine with Tasakone—stone implements (Appendix C.)—an escaped criminal—last visit of Tasakone—his desire for trade—his presents—letter regarding duties to be levied—preparations for departure—contempt for natural-history collections—desire for gun-powder ... ... pp. 287 to 340

CHAPTER XIV.

MOMIEN TO HOTHA.

The Panthays—porters impressed for our luggage—wave an adieu to Tasakone—escort of two officials—a weeping farewell—religious sympathies—adventures on the slippery roads—a little Chinese girl—two dead men on the roadside—halt at hot springs—take their temperature—learn of an ambush of Chinese robbers—the Panthays kill two—get a fore and rear guard—re-entrance into Nantin—our old quarters—the governor's welcome—news of 50 Burmese at Muangla to accompany us back—arrival of luggage—intentional disappearance of some—annoyance of Momien officers—a night-robbery—our ponies gone—get a loan of ponies and set out for Muangla—greeting of the Tsawbwa-gadaw of Mynetee—welcome of towns-people—escort of Shan guard—slippery ascent to Mawphoo—size of rivers in the rains—a pleasant surprise at Muangla—Mr. Gordon appears—brings money and a guard of Burmese—suggestion to go back to Momien and return by the Yang-tse-Kiang or by Canton—province of Yunan too disturbed to be traversed—our party too large—loss of thermometers—investments in Shan products—Gordon's estimate of the Hotha Tsawbwa—Panthays leave us regretfully—numerous peoples and dialects in Sanda valley—our ponies offered at a ransom—authorities decline assistance—our advance—ferry on the Tapeng—exorbitant demands of boatmen—Bloudin exploits over mountain streams—Gordon's pony—beauty of Sanda valley—warm streams flooded so as not to be detected—arrive at Sanda—our old quarters—we are robbed—crowds at the Khyoung—selling articles—priestly propriety shocked—market-day—Kakhyens—Leesaws—attempt at imposition—a Shan household—visit to Shan and Chinese Khyoungs—deities—wooden fish—paintings—excursion to the limestone hill—the Tsawbwa's idea of the capabilities of our telescopes and field-glasses—my shooting hindered—dread of the evil nât—application of medicine to exorcise him from the Tsawbwa—interview with Kakhyens—a night alarm and robbery—a Phoongyee suspected—visit to hot-springs—our guide's explanation of their heat—encounter Kakhyens and Leesaws—wild glen of the Chalktaw—Guadama's footprint and tablets—coax a Leesaw girl to part with her beads—permission to go direct to Hotha refused—go by Manwyne—offer to take us by the Molay river—council of headmen to investigate the theft—Phoongyee charged and ordered to confess—Manhleo Poogain to conduct us to Manwyne—superstition of the Tsawbwa and villagers against survey measurements—distressing scene with the Phoongyee's mother—his excommunication from the priesthood—his further disgrace—crowds of sellers—farewell visit of the Tsawbwa and his grand-child—exchange of presents—a salute—an escort—road along the bunds—devastation from the floods—fields buried in silt—land-slips—village buried—Manwyne—our old residence—Phoongyees become more religious. Death's-head appears—interesting conversation with Phoongyees—Hotha Tsawbwa arrives—objects to our going by his valley—a Kakhyen chief's necklace—whence procured—we determine to go by Hotha—Kakhyen female slave—dine at the Tsawbwa-gadaw's—Hotha, a guest—received by the ladies—spectators of the feast—a practical illustration of the art of dyeing the finger-nails—Hotha's skill in music—The nuns and waiting-maids bring presents to the Khyoung—our arrangements to depart—a message from the nuns—visit their Khyoung—their dwelling-house—industry—mangoes and woman's tobacco—friendliness—the Tsawbwa-gadaw's desire for a portrait of the Queen—expressions of good will on our departure—difficulty of crossing the river—a slough of despond—enormous deposit of silt—arduous ascent—toll at Kakhyen villages—magnificent prospect—a Leesaw village—view of Hotha valley—party divides—lose our way—sleep at Mentone—a devout but inhospitable Phoongyee—Hotha vale—paved roads—bridges—covered wells—Manloi—pagoda of Burmese type—official reception by Hotha—accommodated in his residence—arrival of the rest of our party—extortion at a Leesaw village—evil reports circulated about us—description of Hotha village—two Tsawbwaships in the valley—Hotha and Latha—the Tsawbwa learning Burmese—Poogain and Kingain leave—ask certificates from Sladen—the Tsawbwa's ideas of modern inventions—his domestic economy—arrival of the Namboke Tsawbwa and his Pawmines—Hotha's liberality and friendliness—the bazaar—purchase of dâhs—English broad-cloth—liking for red flannel—indigo—picturesque costumes—appearance of women—teeth dyed black—fire-festival of Shans—search for the fire nát—the Tsawbwa's ladies traffic in their ornaments, &c.—excursion to Tsayeow or Old Hotha—pagoda of Comootomy—a Shan and a Chinese temple, built by the Tsawbwa—description of—solar eclipse—visit to the head of Hotha valley—Burmese surveyor goes to survey Musngwan route—the Tsawbwa dines with us—his favourite soup—his questionings about religion—a Phoongyee's remark—Hotha takes us to Tsenlong—fine Bhuddist Khyoung—deceased Phoongyee lying in state—return by Katcow—temple dedicated to náts—the Mantsi Tsawbwa arrives as a messenger from the Woon of Bhamô—purpose of visiting Latha frustrated—the old chief's dread of us ... ... pp. 341 to 376

CHAPTER XV.
HOTHA TO BHAMÔ.

Affectionate leave-taking of the Tsawbwa's family—general good-will manifested—the Tsawbwa escorts us to the boundary of his estate—makes us over to the Kakhyen Tsawbwa of Namboke—aspect of Latha valley—cross the Namsa—*Namboke*—bad provision for the night—restless companions—our detention—interchange of presents with the Latha chief—reach *Ashan*—put up in Kakhyen houses—foot-path specially opened for us—extensive prospect—Ashan belongs to the Ponsee Tsawbwa—slippery descent to the Namkong—enter another valley—ascend to *Muangwye*—the Tsawbwa's house—his hospitality—descent into the Muangkah valley—crossed a ridge to *Loaylone*—its size and importance—attention of the Tsawbwa—the Mutthin Tsawbwa—muster of Tsawbwas to accompany us to Bhamô—Loaylone, a principal stage on the embassy route—once a Chinese garrison—remains of fort—on the usual route to Momien, *via* Muangwan—Kakhyen tactics delaying departure—meet mules laden with cotton and salt from Bhamô—pass direct road to Hoetone—Mutthin Tsawbwa takes us round by his village—a noisy reception—village large and thriving—*Hoetone*—the Tsawbwa's house—altars to the nâts—compensation asked for the death of the petty chief at Momien—the Mantai Tsawbwa allures us to go by his village—splendid views from the road—liberal hospitality of the Tsawbwa and his ladies—unsafe descent—primitive bridge over a roaring torrent—the flooded Tapeng—the Namthabet—encamp on its banks—extemporise tents for the night—build a raft in the morning—met by the Choungsa of Sit-nga and followers—conduct us to Nampung—aspect of country—reach the Tapeng—two large boats prepared for us—war-boats tow us across—met by the Woon's private Secretary—pavilion erected for us—overburdened with supplies—a contrast—harmonious settlement with our Kakhyen porters—leave Sit-nga—Chittie-doung—Kad-doung—met by the Sayay-dawgyee—breadth of Tapeng—arrival at our old quarters at Bhamô—presents from the Woon—provisions given to Kakhyen Tsawbwas—Kakhyen ceremony of swearing eternal friendship—objections to its celebration—over-ruled—presents distributed to the Tsawbwas—they retire to the hills—exploration of the Molay river—size of the Irawady in September—dolphins—pelicans—bid farewell to Bhamô—return to Mandalay ... pp. 377 to 388

APPENDICES.

Appendix A.—Routes to China—routes from Bhamô to the eastward. pp. 391 to 399.

Appendix B.—Vocabulary of five languages, Kakhyen, Shan, Hotha-Shan, Poloung, and Leesaw. pp. 400 to 409.

Appendix C.—Stone Implements from Yunan, and a notice of a bronze axe-like weapon from the Sanda valley. pp. 410 to 415.

Appendix D.—Meteorological observations. pp. 416 to 429.

Appendix E.—Note on maps.

Illustrations.

Plates I, II, III, IV, Stone Implements.

Plate V, Bronze implement.

Map of the district visited by the Expedition and of the surrounding country, specially prepared for this Report.

Map (skeleton) to illustrate the supposed sources of the Irawady, Salween and Cambodia Rivers.

ERRATA.

Page 6, line 17 of note; *for* " Tsawship" *read* " Tsawbwaship."
,, 24, last line; *for* " 30" *read* " 20."
,, 85, line 26; *for* " Appendix B." *read* " Appendix D."
,, 86, line 2; *for* " Moungtee" *read* " Muangba."
,, 116, line 21; *for* " Bhagariti" *read* " Bhagavati."
,, 116, line 22; *for* " Dhener" *read* " Dhenu."
,, 118, line 33; *for* " Hakhyen" *read* " Kakhyen."
,, 159, line 14; *for* " valley" *read* " village."
,, 182, line 18; *for* " postion" *read* " position."
,, 198, line 3; *for* " so-called first" *read* " first or lower defile."
,, 202, last line; *for* " Pycnontous" *read* " Pycnonotus."
,, 211, line 18; *for* " Cirsaen" *read* " Casarca."
,, 211, line 20; *for* " Haliaster" *read* Haliastur."
,, 242, line 4; *for* " phillippensis" *read* " philippensis."
,, 243, line 31; *for* " from" *read* " for."
,, 250, line 24; *for* " eastern" *read* " western."
,, 256, line 17; *for* " pruniosus" *read* " pruinosus."
,, 259, line 30; *for* " Leucurca" *read* " Leucocerca."
,, 323, line 17; *for* " coolies" *read* " ladies."

REPORT.

REPORT

ON THE

EXPEDITION TO YUNAN.

CHAPTER I.

THE KINGDOM OF PONG.

In order to bring prominently forward the very important part which Bhamô and Western Yunan have played in the political and commercial relations of Burmah and China, I propose to record all the information I have been able to gather regarding their early history. But, before doing so, I will give a brief sketch of an extensive and powerful kingdom which existed, in Upper Burmah, from the 1st to the close of the 18th century of our era; and I am led to do so, because its history is intimately associated with that of the empire of Ava, and with Chinese aggression in the Shan states (Koshanpyi) and Upper Burmah. I refer to the ancient Shan kingdom of Pong, first described in detail by Captain Pemberton.[1]

Captain Pemberton's information was derived from an ancient Shan manuscript chronicle, which he obtained during his residence at Munipore, and had translated into the Munipore language. From this document it appears that the kingdom of Pong, in the 14th century, occupied the country between the frontiers of Yunan and the hills separating the Kubo valley from Munipore, extending north apparently to the mountains which bound Assam on the south-east, and south, as far down as the parallel of 23° 35′. Tradition places the ancient capital on the Shuaylee,[2]

---

[1] Report on Eastern Frontier of British India, by Captain Pemberton.

[2] The *locus* of the ancient capital of this kingdom is obscured by the mists of antiquity, but the fact that the Chinese were in the habit of designating the Mogoung chief after his possessions on the Shuaylee, lends a certain weight to the tradition which assigns it to the banks of that river.

but it appears that after its capture by the Chinese, about the middle of the 14th century, a new city was founded on the banks of the Namkong, on the western side of the Irawady, to which the name of Muangkung was given. According to the chronicle quoted by Pemberton, the ancient capital existed as far back as the 80th year of our era.

The influence of the Pong kingdom, on the neighbouring states, began to be most felt in the reign of Sookampha, who ascended the throne in 777 A.D. He subdued all the countries to the east of his capital, up to the confines of China, and carried his arms into Cachar, Tipurah, and Munipore. His brother, Samlongpha, who commanded his armies, appears to have been a humane and enlightened prince, for we are informed that he pitied the wretchedness of the Muniporeans, remitted their tribute, and devised means for the amelioration of their social condition. He invaded Assam,[1] and succeeded in establishing his brother's supremacy, but he did not return to Pong, as a conspiracy was formed to destroy him. He was joined by his wife, and son, Chownakhum, and the latter is said to have been the head of the subsequent dynasty of Assam. From these facts, it is evident that, even at this early period, Pong was recognized as a powerful Shan kingdom with a large territory.

Captain Pemberton states, "that although the Siamese, and the people of Lowa Shan who speak the same language, unite in representing themselves as descended from the Taee-lon or great Shans who formed this kingdom, that scarcely even its name has hitherto been known." I find Du Halde, however, making the following reference to a great Shan kingdom. He says :—" The Siamese have often been heard to say, that to the north of Siam there was a nation which had the same religion, customs, and language with themselves, and that they received their own from them, and even their name, since the dominions of that people were called the great kingdom of Siam.[2]" Du Halde, however, referred this kingdom to Lassa, on what appears to me to have been very insufficient grounds. His only reasons for conveying it into the very heart of

---

[1] McCosh, in his Topography of Assam, in accounting for the origin of the Assamese, suggests that they migrated early in the 13th century from some mountainous country on the borders of China, and took Assam by conquest. "They were called Ahoms, and spoke and wrote a language different from that of the conquered, and had a system of religion peculiarly their own. They ate beef to the horror of the Hindoos, and pork to the execration of the Mussulmans ; cats, dogs, rats, and locusts were considered as dainties, and spirituous liquors formed an essential article of fare." P. 14.

[2] A Description of the Empire of China, by Du Halde, vol. i, p. 62.

Tartary were, that the Siamese considered themselves to be the same people as the Tay-yays[1] of the Chinese, and because the kingdom was said to be governed by priests, and Lassa being under the supreme pontiff of the Lawas, he considered it likely that the country which the Chinese call Tay-yays was the Lassa of the Tartars. The authors of the Universal History, in treating of this subject, remark that "there is no manner of occasion for removing Tibet out of its place, in order to account for this singularity, since it is enough to suppose that one of the *khutaktas* or deputies of the Great Lama resided formerly in these parts.[2]" But even this supposition is uncalled for, as the country of the Tay-yays or great Shans is the Koshanpyi, or nine Shan states, which are described as lying to the west (north-west and north) of Mohung-leng (Muangleng), the capital of one of the chief Laos states, to the east of the present capital of Burmah. Du Halde describes it as situated on both sides of the Menan-tay or Menanlay[3] river, which, he supposed, emptied itself into the Menankay or river of Siam. The Laos city, Mohung-leng of Du Halde, appears to be the Muanglam or Maingleng-gyee[4] of the maps, 3 degrees of longitude to the east of Ava, and nearly on the same parallel, 22 degrees of latitude, with that city. On the most recent map of this part of the Burmese frontier, compiled at the Surveyor General's Office, Calcutta, in 1867, Muanglam is situated on both banks of a stream called the Melam, which falls into the Cambodia. If I am correct in hazarding the opinion that Du Halde's Mohung-leng is the Maingleng-gyee of the maps,[5] the kingdom of the great Siams probably comprised that extensive tract of country to the north-west and north of Maingleng-gyee, on the right and left banks of the Irawady, between the 21st and

---

[1] Tay-yays in the Universal History, vol. vii, p. 135, is interpreted as the Great Freemen or Franks.

[2] Loc. cit vii, p. 136.

[3] Du Halde was in error in making the Menanlay fall into the Menankong. He describes the Menanlay as descending towards Mohung-Kimarat, and then towards the river of Siam. Now, the position of Mohung-Kimarat (Kiangtung) is well established. It is situated to the south of Mohung-leng (Maingleng-gyee) at some distance to the west of the Cambodia, and the river, on which Mohung-leng stands, first flows to the south, in the direction of Mohung-Kimarat, and then to the east to reach the Cambodia, into which it falls on the same parallel as Kiangtung (Mohung-Kimarat).

[4] In connection with the Siamese tradition that the ancient kingdom was governed by priests, it is worthy of remark that the Sanscrit name of Maingleng-gyee, *Beikkarato*, has been rendered Bhikshurashtra,—"The realm of Saints." Yule's Ava p. 314.

[5] I find that Yule and Macleod have arrived at the same conclusion.

26th parallels of latitude, and stretching from the 95th to the 100th degree of east longitude. The whole of this area supports a Shan population. It appears to me that Du Halde had this large territory in view when he speaks of the Mohung Koshanpyi as lying to the west of Maingleng-gyee. Mohung is evidently the Shan word "Muang," meaning a city or country, and "Koshanpyi" may be translated as the nine Shan states, and he proceeds to say that this Mohung Koshanpyi, to the west of Maingleng-gyee, "was formerly inhabited by a certain people called Tay-yay, who possessed a kingdom of so great extent that it required three months to travel round it." After the middle of the eighth century, the Pong kings extended their conquests far to the east, and this, along with such other considerations as these—that the Shan principalities extend as far as the Cambodia, that all the cities and towns, as far as that river, have Shan names, and that the Chinese conquest of the Cis-Cambodia states dates from the middle of the 13th century, entitle us to conclude that the Cambodia, prior to the 13th century, was the eastern limit of the Pong territories. It would include, therefore, all those states which are known as the Koshanpyi, and which do not lie to the west of Maingleng-gyee as stated by Du Halde, but nearly due north. But as the territory to the west of Maingleng-gyee formed part of the same kingdom with the Koshanpyi, Du Halde was not in error in describing it as the Muang of the Koshanpyi. Up to the middle of the 15th century, we find the Chinese styling the Pong kings after their possessions, Muangmo, on the Shuaylee, one of the nine Shan states.[1] Now, as I have already stated, tradition assigns the ancient capital Manlong (Muanglong) of the Pong kings to the banks of the Shuaylee, and this, taken in connection with the fact that a town of that name still exists in

---

[1] The following states appear to have formerly constituted the Koshanpyi of the Chinese:—Bhamô (Tsinggai), Muangmo, Muangwan, Muangmah(Kaingmah, Maingmah), Latha, Hotha, Sanda, Muangla, Muangtee. Yule, in his enumeration of the Shan states, mentions one which he writes Tsiguen. The similarity between Tsiguen and Tsinggai or Singgaitswn, as it is sometimes written, the Chinese name for Bhamô, is remarkable, and as I am not aware of any Shan state called Tsiguen, I am inclined to believe that it refers to Bhamô. Buchanan Hamilton, I find, who is my only other authority for the Chinese name of Bhamô, spelt it exactly as I have done, affixing, however, *tsuen*. That Bhamô was once a Shan state is evident from the fact that the territory of the Shan states extended as far south as Katha on the Irawady. But we have better evidence than this, for the Tsawbwa of that district described it to Buchanan Hamilton as one of the nine Shan principalities of Upper Burmah. As a consequence we have the term Koshanpyi extended to that part of the valley of the Irawady, which, there can be little doubt, was at one time a portion of the Pong kingdom.

that valley, in the Muangmo state, suggests that there must be some truth in the tradition.

The inhabitants of these small semi-independent states are one in race and language with the Shan population on the western bank of the Irawady,[1] which seems to me to be evidence of a kind entitling us to infer that the Cis and Trans-Irawadian sections were once the members of a common kingdom.[2] It is true that the western Shans, residing in the open valley of the Irawady, have lost many of the distinctive customs of their ancestors from their intimate association with their Burmese conquerors, and the fact is recorded that they adopted the manner of tying the hair and the dress of the latter people so far back as 1596 A.D. On the other hand, however, in the high secluded valleys to the east of Bhamô, some of which are almost walled in on every side by high mountain ranges, we find the Shan race in its purity, preserving its ancient civilization, and the peculiar national costumes which are in such marked contrast to those of the Chinese and Burmese. The position of those people in high mountain valleys has been their safeguard against the introduction of Chinese and Burmese influence in sufficient force to modify the race.

There is one fact mentioned in the Shan chronicle which favours the view I have taken regarding the probable eastern limits of the

---

[1] In opposition to the above statement I have to reproduce Buchanan Hamilton's opinion which is diametrically opposed to it. He writes,—" I have strong reasons (which, however, are never stated) to think, from verbal information received through the slave to the heir-apparent, that all the Shans on both banks of the Irawady, as well as of the Kyendwen, were originally of the same race calling themselves Tailung, and differing somewhat from the Shanwas who inhabit the country between the proper territory of the Burmans and the Salween river." My own experience is that the Tailungs are only a fraction of the population to the east of Bhamô, and that, physically, they have a greater resemblance to the Burmese than to the Shans. The Poloungs occur chiefly to the south and east of the Shuaylee.

[2] Martini, writing about the town of Yunchan, mentions a great kingdom of Kinchi, which formerly existed in the Trans-Irawadian Shan states, and of which Yunchan was formerly the capital. Marsden's Marco Polo, p. 457, note 852. The same author refers to a remarkable custom, which the inhabitants were said to have, of covering their teeth with plates of gold; and he observes " qu'on appelle Kin-chi, c'est à dire, aux dents d'or ;" and he further remarks, "d'autres qui se plaisent à avoir les dents fort noires, qu'ils peignent avec du vernis, ou bien avec quelque autre droque." Now, it is highly interesting to observe that the custom of blackening the teeth is still universally prevalent among the women of the Shan valleys, as it is thought to add greatly to their charms. It must be borne in mind, however, that a similar practice was in vogue in Burmah up to within the last few years, and may still exist in some places.

Pong kingdom,[1] *viz.*, that in 1332 A.D., they were conterminous with the Chinese frontier. About that year, Captain Pemberton states, "some disagreements, originating in the misconduct of four pampered favourites of the Pong king, led to a collision between the frontier villages of his territory and those of Yunan. An interview between the kings of Pong and China was appointed to take place at the town of Mongsee, which is said to be five days' distance from Mongmaorong, the capital of Pong.[2]" We cannot overlook the circumstance that Muangsee (Maingsee, Burmese) is the Shan name of Yunan city, the capital of the province of that name, distant about seven days' march from the Cambodia, and the head-quarters of the viceroy.[3] It seems probable, therefore, that Yunan city was the scene of the interview, and what could be more likely than that the weaker prince should repair to the capital of his more powerful neighbour to arrange the misunderstanding which had arisen between the two kingdoms by the aggressive acts of his own

---

[1] It was not till after I had formed this opinion, and written the above, that I discovered the following passage in Captain Pemberton's Eastern Frontier:—"Of that portion of Yunan extending from Talifoo in latitude 25°44'24" and longitude 100°13'36" east of Greenwich, to the Burmese frontier, little or nothing has been added to the notices found in the hands of Marco Polo, and from his accounts, there can be little doubt that all that portion of the province west of the Lu Khyoung, or Salween river, originally formed part of the Shan dominions, from which it was probably wrested during the early part of the thirteenth century; even beyond this line traces of Shan influence are found in the term 'Muang' applied to many of the cities east of the Lu Khyoung, and which is the pure Shan word for city. The name Karazan which Marsden justly supposes would be pronounced Kala Shan by the Chinese, and which Marco Polo applies to the country between Talifoo and Yunchanfoo, tends greatly to strengthen this belief of Shan supremacy; and in describing the manners and habits of the inhabitants of the next province of which the capital is Vochang or Yunchan, many most striking coincidences are found between them and those of the Shans of the present day, living in the valleys between the Irawattee and Ningthee rivers," pp. 136-137. There is a Shan Tsawship a short way to the south of Yunchan called Tumkhun, and while we were at Momien, the chief was introduced to us as a person of importance.

[2] Pemberton identifies Mogoung with Mongmaorong, but it appears to me that the latter word is so much more closely affined to Muanglong that his identification cannot well be adhered to, and that it is much more probable that Mongmaorong and Muanglong refer to the first capital, and Mogoung to the last metropolis of Pong.

[3] The city of Momien was stated to me to be between 400 and 500 years old, and to have been built by the governor of Yunchan by the order of the king of Manshi. Manshi, I think, can be no other than Manji, the southern division of the Chinese empire mentioned by Marco Polo, and which Marsden supposed to have embraced the eastern part of Yunan. This city was therefore built, in all probability, immediately after the Chinese conquest of the Trans-Irawadian frontier of Pong.

subjects; for, however powerful the Pong kingdom may have been at this period, it was less than some of the provinces of the great empire of China.

Any attempt to map out the probable southern limits of Pong on the left bank of the Irawady, during the reign of Sookampha, is beset with almost as much conjecture as has attended the investigation into its likely eastern range. It is worthy of note that Old Pagan, the Burmese capital, which had been built in 107 A.D., almost on the ruins of the ancient city of Tagoung,[1] and after the fall of Prome, appears to have been removed about this time to Tsagain, on the right bank, about 115 miles further south. The explanation may be hazarded that it succumbed to this Shan king when he was carrying his victorious arms from the eastern countries bordering China to the conquest of the western independent states. The proximity of Old Pagan to Pong, and the circumstance that the destruction of the former happened while the latter state was in the height of its ascendancy, is suggestive at least of the interpretation which I have put on the coincidence of the two events. The Shans, however, did not annex Tagoung, for it is mentioned in the Burmese chronicle as a jaghir of the Tagoung kingdom in 1363 A.D., and governed by a lineal descendant of the Tagoung and Tsagain kings. The Shuaylee was in all probability the southern limit of the Pong kingdom[2] at this period, although in after years the Pong kings are said to have invaded Siam on two occasions. On the right bank of the Irawady, it stretched from the Kubo valley in the south to the borders of Assam in the north.

About the middle of the 14th century (1333 A.D.?), according to the chronicle, this extensive kingdom became embroiled in wars with China and Burmah. The Chinese, after a war of two years' duration,

---

[1] Mweyen, a town a short way to the south of Bhamô, was the capital of the Shakya kings prior to Tagoung, and it has been identified with the ancient city, Manroya.—Yule's Ava, p. 15.

[2] I am borne out in this conjecture by the fact that Katha on the right bank of the Irawady was once the southern limit of the Shan states (Pong). In after times, however, it appears even to have been carried as far south as Tsampenago. I believe that even so recently as 1835, we find a kind of recognition of the old boundary line between the two kingdoms of Pong and Ava in what Captain Hannay relates regarding the navigation of the Irawady between Ava and Bhamô. He mentions that no foreigners except the Chinese are allowed to navigate the Irawady above the Choki of Tsampenago, situated about 70 miles above Ava, and no native of the country even is permitted to proceed above that part, excepting under a special license from the government. Buchanan Hamilton also states that the Shan who supplied him with the materials for his map reckoned Tsampenago as the uppermost Burman town on the Irawady.—*Ed., Phil. Journ.*, vol. iv, p. 84.

captured the capital, and the king, Soognampha, and his eldest son, fled to Ava for protection, and his queen, with two of her sons, sought refuge among the Kamptis to the north. The queen returned after two years and established another capital, and the circumstance that the chronicle is careful to record that it was founded on the Namkong or Mogoung river, seems to imply that the locality was a new one. This supposition is strengthened by the fact that the Burmese chronicle, in referring to the conquest of Pong, which it claims to have been effected by Burmah in 1442 A.D., states that the Chinese had been at war with the Muangmo (Shuaylee) chief for several years before the latter event. There can be no doubt, however, regarding the identity of these events, although there is the discrepancy of nearly a century between the two accounts. There is the distinct statement in the Shan chronicle that about the period above-mentioned, the capital of the Pong kingdom was captured by the Chinese, and in the Burmese chronicle that, prior to the conquest of Mogoung by Burmah, the Chinese had been at war with the Muangmo chief for several years. If my determination of the locality of Muanglong be correct, the war, in which Pong was engaged with China shortly after 1333 A.D., was carried on in the Shan states to the east of Bhamô. Viewed in this light, we appreciate the details which the Shan chronicler has recorded regarding the rise of the new capital, Muangkung, on the right bank of the Irawady, on the Namkong river; and the circumstance that the fugitive queen, on her return, selected a site on the right bank of the Irawady for her capital, seems to indicate that her Trans-Irawadian possessions had been irrecoverably lost.

Before proceeding further, I must refer to a discrepancy of 60 years between the Shan and Chinese chronicles, the latter ascribing events to 60 years earlier than the former. I do so, because a Chinese war on the Trans-Irawadian Pong states is referred by the Shan manuscript to about 60 years later than the well-known invasion of Western Yunan and Burmah, recorded by Marco Polo as occurring in 1272 A.D. We have seen that the conference between the king of Pong and the viceroy of Yunan which, according to the Shan chronicle, was held at Muangsee in 1332 A.D., arose from certain aggressions which had been committed on the Chinese frontier by the subjects of Pong. The Chinese, shortly after this conference, determined on subjugating the Pong dominions; and in connection

---

[1] Colonel Phayre.—*As. Soc. Journ.*, vol. xxx, p. 379.

THE KINGDOM OF PONG.

with this and the causes that led to the conference, it is interesting to observe, what Marco Polo relates, "that in 1272 the Grand Khan sent an army into the countries of Vochang[1] and Karazan[2] for their protection and defence against any attack that foreigners might attempt to make." There can be very little doubt but that this was the army which afterwards captured the Pong capital, reduced the Shan states (Koshanpyi) to Chinese subjection, and over-ran Burmah as far south as Taroupmyo (Chinese point) below Prome.

The Koshanpyi, from the time of the Chinese conquest up to the invasion in 1863 by the Mahomedan rebels, appear to have been tributary to China. The Burmese, however, claim to have annexed them with varying success in the 11th century, 1562, and 1765, and they have a tradition that they once held the country as far as Momien.[3] The Chinese, however, have never recognised that the Burmese had any right to the Shan states, and in 1769 when the generals of the two kingdoms were settling the north-eastern boundary of Burmah, and the Burmese general claimed the Shan states as part of his territory on the ground that they were conquered in 1562 A.D. by the Peguan King, Tshenbyu-mya-yen, (the Lord of many White Elephants), the Burmese pretensions were disposed of by the Chinese generals in a very off-hand manner. The latter allowed that the king of Pegu had advanced on that occasion

---

[1] Marco Polo describes Karazan as lying 10 days to the west of Talifoo (Yachi), and Kardandan as 5 days in a westerly direction from Karazan. From the facts that he makes Vochang the capital of Kardandan, and in describing the people of that province enumerates certain customs, such as, the blackening of the teeth, the use of notched tallies, and the practice, in the case of illness, of consulting sorcerers into whom the evil spirit (nât) was supposed to have entered, and all of which are striking characteristics of the Shans and Kakhyens of the present day, I am led to identify Kardandan with Shan states to the east of Bhamô. Marco Polo, however, appears to have mixed up Burmese with Shan customs, for he describes tattooing, which is unknown in the Shan states to the east of Bhamô, and has probably always been so, as they are a well-clad breeches-wearing people. This identification receives further confirmation from the circumstance that Marco Polo makes Kardandan conterminous with Burmah, which, he says, is reached by a vast descent of two days and a half in which no habitations are to be found. This is a wonderfully accurate description of the descent over the Kakhyen hills to the Burmese plain, a journey of two days and a half, in which very few villages are seen.

[2] It is worthy of special note that the lofty range of mountains to the east of Momien is known as the *Kaszan*, which has so remarkable an affinity to *Karazan* that I cannot but regard the two terms as identical.

[3] Martini states that Momien was formerly known to the Chinese as the Fort of Mien—Mien being also the Chinese name for Burmah. He does not say, however, that the fort was comprised in Burmah, but states distinctly that it was anciently included in the territories of "Sinan," but was wrested from that kingdom by the Yuena dynasty. See Yule's Ava, note *, p. 169.

as far as Hotha and Latha, and had built pagodas in that valley, but refused to acknowledge that he ever retained any hold on the country,[1] and facetiously reminded the Burmese that the Chinese army had on one occasion advanced as far as Taroupmyo. In the country I visited to the east of Bhamô there is little or no evidence of Burmese influence, and that language is little understood, while on the other hand every Shan and Kakhyen talks Chinese, eats with chop-sticks, and has a rudimentary or well-developed pig-tail.

But to return to the history of Pong. After the loss of its Koshanpyi provinces, it was sufficiently powerful in 1364 to attack and destroy the Burmese capital of Tsagain. The Pong king at that time was the youngest son of Soognampha, who, with his eldest son, had fled for protection to Tsagain when their capital, Muanglong, had been captured by the Chinese, and to whom they had been treacherously surrendered by the Tsagain king. The sack of his capital was to avenge this treachery. The destruction of Tsagain is fully verified by the Burmese chronicle, which states that the Shans not only destroyed it, but the city of Penya as well.

In 1475, the Pong King, Soohoongkhum, and the Rajah of Munipore, conquered the rebel prince of Khumbat, and re-settled the boundary line between the two countries,[2] selecting the Noajeeree hills between the Kyendwen and Moo rivers as the western limit of Pong, and the Meeyatoung or Meeya range as its southern boundary. A famous mangoe tree between the Noajeeree hills and the Kyendwen marked the northern boundary.

Soohoongkhum was succeeded in 1513-14 by his son, Soopengpha, in whose reign, according to the Shan chronicle, the Burmese, for the first time, invaded Pong, but from subsequent events, it is evident that its vitality, as an independent kingdom, was not much affected by the Burmese invasion.

Soopengpha, in 1526, retaliated on the Burmese, and over-ran Ava as far south as Toungoo and Prome, destroying the capital, and killing the king, and the Burmese chronicle states that Shan princes at this period reigned for 19 years in Ava.

---

[1] Col. Burney, in a note on this subject, states that the ground on which the Burmese claimed Hotha and Latha was precisely the same as that on which they founded, in 1837, their right to the Kubo valley, Munipore, and even to Chittagong and Dacca.

[2] The first Burmese conquest of Pong is stated to have taken place in 1442, but the Munipore chronicle places it 70 years later. There is no doubt, however, that this settlement of territory between Pong and Munipore was made after the conquest of the former state by the Burmese.

THE KINGDOM OF PONG.

Soopengpha was succeeded in 1568 by his son, Sookopha, who, on two occasions, invaded Siam successfully, and captured four white elephants. The tide of good fortune, however, turned against him in following years, and the Burmese were once more in the ascendant in Pong. They invested his capital, and he fled for safety to Kampti, where he was treacherously betrayed to the Burmese by two of his slaves.

His son, Chowkalkhum, is said to have ascended the throne in 1587, with a resolve to avenge the misfortunes of his father. He invaded Ava as far as Myedu, but meeting with a Chinese army which was attacking Burmah at that time, 1592, he was defeated and slain.

The Burmese chronicle records that, about 1601, the Tsawbwa of Bhamô set himself up as an independent chief, and attributes his doing so, to the fall of the empire of Pegu. It appears, however, to be more probable that the gradual decay of the Pong empire was the real cause, for there is no historical evidence to show that Pegu ever retained any hold on the countries it invaded in 1562, and if the events of 1568 and 1587, detailed in the Shan chronicle, are no myths, they corroborate this view of the Bhamô Tsawbwa's independence.

The kingdom of Pong, after the death of Chowkalkhum, degenerated into little more than a Burmese province. Their so-called kings were appointed by the emperors of Ava, between 1662 and 1672, from their own court, but between the latter period and 1734, the succession was again bestowed on the lineal descendants of the Pong sovereigns.

A few years before the distinguished Burmese Emperor, Alompra, (1752) commenced his brilliant reign and conquests, the princes of Pong struck a last but unsuccessful blow for the independence of their country, and with the powerful assistance of the warlike Rajah of Munipore, Gureeb Nuwaz, they proclaimed a Pong prince as king at their capital on the Namkong. He reigned for a few years, and was succeeded by Chowkhoolseng, the last of the long line of kings who reigned over this once extensive kingdom. This prince succumbed before the arms of Alompra, and with his fall the ancient kingdom of Pong ceased to exist.

CHAPTER II.

WARS BETWEEN BURMAH AND CHINA.

I PROPOSE now to give a rapid sketch of the wars between Burmah and China, in order to show the important position which the trade routes hold in the history of the two nations.[1] The first capital recorded in the Burmese chronicles is Tagoung, on the left bank of the Irawady, about half-way between Mandalay and Bhamô. From its position, a little over 30 miles to the south of the mouth of the Shuaylee, it commanded the Momeit route which proceeds up the valley of that river to Muangmo, to which point the stream is said to be navigable for small boats. That city, according to the Burmese chronicles, was destroyed before the Christian era by the Tartars and Chinese, but another, called Pagan, rose almost on its ruins. In the reign of the third king of Pagan, between A.D. 166 and 241, the Chinese again invaded the valley of the Irawady, but were signally defeated by the Burmese.

Little or nothing is known of the history of Old Pagan. It appears to have been founded about A.D. 107 by one of the princes of Prome who fled to Upper Burmah on the fall of the Prome empire.[2] Towards the close of the 8th century, it seems to have been deserted as the seat of government for another city of the same name 200 miles down the Irawady. The foundation of the most ancient pagoda in this city carries us back to A.D. 850. It is worthy of note—and it can hardly be regarded as a mere coincidence—that the apparent desertion of Old

---

[1] The materials for the above accounts are almost exclusively derived from Colonel Burney's Translations of the Burmese Chronicles. *As. Soc. Journ.*, vol. vi, p. 121, et seq.

[2] I visited the site of Tagoung and old Pagan both on my upward and downward journey on the Irawady. On the latter occasion I determined to satisfy myself if any ruins existed, and landed about the middle of the river-face of the ancient city of Pagan with a strong party of men, headed by a Burmese from Tagoung, as our guide. We cut our way for about a mile through a dense low jungle interspersed among fine forest trees. Bricks met us at every step, but with the exception of occasional low mounds of brick-work covered with a luxuriant vegetation, there is no further trace of ruins. The sites of the two cities lie side by side. From Pagan we crossed an immense mass of ancient brick-work said to be the wall of old Tagoung. The ruins of the latter city, we were assured, were in the same condition as those of Pagan, mere brick heaps overgrown by dense jungle. It is a matter of great regret to me that I had neither the time nor the appliances to open any of the mounds, for they, in all likelihood, contain objects of great historical and antiquarian interest.

Pagan for another city of its own name, so far to the south of it, should have happened at the time when the Pong kingdom, in Upper Burmah, was in the zenith of its power. I cannot but connect the events, and explain the forsaking of old for New Pagan on the theory that it was brought about by the conquests of the Pong kings.

In the 11th century (1017—1059), the wars between Burmah and China originated from a desire of the king of New Pagan, Anôrathá-mengzô,[1] to possess a tooth of Guadama, which was preserved with great veneration in a shrine in China,[2] and the chronicles state that he invaded China for the object of appropriating it. The souvenir of the saint, however, declined to leave the celestial empire, and its declinature marks the date of the commencement of a series of devastating wars between the two countries. The statement that the Burmese king invaded China appears to be inaccurate, for he is recorded to have resided with the emperor of China on the most friendly terms, and to have been feasted daily with viands, served in vessels of gold and silver, which he presented on his departure to the teacher of the emperor, with the pious request that offerings should be made in them daily to the venerated tooth. It is difficult to arrive at a correct estimate of the nature of the visit of the Burmese king to China, but it is remarkable that the emperors of China, in after years, demanded vessels of gold and silver from the kings of Pagan as tokens of their tributary subjection, and that when they were refused, they invariably enforced their demands by an appeal to arms. Nearly all the wars between the two kingdoms are to be attributed to the determination with which China exacted the presentation of these tokens of tributary subjection.

The first of these wars occurred in A.D. 1284, when a Chinese-Tartar army marched against Pagan to enforce the tribute which had been

---

[1] He founded the Shuay-zeagong pagoda at New Pagan.

[2] The Chinese appear to have had many relics of the kind in the 9th century, for Gutzlaff mentions that Heën-tsung, A.D. 819, a very wise emperor of the Tung dynasty, having heard that there was a finger of Buddha in Shensi, caused the precious relic to be transferred in great state to his capital; and sixty-five years later, E-tsung, another king of the same dynasty, discovered another bone of Buddha, and brought it to his capital. Mr. Beal, in his introduction to the travels of Fah-hian and Sung-yun, the Buddhist pilgrims (London, 1869), mentions that when this bone was being escorted under the care of mandarins to the capital by the order of the emperor, one of the Chinese ministers remonstrated with his royal master as follows:—" Why should a decayed bone, the filthy remains of a man long dead, be introduced to the imperial residence? As for Buddha, he braved his vengeance, and defied his power to inflict punishment." The minister was banished to the province of Canton, but he was ultimately converted, and became a sincere disciple of Buddhism. See Du Halde, vol. i, p. 200.

refused by the Burmese three years before, when they put to death the members of the Chinese embassy who had been sent to receive it. From the position of Pagan and the history of the routes followed by the Chinese armies of invasion in after years, we might be led to suppose it probable that this force advanced by Theinnee, but bearing in mind that the Chinese had resolved at the same time to subdue the Trans-Irawadian Pong states, and that they succeeded in doing so, it seems more likely that the Tartar hordes reached the Burmese plain by the valley of the Shuaylee. Their army was commanded by the Mahomedan General, Nestardin; and Marco Polo relates that when the king of Bengala and Mien[1] (Ava) heard of the arrival of the Tartar force at Vochang and Karazan, he sent a large army against it, but the Tartars, having reached the plains before the Burmese had been put in motion, intrenched themselves in a strong position, and ultimately defeated the king of Mien, and annexed the whole of his dominions.[2] The Burmese chronicles, on the other hand, while they acknowledge that the country was devastated as far as Taroupmyo to the south of Prome, make it appear that the Chinese only over-ran the country, and then retired, hard pressed for supplies. There are no facts besides these, as far as I am aware, to prove that Burmah ever was tributary to China in the ordinary acceptation of that term, but it should be remembered that the Chinese emperors have always asserted their superiority to the Burmese kings, by insisting that the two countries should "transmit and exchange affectionate letters on gold once every ten years," supporting their pretensions by force of arms. Besides, in all the communications which have passed between China and Burmah, the kings of the latter country have been addressed as younger brothers.[3] The relations

---

[1] In a note in Marsden's Marco Polo, it is stated that in the Basle edition of the great traveller's work, the words are "rex Mien et rex Bengala," but Marsden inclines to the opinion that only one personage is intended, who might at that period have styled himself king of Bengala as well as of Mien, from the circumstance of his having conquered some eastern districts belonging to Bengal. The fact that the Burmese have, on more than one occasion, claimed territory so far west of their capital as Dacca, supports Marsden's supposition.

[2] It is highly probable that this refers to the conquest of that part of the Shan kingdom to the east of the Irawady.

[3] The Chinese, during Lord Macartney's mission to Pekin, informed Sir George Staunton that Siam, Ava, and Pegu were tributary to China. It may prove of interest to note, in connection with the position which the Chinese assigned to Ava in 1787, that even the Burmese government itself was afraid that the Chinese might betray it into a position which might be construed into one of tributary subjection. What gave rise to this suspicion was that the emperor of China presented the Tsawbwa

of Burmah to China, at the period of which I am writing, are further illustrated by what followed in A.D. 1300. In that year, Kyô-zuá, the son of King Nara-thì-padé, who had been defeated in 1284, was treacherously betrayed by his queen into the hands of three brothers, the most powerful chiefs in his kingdom, who resided at Myenzain to the south of Ava. They first forced the unfortunate monarch to become a phoongyee, and then murdered him, and assumed the government. Before his death, a Chinese force marched on Pagan to assist in his restoration,—a fact which shows that the Chinese emperors took a special interest in the internal affairs of Burmah. When the Chinese had advanced as far as Myenzain, the three brothers decapitated the king, and showed the head to the Chinese, who promised to retire, provided the brothers would send presents to the emperor. They agreed to do so, on condition that the Chinese would first construct a canal, and the chronicle records that the Chinese generals, to show the great strength of their army, completed it in one day. It was 4,900 cubits long, 14 broad, and 14 deep.[1]

According to the Burmese, the Shan states of Muangmo, Hotha, and Latha were separated from the Pagan empire in the reign of Kyô-zuá, but as the Muangmo chief was the king of Pong and an independent prince till he was conquered by the Chinese in 1284 (Shan chronicle, 1333 A.D.), I am inclined to believe that the Burmese claim to his territory has no other explanation than that which was given of it by the Chinese generals in 1769.

Pagan appears to have been destroyed by the Chinese-Tartar army under Nestardin. The new capital, Tsagain, on the right bank of the Irawady, about 100 miles above Pagan, and opposite to where the Theinneé route from China opens on the Burmese plain, was founded in A.D. 1332,[2] and destroyed in 1364, according to the Shan chronicle, by the Pong King, Soo-oop-pha.[3] The capital of Augwa (Ava) was founded in

---

of Bhamô with a seal, which, he was informed, would confer on the king of Ava the same power and authority as the emperor himself possessed over every part of the Chinese empire. The Burmese government questioned at first the propriety of retaining such a gift, as its acceptance might afterwards be construed into an admission that the king of Ava derived his power from the emperor of China, or that the latter confirmed the former's title to the throne of Ava. The value of the gold, however, of which the seal was made, is said to have decided the Burmese to keep it. *As. Soc. Journ.*, vol. vi, pt. i, p. 434.

[1] Colonel Burney mentions that this canal was in existence when he wrote, and used for irrigation; it was known as the Theng-dué-myaung.

[2] Crawford's Ava, Ap. no. viii, p. 34.

[3] Pemberton's North-East Frontier, p 112. Crawford's Ava, loc. cit.

the latter year on the left bank of the Irawady almost opposite to Tsagain. Pemberton[1] states that Major Burney discovered the record of the destruction of Tsagain (Chitkaing) and Penya, recorded in the sixth volume of the Maha Yazwen, or great history of Ava, where the ruin of both cities is said to have been effected by the Shan King, Thokyenbwa. From its position the new capital was exposed to the inroads of the Chinese and Shans by the Theinnee route, which has been recognised for centuries as a highway from China to Burmah.

From the events which happened in the beginning of the 15th century, it appears that the Shan state of Theinnee was not at the time tributary to Burmah, for it is recorded in the Burmese chronicle that a Chinese army advanced, in 1412, along the Theinnee route to assist the Tsawbwa of that town to repel an attack by the Burmese. The Chinese, however, were defeated and compelled to retire. The causes which led to this war are conclusive evidence that Theinnee was an independent state at that time. The father of the chief, who had invited the aid of the Chinese, had marched, in the early part of 1412, with a force to attack Ava, but had been defeated and killed by the Burmese, who followed up their success, and captured the city of Theinnee, from which his son had thought to drive them by the assistance of the Chinese. The incidents of the following year indicate that Theinnee was not the only Shan state to the east and north-east of Ava that lost its independence at this period of the 15th century, and became tributary to Ava, for we read that the Chinese, in 1413, taking advantage of the absence of the Burmese army, which was engaged in a war against the Talains in Lower Pegu, had marched their troops against Ava, and invested the city, demanding the liberation of the families of some Shan chiefs who had made a raid on the Burmese town of Myedu, had been defeated by the Burmese, and had fled to China, leaving their states to the mercy of their conquerors. The Burmese refused to accede to the pretensions of the Chinese, who, being hard pressed for provisions, proposed to settle the dispute by single combat between horsemen chosen from either army. The king of Ava, who had returned victorious from his campaign against the Talains, selected one of his prisoners, Thamein-puran, as the champion of the Burmese army. This redoubtable warrior slew his adversary, and the Chinese retreated to their own territory.

---

[1] Loc. cit., p. 112.

In 1442, a Chinese mission came to Ava to demand vessels of gold and silver which, they alleged, had been presented by Anôra-thá-zô as tribute when he visited China in search of Gandama's tooth. The Burmese refused, and in the following year a Chinese army invaded the kingdom, now demanding the surrender of the Shan chief of Mogoung. There can be little doubt but that this person was Soognampha, of the Shan chronicle, who fled for safety to Ava, after the capture of his capital by the Chinese. On this occasion the Chinese appear to have advanced by the valley of the Shuaylee, for it is stated that the Burmese king went out with a strong force to the north of his capital, and drove the Chinese back to Muangwan. The Chinese, however, renewed their demand for the surrender of the Mogoung chief in 1445, and advanced upon Ava. The king opposed them with a powerful army, but returned to Ava on the representation of his officers that the Chinese would not desist from invading his territories until the Shan chief was surrendered. He resolved to follow this advice, on condition that the Chinese would first subdue Yamitheng, a Burmese town, then in revolt. The Chinese army had followed the king to his capital, and invested it, and improbable as it may appear that a victorious general would accept a conditional surrender, we are told that he acceded to the Burmese stipulation, and reduced the rebel town. In the meantime, however, the unfortunate Mogoung prince had destroyed himself by poison, but his body was given to the Chinese who, after disembowelling it, and drying it by roasting, retired with it to China.

It appears that, in 1449, the Chinese attempted the conquest of the Mogoung or Cis-Irawadian provinces of Pong, but were successfully resisted by the then reigning prince. In other attempted invasions by the Chinese of this part of Upper Burmah, their armies advanced by routes which run through the Momien and Sanda districts of Yunan to Kakhyo and Maingla on the Irawady; but there is no evidence that the Chinese armies have at any time succeeded in crossing the river.

In 1477, an army from the neighbouring empire of Pegu marched through the territories of the king of Ava to the borders of China, and erected a pillar at the town of Khanti to mark the boundary of the empire. On its return, it was attacked by the Burmese, and the Talain General, Thamein-puran, was carried a captive to Ava. The Chinese emperor sent an army to remove the pillar, and his general invaded Ava, and demanded tribute in gold and silver vessels according to established custom.

The Burmese chronicles again reproduce an incident, similar, in all its details, to the one which decided whether the families of the Shan chiefs were to be surrendered. In the combat which, in the present instance, was to determine whether tribute was to be paid or not, the Burmese champion is again said to have been the Talain Chief, Thameinpuran, and Colonel Burney justly remarks that from the fact, that the name and description of the Burmese champion were the same as on the former occasion, a strong suspicion is excited as to the veracity of the Burmese historian.[1]

In 1562, the empire of Pegu had conquered Ava and all its dependencies, and had carried its arms into the Shan states to the north-east of Ava, and up the Shuaylee into the neighbouring valley of Hotha and Latha, into which it introduced Buddhism, and built pagodas and monasteries.[2] In passing, it is worthy of note that two centuries later, the existence of these pagodas in the Hotha and Latha valley was advanced, by a wily Avan diplomatist, as a reason why that valley should be regarded as a part of the territory of his king, ignoring the fact that they had been built by the conquerors of his own country.

In 1601, after the downfall of the Peguan empire, the Tsawbwa of Bhamô established himself as an independent prince. The restoration, however, of the kingdom of Ava happening about the same time, an army invaded his state, and annexed it to the empire. The chief escaped to Yunan, but the king of Ava sent his son to the governor of that province, demanding his surrender, and threatening him with invasion in the event of refusal. The Chinese agreed to deliver up the chief, but he was killed in an attempt to escape: his body, and family, nevertheless, were faithfully transmitted to Ava.

The anarchy which prevailed in South-Western China after the third Tartar invasion,[3] which took place in 1644, shortly after the reign of the Emperor Zonchi,[4] was the cause of another Burmo-Chinese war that lasted nearly three years. After the Mantchoo Tartar rule had been established throughout Eastern China, under the wise government of the boy-king, Chun-chi, with his uncle, Amavan, as regent, the

---

[1] Journ. As. Soc., vol. vi, p. 124.

[2] Pagodas ascribed to this period still exist in the Hotha valley in wonderful preservation. They have all the characters of the Burmese pagodas, but the highest of them, the Comootonay pagoda, does not exceed 50 feet. The monasteries, too, resemble those of Burmah in their architectural style, but they are much more substantial structures, being built almost entirely of stone.

[3] Tartar Conquests of China. Haklyut Soc., 1854, p. 15, et seq. Du Halde's China, p. 227.

[4] Hwae-tsung of Gutzlaff's Chinese History, vol. i, p. 431; the Khaytsong or Tsoung-ching of Du Halde.

Tartar armies were fully occupied for some years in subduing the south-western parts of the empire, in which certain Chinese princes had attempted, with the support of the princes of the Taimin family, to establish independent kingdoms. Notable among these was Yunlie,[1] who was prolaimed king at Canton. He was attacked, however, by the victorious Tartar forces under the able Amavan, and forced to abandon his kingdom. He escaped to Yunan, and arrived at Momien (Theng-ye-chow); he made overtures to the Tsawbwa of Bhamô to reside at that town, promising to pay 100 vis of gold to the king of Ava, if he were allowed to do so. As the Tsawbwa declined to forward such a proposition, the fugitive sent back to say that he would become a subject of Ava, and this being approved by the court, he arrived at Bhamô along with the governor of Yunan, and a retinue of 600 men, among whom were many of his nobility. They were all disarmed and forwarded to the capital, and the king gave them the town of Tsagain to reside in. Colonel Burney remarks[2] that the Burmese chronicles endeavour to create the impression that Yunlie was treacherous, and ambitious to found a kingdom for himself in Burmah, and that he was followed by an army which was advancing in two divisions,—one by the Momeit and the other by the Theinnee route. But we have the authority of the Jesuit Father, P. Joseph D'Orleans, that Yunlie's party was so weak that it had to abandon him to his fate, and of Du Halde, for stating that he had not sufficient forces to resist the Tartar Regent, Amavan. It is highly improbable, therefore, that the apparently powerful army, which advanced upon Ava during Yunlie's residence at Tsagain, was the remnant of his scattered forces. Yunan at this time, however, was the asylum of the

---

[1] The Jesuit, Pierre Joseph D'Orleans (Haklyut Soc., Tartar Conquerors of China) states that Yunlie was not far from the kingdom of heaven, and that his wife and son were baptised by the names of Helen and Constantine, and that he had the Jesuit Father, Cofler, attached to this court, and that he sent another priest to Rome to give in his alligeance to the Vicar of Jesus Christ, loc. cit., p. 24. Du Halde says that the Father, Andrew Cofler, instructed the emperor's mother, his wife, and eldest son in the truths of Christianity, and baptised them. "It was expected," he continues, "that this emperor would one day be the Constantine of China, which name was given to him when he received the sacrament of spiritual regeneration;" loc. cit., p. 228. Gutzlaff, who was not very accurate, mentions that the emperor himself was a convert, and that his general officers were all Christians, and that his court was filled with converts. Du Halde relates that he kept his court at Shanking, the capital of the province of Queychew, loc. cit., p. 229. Gutzlaff's History of China, vol. ii, p. 19, et seq.; Du Halde, vol. i, p. 228, et seq.: Universal History, vol. viii, p. 494.

[2] Loc. cit., p. 126.

rebel army of the incarnate fiend, Chamienchou,[1] a robber chief, who had committed the most revolting barbarities in the provinces of Honan, Kyangnan, Kyangsi, and Sechuen, and had proclaimed himself king in the latter under the name of Lewang. He was shot by a Mantchoo arrow in an expedition against the province of Shensi, and his army was dispersed, and fled in great haste to Yunan; and it is probable that this army of robbers, being aware by bitter experience that it was powerless against the Tartars, may have tried its fortune by a raid on Burmah,[2] but whatever may have been its source, it appears unlikely that the army, which followed on Yunlie's retreat to Burmah, was a remnant of his regular forces. The Burmese historian records that it twice advanced on Ava, and besieged the capital, but was forced to retire on both occasions. In the first attack, a foreigner, Mithari Katan,[3] along with some native Christians, rendered good service to the Burmese, and were the means of the discomfiture of the Chinese. Notwithstanding the presence, on these two occasions at Ava, of this so-called army of the fugitive Chinese emperor, he remained inactive at Tsagain,—conduct which we can hardly reconcile with the theory that it was his, and that he was ambitious to found a kingdom in Burmah.

Yunlie, while a fugitive in Burmah, retained the title of emperor, and the Tartars, fearing he might attempt to regain a position in China, resolved to demand his surrender. For this object an army of 20,000 men, under the command of the governor of Yunan, advanced as far as Yung-peng-long, and sent a mission to the king of Ava, demanding Yunlie, and threatening, on refusal, to attack Ava. The Burmese, fully aware of the power of the Tartars, and anxious to escape another war, were glad to avail themselves of the surrender of the Pong king to the Chinese, and the Tsawbwa of Bhamô by the Chinese to Burmah, as precedents, which would justify their king in complying with these demands; and Yunlie, along with his two queens,[4] was accordingly delivered up

---

[1] Universal History, vol. viii, p. 499. D'Orleans' History. Tartar Conquerors. (Haklynt Soc.) p. 26. Gutzlaff, p. 20, et seq. Du Halde, loc. cit., p. 228, quoted by Burney. As. Soc. Journal, vol. vi, note to p. 126.

[2] In the Universal History it is stated, evidently on the authority of Du Halde, that at the above period a great number of Chinese fugitives out of Yunan fell upon, and reduced, the neighbouring territories: vol. vii, p. 153.

[3] Burney, l. c. In connection with an European manning the guns in Ava, along with certain native Christians, Colonel Hannay mentions a village, called Tsa-khyet, in the Madeya district, in which there are people called the king's gunners, and that several of them have light hair and eyes.

[4] His queens, however, were honourably treated, and separate palaces allotted to them. When D'Orleans wrote, he mentions one queen who was still alive, and that the loss of her liberty had in no way affected her faith.

to the Tartars on the 15th January, 1662, and taken to Pekin and strangled,[1] after more than eleven years had elapsed since the loss of his kingdom.[2]

As the history of Yunan is so intimately connected with the wars between China and Upper Burmah, it may be as well to indicate the position in which this province stood to the government at Pekin, at the period which I am now describing. In 1651 A.D., or thereabouts, the Chinese General, U-san-ghey,[3] who had been the means of bringing the Tartars into China to assist him in dethroning the usurper, Licon, was rewarded by Chun-chi, when he ascended the throne, at the age of fourteen years, on the death of his uncle, Amavan, in 1651, with the title of king of the province of Yunan.[4] He does not appear to have been a person of distinguished family, for D'Orleans speaks of him as an individual who had raised himself, by his great talents, to the very first place among the Chinese as a general. He describes him as a patriot passionately devoted to the Chinese dynasty and to his country. It was his intense devotion, to the interests of the royal family, that prompted him to call in the aid of the Tartars to quell the rebellion raised by the usurper Licon, but when this was accomplished, and the Tartar Chun-chi was proclaimed as emperor, under the guardianship of his uncle Amavan, no one was more sincere than U-san-ghey in regretting the great mistake he had committed, in seeking assistance from such a quarter, and he used to say that he had sent for lions to drive away dogs. For a time, however, he became reconciled to the Tartar rule, as he was highly esteemed at the Tartar court, and had won the friendship of the great Amavan. He

---

[1] According to Gutzlaff, whose account of Yunlie's fate differs from every other record of it that I know of, "Woosankwei (U-san-ghey) was the governor of Yunan and Kwei-chew (Quey-chew), which he had received from the Mantchoo emperor under the name of a principality. A rebellion had been organised in Quey-chew, and Yunlie was called to take possession of the province; but he was intercepted by the treacherous U-san-ghey, who strangled the unhappy emperor, and dispersed his small army;" loc. cit., p. 25.

[2] The Tartar General, Amavan, who had destroyed Yunlie's power in Canton, died, according to D'Orleans, in 1651, some years after that event; and as Yunlie arrived in Burmah in 1658, he must have been more than seven years a fugitive in Yunan during the reign of U-san-ghey; D'Orleans, loc. cit., p. 67.

[3] Du Halde, loc. cit., p. 227. D'Orleans, loc. cit., p. 18. Modern Universal History, vol. viii, p. 484.

[4] D'Orleans, p. 54. Du Halde, p. 227. Du Halde, who makes him king of Shensi, is quoted in Universal History, p. 483, and Gutzlaff, evidently deriving his information from the former source, commits a similar error.

reigned in Yunan for 28 years, and made Yunan city his capital, but the last seven years of his life were spent in open rebellion against the Tartar monarchy. He issued a proclamation[1] in 1672, calling upon all brave Chinese to join themselves to him to drive from the heart of their country the common enemy which oppressed her. He was at first joined by the kings of Fokien and Canton,[2] and he also succeeded in attaching to his cause the powerful and warlike Mongsan, Tartar Lamas, by ceding to them part of his territory in Tibet, lying between the Irawady and Va-young-ha[3] rivers. With such powerful allies, the success that attended his arms was so great, that it was thought that the Tartar emperor would have had to retire to his native country. The tide of fortune, however, in the long run, flowed in favour of the Tartars, and the Fokien and Canton princes returning to their allegiance, left the brave old patriot to fight single-handed for the independence of his country. All his family, except one grandson, had been kept at Pekin as hostages for his fidelity, and when he rebelled, they were put to death. After that event, to show his party that he never meant to be reconciled to the Tartars, and not choosing to take the name of emperor himself, because he said he was too old to change his condition, he caused it to be assumed by his grandson.[4] According to D'Orleans, he retained his dignity and reputation to the last, in 1679, against all the efforts of the Tartar power. The guardianship of his successor had been

---

[1] The following translation of the proclamation is given by the Jesuit D'Orleans:— "When I summoned the Tartars to the assistance of the emperor, my master, against the rebels who attacked him, and who endeavoured to usurp the monarchy, I gave an opportunity, without intending it, to these nations to seize upon it themselves. It now causes me the most painful regret, and my conscience reproaches me continually for the evil I have brought down on my country, by reducing it beneath this tyrannical yoke. I am afraid that heaven will be irritated against me, and will punish me severely if I do not make any effort to repair my fault. I have been a long time reflecting (he was now about eighty years of age) upon the means, and making the necessary preparations for the execution of this enterprise. If my fellow-countrymen will assist me in the smallest degree to carry out my design, we shall accomplish it with ease. I have men devoted to me, without reckoning the auxiliary troops which are provided me from various kingdoms; I am in no great want of money to maintain them: I therefore invite all brave Chinese to join themselves to me to drive from the heart of our country that common enemy which oppresses her." Loc. cit., pp. 55-56.

[2] The so-called kings of the large provinces of China were kings only in name, for the government was entrusted solely to mandarins appointed by the emperors, whose policy it was to provide empty titles for the princes of the blood, and not to permit them to reside at court, or take any part in the administration of state affairs. D'Orleans, loc. cit., p. 54.

[3] Du Halde, vol. ii, p. 385.

[4] D'Orleans, loc. cit., p. 59.

entrusted to one of his generals, who was defeated in 1681 by the Tartars, and the youthful emperor in his extremity died by his own hands, and with him ended the war of independence in Yunan.

After the surrender of Yunlie in 1662, the Burmese and Chinese appear to have continued in peace for more than a century, and no sooner was the war at an end than the highways from China to Bhamô were frequented by traders and travellers. Immediately before the outbreak of the next war in 1765, the trade appears to have been of considerable importance. We read [1] of large caravans of three and four hundred oxen, and others of two thousand ponies, carrying silk and other merchandise between China and Bhamô. Moreover, from the circumstance that four Chinese travellers,[2] who visited Ava about the middle of the 17th century, probably soon after the cessation of the war, mention that there was a Chinese custom-house at the last village on the borders of Yunan, five days from Momien,[3] it is more than likely

---

[1] Colonel Burney, loc. cit., pp. 128-129.

[2] Modern Universal History, vol. vii, p. 129. Edin. Phil. Journ., 1820, vol. iii, p. 34.

[3] These travellers came from the city of Yunan, first to Yungchan in eighteen days, from thence to Momien in four, and in five more to the last village on the borders of Yunan and China, a fatiguing way through woods full of tigers, but no elephants. At this village, where there were a custom-house and garrison, they embarked on a river, and in twenty days reached Ava. The river could have been no other than the Irawady, but the author of the Modern Universal History makes it the Lu-kyung or Salween, which is absurd. The distances given by these travellers are wonderfully accurate, and from the fact that they describe their way as lying through a forest, I suppose them to have followed the hill road. Tigers are not uncommon in the thickly wooded parts of the country. Buchanan Hamilton (Edin. Phil. Journ., 1820, vol. iii, p. 35) supposes the Chinese travellers to have embarked on the Tapeng. If they did so, it must have been to the west of the Kakhyen hills in the Irawady valley, because the former river is not navigable to the east of those hills. But this supposition of Buchanan Hamilton's was due to the circumstance that he believed the Tapeng to be the river which flowed past Muangwan. Now, however, from our advanced knowledge of the geography of the country through which the travellers passed, we are aware that the Tapeng does not approach Muangwan, which is situated on one of the affluents of the Shuaylee. But unfortunately for his hypothesis, the Shuaylee itself is not navigable for boats above Muangmo. There is this fact also to be taken into consideration, that the river on which the Chinese embarked is described as larger than that of Siam, which both the Tapeng and Shuaylee are not. I have no doubt that the custom-house and garrison were in the Kakhyen hills, as they were prior to the Mahomedan rebellion, and, if so, the garrison village could not have been on the banks of any navigable stream, for the Kakhyen affluents of the Irawady are, as a rule, mountain torrents. The explanation I would offer is this—that the village spoken of must have been so near the exit of the Tapeng from the Kakhyen hills where it is navigable that the village and the river were reached in the same march, and were described as one incident.

that a trade had flourished prior to 1662. It is improbable that the few years, which elapsed between the conclusion of the peace and the date of their travels, could have sufficed for the development of so much mercantile enterprize. It is unnecessary, however, to search for arguments to prove that a commerce of a kind had thriven in the neighbourhood of Bhamô before the war of 1662, if we accept Marco Polo's account[1] of South-Western China, which carries us back to near the end of the 13th century.

The next disastrous war[2] with China, which began in 1765, arose out of a misunderstanding between certain Chinese traders and the Burmese officials at Bhamô.[3] An enterprising Chinese trader, Loli by name, requested permission of the Bhamô officials to throw a bridge[4] across the Tapeng at the village of Namba, a few miles from the town where the road to China, by Ponline, Ponsee, and Manwyne, reaches the right bank of the Tapeng. The officials declined to sanction the proposal on their own responsibility, but offered to refer it to the ministers at Ava. Loli, annoyed at their obstructiveness, became disrespectful and impertinent, and they, suspecting that he was a Chinese officer in disguise, seized him, and forwarded him as a prisoner to Ava, with a report of his conduct. He was imprisoned, but the ministers, failing to detect that he had any political object in making the proposal, released him, and sent him back to Bhamô, with instructions that he was to be allowed to trade as usual, and to construct a bridge if he wished to do so. On his return to Bhamô, he complained to the officials that his goods had been tampered with in his absence, and demanded compensation, which was refused. On his arrival at Momien, he complained to the governor that Chinese

---

One of the old Chinese garrison villages is Nampung, distant four hours' march from where the Tapeng debouches on to the Burmese plain. We made eight marches from the foot of the Kakhyen hills to Momien, but the journey might be easily accomplished in five or six by men untrammelled by mules and heavy baggage. The Chinese took five days from Momien to reach the river on which they embarked for Ava.

[1] Marsden's Marco Polo, p. 447.

[2] Gutzlaff ascribes its origin to the inroads of the Burmans on the Chinese frontier; loc. cit., vol. ii, p. 55.

[3] This was during the reign of the Chinese Emperor, Keen-lung, who ascended the throne in 1736, and reigned for sixty years, at last abdicating in favour of his son Kew-king. The Mahomedans of the western frontier and those near Kansun successively revolted during Kew-king's reign, but were finally subdued.—Chinese Repository, vol. ii, p. 127.

[4] Our expedition went by the Ponline route across the Kakhyen hills, and one of the first improvements in the road that suggested itself to us was a bridge across the Tapeng, at the same village at which the enterprising Loli had offered to construct one a century ago.

traders were ill-used at Bhamô, and that the officials had falsely accused him with the object of appropriating his merchandize. He then proceeded to Yunan city, and made a similar complaint to the Tsauntû, who declined to interfere, until his statement was further substantiated. He had not, however, to wait long for additional proof, for another trader, who had arrived at Kaungtoung-myo,[1] a short way to the south of Bhamô, at the head of a Shan and Chinese caravan of 2,000 ponies, and sold some goods on credit to the Burmese, was refused payment. A feud ensued in which a Chinaman was killed, and the surrender of the murderer to the Chinese chief being declined, the latter returned to the Tsauntû accompanied by some of the principal traders, and laid a formal complaint before him. A number of Burmese refugees were at this time resident in Yunan, among whom were the ex-Tsawbwas of Bhamô, Theinnee, and Kaungtoung, who used their influence with the Tsauntû, and urged him to report the ill-treatment of the Chinese traders to the emperor. This had the desired effect, and an army advanced upon Burmah, and besieged Kaungtoung, the Tsawbwa of which rebelled, and joined the Chinese. The king of Ava sent an army against the invaders, and dislodged them from before Kaungtoung. The Chinese retired to some earth-works which they had thrown up on the banks of the Tahô,[2] but they were again forced to retreat before the Burmese, who are reported to have followed them up as far as the Mekhaung or Cambodia.

Another Chinese army advanced in 1767, and took up its position on the Shuay-mue-loun[3] mountain at the head of the Hotha valley, and opposite to the Mawphoo hill, at the eastern extremity of the valley of Sanda. From this point it advanced on the Burmese territories in three divisions. One proceeded by the Nuaylet and Muangwan route against Bhamô, and another by Nantin and Sanda, and from the latter town it marched in a north-westerly direction to the Lizo mountain, to the east of Kakhyo and Wainmô,[4] on the left bank of the Irawady; the third

---

[1] Kaungtoung appears to have been of quite as much importance as Bhamô.

[2] At Momien the Tapeng is known as the Tahô, or Talô.

[3] The Burmese chronicle describes this hill as lying to the westward of the Cambodia, which it is, but in the same way that the town of Nantin is to the west of that river, from which it is separated by the Salween and Shuaylee. It is now the head-quarters of the Chinese chief, Leesetai, who, we suppose, instigated the attack made on our party between Nantin and Momien.

[4] In Colonel Burney's translation, he says the Burmese general crossed the Kakhyo-Wainmô, but what he meant was that he crossed the Irawady at Kakhyo and Wainmô, two Shan towns on its left bank.

division was sent to support the troops that were advancing on Bhamô, and it took up its position on the Thinza-nuay-lein mountain. Another and independent force of upwards of 50,000 men was posted on a high mountain near Theinnee to threaten the capital. The king of Ava despatched two armies to oppose the two main divisions of the Chinese forces. One proceeded by the land route to Mogoung on the right bank of the Irawady, with instructions to cross the Irawady to the north of Mogoung, and march by the Sanda route against the Chinese. The other proceeded up the river in boats to the relief of Bhamô. In the mean time, however, the first division of the Chinese army had reached Bhamô, where it stockaded itself along the bank of the river; and after leaving a sufficient force for the defence of the stockades, it advanced and besieged Kaungtoung, which was ably defended by its governor, Balamenden. The Burmese general, in his advance up the Irawady, having heard of the siege of Kaungtoung, resolved, if possible, to assist the governor with ammunition. Three Burmese officers volunteered for this hazardous undertaking, and successfully accomplished it. They arranged with the governor of Kaungtoung that the river army should first proceed to the relief of Bhamô, and afterwards fall on the rear of the besieging army before Kaungtoung, and that the governor should make a sortie at the same time. The stockade at Bhamô was carried by the Burmese, and a troop of 1,000 cavalry, which the Chinese general before Kaungtoung had despatched to the assistance of his force at Bhamô, was prevented from advancing by a strong body of Burmese horse, which had been posted along the banks of two streams to intercept communications between Bhamô and Kaungtoung. The Burmese general informed Balamenden of the capture of the Bhamô stockades, and appointed a day on which he would attack the besieging army in the rear. This preconcerted assault on the Chinese position was a brilliant success, and the Chinese fled in disorder to their stockades on the Thinza-nuay-lein mountain, from whence they were driven by the Burmese as far as Muangwan, losing a large number of men, horses, and arms. The western division of the Burmese army marched from Mogoung to oppose the Chinese advancing by the Sanda route. They crossed the river at Kakhyo and Wainmô, and sent a reconnoitering party forward to discover the position of the Chinese. They were met by 1,000 Chinese horse, and the Burmese, decoying them into a narrow defile, attacked and defeated them. The army halted on the right bank of the Tapeng to wait the return of their scouts, who reported the

Chinese army to be stockaded on the Lizo mountain.[1] The Burmese threw the two wings of their army round the mountain to attack the Chinese in the rear, and the Chinese general, unaware of this movement, marched the greater part of his army to the left bank of the Tapeng. His stockades on the mountain were captured shortly after he left by the wings of the Burmese army, and the Chinese who defended them fled precipitately to their general. The two Burmese wings then marched on the rear of the Chinese position on the Tapeng, and the main body of their army crossed the river to attack it in front. The Chinese general, discovering the danger of his position, retreated to a spot beyond the Lizo mountain, where he was again defeated by the Burmese. He fell back upon Sanda, and intrenched himself on a hill overlooking that town.[2] The Burmese army marched to Muangla at the head of the Sanda valley, with the object of intercepting the retreat of the Chinese. The Burmese commander fell sick, and was relieved by the Bhamô general who joined his forces to those at Muangla, and attacked the Chinese, and defeated them, taking a great number of prisoners and horses. He took possession of the eight Shan states of Hotha, Latha, Muangla, Sanda, Muangmo, Tsiguen, Kaingma, and Muangwan, which the chronicle states had heretofore thrown off their allegiance to Ava. He then effected a junction with a Burmese general who had been despatched by the Lú-ta-tshay-nhít-paná route, and advanced on the Chinese army that had been sent by way of Theinnee, and defeated it, and the victory of the Burmese was so complete that only one-third of the Chinese escaped. The generals returned in triumph to Ava in the May of 1767.

But the Burmese had not enjoyed the blessings of peace many months, when their country was again invaded, in 1767, by a powerful Chinese army, which advanced in two divisions, one by the Thinza-nuay-lein (Loaylone) route upon Bhamô, and the other by the Theinnee route, threatening the capital. A Burmese army was sent out in three divisions to oppose the invaders, the main body marching to Theinnee, the left wing by the Momeit route to join the former, and the right wing by the valley of the Myitnge to attack the Chinese in the rear. At first, the Chinese carried everything before them, and the Burmese king had begun

---

[1] This mountain may be one of the high peaks of the Kakhyen hills, probably the one above Ponsee, on which the Kakhyens say the Chinese army once suffered a severe defeat from the Burmese.

[2] The cutting on the hill side overlooking Sanda is ascribed by the Shans to this war.

to despair of success, and to fortify his capital, when the right wing of his army, in the rear of the Chinese, turned the tide of victory. His generals were victorious at all points, and the Chinese retreated in disorder after disastrous losses. The Thinza-nuay-lein division of the Chinese army vigorously attacked Bhamô, which was ably defended by its valiant governor, Balamenden, but as soon as the news of the defeat of their main army reached the Chinese general, he raised the siege, and retreated in haste to Yunan.

The Chinese, however, were not deterred from prosecuting the war, and in the end of the following year, 1769, they marched another army against Mogoung and Bhamô. The army proceeded, in the first instance, to mount Yôyi to the north of Lizo, where the three Chinese generals detached 10,000 horse and 100,000 foot against Mogoung. They then cut a large quantity of timber, and carried it to the banks of the Irawady, and left 10,000 carpenters and sawyers to construct large boats.[1] The main body of the army then advanced upon Bhamô, but we have no clue to the route it followed. Having reached the neighbourhood of that town, it stockaded itself at Shuay-nyaungbeng, 12 miles to the east of Kaungtoung, and leaving a strong body of men to defend this position, two of the generals advanced upon Kaungtoung, and invested it on the land side. They were joined by 500 boats which had been constructed on the upper Irawady, and by means of them they blockaded the town on its river-face. The bold soldier, Balamenden, however, who was still governor of Kaungtoung, successfully resisted

---

[1] Gutzlaff, in his account of this war, records that the Chinese army embarked on the Yang-tse-kiang, which he connects in some mysterious way with the Irawady, and makes the army reach the latter river by boats from the former; loc. cit., p. 53. Dalrymple mentions that he had been informed that "there is a kind of aquatic land carriage; between the Ava river and another large one which traverses part of China, there is a narrow tract of low land; this being overflowed in the floods, much is left behind by the stream over which the carts with goods are transported from one river to the other. This transportation, from leaving one till launching into the other river, takes up about a week. As there is strong reason to presume the river here mentioned is what runs from Yunan through Lassa or Camboja, the trade thither may be commodiously carried on by this track."—*Oriental Repository*, p. 114. The Molay river, about four miles to the north of Bhamô, is navigable for boats during the rains almost as far east as Sanda, from which it is separated by high mountains, and its highest navigable point is about a week's march, of 16 miles a day, from the Cambodia over a mountainous country, and the latter river is 10 days' journey from the Yang-tse-kiang. Gutzlaff's supposition, therefore, of a communication between the Irawady and the Yang-tse-kiang is palpably incorrect, and Dalrymple's account is so vague, in every respect, that it is impossible to say at what part of the Irawady the communication he speaks of diverges to China.

every attack on his position. In the meantime, the Burmese armies had advanced from Ava by three routes: one division had proceeded by the western land route to Mogoung to fortify it, and march against the Chinese forces coming in that direction; another, in two sub-divisions, took the eastern land route; and a third went up the Irawady in boats to Bhamô. When the river force had reached Tagoung and Mali, it fell in with the army advancing by the eastern route, and the general commanding detached a division with orders to proceed to Momeit, and fortify it, and then to watch the course of events, and to take advantage of any opportunity that might offer for attacking the Chinese. Before this, the general directing the river force, having heard of the siege of Kaungtoung, had sent forward four of his officers, with a strong fleet of boats, to throw in provisions and ammunition to the relief of the besieged, which they accomplished, capturing a number of the Chinese boats. One of these officers also landed and stockaded himself with 5,000 men in the rear of the Chinese, to the south of Kaungtoung, while two of the others took up a position, with their boats, behind the island of Kyundo, on the western side of the Irawady, opposite to Kaungtoung, where they were joined by the main body of the river force. A detachment of this division of the army was landed at Bhamô, and cut off the supplies of the Chinese coming by the Nantin road. It then proceeded to attack the Chinese in the rear, but the latter, hearing of this and of the advance of the army from Momeit, sent out two divisions to oppose them, but they were both signally defeated. The Burmese now joined the Bhamô and Momeit divisions, and carried the Chinese stockade at Shuay-nyaungbeng, which is described as having been as large and extensive as a city. The Chinese besieging army was now enclosed on every side by the Burmese, and its fleet of boats being destroyed, and the generals, perceiving the dilemma, began to open negotiations for peace. The Mogoung division of the Burmese army, discovering that the Chinese had halted on the east bank of the Irawady near Naungtálô island above Kakhyo, and that the intention was to construct a bridge across the river, which is described as being narrow there, advanced and took up a position on the right bank, and thwarted the designs of the Chinese.

In the letter containing the terms on which the Chinese generals proposed that peace should be concluded, they attribute the war to an invitation addressed to China by the Tsawbwas of Theinnee, Bhamô, Mogoung, and Kyaing-young, on the Cambodia, advocating an invasion of Ava.[1] It was to this effect:—"We will deliver up the Tsawbwas,

---

[1] As. Soc. Journ., vol. vi, pt. 1, p. 144.

subjects of the descended king, who are now in China; let them be restored to their former towns and situations. And after the Burmese general has delivered up to us all the Chinese officers and soldiers who are in his hands, let him submit to the sun-descended king and great lord of righteousness, and we will also submit to our master, the emperor and the lord of righteousness, that the two countries may continue on the same terms as they always were before; that all sentient beings may be at rest; that there may be no war; and the gold and silver road may be opened." This letter was delivered on the 3rd December, 1769, and was received by certain officers deputed by the Burmese general, but one of these officials, becoming aware that the purport of the letter was a negotiation for peace, told the bearer of it, a Chinese officer of high rank, that it ought to have been delivered on the boundary line between Ava and China, to which the Chinaman assented, but enquired where the boundary line was. He was asked if the Burmese had not built Buddhist pagodas in Hotha and Latha, Muangla, Sanda, Kaingma, Khanti, and Khannyen, and in this he also acquiesced, and mentioned that they were still in existence. The Burman, imagining that he had the advantage, proceeded to point out that the Chinese neither built nor worshipped Burmese pagodas, and that the existence of these religious edifices in these towns was, therefore, conclusive proof that they belonged to the king of Ava; and from this he deduced that the Chinese army ought first to retreat beyond these Tsawbwaships[1] to Momien,

---

[1] From what Buchanan Hamilton states, it would appear that the Chinese had hoped to secure possession of the silver mines at Ponsee in the Kakhyen hills. He remarks that in the above war, 60,000 captives put an end to the Chinese hopes of conquest, and gave the Burmans possession of the valuable mines of Bodwan. These mines are situated in the valley of the Tapeng in the very heart of the Kakhyen hills, about fourteen miles to the east of the Shan valley of Sanda. I doubt very much whether the Burmese ever had any real authority among the wild tribes of these hills, and judging from what I saw, when I lived among them, and when Burmese influence was at its height, it seems to me that the Burmese were as much, if not more, in dread of the Kakhyens, as these hill-men were, of their would-be superiors. Burmese influence is tolerated, not because the Burmans could do much injury to the Kakhyens in their own hills, but because they can bring unspeakable misery upon them by stopping their trade with the plains, from whence they derive nearly all their salt. The king of Burmah keeps up a show of influence before his subjects by giving titles and gold umbrellas to the chiefs, but these wild hill-men, although they have a secret pride in their decorations, are sufficiently far-sighted to understand that they are bestowed as peace offerings. Everything I observed convinces me that Burmese influence in Kakhyen land is merely nominal, so far as the internal affairs of the tribes are concerned; and that although the Burmese are allowed to work the mines to the present day, their presence is merely tolerated for the reasons I have mentioned, and because the Kakhyens have neither the unity of action nor the appliances necessary for mining work.

before it sued for peace. The Chinaman, after listening to these specious arguments, humourously asked the Burman if there was such a place as Taroupmyo in the king of Ava's dominions, and as the latter had a sufficient acquaintance with the history of his country to understand the allusion, the Chinaman followed up his advantage by allowing that the king of Pegu had advanced as far as Hotha, Latha, &c., and built the pagodas, but held that it was analogous to the march of the Chinese army through Burmah as far as Taroupmyo. His adversary had no argument to offer, in return, and the letter was carried to the Burmese general, who summoned thirty of his principal officers to consult on what answer should be returned to it. It was agreed that terms should be granted to the Chinese, but not until the Burmese general, in the absence of all instructions from Ava, and the opposition at first of his own officers, had declared that if his master disapproved, he would take the whole responsibility on himself. The result of the deliberation was communicated to the Chinese who, in return, requested that officers of rank and intelligence from each side should be appointed to settle all points of difference. The representatives from either camp met on the 13th December, 1769, in a large building, with seven roofs, which had been erected for the purpose on the south-east angle of Kaungtoung, and concluded this memorable peace[1] which has derived its name from the

---

[1] "Wednesday, 13th December, 1769, in the temporary building to the south-east of the town of Kaungtoung, His Excellency the General of the Lord who rules over a multitude of Umbrella-wearing Chiefs in the Great Western Kingdom, the Sun-descended King of Ava, and Master of the Golden Palace, having appointed [here follow the names and titles of fourteen Burmese officers], and the Generals of the Master of the Golden Palace of China, who rules over a multitude of Umbrella-wearing Chiefs in the Great Eastern Kingdom, having appointed [here follow the names and titles of the thirteen Chinese officers], they assembled in the large building erected in a proper manner with seven roofs, to the south-east of the town of Kaungtoung, on the 13th December, 1769, to negotiate peace and friendship between the two great countries, and that the *gold and silver road* should be established agreeably to former custom. The troops of the Sun-descended King and Master of the Golden Palace of Ava, and those of the Master of the Golden Palace of China, were drawn up in front of each other, when this negotiation took place, and, after its conclusion, each party made presents to the other, agreeably to the former custom, and retired. All men, the subjects of the Sun-descended King and Master of the Golden Palace of Ava, who may be in any part of the dominions of the Master of the Golden Palace of China, shall be treated according to former custom. Peace and friendship being established between the two great countries, they shall become one like two pieces of gold united into one; and suitably to the establishment of the gold and silver road, as well as agreeably to former custom, the princes and officers of each country shall move their respective sovereigns to transmit and exchange affectionate letters on gold once every ten years." As. Soc. Journ., vol. vi, pt. 1, pp. 146-147.

town of Bhamô. After these negotiations were completed, the Chinese army retired by one of the Bhamô routes, for we are informed that when the Burmese demanded the surrender of all their remaining boats, they promised to comply with the request after they had conveyed their provisions to that town. This answer, however, appears to have been resorted to only as an escape from a humiliating exaction, for they burned them as soon as they reached Bhamô. The Chinese were followed to their frontier by two divisions of the Burmese army, and it is recorded that "only the able-bodied men succeeded in reaching China alive, and that the forests and mountains were filled with countless numbers who died of starvation." The Mogoung division of their army also retired without having accomplished anything, beyond attempting to construct a bridge across the Irawady.

The king of Ava was much dissatisfied with his generals for permitting the Chinese army to escape, and some considerable time elapsed before he would allow them to return to the capital. The conduct of the Chinese generals met with the full approval of their master. With the conclusion of this important peace, the trade between the two countries was re-established, and large caravans of merchandize travelled, as of yore, over the golden road from Bhamô to South-Western China.

The history of the intercourse between Burmah and China, after 1770, is one of peace. Eleven years after the conclusion of the war, and, I suppose, in accordance with the provisions of the treaty of Bhamô, a small party of Shan Tsawbwas was sent by the Burmese as an embassy to Pekin. All the members of the mission, however, were seized and sent to the north of the capital, where they were detained to the end of 1788. Their return to Bhamô was effected by another embassy which started from Ava, by the Theinnee route, in June, 1787, with a letter to the emperor, in answer to one he had sent by an embassy, in the beginning of the same year. In that communication, he had expressed his regret that seventeen years had elapsed since the gold and silver road and gold and silver bridge had been traversed by the ambassadors of the two kingdoms, in accordance with the agreement of 1769, that officers of high rank should pass between the two great countries, in order to foster sincere friendship and esteem.[1] The head of this mission, on its arrival

---

[1] The Woongyee, to whom Sir A. Phayre mentioned the existence of the treaty of 1769, denied that it was more than a mere convention between the generals of the two armies. The fact, however, that the above embassy was sent on the strength of it, seems to indicate that the Burmese of those days regarded it in the light of a binding agreement, the infraction of which might lead to war.

in China, had a conversation with Hoochungtung,[1] the first minister of the empire, on the subject of the Shan Tsawbwas who had been sent as envoys in 1781, and of the danger to life and property that existed on the eastern frontier of Yunan from robbers and escaped criminals, a description which is equally true of the country at the present day. The minister assented to the correctness of the ambassador's observations, and promised to exert himself to have these matters settled as speedily as possible. The Shan Tsawbwas were ordered to be brought back from Kuan-toun in Tartary, and to be forwarded to Yunan, and a promise was given that when the Tsawbwa of Bhamô was found he would be surrendered. This embassy returned, after a journey of 123 days, by the Theinnee route, over which they had travelled to Pekin.

In 1790, a Chinese embassy arrived in Burmah by the Bhamô and Muangwan route, accompanied by several officers of high rank, with presents, and three Chinese princesses for the king of Ava. These so-called princesses were natives of Malong, a town in Yunan, and from the circumstance that their feet were not deformed, after the custom in vogue with Chinese ladies,[2] it is evident that they were women of low rank, and whom the Chinese had imposed upon the amorous propensities of the sun-descended king.[3]

Two years after the arrival of this embassy, a Burmese mission was sent to Pekin, by Bhamô, headed by the Tsawbwa of that district as chief ambassador. Gold plates (vessels of gold and silver) were among the presents sent for the acceptance of the emperor. Buchanan Hamilton[4] has given an account of this mission from materials derived from Colonel Symes, who received them from the Bhamô chief. Bhamô is described as the capital of the ambassador's territory, and as one of the nine principalities of the Shanmas or Mrelap Shans, the Koshanpyi of the Chinese.

We read of embassies arriving at Amarapura, from China, in 1795 and 1796, with presents from the emperor, and Colonel Burney suspects

---

[1] Hoochungtung was the chief minister during Lord Macartney's embassy. The above embassy appears to have been at Pekin during the formal introduction of Lord Macartney, for the Chinese informed Sir George Staunton that ambassadors from Pegu were present.

[2] I was informed by a Panthay official of high rank at Momien, that the feet of the female children of domestic servants and slaves are never dwarfed, and I had a practical illustration of the truth of his statement in the natural feet of his wives' serving-maids.

[3] Colonel Burney mentions that this was not the only occasion on which that king had been imposed upon, for women were also presented to him as daughters of a king of Ceylon and a king of Benares, loc. cit., p. 433.

[4] Edin. Phil. Journ., 1820, vol. iii, p. 32, et seq.

that two or more must have passed between 1796 and 1819. Colonel Symes[1] met the Chinese ambassadors of 1795 at Amarapura, and he mentions that they were represented to him as composing a royal mission from Pekin, but that circumstances led him to suspect that their real character did not rise higher than that of a provincial deputation from Yunan city, a conjecture which, he says, was afterwards confirmed. Colonel Burney,[2] writing on this subject, even goes so far as to state that none of the members of the Chinese embassies, which visited Ava at that period, ever came from Pekin; the letters on gold and some of the presents, he considered, were sent to the viceroy of Yunan, who forwarded them by some of his own officers, who, on their return, did not proceed beyond Yunan. When the Burmese accompanied the Chinese envoys to China, they were made to believe that the reason why these officials did not go as far as the capital was that their presence was required in Yunan, as additional rank had been conferred on them in their absence. No mention is made of the routes by which these embassies travelled.

A Burmese mission proceeded to China in 1823, by Bhamô, over the hills forming the southern side of the Tapeng valley to Muangwan, and from thence through the Nantin valley to Momien, and from this city by Yungchan and Yunan to Pekin. It returned with a Chinese mission which had arrived at Ava in the previous year with presents[3] to the king. Besides numerous valuable gifts, five elephants were sent to the emperor, a fact that seems to indicate that the route presents no great physical difficulties. We gather from the Burmese itinerary of this journey that the Chinese had their garrison stations in the Kakhyen hills to the east of the Shan states, and overlooking Burmese territory. I passed two of these old frontier out-posts, one on the Nampung stream, a few hours' march from the Burmese plain, and another at the village of Loaylone in the very heart of the Kakhyen hills on the embassy route. The head of the mission of 1823, on his return to Ava, was appointed governor of Bhamô.

An embassy from China arrived at Ava in April, 1833, and returned the same year, accompanied by one from Burmah, with valuable presents, among which were five elephants, which were made over to the governor of Yunan to forward to Pekin. This was necessary, as the mission had to proceed a considerable way down the Yang-tse-kiang in boats,

---

[1] Symes's Ava, 1827, vol. ii, p. 18.

[2] As. Soc. Journ., vol. vi, p. 434.

[3] Among the presents we read of a male and female *lo*, a large description of mule, which the Burmese assert to be prolific. Colonel Burney, loc. cit.

It followed the same route from Bhamô as the previous embassy, and from the circumstance that this road has been so frequently used by the ambassadors of the two countries, it is now commonly known as the embassy route to China.

From this brief review of the more important events that have occurred in the Bhamô district, in connection with its routes to China, during the last six centuries, it is evident that they have always been recognised as the chief western highways to that great empire. The only route which has attempted to compete with them is the one by Theinnee, but it has to contend with two insuperable disadvantages, which will always operate against its ever becoming a trading route of importance. I refer to the great distance over which it has to pass before it reaches the Irawady, and to the difficult nature of the country through which it runs, from the point where it reaches the Cambodia, on to Ava. Taking Talifoo as the terminus of our journey, we find that, leaving the Irawady at Bhamô, we can reach that city in twenty-two marches, whereas, following the Theinnee route, we could not arrive at it within thirty-five days. One of the roads (Sanda) from Bhamô to Momien, after 25 miles of the Kakhyen hills have been crossed, runs through a level valley in which there are only two insignificant ascents; and beyond Momien, as far as the Cambodia, the only difficulties it has to contend with, are the mountain ridges which define the courses of the Shuaylee and Salween. By the Theinnee route, however, the case is very different, and consulting the Burmese account of this route drawn up in 1787, we find that forty-six hills and mountains, five large rivers, and twenty-four smaller ones are encountered between Ava and a point on the Cambodia, about 40 miles to the south-east of Yungchan. It appears to me, then, to be beyond all dispute, that the Bhamô routes offer the greatest facilities for travel, are the shortest to the Irawady from the great trading centres of Yunan, and will certainly command the greatest traffic, although they may not absorb it all.

The importance of Bhamô, as one of the gate-ways to China, appears to have been early recognised by those keen traders from Western Europe, who visited the east in the 16th and 17th centuries; and this leads us to another short chapter in its history.

CHAPTER III.

EUROPEAN INTERCOURSE WITH BHAMÔ.

MARCO POLO appears to have been the first European who visited the countries neighbouring Bhamô, and as he seems to have been an eye-witness of the massing of the troops at Yungchan for the protection of the Chinese frontier, he could not have been more than eleven days distant from Bhamô itself.

In his account of the province of Kardandan,[1] as I have already noticed in passing, he has described certain peculiar customs of the inhabitants, which coincide so remarkably with some of those of the Shan and Kakhyen population intervening between Yungchan and Bhamô, that it is hardly possible to avoid the conclusion that the country through which our route lay must have formed part of Marco Polo's Kardandan. The use of tallies, to which the great traveller refers, is still prevalent among the Kakhyens and Shans. A slip of bamboo, about eight inches long, is fractured at intervals. The fractures are simple, and the pieces do not separate from each other. Our mule-men always used this form of tally in reckoning up the number of their mules, and the plan they followed was this: they first prepared a number of bamboo slips, and then passed from mule to mule, making a fracture in the tally for each beast. When we came to settle the payment of the mule-hires, the tallies were produced, and afterwards destroyed. Some of the Shans in our service used to check the number of the mules in the same way, so that there was no necessity for exchanging the tallies if the two numbers agreed. Marco Polo mentions that the tallies are divided, and each party receives one of the corresponding pieces, and it is quite possible that, in transactions among themselves, they may follow that practice, for nothing could be simpler than the longitudinal division of one of these primitive vouchers.

---

[1] In the Jámíut Tawárikh of Rashi-du-d-Dín who has largely copied from Al Bírúní, who wrote between 970 and 1030 A.D., the author enumerates the places met with, in an easterly route from Cabul to Tibet, and mentions Zardandan. He says it is so called because the people cover their teeth with gold. They puncture their hands, and cover them with indigo, and eradicate their beards.

The other custom recorded by Marco Polo, as a characteristic of the inhabitants of Kardandan, is that of consulting, in cases of illness, persons who were supposed, for the time being, to be possessed with a devil. To the present day, the Shans consult sorcerers in all matters of importance, and the Kakhyens resort to the Toomsah in cases of sickness, and to the Meetway when matters of public importance have to be decided. The Toomsah is supposed to stand in some peculiar relation to the nâts,[1] who are believed by the Kakhyens to exercise a powerful influence for good or evil on the every-day incidents of life. When he is employed in a case of sickness, he calls all the nâts together, and the spirit, by whose evil influence the disease has arisen, makes itself heard through him, as to what offerings are necessary for the recovery of the patient. The Meetway, when he is consulted, becomes like a person possessed with a devil. He seats himself in a corner of the house on a small stool, surrounded by the anxious chiefs and their headmen, and with his elbows resting on his knees and his face buried in his hands, his body begins to quiver from head to foot, and piteous yells and groans announce that the nât is entering into him. When the demon has gained possession of the priest, he then communicates the line of action that the chiefs are to pursue, and how many buffaloes or pigs it will be necessary to offer to secure the good-will of the nâts. The similarity of these ceremonies to those described by Marco Polo as prevailing during his time in Kardandan requires no remark. Moreover, the way in which the sacrifices are offered to the nâts by the Kakhyens agrees so closely with the Venetian's description of the Kardandan sacrificial rites that I will here briefly relate what I have seen.

At Bhamô, two buffaloes were sacrificed to the nâts, over two separate but primitive altars of bamboo that had been specially erected for the purpose, and consecrated by the Toomsah. During the latter ceremony, he stood in front of each of them for more than an hour, waving a bunch of long grass, and muttering an incantation, inviting the nâts from all parts of the world to be present to witness the sacrifice, and receive the offerings of flesh which were to be

---

[1] The Kakhyens are not Buddhists, but propitiate the spirits of evil, nâts, by offerings of pigs, buffaloes, rice, and sheroo. They recognize good nâts, but never worship them. The nâts of the Burmese are, in all probability, a remnant of this form of worship that prevailed in Burmah before the Burmese were converted to Buddhism.

given. The buffaloes were slain, not by the priest, but by one of the bystanding Kakhyens, but before the death-blow was given, water held in a plantain leaf was thrown over the sacrificial buffalo, and when the animal had received the fatal gash from the dâh, water was poured into the wound, and the blood collected in bamboos. The carcass was then cut into pieces, and distributed to the chiefs and their attendants. The entrails and viscera were reserved for the special use of the nâts, boiled along with some of the blood in a large iron pot, and a cut off the breast as well was roasted on sticks placed crosswise over a fire. These parts, along with some cooked rice, were placed on plantain leaves, and laid out reverently on a high bamboo scaffolding, in front of which the Toomsah waved his bunch of grass, and chanted an incantation, in a low musical strain. No Kakhyen dares to eat until this part of the ceremony has been completed, and so particular were the chiefs on this subject that they made a special request to us, that we would abstain from food while it lasted, so that the nâts might have no cause of offence. This is a remarkable comment on Marco Polo's statement that the Kardandaners believed, that if a man died after a sacrifice had been offered on his account, it was due to the fact that those who had dressed the victuals must have presumed to taste them before the deity's portion had been presented to him. It appears to me, too, that the elevation of the flesh on the high platform corresponds to the sprinkling of the blood towards the heavens, and to the casting into the air of the water in which the flesh had been seethed, so carefully described by the distinguished traveller as a part of the sacrificial rites of the inhabitants of Kardandan. With the completion of the ceremony of the elevation of the flesh and its juices, the Kakhyens retired to their temporary quarters to eat and drink, and I have been informed that when a sacrifice of the kind I have described takes place in a Kakhyen village, it is followed by a great feast and carnival; and Marco Polo relates that in his time, the Kardandaners completed their sacrificial rites by a feast on the meat that had been offered in sacrifice, and by drinking with signs of great hilarity.

The Shans, unlike the Kakhyens, have accepted Buddhism, which knows nothing of sacrifices, and is utterly opposed to the taking of animal life by its disciples, although they are at liberty to partake of what has been slain by others. But it is highly probable that before the introduction of Buddhism from Pegu, the Shans, like the Burmese, had the same respect for the principle of evil in everything that was opposed to their self-interest, as marks the Kakhyens of the present day. Apart from these coincidences, we find other facts recorded by Marco Polo, in his chapter on Kardandan, which strengthen my position regarding the identity of Kardandan and the Shan states to the east of Bhamô, and the country beyond it, as far as Yungchan. In his day, an ounce of gold was exchanged for five ounces of silver, and a saggio of gold for five saggio of silver, the reason assigned being that there were no silver mines in the kingdom, but much gold. And in his account of the trade that existed between Kardandan and the Burmese plains, he mentions that the inhabitants took their gold to the mart on the Irawady to be exchanged for silver, one saggio of gold being given for five of silver. My observation on this is, that silver now is the most highly-prized metal in the Shan states, and that gold is at a discount at Momien. I am well aware that a mere coincidence of this kind, between the monetary affairs of a people separated from each other by centuries, is not of itself sufficient to establish their identity; but it is unnecessary for me to resort to any such extreme argument in this instance, for the great traveller has so sufficiently indicated the geographical position of the province of which he was writing, that it is impossible to doubt that his Kardandan, and the country in which we experienced this anomalous disproportion between the values of the precious metals, are one and the same. Marco Polo describes Kardandan as the Chinese province of which Vochang is the capital, but as Marsden[1] justly remarks, we would have been unable to localise the province itself if this town had not been mentioned, and proceeds to say that "the name, indeed, of Vochang (or Voccain in the old Italian orthography) would have been equally unascertainable with that of the province itself, but that we are assisted in this instance by the readings of some of the other versions."[2] It is certainly a remarkable circumstance that little or no change should have taken place between the relative values of the metals in the course of the five centuries; but so far as my knowledge goes, Marco Polo's assertion that there were no silver mines does not apply to the present time. There are two mines within a few miles of the western end of the Sanda valley, and another exists a short way to the west of the Shan town of Kaingma. But the two former lie on the now debatable territory of the Kakhyen hills, and have for many years been almost exclusively

---

[1] Marsden's Marco Polo, p 437, note 852.

[2] In the early Latin edition the word is "Uncian;" in the Balse, "Unchian," and in the early edition of Venice, "Nocian," which point out the city to be Yungchan in the western part of Yunan. Marsden, loc. cit.

worked by the Burmese, who carry the silver into Burmah, and the one at Kaingma as well appears to have been worked by them. The Shan states, therefore, derive little or no benefit from the proximity of these mines. Another mine, however, exists to the north-east of Momien, but the silver from it is chiefly absorbed by the country beyond. It appears to me that the real cause of the disproportionate value of the two metals is to be sought for in the inordinate love of the Shans for every variety of silver ornaments, and which leads them to convert all their surplus silver into trinkets of some kind, and with this result, that the amount of this precious metal in circulation never has an opportunity to increase. I cannot leave this subject, without mentioning that a Kampti Shan from the country above the junction of the so-called main branches of the Irawady, at the Mainla of the maps, on the 26° parallel of north latitude, informed me that the tribes of that part have no silver, and that they trade with gold, and that 50 ticcals of salt are purchased for a four-anna piece weight of gold. While I accept the general fact, I doubt the details, which are probably grossly exaggerated.

Marco Polo refers to a custom which the men and women had of covering their teeth with plates of gold, but which does not now exist, although the nearly allied one, as I have already mentioned, of blackening the teeth, prevails among Shan women, but the custom also extends to Burmah, and even to India. He also describes a curious usage of the husband taking the place and duties of the wife for forty days after her delivery; but I could detect no trace of any such custom among the Kakhyens, neither am I aware of its existence among the Shans, nor in any of the hill tribes we were brought in contact with. His general statement that "they (the people of Kardandan) have no knowledge of any kind of writing," while it does not apply to the Shans, is perfectly true of the Kakhyens (Singphos), Leesaws, and Poloungs, who form a large portion of the hill population between Bhamô and Yungchan.

It is interesting to note that the description which Marco Polo has given of the summer season of Kardandan, that it is so gloomy and much obscured[1] that strangers are glad to escape from it, was exactly our experience of a June and July residence at Momien. The inhabitants themselves, too, recognise that new-comers invariably suffer, and one of the first monitions we received from the governor related to the

---

[1] Marsden, in a note on this statement, seems to have been under the impression that his author was describing a country like the Terai land of the Himalaya, while his discourse referred to a country at least from 1,700 to 5,000 feet above the sea.

preservation of our health, accompanied by a warning that it would certainly be injured if we bathed in the river water. The inhabitants of Momien attribute the prevalence of goitre among them, and the ill-health which strangers experience when they visit their city, to the use of the water of the Tahô. We were dissuaded against its use in such strong terms as to create the impression that it was the fountain-head of all the ills that flesh is heir to, in this sequestered and now almost deserted valley, the desolation of which, however, is due to an entirely different cause, the Mahomedan rebellion. The mist and gloom, which prevail at Momien during the summer months, are proverbial; and the best comment I can offer on our traveller's description of the climate is our own experience. During a residence of a month and a half, we had only two or three fitful gleams of sun through dense clouds, which were incessantly discharging themselves, either in vapoury drizzle or in heavy showers. The depressing influence of such a climate soon made itself felt on all, and nearly every one of us suffered more or less from an obstinate diarrhœa. The proportions of some were sensibly reduced, and in one case it led to the development of serious symptoms that called for an immediate change of scene, and for a residence at a lower altitude. But the most striking proof of the trying nature of the summer climate of Momien to strangers was evinced, in the rapid and marked improvement that took place in the health of the men, when we reached the lower valleys.

Marco Polo, in his chapter on Karazan, which probably corresponds to the district to the north-east of the Kananzan mountain, north-east from Momien, relates that the inhabitants docked the tails of the horses, depriving them of one joint, to prevent their being whisked from side to side, and to occasion their remaining pendant, as the whisking of the tail in riding appears to them a vile habit. Now, the Shans and Chinese to the east of Bhamô hold the same views on tail-whisking, but they do not resort to the custom described by Marco Polo to obviate it. Their practice is simply to tie the long hair at the end of the tail into a knot, as is done in Persia.[1] The nature of the country and the character of the roads have originated this custom. During the rains, the whole of the valleys are more or less under water, and the roads are frequently flooded; so the traveller has to pick his way, as he best can, over the highest ground, and along the banks which define the fields, and with this result that the pony is frequently up to its middle in water. A well-draggled tail is the consequence, and to prevent its being whisked

---

[1] Malcolm's Persia, vol. i. p. 358, note.

about to the discomfort of the rider, it is tied up into a large knot. Marco Polo describes the horses of large size, and that they are ridden with long stirrups, which is the opposite of what I found in the Shan states, where only ponies and mules occur, and where the short stirrup is used. He mentions also that the men wear complete armour of buffalo-hide, and carry lances, shields, and crossbows, and that all their arrows are poisoned.[1] These are the familiar weapons of the country, but armour and shields, as far as my observations go, are not in use.

Turning now to Marco Polo's description of the country intervening between Kardandan and the Burmese plain, we are struck with the remarkably accurate but brief account which he has given of it. His words are,—"Leaving the province of Kardandan, you enter upon a vast descent, which you travel without variation for two days and a half, in the course of which no habitations are to be found. You then reach a spacious plain." I do not know of any more correct description that could be given of the descent from the Shan states over the Kakhyen hills to Burmah than this of the great traveller's. The words, "vast descent," convey a truthful picture of the road; and the valley of the Irawady, when viewed from the Kakhyen hills, appears as a spacious plain. Moreover, starting from the Shan-Chinese town of Manwyne at the eastern end of the Sanda valley, where the descent begins, the journey occupies exactly two days and a half. So closely does his account of the route to Burmah coincide with the two roads that follow the valley of the Tapeng over which I travelled, that I cannot but conclude that it referred to one of them; but his description being devoid of details, it is impossible to say which of the two routes he had in view. I have no personal experience of the only other route to Burmah from this quarter of the Shan states, which opens on the Burmese plain; but I can adduce the evidence of our surveyor, who travelled it, to show that it is not a vast descent. The latter, speaking of the Sawaddy and Muangwan route, says,—"It is smooth and even throughout, and there are no difficulties of a nature to induce fatigue or wretchedness." This was evidently written in vivid remembrance of his journey by the "vast descent." As the Muangwan route, therefore, can in no way be described as a vast descent, it must be disregarded, and Marco Polo's description must be held as applying to one of the two roads that follow the Tapeng valley to Bhamô. Moreover, that it could not have been any other route further to the south is evident from the fact that it

---

[1] The poison used by the Kakhyens and other wild tribes is the Aconitum ——? known also to the Lepchas and other hill tribes of Nepal, Sikkim, and Assam.

reached the Burmese plain fifteen days' march north of the capital. Marsden has pointed out that from the early Italian versions, it is to be understood that, on descending from the heights of Karainan or Yunan, you do not immediately enter the country of Mien or Ava Proper, but, after a journey of five days, reach a province which he supposed to be the Mekley of the maps; and from thence, after travelling fifteen days through forest, arrive at the capital. Mekley, however, is about three degrees further west, so that Marsden's supposition must fall to the ground. Reverting, however, to the history of Pong, and to the indication I have given of its southern limits on both banks of the Irawady, we are entitled to conclude that it was the province referred to in the early Italian editions, as intervening between the trading mart and Pagan, the capital of Mien. The distance from Old Bhamô, in which neighbourhood the mart appears to have been situated, to the capital, by land, in a straight line, is about 250 miles,— a journey which, after making allowances for the windings of the road, could be easily accomplished in fifteen days. He describes the road as lying through a country much depopulated, and through forest abounding with elephants, rhinoceroses, and other wild beasts, where there is not the appearance of any habitation. On the likely supposition that all Marco Polo's information regarding Burmah was derived from Chinese traders, who had doubtless been much struck by the scanty population of Pong and Burmah, as contrasted with their own densely-peopled provinces, we can easily understand how they came to describe it to him as one much depopulated, whereas they were only delineating what appears to have been always a characteristic of Burmah, its paucity of population. Even at the present time, a large tract of the country between Bhamô and Mandalay is covered with forest, and from enquiries I made on my way up the river, and from personal observations in the neighbourhood of the latter town, wild elephants are not uncommon, and I was informed that rhinoceroses were occasionally met with.

With reference to the probable position of the mart described by Marco Polo, it follows, from the position which I have assigned to his route to Burmah from Kaudandau, that it must have been situated somewhere in the Bhamô district, and I believe we must look for it in the direction of Old Bhamô, on the right bank of the Tapeng, at the foot of the Kakhyen hills, 30 miles to the north-east of the present town of that name.[1]

---

[1] Pemberton placed Bhamô on the left bank of the Tapeng river some distance above its confluence with the Irawady, and not on the banks of the latter river. From the present position of the town on the left bank of the Irawady, it is evident that the courses of the two rivers have been materially altered since Pemberton wrote.

I passed close to this old town on our way across the Kakhyen hills by the Ponline route, and although I did not stop to visit it, it bore evident marks, in its ruined pagodas and general appearance, that it had once been a place of considerable importance. We have no facts to guide us, as to when Old Bhamô was abandoned as a trading station for the other town of the same name on the Irawady. The circumstance, however, that the first mention of the rival mart of Kaungtoung occurs after the long peace of a century, which ensued on the surrender of the Emperor Yunlie in 1662, suggests that the rise of that mart may have been the cause of the change. I think we are entitled to conclude that the desertion of Old Bhamô took place before the outbreak of the war, because it is stated in the Burmese chronicle, that when the Burmese fleet was proceeding to invest the town, the boats moved from the island opposite the beleaguered mart of Kaungtoung, along the western bank of the Irawady, and then crossed to Bhamô, implying that it was on the opposite side. This description is quite inapplicable to Old Bhamô, 20 miles up the Tapeng, a river which is besides not navigable for very large boats in February and March, the months in which the Burmese fleet performed this manœuvre. It appears that the abandonment of Old Bhamô was brought about in this wise. Continued peace had given a great impulse to trade, and the merchants naturally resorted to that route which presented the fewest difficulties to travellers. The surveyor who journeyed by the Sawaddy route on his return from Yunan, and who, it must be remembered, had accompanied the expedition by the Ponline route, pronounces it not to be beset with the difficulties encountered on the latter, and that it is smooth and even throughout, as far as Muangwan. Moreover, from personal experience I can state that the embassy route by Hoetone and Mutthin is almost on a par with that by Ponline. We have thus one route surpassing all the others in facilities for travel,[1] and it is reasonable to believe that in the case of a well-established trade, the easiest route, and the one in which the goods of the merchants would be least liable to injury, would be the one generally resorted to; and I do not see how we are to account for the rise of Kaungtoung on any other ground, and I believe that the whole explanation of it may be summed up in these few words, that it was the point on the Irawady nearest to where the Sawaddy and Muangwan (Mynewan) route opens on the Burmese plain. Turning to Bhamô we

---

[1] It must be understood that I speak entirely on the authority of a Burman surveyor.

have now to apply these facts to it, and the application is this, that its merchants found that as the trade began to flow in great measure by Kaungtoung, it was necessary that they should move near that mart, and I daresay they were under the impression that a position like that of Bhamô, occupying, as it does, a site nearly equally distant from the exits of all the routes, would be certain in the end to secure the greatest custom, and if these were their views, they are fully borne out by the experiences of the two marts.

I will now turn from Marco Polo, and relate the little that is known regarding European intercourse with Bhamô after his day, but much of which is simply conjecture. The old documents of Fort St. George record that the English and Dutch had factories in the beginning of the 17th century at Syriam, Prome, and Ava, and at a place on the borders of China which Dalrymple supposes to have been Bhamô.[1] According to this authority, some dispute arose between the Dutch and the Burmese, and on the former threatening to call in the aid of the Chinese, both the English and Dutch were expelled from Burmah. Valentyn, however, in his great work on the East Indies, ascribes the breaking-up of the Dutch trade in Burmah to the constant wars that were going on in those regions, which seems to be a much more likely explanation of its dissolution, especially in view of the facts I have recorded of the great war that took place in Upper Burmah from 1658 to 1661. A telling instance, in support of Valentyn's statement, is the fact that the guns on the walls of Ava in 1658 were manned by a foreigner, who was in all likelihood a trader driven to fight for the protection of his property, which would certainly have been pillaged if the Chinese had carried their assault on the city. Such conditions and occupations were certainly inimical to trade, and it is not to be wondered at, that the first English and Dutch establishments in Upper Burmah were short-lived.

However, after the peace of 1662 had been concluded, as a natural consequence we find a revival of trade. I have on two former occasions referred to the thriving traffic that appears to have existed at Bhamô between 1662 and 1765, while Burmah was at peace with China. In 1680, the reputation of this field for mercantile enterprise appears to have again attracted the attention of the authorities at Fort St. George, and

---

[1] Bayfield describes the remains of an old brick godown at Old Bhamô, of which the people did not know the history, and Yule suggests that it possibly may be the relic of the old British factory of which Dalrymple wrote. Yule's Ava. p. 280.

four years afterwards, letters were sent by one Dod, trading to Ava, who was instructed to enquire into the commerce of the country, and the terms which might be sanctioned, and to express a strong desire that a settlement might be sanctioned at Prammoo on the confines of China. Dalrymple, who records these facts, states that he was unable to determine the situation of Prammoo, but was induced to suppose that it was the place at which we had formerly an establishment. The strong likeness of Prammoo to Bhamô leaves little doubt regarding their identity.[1] This mission proved unsuccessful.

In the end of the 17th century, the Jesuit, Du Chatz,[2] appears to have been in the neighbourhood of Bhamô, and to have entered Burmah from Yunan, a feat which has been accomplished by no other European. He is recorded to have reached Burmah by the same route that the five Chinese travellers had followed in the same century, after the conclusion of the peace of 1662. He has given an account of the Irawady from Ava to the sea, but little or nothing concerning the country and its inhabitants.

The Jesuit missionaries, P. Fridelli and P. Bonjour, were ordered by the emperor of China, in the early part of the 18th century, to proceed to Yunan to complete the map of that province. On the death of P. Bonjour, which happened on the confines of Ava and Pegu, on 25th December 1714, Père Regis was sent to the assistance of P. Fridelli who was sick. We have evidence, in the table of observed latitudes, that they visited the extreme frontier, and from the fact that they inform us that the position of Sanda on their map was the result of several triangles, they must have been in sight of it, if not at the town itself, and within

---

[1] I find that Marsden, Symes, Burney, Yule, and Griffith write Bhamô without the h, and that Burney and Yule correctly place the accent on the last syllable, which Symes, Marsden, and Griffith did not. Pemberton, Bayfield, Buchanan Hamilton, and Crawford all use the h in the first, but Crawford alone accentuates the last syllable. Dr. Bayfield and Buchanan Hamilton are the only two travellers who use the n before the m, and in doing so they adhere strictly to the manner in which the word would be trans-literated into English by a Burmese conversant with our language. But the n sound is so slight that for all practical purposes it is better to leave it out, as the tendency would be to pronounce it, while in practice the n and m are run into each other. With reference to the terminal syllable, after a careful analysis of the pronunciation, I concluded that the sound is best expressed by au or aw instead of simple accentuated ô; but, in deference to established custom, have spelt it after the received fashion. In connection with Dalrymple's word Prammoo, it is worthy of note that Buchanan Hamilton not only writes Bhanmo but also Panmo.

[2] Modern Universal History, vol. vii. p. 121. Du Chatz, Ap. Mem. Acad. Scien., 1692, p. 399.

70 miles from Bhamô. There is no allusion, however, to the latter place in any of the memoirs. They also found the position of Momien by personal observation, and must have, therefore, remained in that city for some time.

The able and versatile Dr. Francis Hamilton Buchanan was the next European traveller to contribute largely to our knowledge of the geographical features of Upper Burmah. This distinguished man accompanied Symes on his mission to Ava in 1795, but the results of the geographical enquiries he instituted, while at the Burmese capital, were not published till 1820. He did not proceed beyond the capital, but so well did he occupy his time, while there, in amassing information from travelled natives, on the course of the Irawady and its principal affluents, on the position of Bhamô, on the physical characters of the country to the east of it, and on the routes from Upper Burmah to China, that he was enabled to speak with considerable accuracy on these interesting geographical questions. He fell, however, into the fashionable error of his time, and connected the Irawady with the Sanpo of Tibet.

In his account of the route followed by the Burmese embassy of 1792, the materials for which were given to him by the Tsawbwa of Bhamô, who had accompanied it as chief ambassador, he describes Bhamô as the capital of the ambassador's territory, and one of the nine principalities of the Shanmas or Mrelap Shans as they are called by the Burmans, or the Payæ (Tay-yay) of the Chinese, a statement the accuracy of which we can hardly doubt when we remember it was made on the authority of the chief himself. He also mentions that Tsampenago[1] was the Burmese town highest on the Irawady. The natural inference

---

[1] With reference to Tsampenago, it is worthy of remark that two cities of that name formerly existed in the neighbourhood of Bhamô, one evidently of great age, and the other of more recent date. The ruins of the former were accidentally discovered by me, in a ramble in quest of birds through the jungle about one mile to the north of the town of Bhamô. I am not aware that its existence has been noticed by any previous traveller. It lies buried under a dense vegetation, and the ruined walls and brick mounds support splendid forest trees. I doubt much, if I had not been fortunate enough to cross the wall, that I would have ever suspected the existence of ruins in the mass of jungle-covered mounds which it encircles. But when the wall is once seen, there is no mistaking its true nature. A very good view of it is obtained on the eastern side of the ruins where the underwood is light. It is surrounded by a deep broad ditch and a high earthen mound, and in some places where I measured it, it varied from 12 to 20 feet above the bottom of the ditch. It is of great thickness, and, as far as I observed, composed entirely of bricks. I traced one side of it for three-quarters of a mile, cutting my way along the top through a dense tangled thicket of bamboos and climbing plants.

The old phoongyee at Bhamô informed me that the ruins were the remains of the ancient city of Tsampenago, which, according to him, had flourished in the days of

from these facts is that, in 1795, the Shan principality of Bhamô was only tributary to Burmah, and that its complete absorption into the empire was an event of after years.

Hamilton, Buchanan, in one of his contributions to the geography of Upper Burmah, informs us that he met in Calcutta a Mahomedan, who had been present at the battle between the Burmese and Chinese. This man informed him that the famous silver mines of Bodwan were six days' journey from Bhamô, and fifteen from Amarapura. I visited these mines during our detention at Ponsee, and can confirm this statement as to their distance from Bhamô; and, moreover, as they are only 200 miles from the capital, fifteen days appear to afford ample time for the journey between the two places.

These mines are situated north-east of Bhamô, in the midst of the Kakhyen hills, only 500 yards from the left bank of the

---

Guadama. He stated that they are well seen after the burning of the jungle in March. It is curious that the northern extremity of the ruins should have become a favourite site for pagodas, and I was at first inclined to believe that it had been selected on account of traditions that associated it with the city, but an intelligent Shan, who built the chief pagoda, assured me that such was not the case. I would not regard his opinion, however, as final, for many of the other pagodas are of considerable age. It is desirable that our officials, now stationed at Bhamô, should enquire into the history of the Shuaykeenah pagodas, as it may tend to throw some light on that of the old ruins, which also merit further investigation. The importance of the site is indicated by the fact that the pagodas number from two to three hundred. If I may venture an opinion as to the probable age of the city, derived from its appearance as compared with Tagoung, I would ascribe to it an antiquity equal to that of that ancient capital.

The other town of Tsampenago stands on the right bank of the Tapeng, below where it is joined by the Manloung. It is apparently of no very great age, as the outline of the pagodas is still more or less intact, but it is in every way a ruin.

The present town of the same name is situated on the left bank of the Irawady, about 60 miles above the capital, at the head of the first defile, or Khyoukdweng. Opposite to it is the town of Manlay, sometimes written Malé. I satisfied myself that the former pronunciation is correct, and it appears to me that the first syllable is the Shan word *muang*, a term corrupted by Burmese influence to *man* or *ma*. This of itself is a kind of evidence which supports the view I have adopted of the southern extent of the Shan principality of Bhamô in former times, and the fact that Tsampenago was originally the name of a Shan city, is a further proof of the correctness of my supposition.

From the extent of the ruins at Bhamô, it is evident that the old city must have been one of considerable importance; and the circumstance that, after its decay or fall, the name was perpetuated in another town, and that when the latter had also become a heap of ruins, we still find it preserved in Tsampenago of the present day, leaves scarcely a doubt that the ancient city must have had some important historical associations that made its name a household word which the Shans were loath to lose.

Tapeng, below the village of Ponsee. Hamilton Buchanan supposed them to be the mines referred to in the Universal History, as lying five days to the north of Mohungleng (Maingleng-gyee), formerly the capital of the Shan states to the east of Ava, but in this he was mistaken, because the great silver mines, the Bodwan-gyee of the Burmese, lie to the north of Maingleng-gyee, half-way between Kaingma and Muangting, 160 miles to the east-south-east of Bhamô. I failed to discover that any other mines existed in the country intervening between those of Bhamô and Kaingma, so that the other Bodwan, which occurs on the map of the north-eastern frontier, published at the Surveyor General's office, Calcutta, in 1867, comprises the mines which are situated on the banks of the Tapeng.

By a reference to the map on which Dr. Buchanan founded his deductions as to the position of Bodwan, it is evident that the native who delineated the country could never have visited what he professed to map, for we find him placing the Shuaylee on the right bank of the Irawady, and making the Tapeng flow to the north-west, instead of in the opposite direction, and locating Muangwan to the north of the latter river. Bodwan is placed beyond the source of the Tapeng, and to the west of Theinnee. Under such a false guide, it is no matter of surprise that the able geographer was misled as to the position of the silver mines of which he was writing, and that he confounded those of the Tapeng with the Kaingma mines. The former lie in the centre of the Kakhyen hills, and the latter in a Shan state a long way to the east of them, remote, if my authorities are correct, from the Kakhyen population of Upper Burmah. These are the only two special references to Bhamô and its immediate neighbourhood, which occur in Hamilton Buchanan's valuable contributions to the geography of Upper Burmah.

Col. Symes states that an extensive trade existed, in 1795, between the Burman dominions and Yunan in China, and that cotton was the chief article of export from Ava. "This commodity was transported up the Irawady to Bhamô, where it was sold to the Chinese merchants, and conveyed, partly by land and partly by water, into the Chinese dominions. Amber, ivory, precious stones, betel-nut, and the edible nests brought from the Eastern Archipelago were also articles of commerce. In return the Burmans procured raw and wrought silks, velvets, gold-leaf, preserves, paper, and utensils of hardware." In connection with Col. Symes's statement that the goods were transported from Bhamô, partly by land and partly by water, it must be observed that all the routes from thence are exclusively land journeys, the merchandise being carried on mules, ponies, and, rarely, on pack-oxen. It may be that "partly by water" may refer to the Shuaylee and Molay rivers, along which there is a small boat traffic during the rains.

The next reference to Bhamô occurs in Captain Wilcox's valuable memoir on Assam and the neighbouring countries,[1] in which he indicates the route to Momien, *viâ* Muangwan and Muangtee (Mynetee). His information was derived from a Kampti who had been a resident in Yunan for eight years, and a few Chinamen who had been with him for some time. These men, however, gave Wilcox a very inaccurate account of the size of the Namkho (Tahô, Tapeng), and of its relation to the towns along its course. The Kampti described it as being as large as the Irawady, and as the boundary line between a Shan province and China, neither of which it is, nor ever has been. From this mis-statement of facts, Wilcox was led to identify the Namkho (Tapeng) with the Lu-kyang, Loakyung, or Salween; and from the ignorance of the Chinamen to regard Muangtee and Tengye-chew as one and the same place. As he did not extend his observations beyond Momien, it is evident that the Namkho could not have been the Salween, which is considerably to the west of that city, and it is equally apparent that the river the Kampti crossed between Muangtee and Momien was the Tahô, the only river in those parts.

Turning now to the journal of an embassy to the coast of Ava in 1826, by Crawford, the distinguished historian of the Malayan Archipelago, it is stated that the Irawady, the largest river in Ava, is navigable only for canoes at the town of Bhamô; while the fact is, that large river steamers can reach that place with ease, and that it is probable that the channel of this magnificent river will be found deep enough for them even for 150 miles further. In the light of such facts, Crawford's deduction that it is a stream of no great magnitude above Ava, and that its source cannot be very remote from the capital, of necessity falls to the ground in the light of recent research. Crawford unfortunately fell into another error, in stating that the goods from Bhamô to the capital were conveyed overland, and it is difficult to say whether this mistake into which he unwittingly fell, or his explanation of it, is most opposed to fact. All the trade from Bhamô to the capital appears to have been conducted by boats from time immemorial. He gave, however, a very accurate description of the character of the trade between the capital and China, but erred in applying his description to Bhamô. "The traffic with the capital," he says, "although

---

[1] Asiatic Society Researches, vol. xvii, p. 349.

probably subjected to less restraint, resembles, in a great measure, the commerce which is carried on, on their mutual frontier, between the Russians and Chinese. It is not a continued trade conducted throughout the year as between two friendly nations, but one carried on at annual fairs. The caravan from China, composed entirely of Chinese, commonly arrives at Ava in the beginning of December, and is said to take about six weeks in travelling from Yunan. It is probable, indeed, that it cannot quit China until the cessation of the periodical rains in the middle of October, which would limit the journey to the period mentioned. No part of the journey is by water, nor are the goods conveyed by wheel carriage, but by small horses, mules, and asses." All the facts in the foregoing extract are accurate, but I do not think he has rightly interpreted them. The mere circumstance that the caravans arrive at the capital only once a year, seems to me to admit of an altogether different explanation from that given of it by Crawford. It appears that the great distance and the difficult character of the country to be travelled; the preparations for the journey there and back, such as the collecting the merchandise for the Burmese market, and the disposing of it, and the purchase of goods for the return journey occupy so much time, that only one journey can be overtaken, and that the dry months are selected because they are the most convenient. The danger to life, and almost certain loss of property from flood and fell during the rains, would far outweigh all other considerations. These remarks apply only to the trade with the capital by the long difficult route *viâ* Theinnee, for small trading caravans visit Bhamô at all seasons of the year, although, as a rule, all the large caravans arrive during the dry weather. Bhamô is commercially linked to Yunan by a chain of Chinese merchants who have settled in it, and in the Shan towns of Manwyne, Sanda, and Muangla, and who maintain a constant but petty trade with the more extensive Momien merchants, who, in their turn, are linked with the great trading town of Yungchan, the mart to which the products of Western Yunan find their way. The result is, that there is a steady and constant flow to Bhamô of the produce of a part of Western Yunan, largely in excess of the requirements of the inhabitants of that town and district; and all the surplus trade finds its way down the Irawady to the capital, and to the various large trading towns along the river. This traffic is entirely in the hands of the Chinese at Bhamô and Mandalay, and from its thriving and continued character and great age, and from the facilities for transit which it can command at all seasons of the year, it is greatly more important in every respect than that which finds its way once a year by Theinnee to the capital. Bhamô is, to all practical purposes, the mart which supplies the Burmese markets with the products of Yunan, and that province with the cotton of Burmah.

In a paper read by Sir J. F. Davis [1] before the Royal Asiatic Society of London in December 1827, it appears that the interest which attaches to the geography of the Burmese empire, and to its relations with China, was beginning to attract the attention of those in England, who were most deeply conversant with the commercial and political requirements of our eastern possessions, and especially with their relations to the great *terra incognita* of South-Western China. The authorities in India, as well, seem to have been duly alive to its importance, for we find that the Bengal Government published about that time a map, containing all the latest information on the Burmese country and its Chinese frontier. In the paper above referred to, Sir J. F. Davis set himself the task to compare this map with a manuscript one compiled from the labours of some Jesuit missionaries, confining his remarks to the tract of country along which our expedition travelled. A considerable degree of correspondence was found between the two maps, but although he inclined to the Chinese one as his guide, there can be no doubt that the Calcutta map was the most correct; indeed, its only error was in placing Muangmo (Long-chuen) on the Tapeng instead of the Shuaylee. The former map, however, located that town correctly, but erred in transferring Nantin and Tengyechew (Momien) to the banks of the Shuaylee. Sir J. F. Davis, having committed himself to the Chinese map, concluded that as it had correctly placed Long-chuen, therefore Nantin and Tengyechew were properly located on the Shuaylee; and then, by some mysterious philological process in which vowels and consonants were ignored, he detected a resemblance between Muangmo and Bhamô or Panmô, and arrived at the conclusion that Bhamô was situated on the Shuaylee. Following up these erroneous deductions, he doubted the existence of a route to Yunan along the northern river or Tapeng, and the correctness of the English map in laying down a route from Bhamô through Yungchan and Talifoo towards Yunan city, as he thought it unlikely that the natives of Ava were allowed to enter so far into Chinese territory.

He mentions one interesting fact, however, that the Jesuit Father, L'Amiot, who had resided for thirty years at Pekin, informed him that the Chinese considered the western part of the province of Yunan

---

[1] Trans. Roy. As. Soc., vol. ii, p. 90, et seq.

as unhealthy. It had been the fortune of this missionary to meet a Tartar officer who had been engaged in the Burmese war of 1767, and who attributed the failure of that great enterprise to the unhealthiness of the climate. L'Amiot also supplied him with some detached notes relating to the province of Yunan which are given in his paper.

Colonel Burney, who was appointed Resident at the Court of Ava on the 31st December 1829, published a large number of very valuable contributions to the history, geography, and resources of Upper Burmah, and accurate itineraries of the Theinnee and Bhamô routes to China, from materials derived from the chronicles and records kept by the Burmese court. The great use I have had occasion to make of his history of the wars of Upper Burmah shows how much I am indebted to his labours for the materials on which that part of this report rests. I can vouch for the accuracy of the Burmese itineraries from Bhamô to Momien, and I am consequently led to infer that the others will be found equally reliable as guides to the country beyond, and to the route which proceeds to Pekin by Theinnee, for they are all drawn up after one plan.[1]

Pemberton, in his Report on the Eastern Frontier of British India, published in 1835, gives a clear *resume* of all that was then known regarding the trade of Bhamô and of the Shan valleys to the east of the Kakhyen hills. He was the first who fully realized that "the province of Yunan," to use his own words, "to which the north-eastern borders of our Indian empire have now so closely approximated, has become, from this circumstance, and our existing amicable relations with the court of Ava, an object of peculiar interest to us;" and he proceeds to say that he has "every reason to hope that if the attempt be judiciously made, a flourishing branch of trade, which is now carried on between its industrious inhabitants and those of the northern Shan provinces of Ava, may be extended across the Patkoi pass into the valley of Assam," and, I would add, down the great natural highway of Burmah, to Rangoon.

In 1835, the Dupha Gaum, a feudatory Singpho chief of Ava, residing on the southern foot of the Patkoi pass leading from the Hukong valley to Assam, headed a strong party, and, crossing the mountains, ravaged and plundered the village of the Bisa Gaum, a Singpho chief, who had tendered his submission to our Government. These circumstances becoming known to Colonel Burney, the British Resident at the court of Ava, an enquiry was demanded, and security against the recurrence of similar acts of aggression. The Burmese appointed a mission to insti-

---

[1] See Appendix A. Routes to China.

tute the necessary investigations, and the enlightened Resident at their court at once availed himself of the opportunity, so unexpectedly offered, to appoint an English officer to accompany it, and he selected for the duty Captain Hannay, who commanded his escort.

Captain Hannay proceeded from Ava in the end of November 1835, up the Irawady to Bhamô and Mogoung. His journal was never published, but Pemberton, who gave an abstract of it, remarks that "many geographical points of extreme interest were determined by the personal observation and enquiries of that meritorious officer. Bhamô was for the first time accurately described, and much valuable information was gained respecting the trade carried on between Ava and China in that remote part of the Burman empire. The habits and localities of some of the principal tribes occupying the mountainous tracts bordering on Western Yunan were successfully investigated; the position of the very remarkable valley of Hukong was determined; the Payendwen or amber mines were for the first time examined by the eye of European intelligence; the latitudes of the principal towns between Ava and Muangkhong were ascertained by astronomical observation, with a degree of accuracy sufficient for every purpose of practical utility, and they may now be regarded as established points."

In February 1837, the distinguished botanist and traveller, Dr. Griffith, started from Suddyah, and, crossing the Patkoi range, travelled along the Hukong valley to Mogoung, and down the river of that name to the Irawady and Bhamô. His journal is replete with minute details of the physical characters of the country, the height of its mountains and hills, the general elevation of its valleys or plains, and the temperature of the air, and elaborate descriptions of its vegetation, and interesting notices of its fauna, and geological features. Dr. Griffith had Captain Hannay as his fellow-traveller as far as the Patkoi range, where they were joined by Dr. Bayfield, who had been sent by Colonel Burney from Ava, viâ Bhamô and Mogoung, to meet them. Captain Hannay was left behind on the Patkoi range, unable to go on or retreat, owing to his having no coolies.

There is a marked discrepancy between Hannay's and Griffith's account of the extent and social condition of the population of Bhamô. The former traveller, who had visited the town in the year before Griffith and Bayfield, described it as one of the largest towns he had met with in Burmah next to Ava and Rangoon, and certainly the most interesting of all. He considered that it contained about 1,500 houses, and if we allow four persons to each house, which is not a high average, he would have given it a population of 7,000. The houses impressed him as being large and comfortable, and when he landed, he found himself amongst a fair-complexioned people wearing jackets and trowsers. After being accustomed to the harsh features and party-coloured dress of the Burmans, he felt as if he were almost in a civilized land again. In connection with the foregoing account, it is curious to find Griffith stating that the town scarcely contained 400 houses, and that it had only one long street; and that neither were the houses good nor large, and that the population could not be calculated at more than 3,000.

All the inhabitants of Bhamô are Burmese-Shan, or Shans who have adopted the Burmese style of dress, and who intermarry with that people; and as they have been similarly attired for nearly three centuries, Captain Hannay's jacketed and trowsered people must have been the sprinkling of eastern Shans who yearly reside in Bhamô, from November to March, to make sun-dried bricks for the Chinese, and dâhs for the townspeople, and for the Kakhyens who trade with the place. As far as my own observations go, I did not detect any difference in the style of dress of the inhabitants as compared with other towns in Upper Burmah. Hannay's description of Bhamô has been quoted by more than one author, but it certainly produces an exaggerated impression of the place, while Griffith's description is certainly more in keeping with Bhamô of the present day.

It is much to be regretted that Colonel Hannay's and Dr. Bayfield's journals[1] were never published in full, for, with the exception of Griffith, they are the only travellers who have visited these little known regions. Those who have seen the journals have pronounced them to be most valuable records of travel.

Mr. Kincaid, an American missionary, visited Bhamô, as far as I have been able to discover, about the time of Griffith's and Bayfield's march down the Hukong valley, but I have not been able to ascertain that he published any account of his journey.

In 1848, Baron Otto des Granges published[2] "a short survey of the countries between Bengal and China, showing the great commercial and political importance of Bhamô, and the practicability of a direct trade overland between Calcutta and China." In this valuable paper,

---

[1] Colonel Hannay's journal had only extracts published from it. It was deposited in the Foreign Office, and ought to be there still. Dr. Bayfield's was never published, even in extracts, as far as I am aware. I have seen it, but found it illegible in many parts from the fading of the ink. It is surely worthy of a better fate.

[2] Asiatic Society's Journal, vol. xvii, p. 132.

the far-seeing author describes it as the most important town in Upper Burmah, and as the emporium of trade with China from the earliest centuries, and that it commands the only route which leads from India to China, on which any direct intercourse between both countries ever can take place, since in all other directions they are separated by the highest mountains and far greater distances. Duly impressed with the great advantages that would accrue to Indian commerce by its extension to Bhamô and Yunan, he advocated the equipment of a small expedition to ascertain the mercantile relations of the country about Bhamô, to examine the geological formations and mineral wealth of Yunan, and to enter into negotiations with the Chinese merchants at Bhamô; and suggested that the mission should either proceed by way of Rangoon and Ava up the Irawady, or by Sylhet and Munipore, which he proposed as the overland route to China *viâ* Bhamô.

Bishop Bigandet, the learned author of the Life of Guadama, visited Bhamô in 1857, but I am not aware that he ever published an account of his trip; but in a memorandum by the Vicar Apostolic of Tibet, on the countries between Tibet, Yunan, and Burmah, communicated to the Asiatic Society in 1861 by the bishop, we have the benefit of his Bhamô experience cropping out in foot-notes, and in a letter to Sir A. Phayre. This paper is a revival of the wild hypothesis that the Sanpo was the stream that entered the Irawady at Bhamô, not, however, as far as I am aware, with any new facts favouring the possibility of D'Anville's vagary, but simply a re-statement of it founded on Klaproth's map, and on information derived from Chinese sources.

In 1862, the Government of India, in the prospect of a treaty being negotiated with the king of Burmah, directed their Chief Commissioner, Sir Arthur Phayre, to include in it, if possible, the re-opening of the caravan route from Western China by the town of Bhamô, and the obtaining facilities for the residence of British merchants at that town, as well as their free passage to Yunan, and free passage of Chinese from Yunan to British territory, including Assam. Sir Arthur Phayre was also instructed to try and bring about the re-opening of the caravan route from Ava *viâ* Bhamô to Yunan, by obtaining the king's sanction to the despatch of a joint British and Burmese mission to the frontier. A treaty was concluded wherein the British and Burmese Governments were declared friends, and trade in and through Upper Burmah was freely thrown open to British enterprise, and arrangements were made that a direct trade with China might be carried on through Upper Burmah, subject to a transit duty of one per cent., *ad valorem*, on Chinese exports, and *nil* on imports. The proposal, however, regarding the mission, was unsuccessful.

Dr. Williams, formerly Resident at the court of Mandalay, in his lately published work on Upper Burmah, informs us that having resolved on testing the practicability of a route through Burmah to the western provinces of China, he addressed, early in January 1863, a formal petition to His Majesty the King, craving for the necessary permission and protection while journeying through his territories. He received the royal consent to his proceeding as far as Bhamô, and started on the 24th January, and arrived at his destination on the 16th of the following month. The result of his observations was communicated to the Asiatic Society of Bengal, in September 1864, in a paper in which he reviewed the political state of the several countries between the Bay of Bengal and Central China, the physical geography of the district proposed to be traversed by the various lines of communication, and their commercial conditions and capabilities, including their population, products, and former and existing trade. He arrived at the conclusion that the Bhamô routes to China, which have been sanctioned by ages of use, are politically and physically the most feasible to follow, and commercially the most likely to give the highest returns for the least expenditure. Ever since his return, Dr. Williams has energetically advocated the claims which these routes have over all the others to the south, by which it has been proposed to reach China. There can be little doubt that his exposition of the facilities which they offer, and of the resources of the country to the east of Bhamô, have led the mercantile community of Rangoon to appreciate the importance of their own position in commanding, through the Irawady, the most ancient highway to Western China; and, in doing so, he has done good service to the interests of that thriving community. The merits of the claim, however, which has been advanced in the preface to his work on Upper Burmah, that he was the first to suggest a trade route from Bhamô to Yunan, will be fully appreciated after what I have stated regarding Pemberton, and the Baron Otto des Granges; and the further assertion that he was the first Englishman, if not, indeed, the first European, to visit this portion of Upper Burmah, requires no remark, after the notice I have given of the labours of Hannay, Bayfield, and Griffith, and as we are now familiar with the names of Kincaid and Bigandet, leaving out of view the traders of two centuries and a half ago, whose presence at Bhamô was in itself a recognition of the commercial importance of that town.

Looking back on those two centuries and a half which have passed since the first Englishmen visited Bhamô on their peaceful and humanizing mission as traders, it is evident that, notwithstanding the professions of the Burmese Government, our position in Upper Burmah has little advanced through these long years. I know of no more telling instance of Burmese conservatism than this, which is almost on a parallel with the tenacious exclusiveness of China. But it is in both cases the grasping conservatism of an almost effete power that mistakes every novelty for an infringement of its rights, and rejects it as such.

It is curious that the first really practical test of the rights conferred on the English Government, by the treaty of 1862, should have been suggested and carried out by General Fytche, a descendant of Fitch, who was one of the first English merchants who visited Pegu, and who has bequeathed to us his impressions of that country through which he travelled so long ago as in 1586.

General Fytche's proposal, that an exploring party should attempt the passage of the Bhamô route, was submitted to the Government of India on the 21st June 1867, and received its sanction in the following September.

CHAPTER IV.

PHYSICAL FEATURES, GEOLOGY, &c., OF BHAMÔ DISTRICT AND WESTERN YUNAN.

THE great valley and alluvial plain of the Irawady may be described as extending from the 17th to the 26th parallels of latitude, between two mountainous regions—Arracan, Munipore, and Assam to the west, and the Southern Shan states and Yunan to the east—abruptly defined between two degrees of longitude. The surface of this enormous valley is broken up at intervals by comparatively low isolated ranges, running nearly north and south, the frequent occurrence of which confines the waters of the Irawady, in a great part of their course, to comparatively narrow but deep channels, to a greater extent than happens either in that portion of the Brahmaputra below Suddyah, or in the Ganges generally, and in this respect the great river of Burmah resembles the Yang-tse-kiang. There are, however, long open tracts of country devoid of hills, and in these localities the valley presents the appearance of an immense level plain extending away from the banks of the river as far as the eye can reach, the Irawady opening out into a noble expanse of water which, even at Bhamô, 600 miles from the sea, is $1\frac{1}{2}$ miles in breadth during the rains, and about 1 during the dry weather. The hill ranges, as a rule, may be said to be composed of metamorphic and crystalline rocks, and they were, in all probability, islands when the eocene and miocene strata were deposited around them. These consist chiefly of limestone, sandstone, clays, coal, and ferruginous conglomerates, with interbedded traps. The only bed of limestone, observed by me, occurs below Bhamô as an enormous cliff overhanging the river, and estimated by different travellers at from 600 to 1,000 feet in height. Coal mines have been opened out at three localities along the upper Irawady, and Dr. Oldham is my authority for the statement, that they hold out a fair promise of good fuel, in sufficient quantity for the river navigation of the upper Irawady, and for any demand that may arise in or about the capital of Burmah.[1]

---

[1] Oldham's Notes on the Geological Features of the Irawady; Yule's Ava, App. p. 42.

My object, however, is not to describe either the resources of the Irawady valley, or its physical aspect, except in so far as the latter will contribute to an understanding of the appearance of that part of it in the neighbourhood of Bhamô, to which my observations and researches were chiefly confined.

Bhamô is situated on the left bank of the Irawady, in lat. 24°16′, long. 96°53′47″, about a mile below where it is joined by the Tapeng. From 10 to 12 miles to the east of it, a range of hills (Kakhyen), varying from 5,000 to 6,000 feet in height, runs like an unbroken wall north-east and south-west, probably the continuation of the hills which begin to the east of the capital of Upper Burmah. Low undulating land stretches from the Irawady to their base, covered with a dense forest in some places, and in others with small trees and thick bush jungle, marking in all likelihood the site of old clearings. It is much cut up by deep hollows, usually containing a fair amount of water—long, narrow, canal-like excavations, exactly resembling the old river channels that are found in large islands. The town lies half-way between the first and second defiles of the Irawady, which are separated from each other by about 15 miles of comparatively level country, but connected on the western bank by a belt of low hilly land, separated from the river by a moderately broad alluvial flat, covered with dense forest. The undulating, almost level country about Bhamô stretches to the south between the Kakhyen mountains and the range of hills defining the eastern side of the second defile, and to the north of the Tapeng it is closed in by a low ridge of hills running east-north-east from the southern end of a range on the right side of the first defile. This east-north-easterly range has the Molay river running close to its northern face, and the Tapeng about 2 miles from its southern aspect. The population of the level country about Bhamô is almost entirely Shan, with a small intermixture of Burmese and Chinese; but to the north of the Tapeng, the Phwons occur on both banks, and at Mogoung there are a few Assamese and Chinese. The hill ranges, high and low, on both sides of the river, above and below Bhamô, are inhabited by Singphos of the Khanlung tribe. Their chief seat is in the Mogoung district, but of late years they have been spreading southward, and are now found below the second defile.

The towns of most note about Bhamô are Sawaddy, which is 3 miles down the river, on the same side with the once famous mart of Kaungtoung, which is about a mile below it. A number of small villages occur along the Tapeng, chiefly on its right bank, on the line of road leading to the Shan valleys, and the most noted among them is Old Bhamô, at the head of the Tapeng plain, where the English and Dutch are supposed to have had factories as early as 1658. The small towns of any extent above Bhamô on the Irawady are Tsenbo and Mogoung, but any importance that may attach to the former depends entirely upon the circumstance that it is situated at the mouth of the river on which the latter is placed, which is the head-quarters of the trade in jade and amber, the two principal products of that part of Upper Burmah. Two other towns, still further up the left bank of the Irawady, were once important places, as they lay in the line of trade between Yunan and Mogoung; but since the disturbances in that province, the trade is only the ghost of its former self, which is equally true of the two towns, Kakhyo and Wainmô. Although I use the term town in speaking of these places, it must be borne in mind that many villages in England are much larger. Even Sawaddy and Kaungtoung are not larger than moderately sized villages, and when Griffith visited Tsenbo, it had only 30 houses; and Mogoung itself, with the hamlets outside it, only numbered 300 houses during Captain Hannay's visit.

The Irawady is navigable by large boats for 150 miles above Bhamô, and it will, in all likelihood, be found to be so even for a much greater distance. From a survey of the first defile, in February 1870, by Captain Bowers, this officer is of opinion that no difficulty would be experienced in taking large river steamers through it; and he states that he seldom found it to be under 80 yards in width, and with a depth in some places of 100 fathoms, and at the south end of the defile his soundings gave 168 feet with a current of one mile an hour.[1] My impression is that Captain Bowers has under-estimated the natural difficulties which would have to be contended against in the navigation of this part of the Irawady. All below is comparatively smooth sailing, but it appears to me extremely doubtful that any steamer, except of the very smallest size and draught, could pass through the narrow channels between the rocks in the upper defile. A rock barrier stretches across the whole breadth of the river with only two channels, about 50 feet in breadth, between the rocks, and as the rise of the river in the rains appears never to exceed more than 30 feet, it would only serve to hide the numerous rocks, and to increase the danger to any vessel attempting the navigation at that season. But the barrier is of such a nature that a few pounds of gunpowder, used

---

[1] I doubt the accuracy of these soundings which were communicated to me by Captain Bowers.

in two or three places, would throw open the navigation of this splendid river, as far at least as the mouth of the Mogoung stream, if not to the 26th parallel of latitude.

According to information communicated to me while in Upper Burmah, the Irawady is said to be subject to regular floods, which the Burmese ascribe to the full moon, and which occur in the height of the dry weather as well as during the rains. While at Bhamô I had an illustration of one of the sudden rises of the river due to the latter cause. On the 7th September, it rose 1 foot in six hours, and on the 9th 2 feet more. On the 11th it had fallen 18 to 29 inches, and on the 12th it had subsided fully 10 feet. This flood was doubtless due to heavy rain on the mountains at the head of the Kampti plain, which appear to be subject to a heavy rainfall at seasons when it would be least expected. Wilcox, on his visit to the country east of the Brahmakund, experienced heavy rains in the month of April for days together, and this, with the melting of the snows, which he also mentions, fully accounts for the floods of the Irawady during the dry weather in the south.

The branches of the Irawady which deserve a passing notice are, proceeding from below upwards, on the left bank—first, the Shuaylee, about 40 miles in a straight line to the south of Bhamô; second, the Tapeng, about one mile and a half above that town; third, the Molay, about 4 miles above the latter stream; and, lastly, the Mogoung river, about 50 miles above Bhamô on the right bank. The Shuaylee rises 40 or 50 miles to the north-east of Momien, and has a course of about 260 miles, in the latter part of which, before it reaches the Burmese plain, it flows through a broad fertile valley inhabited by industrious agricultural Shans and Chinese. The Kakhyen mountains, where the river debouches on the plain of the Irawady, describe a great bend to the east, so that the Shuaylee flows through a greater extent of level country on the Burmese side than its fellow, the Tapeng, to the north. Its descent to the plain, too, is not so rapid nor violent as in the case of the latter river, which precipitates itself through 25 miles of the Kakhyen hills as a roaring torrent. It is about 300 yards broad at its mouth during the dry weather, and has been stated to be navigable by large boats, about three days' journey from the Irawady, and to be a fine, broad, quiet, flowing stream in the valleys of Yunan. I can well understand this, for the Tapeng, which is smaller than it, is deep enough in the Sanda valley, 50 miles from the Irawady, to admit of a boat traffic with the Burmese plain, if the Kakhyen hills did not intervene; and this being the case with the Tapeng, the capabilities of the Shuaylee must be proportionately great, and indeed some Kakhyens described it to me as a fine and deep river at Muangmo, flowing through a richly cultivated valley about 25 miles in breadth. If this prove to be true, and it is navigable by large boats as far as has been represented, the Shuaylee is certainly the most important branch of the Irawady in Upper Burmah, because it leads to the most feasible and most universally recognized trade route to the town of Momien, and which will be spoken of in its proper place as the Sawaddy route. A survey of this river would be one of the first subjects to deserve the attention of any future expedition to Upper Burmah.

The Tapeng may be said to have a course of 145 to 150 miles. Rising about 10 to 12 miles to the north-west of Momien in the Kananzan mountains, it is a continued succession of water-falls and rapids till it reaches the Sanda valley, where it spreads out into a fine river. It enters the Kakhyen hills by a narrow gorge, and, in its course through them to the plains, is an irresistible mountain torrent, whose deafening roar is heard high up the mountain sides. It flows for 20 miles through the Burmese plain as a placid river before it reaches the Irawady, and is navigable by heavily-laden, large boats during the dry weather, and by river steamers during the rains.

The Molay river, 4 or 5 miles to the north of the Tapeng, is a narrow, shallow stream during the dry weather, with a course of about 90 miles. During the rains it appears to be navigable for about 30 miles from the Irawady, but it is so narrow that a large boat cannot turn in it after it gets up a short distance. It rises to the north of Sanda, and flows through a hilly country, and valleys parallel, or nearly so, to those of the Tapeng and Shuaylee.

The Mogoung river is navigable by small boats as far as the town of that name. It is a slow flowing stream, much obstructed in the dry weather by sand-banks and snags. It is about 70 yards broad at its mouth, which is deep, and has a course of about 80 miles through a hilly country, containing amber, jade, gold, coal, and limestone.

The country above the first defile has been described to me as again opening out into a wide plain, richly cultivated by Kampti Shans, Phwons, and Kakhyens. A good deal of cotton is grown, which is more highly valued at Bhamô by the Chinese merchants than the cotton that finds its way to that mart from the districts to the south. Tobacco also, of good quality, is largely cultivated. At the junction of the small Shuaymai with the main stream of the Irawady, at about the 26th parallel, the country again becomes hilly; but beyond this point, we have no certain information, although it is stated that there is another plain still further to the north.

The soil, on the level country about Bhamô, is very rich, especially in the hollows. It rests on a yellowish and greyish clay of great thickness, some sections of which along the river's bank are fully 50 feet in depth. It is used in making rough earthen-ware vessels and sun-dried bricks.

The chief grain is rice, of which two crops are raised during the year. The first is grown in the hollows which never completely dry up, and is planted in the beginning of February, and the second on the level flats during the rains. Numerous legumes, yams, and melons are cultivated, as well as a little cotton, and the sandy islands of the river produce capital tobacco. The edible fruits at Bhamô are jacks, tamarinds, lemons, citrons, peaches, and a small purple plum; cocoanuts are very scarce, but plantains are plentiful. The wild tea plant *(Camellia thea)* is found more or less on all the hills about Bhamô. The whole of the Tapeng plain in the month of February was literally covered with a carpet of the wild strawberry *(Fragaria Indica, Andr)*.

Buffaloes are numerous, but oxen are not so common, and all the ponies at Bhamô came from the Shan states to the east. There is a capital breed of pariah dogs, with longer hair and more pointed ears and muzzle than the Indian race, and the tail is bushy and curled over the back, somewhat in the fashion of the true Chinese breed. The reddish colour that characterizes the wild dog is the prevailing tint of the hair, but piebald dogs are not uncommon. A breed, black, with tan points and longish hair, is said to be universally born with a short tail about three inches long, and sometimes much shorter. I have seen a number of specimens, but had an opportunity to examine only one, and, as far as I could make out, the peculiarity seemed to be a natural characteristic; the natives, too, strongly assert that the tails are never cut. Fowls, ducks, and geese are abundant.

The river is rich in a great variety of edible fish which are chiefly converted into "gnape," or dried.

During the month of February, the mean maximum temperature by the dry bulb was $80°9$, and the minimum $74°7$, and the mean of observations with the wet bulb, maximum $54°2$, minimum $53°3$. The means of the dry bulb thermometer at 7 A.M., 4 P.M., and 9 P.M. were, respectively, $55°7$, $75°4$, and $61°2$; and with the wet bulb at the same hours $54°9$, $69°$, and $61°8$. During the first twelve days of February, the little wind that there was, blew chiefly from the south-west, and occasionally from the north-east and north-north-east; but, as a rule, the atmosphere was very calm, and the sky unclouded; towards the middle of the month, the lower current gradually veered to the north-east, while the upper current still travelled from the south-west, but by the end of the month, the latter was from the north, and occasionally from the north-west. In the morning the country was usually wrapped in thick fogs that disappeared with the rising sun. About the latter third of February, there were occasional heavy showers with thunder and lightning. From what Griffith states, it appears that even the first part of May differs little from the latter part of February, except in the higher temperature, for he mentions that north winds are common in that month, and that they are accompanied with a little rain and unsettled weather. On my return to Bhamô in September, I had no proper instruments to take observations, as they had been stolen on the homeward journey from Momien, but the maximum temperature varied between 76° and 91°, and the wind between south-west and north-west. The atmosphere was generally so calm that it hardly stirred a leaf, and the heat was very oppressive, more especially to us who had suddenly reached the plains after a seven months' residence at an elevation of from 3,000 to 5,000 feet above the sea. The district appears to be a healthy one, and although fever occurs during the rains, it is far from prevalent. There are certain swampy districts, however, a short way to the south-east of the second defile, which are said to be very unhealthy. The disease most dreaded is small-pox, which sometimes commits dreadful ravages among the population of the whole of that part of Upper Burmah.

Although there is no very striking feature in the natural products of Bhamô itself, we learn from Hannay and Griffith that when we cross the Irawady and make our way to the north-north-west about 80 miles, we find ourselves in a district producing amber, jade, gold, and salt, with indications of the existence of a fair supply of coal. The occurrence of the latter mineral, at the very terminus of the steam navigation of the Irawady, is a fact of the greatest importance, and augurs well for the future commercial history of Upper Burmah. It is said to occur in the Hukong valley, and from the circumstance that the Mogoung river is navigable to boats as far as Mogoung, the coal could be landed at Bhamô with comparative ease and at no great cost, and with the other three coal-yielding localities, further down, the Irawady has every condition in itself for its successful navigation. The extent, however, of these coal-bearing strata at Mogoung is unknown.

The amber mines are situated at an elevation of 1,050 feet above the sea, in a low range of hills to the south-west of the Meinkhoom plain in the Hukong valley, or Payendwen, as the Burmese call it, in allusion to the amber, which is procured by digging holes about three feet in diameter, and varying from six to forty feet in depth. Fifteen to twenty feet of the superficial soil is clayey and red, but the remainder consists of a greyish-black carbonaceous earth. Foliated limestone, serpentine, and coal are among the other strata.[1] The amber is found in both of the former, and its presence is indicated by small pieces of lignite which are easily detected, so that the search is comparatively simple. The out-turn, however, is not very great, but the people appear to have no guide to the selection of favourable spots, and their tools are of the most primitive kind, consisting of wooden shovels, a wooden crowbar tipped with iron, baskets for removing the earth, and buckets made of the bark of a *Sterculia* for heaving up the water that accumulates in the pits. Captain Hannay mentions that newly-opened pits have a fine aromatic smell. The amber most valued at Momien is perfectly clear, and of the colour of very dark sherry, and is sold by its weight. A triangular piece of this kind, about one inch long and one inch its greatest diameter, cost about five rupees at Momien. It is made into Buddhistic rosaries, finger-rings, pipe mouth-pieces, and buttons, and carved into small figures as ornaments for the Shan and Chinese chatelains. Many Kakhyens, Shans, and Chinese from the hills and valleys to the east of the Irawady trade in it. Amber-workers used to be very numerous at Momien, but very few now exist.

The jade[2] mines, the most important feature of the Mogoung district, occur in a semi-circular valley in the vicinity of a hill, 25 miles to the south-west of Meinkhoom. The surface of this valley is broken up with the excavations which have been carried on from time immemorial. The stone is found in the form of more or less rounded boulders, associated with others of quartz, &c., imbedded in a reddish, yellow-coloured clay. The pits are not dug after any particular plan, and none exceed 20 feet in depth. They occur all over the valley and at the base of the hill. The masses which are removed are of considerable size, and I saw some in the godown of a merchant at Rangoon so large that they required

---

[1] Griffith's posthumous papers, p. 82.

[2] Captain Pemberton states that Abel Remusat, in the second part of his history of Khotan, is said by Klaproth to have entered into a very learned disquisition, proving the identity of the *yu* or *yueesh* of the Chinese with the *jasper* of the ancients. James Prinsep observes that *yu* is a silicious mineral, coloured with less intensity, but passing into heliotrope, and that it is therefore *phrase* rather than jade or nephrite.—*Journ. As. Soc.*, vol. vii, p. 265.

three men to turn them. During certain seasons of the year, as many as 1,000 men are engaged in digging for jade; they are Shans, Chinese, Panthays, and Kakhyens from the east of the Irawady, and a large trade used to be carried on in it, by the Kakhyo and Wainmô route, and also through Bhamô. It found its way chiefly to Momien, where it used to be largely worked in former days, and where there is still a bye-street in the town, in which the majority of the houses are devoted to the manufacture of small discs for ear-rings about the size of a shilling, armlets, buttons, pipe mouth-pieces, &c. I purchased for Rs. 4, at Bhamô, finger-rings of this substance which sell at Canton for £2. Each digger pays one ticcal a month for the privilege of being allowed to work at the mines, and all that he finds becomes his own, and those who purchase the jade pay $1\frac{1}{2}$ to $2\frac{1}{2}$ ticcals for permission to proceed to the mines, and $1\frac{1}{4}$ ticcal a month so long as they remain; and on their return the jade they have bought is taxed 10 per cent. on its value. The ponies employed in carrying the jade are also taxed, and each trader, on his return to the village of Tapo, is subjected to a small duty of a quarter ticcal, and has to return the certificate granting him permission to proceed to the mines. The revenue from these mines, in 1836, was Rs. 40,000.

Gold is found in the channels of the majority of the rivers, both in fine grains, or in pieces as large as a pea, but the streams that are richest in it, and yield the best quantity, are the Kapdup and Namkwún, and Captain Hannay was informed that large pits were sunk in the banks of the former river by the natives in search of the metal. I was told by a Kampti Shan, and by the Chinese at Momien, that gold is found in considerable quantities in the Kampti country, north of the junction of the two supposed main streams of the Irawady, and that the people there barter it for salt, and for the merchandize which is taken over to them by the Shans and Chinese from Sanda and Muangla. Although I may be wandering in my remarks from the neighbourhood of Bhamô, I cannot but refer to the silver and iron mines that are said to exist in the Muanglan country, north-east of the Kampti district, for, in the event of Upper Burmah ever being opened up to western enterprize, the products of these mines, if they should ultimately prove of sufficient value to be worked, would assuredly find their way to Bhamô along the great water highway of the Irawady. Salt, on the authority of Captain Hannay, is said to be procured on both sides of the Hukong valley, and the rivers Namtwonkok and Edi are quite brackish from the presence of numerous salt springs in their beds.

Leaving Bhamô, and crossing the Tapeng at its mouth, we follow the left bank of the river for about 25 miles over a level plain, and reach the Kakhyen hills, which it will be my object now to describe.

As seen from the Burmese plain, they appear to run nearly due northeast and south-west, preserving an average height of 5,000 to 6,000 feet, with a long undulating outline broken up here and there by pointed and dome-shaped peaks. To the east of this range, which is about 25 miles in breadth, the country is a succession of hills and valleys, the general elevation of the latter varying from 2,000 to 4,500 feet above the sea. The portion of the part of the country I travelled over may be divided into two belts, the most westerly one extending about 70 miles to the east of the Kakhyen hills, and succeeded by another which is defined to the east of Momien by a lofty range of mountains running nearly north and south, marking the western side of the valley of the Shuaylee, and corresponding in direction to the Kakhyen hills. These two belts, as we shall presently see, are markedly distinct in physical appearance and geological structure. First, however, with regard to the Kakhyen range, running north-east and south-west.

As far as my observations go, these hills appear to be largely composed of metamorphic and crystalline rocks. A dark bluish grey fine-grained gneiss, with white layers of felspar in it, forms a great part of the range, and in a section in the gorge of the Nampung, 953 feet above Bhamô, the mass of this rock is seen following the trend of the hills, and the line of cleavage is nearly vertical. The varieties of structure are very numerous, and beds of the very finest grain are found lying alongside others resembling porphyry, while others are schistose, felspathic, and granitoid forms of gneiss. Granite was never observed *in situ* along our route, but we had ample evidences of its existence in the boulders in the larger hill streams. Quartzose rocks alternate with the gneiss and with a white crystalline limestone, with iron pyrites disseminated through it. The marble has all the characters of the beds found in the neighbourhood of Mandalay, and the galena ore, which is rich in silver, is extracted from the spur in which one bed crops out. Although I have never observed the ore in position, it occurs, in all probability, as a vein in this crystalline limestone, which is found on the left bank of the Tapeng opposite the village of Ponsee, about 15 miles from the Burmese plain, and as the silver mines are in the territory of the Ponsee Tsawbwa, which runs transversely across the valley from ridge to ridge, they may be termed the Ponsee silver mines.

Professor Oldham[1] has made two assays of this ore, and informs me that it contains ·191 per cent. of silver in the galena, and 0·225 per cent. of the precious metal in the lead, and has favoured me with the following comparative table of the maximum results of assays of galenite from the under-mentioned mines, by which it will be seen that the Ponsee ore is richer than any of them:—

Hartz	0·03 to 0·05
English	0·02 to 0·03
Scotch (Lead hills)	0·03 to 0·06
Tuscany	0·32 to 0·72
Ponsee	0·191

No detailed information regarding the productiveness of these mines could be obtained from the Kakhyens, but they have the reputation of being very rich in ore, and if this be so, the large percentage of silver would make them very valuable. They are of easy access, and from their close proximity to the borders of China, little or no difficulty would be experienced in finding labourers to work them. They have been periodically worked by the Burmese, who have no claim whatever to them beyond what they may have paid the Kakhyen Tsawbwas of Ponsee and Ponlyne for permission to remove the ore. They have, however, been abandoned since the outbreak of the recent Mahomedan rebellion in the Momien district, now fifteen years ago, but a few Kakhyens occasionally remove some of the metal for their own wants. As has been already stated, they appear to be the mines of the maps incorrectly placed a short way to the north-east of Muangmo, and to the south of the Shuaylee.

Silver is said to be found also on the right bank of the Tapeng, high up the hill sides to the west of Ponsee, in a bed similar to the one we have just indicated as the probable site of the galena vein of the principal mines. The existence of a white argentiferous crystalline limestone, on both banks of the Tapeng, at different elevations, renders it highly probable that this portion of the valley of the river is an immense faulted cynclinal. Another mine is said to exist to the east of Muangmo, in the remote valley of Kaingma.

Gold is found on a hill to the north of the village of Ponline, and I was shown at Bhamô a small quantity of this metal in grains as large as small peas, which was said to have come from these hills.

---

[1] A galena, very rich in silver, is mentioned by Dr. Oldham as having been procured from the Kuenapa range to the east of Mandalay, the percentage of the two metals being lead 63·000, silver 0·0625 per cent. Notes on Geological Features of Irawady, Yule's Ava., App. p. 60.

A striking feature of the Kakhyen range is the number of large water-worn boulders that lie scattered all over its surface, even to its highest peaks. There they have lain through the long æons that have elapsed since that great hilly area rose, surely but imperceptibly, from the ocean that rolled them into their present forms. Then, doubtless, the immense valley of the Irawady was yet a thing to be, and the waves of the wide Pacific broke in white spray at the foot of the giant Himalaya, the sea and land being tenanted by the mammals and reptiles whose remains are now familiar to us in the Sewalik and Ava fossils!

The sides of the Tapeng valley are very precipitous near the river, and consist of long spurs with intervening hollows, and with level flats devoted to rice-fields, but from half-way up the hills to their summits, we meet with Kakhyen villages in the neighbourhood of long, gentle, well-cultivated slopes.

The vegetable products of these hills are chiefly rice, Indian corn, a little cotton, opium, and tobacco. Among the cultivated fruits we find the peach *(Persica vulgaris)*, the pomegranate *(Punica granatum)*, the love apple *(Lycopersicum esculentum)*, the guava *(Psidium guava)*, and the plantain; and among wild fruits, *Pyrus Indica, Pyrus pashia, Juglans regia, Engelhardtia spicata, Prunus puddum, Castanea vesca, Fragaria Indica*, and a variety of brambles. The tea plant, *Camellia thea*, is indigenous, but is confined chiefly to the eastern side of the hills, but becomes more abundant in the secondary ranges defining the eastern valleys. Extensive clearings for the cultivation of rice and Indian corn occur at all altitudes, the latter crop being reared chiefly in the higher slopes. There are still, however, extensive tracts of forest with a fair proportion of valuable timber trees, and on the heights we meet with oaks, *Quercus spicata*, and *Q. fenestrata*; birches *(Alnus Nipalensis)*, and a variety of other less important temperate species, and at the same altitudes, considerable areas restricted to such trees, as *Cinnamomum cassia*[1] and *C. caudatum*, which are being felled every year in thousands, and burned where they lie, to provide fresh ground for the rice and Indian corn crops.

The mention of opium, as one of the vegetable products of Yunan, suggests the remark that the circumstance of the cultivation of this drug having spread across China from the east, to within 100 miles from our own frontier, is a subject inviting serious attention from those who have the direction of the monetary affairs of our Indian possessions,

---

[1] The oil of this tree is commonly sold under the name of the oil of cinnamon.

which have derived such a large portion of their revenue from the monopoly of opium.

There can be little doubt that opium was cultivated in China long before its importation was legalized by Hien-Kiong in 1858, as small quantities were secretly grown, in 1821, even so far west as Talifoo. The legalization, however, of the import trade seems to have given an impetus to the cultivation, for we are informed by eye-witnesses that it has now spread over many of the northern provinces of the empire, such as, Shensi, Sechuen, and Yunan, all of which have been more or less independent for many years of the authority of the central government at Pekin; and we have now to meet the additional fact that it has even found its way as far west as the Shan valleys and Kakhyen hills. Such a result was never contemplated when the British, French, and American Governments pressed for the legalization of the import trade, but the very circumstance that the drug was removed from the category of contraband goods, and entered the empire on the same footing, or nearly so, as the articles of legitimate trade, doubtless suggested to such enterprising agriculturists as the Chinese some such reasoning as this:—This hitherto forbidden drug, which finds such a large and remunerative sale among our people, is now declared a legal import; why should we be dependent on a foreign market for a substance which we can grow equally well ourselves, and which we will be able to sell at a profit, and at a much lower rate than the imported drug? Why should all the fortunes that are to be made by its sale go to the merchants, and the agriculturists be denied any participation in them? There can be little doubt that the legalization contributed to increased consumption, while at the same time it excited competition. That there has been a remarkable increase, within the last few years, of the quantity of opium consumed in China, is self-evident, because there has been a wonderful extension of the cultivation throughout the length and breadth of the empire, with no commensurate falling off in the amount of the imports from India. But with a rapidly extending cultivation, this state of matters cannot last for any length of time. The opium which, within the last few years, has supplanted rice cultivation in many a district of Sechuen and Shensi, would not have been grown unless there had been the prospect of its finding a ready market. The extent to which the cultivation has spread is a speaking proof to the immense quantity of the drug consumed by the population of China, and also to the inability of government to put a stop to the growth of the poppy; for it so happens, as I have already stated, that the great opium districts lie in the rebel provinces of Shensi, Sechuen, and Yunan, in the first and last of which the imperial authority is all but annihilated. But it is also cultivated in the royalist provinces, and the mandarins are either powerless or unwilling to interfere with it; it is extending every year, and the probability is that the government, however loath it may be to recognize the fact, will ultimately be driven either to shut its eyes to it, or to legalize the cultivation. In such an eventuality, our opium revenue will dwindle, in a few years, to a mere pittance, and ultimately disappear as an item in the budgets of our financiers, who will have to discover some other and more reliable source of income, and one more in accordance with the principles of an enlightened political economy, having in view the good of humanity at large, be it Mongolian or Aryan.

The opium at first grown in China was so inferior that there was no immediate chance of its soon replacing the Indian drug, but it has improved of late years. Colonel Burney, in speaking of the opium brought to Mandalay in 1831 from Medoo, two days' journey from Tali, describes it as very inferior to Bengal opium, but the following comparative table of Western Yunan (Shan) and Bengal opium, drawn up by the Opium Examiner to Government, shows that the former is not so far behind the latter in point of quality:

Analysis of Yunan opium as compared with that of Benares and Behar opium manufactured in 1869.

		Quantities used for morphia.	Morphia obtained.		Quantities used for extraction.	Extraction obtained.		Pro.	Revenue.	
			Grains.	per cent.		Grains.	per cent.		Morphia per cent.	Extraction per cent.
Benares	76°	Grs. 1,000	39	3·9	Grs. 300	130	43·33		2·9	43·33
Behar	75°	,, 1,000	37	3·7	,, 300	184	41·66		3·7	44·66
Yunan	70°	,, 1,000	35	3·5	,, 300	126	42·		3·5	42·

Before leaving this subject, I would press this consideration, that the cultivation of the plant is firmly established in the three provinces of Shensi, Sechuen, and Yunan, and that should these, with Khansi, ultimately become one independent kingdom, which passing events would lead us to believe to be a possible, if not a probable contingency, we should have to contend against a great opium-producing country, in which imperial Chinese legislation would be utterly powerless to prevent the growth of the poppy.

PHYSICAL FEATURES, GEOLOGY, &c.

But to return to the sketch of these hills. A few buffaloes are occasionally seen, and used for ploughing in the more level spots, but they are far from being plentiful. They are not unfrequently stolen from the plains as offerings for the nâts, and secreted on some retired spot till they are required. Each village usually owns a few Shan ponies, and sometimes a mule or two, either stolen from the Shan-Burmese, or purchased in the neighbouring valleys; for the Kakhyens never attempt to breed any other animals besides pigs, fowls, and ducks. A small goat, with long fine hair, and flat spiral horns directed backwards, and somewhat resembling those of the *markhor*, is not unfrequent; a good breed of dog, usually black, with pointed ears and the tail curled over the back, is of rare occurrence. Every village owns a few black or piebald pigs of moderate size, but they cannot be said to be plentiful.

The majority of the observations on the climate were made at an elevation of 3,185 feet, at the village of Ponsee, in the heart of the Kakhyen hills. The most important extended over the months of March, April, and part of May, and the mean temperatures of the three months were as follow :—

Dry Bulb Thermometer.

March	7 A.M., 60·6	4 P.M., 73·4	9 P.M., 58·9	Maximum, 79·3	Minimum, 53·6
April	" 64·7	" 79·2	" 62·8	" 82·9	" 68·2
May	" 66·7	" 81·7	" 63·5	" 86·3	" 60·9

Wet Bulb Thermometer.

March	7 A.M., 57·2	4 P.M., 67·8	9 P.M., 56·6	Maximum, 76·2	Minimum, 51·6
April	" 63·3	" 70·4	" 60·2	" 74·9	" 56·6
May	" 62·5	" 71·6	" 61·8	" 79·6	" 58·

Mean Dew point—March 54·4; April 60·5; May 61·30.

In March, the general direction of the wind, up to sun-down, was usually south-west or west-south-west, but at sunset it almost invariably changed to the north-west, when we found a fire requisite to our comfort. There can be little doubt that these cold currents of air which roll down the valleys of the Kakhyen hills to the plain of the Irawady explain the frequent, almost daily occurrence of morning mists in the latter locality, throughout the cold weather. During the day the sky was generally cloudless, and the air clear and bracing. Rain fell only on four occasions in March, either over the night or in early morning. In April, the north wind which set in at night, usually lasted till morning, when it changed to the north-east, with a south-westerly upper current, which was also the prevailing direction of the lower current, after the sun had been up a few hours. The temperature sensibly increased during this month, and the sky was frequently overcast. Rain fell on twelve occasions, accompanied by high winds, generally from the north-west, with considerable electrical disturbance. These storms occurred, as a rule, either immediately before or after sun-down, and frequently lasted to the following morning, and on one or two occasions till the afternoon. A heavy hail-storm fell on the 12th of April, and some of the stones were nearly an inch in diameter. The centre of each was occupied by a white nucleus 3''' in extreme breadth; considerable barometrical disturbance characterized the storm, and it was issued in by a calm, and a rise in the barometer from 26°62'—attached thermometer 74°—to 26°63', and in a few minutes afterwards the barometer rose to 26°65' with a falling thermometer. Five minutes after it had reached its maximum, and during the height of the storm, it fell to 26°63', and in three minutes afterwards it rose to 26°64', again falling to 26°63', rising in five minutes afterwards to 26°65', and falling once more in five minutes to 26°63', with the attached thermometer at 70°. The storm came up from the south-west as a deep black cloud, but the wind afterwards veered to the north-west. The day had been cool and pleasant with fitful gusts from the south-west, with detached clouds flying about. The observations for May extended over only nine days, and during that time we had thunder showers on four consecutive days, from the 6th to the 9th, and it is interesting to remark that all of them occurred with a northerly wind and between sunset and sunrise. On returning through the Kakhyen hills in September, the rains were evidently drawing to a close. We made five marches, and three of these were unattended with rain, while in the other two we experienced only heavy showers; we had incessant rain for one day at Namboke, and for another at Loaylone in the centre of the hills. The rainfall, however, must be considerable during the truly wet months, and the flora leads me to conclude that the climate of these hills partakes of the moist character of the Khasya range, modified by their remote position from the direct influence of the south-west monsoon, which loses a great deal of its moisture on the southern hill ranges of Burmah before it reaches them. Snow is said to fall in the cold weather on the summits of the highest peaks, but is of rare occurrence, and melts as fast as it falls. The climate appeared to be healthy, and there is a plentiful supply of water from the numerous mountain streams. During our residence at Ponsee, our men had to endure considerable hardships from exposure, and the reduction of their rations, but although they were housed only in huts, which they had constructed for themselves in a few hours from bamboos and leafy branches of trees, we had not a single case of fever, and had only a mild case of dysentery, which speaks well both for the physique of our guard, and for the healthy character of the climate.

There can be little doubt that the tea plant would thrive if cultivated, as it is indigenous, and largely grown by the Poloungs to the east. Like Assam, however, the Kakhyen hills are thinly populated, and the inhabitants are little given to manual labour; on the other hand, these hills are in the immediate neighbourhood of a Shan and Chinese population of agricultural habits, and within easy reach of the tea-growing Poloungs, so that little or no difficulty would be experienced in procuring skilled labour at a cheap rate. The tea grown by the Poloungs finds a market among the Shans and Chinese of the valleys, and the almost exclusively Chinese population to the east of Nantin. The consumption must be considerable, as it is largely and universally used. A sample, unfortunately out of condition, due to its having got thoroughly wetted in our march across the Kakhyen hills, has been reported on by one of the best judges of tea in Calcutta, who describes it as a large, lumpy-leafed article, with some flat open leaves, mixed with small dull yellow dust, very thin liquor, out of condition, but worth about 6*d*. per ℔.

In the event of any mercantile caravans proceeding from Bhamô, it would be interesting to ascertain by experiment how the coarser and cheaper kinds of Assam teas would be received by these people. This may appear as if I were advocating taking coals to Newcastle, but such a proceeding would not be more remarkable than what happens every day in these valleys, in which the round cakes of tea that come from the Trans-Yang-tse-kiang provinces of the empire, are exposed for sale in all the large bazaars, and find a ready market among the Chinese. They consist of mixed dark and yellow leaves, very thin and extremely coarse, valued in Calcutta at 3*d*. and 1*d*. per ℔.; these rounded cakes are piled in heaps of one size, and covered with the large dry leaves of some tree.

We come now to consider the country to the east of the Kakhyen hills, but as the Nantin valley and a broad tract of country from thence to Momien belong to an entirely different geological age from the Hotha and Sanda valleys, I propose to treat of the two separately. A line drawn north-west across the range of hills closing in the Nantin valley to the north, intersected at the town of that name by another drawn east and west, along with the range of hills, would define an angular space over which there has been a comparatively recent outflow of trappean rocks, while the country to the west is exclusively granitic and metamorphic. My observations of the latter country were limited to the valleys of Sanda and Hotha. I select the former town to designate the valley in which it is situated, from its being the well-known Sanda-Foo of the maps. It must be borne in mind, however, that so far from being a Foo or city, it is little larger than a small village in England, and that Muangla in the same valley, although a place of greater consequence, is about the size of a small English country town.

Before describing these two valleys in detail, I shall glance at the general features of the country between the Kakhyen hills and the Cambodia, and I am enabled to extend my remarks thus far from a careful consideration of the Burmese itineraries of the embassies to Pekin.

The Kakhyen hills, in the Tapeng and Hotha valleys to the east, send off long high secondary ranges running nearly north-east and south-west, and the country to the north and south is described as partaking of the same character, which is probable, and almost certain to occur in the ranges defining the Shuaylee and Molay. The relation of the Hotha to the Tapeng valley is simply a repetition of the relation of the latter to the great valley of the Irawady itself. It is an affluent valley to the Tapeng, and the name of its river is the Namsa. This stream flows in a north-westerly direction to reach the Tapeng, and the probability is that there is a valley to the south corresponding to that of the Hotha one, and that its stream flows to the south-west to reach the greater valley of the Shuaylee. The conception, then, that may be formed of the country is this—that such large rivers as the Irawady, Salween, and Cambodia are defined by high primary ranges of granitic and metamorphic rocks, running nearly north and south, the Kakhyen hills being the range that bounds the eastern side of the first-mentioned river; and that the Shuaylee, Tapeng, and Molay indicate the existence of large secondary ranges to the Kakhyen mountains, running east-north-east and west-south-west; and that the interval between two such rivers as the Tapeng and Shuaylee is occupied by a more elevated country than the great valleys of the secondary ranges which again are divided by small tertiary ranges quite as high above the sea as the secondary ones, but instead of enclosing broad valleys, they define only short comparatively shallow valleys, elevated from 1,000 to 2,000 feet above the greater valleys, and all draining into the larger valleys on either side of them. Such are the general relations of the Hotha to the Sanda valley, and from the top of Chittie-doung, above Ponsee, it was apparent that a similar arrangement prevailed to the north between the Molay and its subsidiary valleys. The occurrence of such streams as the Myitnge, to the south of the Shuaylee, renders it highly probable that this distribution of hill and dale holds good along the course of the large rivers wherever they receive affluents.

Another range, almost parallel to the Kakhyen hills, occurs to the east of Momien. It is a lofty jagged line of mountains with the Tapeng rising on one of its sides, and the Shuaylee on the other, but it does not extend any way to the south between the two rivers, but loses itself in the surrounding mass of hills; it is very elevated as we trace it to the north, and I estimated the highest points visible from Momien at about 8,000 to 9,000 feet above the level of the sea. To the east of this, again, I am informed that another ridge is crossed before the Salween is reached. The first of these ranges, Kananzan, as seen from Momien, has all the appearance of being composed of primitive rocks, and is in strong contrast to the grassy trappean hills that form the country round about that town.

The general direction of the rivers, from the Irawady valley as far east as the most eastern branch of the Cambodia which flows out of the lake of Tali, indicates that the lay of the country, from the Kakhyen hills to the centre of the province of Yunan, is nearly north and south, with subsidiary ranges diverging generally to the east-north-east; but some have even more easting in them, and it is the occurrence of these secondary ranges, and their latter modifications, that have doubtless contributed to give the Bhamô routes their high place as the easiest and most direct highways to Western Yunan.

With regard to the distances that exist between the Irawady and its affluent the Shuaylee, the Salween, and the Cambodia, and consequently the approximate intervals between the various ranges defining their water-sheds, it may be stated that Momien is 120 miles from the Irawady valley by the ups and downs of the road, and that the Shuaylee is 32 miles to the east of the Momien valley. In the Burmese itineraries on which I place considerable reliance, as I have been able to test their accuracy from Bhamô to Momien, and have found them remarkably correct, the Salween is stated to be 14 miles eastward from the Shuaylee, and as the latter river is crossed by an iron suspension bridge, the probability is that it is there confined to a narrow valley, and only separated from the Salween by a mountain ridge. The Salween is 36 miles from what the Burmese regard as the main stream of the Cambodia; and 46 miles still further to the east, a considerable affluent is encountered entering another large branch of the Cambodia yet further to the east, flowing from the lake of Tali. The last-mentioned is called the Hokyan, but as the Burmese state that they halted at the village of Yanpyinhein after crossing the former, and then crossed the Hokyan, I conclude that the two streams are bridged immediately above their union, for no mention is made of the distance between these two points, whereas the distances generally in the itinerary are carefully noted. The general character of the country, then, between the Burmese valley and a line drawn north and south through Talifoo, is a succession of main mountain ranges running nearly north and south, defining the course of certain large rivers, and giving off a series of long secondary ranges extending, more or less interruptedly, a long way to the east-north-east.

In the instance of the Tapeng, the secondary ranges form a valley about 120 miles long, or nearly so; but the Shuaylee, which is a much larger river, after tracing it about 100 miles from the Irawady, comes down from the north round the high Kananzan range, a ridge of mountains corresponding in its course to the hills defining the western side of the Salween, but of limited southward extension. Beyond this, the Cambodia is separated from the Salween by a ridge nearly parallel to the Kananzan range, and I have been informed that a considerable descent is made to reach the former river. The eastern affluents of the Cambodia come down through secondary valleys corresponding to those of the Tapeng and Shuaylee.

With regard to the general elevation of the country, it may be said to be at a considerable altitude above the Burmese valley, and from what I observed and learned from the natives, it is doubtful whether any of the valleys are much below the height of the Sanda valley, which aneroid observations, corrected for temperature, latitude, and the diurnal atmospheric pressure, have made to be about 2,200 feet above the level of the sea. This may be taken as a fair average of the height of this valley, which may be said, in round numbers, to be about 48 miles in length. The Hotha valley, which runs parallel to it, on the other side of the high range defining it to the south, is a small valley more than 2,000 feet above it, and enclosed by hills on every side. The valley of Nantin, which is only the eastern continuation of the Sanda valley, is about 1,040 feet higher than it, while Momien is 1,400 feet above the Nantin valley, so that to reach the town of Momien from the plains of Burmah, we first ascend the Kakhyen hills to the Sanda valley, and from thence pass over the high intervening spurs of the Mawphoo hill to the Nantin valley, from the upper extremity of which we ascend to the valley of Hawshuenshan, and rise from thence to that of Momien at an elevation of nearly 5,000 feet, which appears to be the average height of the country to the east of Hawshuenshan.

The Sanda valley is about 48 miles long with an average breadth of from 3 to 5 miles, and although the difference of altitude between its extremities is considerable, its great length makes it appear to be almost level. It is defined on either side by a range of hills, which I estimated by the eye to have an average height of 2,500 feet above the valley, but one high mountain occurs behind Sanda, to the north, which Mr. Gordon considered to be close on 4,000 feet in height. The highest peak, Shuemuelong, of the southern range, situated to the east south-east of Muangla, appears to rise above 3,000 feet. I had, however, no means at my disposal for ascertaining the actual heights, and as the apparent altitude of mountains is much influenced by the state of the atmosphere, it is quite possible that I have over-estimated some, and under-estimated others. I believe, however, that the limit of error will be under 500 feet in the case of the loftiest hills. The two ranges are very precipitous, and have a markedly peaked outline where they are highest, and their summits are covered with patches of dense forest, while their steep slopes below are overspread with grass. The almost inaccessible heights of their bold projecting shoulders are dotted with Kakhyen villages which are connected to the valley by narrow, zigzag paths winding down the giddy declivities.

So much for the general appearance of this lovely valley, but when we come to examine its northern wall in detail, we find that there is a remarkable break in it at the town of Muangla, and that it bends across to the north-east to form the western boundary of a vale that opens out into this portion of the Sanda valley. Its place, however, is taken up by another and lower range of tree-capped, grassy, peaked hills, defining the eastern end of the valley beyond Muangla. The gap between these two ranges gives passage to the main stream of the Tapeng, which flows down to join the Tahô below Muangla. A somewhat similar vale to this, but on a much smaller scale, occurs at Sanda, where it forms a bay, as it were, in the main valley, and is continued to the north-east as a high steep glen between two ranges, through which the Nam Sanda or Sanda river flows to join the Tapeng. The town of Sanda is situated at the mouth of the bay.

Another feature remains to be mentioned, and that is, that the northern range sends out long spurs in two places which almost divide the valley into three basins, and their occurrence has, in all probability, brought about the three divisions of the valley into as many states— Manwyne, Sanda, and Muangla. Sanda is situated between the two spurs, and is so shut in that on looking from the hills above the town, neither the Muangla or Manwyne basins can be seen. The spur separating it from Muangla is only 2 miles distant to the east, and runs right across to the opposite hills as a low grassy ridge, confining the Tapeng to a narrow, deep channel. The other spur is not so marked, and is half-way between the two towns. The southern range is unbroken throughout its whole extent, but is cut into by deep glens and gorges, down which mountain streams fall over rocky precipices to the valley.

The part of the valley above Muangla is much contracted, and consists of the undulating ground of the low ends of spurs. The Tahô runs along the base of the southern range in a deep narrow channel. At the upper end of the valley, where the river debouches from the Mawphoo gorge, it has cut away an area of the superficial deposits, which are more or less peaty in their upper layers, about a mile in length, two hundred yards broad, and 60 feet in depth, and the whole of this denuded spot is a barren waste of rubble. A similar denudation has taken place at Muangla, below where the river leaves that part of the valley. Here, too, the superficial deposits have been gradually washed away even on a larger scale than in the former locality, the tract being about $2\frac{1}{2}$ to 3 miles long, and 2 broad. The Tahô, in its course over it, is broken up into a number of small channels partly natural, while others have been made for the irrigation of the rice crops that are grown on the northern side below Muangla, where there has been a greater deposit of silt than in the other parts. By far the larger portion of the expanse is covered with large pebbles and sand. The old river banks are well defined on either side of this gorge, at the western end of which the main stream of the Tapeng is joined by the Tahô. No more instructive illustration of denudation by running water could be wished for than these two examples furnished by the Tahô.

The rocks constituting the mass of the hills are simply a repetition of those I have described as occurring in the Kakhyen hills,—varieties of forms of gneiss, crystalline limestone, quartzose rocks, and granite. Opposite to Manwyne a white crystalline limestone shows itself in a brown-weathered cliff on the hill side, capped by thick beds of quartzose rocks. The transverse spur above Sanda runs down from a high, rather peaked hill, consisting chiefly of blue crystalline limestone; and on the other side of the bay-like vale, the hill behind Sanda is composed of a very hard, splintery, slightly pinkish, quartzose rock, which disintegrates into a rich red soil. A number of spurs of this colour occur all along the base of the northern range, and as the one at Muangla consists of a rock strongly resembling that at Sanda, it is probable that the whole of these spurs are made up of varieties of the same rock. These spurs are peculiar in this respect, that few trees will grow on them, and that their soil is only adapted to tobacco, and one or two minor crops.

In the range that takes the place of the other, which extends from the Kakhyen hills to the right bank of the Tapeng at Muangla, a micaceous granite is found associated with a finely micaceous bluish gneiss, and this is the only spot I observed granite, in position. Below the Mawphoo gorge, the boulders are chiefly quartzose granite, and a dark earthy slate which was not observed *in situ*.

The superficial deposits consist chiefly of yellowish and bluish clays, and sandy loam, with interbedded river gravels. An elephant's molar, said to have been found in the channel of one of the streams about Muangla, was offered for sale, but was a long way beyond my means, as £50 were demanded for it. The natives considered it to be the tooth of a dragon, and endowed it with wonderful curative and protective power: it is highly probable that it was washed out of some of the river deposits. It was certainly not a recent tooth. A few peaty beds occur in the upper or Mawphoo portion of the valley, and in that locality the channels of the mountain torrents that enter the Tahô from the east are strewn with fragments of imbedded peat, and the occurrence of this deposit originated, no doubt, the statement, made by a Chinaman from Mandalay, that coal was to be found in the Shuemuelong mountain.

Hot springs occur in the centre of the level flat of the bay-like vale close to Sanda, but although the locality has limestone hills on either side of it, the analysis of the water, as made by Dr. Macnamara, the Chemical Examiner for Government, does not show the existence of lime, and only a trace of carbonic acid. The following are the results of Dr. Macnamara's examination of the water:—

1 Gallon
$\begin{cases} 49\cdot7 \text{ grains, solid matter.} \\ 3\cdot9 \quad \text{,,} \quad \text{salts of alkalis.} \\ 10\cdot7 \quad \text{,,} \quad \text{silica, earthy salts, and oxide of iron.} \end{cases}$

The salts of the alkalis were almost entirely chloride of sodium. Sulphuric and carbonic acids were present, but no nitric acid. There were traces, however, of phosphoric acid. The water became slightly alkaline after boiling, and had a peculiar smell, which Dr. Macnamara suggests may have been due to the dregs of wine or spirit in the bottles in which the water was kept; but this is unlikely, for every precaution was taken to have the bottles well washed with warm water, and first emptied, and again re-filled with the water from the springs; but failing this explanation, Dr. Macnamara attributes the smell to the presence of some empyreumatic matter naturally present in the water.

The temperature of springs was 204°, but the Shans informed me that it reached the boiling-point during the cold weather, and the feathers of fowls and hair of kids lying about were pointed to as evidences that the water was hot enough to cook the flesh of these animals. The boiling-point of Sanda is 206°, and the diminution of temperature of the springs during the rain is due to the circumstance that they occur in the bed of a stream, the water of which flows into them, reducing their temperature two degrees. As the stream subsides, and the channels become all but dry during the cold weather, they regain the boiling-point. The flow of water is not very great, and it bubbles up through round holes in a blackish micaceous sand; the ground about them is so hot that my naked-footed companions could not stand near the principal one for any length of time. The air, too, in their immediate vicinity, was sensibly warmer than the surrounding atmosphere, and was laden with a peculiar heavy smell, which lends additional weight to Dr. Macnamara's supposition that the water contains some empyreumatic matter. On our way to Muangla from Sanda, we crossed a hot stream, only a few miles distant from these springs, and said to arise from the other side of the limestone hill; and where we met it, on the Muangla side of the spur, it was so hot, although a considerable distance from its source, and diluted by an offshoot from the Tapeng, that its presence was at once recognized, our men shouting out that they were in hot water.

As the valley of Hotha is so closely related, in many ways, to that of Sanda, it may be as well to describe it, and afterwards consider the resources and population of the two at the same time. It lies to the south, and parallel with the Sanda valley, and the two are separated by a common range. The Hotha valley, however, is very much smaller than the one I have just described, and at a considerable elevation above it. It is shut in on either side by a well-defined ridge, the southern end of which is not nearly so high as the northern, the former being only about 500 feet high, while the latter is close on 1,000 feet, if not higher in some places. The northern range, the heights of which are thickly clad with a sub-temperate forest, sends down long grassy spurs, covered with a red rich soil. The ridge to the south is a compact range of wooded hills, terminating abruptly in the valley in a series of steep spurs, with a village usually at their base, the towns and hamlets of the northern side occupying much the same relation to its mountain spurs. The small stream, the Namsa, that flows through the valley, runs close to the southern hills in a deep channel which it has cut out for itself in the dark blue, almost bituminous clays, which, in a great part, constitute the surface of the valley and of the spurs to the north. The valley is about 1 mile to 1½ miles broad, and 25 miles in length, and is closed in at its western end by a sea of rounded grassy hills covered with the common *bracken*, through which the Namsa finds its way to precipitate itself down a steep valley in the Kakhyen hills to the Tapeng, half-way between Ponsee and Manwyne. The eastern end or head of the valley is shut in by a transverse ridge about 400 feet high, connecting the parallel ranges which define its sides. A great part of the ends of spurs from the north range have been washed away by the Namsa, and the level land that has been left consists of a rich black loam on which the rice crops are raised. The red spurs are chiefly devoted to the cultivation of tobacco and culinary vegetables.

The rocks consist of granite and gneiss, and present no features of interest. The ridge connecting the two ranges appears to be composed almost exclusively of the latter rock. The superficial deposits, besides the blue bituminous-like clay, are made of thick strata of a tenacious light yellow clay, with thin beds of rubble and sandy loam. The study of these clayey beds forcibly suggested the conclusion that they had been deposited in still water, and it is probable that the valley was a lake or swamp prior to the time the Namsa found an exit for itself through the hills to the west, or one of sufficient capacity to admit of the free drainage of this mountain basin. If the present exit of that small stream were closed, the whole valley would be submerged several feet.

The staple crops of the two valleys are rice, tobacco, and a little opium, all of which are also cultivated by the Kakhyens and Leesaws on the neighbouring hills, who grow Indian corn in addition to the rice crop. The tobacco grown by the Shans is of a very superior quality. A well-known Calcutta merchant has kindly sent a sample to the bazaar as the best way of getting a fair report upon its mercantile value, and the result is that, if it had borne a known maker's name, it would have brought Rs. 1-8 per lb.; but, without that, it was valued at Re. 1 per lb. for retail sale. In wholesale quantities a lower rate would be given.

Both valleys are covered on their upper halves with a forest in all respects resembling that of the Kakhyen hills about Ponsee, and in the Hotha valley we find the well-paved roads through the villages overshadowed by pear, plum, peach, apricot, cherry, and chestnut trees. I was informed that teak occurred on the low southern range, while, from the ridge at the head of the valley, numerous fir trees (*Pinus khasyianus*) were observed on the hills to the east. The absence of forest on the lower portion of the hills is ascribed to the felling of the trees for cultivation, and firewood: although these causes may have operated in some localities, the feature in question is most probably attributable to the character of the soil, for the natives point to immense tracts, which they say never had any forest. It is on those grassy tracts that the wild indigo grows which is in such request among the Shans for dyeing their clothes of sombre blue, in such marked contrast to the brilliant pink and yellow, so much admired by the people of the sunny plains of Burmah.

The extensive tracts of fine pasture land, surrounding the Shan towns and villages, support considerable droves of cattle and buffaloes, and large herds of ponies and mules. The cattle are not humped, and are of rather slender make, and usually reddish brown or black. The buffaloes are large, heavy animals, and quite as good specimens of their kind as those of the plains of Burmah. Some full-grown individuals of an almost creamy colour were observed, but their occurrence was exceptional. The pack-ponies, as a rule, are small; and white, iron-grey, or pale brownish-buff are the three prevailing colours. In the latter colour there was usually a dark line down the back, and the points were deep brown. The animals kept for riding by the well-to-do classes are of a larger and better breed, and a good serviceable pony costs about £8 to £10. These were the prices put on some offered to me for sale. The mules, as a rule, are even finer animals than ponies. They are usually a dark reddish-brown, with brown tips to the ears, a faint brown shoulder stripe, and black list down the back. They are brought chiefly from the country to the north of Tali, and I could not discover that any were bred in these valleys, in which I am not aware that any asses occur. The swine are kept by the Chinese and Shans; and geese, ducks, and fowls are abundant. Cats, too, are numerous, and of a uniform grey, with faint dark spots. They closely resemble an almost similar breed which is prevalent in the Himalaya, and which is nearly allied in its colouring to that grey variety of *F. Bengalensis*, which is of such frequent occurrence, especially on the plains of India. Dogs are scarce in the Sanda valley, but such as

I saw were powerful animals with shortish hair, pointed ears, and full muzzle; black and white, and brown and white were the usual colours, and their tails were carried erect. They are quite distinct from the breed found among the Kakhyens, which appears to be a cross between the Chinese dog and the pariah of the Burmese. The dogs of the Hotha valley have much more of the Chinese blood, and have long shaggy coats with erect ears, and a tendency in the tail to curl over the back, while some of them, with these characters less intensely developed, have a strong resemblance to the shepherd dogs of England.

The climate of the Sanda valley is known to me only by a short residence in May, and again in the latter end of July and beginning of August. The mean of the maximum temperature for nine days in May was 87°, and the mean of the same number of observations for the minimum temperature of that period was 63°5'. During nine days of July the mean maximum temperature was 88°6', and the mean minimum temperature 72°. In the month of May we had two or three wet days, but on our return the rainfall was very great and lasted for days together; on the former occasion the sky was usually clear and the tops of the mountains visible, but on the latter all the surrounding hills were wrapped nearly half-way down their sides in thick mist.

The maximum temperature for sixteen days of the Hotha valley in August was 82°, and the mean minimum for twenty days of the same month 68°. We had rain during the greater part of our residence, with the wind, as in the Sanda valley, from the south-west. The sky was generally clouded, with a thick mist resting on the mountains. The aneroid observations from the two valleys are tabulated in Appendix B.

With regard to the population of the Sanda valley, the data I have to offer are far from exhaustive, and, indeed, nearly all my information was derived from the Hotha Tsawbwa, but as he had a most extensive knowledge of both valleys, the results I have obtained may be considered as approximately correct. It must be borne in mind, however, that the hill population is not included, and that my calculations only refer to the villages on the comparatively level ground of the two valleys.

The number of villages in the Sanda district were estimated at from 86 to 90, those of Muangla at 200, and the Manwyne Tsawbwaship is said to contain 1,000 houses. The Hotha state numbers at least 90 villages, and the Latha comprises about 30. With these general facts before us, and allowing that half of the villages had not more than 30 houses in each, and the other half have as many as 55, and that five persons to each house may be considered a fair average, we have the following result, to which has been added the population of the respective towns, taking Muangtee at 2,000, Sanda and its bazaar at 1,500, and Manwyne at 700:—

Muangla	44,500
Sanda	20,625
Manwyne	5,700
Hotha	19,125
Latha	6,375
Total Population	96,325

The inhabitants of the Sanda valley are exclusively Shans and Chinese, while those of the Hotha valley belong to two distinct offshoots of the Shan race, a very small proportion belonging to the same stock as the Shans of the former valley; while the bulk of the population consists of what may be appropriately called the Chinese Shans or Shan Chinese, who are a markedly distinct race from the former. The typical Chinese are unknown in the Hotha valley.

The chief interest attached to the physical characters of the narrow belt of country, about 6 miles in breadth, forming what may be called the Mawphoo gorge, arises from its interesting manifestation of the disintegrating force of water. As already stated, the Tahô now runs in a deep narrow channel at the foot of the hills, forming its south-eastern side, but the two river terraces above it are unimpeachable evidence that it has cut for itself its present course; and if additional proof were required in support of this, we have only to turn to the Nantin valley, with its large river terraces, to discover that the denudation extends over a very much larger area than the Mawphoo gorge, and that the latter was denuded at the same time as the former; and as it is impossible to consider the two separately, I will describe at one and the same time what appears to have been their history. The valley of Nantin, to where the two river terraces that form its sides meet, may be said to be about 16 miles in length, with an average breadth of a mile or a little less. It is a slightly crescentic valley, running round from the west-south-west to the north. It is surrounded by grassy rounded trappean hills to the south-east, and by peaked granite and metamorphic hills to the north-west. Its head is closed in by the terraces, beyond which there is another elevated platform, or further continuation of it, devoid of terraces, but as I only obtained a distant view of this portion, I cannot describe it in detail. Its foot is formed by the high land of the Mawphoo gorge, into which the Tahô enters by a narrow deep channel between high rocky banks. The highest terrace of the Nantin valley is almost on the same elevation with the level platform at its head, and corresponds to the heights of the lowest terrace of the Mawphoo gorge. The only explanation of this coincidence in the heights of these very extensive river terraces is this, that the whole of the area defined by them has been denuded by the action of the Tahô, and that the only reason why the elevated tract of country, forming the Mawphoo valley, was not worn down by the action of the river to the level of the Nantin valley, is to be looked for in the fact, that it is largely composed of metamorphic rocks which offered a much more powerful resistance to the disintegrating action of the river than the comparatively recent soft beds of the Nantin section. It is probable also, from the close proximity of the latter to the extinct volcano of Hawshuenshan, that the denuding action of the river may have been accelerated by changes in the level of the country. In looking at this most interesting valley, from the point where the terraces close in at its head to the foot of the Mawphoo gorge, the probability is that the whole of this area was originally a level flat, with an elevation corresponding to the top of the highest terrace in the Mawphoo section, and that at that period the Tahô precipitated itself as a waterfall into the Sanda valley, as it does now from the Momien valley into that of Hawshuenshan. This theory of the origin of the two valleys is borne out by the fact, that there are indications of a third and higher terrace in the Nantin valley corresponding to the highest one of the north-eastern side of the Mawphoo glen, and the likelihood is that the elevated flat at the head, immediately surrounding the extinct volcano of Hawshuenshan, was considerably raised after the formation of the first terrace, and we might even go further, and say that the weight of evidence is to prove that the original upward termination of the Nantin valley was what is now the distinct isolated circular basin of Hawshuenshan, into which the Tahô falls from the higher valley of Momien, and that the most recent outbursts of the neighbouring volcano which closes it to the west were posterior to the disintegration of the Hawshuenshan valley, for the volcanic vent shows little or no evidence of having been subjected to the denuding action of the Tahô, which flows along its eastern side.

A striking feature of the Nantin valley, besides its river terraces, is the entire change that has come over the character of the hills which bound the left bank of the Tahô in this part of its course. Instead of the bold precipitous mountains that define it as far as the head of the

Mawphoo gorge, moderately high hills, running upwards in rounded grassy sweeps, over one another, sparsely covered with occasional clumps of trees, are now met with. Near the head of the valley, they rise into two rounded peaks, the first above the famous hot springs to the north-east of Nantin, and the other a little further in the same direction. The hills to the north-west are much higher, and are the continuation of the peaked tree-capped range that began on the left bank of the Tapeng at Muangla, and which becomes suddenly elevated; and the lower end of the Mawphoo gorge is continued onwards from that point to the north-east as a lofty well-wooded mountain wall, defining the north-western side of the valley. The eastern side of the valley, along which I travelled, is marked by numerous water-courses running at right angles to the river terraces. Their channels are strewn with water-worn granite boulders, and rounded masses of cellular basalt, a rock that can only be described as lava, and large fragments of peat. The only rocks in position that I had an opportunity to examine were those composing the side of the hill from which the hot springs issue. They consisted of two well-marked kinds, a cellular basalt and a hard quartzose rock, the former superficial where I observed it, and the latter the rock through which the springs come. Looking at this hill from the west, its south-eastern side is seen to be marked by an apparently deep nearly circular hollow of considerable size, almost surrounded by an abrupt precipice from the peaked summit of the hill, and forcibly suggesting that it may once have been a volcanic vent, a supposition which is heightened by the almost scoriatious character of some of the neighbouring rocks, and by the evidence of internal heat which the springs themselves afford. These are located on the western face of the hill, but others on a still more extensive scale occur on its other side, some miles to the east. The former issue at about 60 to 80 feet above the level of the valley under the rounded shoulder of the hill. The most important one is an oval basin, about three yards long and two broad, with a depth of about eight inches. It is situated on a level spot immediately below the shoulder; and about six yards distant from it, there are a number of funnels, about six inches in diameter, in the quartz rock, emitting steam; and on the face of the hill higher up, and about fifty yards off, another jet of steam occurs; and on the side of a very narrow gully below the principal spring, there are two other springs which give out a considerable amount of water. The water in the principal spring comes up with great force through a number of circular holes about three inches in diameter, and the bottom of the basin is covered with a thick layer of impalpable white mud. The water is quite clear, but the surface is in violent ebullition, with a temperature of 205°, the boiling-point of the thermometer at Nantin, with the air at a temperature of 71°. Nantin is a few feet below them, so that these springs afforded a verification, as it were, of the observations of the boiling-points of water in the former locality. They give off such a profusion of steam, and the heat is so great, that one can only stand to their leeward side. The ground in the immediate neighbourhood of them and the funnels is intensely hot, and our barefooted companions could not approach them by some yards. It vibrates in a remarkable way, and the sensation was as if one were standing over a gigantic boiler buried in mother-earth, an impression which is heightened by the loud, rushing sound from the funnels, and by the indistinct rumbling noises in the inferno beneath. The funnels are the most remarkable features connected with these springs. There are four or five of them in full activity, about six inches in diameter, giving exit to a rush of steam, which makes the rock intensely hot, and vibrate quite as much as the ground. The two other springs in the gully below, although they give egress to a considerable body of boiling water, are not to be compared to the one just described, as they issue through the earthy face of the hill. It is remarkable that although the stream, flowing down from the springs, is at a scalding heat, and only 8 to 10 degrees below the boiling-point, the stones in it are covered with masses of green jelly, which thrive at a temperature which was much too great for me to immerse my hands into, even for a second. Its channel is also encrusted with a white deposit. The analysis of the water of the chief spring is as follows:—

Nantin springs, temperature 205° (boiling).

1 Gallon
- 120 grains, solid matter.
- 112 ,, salts of alkalis.
- 80 ,, earthy salts, silica, and oxide of iron.

The salts of the alkalis were almost entirely chloride of sodium; very little sulphuric and carbonic acids were present, and no nitric acid was discovered, but traces of phosphoric acid were detected. This water, as in the case of the Sanda springs, was slightly alkaline after boiling, with a peculiar smell, which was sensibly felt in the vicinity of the springs.

Since the Mahomedan rebellion, only a little rice is cultivated in the neighbourhood of the two towns, Muangtee and Nantin, and around some of the half-deserted villages at the head of the valley. The soil is rich, and in the Tahô and its affluents, there is every facility for the irrigation of the fields, which were all under water in the month of May. I observed no other crops.

There is abundance of pasture on the hills, but life and property are so insecure, that the stock of cattle and ponies is reduced to the lowest ebb compatible with the every-day necessities of the few Shans who still cling to the valley, the position of which, lying, as it does, between Momien, the centre of Mahomedanism in Western Yunan, and Mawphoo and Shuemuelong to the west, which have been at different times the head-quarters of imperialism, has made it the scene of chronic warfare and raids which have almost depopulated it, and paralysed the energies of the scanty remnant of its once thriving and industrious Shan and Chinese population. Its capabilities as an agricultural and grazing country are very great, and from the circumstance that Muangtee is the point to which the Sawaddy, Hoetone, and Sanda routes converge, it formed in times of peace the high road to Momien, along which all the trade from thence found its way to Burmah, and was visited by all the embassies that ever passed between Pekin and Bhamô.

In connection with the Nantin valley, and very noteworthy, is the large extinct volcano of Hawshuenshan that occurs at its head, and only separated from the valley of Momien by the little circular valley of its own name. It lies about 300 to 400 feet below the level of Momien, and its base is from 600 to 700 feet above that of Nantin. It runs nearly north and south, and is about 4 miles long, and of an elongated oval form. On its eastern side it is surrounded by flat-topped, grassy hills, which are generally higher than it, and to the west and north it is separated from the base of a lofty range of mountains by an intervening plain about 4 miles in breadth. It is about 300 feet in height, and its summit is an apparently rounded mound, covered with luxuriant grass, while its long flowing sides are a mass of black lava, thrown into long undulations from top to base, or broken up at intervals into heaps, with a few plants growing among the interstices. As my observations were confined to a cursory view of it from horseback on my upward and downward journeys, I am not in a position to enter into the details of its structure, or of that of the plain to the west which was only seen from a distance. The sea of rounded hills to the south and east is forcibly suggestive of volcanic energy, and the occurrence of a small outburst of lava, on the western slope of the Momien valley, indicates that the disturbing influences must have been felt over a very large tract of country. It doubtless rests on a platform of rocks similar to those found in the Sanda valley, and which appear to recur in the mountains to the east of

Momien, so that there has been a comparatively recent outflow of basaltic trap and lava over an extensive area largely composed of granite and metamorphic rocks. One bed of trachyte on the side of Momien hill was above the basalt, but whether the latter may not have been merely a dyke, I cannot say. Earthquakes are said to be of frequent occurrence at Momien, and taken into connection with the "stufas," or boiling springs of Nantin, we have decided indications that the region even now is one of considerable volcanic activity.[1] With these scanty data, any opinion as to the probable age of the volcano must necessarily be of the most vague description, and of little or no value.

The valley of Hawshuenshan is a deep basin-shaped hollow, about 1½ mile long and the same in breadth, and is surrounded on all sides, except the one on which the volcano occurs, by the ruins of numerous villages lying on the gentle slope at the foot of the abrupt grassy hills that close it in. The centre is quite flat, and covered with rice cultivation, and well watered by the Tahô that flows through it. The road runs along the top of an embankment, and has two narrow paved paths for foot passengers, and a rough one for mules between the two. A short steep ascent between the hills leads from its north-eastern side up to the valley of Momien.

The valley of Momien is an elongated oval about 4 miles in length and 2 in breadth, and is perfectly level in its centre, and covered with rice cultivation, irrigated by the Tahô and other streams. It is surrounded by grassy hills on all sides, and the majority of them are rounded and flat on their tops; a few, however, occurring on the northern and north-western sides, are peaked, but supporting only grass. The pagoda hill to the west separates it from the preceding valley, and the Tahô flows round the northern end of the hill, leaving the valley by a waterfall of 100 feet, between two truncated pyramidal hills, which appear to have been once connected together, and to have closed in the valley at this point, a supposition that is borne out by the circumstance that the deposits of the valley are indicative of a lacustrine origin. Below the soil, which is about one foot in thickness, there is a reddish ochreous earth of very light weight and of about eight inches deep, resting on a bed of black peat, about four feet thick in some places, and overlying a light coloured consistent clay of considerable depth, filled with little water-worn particles of white quartz. This clay is largely used in the

---

[1] Burmah has frequently been visited by earthquakes, which have been felt from Bhamô to Rangoon, and as the motion has been observed to travel from the east, it is possible that they may have originated in the volcanic centre of Momien.

manufacture of bricks. The probability is that the Momien valley, through some disturbance in its level, immediately after the formation of the lowest bed, was converted into a shallow marsh; then followed another change in its level, indicated by the reddish ochreous earth, and the valley was once more converted into a lake. There can be no doubt that the Tahô itself has done much in altering the character of the valley, for it is impossible to look at its narrow exit, and at the aspect of the hills between which it flows at that spot, without the conclusion forcibly suggesting itself that the river has done a gigantic work in the way of cutting a passage for itself between them, and that their configuration is in great part to be attributed to its eroding action. A careful examination of the glen below the fall reveals the fact that the river is slowly but gradually bringing the waterfall more and more to the east. Standing to the east of the low conical hills that close in the valley at this point, the theory suggests itself that the valley must have been at one time a deep lake, with a depth corresponding to the conical hills, and that its waters, draining out as a small stream into the valley below, slowly deepened their channel every year, reducing the level of the lake till at last it ceased to exist, and the Tahô, that had fed it, flowed through it, and began to disintegrate the slope to the Hawshuenshan valley, and to form a waterfall when it came in contact with the mass of basalt that forms the Momien plateau. The slow wearing away of the hills at the exit of the lake could have in no way affected the nature of the deposits, the differences in which can only be accounted for by the changes in the relative levels of the valley. The banks at the base of the hills, which slope gradually to the level flat of the valley, seem to favour the foregoing view of its history.

About 10 miles to the north-east of Momien, the primitive and metamorphic rocks appear again in the high range of the Kananzan (Tayshan)[1] mountains, which stands in bold relief as a purple wall running nearly north and south, with the Shuaylee on its eastern face. Limestone and fossiliferous rocks occur near Talifoo, from whence also are derived the chalk, flint, and arsenic sold in the Momien bazar.

Copper is brought from a range of hills near the village of Khyto, where it is melted on the spot, and imported to Momien in flattish lumps. The same hills are said to yield nearly all the iron and salt used in Western Yunan. Tin also is brought to Mandalay in considerable quantities by the caravans from Talifoo. By far the most important product,

---

[1] Is this word in any way connected with the Tay-yay or great Shans?

however, is the galena, and Dr. Oldham has assayed a specimen which he has pronounced to be wondrously rich, among the richest in silver he has ever known, and he informs me that the average percentage of silver in galena is 0·01 up to 0·05—rarely beyond this, although some ores have yielded so much as 7 per cent. The Khyto ore yields 0·278 per cent. of silver in the galena, and 104 ounces of silver to the ton of lead. The following table shows its position with reference to the galena of the following well known mines:—

Hartz galena	0·03 to 0·05
English „	0·02 to 0·03
Scotch (Lead hills)	0·03 to 0·06
Tuscany	0·32 to 0·72
Kakhyen hills	0·191
Khyto (Yunan)	0·278

Gold is brought to Momien from Yonephin and Sherzwan, villages 15 days to the north-east, but I have no information as to whether it is found in any quantity. The precious metal is also brought to Momien in leaf, and imported to Burmah, where it is extensively used in the decorations of pagodas, khyoungs, and images of Bhudda.

Rice is the staple crop of the Nautin, Hawshuenshan, and Momien valleys, but wheat and barley are also grown, but in larger quantities in the country to the east of Momien, and specially in the neighbourhood of Talifoo. The forests in the Talifoo district have been described to me as almost exclusively composed of pines, and the winter is said to be severe. Potatoes appear to be largely cultivated in Western Yunan, and many fields were devoted to them about Momien, where they are reared and planted out in the same way as in England. They were quite as good as English potatoes, and in great vogue among the Chinese, and 3¼lbs. are sold for four pence. The leaf is slightly smaller than the home plant, and the tubers have a thin red skin. They had nearly finished flowering by the beginning of June. Nothing could be learned regarding the history of their introduction. Celery is also largely cultivated, and seems to be in general requisition. The remaining vegetables are carrots, peas, beans, and cabbage; and the fruits are pomegranates, apples, pears, grapes, walnuts, peaches, apricots, and plums, a variety of brambles, and rose hips. Neither tea nor tobacco are cultivated in the Momien valley, but opium is extensively grown all over the province, and sells in the bazaar at Rs. 10 to Rs. 12 for 3¼lbs.

The Momien cattle have no hump, and are rather a small breed but well made, and generally reddish-brown, passing through intermediate darker tints to black. Buffaloes are also common, and chiefly used for agricultural purposes. The sheep, which are numerous, are a very large black-faced breed with convex profiles. Two kinds of goat are also common, one with long shaggy usually white hair, nearly reaching the ground, and with procumbent, flattened, spiral horns directed backwards and outwards; and the other with very short, dark, reddish-brown hair, short shoulder list and largish beard, with the same flattened kind of spiral horn as the former, only not so procumbent. The horns of both have all the characters of those of *C. magaceros*. The ponies are remarkably fine animals, but they are not nearly so much prized as a good mule, and the latter greatly outnumber them. Pigs are numerous, and all that came under my notice were black. Dogs are very scarce, and the few that occur about Momien are all black with thick shaggy coats, and very like the shepherd dog met with in the south of Scotland. Cats are numerous, and nearly all of a uniform grey, with very faint darkish spots. Fowls, geese, and ducks are abundant and large.

It is doubtful whether the population of Momien and its suburbs exceeds 5,000 or 6,000, and with regard to that of the Nantin and Hawshuenshan valleys, it is improbable that together they exceed 3,000. I am not able to offer an opinion regarding the population of the country generally; but there can be little doubt that the rebellion has paralysed industry, and greatly depopulated the land, especially in the neighbourhood of the Panthay centres of action; and that a considerable population still exists among the more inaccessible hills and valleys to which the inhabitants have resorted to escape the evils of war, and the oppression of the Mahomedans; and that in the event of law and right again asserting themselves, and trade reviving, they would return to their villages, which are at present the haunts of owls and bats, and the lurking-places of lawless bandits.

Up to Muangtee, the population of the valleys is almost exclusively Shan, but beyond that town, the Chinese element prevails, with an intermixture of Mahomedans, and in the hills there is a sprinkling of Kakhyens and Leesaws.

The climate of the country beyond the Mawphoo ridge appears to be of a much drier character than that of the Kakhyen hills and the Sanda valley. Prior to our arrival at Momien, there had been such a protracted interval of rainless weather that the authorities were afraid that the long-continued drought would prove injurious to the crops, and were anxiously looking for rain. As will be observed from the weather tables in the appendix, the wind was generally from the south-west, and that during the whole of June and the first twelve days of July, there were only a very few fair intervals. The sky was obscured by thick misty clouds that wrapped the hills in their dense folds. As a rule the rain fell very heavily, but there were days together when it was little more than a gentle drizzle, in a dead calm. Occasional thunder-storms, however, of terrific grandeur burst over the valley, accompanied by strong gusts from the south-west; but the most characteristic feature of the weather was the generally perfect stillness of the atmosphere, the incessant rain, and low leaden clouds, all which, combined, had a most depressing effect on us who were fresh from the clear exhilirating climate of the Kakhyen hills.

The mean maximum and minimum temperatures for the months of June and July were as follows:—

JUNE.			JULY.	
74° 71′	...	Maximum (dry).	79° 95′	... Maximum (dry).
71° 19′	...	Maximum (wet).	70° 65′	... Maximum (wet).
62° 83′	...	Minimum (dry).	67° 64′	... Minimum (dry).
61° 16′	...	Minimum (wet).	63° 24′	... Minimum (wet).

During our residence we had a fire burning constantly in our apartments, and found it necessary for our comfort.

Snow falls during the winter months, but does not lie long, and frost is said to be of frequent occurrence during the night and early morning. The natives strongly assert that the climate is very unhealthy to strangers, and we were frequently warned against its evil influences, from which we did not escape, as the majority of our party suffered from intractable hill diarrhœa which nothing would check. The river water, too, is considered highly injurious, and we were particularly cautioned against using it.

The children semed very healthy, and I did not see a single case of fever, although I must have treated about sixty or seventy persons for other diseases during our visit. The fact that by far the greater part of the valley is under water for six or seven months, and that during three of these, it is little better than a huge morass, would not seem to augur much for its healthiness. We must remember, however, that it is 4,517 feet above the level of the sea, in the 24th parallel of north latitude, and that it is a comparatively dry temperate country, singularly destitute of trees, a combination of conditions which would appear to indicate that it is beyond the range of miasma.

CHAPTER V.

SHANS AND KAKHYENS AND OTHER RACES TO THE EAST OF BHAMÔ.

THE mass of the population about Bhamô and of the country to the west of it, as far as the confines of Assam, and even to the upper portion of the valley of the Brahmaputra, to the east of Suddyah, and of the whole valley of the Irawady, as far north as the base of the high mountains that define it from the southern borders of Tibet, is essentially Shan, with a considerable proportion of Kakhyens, or, more properly, Singphos or Chingpaws, as the members of that tribe to the east of Bhamô designate themselves. The Shans, however, unlike the latter people, extend a considerable way to the south of Bhamô, and from the circumstance that they long ago adopted the customs of their conquerors, and have in all probability largely intermarried with them, they are not separated from the Burmese by any sharp line of demarcation, but have so blended with them that it is frequently very difficult to say whether one is in a Shan or Burmese district, the assimilation having proceeded so far, that the Shan language in Burmah is almost a dead tongue. This implies that there are no very marked physical differences by which the Shan of the Irawady valley can be distinguished from the Burman. This is probably due, in great part, to intermarriage, for the Shans, as they are found in their native valleys, in the elevated country to the east of Bhamô, where they are almost the sole population, are markedly distinct from the Burmese. Those of the Irawady valley, it must be remembered, have formed part of the Burmese empire since 1596, or before that date, and they were even at that time so influenced by the conquering race that they conformed to all the chief peculiarities that distinguish a Burman. A further breaking down of race distinctions, and perhaps of the one, of all others, that most tends to foster the jealousies and to prevent the assimilation of peoples, was removed by the Burmese language being substituted for the Shan in all the schools of the khyongs. As far north as Bhamô, which was once a Shan principality, and in which there are few, if any, Burmese, the language of the latter people has largely taken the place of Shan, and is understood by the majority. A short way above Bhamô, the Burmese influence has not been so markedly felt, and Shan is much more prevalent, although the great majority of the people there also understand Burmese; south of Bhamô, however, the latter language is the one in general repute. Among the unmixed race to the east, the Burmese language is all but unknown, and the Chinese stands in a similar relation to the Shan that the former does to the latter in the Irawady valley, although not to the same extent. This conversion of the Shans of the Irawady into a Burmese-speaking population has been brought about in three and a quarter centuries, and there can be little doubt that the process of assimilation, which was commenced so long ago, is still in full activity, and it may be that another century will find the Shans knowing only of their own language through their chronicles, and in the course of other and following years these may one by one disappear, and the only remaining trace of the language may be the impress it may have made on the Burmese tongue. Facts like these indicate that no sound system of ethnology can be reared on any other foundation than that of history as the interpreter of the facts of philology, and of the modifications of physical form induced by the blending of races. The study of the changes at present going on in the languages of two peoples, such as those of the Shans and Burmese of the Irawady valley, and the accurate recording of the effects of intermarriage, and the crossing and re-crossing of the two tribes, might ultimately result in our being able to cull, from the mass of facts, certain persistent phenomena, which might be proved by further observation to be of universal occurrence under similar conditions. They would be of two kinds, philological and anatomical; but as it is not the study of an isolated organ, or part of the body, that will yield the results that would be necessary to place the anatomical wall of the temple of ethnological science on a sure basis, no more would the results of the simple comparison of vocabularies be accepted by the philosophical philologist as a foundation on which to rear the superstructure of his system of knowledge. The value to be attached to any generalizations founded on the crania of tribes, the histories of which are unknown to the anatomist, may be gathered from an illustration drawn from the Shans and Burmans of the Irawady. Supposing that two centuries hence their history were unknown, an event which is unlikely to happen in the case of these people, but which may, and probably has, occurred in the instance of many tribes, e. g., the Karens of Burmah, the Mechis of the Himalayan Terai, the Lepchas of Sikkim, the so-called Hinduised aborigines of India, and a host of others, how utterly helpless in such cases would craniology be. All that it could possibly do would be to tabulate the measurements and capacities of the skulls, but to give any indication, beyond their relative brachycephalisism or doliocephalisism, would be out of the question, and such comparisons could by no possibility throw any light on the affinities of these races, because, as has been already said, we know nothing of the laws that regulate the blending of tribes, or whether it gives rise to any particular modification, *sui generis*, of the two original types of crania, if such existed in the original stocks. In such a situation, too, the philologist, as an ethnologist, would be completely at sea in his researches, for he would be dealing with a mixed race, one of the constituent elements of which had lost its language.

But to return to the Shans. The Shan or Tai nation forms by far the most important element in the population of that large tract of country comprising the alluvial flats and hilly country of the valley of the upper Irawady, and the elevated mountainous regions lying between it and the Cambodia. Before the Chinese-Tartar kings extended their conquests across the Yang-tse-kiang, the probability is that the Tai nation stretched even as far east as the banks of that river, because their whole history indicates that they are a people of eastern origin. That they existed in Eastern Yunan, in early times, appears evident from the frequent occurrence of Shan names applied to districts and cities. The likelihood is, that they entered Burmah in the first century of our era, and that they were the conquering host that swept down on ancient Tagoung, and destroyed it, and that their capital at that time was Muanglong on the Shuaylee. At that period they brought all the tribes in Upper Burmah under their subjection, and ultimately spread into the valleys of Munipore and the Brahmaputra. The country was not then peopled with Kakhyens as now, and it is probable that the Shans found the Burmese in possession of the soil, and that the two races, even in those early times, began to commingle. The resultant race, however, was destined to receive a fresh infusion of Burmese blood, and to revert to the customs of the people that had been originally conquered, but were now in the ascendant. Intermarriage between the Shans and Burmans was so prevalent even before the subjection of the Shan kingdom to Burmah, that the former people gave two or three kings to the throne of Tsagain.

The states in Western Yunan appear to have been annexed to China about 1285, but the Shans in the valleys of the upper Irawady retained their independence with their capital in the Mogoung district. It is extremely probable—and, indeed, all the traditions of the Siamese and other offshoots of the Shans point to Western Yunan as the site of the kingdom of their ancestors, the great Tais—that the kingdom that appears to have existed in Western Yunan and Upper Burmah before the Chinese had advanced across the Yang-tse-kiang, or had only begun to do so, was the kingdom of Pong. It gradually became broken up, however, into small principalities and states, and one of the last remnants of the kingdom of Pong disappeared from the page of history in 1752 A.D.

There are no means, as far as I am aware, of determining when the Shans embraced Buddhism, which appears to have been introduced into Burmah 241 B.C., but it is probable that the hordes, which overran Upper Burmah in the first century, met with a Buddhist population, which acted as the leaven in their ultimate conversion to the faith of the immortal Shakyha. The claim advanced by the Burmese to have been the first to introduce Buddhism into the Shan valleys of Hotha and Latha is probably without foundation, and they never, in all likelihood, did more than build a few monasteries and pagodas. The frequent intercourse that existed between China and Burmah, a few centuries before its alleged introduction into these valleys, and the circumstance that that marvellous religion had been firmly established in China for many years prior to that event, render it highly improbable that Hotha and Latha, which were all but on the highway between the two kingdoms, were left uninfluenced by it. There is this peculiarity, too, of Buddhism in the Sanda valley, that it is utterly devoid of pagodas of any description.

The Shans inhabit the valleys of Sanda, Hotha, and part of Nantin, and are also found in the country to the north of the first and last mentioned valleys, and although we possess no definite information regarding the extent of their distribution in that direction, it is probable that they reach as far as the 27th or even the 28th parallels. To the south, they may be said to stretch as far as the 11th parallel, and their respective states are tributary either to China, Ava, or Siam. Those tributary to China lie to the north of the 23rd parallel. It is extremely difficult to define the limit of their range to the east, for beyond the middle of the Nantin valley, they appear to blend with a population essentially Chinese in its customs and language. I refer especially to the peasantry who visit Momien on market days, and who are so alike, physically, to the pure Shans of Sanda, that it would puzzle the most keen and accurate observer to separate the two in a mixed assemblage. This general likeness, however, is even of a more extended character, and Kakhyens are often met with so like Shans that they are frequently mistaken for such; and, moreover, one meets with numerous examples among what is called the Chinese population about Momien that would be unhesitatingly referred to the Kakhyen race. The mule-drivers from Talifoo, who accompany the caravans that visit Mandalay once a year, have also a very strong resemblance to Shans, and are markedly different from the typical Chinese who form the merchant class at Momien. These difficulties in arriving at a correct estimate of the eastern range of the Shan race in their purity, and of their real affinities to the surrounding races, are greatly increased from the circumstance that the Chinese, Kakhyen, and Shan languages are commonly spoken by the Kakhyens and Shans, and also by the so-called Chinese population, bordering the Shan states. There is this to be noticed, too, in connection with the Shans in the district visited by the expedition, that they are broken up into two distinct tribes, the Shans proper and the Poloungs. In the Sanda and Nantin valleys the population is exclusively the first, but on the hills on both sides of them, and also on those to the south of Hotha, we find Poloungs intermarrying with the Shans, but never settling in the valleys. They are in every respect hill Shans, whose chief occupation is the cultivation of tea, opium, and tobacco. In the elevated Hotha valley, the mass of the population are Chinese-Shans, but so uncertain am I regarding the affinity of the latter people, that I hesitate to speak with any degree of confidence regarding their origin. They seem to be physically intermediate between the two nations, and might almost, with equal propriety, be called Shan-Chinese, and if we were guided by their customs and dress, their whole affinities are Chinese. The Shans, however, claim them as a tribe, and they speak a dialect of their language. The true Shans also occur in this valley, and the Tsawbwa is a typical example, although his sympathies are largely Chinese.

The Shans proper of these valleys are a fair people, with a very faintly darker hue than Europeans, with the somewhat sallow tint of the Chinese. These remarks apply to the higher classes, for the peasantry, as a rule, are much browned by exposure. The young people and children have the peculiar waxen appearance of the Chinese, but to a less extent: they have usually red cheeks and dark brown eyes and black hair. The Shan face, generally, is rather short, broad, and flat, with prominent malars, and a faint obliquity and contraction of the outer angle of the eye, so markedly developed in the Chinese. The nose is well formed, and there is not that breadth and depression that is so characteristic of the Burman, and the bridge is usually prominent and almost aquiline. The lower jaw is broad and well developed; but pointed chins, with protuberant heavy lips, are not unfrequent.

Oval, rather laterally-compressed faces, with retreating foreheads, high cheek-bones, and sharp rather retreating chins, are of frequent occurrence, and it struck me that the majority of the better classes had more elongated oval faces than the generality of the common people, and that the cast of countenance among the higher ranks was decidedly Tartar. The features of the women are proportionally rounder and broader than those of the other sex, but they are more finely chiselled, with a very good-natured expression, and generally large brown eyes, with very sparse eyebrows and eyelashes. They become much wrinkled with age; and from the number of old people we observed of both sexes, they appear to be a long-lived race. They are not a very tall people, and the average height of the men does not appear to exceed 5 feet 8 inches, if so much. The women, as a rule, are smaller and more squat. The only difference between the Poloungs and Shans seems to be in the darker skins of the former, and their more uniformly smaller size. There may be other and more marked distinctions, which did not come under my observation, for I only saw a few of these people.

The Hotha Shans in no way differ from those we have just described, but this cannot be said of the Chinese-Shans or Shan-Chinese. They are a much smaller race, almost reminding one of Laplanders in their little squat figures, and broad, short, round, flat faces, characters which are much more intensely and generally developed than among the Shans. The colour of their skin, too, is more that of the Chinese than the last-mentioned people. The cheek-bones are very prominent, and their faces much flatter and shorter than any among their alleged kindred of Sanda, and the breadth between their eyes is considerable, and their mouths are generally heavy, and the lips more or less protruding. The women have all of these characters more pronounced, and their eyes the decided obliquity of the Chinese.

A striking idiosyncrasy of the Shan population to the east of the Kakhyen hills is their fondness for dark blue. There is one prevailing tint, and so universally is it adopted, and so great is the uniformity in their style of dress, with the exception of the Chinese-Shans, that it is questionable whether any regiment of regulars is equipped with more uniformity than these people. In full dress, however, the Shan women exhibit an appreciation for colour that would please the taste of the most fastidious art critic. Their ordinary garb is very sombre, but their peculiar head-dress, like an inverted pyramid, gives them an *outré* appearance in the eyes of a stranger. It consists of a long band, or rather a series of long blue scarfs, about 1 foot broad and of a total length of 40 to 50 feet long, wound round the head with great regularity, and towering upwards and backwards in a large pile, the free end of which is usually fringed, and embroidered with pretty devices in gold and silk thread. The folds are arranged in a crescent over the forehead with the greatest precision and neatness, and occasionally a few silver ornaments are fastened to the front of the turban, or attached to the embroidered end, which is allowed to hang a short way down the neck. The top of the head is left uncovered in the centre of the turban, and the hair is ornamented with silver hair-pins, with flat heads with richly enamelled representations of flowers and insects. The jacket is short and moderately loose, and has a narrow erect collar. It is fastened at the neck, and down the centre, by a number of thin, square, enamelled plates of silver; and in full dress, the shoulders, and a line down the back, and another in front, are covered with large hemispherical silver buttons, richly embossed with figures of birds and flowers, enamelled in various colours. The sleeves are rather loose from the elbow, and usually folded back, showing a massive silver torque-like bracelet. A tight, thick cotton skirt, frequently ornamented round the lower third with squares of coloured silk and satin or embroidered work, with a pair of close-fitting leggings made of the same material, and handsomely embroidered shoes, with slightly turned-up toes, complete their external attire. On particular occasions, a richly embroidered cloth is worn over the skirt. The women are seldom seen without the long-stemmed pipes, which have very small clay bowls covered with a dark brown glaze. Girls, up to the age of thirteen or fourteen, wear trousers like the boys, with small aprons in front, and a simple scarf of blue cotton cloth wound round the head.

The costume of the male peasantry is a double-breasted loose jacket reaching to the loins, and buttoned down the right side. The buttons are frequently jade, amber, or silver. Their turbans are thick blue cotton cloth, with a long fringe at the free end, which is usually wound up with the pig-tail, and brought round the outside. In rainy and sunny weather a very broad straw hat, covered with oiled silk, is worn over the turban. Their trousers are very loose, and reach only a short way below the knee. The shins are bound round with long stripes of blue cloth to protect them against injury, a fashion that seems to prevail not only among the Shans and Kakhyens, but also among the Chinese peasantry generally. Their shoe uppers are made of thick blue, almost felt cloth, embroidered with narrow braid, and with thick leather soles. The better classes, such as the headmen of the towns, wear black satin skull-caps, ornamented with Chinese figures in gold braid, and long blue coats reaching to the ankles. The little boys don blue cotton skull-caps, braided in the same way as those worn by adults, but with a red top-knot, and a row in front of silver figures of guardian nâts.

The costume of the Shan-Chinese or Chinese-Shan women is markedly different from the dress of their neighbours in the Sanda valley, and is intermediate, to a certain extent, between it and the general style of attire that prevails among their Chinese sisters. They wear the Shan jacket, and loose trousers like the men, but with the ends unhemmed. The back half of the jacket is prolonged downwards to below the knees like a long undivided coat-tail, and a double Chinese apron is worn in front, and with the tail completes a kind of skirt. In addition to the silver plate-like brooches, the shoulders are ornamented with an epaulet of small hemispherical discs, the one on either side being connected by a line of silver buttons passing round the shoulders. The waistband of the apron is about six inches broad, and dilates behind into a richly embroidered piece that forms a distinctive feature in the dress of that peculiar people. They seldom wear shoes. Their headdress, however, is the most striking feature in their attire, and consists of a hoop about six inches in diameter, made of cloth wound round a ratan, and placed on the crown of the head, with the hair in front transversely divided and gathered up, with that of the back, into the centre of the hoop, and plaited into the ends of a flat chignon of the dimensions of the internal diameter of the hoop. The latter is kept in position by about 25 to 30 silver pins fastened into the chignon and mass of hair, with their heads resting on and completely hiding the hoop. The pinheads are large, thin, flat plates of silver, placed longitudinally to the length of the hair, and either embossed or engraved with figures of leaves or of flowers. The result of this arrangement is that the crown of the head is encircled with a silver wreath of the diameter of the hoop; and outside it, is wound a scanty blue turban, to the fringes of which a number of silver finger-rings are usually tied, and allowed to hang down behind. In full dress, in addition to the ordinary hair-pins, four much larger, usually richly enamelled, ones are worn at the front, back, and sides of the circle. These are three inches or even more in their greatest breadth, and vary from one and three-fourths to two inches in their least diameter. They are overlaid with silver wire fastened in graceful windings to represent the stems and leaves of plants, and are enamelled green, brown, and yellow, with figures, in the same material, of full-blown composite flowers, the petals being produced by red and blue round stones, and the unopened buds by little silver spheres. The heads of the ordinary pins are slightly convex, and one and three-fourths of an inch in their greatest, and one and a quarter inch in their least diameter. Their convexity is to allow of their overlapping, and their general form is a round lobed figure. The decoration of these curious chignons is sometimes carried even further, and three or four smaller pins, with each head composed of four hemispherical discs, are placed opposite to each other in an inner circle. Full-dress chignons and their pins are a foot in diameter. The head of a pin of this kind is eight inches in length, by two in breadth, and of the most intricate construction. They are of different descriptions. The simplest is made chiefly of silver wire, and flat pieces of the same metal cut out into fantastic figures and representations of trailing plants, in full flower, the colours being given by various enamels, of which green, blue, purple, and yellow are the chief. In some, the leaves are worked out in the finest filagree, and in one specimen I purchased, there is a figure resembling a swan resting on its outstretched wings among a bed of flowers. It is made wholly of silver wire, and the feathers of the wings have been most effectively brought out by simply folding a wire upon itself in the case of the quills and lesser coverts, and a double one in that of the greater coverts. Interspersed among this maze of flower and leaf, a number of mobile coils of silver wire stand up erect, each terminating in two little square discs of silver, with a hemispherical convexity in the centre of each. They have a strong resemblance to the capsuled stems of some mosses, and, indeed, the general appearance of one of these pin-heads suggests that the artist may have derived the idea, in the first instance, from the close study of a patch of grassy sward covered with flowers and moss, a supposition that seems plausible from the circumstance that the complicated and most prevalent form of full-dress pin-head consists of two tiers, one placed above the other, with an interval of half an inch between them, the uppermost being supported on fine silver wire, and the capsule stems rising from the inferior one, and passing upwards through the interstices of the one above it as flowers, show their heads above the grass.

The principal every-day ornaments of the women are a needle-cushion, earrings, neck-hoops, finger-rings, and bracelets. The former among the Shans is a silver tube three inches long, and narrower at one end than the other. It is usually richly ornamented with bands of green, purple, and yellow enamel, separated from each other by lines of twisted silver wire, rounded knobs, and scrolls. The tube encloses a cushion of the same length and form as itself, attached by a hoop at its upper end to a cord that passes round the waist. Whenever a needle is wanted, the tube is pulled up over the cushion.

The earrings of the Sanda and Hotha Shan women are of four kinds. The first is three inches and a quarter in length and five-eighths of an inch in diameter, and made of silver foil rolled round a piece of bamboo three-quarters of an inch shorter than the silver. The length of the bamboo is made equivalent to that of the earring, by a piece of red cloth wound round its anterior extremity, which is ornamented with the elytra of a green beetle, red seeds, and gold thread worked into Chinese talismanic figures. The red lining inside the cylinder, and shining elytra beyond, are decidedly effective. To prevent the earrings slipping out, red silk thread is wound round them. The diameter of these tubes necessitates a considerable hole in the lobe of the ear, but it is nothing compared to what prevails among the beauties of Burmah, among whom an earring of amber, an inch and half in diameter, is in common use. The second form is the short cylinder, an inch in length, of very thin silver, but with a transverse septum close to its anterior end ornamented with Chinese devices. The third kind is very different; it is two inches long or nearly so, and is dilated anteriorly into a disc fully an inch in diameter, abruptly shelving down to a rounded silver knob. The front is composed of open filagree work in silver wire. The Poloung women wear a form nearly akin to this, but without the open work. The fourth and simplest kind is the girl's earring made of silver wire, the pendant portion coiled into a flat spiral, a favourite style of ornamentation during the Roman period in Europe, hanging down a considerable way, owing to the large circle that suspends it from the ear. Those in use by the Shan-Chinese and Chinese married women are of one type, and consist of a silver ring, either plain or gilt, with massive enrichments in rope wire, studs and filagree, suspending, by a hole in its centre, a little jade or enamelled silver disc, one inch in diameter. The Shan-Chinese girls wear a very handsome earring,[1] consisting of two parts, the upper corresponding to the one worn by their Shan sisters, from which there is suspended an inverted rosette of silver wire, concave below, with an open looped margin, from which

---

[1] This earring has a most remarkable resemblance in every particular to that figured by Dr. E. F. von Sacken at pl. xiii, fig. 4; indeed, so much so that it stands for the European ornaments of that early period. *Das Grabfeld von Hallstatt in Oberösterreich und Dessen Alterthümer.*

drops a circle of long club-shaped pendants, hung on fine silver wire. An open wire-work ball, with a rosette below it holding a garnet, hangs down from the roof of the umbrella-like flower, surrounded by other pendants.

The neck-rings or *torques* seem to be more prevalent among the Hotha than the Sanda Shans. They are of two kinds, and usually twelve inches across. The one in common use is a four-margined, hollow, imperfect circle, with its free ends about two inches apart, three-quarters of an inch in its greatest thickness which is in front, and about a quarter of an inch thick at its extremities. It differs only from the torques found in Ireland and other parts of Northern Europe in its more rounded form, and in its free ends being pointed and bent outwards and forwards, instead of being dilated into cymbal-shaped faces. It is impossible to overlook the similarity that exists between these ornaments and those which appear to have been in general use among the Romans, Irish, Celts, Gauls, and early Britons. It is curious also to observe that the rounded stud and rope-shaped fillets that are so prevalent, as forms of ornament, on the diadems and armlets of the early historical periods of Celtic and Scandinavian art, should be found at the present day in their full intensity among the Shans; and when we come to consider the Kakhyens, we will find them, although they are situated between two such comparatively civilized nations as the Chinese and Burmese, using at the present day the very forms of decoration employed by the early tribes of Western Europe in the ornamentation of their sepulchral urns.

The other kind of penannular torque is a flat ring of silver of the same breadth and size as the foregoing one. Its anterior surface is covered with foliaceous ornaments with their outlines defined in rope-like wire, and the enclosed spaces enamelled in green, purple, and brown. Cones in rope-wire filagree, surmounted by a stud resting on an enamelled surface, alternate with large red and blue stones on pieces of glass, surrounded with a sepal-like setting of rope-like silver wire.

Many of the finger-rings are jewelled, but none that I observed were of any value. Garnets of a very inferior kind, moonstones, and pieces of dark green jade appeared to be the stones in greatest repute, but the majority of the rings are not set with stones. A filagree cone of rope-wire, capped by a stud, is a common form, while others are simple spiral coils of rope-wire, resembling the so-called torque finger-rings of antiquarians. There is another kind in which the upper half is a thin oblong plate of silver, an inch in length, and the breadth of the upper surface of the finger, with its anterior and posterior margins slightly reflected, with two eminences surrounded with scrolls and floral enrichments. Each side sends down half a circle with a free end to admit of the easy adjustment of the ring to a finger of any size. Jade and amber rings of the stereotyped Chinese form are in common use with the men.

The prevalent form of bracelet is a torque-like hollow ring, two and a half inches in internal diameter, having the ends separated about half an inch to admit of its adjustment to the arm. The side opposite the free ends has an oval section, while the other is pentagonal, and three-quarters of an inch to one inch in thickness. The outside is covered with floral enrichments in relief, with the ground-work punched all over with small indentations to give it a frosted appearance. This form is frequently gilt with very red gold, and the decorations brought out in enamel, a jewel being usually let into the outside of the ring facing the free ends. The most handsome bracelet, however, is a hoop of silver, one inch and a half in breadth, and the eighth of an inch in thickness, and two inches and a quarter in diameter. The margins are thick and rounded, and project outwards beyond the general surface, with three lines internal to them of knotted and twisted wire. The flat surface is seven-eighths of an inch in breadth, and there are frequently two other ornaments, the exact repetitions of each other, flanking the central one. They consist of a rosette of three concentric rows, the outlines of the leaves being formed by silver wire, and their surfaces covered with enamel. The centre of the middle rosette is occupied by a large silver stud encircled by wire-rope, and the inner circle of leaflets is brown, the one external to it green, and the outer row dark purple. Two leafy enrichments occur on each side of the compound rosette, the centre of each carrying a solid silver ball, and the rounded and pointed leaves being coloured with green, purple, and brown enamel. The general surface of the hoop may be either perfectly smooth, or encircled with grooves externally and internally, giving it the appearance of a number of rings of fine silver wire welded together. The Poloung women wear this form, but the enrichments, as a rule, are simply flattened spiral coils of silver wire welded to the flat surface of the bracelet.

In full dress, the women of the Sanda valley usually wear, suspended from the jacket, silver flask-shaped scent bottles[1] about three inches in

---

[1] The resemblance of these ornaments to those figured by Dr. von Sacken at pl. xiv. fig. 16, &c., is most striking.

diameter, and two in height, decorated on the outside with figures traced in rope-wire, and set with small studs. A number of elaborate pendants, about eight inches long, hang from the bottom of the flask, and terminate in round silver bells that jingle with every movement of the body. Variously formed chatelaines are also favourite ornaments with the belles of Shandom.

A silver chatelaine,[1] with a number of little instruments suspended from it, is a frequent and useful ornament with the men. It hangs by a long silver chain from the jacket button-hole, ornamented at intervals with jade, amber, or glass beads, or with grotesque figures of animals or plants cut in the two former stones. Their forms are very various, but the little instruments are always the same, and number among them such articles as tooth and ear picks, and tweezers; the latter is an essential to every Shan, as he only suffers his moustache to grow, and depilates the rest of his face, an occupation which gives him frequent employment in his idle hours.

The description of the costume of the Shans generally would be very incomplete, were the dâh and tobacco pipe unnoticed. The former has a blade $2\frac{1}{2}$ to 3 feet in length, gradually expanding from the hilt towards the almost square point, which is about $2\frac{1}{2}$ inches in breadth. The handle is wood, bound with cord, and ornamented with silver foil, with a tuft of red goat's hair stuck in the hilt. The wooden scabbard covers only one side of the blade, and a hoop of ratan, bound with red cloth, is attached to its upper third, and worn over the right shoulder. The tobacco pipes are remarkable on account of their elaborate silver stems, which are frequently a yard in length, and enriched with floral tracings in rope-wire, ornamented with little silver balls. The tracings are generally filled up with the usual kinds of enamel. There is another handsome form, in which the stem is dilated at intervals into a series of elongated spheres, composed, as it were, of a number of many-spoked rings, increasing in size from the poles to the equator, and placed side by side. At either end there is a portion of the stem adorned with tracings in wire, many of the flat spiral coils centred with a silver ball. A long bamboo stem intervenes between the silver and the small bowl, which is made of brown glazed earthen-ware. The poorer peasantry use brass and iron pipes with very small bowls, and of a form which appears to be common to Tibet and the greater part of China. The wealthier Shans frequently use the Chinese hookah as well.

---

[1] The style of art of this chatelaine is, I may say, identical with the body of the ornament figured and described by Sacken, p. 56, pl. xiii, fig. 1.

Long matchlocks, with very small stocks, are the only firearms, besides the short broad cannon used in salutes. The former carry a long distance, and are not fired from the shoulder, but from the side of the head, nearly on a level with the ear. Attached to the small square embroidered bag that every Shan carries over his shoulder, is a small powder-flask of the shape of a miniature horn, but flattened and distended at the point, which is open, but has a flat piece of horn which fits into it, and is prolonged backwards across the curve of the flask, to the base of which it is firmly fastened. Downward pressure on the free portion over the curve raises the lid-like anterior extremity of this primitive spring, and allows the powder to run out in driblets. More capacious powder-flasks are made of the horns of cattle, but they are only used on a long expedition. They are suspended from a broad red belt, ornamented with lines and rosettes of cowries, and with tufts of red hair round the margins. The horn of the serrow (*C. bubalina*), artificially sharpened at the point, is usually found attached to the shoulder-bag, and is used as a borer, while its base may be bound with brass, and closed with a lid as a lime or opium box.

Strange to say, the phoongyees in the Sanda valley have their clothes cut in the same fashion as the laymen, but made of the orthodox orange-yellow cloth of the Buddhist priesthood. They wear a very ample turban, brought so far down behind the back of the neck that it encircles the head like a glory, and the very long fringe is coiled round the outside. All the rest of their dress, even to the shin bands and shoes, is that of an ordinary Shan, but is orange-yellow instead of blue. They are usually laden with silver ornaments, even to bracelets like women, and carry round their waists purses studded with enormous silver buttons. The priests, however, of Hotha and Latha do not conform to the vanities of this life, like their brethren in the valley below them, but dress in the simple robe of the true Buddhist priesthood.

The Shans generally are a flesh-eating people, and numbers of cattle and pigs are slain every day at the markets. But milk is used in no form. All kinds of poultry are among the articles of diet, of which rice and vegetables also form an important element. The Shans, however, have some peculiar tastes, and they affect to have a decided failing for the large larvæ of a giant wasp, and for the still more repulsive dish of stewed centipedes. The entrails of animals, too, merit an important place in the Shan *cuisine*, and in this they resemble the Burmese. Samshu is their chief stimulant, but they appear to be a very temperate people, and seldom or ever go to excess. Both men and women are most inveterate smokers, and are rarely seen without their long pipes. The tobacco is carried in small round boxes made of buffalo hide, covered with red varnish, and margined round the edges with brown. They consist of two corresponding halves, the margin of the one overlapping the other. The hide is moistened and stretched over a wooden mould, from which it is removed before it becomes quite hard.

Their towns are always surrounded by a brick wall about 6 to 9 feet high, and the villages are enclosed by a bamboo fence. Both are built on spots above the floods of the river, and the latter are usually embowered in trees and bamboos. The houses are not raised on piles as in Burmah, but built after the same fashion as the Chinese houses at Momien, which exactly agree with those prevalent throughout China, and each is enclosed in a court-yard of its own. The streets are always laid either with slabs or water-worn stones, and have drains running along the sides, but the latter are sometimes extremely filthy, especially when the Chinese population of a town is large.

Agriculture is the principal occupation of the great body of the Shan population, and as cultivators they are perhaps unrivalled. Their principal crop is rice, which is grown in square fields shut in on all sides by small bunds for irrigation. The nearest stream, during the dry weather, has its waters diverted and re-diverted, so that the flooding of any block, or little square of rice, can be accomplished with ease. In the Tapeng they have an unfailing supply of water, and when the streams from the hills run dry, advantage is taken of the slope of the valley to construct canals for the watering of fields that may be miles below the point of divergence. The rice was being planted out in the beginning of May, and the cultivation was so extensive that the valley, from one end to the other, may be said to have been an immense ricefield. The land is tilled by means of a wooden plough tipped with an iron share, and drawn by a single buffalo guided by a ring through its nose. The men and women work together in the fields, but the planting out of the crops is chiefly done by the men, while the women are employed in weeding and thinning. Opium, tobacco, and cotton are important crops to the Shans. They are all grown on the well-drained slopes at the base of the hills; and only in sufficient quantity, in the case of the two latter, to meet the daily wants of the people. The white variety of poppy is the one cultivated, but as the Shans are not, as a rule, opium-smokers, the growth has reference to the wants of the Chinese, Leesaws, and Kakhyens, and to the requirements of the Bhamô and Mogoung markets. A considerable quantity of the drug finds its wa to these two marts, and the Chinamen who purchase it send a fair proportion to Mandalay, where there is a large Chinese population. The drug carried to Mogoung by the Shans and Kakhyens is purchased by the tribes of the latter people along the upper waters of the Irawady, and between that river and Assam; and it is very probable that Yunan-grown opium finds its way as far west as the Singphos to the east of Suddyah.

The Chinese-Shans are expert blacksmiths, and all the dâhs used by themselves and the neighbouring tribes are forged by them in the Hotha valley, and they resort annually to Bhamô, and to the villages in the Kakhyen hills, for the purpose of manufacturing them. The iron is procured from the east, and, from what I gathered, is brought to Momien from Talifoo. The caravans that visit Mandalay, and those also which go to Bhamô, have always a considerable supply of iron pots said to come from Tali. They use charcoal as fuel, and the segment of a large bamboo, placed horizontally, with a piston, and valve at each end, as a bellows. Their proficiency as silversmiths is well illustrated in their ornaments. Their instruments are very simple, consisting of a small cylindrical bellows, a crucible, punch, graver, hammer, and a little anvil. In the Sanda valley, as has been already observed, the phoongyees are the silversmiths, but in the valley of Hotha, where Buddhism has not been corrupted by contact with the Chinese, the trade is confined to the laymen. The Shans are also excellent workers in straw, and produce broad-brimmed hats that would compete with the finest Tuscany.

The women are largely engaged in weaving and dyeing with indigo, as the Shans generally are clad in home-grown, home-spun, and home-dyed cotton cloth. The cloths are of all degrees of texture, and the finer kinds used for jackets are soft, and usually figured with large lozenge-shaped patterns of the same colour as the ground-work. They are also adepts at silken embroidery and needle-work, and make all the clothes for their families. There is still another art in which the Shans excel, and that is, the fabrication of elaborate hair ornaments from the blue feathers of the *Coracias affinis*, which they appear to have derived from the Chinese. A number of pieces of paper are pasted together, and shaped, for example, into the form of a wreath. A series of claw-shaped holes are cut out on either side at regular intervals leaving the margin entire, which is also cut into a continuous series of three-lobed figures corresponding to the pieces separating the claw-shaped vacuities. A thin copper wire is then fastened on to the back of the wreath, from end to end, and another is run along the margins with V-shaped pieces to strengthen the portions between the claw-shaped perforations. The margins of the wreath, generally, have gold thread run along them, and their outer surfaces covered with portions of fine blue feathers of the roller laid on with the greatest nicety, indeed, so much so, that all the barbules are left undisturbed. Another slightly smaller but similar piece of paper is cut into an elaborate floral figure, and treated in the same way with wire, gold thread, and feathers. Figures resembling the sepals of flowers are then cut out, and decorated the same way as the rest of the wreath, and fastened on to its surface by means of short cylinders of paper. The corolla, and last of all, a mass to represent stamens, are fastened one over the other in the same way, and the result is a very pretty simple ornament, which is frequently brightened by a ruby or some other gem.

The marked feature of the woven and embroidered fabrics of the Shans, and also of their enrichments, and, indeed, of Shan art generally, is the persistency with which certain conventional patterns are reproduced without the slightest variation, or any attempt, on the part of the artists, to improve on the works of their forefathers. In this respect the Shans resemble the Chinese, and the probability is that the absence of progression in the arts is to be ascribed in great part to their comparative isolation as a people, for the nations who have made the greatest advances in art have been those who have had the bent of their genius influenced and modified by accretion from without as well as from within. The Shans have been shut up, however, for many centuries in their own valleys, which contained all that was requisite for their every-day life; and as each household manufactured all that was necessary for its wants, the stimulus of competition between members of different trades, which is a powerful means of advancing art in all its departments, did not exist, so that the children followed in the footsteps of their fathers, and generation after generation repeated the very same devices which came down to them, and were regarded as the heirlooms of their ancestors. The probability, therefore, is that Shan textile art, in the 19th century, is much at the same stage that it was four or five centuries ago. In its designs, it has all the elements of primitive art, and if we analyse these, in modifications of the woven and embroidered fabrics, they may be reduced to a very few elementary figures, among which are the lozenge, square, and stripe. The former frequently encloses zig-zag lines, but when we examine them, they are found to be only the outlines of the parent figure connected together in various ways; or lozenges may be built up of similar minute figures, or segments may overlie segments. The pattern may be either simple blocks, or contain peculiar cross figures, the upright portions of which are formed by the inverted halves of lozenges separated from each other by a transverse oblong, dividing at its ends which bend upwards and downwards towards the centre of the device. This cross figure, however, may have the ends of the transverse oblong composed of one or more segments of lozenges, either in a convex or concave outline, and it is frequently so enlarged as to contain a square in its centre, holding another like itself, with four smaller ones external to its sides. The modifications of this figure are almost endless, but the foregoing will suffice to illustrate the character of the art. The groundwork of fabrics with this style of ornament is usually covered over with a profusion of small truncated, almost rounded lozenges, with figures of the sacred *Henza*, or Brahminical goose, scattered over it. Squares are of frequent occurrence, but the distinctive figures of Shan textile art are the lozenge and stripe. Although both are characteristic of a primitive state of art, we are not entitled to conclude that the Shans lack the genius to advance beyond the stage in which we now find them; the probability is that when they are brought in contact with foreign nations, the change will act as a powerful stimulant to the progress of art among a people of great natural abilities that have only lain dormant, there having been hitherto no field for their exercise. The chief beauty of the textile fabrics of the Shans is undoubtedly the wonderful grouping and harmony of the colouring, and in this respect they are all but unrivalled artists. Their principal colours are blue, orange, yellow, green, red, and pink, in full and half tints.

As a people they are very fond of music, and possess a number of simple wild airs of their own, which they play on stringed and wind instruments. The most prevalent form of the latter is the segment of a bamboo, with a small flask-shaped gourd as a mouth-piece; it is constructed like a flute, and its sound is full, soft, and pleasing. The stringed instruments are formed on the principle of the guitar: one is about three feet in length, with three strings, over a broad sounding-board; while another is only about half the size, and the sounding-board is a small, short, drum-like cylinder at the far end, with a snake's skin stretched across it. This is a Chinese as well as a Shan instrument, and is also in great favour with the Panthays at Momien.

The Shans, as a rule are monogamists, but among the higher classes who can afford the luxury of more than one wife, polygamy is not uncommon. Marriage is devoid of any religious ceremony, and all that is required is the sanction of the parents, the consent of the bride, and the interchange of certain presents between the two contracting parties.

The wives and daughters of the chiefs do not appear much in public, but they are regular attendants at the khyoung. No restriction, however, appears to be laid on the movements of the middle and lower classes of women who move freely about.

The diseases that came under my observation were various forms of ophthalmia, and injuries to the eyes from the ravages of small-pox, ulcers of the lower extremities, and eczema. White swelling of the knee occurred in two young people, and disease of the hip-joint in a young lad, and two cases of necrosis of the jaw in strumous children. No cases of syphilis or phthisis presented themselves, and by the far greater proportion of cases that came to my notice were eye and skin diseases. The pharmacopœia of the Shans is anything but an extensive one, and many of their nostrums come from most unlikely sources. We find them placing implicit faith in the curative and strengthening qualities of decoctions of the dried and pregnant wombs of the sambur, tiger, and porcupine, and relying on the dessicated stomachs of these animals for relief in the worst forms of disease. The leg-bones of the tiger and the pounded horns of the sambur and serrow are in great repute as medicines that give tone and strength to the frame, exhausted by disease or excess. They place great faith in the restorative powers of bronze and stone implements, which are frequently carried about the person as charms, in small bags. They are also said to be most useful in tedious labour, and to ensure the immediate birth of the child after the mother has been given a glass of water in which one of them has been placed beforehand.

They bury their dead, and the graves are rounded off into oblong mounds, and a God's-acre in Shandom, with its numerous little headstones, forcibly recalls to the traveller the country church-yards of English villages. The priests, however, are burnt after they have lain in state for some months, or it may be for a year.

The Shans are all Buddhists, but the simplicity of that religion is much obscured and defaced in the Sanda valley by the engrafting of numberless superstitions borrowed from the Chinese and the surrounding tribes, the only religion of the latter being the recognition of the spirit of evil, which is propitiated with offerings of animals and the fruits of the earth. We could have no better indication of the low state of Buddhism in that valley than what has been stated regarding the habits of the priesthood, who work in silver, and allow themselves all the ordinary comforts and luxuries of their lay brethren. Instead of dressing regularly in the tsiwaran or yellow robe, the distinguishing costume of a rahan, they put it on only when they perform their devotions, and, at other times, clothe themselves in comfortable warm garments. No phoongyees were seen in the Sanda or Hotha valleys going about begging their food from door to door, as in Burmah and Ceylon; but in the former valley, they met the requirements of the law half-way, the women bringing the food to the outside of the khyoung, from whence one sallied when all the pious donors had arrived, and received a handful of rice from each in his patta or mendicant's pot. The absence, too, of pagodas is even, perhaps, a more telling illustration of the indifference that prevails regarding matters of religion. The system has become so corrupted that the priests are inveterate smokers, and use pipes with long silver mouth-pieces, in direct opposition to one of the first principles of their order, which requires that no rahan should touch one of the precious metals; but so little is this regarded that, as has been remarked, they even work in silver, and take payment for their labours. It is curious that with this laxity among the priesthood, the rahanees or religious sisters conform much more strictly to the duties entailed on them by their vows, and are always seen in their white robes, barefooted, with clean shaven heads, usually telling their beads, and are most regular in all the observances of religion. A fair proportion of this order are young women of good birth, but both the young and old are most devout, and as they have generally travelled more than the majority of their fellow-countrymen, they have less reserve, and usually a good deal to say. Two old rahanees at Manwyne had been as far as Rangoon, and evidently treasured a lively and pleasant recollection of their visit, and of the kind reception they had experienced at the hands of Sir Arthur Phayre, the remembrance of which led them to say many a good word for the Expedition to their people, by whom they were much respected. They have religious houses in Manwyne and Muangla, and are waited on by a number of female lay-attendants. They employ their time, not only in devotion, but in such useful occupations as weaving and dyeing. They are entirely dependent on the charity of the people, but are liberally supported, as they lead blameless lives, inspired by only one desire, to follow in the footsteps, and imitate the life of Buddha, by the practice of the highest virtues.

The children, as in Burmah, are educated by the priests, and many are taken into the monasteries as shyins, and remain in them till their education is completed, and while in this capacity, they wait upon the priests, and thus acquire merits for future existences.

One of the most interesting facts, noted in connection with Buddhism in the Sanda valley, was the occurrence of the wooden figure of a horse in one of the niches of the Manwyne khyoung, to which offerings of rice were made every morning by the numerous visitors who bowed before it in the act of devotion. On my upward visit, I happened to take up my position in front of the figure, and my people, never suspecting that it had any religious significance, filled up the niche with some packages, and made my bed there; but I had soon to move off, for the head phoongyee informed me that the people came every morning to worship the horse, and that it would be impossible for them to do so if I did not remove my goods and chattels to another place. The next morning gave me a full verification of the truth of the priest's remonstrance. The only plausible explanation of the occurrence of this ancient form of worship as an adjunct to Buddhism is, that it is a parallel instance to nât worship among the Buddhistic Burmans. The probability is that nât worship was the Pre-Buddhistic religion of the Burmese, as it is of nearly all the Indo-Chinese tribes who have not embraced the religion of Guadama, and that it retained its vitality, as a system, in the ignorance and superstition of the masses. Horse-worship was one of the phases of that prehistoric reverence for plants and animals, which seems to have been universally prevalent throughout the east, in early times, and appears to have been the most primitive recognition of the principles of good and evil, or of the useful and of that which was inimical to man. The Hindoo still worships the cow as *Bhagariti*, or the goddess of prosperity, and the Sanscrit name, *Dhener*, or wealth, sometimes applied to her, is only a further indication of how essential she is to his comfort, and of the high estimation in which she is held for the temporal benefits she confers on him. It is probable that even horse-worship, among people like the Shans, who are essentially a race of horse-breeders, and whose wealth is estimated by the number of these animals, may have originated from the same principle of gratitude that led the Hindoo to regard his chief domestic animal as the symbol of wealth and prosperity, and to reverence it as such. In the Buddhist khyoung at Muangla, two life-sized figures of horses were stationed on either side of the entrance to the inner court, and it was evident that they were in some way related to horse-worship (asvamedha.) Each was tended by a man in Tartar costume, suggesting the other alternative, that the Shans may have also some horse fable, the equivalent of the *avaloketeswara* of the Tibetans.

The Shans in Burmah, when laying the foundations of their pagodas, make offerings to the great earth-snake, a ceremony which I have described elsewhere, and which appears to correspond to the Hindoo rite of *vastu-yaga* in which we have snake-worship strongly pronounced.

The occurrence of many-headed snakes, on the back-grounds or canopies to the heads of Buddhistic figures in the khyoungs of their valleys, seems to be a further illustration of the remains of this form of worship. Ignorance of the language, and the circumstance that my so-called interpreters had only a smattering of English, prevented me investigating these most interesting topics.

I observed nothing during my residence among the Shans that would lead me to believe they were other than a simple living people, among whom drunkenness and licentiousness were all but unknown. They are very superstitious, and believe in ghosts, fairies, náts, and evil omens. They are a good-natured, contented race, but without the joviality of the Burmese, and the term gay, as has been applied to them, is entirely out of place, for they are a quiet and rather sedate people.

The Shan states of Sanda, Muangla, and Muangtee each pay five thousand baskets of rice as tribute to the Mussulmans. There is no active interference, however, in their government, which is purely patriarchical, and vested in the Tsawbwa or chief of each state, who is usually counselled by a number of his near relatives and by the heads of the leading families, and his decision is final on all questions that may come before him for consideration. All the land is the property of the Tsawbwa, but each family holds a certain extent which it cultivates, paying the chief an annual tithe of the products. These settlements are seldom disturbed, and the majority have passed from father to son for generations. The chief, however, has the power to resume any land that fails to pay the recognized tithe. The youngest son inherits, and when the land is not sufficient for the wants of a large family, the elder sons look out for other plots that may have become vacant by the death of ryots, or they turn traders. The residences of the Sanda, Muangla, Muangtee, and Hotha chiefs, although they are now almost in ruins, owing to the frequent raids of the Mahomedans and Kakhyens, still indicate that those chiefs must have been men of considerable wealth in the palmy days, before their estates were laid waste by the ruthless Mahomedans. But now they appear to be very poor, and there can be little doubt that many of the best articles of clothing and jewellery offered to us for sale belonged to them, and that their poverty was the sole reason why they were led to part with their heirlooms for hard cash. The chronic warfare that has existed in Western Yunan, now for so many years, has rendered property so insecure that there is no inducement to accumulate wealth, because it might be lost at any moment in a Kakhyen or Mahomedan raid; and, moreover, the latter people are so poor themselves that if they found a man growing wealthy, they would be sure to relieve him of some of his riches; and this uncertainty that attends wealth may be one reason why so little is seen of it, it being the interest of the people to appear poor. I cannot help thinking, too, that the nearly incessant turmoil that has prevailed in Western Yunan, almost since the days of Marco Polo, and the consequent uncertainty attending property, may have given rise to the remarkable custom, prevalent among the mule-men who accompany the caravans to Mandalay, of converting their property into gold and precious stones, and burying it under the skin of their chests and necks. While at Mandalay, I examined a number of men who had recently arrived from Yungchan with a caravan from Talifoo, and found some of them with as many as ten or fifteen stones and coins below the skin of the parts mentioned; and, on asking their reason for doing so, was told that they did it for the greater security of their property and persons. A slit is made in the skin, and the coin or stone is forced below the cut, and the orifice is then closed, and heals up. When a man wishes to use some of his accumulated wealth, all he does is to cut down upon the valuable, and remove it.

I now turn to the consideration of the Kakhyens who inhabit the hill tracts to the east and west of Bhamô. They belong to the race of Chingpaws (Singphos), who are distributed all over the mountains that define the valley of the Irawady north of Hotha, and on the hills that occur between them, as far as the wall of mountains that closes in the Kampti plain to the north. They may be said, in general terms, to be confined, as far as our present knowledge goes, between the 23rd and 28th parallels of north latitude, and the 95th and 99th degrees of east longitude. They claim originally to have come from the mountainous country along the main stream of the Irawady to the north-east of the Mogoung, and I have been twice informed by intelligent Shans that the Kakhyens were unknown in the valleys of Sanda and Hotha 200 years ago, and one of my informants stated that they have been gradually driven south by scarcity of food. Hakhyen is the Burmese term applied to them, but they call themselves Chingpaws, which is their word for man. The tribes always speak of themselves under their own names, without the use of the generic term. The clans are very numerous, and are found as far as Momien, but from information obtained at that town, they do not appear to extend much to the east of it, where their place is taken by the Leesaws and Myautze. Between Momien and the Irawady, we find the Karahs, Nurans, Pungans, Murrows, Atsees, Tsingmahs,

Lahones, and Kakoos; and on the hills near Sanda, Lakones, Laphais, Cowries, Murrows, Moulas, Lasangs, Mumuts, Yoyins, and Mimsahs; and on those about Hotha, we meet with the Khangs. The Chitans or Khanlungs of the Burmese-Shans occur on both banks of the Irawady about and above Bhamô. Colonel Hannay, on his visit to Mogoung, was among the Kakoo Chingpaws, whose country embraces not only Mogoung itself but the district to the north-east of it, on both banks of the Irawady above Kakhyo. He applied the term as synonymous with Kakhyen, but erred in so doing, for it is restricted in its use to the tribes he was among. Believing in the identity of the two names, he states that the Chingpaws of Hukong considered it an insult to be called Kakhyens or Kakoos, whereas they only object to the former term, which is also the case with the Lahones, Laphais, and Cowries to the east of Bhamô, who despise it for some reason or other unknown to me. Colonel Hannay restricted the term Kakoo to the tribes of the south and east of Hukong, but this also arose from his belief in the identity of the two names, and the probability is that enquiry would have proved that they had no objection whatever to being called Kakoos. I met at Sanda some of that clan from Mogoung, and pointedly ask them the question whether they were Kakoos, and was answered in the affirmative. They, along with the Chitans or Khanlungs, are the two clans that have settled most extensively in the valley of the Upper Irawady, whereas nearly all the other tribes are restricted to the hills, and are seldom found even in the high valleys to the east of Bhamô. At the latter town, the so-called Kakhyens bear a very bad character among the Burmese officials, and on our way up the Irawady, they were described to us as blood-thirsty, treacherous savages, lurking in the dense jungle, and killing wayfarers and villagers with their poisoned arrows, for the sake of their clothes: a picture utterly false in all its features and details. The real secret of the evil reports of the Burmese is, that the intolerable oppression and extortion to which they have been subjected, when they are driven to visit Bhamô for salt and some of the other necessaries of life, have so maddened them that they retaliate on the Burmese-Shan villages in the district, whenever an opportunity of spoil presents itself. Only the villages near the head-quarters of oppression are the ones that suffer, and the best proof of this is that those close to Bhamô and Kaungtoung are fortified, while those up the first defile, which are never interfered with, are left unprotected. In the Sanda and Hotha valleys, where they are treated with the same consideration as the Shan population, they are seldom or ever guilty of the excesses that the tribes on the Burmese border have been driven to, and the majority of them are keen traders, and always present in large numbers at the markets. In character they are an impulsive and excitable race. I observed nothing in their demeanour that would lead me to regard them as a courageous people, and, indeed, their prevalent method of attack, surprising unsuspecting villages during the darkness, would rather indicate that they are treacherous and devoid of courage. Before one of these raids, they have usually drunk almost to the point of intoxication, and were it not for the influence of the samshu, sheroo, and opium, they probably would be of rare occurrence. Lacking courage, it is not the character of a Kakhyen to openly remonstrate when he thinks he is wronged, but he will go away from a dispute treasuring up revenge, which he gratifies when his enemy is at a disadvantage. So much for the dark side of his character, but the other and bright one has many pleasing features. His hospitality is proverbial, and every house of any pretentions has always its strangers' hall, in which the guests sleep, and are fed by the household, which speaks to a kindly and liberal disposition, and, under considerate and just treatment, he might be relied on as a true friend. Although not of a very lively disposition, he is fond of company, and can enjoy a joke.

I was much struck with the variety of faces that are met with among them. They may be referred to two types, one with very coarse features, and the other with a finely sculptured outline. The former is a rather short round face, with very prominent malars, heavy protruding lips, broad nose, with a considerable breadth between the eyes, and rather low forehead, and broad square chin; while the other, in the fineness of its features, forcibly recalled to me the womanly face of the Cacharies and Lepchas of Sikkim. In it, the oblique eye is much more intensely marked than in the first, and the face is a longish rather compressed oval, with pointed chin, well-hooked nose, and prominent malars, the outlines, however, having all the delicacy of the face of a woman. Both types are found among the latter sex, but the first is the one most prevalent in both. The obliquity of the eye in the second type is sometimes very feebly marked, and I saw a young girl at Bhamô with large lustrous eyes, and so moderately prominent malars, and fair skin, that she might almost have passed for an European. This, however, was an extreme case, but, at the same time, I frequently met with faces approaching it. From the prevalence of the first type among the women, they are anything but pretty, but they have a good-humoured expression. The hair varies between black and brown, and the eyes between dark and light-brown, corresponding to Nos. 1 and 2 of Paul Broca's tables, and the skin is a buff, agreeing to No. 23 of the same tables. The average height of the women, deduced from a series of measurements, varies from four feet nine inches to five feet, and that of the men from five feet to five feet six inches. I observed men who exceeded the maximum, but they were rare instances compared with the great number who did not come up to it. The average weight of the women who yielded the above results was 6 stone 1 pound: the weight of the men varied from 6 stone to 8 stone 12 pounds; their ages being from 25 to 30 years. The moustache and beard are very sparse, but as the men resort to the Chinese habit of depilation, it is difficult to say what their natural condition is.

The dress of the men is a blue jacket, short loose breeches, supported by a blue cloth wound round the loins, a blue turban in which the long hair is coiled up, an embroidered bag worn over the right shoulder, containing opium, tobacco, betel, pawn, and lime, besides their pipes, and a bamboo filled with sheroo or samshu. A dâh in its half-scabbard, fastened to a bamboo hoop, decorated with charms, such as, the canine or molar of a leopard or tiger, and suspended to a red cloth band ornamented with cowries, is also slung over the right shoulder. A number of fine ratan hoops below the knee, and a leek, flower, or small piece of bamboo worn in a large hole in the lobe of the ear, finishes the description of the costume of the ordinary Kakhyen. The Tsawbwas are more comfortably clad, and usually treat themselves to well-padded Chinese jackets, to shoes, and to rolls of blue cloth round their shins, or to leggings. They are frequently distinguished, especially in the case of those who adhere rigidly to the Kakhyen costume, by a wide silver hoop worn round the neck, and by a necklace of long beads made from an ochreous earth found in the Mogoung districts, and highly valued, as it is supposed that the beads are dug out of the soil ready formed by the nâts. The dress of the Kakoo men is very different from the foregoing; they wear the Shan jacket, but instead of the trousers, a broad piece of thick blue cloth, with a wide red embroidered woollen margin, wound round the loins like a kilt. They have these other peculiarities, that they wear no turban, and that the hair of the head is cut in the same style as among the Kakhyen women to the east of Bhamô, who wear it cut short over the forehead, but allow it to grow moderately long behind. The Kakoo women have adopted the dress of their Burmese sisters. They have a kilt similar to the Kakoo men, but it is always worn so low as to expose the navel, and is supported by a profusion of ratan and bamboo girdles with primitive designs scratched on them, or ornamented with lines of white seeds.

The unmarried daughters of the Tsawbwas and Pawmines have in addition a girdle of large black seeds, each alternating with a small hollow brass sphere, with a free metal pellet in its interior, that tinkles like a bell at every movement of the body; and a broad girdle of cowries. They have adopted the Shan jacket, and the turban of the Shan women, but on a more modified scale. The long cylindrical earring (*laykan*) of the Shans is prevalent among the matrons, who wear in their ears long flat pieces of embroidered cloth which hang down the shoulders, with a fringe of beads of different colours. They have two holes in the ears, one through the lobe, and another through the concha, the long cloth ear pendants being usually worn in the latter opening. They have also a profusion of ratan rings below the knee. The wives and daughters of Tsawbwas are alone entitled to wear the silver hoop (*geree*) round the neck, and the necklace of ochreous earth (*komoong*.) A Kakhyen never thinks of changing his clothes from the day he puts them on until they are worn out; and as a suit lasts for more than a year, and the ablutions of these mountaineers are confined to their faces, hands, and legs below the knee, they are proverbial for their dirt.

Although there is a marked difference between the dress of the Kakhyens and Kakoos, the two tribes of the former that occur along the north and south banks of the Tapeng, in the Kakhyen hills, claim to have come originally from the Kakoo country, and the Lahones appear to have been gradually driving the Cowries to the south. The former clan inhabits the north side of the valley, and the latter the south, but before the advent of the Lahones, the Cowries held the north. A Lahone Tsawbwa having married the daughter of a Cowrie chief, and the latter refusing to give his son-in-law some land that he asked to be allowed to cultivate, took forcible possession of it, and drove the Cowries to the south side of the Tapeng.

The houses are long, narrow structures, usually 150 to 200 feet long, not built on the steep hill-sides as is the custom of the Nagas of Assam, but on the comparatively level ground of a long slope, so that they are usually accessible from every side. They are built on piles, about 3 feet high, and have an average width of about 30 to 40 feet. There is a deep portico in front, in which all the cattle, pigs, and poultry are kept at night, and the house itself is divided longitudinally by a long partition, on one side of which are the apartments of the different members of the household which is always restricted to relations. As many as half-a-dozen families may be found in one of these barracks. There are two or three cooking-places in the long passage that communicates with all the apartments, but as there are neither chimneys nor windows, and as each separate room has its fire-place, the atmosphere is anything but agreeable to a stranger, and the walls are black with soot. There are only two doors, one opening from the portico, and the other at the far end of the building, sacred to the nâts, and only used by the inmates. The strangers' room is immediately within the first doorway. The property is common to all the members of the household, and the purchasing and cooking of the food are entrusted to one or more individuals, according to the size of the establishment. In the event of any of the members wishing to separate their connection with the community, the property is divided, and each receives his share. The young men and women have separate rooms, but as no restraint is laid on their movements, they frequently pass the nights in each other's quarters, and the result is that illegitimacy is very prevalent, and as it is not considered a disgrace for an unmarried woman to be a mother, morality is at a very low ebb among them. The father is not bound to marry the woman whose affection he has gained, and is only called to support her until the child is a month old, and after that, it is usually cared for by her parents. Her position, however, as a mother, is no drawback to her future marriage, but in the event of her dying before the birth of her child, her lover is bound by Kakhyen custom to compensate the loss to her parents by providing them with a male or female slave, a buffalo, a dâh, a piece of cloth, a spear, a gong, an iron vessel for cooking rice, an iron hearth, and to feed all the inmates of the house in which she resided; and in the event of there being no prospect of his being able to do so, he can be taken and sold as a slave. This high value set by the Kakhyens on the loss of one of their daughters arises, not so much from any desire to intimidate immorality, but is simply indicative of the high estimation in which woman is held, by reason of her usefulness, to the community. The comfort of a household depends on the number of daughters, and, as they are regarded as little better than beasts of burden, the death of one of them is a serious calamity, and is felt as a pecuniary loss. The first duty of a woman in a Kakhyen household is to rise early to clean and husk the rice which is only prepared as it is required, and her last duty late at night is to do the same. It is pounded in a large cup-shaped cavity scooped out of the trunk of a tree, and two women stand, facing each other, each with a long wooden pestle, and accompany the alternate dull thud on the grain with a suppressed wild cry; and when the Tsawbwas' and Pawmines' daughters are so engaged, we have the two sounds enlivened by the pleasant tinkle of their girdle bells. Collecting firewood is a most laborious occupation, and employs many hours every day, as the women have to search over the hill-sides for dry timber, which they cut with long knives into faggots, about a foot to a foot and a half in length, and carry to the village tied up in large bundles on their backs. As they have frequently to look for it among almost impenetrable thickets of ratan and thorny shrubs, their bare legs are often torn and lacerated to a painful extent; and the number of intractable ulcers that came under my observation among these poor creatures, could be attributed to no other cause than this. But they have never known other treatment, and are contented and happy with a position which is but little elevated above the brutes. As a rule, the firewood is collected from the old clearings, and is cut from the three or four feet of the old trunks left standing, that are as a kind of store for yearly use. The women are also employed in felling the jungle, which takes place about the beginning of April, and is allowed to dry for a fortnight or so before the men set fire to it. After the fire has burnt itself out, the huge stems are rolled down the hill-sides, and the ground cleared by women. They also weave all the cloth for their husbands and children from home-grown cotton which they have prepared and dyed themselves. The men do little or no manual labour, and only a few of the more industrious among them plough the ground required for the cotton crop and the rice on the terraces, and tend the cultivation of the opium and tobacco, all of which are usually grown in the immediate vicinity of the villages. Their time is chiefly spent in wandering from hamlet to hamlet among their friends, smoking opium, and drinking sheroo or samshu, and as the sheroo is an important element in a Kakhyen household, it also falls to the lot of the women to prepare it. Nearly every village has a few mules of its own, on which the men carry the surplus supplies of cotton, Indian corn, rice, and opium to the plains of Burmah, where they barter them for salt, dried fish, and cloth; but when the village is too poor to own mules, the women carry the heavy loads.

Their language is monosyllabic, and is spoken in an undulating tone, each sentence terminating in a high key, and in the vowel "ee," thus—"Chingpaw poong doon tan-key-ing-ee?—Do the Kakhyens dance?" "Indai poon cadong cowtai-ee.—He has cut down that tree." They have no written language, but some of their chiefs, such as Mutthin, Loaylone, Namboke, and Seray, could read either Chinese or Burmese.

Although hemmed in on either side by Buddhist nations, their religion has not been affected by their position, and they still adhere to the propitiation of good and evil spirits, whom they call nâts, and who were worshipped by their forefathers. They have a very confused idea of what can be only regarded as a most rudimentary conception of a Supreme Being, in a nât, whom they call Shingrawah, and who, they hold, created everything. They call him both man and nât, and deny that they worship him, but hold him in reverence, as they say he is very big. They appear to have glimmerings of a future state, and of a place of rewards and punishments. All good men, and women who die after childbirth, go to Tsojah, or Muangphee, the Shan word for heaven, but all women who die pregnant, and men who have been killed by the dâh, and all bad characters, are consigned to Marai, the Shan word for hell. On asking an intelligent Kakhyen his belief regarding this heaven and hell, he answered, how could he say anything about them, as he had never seen them, and continued, all nations have a similar belief, although they know nothing about them.

The good nâts are those who cause the sun and moon to rise, and the Kakhyens assign as a reason for worshipping them that they were told to do so by their forefathers who said they were good. The sun is worshipped as Chan, and the moon as Shitah, and besides, there is the spirit Sinlah, the nât of the sky, who gives rain and good crops. Agriculture, however, is under the special protection of Cringwan, whose good intentions are apt to be defeated, unless certain spirits of evil dispositions are propitiated at certain seasons. For example, after the fields have been cleared of jungle, and are ready for the seed, the nât Masoo has to be won over by offerings of the flesh of pigs and fowls, which are buried in the earth in front of the village altars, which are called *lamshan*. These structures are always situated at a few hundred yards from the villages, usually in an open spot, among a grove of trees, and consist of a number of small bamboo platforms supported on poles, about six feet from the ground. Again, when the paddy comes into ear, buffaloes, bullocks, pigs, and fowls are slain, and their flesh cooked and buried as a peace-offering to the nât Cajat, in front of the *lamshan*, in the hope that he will be induced to desist from injuring the swelling grain. A Kakhyen regards the possession of silver, or *compraw*, as he calls it, as the greatest good that can befall him, and we find, therefore, a nât Mowlain, who is believed to take a special interest in his monetary affairs, and to whom offerings are made, so that the coveted metal may find its way into his coffers. Then there are the ten brothers—Shitah, Chan, Chitong, Muron, Chambroo, Chinoo, Phee, Pahan, Masa, and Chaga—who take a lively interest in everything affecting the welfare of the Kakhyens, and to whom offerings are made of rice and fowls.

Phee has them under his special care during the night-watches, and a fowl is frequently presented to him in grateful recognition of his protection. Chitong is the hunter's nât, and unless he receives an abundance of good things, such as the flesh of dogs, pigs, and fowls before the chase is begun, some one of the hunting party is certain to be either gored by stag, or killed by tiger. Muron is the spirit who follows a traveller on a journey, and protects him according as his good-will has been secured by offerings before the journey was entered upon. Fowls, pigs, and buffaloes are offered in front of the house of the traveller before he departs from his village, and the Toomsah or priest, addressing Muron, says, pointing to the man,—"That man sitting there is going on a long journey; you will look after him wherever he goes, and acquaint all the other nâts of his progress." Shitah is the guardian spirit of the houses of the Lahones, and none of any other tribe is allowed to go through the door sacred to him without having first presented a peace-offering to the nât. Besides believing in nâts, these ignorant hill people have a particular dread of ghosts, *munla*, that wander about the hills, and are supposed to be the spirits of people who have either been cut down by the dâh, pierced by the spear, or shot. They have the power of entering into people, and of acquainting them of events that may be happening similar to those by which they met their death.

An incident that happened to me would seem to indicate that nât worship is in some way mixed up with a belief in witches. Four Kakhyens, who accompanied me to Calcutta, when they were shown the hairy woman of Mandalay, and her son and daughter, shuddered when they saw them, and, asserting they were nâts, hastily left the verandah of the Residency.

As I have already had occasion to mention, there are two kinds of priests, the Toomsah and the Meetway, but there is no regular priesthood, in the sense of its being a distinct class, existing either by hereditary transmission, or training. A youth exhibits certain qualities and phases of character which seem to fit him for the office, and the recognition of these by his villagers leads him to cultivate them, and when the old priest dies, he finds himself his successor. The Toomsah attends on all occasions on which sacrifices have to be offered; and in cases of sickness, resulting either from natural causes, or from the influence of bad nâts, he is called to ascertain from the spirits the kind of offerings required for the removal of the spell, and assists at the sacrifice to which he has to invite the presence of the nâts. The Meetway is not a sacrificial priest, and his services are only called into requisition when it is desirable to ascertain the mind of the nâts on questions of importance. He fortells future events by the occurrence of certain natural phenomena, such as the peculiar appearance on fowls' bones, and from the character of the fracture of pieces of "nul" grass which have been held over a flame. As a rule, offerings are made to the nâts twice a year by all the villagers, who place them on the altars of the *lamshan*, the Toomsah determining the nâts that are to be propitiated; but if an epidemic of small-pox or any other disease should happen at any other period of the year, immediate recourse is had to nât offerings. Besides the two annual sacrifices, the occurrence of which are made the occasion of a general holiday and feast, the Tsawbwas are bound to offer buffaloes, bullocks, pigs, and fowls to the nâts twice a year. At these times, the population flocks to the principal village, and after the sacrifices have been offered, and the nâts have received their pittance of the rejectamenta, the people retire to the houses, and the next few days are devoted to feasting, in which sheroo, samshu, and opium are ungrudgingly distributed to all present, and dancing is the chief amusement. These feasts have been described to me by a number of independent authorities as the occasions of much debauchery and licentiousness. The skulls of the buffaloes and pigs then killed are always carefully preserved in the portico of the Tsawbwa's house, to the pillars of which they are fastened, and a chief always prides himself on the number of these trophies of his past carousals.

With regard to marriage, as it exists among these people, when the parents of a girl discover that she has committed herself to some one of her male friends, an effort is always made to get them married, but, as has been already said, public opinion among the Kakhyens does not consider it an imperative duty on the part of the man to marry a girl so situated, and I have been credibly informed that even the women think it no shame to forsake their lovers, and marry another if they dislike the first. Among the wealthy Kakhyens, marriage is an important event, and in the case of a Tsawbwa, the Meetway is always consulted as to the village from which he should select his bride. The match being made up, and all the preparations for the marriage having being completed, two messengers are sent from the bridegroom's village to inform the bride's friends that they are prepared for the marriage on a certain day. They are liberally feasted, and return with the messengers from the bride's household, who inform the future husband that they are ready for the ceremony. When the day arrives, five young men and women from the bridegroom go and remain in a house adjoining the bride's till night comes, when she is brought to it by one of the girls, without the knowledge of her parents, and informed that five men have come to claim her for her lord. They set out the same night for the bridegroom's village, and put up in a house adjoining his. In the morning she is conducted by her female companions to a canopy, closed in with cloth, outside her future husband's house, and there she remains. The same morning three or four old men arrive from her village, and entering her lover's house say, they have come to seek for one of the girls of their village who has been missed since the previous night. They are then invited to inspect the canopy, and see if their lost girl is there, and on recognizing her, they are requested by the bridegroom's party to take her back to her parents, but they reply,—"All is well, let her remain where she is." The preparations for the marriage now begin. On one side, the sacrifices are offered; and on the other, all the friends of the happy couple collect to settle their pecuniary affairs. A wealthy bridegroom is required to give the parents of his bride a female slave, ten buffaloes, ten spears, ten dâhs, ten pieces of silver (25 rupees), one gong, two suits of clothes, one matchlock, an iron pot for cooking rice, and one iron hearth, and to exhibit, at the same time, all the clothes and ornaments he intends for his future wife. In addition, he is bound by Kakhyen custom to present the bridesmaids with clothes and silver, and to feast all his guests. The Toomsah now places bunches of freshly cut nul grass in the earth, at regular distances from each other, between the canopy and the bridegroom's house, and presses them flat to the earth, to which they are kept down by bamboos laid crosswise. A grassy path is thus made. The household nâts are then called together by his waving nul grass in front of the altar, and on their arrival they are propitiated with bamboos of water and sheroo, and then the buffalo or ox and some fowls are sacrificed, and the blood sprinkled over the path of nul grass. This done, the bride and her maids pass over the bloody way to the house, where they propitiate the nâts with offerings of boiled eggs mixed with ginger and dried fish, and this ends the ceremony in which the bridegroom or parents of the bride have taken no part. All the guests now collect in the house, and dancing, drinking, and merry-making are the order of the day.

The custom prevails among the Kakhyens that a widow becomes the wife of one of the brothers-in-law. In cases of breach of promise, the friends of the injured fair one make it a point of honour to attack the village of the faithless swain, and to carry fire and sword into its midst, not sparing even the helpless and unoffending women and children; and not content with this fell revenge, they proceed to the destruction of any other hamlet that may have connived at the breach.

Women are able to go about their ordinary duties about the third or fourth day after their confinement; on the day after the birth, the household nâts are propitiated with offerings. Those that take a special interest in the domestic arrangements are offered sheroo within the house, and then a hog is sacrificed to the nâts generally. The flesh is cooked and divided into three portions,—one going to the Toomsah, another to the man who acts as slayer and cook, and the third to the head of the household. The nâts' portion and an offering of two bamboos of sheroo, boiled eggs, dried fish and ginger cut into small pieces are carried out to the lamshan, and placed on the altars. The ceremony is then concluded by a feast to which all the villagers are invited. Sheroo is handed round first to all the old men, and then to the younger ones, and after all have drunk, one of the former rises and pointing to the child says, that boy or girl is named so-and-so.

When a Kakhyen dies, the fact is announced to the neighbouring villages by the firing of guns, which is a signal for the people to repair to the house of the deceased. When all the relatives and other villagers have assembled, some go to the jungles to cut bamboos and prepare a coffin, while others remain to make the necessary preparations for the propitiation of the nâts. A circle of bamboos is driven into the ground so that their upper ends form a much larger circle than those in the earth. Small flags are tied on to each, and a bundle of nul grass is stuck into the ground between them and the house. The Toomsah then takes a small bunch of nul grass from before the circle, and waving it over the remainder, allows it to fall upon it. Sheroo is then held up before the circle, and after a little is poured on the ground, it is handed to the bystanders. A hog is then killed and cooked, and the skull fastened on to one of the bamboos, the flesh being distributed among the assembled friends. The men who go to prepare the coffin select a large tree which they fell with their dâhs, and when it is on the eve of falling, they kill a fowl by dashing it against the tottering stem. The coffin is hollowed out of the trunk, and the spot on which the head of the deceased is to rest is blackened with charcoal. A lid is also constructed for it. The body is then washed by the men in the case of their own sex, and if a woman, by the matrons. It is habited in new clothes, and some of the flesh of the hog, boiled rice, and sheroo are placed before it, and a piece of silver is put in its mouth, so that the spirit of the deceased may be able to pay its passage over the river it has to cross; and in the case of Tsawbwas, a precious stone is placed in each armpit. After this, the body is deposited in the coffin, and carried to the grave amidst the firing of guns, the women accompanying it with bamboos of sheroo, some of which they pour on the grave, while the rest is drunk by the friends. The grave is about three feet deep, and before the deceased is lowered to his last resting-place, three pieces of wood are placed in the bottom for the coffin to rest on, and branches of trees are strewn over the bier before the earth is filled in. The old clothes of the deceased are left on the grave, and as the people return, they strew ground rice at intervals along the path. Nearing the village they cleanse their legs and arms with the leaves of trees, and before entering the house of the deceased, they are sprinkled with water from a bunch of nul grass, and have to pass over a bundle of the same grass on which the blood of a fowl, sacrificed by the Toomsah in their absence, as an offering to the spirit of the dead man, had been sprinkled. The proceedings of the day are concluded with eating and drinking. On the following night, the people again assemble in the house of the deceased, and dance so long as the supply of sheroo lasts. This forms part of the ceremony that is gone through to induce the spirit to leave the house, and in the morning the household nât receives an offering of sheroo in the room in which the man died, and the spirit of the dead receives nul grass, sheroo, and a hog. A general feast ensues, and is concluded by a dance in a circle outside the room of the dead, and it lasts well through the night, and in the morning it is again continued for a short time, and those who have muskets fire them off. An altar is now erected outside the house, and the posts are barked, and covered with leaves, and a buffalo is sacrificed to the household nât, and the cooked flesh, along with rice and sheroo, are offered to him within the room to induce him to remove the spirit, and make it a nât. Then the Toomsah with his dâh breaks down the circle of bamboos to which the flags and the skull of the first hog had been fixed, and all the friends once more resort to the house, and conclude the final dance that is to drive the spirit forth to nât-land. In the afternoon, the men go to the grave, dig a trench around it, and erect a high, conical thatched cover over it, surmounted by two diverging arms, with an erect piece of wood between them. The skulls of the two hogs and buffaloes are fixed on posts around it, and the people return to the village, performing the same ceremonies they had gone through on their return from the burial. The bodies of the Tsawbwas are sometimes kept for years in varnished coffins, but such cases usually arise from the death having taken place in a village remote from his own, for the usual custom of the Kakhyens is to bury their chiefs like any other of their dead. The death ceremonies take place in the village in which he died; but instead of the body being buried at once, it is taken out to the jungle in its hermetically-closed case, and placed on a bamboo platform, to be removed at some more convenient time, and in such cases a hole is made in the bottom of the coffin, and a bamboo inserted into it and the ground, to allow the decaying fluids to escape. The usual burial services are not observed on the death of a man who has been killed by a dâh, or been shot. The body is merely wrapped in a mat, and buried in the jungle as quickly as possible, and a small open hut is built over the spot for the spirit to dwell in, and a dâh, bag, and a basket are placed in it for the use of the deceased. The ceremonies, however, of driving the spirit out of the house are religiously gone through. Small-pox deprives a Kakhyen of the usual death-rites, and also women who die *enceinte*. In the latter case, they are supposed to become evil spirits, and all the young women have a horror of such a death, and for the time being forsake the house in which it has happened. The Toomsah is called in, and consulted as to what animal is to be sacrificed to appease the compound devil-nât of woman and child. Some animal that the evil spirit likes to eat is named, and another into which it would be disposed to transfer itself is also determined. The latter is hanged by the neck, and the woman is buried in the direction in which the head of the animal pointed, after it was dead. The former, however, is first sacrificed to the nâts, and the flesh cooked and some of it set before the dead woman. The body is only rolled in a mat, and, along with the food and property of the deceased, is carried to its resting-place, when, after it has been laid, a bundle of burning straw is thrown on to the face, leaves are scattered over it, and the grave is closed. All her property is burnt on the spot, and a thatched hut is erected as a residence for her evil nât. The usual ceremonies are observed on the return from the burial. The practice of throwing a burning wisp of straw over the face is also practised in violent deaths, and deaths from small-pox, and, along with the custom of burning the property, may have given rise to the statement that the Kakhyens burn the bodies of their relatives who may have died from these causes.

The affairs of a Kakhyen Tsawbwaship are conducted by the chief, and by his lieutenants, or Pawmines as they are called. The Tsawbwa receives one large basket of rice annually from each house on his estate, and when a bullock or buffalo is killed, he is always presented with a hind-quarter. He is usually a trader, but also derives a revenue from duties levied on each mule-load that passes through his territories. The youngest son, from the Tsawbwa to the meanest peasant, always inherits, and the other sons are left to provide for themselves, which they do by collecting their followers, and settling in other parts. When a Tsawbwa dies childless, any of his brothers may succeed him, and if he has none, the nearest relation becomes the chief. The land is held by inheritance, but the eldest sons are allowed to clear any place that has not been previously cultivated. No Tsawbwa has the power to deprive a villager of his land; and on suggesting to a Kakhyen that his chief had a right to do with his own property as he chose, he indicated what his fate would be, if he did so, by a significant sawing motion across his own throat.

The office of Pawmine is hereditary, and descends to the eldest son, and the usual practice is to have only one; but at Ponsee where the Tsawbwa was a mere youth, with little or no force of character, three brothers had assumed the title, and as they were jealous of each other's authority, they were always acting in opposition to each other, and this was one of the causes of the many difficulties the Expedition had to contend against in that Tsawbwaship. The duties of a Pawmine are to settle the disputes that may arise in the villages.

Slavery is prevalent among the Kakhyens, and nearly all the victims I met with, had been stolen in youth in some raid on their native village. Almost all of them were from the most outlying portion of the eastern frontier of Assam, but they had been so long in captivity that they had lost nearly all knowledge of their own language. However, the case of Deen Mahomed, the petty trader from Midnapore, shows that they do not confine their attentions to children, but capture adults when they have the opportunity. The women, as a rule, become concubines, but a rich man, who cohabits with a slave, is despised. The men are usually presented with a Kakhyen wife, and when they are supposed to have given up all hope of escaping, they are allowed to accompany traders to the plains of Burmah, but never are permitted to go alone. The children of a slave become the property of his master, and are theoretically slaves, but they are treated much as the members of his own family. The lot of the slaves generally is not a hard one, and they are well treated if they are industrious and willing workers. A boy or girl costs about Rs. 40, but a man not more than Rs. 20 or 30. As a rule, they belong to the chiefs, and when a Tsawbwa marries, he is expected to present a slave to his father-in-law, among the other gifts that are made on such occasions.

The Kakhyens only know of a period of time, resembling a year, from the cultivation of their rice crops. When the grain has been cut in December, they begin to eat the new rice, and from that to the reaping of the following crop is their year. The jungles are cut in the end of March, or beginning of April, and fired after they have lain for a short time to dry. The ground is then cleared, and the rice and Indian corn are usually sown together, the former in long single lines at intervals among the latter. A certain extent of terrace cultivation is always found in the neighbourhood of villages, and a mountain stream is utilized for its free irrigation. The opium is cultivated in enclosures around the houses, and the juice is obtained by slitting the capsules with a small knife, and carefully scraping it off, and collecting it on tough Chinese paper, or on a hard large leaf. The cotton and tobacco are cultivated in long lines as in the Shan states. Their agricultural implements are a plough, a broad hoe with a short handle, and a bamboo dibble. The former is the same as in use among the Shans, and is employed on the rice terraces, and worked by buffaloes.

They manufacture their own cloth from the cotton grown on their hills, and the labour falls to the women. The loom is a very primitive structure, the same as is in use among the Khyens and Munipoories, and other tribes on the north-eastern frontier of Assam. One end of the warp is held in position by pegs driven into the ground, and the woman, sitting down with her legs straight before her, the other end is kept on the stretch by a broad leather strap fastened round her back. The threads of the warp are kept so far asunder by a long flat piece of wood turned edgeways, that there is sufficient space for the shuttle to pass easily from side to side. The general colour of the cotton cloth is blue, but there is usually a broad checked margin, the colours of which are Indian red, green, and yellow. The fine long hair of the domestic goat is almost invariably used in the manufacture of the coloured border. The custom appears to be, never to weave more than is required for their yearly use, and hence I experienced great difficulty in procuring specimens of the cloth, and had to give extravagant sums for it. It is very strong and thick, and of great durability. The finer kinds, used for jackets and for the trousers of the men, appear to be almost wholly of Shan manufacture. The females, like the Shans, are adepts at silk and cotton embroidery, but they seldom attempt more than the decoration of the cotton bags or haversacks worn by the men. From the similarity of their patterns to those in use by the Shans, it appears probable that they have borrowed the art from them.

Their tobacco pipes are nearly all of Chinese manufacture, and are either of iron or brass with very small bowls. The opium pipe or hookah is made by themselves, but the copper spoon for evaporating the solution of opium which is taken up by long stripes of plantain leaf, and the long forceps for holding the live ember for lighting the pipe, are of Shan manufacture. The bulb of the hookah for holding the water is not made from a cocoanut as in India, but from the segment of a hill bamboo with a green and yellow variegated stem. Although opium-smoking is very general among the men, it does not appear, as a rule, to be carried to excess.

The weapons of a Kakhyen are his dâh, spear, matchlock, crossbow, and poisoned arrows. The dâh is the favourite weapon, which they wield with great dexterity, and use in the most varied offices, felling men and trees alike, and in executing the fine but primitive carvings on their opium pipes and bamboo fau-cases. The spear, too, is a favourite weapon with the mountaineers, but as it is contrary to Kakhyen tactics to come to hand-to-hand encounters in open daylight, it is used as a projectile on such occasions, and thrown with unerring aim. The matchlock has a very long barrel, and a very small stock, which is held at the side of the cheek in firing. The match is a long coil of slow-burning rope, and the powder flask the same as that used by the Shans. The Kakhyens have a very ingenious way of striking fire by the sudden and forcible descent of a piston in a closed cylinder. There is a small cup-shaped cavity at the end of the piston-rod into which a little tinder is inserted. The piston is then introduced into the cylinder into which it tightly fits, and by a blow is made to descend with great rapidity and force, and is as rapidly withdrawn, when the little pellet of tinder is found to have become ignited: a beautiful but simple experiment illustrating the evolution of a very large amount of heat by the sudden compression of the air in the piston. These instruments are not more than four inches long, and are in general use. The crossbow is the same as the Chinese. The arrows, which are poisoned by the juice of an *Aconitum*, which occurs on their hills, are about a foot in length, and are carried in a quiver made either of a bamboo or of the skin of the barking-deer. They are much used in killing game, and if the wound is cut out, no evil ensues from eating the flesh of animals slaughtered by them.

A study of Kakhyen art, as it occurs in the patterns on their opium pipes and horn punches, leads to the conclusion that it is of the same primitive type that distinguishes the carvings on the implements of uncivilized man in distant regions and widely separated periods. We might find almost the exact fellow of a Kakhyen punch in some of the implements of the stone age, and carvings of the very same type among the relics of the neolithic period.

Their chief amusements are music and dancing. Their only musical instruments are the drum hollowed out of the stem of a tree, and covered at either end with the skin of the barking-deer, and a single and double flute from which the sound is produced by a piece of tinsel leaf inside a long slit which is covered by the mouth. While the flute is being played between his teeth, it is customary for the performer to produce at the same time a wheezing sound in his throat, which adds to the wild character of the music, which has only the compass of a few notes. The double flute is occasionally played through the nose, and then the performer has a better opportunity to indulge in his guttural sounds, which are so pleasant to him. A Jew's harp, made of bamboo, gives a wonderfully clear, almost metallic, sound.

The food of the Kakhyens consists chiefly of pork, dried fish from Burmah, the flesh of the barking-deer, the bamboo rat, rice, and vegetables, with beer or sheroo made from fermented rice. They cook in iron pots manufactured at Talifoo, and eat with chop-sticks from off plantain leaves. The men and women do not eat together.

Between Tsitkaw and Manwyne, the following chiefs are met with, viz.—Latong, Talone, Ponline, Ponsee, Hosong, Nanken, and Pongwah, and a short way off the road, between Ponsee and Manwyne, is the territory of the Seray chief, who is almost a Shan in his habits of thought and way of living. On the opposite bank of the Tapeng, between Burmah and Namboke, at the foot of the Hotha valley, the following large states are passed:—Mantai, Hoetone, Mutthin, Loaylone, Muangwye, Ponsee, and Namboke, with a number of smaller ones of little importance. A tariff of four annas a mule-load is levied by each of these chiefs on all merchants passing through their districts.

The Leesaws are an uncivilized tribe occurring on the hills about the Hotha and Sanda valleys, and they appear to be the same people that Mr. Cooper met with, under the name of Leisus, on the northern extremity of Yunan, if not in Tibet itself. A Shan informed me that they extend as far south as Kianghung-gyee, and the Hotha Tsawbwa mentioned that they are also found on the mountains to the east of Yungchan. They are not numerous about the valleys, but are said to occur in greater numbers in these than other localities. They live in villages of their own, apart from the Kakhyens, who regard them as an inferior race, and in some localities exact tribute from them. As all my information regarding them was gained on the market days from the few men and women who visit Sanda and Muangla on these occasions, it is necessarily of the most meagre kind. They are a small hill people, with fair, round, flat faces, high cheek-bones, and some little obliquity of the eye. The dress of the women resembles the costume of the Chinese-Shans, with the exception of the turban, which is made of coarse white cloth, patched with blue squares, and trimmed with cowries. One end is allowed to hang down the back of the neck, while the other is thrown over the top of the head. They also wear close-fitting leggings, made of squares of blue and white cloth, and a profusion of ratan, bamboo, and straw hoops round the loins and neck, in addition to necklaces of large blue beads, and others of seeds, and large brass earrings. A white embroidered bag is slung over the shoulders from a broad red band, ornamented with a profusion of cowries. The men are dressed like ordinary Shans.

The most interesting circumstance, however, connected with the Leesaws is the strong affinity of their language to the Burmese, but I was not in a position to collect any information regarding their history, or to learn any of their traditions; still the similarity of the two languages is so great that it is hardly possible to avoid the conclusion that the two people, Burmese and Leesaws, have sprung from one stock. These little-known Leesaws appear to have a wide distribution over the mountains of Yunan, and it is probable that their traditions, when investigated, may throw some light on the early history and spread of the Burmese race.

Manwyne, the first Shan town that is met with on the eastern side of the Kakhyen hills, and Sanda and Muangla, have all a large Chinese population, not, however, of the changeable character of the one found at Bhamô, but constituting a portion of the natural population of the valley. On reaching Manwyne, the traveller immediately recognizes that he is on the borders of China, and when he proceeds 60 miles further to the east, he finds himself in the midst of a population whose only language is Chinese. To put the fact broadly, but consistently with the history of the country to the east of Bhamô, the borders of China, in the Sanda valley, are now only 30 to 35 miles distant from Tsitkaw on the Tapeng in Burmese territory, but prior to the Mahomedan rebellion, they were within 9 miles of Burmah. I mention this, for we have not been in the habit of recognizing how close our own territory lies to the Chinese frontier.

At Manwyne, the Chinese form half of the population, and the women dwarf their feet, and dress in the national costume; and between that town and Sanda there is a considerable trading village of Karahokah solely inhabited by the same people; and outside Sanda there is a large Chinese quarter enclosed by a wall as a distinct village. At Muangla they occur all through the town and neighbouring villages, and at Nantin we meet with a town that was originally essentially Chinese, although it is now largely inhabited by Panthays. From the latter town eastwards the prevailing language is Chinese. The typical Chinese, as a rule, are a taller race than the Shans, and physically differ but little from their brethren on the east coast of the empire. Their language, however, appears to be a well-marked dialect peculiar to Yunan, and I make this statement on the authority of certain Panthays, who had travelled as far to the south-east as Canton. The peasantry have a strong resemblance to Shans and Kakhyens, and dress like these people, as I have observed on a previous occasion; and the probability is that they have a strong infusion of Shan blood, if they are not entirely Shan, modified by Chinese influence, in the same way that their brethren to the west have been influenced by the Burmese. But owing to the restrictions that were placed on my movements, I had no opportunity to make any personal observations on the habits and customs of the peasantry, and as the town populations exactly resembled, in their habits and customs, the Chinese of other parts of China, I shall conclude this chapter by directing attention to the vocabularies which are appended to this Report, and which will serve to give some indication of the characters of the languages spoken by the various tribes with which the Expedition was brought in contact, with the solitary exception of the Chinese itself.

CHAPTER VI.

MAHOMEDANS IN YUNAN.

THE earliest authentic notice of the introduction of the Arabs (Mahomedans) into China[1] carries us back as far as the 125th year of the Hejira, A.D. 757.[2] Sutsung, the then reigning emperor of the Tung dynasty,[3] while in the deep difficulties of a rebellion which had begun in his father Hiuntsung's reign, and had assumed such proportions that the rebel leader, Ngan-loshan, had dignified himself with the title of emperor,[4] was rescued from his embarrassments by the arrival of an embassy from the Kaliph, Abu Jafar al Mansûr, the founder of Bagdad, accompanied by auxiliary troops, which were joined by Ouïgours and other forces from the west, and which enabled him to crush the rebellion.

The reign of Tetsung[5] (Sutsung's grandson) was even more unsettled, and there was nothing heard of but insurrections which he had difficulty in quelling, the military power of the empire having doubtless been greatly crippled by the huge Tartar invasion which had occurred while his father Taytsung was on the throne. To meet those rebellions, he was forced to augment his army by a great number of fresh troops, some of which he received from the Abasside Kaliph, and to maintain which he had to double his taxes, and impose one on tea. The

---

[1] I much regret that I had no opportunity to consult Yule's learned work on "Cathay and the Way Thither," until the above chapter was in type.—J. A.

[2] Yule, quoted in Edinburgh Review, vol. cxxvii, p. 360.

[3] It is stated in the Universal History, but with no quoted authority, that "the Mahomedans are believed by some to have first settled in China in the reign of the first Emperor of the Hew-chew dynasty, whilst others place it much earlier, even as high as the 13th dynasty" (Tung). *Univ. Hist.*, vol. viii, pp. 122-123. *Gutzlaff*, vol. ii, pp. 199-200.

[4] *Description of the Empire of China*, Du Halde, vol. i, pp. 199-200.

[5] The Chinese annals report that in the eighth year of the reign of Tetsung's father (Taytsung), ambassadors arrived from foreign nations whose air, form, and habit were altogether new to the Chinese, and that the emperor himself rejoiced that in his time, men with fair hair and blue eyes arrived in the empire. In the Imperial Library at Paris there is an old Arabic manuscript, which states that at this time the Catholic Patriarch of the Indies sent preachers of the gospel into China. *Renaudot, Ancient Accounts.*

rebellion was ultimately stamped out by the energy of his general, Kotsui, who had also been the faithful servant of his grandfather, Sutsung.[1]

The account given of China by Abu Zaid,[2] who in the middle of the 9th century compiled a description of the countries to the east of Arabia, from materials derived from the Arab traders of his time, would lead to the conclusion that China had been resorted to by his countrymen long before he wrote. Even in these early days, the Arab community of Hang-chew-foo (Khanfu) was one of considerable importance, for it had a judge or hadji appointed over it by the emperor of China, and we are told that the Christian, Mahomedan, Jewish, and Parsee population put to the sword, in A.D. 878, amounted to 120,000.[3]

The rebellion of Whantsyaw,[4] Hwangchoa, or Banshoa, in the reign of Hitsung of the Tung dynasty, A.D. 878, may have been instrumental in introducing a Toorkish element into North-Western China. That emperor had been driven from his capital, and had fled to the frontier of Tibet, where he begged the assistance of the king of Tagazgaz,[5] who sent his son, at the head of a numerous army, to quell the insurrection, which was suppressed, after many battles, and the emperor was reinstated in his capital.

Mahomedanism was little known among the Tartars before the time of Chengiz Khan, but his conquests were the means of bringing a considerable population of Ouïgours and Toongances into the provinces of Shensi and Kansu. The former tribe had abjured Buddhism, about two centuries and a half before the conquest of China by the Tartars. The religious life, and, indeed, the individuality, as a race, of these newcomers, were kept alive by the vigorous trading and political intercourse that subsisted in these early times between China and their mother-country, and other Mahomedan lands to the west.

With this large increase of Mahomedan population to that already introduced by the Arab traders, and the contingents of the Abasside Kaliph, it is not to be wondered at that the distinguished traveller, Marco Polo, was struck, while residing in China (1271 to 1295), with the number of Mahomedans. In his description of the people on the western verge of Shensi, where the celebrated mart of Singui (Selin of Pallas) was situated, on the way between Tibet and Pekin, and in his account of the

---

[1] Du Halde, l. c.
[2] Ancient Accounts, Renaudot.
[3] Ancient Accounts, p. 183.
[4] Du Halde, l. c., p. 202.
[5] Ancient Accounts, p. 43.

city of Singan, the capital of the province, and of Karazan, part of Yunan, he describes the Mahomedans as forming a considerable part of the foreign population, but does not offer any opinion as to how they were introduced into the empire. The position which this religious sect had attained in China during his time (the reign of Kublai Khan) was considerable, for Polo informs us that the provincial governments and magistracies were entrusted to the Tartars, Christians, and Mahomedans. The latter, however, misabused their trust, so much so, that the emperor, reflecting on the principles of these accursed Saracens, forbade them to continue many practices conjoined on them by their laws. This interdict, however, does not appear to have affected their loyalty, for we find them praying for the welfare of the Great Khan on his birth-days; and some of their leading men, in accordance with Chinese principles of religious toleration, advanced to positions of considerable trust in the civil, military, and scientific departments of the empire. For many years, the emperor's first minister of finance was an Arab, and we find the invasion of Burmah and the sieges of Singan and Funtching entrusted to Mahomedan generals, and another of their sect promoted to the distinguished office of president of the mathematical board. Facts like these, and others of a similar nature which might be adduced, afford ample evidence to show that they had gained a firm hold in many parts of China by Marco Polo's time, more especially in the provinces of Shensi, Kansu, and Yunan. Rashid-ood-deen, the vizier of the Persian empire, in the early part of the 14th century, mentions Yunan province, and states that the inhabitants were all Mahomedans.[1]

Ibn Butata is our next authority on the extent to which they had increased by about the middle of the 14th century. He reached China by sea, and states that in every large town he found Mahomedans, who were mostly rich merchants, and that in all the provinces there was a town for them, each of which had usually a mosque, market, a cell for the poor, and a judge and sheikh of Islam; and that in some districts they were exceedingly numerous.

The Jesuit fathers, who were in China about the middle of the 17th century, make frequent mention of the Mahomedan population. Louis Le Compte,[2] writing to the Lord Cardinal de Bouillon (1680 A.D.), mentions that they had been about 600 years in the country, and that they were never disturbed, because they never disturbed any one

---

[1] Edin. Review, 1868, vol. cxxvii, p. 359.
[2] Le Compte's History of China, pp. 339-341.

MAHOMEDANS IN YUNAN.

else on the score of religion; but quietly enjoyed their liberty without studying to propagate their doctrine even by marriages out of their own kindred. At that time they were neither considerable enough from their numbers or wealth to have any such views.[1] And even in places where they were most numerous, and made the best figure, as in the provinces to the north of the Yellow river, where they had been settled for many generations, and in some of the towns along the canal, where they had built high mosques differing entirely from Chinese ideas of architecture, they were still looked upon as of foreign extraction, and had frequently been insulted by the Chinese.

The oppression to which they were subjected after the second Tartar conquest, began to show itself so early as the beginning of the 18th century, when the populace in the city of Hang-chew, in the province of Huquang, upon some dislike taken at the indiscreet behaviour of some of them, destroyed their mosques, notwithstanding all the endeavours of the magistracy to save them. The earlier incident, however, about 1651, when they were deprived by the Tartar Emperor Chunchi of the high honours they had enjoyed for nearly thirty years in connection with the tribunal of mathematics, seems to have inaugurated that change of policy that drove the Mahomedans to open rebellion in after years. The first of these rebellions occurred in 1765 or 1767 on the western frontier (Yunan?) in the reign of Kienhung, and spread also to the province of Kansu. The rebels resisted the imperial forces with great valour, but were ultimately subdued.

The Abbé Grosier,[2] writing after this event, but without reference to it, says that "for some time past the Mahomedans seem to have been more particularly attentive to the care of extending their sect, and propagating their doctrine," a course which appears to me to have been forced upon them, in order to enable them to withstand the oppression from which they were evidently suffering at the time the Abbé wrote. As the breach widened between them and their Tartar governors, for they appear to have been always on good terms with the Chinese, they became so exclusive that they would not suffer any one to live among them who did not attend mosque. The method they now resorted to, to add to the number of the faithful, was not the rallying cry of the west, but the free use of their wealth in purchasing children, whom they circumcised, and educated as Mahomedans. In the frightful

---

[1] Universal History, vol. viii, pp. 122-123.
[2] Grosier's China, vol. iv, p. 270.

famine which devastated the province of Quangtong, 1790, they purchased ten thousand children from poor parents, compelled by necessity to part with them. These they educated, and as they grew up, provided wives for them, and gave them houses, and even formed whole villages of these bought converts.[1] This system is still prevalent in Yunan, and I had numerous instances of it brought under my notice while at Momien, the most westerly stronghold of the Panthays; and the following may serve as an illustration. The native officer in charge of our police guard, and a most rigid Mahomedan, was accompanied by his Burmese wife, and, owing to his intimate acquaintance with the ceremonial details of their religion, was in great vogue among the Panthays. He was childless, and accordingly a little Chinese girl who had been lately purchased from poor parents was made a Mahomedan, and given him as an heir, as one of the most appropriate gifts they could think of making, in return for the many prayers he had offered up for them in their mosque.

Yunan[2] appears to have been the scene of almost incessant insurrection from 1817 to 1834, wholly attributable, in all probability, to the Mahomedans. The first of these revolts lasted from 1817 to 1818, when the rebels seem to have had some organization, for they attacked the capital in which the Chinese commander had shut himself up. A force, however, coming to his assistance, he routed the rebels, who sought refuge among the tribes on the western frontier, leaving their leader in the hands of the imperialists. A proclamation was issued, promising the tribes protection if they discountenanced the rebels, and threatening them with destruction if they harboured them.

The Pekin gazettes notice a disturbance on the western frontier of Yunan in 1826, and another in the following year. A more serious revolt broke out in the same quarter in 1828, and the leader had an imperial seal engraved, under which he published manifestoes on the frontier of China, insisting on people to join his standard; but this rebellion was also suppressed. The governor of Yunan quelled another insurrection in 1826, and again in 1834. The Pekin gazettes contain notices of other disturbances in the provinces, but there is no distinct statement that they were Mahomedan, although it is probable that all were so.

Gutzlaff[3] mentions that during his residence in China, 1825-1832, they had several mosques in Che-kiang, Pichile, Shensi, and Shanse, but

---

[1] Du Halde, vol. i, p. 678.
[2] Chinese Repository, vol. ix, p. 490, et seq.
[3] Gutzlaff's China, vol. ii, pp. 199-200.

that as they had occasionally joined the rebels of Toorkistan, the government viewed them with a jealous eye. Nevertheless, some of their community were in offices of high trust. Notwithstanding the great distance they lived from the native country of the prophet, he informs us that many of them made pilgrimages to Mecca, and returned with Arabian manuscripts, and wonderful stories about the grave of Mahomed; that a few could read Arabic imperfectly, and perhaps repeat the first Suraj; that they were by no means bigoted nor proselytizing, nor scrupulous in their ancestral rites; and that they venerated Confucius.

In the present century, they appear to have increased more rapidly in Yunan than in any other province to the north, and the population seems to be possessed of considerable trading enterprise. Caravans from Yunan visit Mandalay regularly once a year, and Colonel Burney[1] relates that, in 1831, almost the whole of the Chinese traders to that city were Mahomedans, a circumstance that struck him as very extraordinary. They refused to eat with the Burmese, and killed their meat according to Mahomedan rites; the few only who imported hams were not Mahomedans. Several of them, he states, could read a little Arabic, and one in a loud chanting voice read a passage to him from some religious book in that language. They could, however, give him no account of the time when, or the manner in which, they were converted to the faith.

The first detailed account of the Mahomedans of Yunan, who have given rise to these remarks, was communicated by Major-General Fytche,[2] on information supplied partly by Major Sladen, the Resident at the court of Mandalay, and partly gleaned by himself from a few Panthay traders he met at Moulmein. This communication has since been referred to in an able article in the *Edinburgh Review*[3] on Western China, in which the facts in General Fytche's paper have been reproduced, and commented upon. Two accounts of the origin of the Mahomedans were given on the authority of General Fytche, one derived from Chinese, and the other from Panthay sources. The former has about it all the air of circumstantiality, but the latter is overladen with the mythical and oriental trappings of a religious tradition; but when divested of these, it is identical, to all practical purposes, with the Chinese narrative, and may be briefly stated as follows: about one thousand years ago, a rebellion threatened the safety of the government of the reigning Emperor

---

[1] Gleanings of Science, vol. iii, p. 184.
[2] As. Soc. Proceedings, 1867, p. 176.
[3] Edinburgh Review, cxxvii, p. 357.

Oung-loshan, who sent for assistance to a Mahomedan king, called Kazee or Khazee, who governed the countries to the east of China. The appeal was successful, and a body of 10,000 fighting-men was despatched to his aid, and the rebellion was quelled. A new difficulty now presented itself as to the disposal of the contingent which was much reduced in numbers, and because the members of it refused to return to their own country, as they had learned that they would be despised on their return, on account of their long association with an infidel population; they were, therefore, sent to the province of Yunan, where they settled, and became peaceful subjects of the Chinese empire. With this account before us, our first endeavour is to identify the dynasty in which these events are said to have occurred, but a difficulty meets us at the very outset of the enquiry, for the first part of the so-called emperor's name is not that of any Chinese dynasty we know of, and the difficulty increases when we come to the name itself, for there is no record in history of an emperor called Loshan. We find ourselves in equal perplexity when we attempt to locate the king, Kazee or Khazee. I am, therefore, inclined to suspect that General Fytche's informants had little acquaintance with their early history, and this suspicion is fully justified by the information I received from Tahsakone, and the hadji at Momien,[1] which has this to recommend it, that it agrees with the records of the Chinese dynasties, as given by Du Halde, and other Jesuit fathers, whose materials, I believe, were derived from the imperial chronicles. My informants stated that their forefathers came from Arabia to China 1,000 years ago, in the reign of the Emperor Tung-huon-tsong, who had sent his chief minister, Khazee, to Tseeyoog (?) to implore aid against the rebel Oung-loshan, and that they numbered 3,000 men.[2] When we compare the leading facts in this statement with Du Halde's narrative of the Tung dynasty to which Huon-tsung belonged, we cannot fail to be struck with the remarkable agreement between the two accounts, although the historian of China makes no allusion whatever to the employment of a Mahomedan contingent for the suppression of the rebellion. Du Halde

---

[1] I may state that I took the precaution to write all my questions, and had them translated into Chinese, and that each question had its answer written opposite to it, and that the answer was founded solely on the original questions which were put pointedly, thus: *Question*—In the reign of what emperor did the Panthays arrive in China? *Answer*—In the reign of Tung-huon-tsung.

[2] Major Sladen procured, unknown to me, a short document giving an account of the introduction of the Mahomedans into China, agreeing in every particular with the above account, which I obtained direct from the governor and hadji, quite independently of Major Sladen, or any printed documents.

writes the name of the emperor, Tung-hiun-tsong, but the similarity of Tung-huon-tsong is so striking that we cannot question their identity, especially when we consider the names in conjunction with the events recorded by the historian and my informants. The former mentions that Hiun-tsong was a prince of singular temperance, and zeal for the public good, but that the last fourteen years of his reign were disturbed by an insurrection which had been raised by a foreign prince, Ngan-loshan, to whom he had entrusted the command of his army. This traitor made himself master of a great part of the north, and ultimately routed the imperial army. A company of robbers, encouraged by these disasters, also attacked it, and compelled the emperor to seek for safety in the province of Sechuen. After this retreat, Sutsung, his son, took possession of the government, although his father was still alive, and with the aid of his prime minister, Kotsûi, he dispersed the robbers, restored public tranquillity, bringing his father back from Sechuen to his palace. Insurrection, however, does not appear to have been finally quelled, for we are informed that Ngan-loshan looted the palace of Chang-ngan. In the end his treachery to his king did not go unpunished, for he perished by the hand of his own son. If there can be little difference of opinion about the similarity of Hiun-tsong and Huon-tsong, there must surely be quite as little regarding the identity of Ngan-loshan and Oung-loshan, the only rebel of this name in Chinese history. Hence it seems probable that General Fytche's Oung-loshan was the rebel and not the emperor, and that the certain king, Kazee or Khazee, was the prime minister, Khazee. The circumstance also that Ngan-loshan's insurrection is mentioned by Du Halde, as having been protracted into the reign of Sutsung, is indisputable evidence that the incident related to me by the Mahomedans at Momien is the same as the one given by Yule in his work on Cathay. Although my informants stated that their forefathers had come, in the first instance, from Arabia, they mentioned with equal clearness that they had settled in Yunan, from the provinces of Shensi and Kansu, about 150 years ago, a fact which would make us doubt the purity of their boasted Arab descent, for the whole weight of historical evidence is to prove that these two provinces derived the greater part, if not the whole, of their Mahomedan population from the tide of Toorkish conquest that overran the northern provinces of China. We have, however, Marco Polo and Rashid-ood-deen's authority for the existence of a large Mahomedan population in Yunan in the 14th and 15th centuries, 440 years before the date assigned by my informants for their arrival in the province.

I am led, therefore, to suppose that the ranks of the original Mahomedan population in Yunan, which may have been of Arab descent, were augmented about the beginning of the 18th century by a number of Toorkish Mahomedans from the northern provinces of Kansu and Shensi, that the two elements rapidly amalgamated, and that their fusion was so complete, that their respective traditions became as much blended together as the races themselves.

And here I cannot avoid remarking that the origin of the original Mahomedan population of Yunan and other provinces, leaving out of sight for the present Sutsung's contingent, as it is usually accounted for, *viz.*, on the theory that it found its way in from the sea-board, seems to be a one-sided explanation, when we remember that the Nestorian Christians had made their way overland to the province of Shensi as early as A.D. 636, and that it has never been claimed for them that they necessarily percolated into China from the coast. What the Nestorian Christians achieved could also be accomplished by the devotees of the prophet.

And the mere coincidence that the more learned among them, such as the hadjis, know a little Arabic, appears a frail basis on which to rest their claim to an Arab descent, the more especially seeing that the Mahomedans of the northern provinces are quite as familiar with this language as their southern co-religionists. The great charm Arabic has to these people is bound up in the circumstance that the prophet spoke it, and that it is the one in which all the religious books brought back by their pilgrims are written.

The fact that these Mahomedans of Yunan claim kindred with those of Kansu and Shensi is one which seems destined to exercise a powerful influence on the future of the Chinese empire; and the present course of events points in the direction of the establishment of a Mahomedan monarchy, which will comprise the provinces of Yunan, Sechuen, Shensi, and Kansu. This probable result was forcibly suggested to me by the facts I gathered, while at Momien. The whole of the province of Yunan, I may say, was then in the hands of the Mahomedans, who were turning their attention to the southern portion of the province of Sechuen, which they had overran, about six months before the visit of Colonel Sarel, in 1861. The northern division of the province was devastated by Mahomedan rebels from Shensi and Kansu in the early part of 1868. The Toonganee rebellion in Dzungaria is so intimately bound up with Russian interests in Central Asia, that we may look for its suppression by that power.

I come now to speak in detail of the Yunanese Mahomedans. The term Panthay, applied to them by the Burmese and adopted by the English, means simply Mahomedan. On the authority of General Fytche, they are known to the Chinese as "Quayzay," which the writer in the *Edinburgh Review* conjectures to be identical with "Houi-houi," the generic term applied by the Chinese to all Mahomedans. Mr. Cooper, the Chinese explorer, informs me that there are two Chinese words very similar in sound, but with entirely different meaning, "Quayze" and "Houize," and that the use of the first, as applied to the Mahomedans, is incorrect. "Quayze" means a foreigner, and is not used when speaking of them, whereas "Houize" is constantly applied. Before the rebellion "Houi-houi" was the term in use, but now in rebel districts they are only known as "Houize," the affix *ze* meaning independent of Chinese authority. It is the same termination that occurs in Matze, Tibetan; Tatze, Tartar; and Miautze, all of which are independent tribes, and are indicated as such by the terminal syllable *ze*.

The rebellion in Yunan seems to have been brought about solely by the oppression to which the Mahomedans were subjected by their rulers. Riots occurred in which their mosques were despoiled, and this roused their religious hate, and ultimately led to the complete destruction of nearly every Buddhistic temple in Yunan. As the insurrection spread, the Chinese towns and villages were pillaged, and indiscriminate slaughter overtook the male population, the women being spared to minister to the passions of a brutal, undisciplined mob, while the unresisting children were eagerly preserved to be educated as Mussulmans. The desolate and ruined villages between Nantin and Momien, and the almost unbroken line of deserted towns and hamlets encircling the once smiling and busy valley of the latter town, are incontrovertible evidence of the relentless ferocity with which the Panthays prosecuted the rebellion. They met with little direct resistance from the imperial government; and in time the Chinese officials in the provinces, with a remnant of adherents, were gradually driven from the high fertile valleys to seek refuge in the smaller and more inaccessible valleys among the mountains, to which they were followed by other adherents of the imperial cause. As years passed on, and the Panthays extended their power throughout the principal valleys, a constant guerilla warfare was maintained between them and the Chinese officials, whom the Panthays now style robber-chiefs, from the circumstance that they take every opportunity to pillage Panthay villages, petty traders, and caravans, and to make forays even to the very walls of Momien. Prominent among the so-called dacoit leaders is the famous chief, Leesetai, who till lately had his fortress at Mawphoo, half-way between Muangla and Nantin; and Lowquangfang, who occupied the hills to the north-west of Momien. The hatred that exists between these two chiefs and the Panthays is constantly making itself felt in raids that have effectually paralysed trade, and reduced the cultivation of the valleys to the lowest ebb compatible with the small wants of a miserably impoverished population. At Momien and its neighbourhood, and from what I observed in the Shan states, it is evident that the fury of the Mahomedans was ultimately directed against the Buddhistic temples and monasteries, and I may safely say, from personal observation, and information gained at Momien, that very few have escaped destruction. The Shans, although they did not side with either party, were not exempt, and their temples, and the palaces of their Tsawbwas as well, were looted, and either burnt or rased to the ground.

While mentioning the Shans, it may be as well to state that it does not appear that either they or the Kakhyens ever joined or gave any assistance to the Panthays during the height of the rebellion, for the sympathies of these people are entirely on the side of the Chinese; and it is only within the last two years that the Shan states in the Sanda and Hotha valleys, and the Kakhyens on the neighbouring hills, have been forced by the course of events to give in their adherence to the Panthay cause, and consent to pay tribute to them instead of to China.

The rebellion was still active, while we were at Momien, and the capital of the province fell to the insurgents during our residence among them. If the account they furnished us of the taking of that great city, Yunan, is to be relied upon, it was conducted with the utmost moderation, and suggests the hope that the Panthays are beginning to realise their position in the province, as so far established, that it is both politic and expedient for them to gain the favourable opinion of the people, by a just consideration for the conquered, and by a laudable moderation. Vigorous hostilities were being carried on, on the road between Momien and Yungchan which was quite impassable. Two, out of three messengers, with despatches from Tali, were killed, and the other escaped with difficulty.

In order that there may be no misconception as to the position of the Panthays in such outlying districts as Momien, I will further describe affairs as we found them in that city. During our residence, two thousand men under the command of the chief military officer marched against a body of Chinese who were threatening the Panthay town of Khyto, about 30 miles north-west of Momien, and 200 of the ears of the Chinese were secured as indisputable vouchers of the victory gained. Over 15 executions took place during the 1 month and 17 days we were there, and 30 mules that were grazing on a hill-side close to the city were carried off by a body of Chinese before the eyes of a Panthay armed guard in charge of them; and, moreover, so great was the insecurity to life that we were not allowed to go beyond half a mile from the city, without the protection of an armed escort, under the charge of some responsible Panthay officer.

Before the fall of the capital, the district in its neighbourhood had been the scene of great devastation and bloodshed. One hundred villages, besides 37 towns and cities, had been captured, and it is significantly stated in the proclamation from which I derive these particulars, that the inhabitants of those that tendered their submission were spared, leaving us to infer that those who resisted were either put to the sword, or perished in the flames of their burning homesteads. Twenty-one thousand are stated to have been killed, and it is also mentioned that 40 towns were taken and destroyed, that 300 persons were burnt to death, and that there were innumerable killed and wounded besides. The Panthays were opposed at the capital by fifty or sixty thousand imperial troops, against which the Chinese were unable to contend, and the surrender of Yunan city by its officials was a telling recognition of the invincible progress of the Mahomedans. The fighting, however, at this time, 1867-1868, was not confined to the Momien and Yunan districts, for Mr. Cooper informs me that while he was at Weesee, on the left bank of the Cambodia, in the north of the province, in July 1868, that the Panthays and Chinese were engaged in active hostilities at Tseegooshan and Tseejanfoo, almost on its extreme northern outskirts. During the same month, I learned at Momien that the Mahomedans had spread into the neighbouring province of Sechuen, into which they had formerly made a raid, along with the Miautze, so far back as 1860. On that occasion they crossed the river at Pingshan. They have also spread as far as Theta in the south of the province, 4 or 5 days' march to the north of Kiang-hung on the Cambodia. The whole of Yunan is in open rebellion, and as this is not an event of yesterday nor to-day, but has existed for the last fifteen years, and even before that, I leave it to those most interested in the scheme for opening up a trade between China and Burmah *via* Yunan, to form their own conclusions as to its practicability, in the present unsettled condition of the country.

With reference to the internal affairs of the Panthays, it is now well known that a hadji, Ma Yussu by name, was elected, a few years ago, to the responsible position of king, and that he holds his court at Talifoo. He is known to the Mahomedans as Sooleyman, and to the Chinese as Tuwintsen. Four military and four civil officers, or what the Chinese call mandarins of the first class, are associated with him in the government, and the former have certain districts allotted to them, but every matter of importance is referred to Talifoo where the king has the advice of a civil council of four chiefs. The governorship of Momien is one of the most important offices in the state. This official wears the robes of a Chinese military mandarin of the first class, and keeps up a show of state in a small palace within the city, which was almost entirely destroyed at the outbreak of the rebellion. Tasakone, the present governor, is always attended by a number of military officers, all young men devoted to his service. As is the case generally with governors, he is supreme in all matters, civil and military, but the command of the troops at Momien is entrusted to an officer with the title of Tahzyungyee.

All criminals, and persons suspected of Chinese sympathies, are brought before the governor for judgment, and his sentences are carried into effect by the military who have charge of the prison. If the sentence is capital, the uncompassioned criminal is at once led to the outskirts of the bazaar by a small escort, with music and banners flying, and, with his hands tied behind his back, is made to kneel by the side of the road, and has his head struck off by one fell swoop of the executioner's dâh, and is buried on the spot. If taken in the act of dacoity, he is executed without any trial, and the ghastly head is usually hung up by the side of the gate of the city, as a terror to evil-doers.

The male portion of the Panthay population is almost exclusively military, and resides within the city. A constant watch is kept from guard-houses over the gates, two of which have been built up for greater safety; and the bazaar outside, in which the Chinese population which has given in its adherence to the Panthay cause resides, is also enclosed by a low brick wall with a number of gates that are closed at dark, and are under the care of sentinels. It neither requires any very lengthened observation nor enquiry, and indeed a few days' residence at Momien sufficed to impress me with the fact, that the government is entirely in the hands of the soldiery; that the hold the Panthays have in the district is still so precarious that they are liable to be attacked at any moment; and that the feeling among the Chinese traders and merchants, and of the peasantry, is unfavourable to them.

The Panthays at Momien are generally well-made athletic men, of moderate height, and all are fair-skinned, with slightly oblique eyes and high cheek-bones, with a cast of countenance quite distinct from the Chinese. Their general type of face recalled to me those one meets with among the traders who come down to Calcutta from Bokhara and Herat. They usually wear a moustache, but pull out in Chinese fashion all the rest of the hair on their faces. The hadji, however, at Nantin went unshaven in true Mahomedan style. The hair of the head is usually allowed to grow long behind, and is coiled in the folds of their ample white turbans, which project outwards nearly on a line with the shoulder. They wear the Chinese jacket and short trousers, and have the lower part of the leg above the ankle bandaged with blue cloth in the same way as the Shans. A bright orange yellow waist-band, in which they usually carry a silver-mounted dagger, completes the costume. Their women dress after the fashion of their Chinese sisters, and those of the better classes have small feet.

The governor has four wives who are carefully excluded from gaze. He is fully 6 feet 2 inches in height, and of commanding appearance. His face and hands are very dark from exposure, but the general colour of his skin is quite as light as the fairest Chinese. He has the oblique eye; his lips are heavy and rather protuberant; while his face is a decided oval, with high cheek-bones. His head is not large, and his forehead is small and retreating. He may be said to be the hero of a hundred fights, and his numerous scars are speaking proofs of his courage. A deep indentation between his eyes marks where he was hit by a spent bullet; a round hard thing like a small marble over his ribs, and another in one arm, are two other gun-shot wounds. Scars on his legs and arms testify to hand-in-hand encounters with the formidable dâh. He is quiet, self-possessed, with a determined will, sound sense, and great natural dignity of bearing, with the impress of one born to command.

The Panthays profess to be strict observers of the laws of the prophet, and abstain as a rule from strong drink, tobacco, and opium, but on one occasion when we were feasted by the Tahzyungyee, he drank with us out of a large jug containing a peculiar but pleasant warm preparation of spirit, and kept the bowl circulating, until we had drained it to the dregs. My curiosity prompted me to examine into the components of this decoction, and I was rewarded with the unpleasant discovery that they were largely composed of small pieces of pork-fat and walnuts. Our host had a particular *goût* for the beverage, and, I suppose, with more wisdom than his guest, was careful to avoid any enquiries into its composition.

Before the rebellion they had a mosque built in a style quite distinct from the Chinese, and after plans brought home by their hadjis; but now the prayers are said in a building thoroughly Chinese in all its details. In the verses from the Koran written in Chinese, there is evidence that Arabic is not very generally cultivated; indeed, there was only one hadji at Momien who made any pretentions to be able to read it.

The presence of our jemadar was a great god-send to them, and the demand for his services at the mosque was so great, that he entirely lost the use of his voice, to the grievous disappointment of the celestial Mahomedans. He frequently lamented to me the laxity that prevailed among them, and my native doctor held them in extreme contempt, and used to assert that they were no Mussulmans. They were full, however, of kindness to their fellow-religionists in our guard without distinction, and did everything for their comfort. On our departure a few of the officers accompanied us nearly a mile from the city, weeping bitterly as we left them, and our last sight of Momien embraced these tender-hearted men anxiously looking after us from the spot on which we had parted from them.

I will refer to only two other aspects of the Panthay character, which are encouraging when we contemplate the possibility that they may ultimately become a distinct nationality in Asia, strange to say, on the very soil of the most exclusive and conservative people that the world has ever known: I refer to their strict honesty in all trading transactions, to their abilities as traders, and to the keen appreciation they appear to have of the benefits which are likely to accrue to them from commercial intercourse with other nations. Their honesty requires no comment; and to illustrate their consideration for traders, I may mention that I was informed by a Chinaman, who was travelling in the north of Yunan during the rebellion, that a large caravan, on its way to Eastern Tibet, had occasion to pass where the Panthay and Chinese forces were opposed, and as my informant put it, the Mahomedan general desisted for a day from attacking his adversary, in order that the caravan might safely pass. He mentioned as well, that the Mahomedan mandarins, in those northern portions of the province which have had occasional periods of peace, are not nearly so much dreaded by the merchants as the imperial officers, and that they feel themselves safe from inordinate extortion whenever they reach their jurisdiction.

CHAPTER VII.

THE TRADE ROUTES OF UPPER BURMAH.

Three routes proceed from Bhamô to Momien, *viz.*, Sawaddy, Loaylone, and Ponline. I travelled over the last two, and, therefore, am in a position to give an opinion on their respective merits, and as the first was reported on by a Burmese surveyor who had accompanied us by the latter route, I can contrast his experience of the Sawaddy road with mine by the other two.

Before describing the general characters of these routes, it should be observed that they are more or less hill-paths made by the Kakhyens, who, like other mountain tribes, do not generally select their routes as being the easiest, but the shortest ways. If a steep hill-spur intervenes between a Kakhyen and a point he wishes to make for, he seldom thinks of rounding the spur by the gentle slope along its side, but carries his path right over its crest, and as this principle has been almost universally adopted, the routes, as they at present exist, cannot be regarded as giving any fair indication of the capabilities of these hills for road-making, for it should be no difficult task for an engineer to lay out a road even from Tsitkaw to Manwyne, that would be little more than a gentle gradient that might be travelled with little or no fatigue. The construction of a good cart road from the plains of Burmah to the Shan states would be mere child's play, compared with such gigantic undertakings as the cart road from the Terai to Darjeeling, and those to other hill stations of India. What is at present wanted, however, is to indicate the route from Bhamô to Western China that offers the fewest difficulties to traverse, apart altogether from any contemplated improvements that might be ultimately achieved through engineering skill.

The Ponline and Loaylone routes respectively follow the northern and southern sides of the comparatively narrow valley through which the Tapeng precipitates itself from the Sanda valley to the plains of Burmah; and the Sawaddy, or as it is sometimes called the Kaungtoung route, lies to the south of the Loaylone road. They have all a north-eastern course over the Kakhyen hills, the Ponline route making for the valley of Sanda, the Loaylone either for Hotha, or the valley of Nantin, and the Sawaddy route for the latter valley. The Ponline route runs direct to Momien, past Sanda, Muangla, and Nantin, and the Loaylone and Sawaddy routes join it at Nantin. So much for their general relations to each other.

To reach the Ponline route, the Tapeng is crossed by boats about 2 miles above Bhamô, and the road lies for about 23 miles over a level country along the right bank of the Tapeng to the foot of the hills, and in this distance two other small but unfordable streams have to be crossed. From the base of the hills, it makes a sudden rough ascent till it reaches 2,541 feet at Ponline, about 9 miles from the plains, that is, an ascent of 2,100 feet above the village of Tsihet at the base of the hills, but this part of the road lies over steep spurs which make it very trying to the traveller unaccustomed to the hills. From Ponline a sudden and abrupt descent of 1,766 feet is made to the banks of a rapid mountain torrent, the Nampung, 337 feet above the plains, and barely fordable during the dry weather. It is about 12 miles distant from the foot of the hills. From the Nampung, a tedious ascent of 1,388 feet is met with, extending over 3¼ miles, followed by another descent of 500 or 600 feet, succeeded by an almost continuous ascent of 6 miles to the village of Ponsee at 3,185 feet above the sea, and two marches from the Burmese plains. The road is tolerably level for about one mile and a half beyond Ponsee, when it makes a sudden descent of about 500 feet, followed by a gradual one till it reaches the foot of the Sanda valley, about 2,000 feet above the level of the sea. From the town of Manwyne about that elevation, and 19 miles from Ponsee, it follows the Sanda valley for about 46 miles, passing, as I have said, the towns of Sanda and Muangla. The slight rise that occurs in the Sanda valley, between its western and eastern extremities, is so gradually distributed over its entire length that, when looked down upon from a height, it has the appearance of a plain, which in the spring months is covered with a bright green carpet of young rice. The road at the head of the valley encounters the ascent of the spur of the Mawphoo hill, and tracks along the hill-side, for about 6 miles, over very rough ground broken up by numerous hollows cut out by mountain streams. At its eastern extremity, another descent is made to reach the Nantin valley, where the Tapeng can either be crossed by a suspension bridge, or forded a little further up during the dry weather.

The roads from Loaylone *viâ* Hotha and Momien, and the Sawaddy route, join the Ponline route at the entrance to the Nantin valley, which is nearly level, and about 15 miles in length.

At the head of the Nantin valley, there is another steep ascent of about 700 feet, and a slight descent to the level of the Hawshuenshan valley, followed by a rapid acclivity of nearly 400 feet, from which the traveller follows a gentle ascent for half a mile to the valley of Momien, which is 21 miles from the town of Nantin. From the fact that all the roads meet in the Nantin valley, we are not particularly concerned to describe that portion here, but it may be as well to state regarding it, that a short detour would obviate the necessity of the ascent at the head of the valley, and the descent to the valley of Hawshuenshan; and that a comparatively level road could be made from Nantin to Momien with little or no difficulty, and as the greater part of it already exists, only 8 or 9 miles would have to be constructed to give it a uniform character throughout, and that the cost would not be great, as all that would be necessary would be to carry it round the base of a spur instead of following its present course over the crest.

The Loaylone route, leaving Bhamô, follows the Ponline one as far as the village of Sit-nga on the Tapeng close to Tsitkaw, where the river is crossed by boats, to the small hamlet of Nampung on the left bank, from whence the road crosses a level flat for about 3 miles, beyond which it lies over low hills to the banks of the Namthabet, which is unbridged, and does not appear to be fordable at any season of the year, and in the neighbourhood of which there are few villages. From the right bank of that stream, which is about 50 yards broad, the road skirts the Tapeng for about a couple of miles, over tolerably level ground, till it reaches a small mountain torrent, from which a steep ascent of about 1,800 feet is made to the village of Hoetone, 2,450 feet above the sea, which is considered one day's march from Nampung. From Hoetone, the road ascends gradually for 10 miles along the hill-sides to the village of Loaylone, 4,413 feet above the sea, on the western face of one of the main ridges defining the western side of the Muangwan valley, which can be seen from the hill behind the village. The ordinary route to Momien by Loaylone, known as the Embassy route, does not go by Hotha, but crosses into the Muangwan valley, as is proved by all the Burmese itineraries I have consulted, and as I also learnt from enquiries made on the spot; but I have no personal acquaintance with that part of the route. After the descent into the Muangwan valley has been accomplished in one march, two other marches through it, and over the hilly ground at its head, brings the traveller to Nantin. The route from Loaylone *viâ* Lassa and Hotha is extremely difficult, for a descent has to be made from Loaylone into the Muangkah valley, where a stream of the same name has to be crossed. The road then sweeps over the Muangkah ridge, on the other side of which are two streams, and a steep ascent up the southern face of the main range of mountains defining the southern side of the Tapeng valley, and on the summit of which is the village of Ashan belonging to the Ponsee chief. From Ashan, the path lies along the inequalities of the ridge at an elevation of about 5,000 feet, and then makes a sudden descent to the sea of little rounded and pyramidal hills, among which the village of Namboke lies, at an elevation of 4,675 feet, in sight of the Hotha valley. From Loaylone to Ashan may be accomplished in one long march, and from the latter village to Namboke we have another day's labour, and Hotha is still another march further on, while Nantin is two days distant from Hotha; so that Nantin is five days' march from Loaylone *viâ* Hotha, and only three *viâ* Muangwan. From Namboke to Hotha there is a comparatively easy and level path along the greater part of its extent, but long spurs run down from the Shuemuelong mountain on the other side of the ridge forming the head of the Hotha valley, and intervene between it and Nantin, so that that part of the route is beset with difficulties, and seldom travelled. The usual course, followed by the residents of the Hotha valley, is to cross over the mountains to Muangla, and proceed from thence to Nantin.

The Sawaddy route is known to me only from hearsay, and from a short report by the Government assistant surveyor who was deputed to return from Hotha by that route. He describes it "from Sawaddy to Muangwan as smooth and even throughout, and devoid of difficulties of a nature to induce fatigue or wretchedness." From his rough itinerary, I find that he made eight marches between the two places, but one was a march only of two hours, one of four, and two others of five hours each. He made only three marches of seven, and one of nine hours; and, in all, he took 46 hours to accomplish the journey. If seven hours be taken as an average hill march, the journey from Sawaddy to Muangwan, *viâ* the Loaylone route, does not take more than four days. Although he states the route to be smooth and level throughout, this cannot be accepted in its literal meaning, for he mentions that the greatest altitude was attained in the Phongan Tsawbwaship, and that looking down from the hills at that point, on a clear day, the course of the Irawady can be seen as far as Bhamô, which would appear to indicate that the road runs over tolerably high hills. But although it is longer than either of the other two, it is allowed, by universal consent, to be the one that presents the fewest difficulties to the traveller.

It will be granted that in considering the respective merits of any lines of road, the mere fact that one, in order to reach its destination, has to rise to a greater elevation than another, would not be a sufficient reason why the former should be condemned, for there are many other considerations which would have to be taken into account, and practically the points that most require to be kept in view are the lay and character of the hill-spurs over which the respective roads pass. When we contrast the Ponline and Loaylone routes from this standing point, we find that while the former only rises to 3,185 at Ponsee, at its highest, the latter is 4,413 feet at Loaylone. The Ponline road, after reaching 2,103 above the Burmese valley, descends at Ponline to 337 above the same level, making a descent of 1,766 feet, and again rising at Ponsee to 3,185 feet above the sea, and 2,747 feet above Bhamô. Now, in the Loaylone route there is no equivalent of the descent from Ponline, from the circumstance that that route follows the bank of the Tapeng till it is opposite to Ponline, where the ascent of the hills begins in earnest, and in which no descent of any consequence is encountered until Loaylone itself is attained, at an elevation of 4,413 feet above the sea, or 3,975 above the valley of the Irawady. After the two roads arrive at the valleys of Sanda and Muangwan, they experience no difficult ground, until the Ponline route reaches the foot of the Mawphoo hill, and the Loaylone one arrives at the head of the Muangwan valley, for up to these localities they lie through almost level parallel valleys of equal length. There seems to be little doubt that beyond the towns of Manwyne and Muangwan, as far as Nantin, the merits of the two are about equal. From Tsitkaw to Manwyne can be accomplished in three marches, and from the former town to Muangwan in the same number of days, so that the two distances may be regarded as about equal. From Manwyne to Nantin we have three other marches, *viz.*, to Sanda, Muangla, and Nantin itself, and an equal number from Muangwan to the latter town, proceeding first to the old *choki* of Shuemuelong, afterwards to Muangtong, and from thence to Nantin, and one march from the latter brings us to Momien. The merits of the two then being equal after the Kakhyen hills are passed, the Ponline in its present condition must be rejected for the Loaylone route.

I have no information regarding the heights crossed by the Sawaddy route, but there can be little doubt that whatever its length may be, as compared with the other two, it has those strong recommendations, that the mountains are not so high, and that it passes through a narrow tract of hilly country between the Burmese plain and Muangwan, where it joins the Loaylone route. The Burmese surveyor describes it as free of all obstructions and wonderfully pleasant, terms which are quite inapplicable to either of the other two; and states also that there is a constant stream of trade, and that merchants with mules and pack-bullocks are always passing along. He accompanied the expedition by the Ponline route so that his opinion has considerable weight, for he was in a position to contrast the one with the other; moreover, the Sawaddy route, as I have already mentioned, is recognized by universal consent as the easiest road to Momien.

These remarks are applicable to the routes only as they now exist. In the event of a trade springing up that would repay the re-construction of a new road, there is nothing in the character of either the northern or southern sides of the Tapeng valley that would interfere with its being accomplished with comparative ease. There is this to be said in favour of the Ponline route, in the prospect of such an event, that a road might be constructed along that side of the valley to rise to Manwyne by a gentle gradient to 1,562 feet above Bhamô instead of 2,747, its present height at Ponsee. A road, however, by the Loaylone route, could not be taken by a lower elevation than 3,975 feet above the same level, because it strikes away from the Tapeng valley into the centre of the hills, where it has to cross the ridge of mountains defining the north-western side of the Muangwan valley. The great recommendation in favour of the Ponline route under these circumstances would be that it is the most direct way to Momien, that it need not be carried higher than 1,562 feet above the plains, and that it commands the water carriage of the Tapeng at its entrance to the hills, an advantage which the Loaylone route shares with it. With a good road along the right bank of the Tapeng in the hills, the goods might be sent down in a few hours to Bhamô either in small steamers or boats. The great drawbacks to the Sawaddy route, under these altered conditions, would be, its greater length, and the long march from the mart to the base of the hills over marshy ground, which is much cut up with small streams.

These are the three highways that, leaving the neighbourhood of Bhamô, strike across the Khakyen hills and through the Shan valleys to Momien. They are travelled at all seasons of the year by small bands of traders, but the traffic that passes over them is never, as a rule, directed from one route to another, but preserves an uninterrupted course to its destination. The lay of the mountain ranges is unfavourable to trade between the districts over which they pass, although, at the same time, there are numerous hill-paths passable for laden mules, by which the people of the respective valleys communicate with each other. It was by one of these roads, leading from Sanda to Hotha, that the expedition crossed over from the former to the latter valley to explore the Loaylone route, but it was in no way connected with either of these routes so as to influence their respective merits, as the great trading highways to China.

From Momien to Yungchan is a distance of four marches, or about 64 miles, and it is interesting to note that the first stage is the village of Kanlantsan (or Kananzan) which takes its name from a lofty range of mountains, on the other side of which is the Shuaylee, which is crossed by an iron suspension bridge. A few miles from the left bank of the river is the valley of Paweng, the next stage of the journey, and about 12 miles from Kananzan, which is nearly 20 miles from Momien. The next halt is made at Phupyauk, about 14 miles from Paweng, near the left bank of the Salween river, which is crossed by boats, and another march of about 22 miles brings the traveller to Yungchan. The road to the latter town, which is the principal mart of Western Yunan, must be over a difficult country, for it runs at right angles to the great ridges that define two such important streams as the Shuaylee and Salween.

Talifoo is about 80 miles from Yungchan, and can be reached in from eight to ten marches from the latter town, which is also about nineteen marches, 190 miles, from the city of Yunan, or the Muangsee of the Shans. In proceeding to Talifoo and the latter city, the main stream of the Cambodia, and a large branch which it receives from the lake of Tali, are crossed by iron suspension bridges; but full particulars of the character of this part of the country, and of the various routes to Burmah from these two cities, may be looked for from the French Expedition.

From Yungchan a route proceeds to the south, four days' march to the city of Shuenli, or Muangchan, where it joins the route from Mandalay, *via* Theinnee and Kaingmah. The latter road crosses the Cambodia by an iron suspension bridge on the second march from the city of Muangchan, which is about twenty-four marches from the capital of Burmah. The road from Yungchan appears to join it at the city of Tsankchow, to the east of the Hokyan, a branch of the Cambodia, and five marches from Yungchan and six from Muangchan. The city of Yunan is forty days' journey from Mandalay by the Theinnee route, and only twenty-eight days' from Bhamô *viâ* Momien and Yungchan, that is, the latter route is twelve days' journey by land shorter than the former, which is an immense recommendation in its favour, even although the six or seven of the twelve days saved in the land journey are occupied in going up the Irawady, by boat to Bhamô. In proceeding from China to Burmah, the result is even still more favourable to the Bhamô route, because the downward passage of the Irawady to the capital is made much more rapidly than when proceeding against the stream.

I have no detailed information regarding the Shuaylee route, but, from the circumstance already stated, that the Kakhyen hills take a bend to the east where the river reaches the plain of Burmah, and are much lower than the ranges to the east of Bhamô, while the river is a considerable stream flowing through a broad valley, in the upper part of its course, it is highly probable that this route will be found to present advantages intermediate between those of the Theinnee and Bhamô routes, and to be the line of country most adapted for a railway when the trade between Burmah and China demands such an improved means of carriage, an event, however, which appears to be a very long way off.

There is a small trade carried on between Momien and the Sanda valley and Mogoung. The Chinese, Shans, and Kakhyens who resort from these localities to the latter town usually make for Kakhyo on the left bank of the Irawady to the north-east of Mogoung, which is situated about a day's march to the west of the Irawady on a stream of its own name. The merchants from Momien can either proceed by the direct route from that town to Kakhyo, a distance of five or six marches, over a hill road, or they may take advantage of the comparatively level Bhamô route as far as Sanda, from whence the Shan road to Kakhyo crosses the hills in a north-westerly direction, reaching the Irawady in little more than five marches. The latter route is in all probability the easiest, and since it was the one selected for the passage of a division of the Chinese army that invaded Burmah in 1767, it probably does not present any very serious obstacles to trading caravans composed of mules, ponies, and oxen. Both routes are in daily use, but the one from Sanda is preferred, as it lies through a country that has not been much affected by the Mahomedan rebellion.

Between Sanda and Manwyne another route diverges to the north-west, for about two marches, to reach the Molay river, a narrow stream along which small boats can proceed to and from the Irawady, which would appear to indicate that the fall from its upper waters to the latter river cannot be very abrupt, and that the general elevation of the country to the north of Sanda is somewhat less than what prevails in the latter locality, which favours the view I have expressed regarding the character of the Sanda and Kakhyo route.

Since the trade routes to China through Upper Burmah have been attracting public attention, the claims of certain routes from Upper Assam to Yunan have been advocated by those interested in the development of the resources of the former province, and as the characters of the roads between the upper waters of the Brahmaputra and the valley of the Mogoung river are not generally known, I shall give a brief resumé of our knowledge regarding them.

Dr. Griffith, who was the first Englishman to penetrate from Assam to Mogoung, started from Suddyah on the 7th February 1837, and reached Kidding on the 10th, where he remained one day. On the 12th, he made for Namroop Putar, a cultivated rice tract close to the Naga hills, on the river Namroop, a branch of the Booree Debing, and about 40 miles from Suddyah. Throughout these marches the jungle was low and intersected by ravines, and the Karam, the Noa Dehing, and the Namroop rivers were crossed. He left Namroop on the 19th, and proceeded south-west for 12 miles, halting at Darap Kha, at the foot of the Naga hills, so that he must have kept the Namroop to his left, for he states that it flows from the eastward, and receives the Kamteechick from the south. He again went forward on the 21st, and after a march of 10 miles had ascended to 383 feet above Suddyah, over a winding but good path, except at the foot of the hills. On the 22nd, he marched 12 miles, and halted at 1,029 feet above the sea, after having crossed the Darap, a considerable stream. The road was difficult for elephants, and he had to halt on the 23rd[1] to allow them to come up. On the 24th, he marched for five hours south-south-east, and halted on the Kamteechick at an elevation of 1,413 feet, after having crossed a hill 1,000 feet high. He proceeded 10 miles south-south-east up the bed of the Kamteechick, on the 25th, through heavy jungle, and on the 26th, marched 100 yards up the Kamteechick, and then crossed the Tukkaka, and ascended a high hill of about 1,000 feet above his last camping-place, and halted, after a march of 4 miles, at an elevation of 3,026 feet. He remained at his encampment till the 4th March, when he crossed a low hill and then a torrent, afterwards commencing a very steep ascent to the top of the Patkoi range, at an

---

[1] Griffith was evidently out one day in his time, for he states that he halted till 10 A.M. on the 23rd; and again, under the date of the 23rd, he states that he commenced his march at 7 A.M. I have allowed for this error.

elevation of about 4,526 feet, and after a march of four hours, descended to the Kamyoom or Kammairoan, which forms the British boundary. He followed this stream through some of the rankest jungle he had ever seen, and then ascended a low hill, and again made a continuous descent through dry open tree jungle, encamping in the bed of the stream, after a march of 15 miles in a south-south-east direction. On the 5th March, he again came upon the Kammairoan, and made a most fatiguing march along its bed for 10 miles, crossing and re-crossing it at intervals. It is a small stream with precipitous banks. On the 6th, he proceeded east-south-east towards the same river, a distance of 4 miles, but had to return to his halting-place, 2,138 feet, as there were no coolies nor rice to be obtained, and where he remained till the 14th, when he proceeded still further down it, in an east-south-east course, for 7 miles, passing some remains of old habitations. On the 15th March, he still followed the Kammairoan, but soon left it to cross some low hills, and passed the village of Kammairoan to his right, the first cultivated ground he had met with since leaving Kamteechick, and halted at the Khathing stream, at an elevation of 1,622 feet above the sea. He made a march of 13 miles on the 16th, first proceeding 100 yards up the Khathing, and then, leaving it, commenced an ascent, which lasted, without intermission, for some hours, the whole way being through heavy tree jungle, and the ascent in some places very steep. On reaching the summit, 5,566 feet, the road lay along the ridge for a short way, when he descended, after a longish march, and halted on the Khasse river, at an elevation of 3,516 feet. On the 17th, he reached the Khasse without any material descent, but from thence the declivity was considerable to Namthuga, after leaving which the descent increased. He halted at Kullack Boom, 3,270 feet, after a march of 13 miles in a southerly direction. From thence he obtained a view of the Hukong valley, enclosed by a range of hills, stretching east-south-east and west-north-west, broken in its middle by a gap, through which a river flowed south, and in the distance he saw the Kyendwen or Namlunai winding excessively, especially to the east-south-east, and passing out towards the gap just mentioned, winding round the corner of the hills. On the 18th, the descent from the Kullack Boom was interrupted as far as the Loon-karankha, a mountain torrent, with a bed of sandstone, and from it he continued his course up a considerable acclivity, and then made a uniform descent to the Namtuwa, along which he marched for some distance till he came to the Panglai river, along which his course lay for a short time. Between the two streams, the path was through low wet jungle along small water-courses. He halted, after a march of 10 miles, on the banks of the Namtuseek at an elevation of 1,099 feet. On the 19th he reached the stockaded village of Nampean (1,399 feet) on the right bank of the Namturoon, a stream 270 yards broad, after a march of seven hours and a half, in which he had gone 18 miles. The greater part of the route lay through heavy but dryish tree jungle, and the remainder through portions of cultivated land; but he observes that throughout the march he saw nothing to show that that part of the Hukong valley was inhabited. From Nampean, he proceeded on the following day a distance of 4 miles to Kidding, a stockaded village on the left bank of the Saxsai, a small stream on the left bank of the Namturoon. His course was south-south-east, and on the 23rd, he passed Shelling-khet on the Prongprongkha, 1,340 feet, and proceeded to Culleyang, 1,064 feet, on the same stream, where he halted after a march of 13 miles by a winding path. The whole tract was covered with tree jungle. On the 24th, he passed Lamoom on the banks of the Moneekha, and from thence marched to Tsilone, a Singpho village, on the right bank of the Nam Tunail, a stream of considerable size, with scarcely any rapids, and at an altitude of 1,066 feet. The general direction of his course was now south-west, and the distance travelled 10 miles. Leaving Tsilone on the 25th, he reached Meinkhoom after a hot march of seven hours, or about 17 miles. The first part of his course lay along the bed and banks of the Kyendwen, and afterwards over grassy plains intersected by belts of jungle. Two ranges of hills occurred to the west. The Kyendwen, at this part of its course, measures 250 to 350 yards in breadth, and where he forded it, its greatest depth was 4 feet. On the 28th, he proceeded over the Meinkhoom plain, in an easterly direction, to Wullaboom, 1,066 feet, a large village on the Nampyokha, a distance of 12½ miles, in a south-easterly direction, over low plains, but he passed no villages. On the following day, he marched 22 miles in a southerly direction, first following the Kampyet, and from thence diverged into jungle, and the rest of the march was occupied in crossing low hills, with here and there a small plain, and he halted on a stream that falls into the Mogoung river. He observed no other signs of population than an old burial-ground. On the 30th, he marched in a southerly direction for 15 miles, through the same kind of country as on the previous day, and halted on the banks of the Mogoung river, which is navigable for small boats within 4 miles of where he remained for the night. On the two following days, he marched 13 and 14 miles along the bed of the Mogoung in a south-easterly direction, and through an uninteresting and inhospitable tract of country on the second day. The river is shallow and much impeded by stumps and fallen trees. He observed some cultivation on the low hills to the south-east and east, which are inhabited by the Kakhyens. On the 2nd April, he left the Mogoung river, and marched 14 miles south-south-east over an extensive plain almost free from trees, crossing the Wampama, a stream, beyond which the open ground continued. The plain is surrounded with hills, the highest of which are to the east, and pre-eminent among them was the Shuay-toung-gyee, 3,000 feet, from which the Namlunai (Kyendwen) rises. He halted at the Shan stockaded village of Camein, and from thence visited the amber mines, starting from Camein on the 3rd April, and arriving at them on the 6th. They are situated almost due east or east-by-south from Camein. He left the latter village on the 9th, and reached Mogoung after a march of at least 25 miles, his course being at first due east, and afterwards more southerly. The road lay through a grassy plain; but no villages, nor any signs of such, were observed. On the 19th, he proceeded down the Mogoung river by boat, and arrived at the Irawady on the 24th. He found the former river a slow stream on the first day, and much impeded with fallen trees, but more especially with sand-banks. On the second day, however, it had improved, being deeper and less spread out, owing to its proximity to low hills. On the 22nd, he passed a few rapids, which were rendered worse by the channel being impeded by large rocks. The stream, however, was generally very deep. He arrived, as I have said, at the Irawady on the 24th, where he moored for the night, and, starting next morning, reached Bhamô at 5 p. m.

An unsuccessful attempt had been made by Captain Burnett, some years before Griffith's mission, to reach Mogoung by the route across the Patkoi range, following the course of the Namroop and of its upper tributaries, the Nunnun and Khasse.[1] His course was somewhat to the east of that afterwards travelled by Griffith, but he followed the route by which, it is said, the Shans effected the conquest of Assam, and by which the Burmese army of 1818 and 1822 advanced. It is also the route along which any interchange of population between the valleys of the upper Brahmaputra and Irawady had taken place, which would seem to indicate, as Pemberton[2] observes, that it presents greater facilities for

---

[1] Captain Charlton, writing in 1834, in view of Captain Burnett's report on the character of the country, regretted that no communication existed between Suddyah and Yunan. *As. Soc. Journ.*, vol. iv, p. 47.

[2] North-West Frontier, p. 64.

travel than any other portion of the Patkoi range, and Mr. Jenkins,[1] who appears to have crossed the Patkoi at the same point as Captain Burnett, gives it as his opinion that, as far as he could see, there is a dip in the range at this point. Captain Burnett started from Suddyah, making for Beesa, on the Noa Dehing, a distance of 40 miles, over a level fertile country. The Noa Dehing, along which the road runs nearly the whole way, is navigable for small canoes, almost as far as Beesa. Beesa is a Singpho village, about 10 miles distant from where the Namroop river issues from the hills through a narrow precipitous valley, along which the road lies. The first march is from Beesa, a distance of 16 miles, and some way up the Namroop. On the second stage, 12 miles, two hills are crossed, the Tontook and Nunnun, between which the Namroop flows, but they present no difficulties of a serious nature. The encampment on this march is made on the banks of the Namroop a short distance from where it is joined by the Nunnun, and the ground is tolerably free from jungle. The third stage is to a small stream, the Khasse, at the foot of the Patkoi range, a distance of 7 miles. In this march, a low hill is crossed after leaving Nunnun, and the Namroop is again reached, the road lying along its bed for 5 miles over large boulders and rocks, which make it very difficult to the traveller. The Shan traders, however, of former days avoided the river by cutting roads along the hill-sides above. From the Khasse stream to the summit of the Patkoi central ridge, the limit of Captain Burnett's course, is about 4 miles, and from Khasse to the southern foot of the ridge, where the Loglai stream is met with, is one long march, on which there appears to be a scarcity of water. From the Loglai to Beesa-laum, situated near the head of the Hukong valley, is six moderately long and easy marches. Eight marches from Beesa brings the traveller to Mogoung. Captain Pemberton, writing in 1855, describes this portion of the route as passing over a fertile, populous, and well cultivated country; but Griffith, who wrote only two years afterwards, from personal observation, described it as very thinly populated and all but uncultivated. Small clearings, he writes, may be met with after miles or even days of travel, but they are rare, and villages are equally so.

In December 1868, Mr. Jenkins, of Assam, followed Captain Burnett's route as far as the southern side of the Patkoi range, and found the Loglai draining the Nongyang, a small lake at the foot of the hills. He describes the country intervening between Assam and Hukong as a

---

[1] Proceedings, Royal Geographical Society, vol. xiii, p. 246.

dense jungle of valuable forest trees, and the only paths as the natural beds of the rivers, mountain streams, &c. He ascribes the destruction of the paths that formerly existed, to the desertion by the Burmese of the villages or posts that they used to have along every 12 or 15 miles of this route, and the inhabitants of which kept the paths clear from jungle and fallen trees. This route is now all but forsaken by traders from Hukong, who follow a more westerly one through Naga villages where they can get supplies. If we take Jyepoor on the Booree Dehing as our starting-point, the latter route strikes across the Patkoi range in an almost direct south-easterly course to the Kamyoom or Kammairoan of Griffith, from whence it follows the course of that traveller, and crosses a range of hills, 5,516 feet high, on the third march after it has reached the Kamyoom.

These two routes, proceeding from the Booree Dehing across the Patkoi range, have this to recommend them, in the event of a trade being ultimately developed between Assam and Upper Burmah, that the Booree Dehing is navigable to steamers during the rains for nearly 40 miles of its course, that is, as far as Jyepoor, and that large boats can proceed up it for many miles beyond this point. It is probable that the easiest route will be found to be along the course of the Namsan that joins the Booree Dehing, about 8 or 10 miles to the north of Jyepoor, and which has been already partially surveyed, for its valley leads right up to the Patkoi range, and corresponds to that of the Kammairoan on the southern side. An accurate survey, however, can alone determine this, and whether it is posssible to avoid the high range that is encountered beyond the Kammairoan to the south.

Another route, from Suddyah to the almost extreme limit of Upper Burmah, exists along the Noa Dehing, which enters the great eastern branch of the Brahmaputra above Suddyah. Wilcox, in 1825, was enabled to proceed in boats along this stream to within nine days' march of Manlung on the eastern branch of the Irawady, which he regarded as the main stream of the great river of Burmah. The land journey was accomplished without any great inconvenience or serious difficulty beyond what was due to a mountain road through primeval forest.

Having now described the routes from Bhamô, and indicated their continuations beyond Momien, and their ramifications amongst the hills, and also sketched out the subsidiary routes between Assam and Upper Burmah, I shall proceed to consider the capabilities for improvement of the routes which follow the course of the Tapeng valley.

The great advantages of Bhamô as a starting-point to China are these: its situation on the Irawady, which is navigable to large river steamers up to the town; its close proximity to Yunan; and the fact that it lies at the entrance of a natural break in the hills which separate Burmah from China, and that leads directly into China as one of nature's highways, the like of which is not to be found in any other part of the range to the south, with the exception, perhaps, of the opening of the Shuaylee valley. The capabilities of the Irawady, from Ava to Bhamô, for the traffic of large river steamers, has been frequently and satisfactorily tested since the return of the Expedition, and as coal occurs at intervals along the right bank of the river from below the capital, even as far north as Mogoung, depôts of good fuel might be easily established at Bhamô, Malé, and Mandalay, that would place the navigation of the Irawady on a footing enjoyed by very few of the rivers, not only of India, but of the east generally.

Bhamô is only about 25 miles from the base of the Kakhyen hills, and this tract of country is perfectly level throughout, and a road might be constructed with ease along either bank of the Tapeng; or this stream might be used for boat traffic during the dry weather, and by steamers during the rains. Unless steamers could be constantly used, the road would have the preference in proceeding to China, for the distance could be got over more quickly than by boats going against the stream. To leave the Tapeng perfectly free for steamers and boats, it would be undesirable to bridge it at its mouth as was proposed by Loli, the Chinese trader, in 1765; but the road might be carried along the left bank as far as the foot of the hills, where it might be continued along the same bank as far as the Sanda valley, and a bridge might be thrown across the Tapeng at its entrance to the hills, for it is there defined by high banks. An iron chain suspension bridge, of the kind in use in Yunan, could be put up by the Shans at a very small cost, and in a very short time. Eighteen strong iron chains, about 55 to 60 yards in length, would suffice, and the gneiss buttresses to which to fasten them would soon be forthcoming from the surrounding hill-sides. This, or the other alternative, a bridge at the exit of the river from the hills, would permit of steamers discharging their cargoes within 25 miles from the province of Yunan.

The 25 miles through the Kakhyen hills are comparatively easy travelling compared with the majority of hill roads in India. A road might be constructed, or even a railway carried from the foot of the hills to Manwyne, at a gradient of 1 in 78. It would be unnecessary to carry it more than a few yards above the level of the river, for the present height of the roads, as I have already stated, gives no indication whatever of the capabilities of the valley for engineering, as they have been purposely made to lead past the Kakhyen villages, which seldom occur below 2,500 feet. Arrived at Manwyne, a hardly perceptible rise would lead the road or railway to the head of the Sanda valley at the foot of the Mawphoo hill, and in the case of a railway, it would be unnecessary to cross the Tapeng, for the valley is so narrow that it would be easily accessible to all the towns along the route, each of which might be connected to it by a high wooden bridge for passenger or mule traffic. The objection to taking a railway along the right bank of the Tapeng would be that the river would have to be crossed thrice, once on the Bhamô side, again at Manwyne, and once more at the foot of the Mawphoo gorge. In the latter locality it would be necessary to cross the Tahô to carry it along the left side of the gorge, through which this affluent of the Tapeng flows from the Nantin valley. But if it were considered desirable to take it close to the trading towns, *i. e.*, along the right bank of the Tapeng, the river might be crossed immediately above its entrance to the hills; and, from below Muangla, one of two alternatives would have to be resorted to, either to bridge it below where it receives the Tahô, and to continue it along the left bank of the latter stream, thus leaving Muangla 2 miles to the left, or to cross it above its junction with the Tahô, thus necessitating the bridging of the Tahô at some other point between Muangla and the Mawphoo gorge. The latter locality is a difficulty, for the Mawphoo hill runs down to the stream in steep cliffs on the right bank apparently nearly the whole way through the gorge, whereas the hills on the opposite side sweep down to the stream in moderate slopes. If the railway were carried right along the left bank of the Tapeng, it might start from Bhamô, and be laid to Momien without encountering any stream of importance beyond the Namthabet, which flows through a well-defined channel about 30 or 40 yards broad at its junction with the Tapeng, and seldom or ever floods its banks. A number of small mountain streams, few exceeding 30 or 50 feet in breadth, would be met with both in the Kakhyen hills and Sanda valley, that would necessitate the construction of substantial one-arched bridges.

The difference of altitude between the foot of the Sanda valley and Nantin is 1,040 feet, but this rise is distributed as follows: between Manwyne and Sanda there is a difference of 236 feet, giving a gradient of 1 in 425 in the distance of 19 miles, and in the same distance between the latter town and Muangla, there is a further rise of 244, or a gradient of 1 in 411 feet, and between Muangla and Nantin there would be a gradual ascent, perhaps, on the whole distance, 21 miles, of 660 feet, or 1 in 168. From Nantin to the head of the valley, a distance of 10 or 11 miles, the road is quite level, but beyond this point a railway would have to gain the summit of the river terraces, the highest of which at the head of the valley is about 150 feet above its level; but as the Tahô opens through them, its best course would be a gradual rise for some miles before the head of the valley is reached, so that, when it arrived there, it would be on a level with the top of the highest platform. It would then still make a gradual ascent for 8 or 9 miles, following the course of the Tahô, across the extinct volcano of Hawshuenshan to the valley of that name, skirting round its southern side to reach the valley of Momien. The gradients from the head of the Nantin valley to Hawshuenshan would be considerable.

The most difficult ground for a railway would of course be in the Kakhyen hills, where extensive cuttings would be necessitated in passing round the ends of the long spurs that run down to the river, but they would be trifling compared with those that are undertaken every day in the construction of hill roads in the Himalaya. When, however, the magnitude of the end aimed at is considered, viz., the opening of a direct land route into the very centre of China, the difficulties that would be met with in the line of country visited by the Expedition would hardly merit consideration.

Although I have dwelt on the capabilities of the Tapeng valley, it must not be concluded that I would give it a higher place than the Sawaddy route, for I have dilated on the practical advantages of the former, simply because I have no acquaintance with the details of the latter, which offers, in all probability, far greater facilities for the construction of a railway, although it also may be rivalled by the broad valley of the Shuaylee.

The proposition, however, to construct a railway to China at the present time, before any interchange of the commodities of the two countries worthy of the name of trade exists, seems so premature as to be, as yet, scarcely worthy of serious consideration. In future years, if a trade should spring up between the two countries, on such a scale that the profits likely to accrue from it would be such as to justify the construction of a railway, there would be a reasonable prospect of its being seriously entertained; but now, as little exists either between Rangoon or Bhamô and China, it appears to me that the project at the present day could only emanate from the brains of scheming or interested enthusiasts. It has been, notwithstanding, seriously proposed to carry a railway from Rangoon to Canton over the river of Pegu, *vid* Shuaygyeen, over the Salween, through the long, elevated, and thinly peopled tract of hilly country between the latter river and Kianghung-gyee on the Cambodia, across the Cambodia itself, and the high ranges that define it, past Esmok over the water-shed, and feeders of the Tisien and Hong-kiang, and through the mountainous country that intervenes between the latter and Canton, without any apparent regard whatever to the physical characters of this enormous tract of all but unknown territory. The general lay of the mountain ranges, nearly due north and south, and the large number of formidable rivers encountered along the route, are practical objections to its accomplishment, which must be apparent to all. When the time comes for constructing a railway to China, the most natural course would be to carry it up the great valley of the Irawady as far as Bhamô, from whence it might be taken up the valley of the Tapeng or Shuaylee to Momien, Yungchan, Yunan city or Tali, thus connecting with the Irawady the three great water highways of China, *viz.*, the Yang-tse-kiang, Canton river, and the Mekhong. Arrived at Yunan city, one branch might follow the course of the Yang-tse-kiang, and another proceed down the valley of the Canton river to the sea. The great recommendations in favour of such a line would be in the facts that it was a railway, not only to China, but through the length of the great valley of the Irawady; that it would follow a route that is recognized, not only by the Burmese as the gateway to China, but by the Chinese as the highway to Burmah, and one that has been in constant use as far back as the beginning of the Christian era. The circumstances that only 144 miles of difficult country intervene between Momien and Talifoo by the mercantile city of Yungchan, and that the great city of Yunan is only 190 miles beyond the latter, are favourable to this route, for they indicate, first, that it would lie through a civilized and not thinly populated country; and, second, that the difficulties that would have to be contended against would be restricted to 254 miles, if Yunan city were the starting-point, from whence it would diverge to Canton and Shanghai. Beyond the capital of the province, these branches would follow the valleys of two large rivers; and, indeed, to state in a few words the advantages of the Bhamô route over any proposed route from Southern Burmah, they are these: that it has the full advantage of the natural lay of the country from Rangoon as far as Momien; that it reduces the ground in which the mountain ranges and rivers run north and south to the lowest minimum, 254 miles; and that having crossed this difficult band of country, it again follows to the sea the course of the large rivers and great hill ranges. Whereas the proposed route from Rangoon to Canton, *via* Shuaygyeen and Esmok, lies for a great part of its course of 1,450 miles almost at right angles to the lay of the land, through a thinly peopled country and among semi-civilized tribes.

Supposing a railway were constructed to Yunan or Talifoo, or the more likely and feasible project of a road, what practical advantages would accrue to trade? There are three great water highways from Central and Western China to the sea,—the Yang-tse-kiang, the Canton river, and the Cambodia. The former defines the eastern border of the province of Yunan, and is the most important. It is the great navigable estuary down which the rich produce of the fertile province of Sechuen, and the other provinces along its course, finds its way to the sea-board; and the river of Canton to a less extent fulfils the same function in the country through which it flows. The Cambodia, which is also navigable as far as Kianghung-gyee, is another large outlet for the produce of Southern Yunan, and of the rich tract of country through which it runs to Saigon. Now, in the event of either road or railway being opened out, even as far as has been indicated, it would have a severe struggle with these long-established water highways down which the riches of that immense empire of China have rolled to the sea, generation after generation; and when it is remembered that the sole purpose, or nearly so, of a proposed land communication with China, is to divert a moiety of the trade that finds its way down these splendid rivers to the sea in an opposite direction, and to bring it by a land route to another river, the Irawady, in foreign territory, the immense difficulties that lie in the way of its successful accomplishment are easily understood. In plain language, the project is to divert from the Yang-tse-kiang, Canton river, and Cambodia that which naturally belongs to them, and to bring it to the Irawady by a land journey. I leave it to practical men to judge if such an end is likely to be attained. It is not as if no long-established marts did not exist on the sea-board of China, and at the mouths of the rivers, and that no outlet to the produce of the country existed in that direction, for in such a case it would be possible to understand how the trade might find its way to Burmah, or to any other market that might offer; but with our mercantile interests and those of other nations firmly established along the whole sea-board of China, and daily increasing in importance, since the opening of the Suez Canal, while the Chinese government is most careful to exclude foreign influence from the inland provinces of the empire, who, under such adverse circumstances, would be bold enough to advocate the practicability of a railway to China at the present time? In years hereafter, when the Chinese government shall have become so far enlightened and influenced by western ideas, as to be able to appreciate the great advantages that it would reap from the presence of a locomotive highway traversing the length and breadth of its immense possessions, connecting together the mercantile centres of the east, then, and not till then, will it be expedient or practicable to construct a railway. In the present state of China, and the feeling that prevails among the population with regard to foreigners, the feasibility of even a preliminary survey is extremely doubtful. In our own territory to the south, and in the neighbouring friendly Shan states, it might with caution prove a success, but I doubt the propriety of attempting it among the semi-civilized tribes beyond, who look with suspicion on a foreigner when he attempts to measure or survey their country, and naturally conclude in their ignorance that he has come among them for no good object.

With regard to the special project of constructing a tramway from Kianghung-gyee on the Cambodia to our own territories, it appears that the advantages that are likely to result from it have been much exaggerated, and that it is extremely doubtful that it will succeed in carrying away, from the banks of the navigable Cambodia to Rangoon, that which it is the whole interest of the French government should find its way to Saigon.

To return, however, from these still premature projects, to consider the character of the trade that might be developed by a simple trading route to Yunan, we are met at the outset with the unpropitious fact that the whole of the province is and has been for many years in open rebellion against the authority of the imperial government of China, which has not relinquished all hopes of recovering it. Such a condition of things is most unfavourable to the revival of the trade between Bhamô and Western Yunan; and, indeed, there is little prospect of its being brought about until the rebellion has either been put down, or the Mahomedan power established on a firm basis, and recognized by the empire as an independent state. So long as the province is the scene of constant warfare, throughout its length and breadth, as has been the case for the last fifteen years at least, it is easy to understand the uncertainty that attaches to property, and how nearly all industry and trade are paralysed. There is little hope of a remunerative trade between Bhamô and Yunan until one or other of the contending parties either gives way, or becomes the master. Until this is brought about, the only market that would be open to traders from Bhamô would be the Shan valleys as far as Momien, but as the wants of the Shans are few, and as they wear little beyond the indigo-dyed cotton cloth which they grow and manufacture for themselves, there would be no great opening for Manchester goods. It would be found in all probability that a few bales of cloth of various textures and colours would surfeit the market. There is no trade at present in Western Yunan, so long as it is restricted to the Shan provinces, that would repay our Rangoon merchants entering on it; while petty traders, such as the Chinese at Bhamô, who introduce perhaps half a bale of red flannel or blue or green long cloth, at a time, into a valley like Hotha, and sell it at a high profit, doubtless find the trade remunerative: but, as I have already observed, a bale or two would flood the market, and there would be little or no profit. These remarks also apply to the valley of Sanda, and only on a slightly more extended scale.

Dark coloured yarns would meet with a better and more general sale than cloth; and there would be a small market for drills, woollen cloths, merinoes, handkerchiefs, Turkey red, and carpets; but glass-ware, earthen-ware, lamps, lanterns, buttons, needles, pins, knives, scissors, betel-nut, cutch would find a ready sale, if offered in small quantities. Two or three caravans, however, of such merchandise, following in quick succession, would inundate the market, and so reduce the prices that the profits would scarcely cover the cost of mule-hire, the imposts in the Kakhyen hills, and other expenses. Salt would be a profitable article to import into the Shan states in moderate supplies. It is at present derived from Shienpagah on the Irawady, but it is of inferior quality, and could not compete with Indian salt. At Momien it comes from Yungchan, and the neighbourhood of Khyto, where it is manufactured as a government monopoly, and sold in the bazaar by licensed dealers at Rs. 60 to 100 a viss.

The substances that might be derived from Momien for exportation to Burmah would be gold, silver, lead, copper, and iron, and as extensive and rich mines of all these metals appear to exist in a number of localities, a demand has only to spring up, and they would be forthcoming in considerable quantities. But they will never be fully productive until the disturbances are at an end, and public confidence restored. Even a small trade to the comparatively peaceful Shan states, as far as Momien, might exercise a powerful influence in helping to bring about the latter much-desired result, and lead to the opening up of a traffic that would extend as far as Yungchan and Talifoo. In the event of this happening, a much brighter prospect would be in store for the merchants of Rangoon and Moulmein. Then the population of Western Yunan and the millions of Central China would be reached, and Manchester and Sheffield goods might be poured into the country without much danger of their being in excess of the wants of the people. The great highway leads from Yungchan direct to Yunan, the capital of the province, and from thence it proceeds to Chingtufoo, the capital of Sechuen, so that, the country once settled, English manufactures might be largely introduced into the wealthiest province of China; and without contemplating carrying the trade beyond Yunan city, considerable quantities of the tea and the mineral wealth even of Sechuen itself might eventually reach it.

It is worthy of note that nearly all the trade to Tibet and North-Western China finds its way along the Yang-tse-kiang to Chung-king (lat. 29°38' N., long. 107°5' E.), the great commercial city of Central China. In the event of the re-opening of the trading route between Burmah and Yunan, we may rest assured that the merchants of Shanghai would use all their influence to have Chung-king declared a free port, in order to limit the trade between Burmah and China as much as possible to the province of Yunan, and the probability is that both of these endeavours would be successful, and with these contingencies, the Bhamô routes would never be able to compete with the steam navigation of the Yang-tse-kiang.

The Yang-tse-kiang stands in the same relation to the Irawady that the latter river does to the Brahmaputra, and if I am correct in concluding that the Irawady will never command more than the trade of Yunan, and some indirect traffic with Sechuen, what chance of success would the proposed trading routes from the Brahmaputra to Talifoo have in competing with the Bhamô route, which would be only half their length? It seems most absurd to contemplate carrying the trade of Yunan past the Irawady to the Brahmaputra, by a long and difficult land route, when the goods, if they were despatched from Bhamô, would reach Rangoon in a shorter time than it would take them to arrive at the Brahmaputra.

It appears probable that if we were free to communicate with the country lying along our north-eastern frontier, the routes by the valleys of the Dihong and Brahmakund might successfully compete with those from Chung-king on the Yang-tse-kiang for the trade of Tibet and North-Western Sechuen, for there can be little doubt that these two valleys are the most natural and shortest inlets from the sea into that portion of the Chinese empire.[1] Why, Bathang itself, in Sechuen, on the highway between Chung-king and Tibet, is only 14 days' march by a good road from our frontier.

Little is known of the capabilities of the Dihong, and it is quite possible, if it is the large river that it is represented to be, discharging 56,000 cubic inches of water per minute, that steamers of light draught and weight would be able to go up it a considerable distance beyond Suddyah. During Crawford's time, the Irawady was stated to be navigable only to small boats above the capital, but actual survey has proved it to be deep enough during the dry weather for large river steamers as far as Bhamô. It is quite possible that similar mistaken opinions prevail regarding the Dihong above Suddyah, and a survey will alone settle the question. Even supposing, however, that it is unnavigable, there are the valleys to fall back upon. A route leaves Suddyah, and following the course of the Dihong, reaches the Tibetan town of Bhaloo in sixteen marches, passing the following villages—Kudgin, Lackquee, Laloon Namanoo, Dullee, Omono, Hullee, Sumloy, Hamay, Kumday, and Rheeshah. Four days' march beyond Bhaloo is the city of Rasheemah, containing fine stone buildings, a large population, and a government purely Chinese.[2] This route, however, is described as being very arduous, but it cannot be more so than the road leading from Chung-king to Bathang, which passes over high ranges of mountains covered with perpetual snow. Nevertheless, the latter highway is the scene of a constant traffic between the Yang-tse-kiang and Tibet, and we may conclude that if it pays the Chinese and Tibetan merchants to carry their goods by that long and difficult journey, their profits would be much greater could they purchase and dispose of their merchandise at the much nearer and more accessible marts of Assam.

Hamilton Buchanan describes another route between Assam and Tibet, which shows that a direct communication existed between the two countries during his time, and that the isolation of Assam, from any participation at present in the trade of Tibet, is not attributable to the physical difficulties encountered in the intervening country, but is wholly due to the exclusive policy of the Chinese government and to their hatred of foreigners. He says: "at a place called Chouna, two months' journey from Lassa, on the confines of the two states, there is a mart established, and on the Assam side there is a similar mart at Geegunshur, distant 4 miles from Chouna; an annual caravan repairs from

---

[1,2] Robinson's Assam, p. 247.

Lassa to Chouna, conducted by about twenty persons, conveying silver bullion to the amount of about £10,000, and a considerable quantity of rock salt for sale to the Assam merchants at Geegunshur, to which place the latter bring rice, which is imported into Tibet from Assam in large quantities; tussa cloth, a kind of coarse silk cloth, manufactured by the native women in Assam from the queen downwards; iron and lac found in Assam, and otter skins, buffalo horns, pearls, and corals, first imported from Bengal."

Pemberton[1] has also pointed out that "the Lassa merchants, just before the Burmese invasion of Assam, had visited Durrung," from which, he says, we may conclude "that the intercourse had at that time become more intimate and unreserved than it was at the time described by Buchanan Hamilton." Turner, in his mission to Tibet, states that articles purchased in Bengal were offered for exchange at Silling on the borders of China. During his time, 1782, nearly all the English and Indian products that found their way into Tibet were carried through Nepaul, but the Nepaulese and Chinese invasion of Tibet, which occurred subsequent to his mission, did away with all the commercial advantages that had begun to result from it, and a policy of rigorous exclusion was inaugurated by the Chinese government, which is still in full activity all along our north-eastern frontier to the immense detriment of the interests of Assam.

If these routes to Sechuen and Tibet were once opened to trade *viâ* the Brahmaputra, the success of tea cultivation in Assam would be an accomplished fact, and the province, which is second to no other district in India in fertility, would be in a position which would favour the full development of its great natural resources. As a tea-growing country, with a splendid water communication with Calcutta, from whence it could derive its supplies of Manchester and Sheffield goods, which find such a ready sale in Sechuen and Tibet, Assam has everything in itself which would enable it successfully to compete with the Yang-tse-kiang for the markets of Tibet, and even Western Sechuen; and ultimately, perhaps, to absorb a very large portion of the trade that now finds its way thence by a circuitous course through the breadth of China, and the Brahmaputra would be put in possession of a traffic that naturally belongs to it. At present nearly all the brick-tea for the supply of the Tibetan market, estimated at six millions of pounds per annum, is exported from Sechuen, whilst Assam, from its geographical position, might be the

---

[1] North-Eastern Frontier, p. 176.

fountain-head of this supply, not only to Tibet but to Central Asia generally, were the routes that I have indicated only thrown open. As it is, however, Assam is as effectually debarred from contributing to it, as if it were a remote province of Northern Siberia, and is at present little better than an enormous *cul-de-sac*, without any outlet in the direction in which its staple product should find a ready market, among the large, tea-consuming population of Tibet. No province, thus shut in and excluded from exchanging its natural products for those of the countries around it, can ever flourish, and the more so in the case of a sparsely peopled country like Assam, for the barriers that put a veto on trade effectually stop emigration from the very quarter from which it would naturally flow. From the physical configuration and hilly nature of Assam, it is extremely doubtful whether it would be possible to colonize it from the plains-loving people to the west, but the character of its population and past history render it highly probable that if these barriers, which prevent a free communication with the countries to the north and east, were once and for ever removed, and inducements to emigration held out to the hill tribes in these directions, Assam might yet boast of a large industrious population, and of a thriving trade with Tibet and Sechuen.

CHAPTER VIII.

THE IRAWADY AND ITS SOURCES.

It does not say much for geographical enterprize in the East, in recent times, that the Irawady, a river equalling in magnitude the Ganges of India, should remain unexplored. This noble river flows for many hundred miles through British territory, irrigating its fields, transmitting its merchandize through the country, and leading up to the very doors of China; and yet no one has had the curiosity, courage, or encouragement to search out from whence it comes. It is a subject of much regret to me that I had neither time nor facilities, while at Bhamô, to contribute, by personal exploration of the higher waters of the Irawady, to the elucidation of the interesting problem of its origin, but I hope to throw some light on the subject from the information I carefully collected while in Upper Burmah.

I shall first reproduce, however, all the facts which Captain Wilcox brought to bear on the subject, along with those gathered by his fellow-workers, Captains Burlton and Neufville, but as none of these observers had ever seen the main stream of the Irawady, below the junction of its eastern and western branches, at lat. 26° N., I shall also state what Hannay, Bayfield, and Griffith record of it to nearly latitude 25°, and the opinion they had formed as to its probable origin.

I am no disciple of the theory that the Sanpo is the Irawady, and cannot see how it is possible, in view of Turner's account of the former stream, and the accurate observations made by Captain Montgomery's pundits, that any one could be found prepared to re-advocate its claims. It appears, however, that Klaproth's hypothesis has done good service to the Irawady in as far as it excited an interest in the discovery of its sources, and gave to it an importance to which it is entitled by the enormous body of water which it carries to the sea. The circumstance that so many able geographers have pinned their faith to the theory in question, seems to indicate that there must be some foundation for the opinion that the main stream has its source a long way to the north of the Kampti mountains. This, however, only by the way, for such evidence is of little practical value.

While Lieutenant Burlton was engaged in the survey of the Brahmaputra in March 1825, he considered that its eastern branch had its source in a high snowy range called the Brahmakund, and from what the natives told him, he was inclined to believe that the Siri Sirhit or Irawady rose at the same place.

In June 1825, Lieutenant Neufville learnt that the ranges of the Brahmakund were much further east than were at first supposed, and he was informed by some Kamptis that the Irawady took its rise from the opposite side of the same mountain from which the Brahmakund branch of the Brahmaputra rose; and he gave it as his opinion that this theory of the sources of the two rivers was probably correct, and agreed both with the general accounts and geographical features of the country.

Captain Wilcox, on his visit to the Lúri Gohain's village, some distance up the Suddyah stream, learnt that the Lama country, on the banks of the Brahmakund, was about 15 days distant, and the upper part of the Irawady about the same. On his return to Suddyah, he met from the tract beyond the Irawady, in lat. 25° to 26°, Burmans and Shans, the latter from Mogoung west of the Irawady in lat. 25°, and the former from various parts of their own empire, also many Kamptis from the source of the Irawady. Taking advantage of these opportunities to investigate the connection of the Irawady with the Sanpo, all that he was able to establish was the existence of a large eastern branch of the former river. Wilcox gained his first view of the supposed main stream of the Irawady from the hills which separate the Namlong, one of the affluents of the eastern branch of the Brahmaputra, from the plains of the upper Irawady. The stream winds in a large plain, spotted with light green patches of cultivation and low grass jungle; he states that on reaching its banks, he and Lieutenant Burlton were surprised to find but a small river, smaller even than they anticipated, though aware of the proximity of its sources. It was not more than 80 yards broad, and still fordable, though considerably swollen by the melting snows; the bed was of rounded stones, and both above and below where they stood, they could see numerous shallow rapids similar to those on the Dihing.

As to the general question of the origin of the Irawady, he proceeds to say, he felt perfectly satisfied, from the moment he made enquiries at Suddyah, that Klaproth's theory that the waters of the Sanpo find an outlet through the channel of the Irawady was untenable; and now that he stood on the edge of the clear stream which he concluded to be the source of the great river, he could not help exulting at the successful termination of his toils and fatigues! Before the two travellers, a towering wall of mountains rose to the north, stretching from the west to the east, offering an awkward impediment to the passage of a river in a cross direction; and they agreed on the spot that if Mr. Klaproth proved determined to make his Sanpo pass by Ava, he must find a river for his purpose considerably removed towards China. On the eastward of where they stood, about lat. 27°29″, were peaks heaped upon one another in the utmost irregularity of height and form, and at all distances. Their guide pointed out the direction of the two larger branches uniting to form the eastern branch of the Irawady or Namkiu, by which the Kamptis distinguish the Irawady through its course to the sea. The mountain at the source of the western branch bore 315°, and of the other, which takes the name of the main stream, 345°. They could also perceive the snow to the westward source, continuing as far round to the southwest as 240°. The elevation above the sea was proved to be 1,855 feet; and on the theory that Bhamô was 500 feet above the sea, which would be equivalent to a fall of the river of eight inches each mile, there would remain 1,300 feet of fall in the 350 miles between their position and Bhamô, which he believed sufficiently accounted for by the greater part of that distance being unnavigable excepting for small canoes.

The most important geographical information obtained by Wilcox was the existence of the eastern branch falling in at two days' journey above where the road turns off to Mogoung. This river had hitherto been a stumbling-block in reconciling the accounts of the Singphos and Burmans at Suddyah, for the latter were unacquainted with it, from the fact that their route lay to the south of it by the Mogoung valley, while the former came from the eastward of the Hukong valley. The Kamptis, as well, appear to have been quite as ignorant of the eastern branch as any of the other tribes, and he states that they had no positive information about it. This eastern branch, which no European eye has ever seen, and about which Wilcox professed he was unable to obtain any positive information, he calls the Súhmaï-Kha, Pongmaï, or Sinmaï Kha. It was described to him as rising in the northern mountains at no great distance eastwards from the heads of the Irawady; and the objections to assigning it a very distant source, are, first, its want of magnitude, for it is not described as larger than the Kampti branch; second, the direction of the high range which would require it to break through the most elevated ground in that quarter; and lastly, the want of room. In an appendix to his account, he again repeats what he had already said about having no positive statements to offer regarding the origin of the Súhmaï-Kha; but what is worthy of special note, he records that the Singphos generally were of opinion that it is somewhat larger than the western branch though not materially, and he supposed it not at all improbable that it was the river which had been mentioned to him by an old man, who had been a slave among the Lamas, as rising in the snowy mountains of the Khana-Debas country, and flowing to the south near where the source of the eastern branch of the Dihong turns to the north-west. These are all the facts which Wilcox, from his own observation and research, brought to bear on the question of the sources of this river. He may have contributed to disprove Klaproth's theory, but he certainly did not discover the sources of the Irawady as he seems to have thought.

I shall now examine the estimate he had formed of the river whose sources he thus located, but whose main stream had never been seen by him; and in connection with this subject, he asks himself the pertinent question, what is the magnitude of the Irawady compared with other rivers close at hand? I shall give here the answer in nearly his own words, and with it before us, we will be able to judge whether his knowledge was sufficiently accurate to give his opinion on its probable source much weight. Speaking of the reported difficulty of stemming its current in the rainy season, as a proof adduced by some, of the great body of water which it sends down, he very justly remarks that such statements, to those acquainted with the Ganges and Brahmaputra, amounted to no more than that it resembled those rivers in the periodical difficulties of its navigation. He adverts to the fact that the Irawady is, in one place, contracted in breadth by its high banks to 400 yards, of which we have, he observes, no similar instance in the others; and in view of such a circumstance, he could not consent to allow that the difficulty of stemming its current was a convincing argument of its superior importance. This comparison, however, and deduction from it, would not have been made by one who had had any practical acquaintance with the Irawady, or of the character of the country through which it flows, for the conditions of the river are entirely different from those which characterize the Ganges and Brahmaputra. He reproduces Buchanan Hamilton's statement, that during the dry months of January, February, March, and April, the waters of the Irawady subside into a stream that is barely navigable, and founding his deduction as to the magnitude of the river on this description, which is utterly opposed to the facts, it is not to be wondered at, that he limited its source to the southern face of the mountains bounding the Kampti plain to the north, in latitude 28°. In his accounts, he also enters into a comparison of the Brahmaputra and Irawady, with the object of combating Klaproth's theory regarding the course of the Sanpo, but it does not appear that he succeeded in proving that there was any very great disproportion between the size of the two rivers.

We will now turn to the accounts of Hannay, Bayfield, and Griffith, to give some idea of the true character of the Irawady about 80 miles below where it receives the branch Wilcox visited. Colonel Hannay describes the Irawady, in latitude 24°56′53″, at the mouth of the Mogoung stream, as still a fine river, flowing in a reach from the eastward, half a mile broad, at the rate of two miles an hour, with a depth varying from three fathoms in the centre to two at the edge; and that it is not unnavigable to large boats is evidenced by the fact that his boat required 25 men to row it. In speaking of the first defile below Tsenbo, through which they had taken their large boats, he describes it as the most dangerous part of the Irawady, which I can fully verify from personal observation. This portion of the river commences a few miles above Bhamô, and stretches to within 7 or 8 miles of Tsenbo. Between these two points, it flows under high wooded banks formed by the parallel ranges. At the lower approach to the defile, the channel is as much as 1,000 yards broad, but as we proceed upwards it gradually narrows to 500, 200, 100 and even to 70 yards, according as the ranges approach each other, again increasing in breadth as they recede, till at last, below Tsenbo, it spreads out again into a noble river. Considering all that portion to be defile, in which the course of the river is defined by high hills, it may be stated to stretch over 25 miles in length. It must not, however, be imagined that the whole of this long stretch is equally difficult of navigation, for besides the so-called rapids and the narrowed portion in which the bed of the stream is crossed by huge trap dykes, there are long, deep, lake-like reaches, in which there is hardly any perceptible current, and no rocks. The dangers mentioned by Hannay lie in that part of the defile where the channel is intersected by the green stone beds. There the river has cut a passage for itself through the solid rocks in some places not more than 60 or 70 yards broad, but 10 to 12 fathoms in depth. The current is not so strong in the dry weather as to interfere materially with the passage of boats, when they are kept under the lee of the green stone beds; but I had telling evidences, in the height of the high-water mark, which was about 25 feet in February, and in the shivered trunks of large trees, and in broken logs and branches heaped in wild confusion among the rocks, that all navigation, with the present obstructions unremoved, must be impracticable during the height of a flood, and that the body of water that pours through the narrow gorge must be enormous and of terrific power. Immediately below it, there is a deep, still reach of black water evidently of great depth, and so land-locked that it resembles a mountain lake.

Griffith states that Dr. Bayfield ascertained, during his passage up, at a season when the waters were low, that in many places of the first defile, no bottom was to be found at a depth of 45 fathoms. Griffith's own account of the Irawady above Bhamô is, that it keeps up its magnificent character as far as he went, to the mouth of the Mogoung river, where it is 900 to 1,000 yards across, and he describes the appearance of its vast sheet of water as really grand. He allows that the general characters of the Irawady are very different from the Ganges and Brahmaputra, its waters being much more confined to their bed, and, comparatively speaking, becoming seldom spread out. Generally it is deep, and the stream is not violent; and he states, what experience has proved to be perfectly accurate, that it affords every facility for navigation, although, in one or two places, troublesome shallows are met with. In the first defile, the channel is occasionally impeded with rocks, but it is only in this part of the river that the navigation is attended with danger. Further, in speaking of the tributaries of the Irawady between Mogoung and Ava, he remarks that they are unprecedentedly small, which leads to increase the astonishment with which one regards this magnificent river. He favours the opinion that its source will probably be found to be the Sûhmaï-Kha, and points out the fact that the great body of water comes from the eastward, for between the Mogoung river and Borkampti, in which country Wilcox visited the Irawady, where it was found to be of no great size, no considerable branch finds its way from the westwards, neither are the hills which intervene between these points of such height as to afford large supplies of water. On the whole, he thought it probable that the Irawady is an outlet for some great river which drains an extensive tract of country, for it appeared to him that if all its waters are poured in by mountain streams, a tract of country expansive beyond all analogy will be required for the supply of such a vast body of water. I attach great weight to this opinion, for it was formed by Griffith immediately after his visit to the Brahmaputra, and because he was a man of thoroughly scientific habits of thought, "*très instruit, très zélé, et fort bon observateur,*" as Mirbel observes. Colonel Hannay, while at Hukong, learned from Singphos, from the borders of China, that the Sûhmaï river rises in the mountains bordering the plain of Kampti to the north, and is enclosed on the east by the Goulangsigong mountains which they considered the boundary between Burmah and China. This river was pronounced not to be navigable even for canoes. Several smaller streams were described as falling into it from the Shuedong-gyee hills to the west, and the name of Situng was given to the tract of country through which they flowed.

Dr. Williams, in a book entitled "Through Burmah to Western China," gives it as his opinion that a river steamer of proper construction would have no difficulty in making its way to the Tapeng, and for many miles beyond. My comment on this is, that we proceeded to Bhamô in a large steamer drawing three feet of water, and experienced no difficulty in the navigation, although the captain and all the crew were Burmans, to whom the river above Mandalay was entirely new. This, too, happened in one of the months (January) in which Buchanan Hamilton stated the river to be barely navigable to native boats. While at Bhamô, I took the opportunity to make what I can only characterize as a rush up to the first defile. The visit was necessarily a hurried one, as our leader, Major Sladen, was in the daily expectation of being able to make an immediate advance, so that, if I had gone in for a thorough investigation of the river above Bhamô, I should have certainly seriously interfered with the progress of the Expedition. My visit, however, sufficed to convince me that the Tapeng makes hardly any sensible difference to the volume of this great river.

The Irawady, at the beginning of the first defile, about 5 miles above Bhamô, is about 1,000 yards across, and its course is defined by low wooded hills which run close to its bank. About 2 miles further on, the channel narrows to 500 yards, and the hills become even closer and more abrupt over the stream than before; and about another mile beyond, a higher range of hills from the south-west comes in behind another, and both terminate on the bank as two headlands. At this point, a ridge of rocks runs half across the bed, and at the season (February) I visited it, was eight feet above the water, but the river was so broad and deep that I find myself speculating in my notes made on the spot, on the course a steamer would follow in passing these rocks. The hills still continue on both sides, but they are highest to the west, and as one proceeds for 4 or 5 miles, the number of rocky points running out into the river increases, and opposite a Phwon village, about 10 miles above Bhamô, on the left bank, the channel has narrowed to about 150 yards; and here the first so-called rapids occur. The bank on which the village stands is about 80 feet high, and the country inland is undulating, and running up to low ranges of hills a few miles to the north. Here I moored my boat for the night. Next morning I proceeded about 8 miles further up the defile, or Khyoukdwen, as it is called by the Burmese, still preserving its high wooded banks on either side. After I had gone about 3 miles of this distance, I came to a reach in which the river flows very sluggishly between two high conical hills, which so close in upon it that one is puzzled to detect any outlet. The quiet motion of the water and its deep olive-black are suggestive of great depth. The breadth of this lake-like reach is about 250 yards, and its length about $1\frac{1}{2}$ miles, and passing on, it is found abruptly closing in at its further end, and its channel broken up by numerous rocks which jut out boldly on either side to the stream, in many cases approaching each other so closely, that the channel is reduced to 60 or 70 yards. The height of these rocks averages 30 feet, but many of them are not more than 15 to 20 feet. The current, although strong, did not interfere much with my progress. There is a small isolated rock on the right side of the channel, capped by a pagoda, and another little promontory further on with a similar structure. The first appears to be of great age, and its presence on this rocky island, well into the middle of the stream, and not higher, I should think, than 45 feet above it, gives us some indication as to the limit of the rise of the river, for the pagoda could not withstand the force of the current. The Irawady, however, had not reached its lowest, when I visited the spot.

This rocky reach stretches about a mile in a north-north-west direction, and terminates abruptly in an elbow, from which another reach extends in an east-north-east course, with a clear channel overhung by the precipitous but grassy sides of high hills. This elbow is one of the most dangerous parts of the whole defile, owing to a number of large insulated rocks that stretch across it, exposed about 20 feet or more during February. Owing to the sudden bend, the current rushes between them with great violence, but not so much so as to prevent boats passing; indeed, after I had taken my boat round the point, and had stopped to admire this novel and grand bit of river-scenery, the magnitude of the Irawady in the northern reach, and of the picture generally, was brought out by some boats in the distance that had passed up before me, and which were completely dwarfed amid the grandeur of the surrounding scene. It was a matter of much regret that I could not afford the time to go beyond this, but I learned from the boatmen that with what I had done, and a glance up the reach ahead, I had seen the whole of the defile. The body of water which flows round this corner during the rains must be very great, and its velocity and power tremendous, for all the rocks (greenstone) subjected to its influence are rounded, and shine with an almost metallic glaze produced doubtless by the attrition of the flood. The rocks are all *in situ*, and run across the stream from east-north-east to west-south-west, and through the hills on either side. The softer strata between them have been much denuded, and correspond to the shallow valleys and hollows of the hills.

It should be remembered that two other defiles occur in the Irawady, one immediately below Bhamô, and the other about 40 miles above Mandalay; and another may be said to exist below Thayetmyo and at Prome, where the course of the river is defined by high hills. Throughout each of them, the river is of necessity restricted to a well-defined channel, and its breadth entirely depends on the proximity or remoteness of the hills to one another; so that its breadth is no indication whatever of the body of water which passes through these channels; hence the opinion formed of it by Buchanan Hamilton, deduced from its contraction at one place to 400 yards, cannot be entertained.

The following information was communicated to me by a Kampti Shan from the village of Kakhyo, three days' journey by boat below the junction of the two main streams of the Irawady. He professed to know the country well, as far as one day's journey up the eastern river to a village called Muangla, where his wife came from. He informed me, of his own accord, that the river above the first defile is nearly like what it is at Bhamô; and he stated that if a steamer, as large as the one we had at the latter place, could be got through the rocks of the first defile, there would be no difficulty in taking it as far as the village of Wyesoam, at the junction of the two streams. After the defile is passed, he described the mountains as receding from the river; and in speaking of the country about his native village, he said that on climbing a high tree, it appeared a dead flat for miles around, with the mountains in the distance, but nearing the junction of the two rivers, the hills again close in, though not to the extent to form a gorge. He described the eastern branch as the largest, and that it is navigable as far as the village of Muangla, one day's journey from its mouth, but that above that point the channel becomes rocky and dangerous to navigate; that between the first defile and Kakhyo, the Namsang stream from the east enters the Irawady about one mile above the Mogoung river; and that one day's journey by boat above the former, the Namthabet, another small river, flows into the Irawady from the east.

In the map of the north-eastern frontier of Burmah and Western China, compiled at the Surveyor General's Office, Calcutta, in 1862,

I find rivers corresponding in position to these. The southern one is named in the map Shoomaee, but at one place along its course I find the word Mengzan-khong, which has such a close resemblance to Namsang-hkyoung that I am inclined to regard it as the same. The name, however, is put in almost at right angles to the river, and evidently with some doubt, for it is difficult to say to what it refers. Any one, familiar with the Burmese word hkyoung, would have had no hesitation in referring the name to the river, although the first part of the word is essentially Shan—Nam-sang, the River Sang;—to add hkyoung to this is an apparent tautology, but one which is in vogue among the Shan-Burmese of Upper Burmah, as is instanced, *e. g.*, by the Nam-tapeng-hkyoung. The name by which it goes in the map, Shoomaee, is evidently Burmese, and should be written Shuaymai, or Shuemai-hkyoung.

Now, if we examine the orthography of Wilcox's eastern branch, we find that its name, as given by him, has a wonderful resemblance to that of this eastern *hkyoung*, or rivulet, the Shuaymai, opposite to Mogoung. He writes it Súhmaï, and gives it a Singpho origin, but it appears there can be little doubt that it is closely affined to Shuaymai, which seems a plausible supposition, from the fact that it flows through a country rich in gold. In this case the word is Burmese, and Pemberton, in his map of the eastern frontier, gives the Singpho name Ziumae, and writes the other Shuemae. If two rivers of the same name do not exist, I cannot avoid supposing, from the circumstance that Hannay made his enquiries at Hukong, that his Sginmae was the small stream opposite or nearly so to the Mogoung river, and not the Súhmaï of Wilcox, for the Kakhyens (Singphos) from whom he derived his information came to Hukong from the borders of China. If they travelled by the Bhamô route, it is highly improbable that they knew anything whatever about the affluents of the Irawady above Mogoung; and I think it, therefore, likely that they were some of the many Kakhyen traders who pass between their hills and Mogoung by the Kakhyo and Wainmô route. This would lead them across the Shoomaee (Namsang), and what could be more natural than that these ignorant hill-men, who have little or no acquaintance with the Burmese plain, when questioned about the Súhmaï, an eastern branch of the Irawady, should describe the small stream of that name they had so lately crossed. They were quite correct in describing it as rising in the Kampti mountains, as the Kampti race extends as far south as Kakhyo, and to the east to the neighbourhood of the sources of the small Shoomaee or Namsang, the head waters of which might, therefore, be accurately described as lying in the Kampti country. It flows from the south side of the Siue Shan mountains, which evidently ought to have been written Shuay Shan, and through a country rich in gold; and in the light of these circumstances, we can easily understand how the confusion arose as to the two streams.

According to my informant, the name of the eastern continuation of the Irawady is the Kewhom, and he described it to me more as the upward prolongation of the Irawady than a branch. Menla or Muangla, which is placed in the map at the junction of the two streams, he stated to be only half a day's journey by boat from Wainmô, whereas Wyesoam, which he places at the junction, is two days' journey above Muangla. Wyesoam is evidently the Maintsoung of the maps, situated to the south of the position my informant assigned to it.

I will now detail some information I obtained while at Momien on the course and extent of the rivers in Western Yunan, for the subject is closely connected with the sources of the Irawady. Momien itself stands on the easterly branch of the Tapeng, the river through which Klaproth directed the waters of the Sanpo to the Irawady. It is a small fordable stream about 20 yards broad at Momien, but during the rains it rises to about eight feet in the Momien valley, which is about 125 miles from the Irawady. Its sources lie in the Kananzan range of mountains, about 10 miles to the east of Momien, on the east side of which is the Shuaylee. The latter river was described to me as a comparatively small stream, rising in a range of hills about 40 or 50 miles to the north-east of Momien; and in the itineraries of the Burmese embassies, I have since found it estimated to be about forty yards broad, and it is said to be spanned by an iron suspension bridge, which was mentioned to me in Momien, and described as the exact fellow of the iron bridge over the Tapeng below Nantin, or 25 miles below Momien, where the river is about the same breadth as the Shuaylee to the east of the latter city. The Salween, which flows on the other side of the range of mountains defining the entire watershed of the Shuaylee, I was informed was a larger river than the latter, flowing in a narrow but comparatively level valley, like that of Sanda, and that there was a ferry over it, as stated in the Burmese itinerary. It was further said to be about the size of the Tapeng below Muangla, with which my informant was well acquainted. It is improbable, therefore, that its sources can be more than a 100 to 150 miles to the north of the latitude of Momien.

If we turn now to the Jesuits' map of the province of Yunan, the result of a survey by the Fathers Fridelli, Bonjour, and Régis, in the years 1714-15, and enquire into the data upon which it is founded, it appears to me that the distribution of these rivers, as laid down in it, so agrees with the data I have collected, that it is worthy of our full acceptance until other facts have been adduced to disprove its accuracy, for Père Régis, one of the surveyors of Yunan, gives us the following account of how the survey was conducted. He informs us that they omitted nothing for rendering their work perfect, and that they visited all the places, even those of least consideration, throughout the province; that they examined the maps and histories of each city, made enquiries of the mandarins and their officers, as well as of the principal inhabitants whose territories they passed through; and that by measuring as they advanced, they still had measures ready to serve the triangles formed by such points as were to be fixed, and that they corrected their determinations by triangles, by the meridian altitudes of the sun and polar stars. As a proof of the accuracy of their maps, we have only to compare their distribution of the Tapeng to within 30 miles of the plains of Burmah, with the result of the survey of our Expedition. If we take the postion of Santa (Sanda) as triangulated by the Jesuits and its relations to the branches of the Tapeng, we will find that they agree in every way with the result of our observation, and that the most insignificant branch of the river about Sanda has been mapped with the most marked accuracy. The same remarks are also equally applicable to the river about Momien. Are we not, therefore, entitled to argue that if such accuracy characterizes their work in mapping out secondrate rivers, a like accuracy will be found in their delineation of streams so important as the Salween and Cambodia? They restrict the sources of the former to latitude 27° 10′ north, or thereabouts, and those of the latter to 27° 30′, or nearly so, which gives a course to the Salween of 640 miles from its sources to Moulmein, and to the Cambodia of 850 miles from its origin to the sea. The Salween is a much less important river than the Cambodia, and it may appear that the greater length of the latter, as indicated by the Jesuit maps, is, however, not enough to account for its greater size. And, perhaps, it would be so, if the Cambodia did not possess the immense reservoir that it does in the lake of Tali, which stretches northwards from 25° 27′ north latitude to about 26° 12′, and from which it derives a large body of water through the Hokyan river, which joins it at 24° 45′ north latitude. The mention of the latter river gives me another opportunity to verify the accuracy of the Jesuit fathers, for I find it stated in the Burmese itineraries that the ambassadors on their way to Pekin from Ava, after crossing the

Cambodia over an iron bridge, about 60 yards long, came to a branch of the Hokyan, over which there was another iron bridge 40 yards in length; and that still further on, they came to the Hokyan itself, which flows from the lake of Tali to join the Cambodia, and over which there is an iron bridge with a span of 42 yards. These two streams, each 40 yards broad, must surely represent a large body of water, and with the knowledge that the Cambodia receives through them a supply of this magnitude from a lake fully 35 miles long, we do not expect it to have the same northerly extension that would be necessitated if this reservoir did not exist. It seems reasonable, therefore, to suppose that the three degrees of latitude in the Jesuits' maps, assigned to the main stream above where it is joined by the Hokyan, is an area of sufficient extent to account for a river like that which the Cambodia appears to be, above its junction with its Tali affluents. The result of this argument is then to prove that the Tibetan rivers are in no way connected with either the Shuaylee, Salween, or Cambodia. In the Jesuits' maps of Yunan, they were certainly never connected. It is only when we come to such maps as D'Anville's, which were drawn up for the express purpose of upholding a flimsy hypothesis, that we find them brought boldly down through the most extraordinary series of windings to their desired course.

With these facts before us, we are prepared to examine the position which Wilcox claimed for himself, that he had discovered the sources of the Irawady. After a careful consideration of all the statements advanced by him in his account of the survey of Assam and the neighbouring countries, I cannot avoid thinking that he came with a biassed judgment to the investigation of the sources of the Irawady, for he states that he felt perfectly satisfied as to the origin of the river before he left Suddyah! But from the internal evidence of his paper, it is evident that he knew nothing of the main stream, and had never seen it. We are, therefore, fairly entitled to submit the evidence which he adduces for restricting its sources to the Kampti mountains to a rigid criticism. But to appreciate his position, it must be borne in mind that he had set himself the task to demolish M. Klaproth, and no one had better facilities and information for doing so than this able explorer and geographer, and to my mind he was quite successful in this task; but in carefully reviewing his decision of the question, it appears that in his desire to establish his position, he was led unwittingly to depreciate the importance of the Irawady, and to give it a restricted distribution at utter variance with its magnitude. The error was a likely one, for his whole acquaintance with the river was a few hours' observation of one of its streams, between the 27th and 28th parallels of north latitude, to the east of Assam; and because what he learned of it beyond the spot on which he stood, was derived solely from Kampti Shans, who were, according to his own statement, little given to travel, and from Singphos from the eastward of Assam. He adduced no proofs, however, that the latter had ever been to the eastward of the eastern branch of the Irawady, which they made two days' journey above the Mogoung river; and according to his own account, the former knew nothing of the river beyond the branch on which the villages were placed; yet, notwithstanding all this, and the fact that the Singphos, generally from the sources of the western branch, had informed him that the eastern one was the larger of the two streams, he adhered to the information which he had received at Suddyah, that the western and smaller branch was the source of the river, and this on the authority of the Kampti Shans, who knew nothing of the Irawady beyond their own river. It is unnecessary to recapitulate what he has stated respecting the probable origin of the western or Kampti branch, and I agree with him in judging, from the size of the stream where he met it, that its sources could not be far distant; but, at the same time, I am not disposed to limit its course on the ground he advances, *viz.*, the presence of a high range of mountains stretching to the east and west. We have only to look at the Dihong, Debong, and Brahmakund to find examples of how large rivers find their way through mountain ranges. I have no better example of this than the Tapeng piercing a mountain range, which, in the distance, one never would have imagined it probable that a river flowed through. So apparently unbroken by valleys are the Kakhyen mountains, and such seemingly impracticable barriers to the passage of a river, that I have found myself at 4 miles from their base, speculating on the course of the Tapeng, and puzzled to define it. The passage, therefore, of the Irawady through the mountains to the north, would be no uncommon phenomenon, and indeed it seems to me to be necessitated in order to account for the volume of water which reaches the Kampti plain. If Wilcox had only had the same practical acquaintance with the main stream of the Irawady with Griffith, we would doubtless have had the testimony of both, that the western stream was quite insufficient, even along with an eastern one of nearly the same dimensions as the former, to account for the great body of water in the Irawady above Mogoung. A glance at his description of the stream, and of the weather during his visit to it, will be sufficient to show that the only light he threw upon the sources of the Irawady was to indicate that the weight of evidence pointed in the direction of the eastern branch, as the great channel from whence that splendid river derives its supply from the highlands of Tibet, between the Yang-tse-kiang, the head waters of the Cambodia and Salween, and the two eastern affluents of the Brahmaputra, the Debong and Brahmakund. He says he was surprised to find but a small river, smaller even than he had anticipated, though aware of the proximity of its sources, a statement which has the smack of a foregone conclusion, but he goes on to describe it as 80 yards wide, but still fordable, although considerably swollen by the melting snows. That this, however, was not the only cause of the rise of the river, such as he describes it, is evident from the frequent reference he makes to the very heavy rains he had experienced in the last eight days of his march, but which never occurred to him as the *vera causa* of the flood. Now, with these facts before us, that the river during the height of a flood, caused by the heavy rains and the melting snows, was only 80 yards broad and fordable, the inference is forced upon us that it would be little more than a mountain rivulet during the dry weather. Such, then, was Wilcox's supposed source of a river, which 200 miles further down, measures more than half a mile in breadth, with an average depth of from two to three fathoms, without receiving any notable stream on the way that would account for the unprecedented difference between these two points. The conclusion, therefore, we arrive at, is, that the western branch, as described by him, was only a small affluent of the main stream which flows down from the north-east as described by my informant, and that the sources of the river in all probability lie considerably to the north of the so-called Kampti range of mountains, and that it thus becomes one of the Tibetan rivers; and as I have shown that the Jesuit fathers, our only reliable authorities on the distribution of the Cambodia and Salween, restrict these rivers to the 28th parallel of north latitude, it becomes probable that some of the Tibetan rivers flowing down from the north, in the direction of the Irawady, may be its upper sources, while the others may be branches of the Yang-tse-kiang; and that the Irawady drains part of that area between Lassa and Bathang which has hitherto been apportioned to the Cambodia and Salween.

D'Anville was the first to connect the Tibetan rivers with the Cambodia and Salween, a conclusion which was forced upon him, from the circumstance that he believed the Sanpo to be the Irawady. Bringing the former river in the way he did to the west of Yunan, he considered he had provided an ample supply of water to account for the volume of the latter, and he had therefore to look for some other outlet for the drainage of that area of Tibet between Lassa and Bathang, to the north of the supposed course of his Sanpo, and he hit upon the Cambodia and the Salween as affording the means, and the unnatural and extraordinary course which he gave these rivers has been perpetuated ever since in the maps of Klaproth, Dalrymple, and Berghaus, without a tittle of evidence in its favour. Now that the Sanpo flows in its natural course to the Brahmaputra, as has been almost proved to a demonstration, it is to be hoped that the Irawady will not any longer be allowed to be deprived of its due, as a river far surpassing the Salween and Cambodia in its northern distribution.

Mr. Cooper, in the proceedings of the Royal Geographical Society for November 1869, hazards the remarkable proposition that the Sanpo and another large river to the east of it fall into a river called the Yarlong, which, he supposes, may be either the Brahmaputra or the Irawady, an amount of uncertainty which affords ample field for speculation. I think I have made it sufficiently evident, from the foregoing summary of the present state of our knowledge regarding the upper waters of the Irawady, as gleaned from the materials which I have adduced, that all the information as yet obtained is little more than conjectural. A most important geographical question still remains to be settled, and the interests of science and of commerce alike demand that it should receive the attention which it deserves.

NARRATIVE OF THE JOURNEY.

CHAPTER IX.

MANDALAY TO BHAMÔ.

THE Expedition party left Mandalay, on the 13th January 1868, in the King of Burmah's steamer, the *Yaynan-Sekia*. It was composed of Major Sladen, Captain Williams, and myself, with Messrs. Bowers, Stewart, and Burn as representatives of the commercial community of Rangoon.

Our guard of police, 50 strong, was a mixed one of Burmese and Mahomedans, officered by an inspector and three sergeants. The inspector, a fine tall Mahomedan, with a fair sprinkling of grey hairs, was followed by his young Burmese wife, who, although possessed of few physical charms, won the admiration of all by her deep devotion to her lord, and by the indomitable pluck with which she bore the many hardships to which she was exposed.

A Burmese court official accompanied us as far as Bhamô, to assist in procuring firewood for the steamer, and to provide boats in the event of the river proving unnavigable. A royal order had preceded us to certain towns along our course to have firewood in readiness, and as it was always forthcoming when wanted, and as no difficulties of any moment opposed our progress along the noble river, the duties of the court official were light, and he found ample leisure to indulge in the four delights of a Burman, salted tea-leaves, betel-nut, cheroots, and sleep. A Chinese interpreter, whom the king had made over to Sladen on account of his knowledge of the language, and of the localities we were to visit, also formed one of our party. This individual, Moungshuay-Yah by name, half Burmese and half Chinese by birth, proved eminently useful so long as he abstained from samshu.

Our crew was entirely Burmese, from the captain to the firemen, and bearing in mind the brief experience that Burmans have had of steamers, it was surprising in how thoroughly a workman-like way all the details in the management of the ship were conducted, and especially remarkable, the cool bearing and ability of the captain in the navigation of some of the narrow and shallow channels which were then for the first time traversed by a steamer. His knowledge of the water, that is, his acquaintance with the kind of ripple that indicates deep and shallow places, was almost instinctive, and the secret of the success that followed him in the trip to Bhamô. Although certainly an able captain for a Burman, his disposition was in strong contrast to the jovial open-heartedness so generally characteristic of his race, and he seemed to study to make himself as disagreeable as possible to the despised *Kalas*, and I believe that his hatred of us was such, that it would have given him great pleasure to have consigned us all to oblivion in the Irawady.

Under this *régime*, we left our anchorage at Mandalay on the afternoon of the 13th January, and steamed as far as Mengoon, a short way above the capital, on the opposite bank of the river. Thus far we were accompanied by an Armenian gentleman, who is distinguished by the high-sounding title of *Kala Woon*, or foreign minister, whose chief end is to please his king, and, if possible, to enjoy him for ever.

We moored alongside the bank, and on the following morning I went ashore by day-break to test the abilities of my collectors, who seemed to have quite as much knowledge of their work, and objections to it, as the animals they were in search of, for they returned to me, after having been out two hours, with only one butterfly and two beetles. The rest of the party went to visit the great pagoda, which Yule describes as one of the highest masses of brick-work in the world, and the famous bell, which is fourteen times as heavy as the great bell of Saint Paul's, but only one-third the weight of that at Moscow.

From the rising ground above Mengoon, a good view is obtained of the position of the capital, and of the surrounding valley. The latter is seen to be defined to the east by the long line of mountains, which, commencing from the north bank of the Myitnge, runs to the north-east in an unbroken chain, as far as the eye can reach; and to the south of that stream is the irregularly peaked outline of the Mya-leit-toung, in singular contrast with the long, flowing sweep of the hills on its northern bank. A few miles behind us, the land rises to the dry and treeless Tsagain ridge, which defines the western side of this noble valley, which is here about 15 miles broad. The Irawady comes down under the western hills, but when opposite Mengoon, its channel widens out, and is marked by three or four large islands, on the largest of which one of the king's gardens is situated, and by numerous sand-banks in the dry weather, on which tobacco and other crops are cultivated. The main banks, opposite the capital, are almost three and a half miles apart from each other. Mandalay is situated on the tail, as it were, of one of the low isolated hills, Mandeiytoung, in the middle of the alluvial flat. Behind the city, to the east, is seen the large irrigation reservoir of King Augbenglé. These are the bare outlines of a landscape of great beauty. The splendid river in the foreground, broken up here and there by luxuriant islands, and enlivened by the passage of large timber rafts, canoes, and boats of varied form and size; the rich alluvial plain in the middle distance, glittering with the gold-gilt roofs of the city gates, and numerous monasteries that cluster outside the red walls of the capital, and around the picturesque hill to the north, which is crowned with a gold emblazoned temple; the many-roofed spires of *zayáts*, and the sparkling *tees* of pagodas, unite, with a noble background of mountain and cloud, to produce a picture never to be forgotten!

We left Mengoon about 11 A.M., steaming along under the right bank, and passing numerous sand-banks and islands to the east. On the former I observed large flocks of whimbrel *(Numenius phæophus,* Lin.), and golden plover *(Charadrius longipes,* Temm.), and still more extensive ones of the snake-bird *(Plotus melanogaster,* Gmel). The white-necked stork *(Melanopelargus episcopus,* Bodd) and the dusky grey heron *(Ardea sumatrana,* Raffles) were not uncommon, and stints and green shanks were very numerous. The ruddy shield-rake *(Casarca rutila,* Pallas) and the common teal *(Querquedula crecca,* Pallas) were the most prevalent ducks. An occasional kite *(Milvus govinda ?)* followed us, and a flock or two of the Indian skimmer *(Rhynchops albicollis,* Swainson) were also observed darting over the water.

The right bank of the river as far as Shienpagah, where we arrived at 1 P.M., has an average height of 40 or 50 feet, and is broken up into a series of picturesque headlands, separated from each other by wooded dells, each of the latter, as a rule, supporting a village. Shienpagah lies in one of those hollows, which have a much more luxuriant vegetation than the neighbouring heights, which are covered with clusters of white pagodas approached from the river-face by long flights of steps. The village is a thriving place, containing about 400 houses. The trade is chiefly in salt, which is procured from the swamps behind the Tsagain hills, and in fish and firewood for the capital. The country behind the town retreats to the base of the sterile Tsagain hills in long low undulations cut up into rounded mounds, deep hollows, and dried-up watercourses. The former are clad with dense patches of prickly shrubs, matted to each other by long trailing creepers, and the portions free of this form of jungle are overgrown by a long delicate grass. The soil on these parts is a light yellow sand with pebbles of quartz, and occasional masses of ferruginous conglomerate. In the hollows, however, the soil is rich, and rice and other crops are reared in them, but on a small scale.

We left Shienpagah at sunrise on the following morning, and kept along the right bank for 4 miles, and then crossed to the channel which runs on the eastern side of the long island of Alékyoung. The western channel is broken up by islands, on which the natives were busily preparing the soil for seed time. Opposite the entrance to the eastern channel, the low broken ranges of the Sagyen and Thubyo-budo hills run nearly parallel to the general course of the river, but separated from it by a broad alluvial flat. Nearly all the marble that finds its way to the capital comes from the former hills. Beyond these two ranges to the east, there is another broad alluvial flat, skirting the foot of the Shan mountains, which has a sparse covering of lofty trees, and is richly cultivated. The villages along the eastern bank are small and not very numerous, and are usually embowered among tall trees and groves of palmira palms, and a few cocoanuts, relieved by the bright pale tropical green of the plantain.

Passing up the eastern channel, with Alékyoung town to our left, we found the northern extremity of the island terminating in the rounded flat-shaped hill of Kethung, capped by numerous white pagodas, overlooking a dense grove of dark green trees, in which we detected the little village that derives its name from the hill. On the opposite bank is the small village of Htseezeh (the village of oil merchants) with a fine green sward in front of it, but separated from the river by a belt of bright yellow sand. Noble trees, palmiras, and gigantic bamboos shade it, and form the back-ground to a piece of river scenery of exquisite colouring and beauty.

We stopped opposite these two villages to take in firewood, which was sent off to us in boats, and from the number of villagers who thronged the banks, they seem to be larger than any of the other villages we had passed, with the exception of Shienpagah.

At the northern extremity of the island, the entrance to the eastern channel is marked by a long sand-bank on which a variety of birds had congregated, evidently attracted by the presence of large fishing-stakes. There are a few small islands above Alékyoung covered with long grass and a few trees, but no appearance of villages on any of them. About this point, 2 miles above Alékyoung, the main banks approach each other, and there are no intervening islands. To the left is the short, rather thickly wooded Nättoung ranges of hills, separated from the river bank by a broad strip of level land that sweeps round them, and stretches away to the north-west as a very extensive plain. Their northern end runs down to the river as a low hill, crowned by a white pagoda, and with the small village of Makouk at its base. On the opposite bank is the town of Tsingu, also situated on a headland which, along with the one of the opposite bank, marks the entrance to the so-called first defile of the Irawady. The extensive alluvial plain that stretches north from Mandalay between the base of the Shan mountains and the river, ceases about a couple of miles to the north of Tsingu, where the country becomes hilly. Between this and Shienpagah the vegetation has been gradually becoming more luxuriant, and from the commencement of the first defile to its termination, the country on both sides is hilly and covered to the river brink by forest, in which, I am informed, the teak is not uncommon, especially a little way inland. Tsingu-myo was formerly a fortified place, and the old wall still exists on the east and south. Above this village, as far as Tsampenago, the river contracts to an average breadth of 1,000[1] yards. In the first 10 or 12 miles, its course is west by north, then it takes a sudden bend to the north of east, and continues thus for 2 or 3 miles, and then resumes its general northerly direction, maintaining an average breadth of about 1,500 yards.

Seven miles beyond Tsingu-myo, we reached the fishing village of Tseittha on the right bank. It contains about 30 houses, which are all enclosed by a bamboo fence with two gates. All the fish caught here are converted into ngapé, and the fishermen assert that they get only one kind. On remarking to the villagers that they had very few dogs, I was informed that they were constantly being carried off by tigers, but on cross-questioning them, I found that the culprit was the leopard.

Two species of monkey are found in the forests on either side of the river. Both are said to have long tails, and one was described to me as of a bright sandy colour, with a black face, and the other as a dark blue monkey, almost black, with white eyebrows, evidently *Presbytes*, but I will not hazard an opinion as to the species.

Apart from its scenery, and one or two accessories, such as the stone pagoda of Theehadaw and the remarkable tame fish, the chief interest of the first defile lies in its coal-fields which occur on the right bank. Those which are nearest the river are due west of the village of Kabyuet, 2 or 3 miles to the north of Tseittha, and 6 miles or so to the south of Theehadaw. As I visited them on my return journey, it might not be out of place to record here what I saw. I was accompanied by Mr. Gordon, and we found the headman of Kabyuet and the Burman in charge of

---

[1] This calculation is founded on a number of shots fired from a rifle sighted to 1,000 yards.

the mines very polite and attentive, and they expressed a strong desire to show us everything, and hoped that if we were satisfied with their conduct, we would say a good word for them to the king. Accompanied by these men and three or four others, we set out on ponies at 7 A.M., on the 21st September 1868. The road lay over an undulating rather dry country, covered by a dense jungle of no great height, in which the *Eng* tree predominated. The soil was dry and sandy, and covered by a layer of calcareous nodules *(kunkur)*, and many fragments of fossilised wood. During our ride, the headman of the mines, a jolly Burman, with a special failing for Bass's beer, treated us to his griefs as an official, saying that he never got pay, but only an occasional present, and that his men received only Rs. 10 per month, and that no one was allowed to use the coal. This was said by way of contrast to the pay of our men, and what he considered to be the pleasant places into which they and we had fallen, for he told us that he had been watching us eating on the previous evening, and that few Burmans could fare as we did. He protested he would be glad to go back with us as our *slave*, and would willingly do whatever we wished him, and great was his pleasant astonishment when he learned that we did not indulge in such barbarous luxuries.

Their account of the discovery of the coal was, that it had been found accidentally by some hunters, and that after the king had received specimens, he ordered it to be worked. The first mine we visited is distant about 5 miles in a straight line from the river, and is known as that of Lek-ope-bin. The bed of coal crops out on the surface, in the hollow of one of the long undulations which characterise this part of the country. The thickness of the bed, including all that may be called coal, is 6 feet, and the dip is south-west at an angle of about 35°.

The next mine we visited was the Ket-zu-bin, a little to the north-east of Lek-ope-bin, on the banks of a small stream. It is said to yield the best coal, and has been quarried in three places at short intervals. Two of the openings, however, were flooded, and the other had only recently been commenced. In going to it we passed over a series of sandstones and interbedded greenstones lying evidently between it and the Lek-ope-bin bed. These rocks are exposed in the channel of the stream already referred to, and the one first met with is a greenstone overlying two beds of sandstone of different consistence, and apparently in contact with the Ket-zu-bin coal, below which there is another greenstone bed exposed in another water-course. I examined the sedimentary strata very carefully for organic remains, but could detect only some very faint impressions of plants. Both beds of coal are covered by a layer of bluish ferruginous clay with small calcareous nodules. The upper coaly layer resembles an indurated greyish clay, and I found that the lower aspect of the bed faded away into another of a similar kind.

Not more than half-a-dozen men were working at each pit, and as their only tools were a common wood-axe and a chisel with a wooden handle, it is not to be wondered at that they removed so little coal, and that it is always removed in small pieces. Under proper management, the mines might yield an abundance of useful fuel. They are only six miles from the river, and a very good road leads to them.

The sand in an adjoining stream is washed for gold, and I was informed that it yields about 203 yueys (3 shillings) a day to a single worker. The stream was a mere rivulet, but its channel and well-defined banks indicated that it is liable to heavy and sudden floods, which fall as rapidly as they rise.

While we were eating our lunch in a hut at the Ket-zu-bin, the Burmans proffered the somewhat novel request that they might be supplied with liquor to get intoxicated upon, and when I promised them a few bottles of beer, one of the mine officials, who had joined us at a village on our way, at once said he would return with the others for the debauch, but as each man received only one bottle, their longings after inebriety were not gratified. I mention this beer incident to show that *Bass* is approved by the Burmese palate. At Yenangyoung, on my way down the river, the provost sent one of his officials with a polite message to the effect that he had run out of his supply of beer, and would not receive any till the next steamer arrived, and requested that I would favour him with a dozen or so to meet his wants till then. He afterwards informed me that he drank beer regularly, and that the cause of having run short on this occasion was, that he had of late been entertaining a number of his friends.

But to return to Tseittha. We were under way early in the morning of the 16th, but after we had steamed for about half an hour, we had to lie to, on account of a dense fog, which cleared away, however, with the rising sun. Our course lay between the high wooded banks of the first defile which is very beautiful in some parts, and strongly recalled to me the lake scenery of Scotland. A few miles above Tseittha, we passed the Pon-nah creek, the exit of a small river of that name which I also visited on my return journey. On that occasion we ascended in our large boats for three-quarters of a mile, as there is abundance of back-water from the Irawady up to that point, where the Pon-nah discharges itself in a small cascade at the foot of high cliffs of greenstone. The banks of the creek are precipitous and about 60 feet high, and consist of greenstones and sandstones interbedded; nearly all the boulders in the stream itself are white crystalline marble, but I had not time to trace them to their source. The bed of the stream is chiefly black sand, which is constantly washed for gold during the dry weather by a few miserably poor Burmese, who have taken up their residence on the banks, and who informed me that it was found in much larger quantities at Shuaygyeen, two days' journey further up the stream. Silver is also said to be obtained from the white crystalline limestone, most probably disseminated in galenite.

After Pon-nah, the river runs nearly due south; and at 9 A.M., we reached the little rocky island of Theehadaw about 50 yards off the right bank, not more than 200 feet wide, and approached by a flight of steps. It boasts of the only stone pagoda in the whole of Burmah, and is a favourite resort of the Burmans, who flock to it from all quarters during their great feast in the month of March. The pagoda is of no great size, but is substantially built of a greyish sandstone, which crops out on the left bank a short way above the island, and which has been admirably cut and laid together with mortar. It is said to be of great age, but a Bhuddist priest, who is in charge of it, denied that it had been in existence for more than 50 years. It has a quadrangular base with a chamber on the side, facing the east, but closed with massive wooden doors. The three remaining sides have each a central false door corresponding to the one on the east; and the sides of all and the angles of the building are relieved with Doric-like pilasters. A ricketty wooden *zayát* is attached to the eastern side. But dividing the attention of the pious Buddhists who visit this island, are the remarkable tame fish that come to be fed, whenever they are called. We went provided with rice and plantains, and the boatmen who accompanied us immediately began calling *tit, tit, tit*. In a few seconds we noticed the fish disturbing the water about 50 yards from the island, and after reiterated cries of *tit, tit, tit*, they were alongside, greedily devouring the rice and plantains we were throwing to them. In their eagerness to be fed, they showed their uncouth heads, and even a great part of their backs, and, with their capacious mouths wide open, waited for the handfuls of food which they swallowed with great gusto. They were apparently very fond of plantains, and one I paid special attention to, kept devouring them as fast as I could pass them into his maw. I stroked them down over the head and back, and pulled their long feelers which they seemed to relish as much as a Burman likes shampooing. I put my clenched fist into their mouths and felt their teeth; but on reflection I desisted from this hazardous investigation, for if one had closed his mouth, I would certainly have had to follow him *nolens volens*, and it is difficult to say what treatment I might have experienced, what with their ravenous appetites and their palates fresh from the memory of plantains. After all my stock of provisions had been exhausted, I threw a plantain-skin to one wight who had apparently an insatiable stomach, but he indignantly rejected it, and showed his displeasure by a sudden departure. They are fed daily by the phoongyees, and in the great Buddhistic festival of March they collect in large numbers, as they are fed sumptuously every day by the devout who throng to the pagoda. The fishing for 3 miles above and below the island is carefully preserved, and the phoongyee informed me that the fish never wander more than 6 miles either way. I did all in my power to try and secure one, and offered Rs. 50 for a single specimen, but no one would engage to procure it, as there is a strict order from the king that they are not to be killed.

About 2 miles above the island, we came to the little village of Thingadaw, containing 20 houses, on the right bank; it is one of the depôts for the coal found 6 to 8 miles in the interior, and we stopped to replenish our supply of fuel. We landed after breakfast to visit a new mine which had been recently opened, and which, we were told, was only about 2 miles distant. After walking, however, for nearly two hours over a broken, undulating country, covered by a dense tree and bamboo jungle, and failing to discover it, and having no guide, we resolved to abandon the search. The soil is poor, pebbly, and sandy except in the low hollows which afford good grazing for the ponies and cattle. Fossilized wood is common all over the surface, and white and reddish sandstones crop out in many places, but they are so soft that the wheels of the coal carts cut them into deep ruts. The surface in many places where the sandstones are exposed, presented a very remarkable appearance. It was covered with perfectly symmetrical little solid pillars of sand, about one to two inches high, capped by a hard ashy-grey circular top of the consistence of stone, and of the size of a penny-piece. These little pillars were separated from each other by short intervals. They were composed, as a rule, of light, reddish brown, soft sand, and in cases where they had crumbled away, the surface was strewed with their little round grey coverings which, where numerous, had the appearance of an ash heap. I observed very few birds, and, indeed, I do not remember ever having walked so many miles, and seen so few of the feathery tribe. I found only one *Nectarinia*, a *Phylloscophus*, *Pycnontous*, two *Palæorni*, a *Copsychus*, and a *Dendrocitta*. In a dry water-course, some of our party saw what they took to be the footprints of a sambur, of a smaller deer, and those of a large cat.

We left Thingadaw on the following morning, 17th, at sunrise, and reached Malé on the same bank about 9 A.M. The defile does not extend to the north of this place, and its termination is marked by two prominent headlands, the one on the eastern side being crowned with the pagodas of the old Shan town of Tsampenago, and the western one by those of Malé, which contains about 300 houses, and is the custom-port for the examination of the boats proceeding from Bhamô to Mandalay, and the centre of a considerable trade in bamboo mats, sesamum, oil, and jaggery. Opposite to it, but at some considerable distance from the eastern bank, is the fine peaked mountain of Shuay-toung, about 6,000 feet high, and on which snow is said to lie in the winter months. Our object in calling at Malé was to procure grass for the ponies, and milk. We had sent two men the previous evening from Thingadaw to arrange with the headman for the supply of these articles, and with instructions that they were to be in readiness on our arrival. This, however, was not so, and the official came off and excused himself on the ground that milk was very scarce as the villagers had lost nearly all their cattle in the rebellion; but his explanation was not considered satisfactory, and he was sent back again to make another attempt. He returned in two hours empty-handed, which so excited the wrath of our Mandalay courtier that he ordered him to be flogged on the spot in the presence of his subordinates; a powerful Burman seized him by his top-knot, and threw him on the deck, and then dragged him along by the hair, twisting it round his arm in the most unmerciful way, in order to give him a greater purchase in the bull-dog-like shakes which he inflicted on the unhappy provost. This delicate piece of Burmese brutality accomplished, the unfortunate was ordered to his boat, and we went on our way.

Between Malé and Kyan-Nhyat, a distance of 12 miles, or nearly so, the river is very broad, and we passed several islands and sand-banks. Many apparently round-headed dolphins[1] were sporting in the deep channels between the islands, and they struck me as being the same species which I had observed so frequently near Prome. Like these cetacea, our steamer always followed the deep water, and we experienced little or no difficulty in detecting it, nor any, while in it. Kyan-Nhyat is a considerable

---

[1] Since my return to Calcutta, Captain Bowers has sent me from Bhamô a round-headed dolphin, a new species, which I have described in the Proc. Zool. Soc., 1871, as *Orcella fluminalis*.

village picturesquely situated on the extremity of a broad tongue of land on the eastern bank, running out into the river, and terminating as a low promontory, marked by a conspicuous white pagoda that shows its spire over a dense mass of fine trees, chiefly palmira palms and cocoa-nuts. Beyond Kyan-Nhyat, the main banks are again defined by high wooded hills on the west, and by low undulating land to the east covered by a dense forest, and the channel is about 1,000 yards broad, and entirely free from islands; the hills to the west obtain a maximum height of about 250 feet, and they are said to be covered with a forest which has a fair intersprinkling of teak. We steamed for 22 miles up from Kyan-Nhyat, the river retaining the character which it gains there, and anchored about sunset alongside Tsinuhat on the left bank, about 4 miles below Tagoung and old Pagan. Tsinuhat is a small village of about a dozen houses, situated on the south of a long promontory on the other side of which is Tagoung. Next morning, Williams and I walked across to Tagoung, a distance of 6 miles, where we had arranged to meet the steamer. There is a good track all the way through a dense forest, over level ground for the first 4 miles, but undulating land as we approached the river. There is little or no underwood, but thousands of seedling *Eng* trees, a few bamboos, and a tall grass, resembling the lemon grass in appearance. I observed only one small palm. The forest trees, however, were magnificent, of great height, and with enormous stems, forming a delightful shade against the tropical sun. The villagers informed me that wild elephants, two or three species of deer, and the buffalo, leopard, and tiger were common. In our walk, I saw only a few small birds.

The only indication I then noticed of Tagoung was a mass of brick-work buried under a dense mantle of jungle, said to be the wall of the ancient city. In returning, however, I had leisure to devote a few hours to exploring the sites of the two cities, Tagoung and old Pagan, and I will take the present opportunity to state what I observed. I was accompanied by Mr. Gordon, and a Burmese guide and eight men. Landing about one mile below the village of Tagoung, we first directed our enquiries to old Pagan, where there are still undoubted evidences of the old city wall, in a low rounded line of brick-work two or three feet high, skirting the river's bank. Beyond this point we had to cut our way with dâhs through a dense jungle, and after a fatiguing walk of a mile, in which our search was only rewarded by loose surface bricks, and a few obscure brick mounds overgrown with an impenetrable vegetation, we came upon a narrow forest path leading to Tagoung, and on our way along it, passed an old pagoda, the walls of which were entirely gone, with the exception of one behind a seated figure of Guadama, about 8 feet high; but the pagoda appears to be of no very great age. The path lay through and over large heaps of brick-work almost hidden in the soil, and as we neared old Tagoung, we again crossed what had been pointed out to me on my previous visit as the wall of that city, and which appears to be all that remains of it. Tagoung, according to the chronicles of the kings of Ava, was founded by Abhirája, one of the Thaki or Shakya race of kings, who reigned at Kappilawot, long before the appearance of Guadama, but who retired from Central India to Burmah with his troops and followers after the destruction by the king of Kauthala or Kosala (Oudh) of the three cities of Kauliya, Dewadaha, and Kappilawot, the seats of the Shakya line of kings. The city was first known as Thengat-tha-ratha and Thengat-tha-nago, and stood on the site of a previous city which had flourished in the times of the three preceding Buddhas. On the death of Abhirája, his two sons disputed the succession,[1] but agreed to decide the question in this way, that each should construct a large building on the same night, and he, whose building should be found completed by the morning, should take the throne. The younger son used only bamboos and planks which he covered over with cloth, and whitewashed, so as to give the whole the appearance of a finished building. The elder brother, seeing the other's completed, collected his troops and followers, and went down the Irawady, and ascended the Kyendwen to Kule, south of Munipur. From thence he sent his son, Moodootseitta, to be king of the country between Pegu, Arracan, and Pagan, and he himself built the city of Kyouk-padoung to the east of Guttshapa-nadee, and resided there for 24 years. Ultimately, however, he went and took possession of the city of Arracan (Dinia-wadee), and remained there permanently. Thus the younger brother succeeded his father at Tagoung, and was followed by thirty-three kings. In the reign of the last of these kings, Tagoung was attacked by the Chinese and Tartars,[2] and he was compelled to retire up the Malé river with as many of his people as he could collect, but on his death they were divided into three portions: one proceeded to the eastward, and established the nineteen Shan states; another proceeded down the Irawady and joined Moodootseitta, and the third remained on the Malé river with Nagazein, the widow of the exiled king.

---

[1] As. Soc. Journ., vol v, p. 160.
[2] It is much more likely the Shans were the aggressors.

It has always been the pride of all the kings of Burmah to trace back their progeniture to the Shakya or sun-descended race of Indian kings. After the appearance of Guadama, and the destruction, for the second time, of the three cities of the Shakya kings, one of their race, named Daza Yázá,[1] ultimately established himself at Malé, where he met Nagazein, and finding her to be a Shakya by birth, he married her, and founded the city of Upper Pagan.

Behind the village there were a number of old pagodas in tolerable preservation, but of recent origin, as compared with the ruins of Tagoung, which are said to date from before the Christian era.

I procured a number of small metallic images of Buddha from these pagodas; and impressions of Guadama as the preceding Buddha, Dipenkara, in relief, on a peculiar kind of brick, from the pagoda within the ruins of old Pagan. One of the latter is in every way an exact facsimile of the impression discovered by Captain Hannay in his visit. The pagoda, however, is evidently of no great antiquity, and quite distinct from the surrounding jungle-buried mounds of the ancient city; and it is, therefore, highly improbable that these impressions are of any greater age than the structure in which they are found, if so old. Each bears an inscription in Pali, begining *Ye dhammá*, in the old Devanagri character. The words and even the form of the letters are the same as those which occur on old Buddhistic images and inscriptions in India. Without venturing any opinion as to the probable age of these impressions, it must be borne in mind that the mere fact of their having an inscription in the old Devanagri character is not sufficient reason why we should consider them as very old. I am rather inclined to regard them merely as casts of an old established mould or die, which had been reproduced and handed down through many centuries, and from which fresh casts were being constantly struck off, and widely distributed over the country as articles of trade. From the circumstance that the countenances of the figures in these impressions differ from those in all modern Burmese images, and are nearly of the same character as those found at Saranath, Prinsep has suggested that they may have been made at Gaya for exportation, as is the custom to the present time.[2]

Passing through the little modern village of Tagoung, which does not number more than 30 or 40 houses, we found it almost deserted, and the majority of the inhabitants located in temporary huts on a long

---

[1] The *Yázá* of the Burmese is Raja.
[2] As. Soc. Journ. vol. (v.), p. 157.

sand-bank which had formed in front of it, where they were busily engaged preparing mashed, salted fish, or ngapé. The village stands on a low headland of reddish-yellow sandstone and coarse conglomerate, and is separated from the sand-bank by a deep, narrow channel, across which the fishing-stakes are thrown. Great numbers of fish are caught every morning, and sold by weight on the sand-bank, and immediately converted into ngapé. The entrails are removed by slitting the fish down the back, and the latter are then packed between layers of salt, and trodden down with the feet in long baskets lined with the leaf of the *Eng* tree. I bought fifteen species, and then hurried on board the steamer which was lying off the sand-bank.

The hills opposite Tagoung are very high, and wooded to their summits, and white pagodas occasionally peep out from the dense foliage on their sides. The eastern bank still preserves its undulating and almost hilly character, and about 6 miles to the north of the village, the isolated range of the Tagoung-toung-daw, about 20 miles long and 1,000 feet high, is now seen running almost parallel with the river. When opposite the southern extremity of this range, it is observed to be surrounded by an immense alluvial plateau expanding away to the east, to the base of a range of hills, evidently the northern continuation of the Shan mountains eastward of the capital, and stretching to the north as far as the eye can reach, where it is relieved by a low ridge which appears like an island on its level surface.

About 3 miles above Tagoung, the Shuay-mein-toung hills on the western side begin to recede from the river, and when we are on a line with the Tagoung hills, the two are separated from each other by an interval of about 6 miles, and the channel becomes broken up by large islands covered with long grass and forest trees. These islands are submerged during the rains, and in returning from Bhamô in the month of September, my boat, on a very dark night, was carried over one by the very strong current, to the great danger of our lives, and got fixed in a dense clump of trees and snags, from which we extricated ourselves with the greatest difficulty, and not until two of my boatmen had fallen overboard in their exertions to save their all. Gordon, who accompanied me in another boat, was carried away, at an opposite tangent, into a whirlpool in which he was kept revolving for nearly ten minutes.

Another mile up, the river takes a bend to the east for nearly 2 miles, and then resumes its northerly direction under low banks. The eastern channel, which we followed, turns one point to the south-of-east, running to nearly the base of the Tagoung range. It has an average breadth of 400 yards, and a depth of three fathoms. Dolphins were everywhere numerous, and in large shoals, that kept running at a respectful distance ahead of us.

Thirty minutes after leaving the Tagoung hills, I was greatly astonished to find the steamer again close below them, as it was impossible to have foreseen that the channel could have had such a serpentine course. The eastern and western channels are separated by the large island of Chowkyoung, and by a series of smaller ones to the north of it, and the channel we were navigating winds round their eastern sinuosities. On the western bank a low line of wooded hills rises opposite the former island, with a broad expanse of level land to the north, succeeded by another isolated range from 400 to 800 feet high, running in a north-north-easterly direction. The southern extremity of this range abuts on the western bank as a small rounded hill, on which the little town of Thigyain is situated, with the village of Myadoung almost opposite to it on the low alluvial land of the eastern side. We moored alongside of the former village at 5 P.M. on the 18th January. Dolphins were very numerous in the long clear reach running past those villages. The villages of Thigyain and Myadoung contain only about 50 houses each, and the headman of the former village informed me that each house in either village had received a royal order to supply 50 pieces of firewood to the steamer, and that they were to receive no recompense for so doing; and, moreover, that each house occupied by more than one person pays a tax to government of Rs. 5 a year, and those with a single inhabitant Rs. 2-8 per annum.

Myadoung gives name to the district to the south of Bhamô, and is included in the Woonship of the latter, and the first piece of intelligence that greeted us on our arrival at Thigyain was that the Woon of Bhamô had been lately murdered at Momeit, a Shan town of some importance, 36 miles south-east from Myadoung, and which had been recently placed under his governorship. Momeit derives its importance from two circumstances, its close proximity to the richest ruby mines in Upper Burmah, and to the Shuaylee valley, along which a petty trade finds its way to and from China. Up to a few months before the unfortunate event, it had always been under the government of its own chiefs, but had then been placed under the Bhamô Woon, who was appointed to collect the revenues, and remit them to Mandalay. The Shans and neighbouring Kakhyens united to oppose this innovation of their ancient rights, and the Bhamô governor proceeded to Momeit with an armed force of 300 men to enforce the royal edict. He was surrounded by the insurgents, and lost his life in an attempt to retreat, and many of his brave band perished in the enterprise.

On the 19th January, a thick fog, before and after sunrise, delayed us till 10 A.M. After leaving Thigyain the river is broken up by a number of large islands covered with trees, and nearly all inhabited. Between Thigyain and Katha, the next town we stopped at, a range of hills runs at some little distance from the western bank, the intervening ground being undulating, and terminating at the river in low rocky banks. On the eastern side, the long expanse of country visible is unrelieved by any hills, except a small range that is seen rising to the east-north-east of Katha.

We moored alongside Katha at 4-30 P.M. It is decidedly the largest town after Shienpagah, and the houses cannot be under 200. It is situated on a gently rising low slope on the western bank, and in the distance it much resembles Malé. The range of hills behind it is about 8 miles off, and it is separated from it by long hollows of rich alluvium, closed in by undulating land covered by a dense jungle of valuable forest trees, in which the teak occupies a prominent place. The hollows are all under paddy cultivation, and a little cotton is also grown, and tobacco is largely raised on the islands and sand-banks. The women were busily employed in weaving and preparing the coloured cotton yarns that they obtain from China for the manufacture of putzos and tameins. A number of Shan merchants had recently arrived with their commodities, consisting principally of salted tea-leaves or hlepé. A few Yunanese-Chinese were also in the town selling their merchandise, along with some of their countrymen from Mandalay.

Katha is a long town of two streets running parallel to each other, and the houses are well built of timber, and have a very comfortable appearance. The people, too, were well clad, and evidently in good circumstances. It is surrounded by a bamboo fence, with three gates, which are closed at night. It is the head-quarters of the Woon of a considerable district which takes its name from the town, and whose population is almost exclusively Shan-Burmese.

On my return from Bhamô we stopped for a few hours at Katha, and Gordon, who was with me, and who had been very civilly treated by the Woon on his way up, sent a messenger to announce our arrival, and to thank him for his past kindness. Two men returned with a polite message that the governor would have come down himself, and seen us in our boats if we had had sufficient accommodation, and requested that we would go up and visit him at his house. Gordon went first, but he had not been long gone when a note came from him, saying that the Woon was most anxious to see me, as he was always glad to meet Englishmen, and requesting that I would go. On arriving, I found Gordon seated beside him on a cushion, in an open room, with a verandah in front, in which the town officials knelt at a respectful distance. He is a stout, good-natured, old man, and very politely held out his hand to me as I entered. He seated me on another cushion by his side; and a large metal basin of water, with a gold cup floating in it, was placed before me. The room contained an eight-day English clock, and a few guns and muskets, but no furniture of any kind.

We talked about Bhamô and its Woon, and our friend expressed a strong desire to get that Woonship, and I believe from his marked partiality for Englishmen, as evinced from the hearty welcome he gave us, and the circumstance that his son holds an appointment under our own government at Tongoo, that he would be a good man for the position; and in the event of an English agent being appointed to Bhamô, that he would work well with that official. He informed us that his brother-in-law had been one of the Tsikkays at Bhamô who had been removed and imprisoned at Mandalay on account of their opposition to the mission. His relative, however, had now been set at liberty, and he attributed his release to Gordon's having stated in his diary, a copy of which he had sent to the Chief Commissioner, the substance of their conversation on Gordon's upward journey. How far this had anything to do with the liberation of the offending Tsikkay, I am not in a position to say. On our return to our boats, we were accompanied by a handsome present of rice, ngapé, fish, oil, and vegetables.

20th January 1868—Minimum temperature, 48°5′.—A thick fog set in an hour before sunrise, and delayed our departure until 10 A.M. From day-break, however, till we got under weigh, the steamer had been visited by an eager crowd of men, women, and children who had flocked in from all quarters to see it. We thought of some means to amuse and interest them, and selected a magnetic battery for the purpose with decided success. At first we had some difficulty in finding any one who would try it, but we at last succeeded, and were speedily besieged by applicants of both sexes and all ages, and the grimaces and blank astonishment of those operated upon, elicited roars of laughter from the bystanders. Some stalwart Shans pronounced it very good for the flesh, and coaxed their more timid partners-in-life to a trial, while pretty, modest, young girls who held back, were led forward by the matrons that they might have their share of the physical benefits we were so ungrudgingly distributing. The hearty good nature and frankness of these people were most refreshing, by reason of their strong contrast to the splenetic temperament of the Bengalee.

Above Katha, the river is broken up into a number of channels, and the islands are large, and support many fishing villages; the channels are very tortuous, deep, and narrow, and a favourite resort of roundheaded dolphins. The hills on the west are far from the banks, and separated from them by a broad belt of level country, and to the east an extensive plain stretches to the base of the Shan mountains in the distance. A range of hills is seen right ahead, rising from the plain which spreads away in this direction.

The level land continues as far north as Shuay-goo-myo, which is situated on the southern outskirts of these hills, and alongside of which we moored at 6 P.M. A short way below the town, large flocks of geese kept passing us for nearly an hour, and the sand-banks and shores of the islands were covered with varieties of wild duck, principally *Anas pœcilorhyncha*, *Carsaca rutila*, and *Spatula clypeata*. We passed one enormous flock of *Plotus melanogaster*, which could not have contained less than 500 birds; and a few *Milvus govinda* and *Haliaster indus* were foraging for food in the neighbourhood of the fishing-stakes and villages. As evening closed in, immense flocks of *Herodias garzetta* were seen roosting in the tall grass, and on the high trees, which were lit up like candelebra by their white forms.

21st January.—The minimum temperature this morning was 44°55′; and, as usual, a thick fog delayed us for some hours. We accordingly went ashore, and found the trees dripping with moisture as after a heavy rain. I made at once for the jungle, and on my way passed through a neat little village, shaded by tall trees and feathery bamboos, crossing in my walk a number of small water-courses spanned by substantial teak bridges. Beyond this village I encountered another, but did not enter it, as a man came running out to meet me, and implored me to go another way, as his wife had been confined during the night, and alleging, as a reason why I should do so, that if she heard the report of my gun, she would be almost certain to die. To quiet him and allay his fears, for he was in a very excited state, and evidently firmly believed what he said, I turned to the right through a long swampy flat, into a dense forest of high trees, with an impenetrable undergrowth of bamboo and ratans, and a rich display of orchids and ferns, the first that, I may say, I have as yet seen in Burmah. Wading in mud in a narrow path for nearly a mile through the dense shade of this magnificent forest, I came upon an irregular open flat, covered with young rice plants about six inches high, the first crop of the year, half-covered with water. I went expressly after pea-fowl, but found none, although the air occasionally resounded with their loud, continued cry.

We got under steam at 10 A.M., and the whole village turned out to see us depart, and a number of buxom young women and many boys tried to keep up with us by racing along the side of the river below the high alluvial banks. We at first thought they were attracted simply by the novelty of the steamer, but found afterwards that they were taking advantage of its presence, on their way back to their villages, as a protection against the kidnapping Kakhyens who were in the neighbourhood; and we were further told that it was always the custom of the phoongyee boys, who go from village to village every morning to collect the food for their priests, to creep along under the shelter of the high banks for the same reason.

The mention of Kakhyens reminds me that Sladen and Williams passed through a number of villages at Shuay-goo-myo deserted on account of these hill-men. A Burmese pointed out to them a village which the Kakhyens had lately taken, but as they neared it, their informant got between them for protection, and, stopping short, pointed to a house in which he said some of them were. My friends went up to it, and the Kakhyens, who were quietly seated, started up in mute astonishment at the sight of the two white-faced strangers. Sladen described them as very treacherous-looking, and as having a strong resemblance to the eastern Karens. They were furnished with fine long dâhs, which were manufactured for them by some Shans resident at Shuay-goo-myo. They were invited to come and see the steamer, but, after accompanying my friends a short way, they seemed to think better of their resolution, and begged to be excused, as they said they had to return to a meeting of their chiefs on their native hills. Their real reason, I believe, was a dread of being seized by their inveterate enemies, the Burmese officials.

Last night, a boy, about ten years of age, who had been sold for Rs. 25 by a Kakhyen to the head official, was brought on board. He was evidently of Chinese extraction, and had been kidnapped beyond the mountains, to the east of the Irawady. Nearly opposite Shuay-goo-myo is the large island of Shuaybaw, with its 1,000 pagodas, whose bright golden *tees*, peering over the deep, rich, green foliage, have a picturesque effect. The great centre of attraction round which all are gathered is an ancient gold-gilt pagoda about 60 feet high. A richly carved zayât of teak, with a most elaborately decorated roof, and cornice of small niches, with seated marble figures of Buddha, encloses it on two sides. The pagoda is distant about three-quarters of a mile from the river, and is approached by broad paved ways, enclosed by low balustraded walls. One is known as the Bhamô, and the other as the Shuay-goo-myo entrance. Numerous zayâts cluster round the magnet, piled to the ceiling with Buddhistic figures in metal, wood, and white marble, the offerings of the throng of worshippers who yearly frequent this holy spot, where Buddha left his sacred footprint. The great festival occurring in March, when the river is low and the long sand-banks are exposed, a town springs up on them for the time, and general feasting is the order of the day.

About 3 miles above Shuay-goo-myo, the river runs through the hills we sighted yesterday, and which overhang it for about five miles, and the grandeur of some of the precipices surpasses anything that my pen can describe. Their summits generally are covered with scanty, somewhat stunted trees, but further down, their bold sides are wrapped in a splendid mantle of dark green forest, picked out here and there with the fresh verdure of festooned clumps of bamboo, a few palms, and luxuriant musæ. Little fishing villages, walled with bamboo fences, lie snugly in the hollows between the different hills. The first point we rounded was a many-peaked hill to our right, that rises precipitously over the deep green river to a height of 400 feet, its outline broken by huge black rocks that stand out in bold relief against the clear blue sky. A little white pagoda, Yethaycoo, stands at the entrance of a shallow cave, overlooking a precipice of grey limestone about 150 feet high, and we wondered who the enthusiasts were who had risked their lives up the giddy height to build it.

Nearly opposite to this, on our left, a huge wall of grey limestone rises from the river to a height of 800 feet, with a flat summit sparsely covered with stunted trees, and its sides worn into rounded hollows by the river, and curiously marked, yellow and white, by veins of carbonate of lime. Another little pagoda, that of Sessoungan, is perched on a detached pyramid of limestone at the foot of the giant wall, embowered in fine trees that cling to the sides of its rocky foundation, and hide another little temple behind the rocks. The first is reached by a long bamboo ladder which is repaired once a year at the great festival in March, when many devotees resort to this shrine. Here, instead of having tame fish to feed, as at Theehadaw, at the bye-hours of his devotions, the pious Buddhist amuses himself by calling round him a large band of red-faced monkeys, who have a colony at the foot of the great precipice, attracted doubtless by the good things that fall to their lot during the yearly feast, and at all times from passing boats.[1]

At the next angle of the river, beyond the huge cliffs, we passed another pagoda with a handsome, many-roofed, tapering zayât by its side, embowered in trees on the summit of the precipitous hills to the left; and about one mile further on, we left this noble gorge, and the river again flowed between low banks with a stretch of comparatively level land on both sides, defined to the west and north by low rolling hills, and to the east by the Kakhyen mountains.

It is very difficult to judge of the actual breadth of the defile, as the hills are so high and close to the river, that they make it appear to be much narrower than it really is. I believe, however, that in no place will it be found to be under 300 yards. There are no rocks to impede its course, which is slow and placid compared with many of the channels in the open country below. This is the case also during the rains, and judging from what I observed in September, a steamer would not experience very much difference between the strength of the current then, and in the dry weather. I had no means to take the depth, but its general appearance indicated that it must be considerable.[2]

The rocks are chiefly greenstone and limestone, heading to the east-north-east, and dipping to the west at an angle of 65° in the localities examined. Large limestone cliffs of a similar character occur near Moulmein. A good deal of lime is prepared by the villagers.

Leaving the defile, we soon passed the old mart of Kaungtoung, so noted in the commercial history of Upper Burmah as one of the principal emporiums of trade with Western China, and distinguished for its able defence against the Chinese in 1767. We did not stop to visit the place, but in 1835 Hannay estimated the houses at 200, and describes it as being surrounded by a ditch, and mentions the remains of a brick redoubt, loopholed for armour or musketry, enclosing a pagoda. The village is encircled by a bamboo palisade, as has been the case with all the villages we have passed since leaving Shuay-goo-myo, intended as a protection against the attacks of the Kakhyens. It commands the Mowun or Muangwan route, and the valley of the Shuaylee. Above Kaung-

---

[1] This monkey belongs to the genus *Macacus*, and has a very strong resemblance to *M. rhesus* of India, but it is larger, and has more hair about its neck and chin.

[2] At present, no accurate data exist for a comparison of the volume of the Irawady, above its junction with the Kyendwen, and the Ganges and Brahmaputra at corresponding distances from the sea and above their principal affluents, and it is to be hoped that the Assistant Resident at Bhamô may find an opportunity to give an accurate section of the river below the first defile, above Bhamô.

toung, the river covers a very wide, sandy bed broken up by numerous islands and sand-banks, and in many places it is one mile and a half in breadth.

On a long stretch of sand some miles above Kaungtoung, and in front of the village of Sawaddy, there was a large encampment of Shan, Chinese, and Kakhyen traders, and many boats were lying alongside the bank to receive the goods destined for the capital, and intermediate marts like Katha.

Here we sighted Bhamô in the distance, situated on an elevated bank overlooking the river, the *tees* of its few pagodas glittering brightly in the setting sun. About 15 miles to the right of the town, looking up the river, the high range of the Kakhyen hills is seen stretching away to the east-north-east in an unbroken line; and to the west a low range of undulating hills, thickly clad with trees, bends round to the south to join those which form the western side of the defile. An almost level country, about 25 miles broad and covered by a dense forest, intervenes between these two ranges, and about 10 miles to the north, it is closed in by a low wooded range, the beginning of the first defile of the Irawady. The channels below Bhamô are numerous and generally deep, but we experienced some little difficulty in finding one adapted to the steamer, a long vessel which does not answer its helm as it ought. The delay was certainly much less than I experienced on more than one occasion in some parts of the river between Thayetmyo and Mandalay in a steamer of less size. The channel in front of Bhamô is broad and very deep under the bank, alongside of which we moored on the 22nd January, at 5 P.M., about the middle of the river frontage of the town. Our arrival created a great sensation, that was heightened by the shrill sound of the engine whistle, and by the rush of steam that announced it, and which I am led to think almost frightened some of the fair sex into the belief that discretion is the better part of inquisitiveness, for many of them made a precipitate retreat when the unwonted sounds burst upon their ears.

CHAPTER X.

RESIDENCE AT BHAMÔ.

BHAMÔ, situated in latitude 24°16′ north, longitude 96°53′47″ east,[1] on a high prominence on the left bank of the Irawady, about two miles below the mouth of the Tapeng river, is a narrow town one mile in length. It widens towards its middle, and is enclosed by a stockade about nine feet high, consisting of the halves of trees, six to eight inches in diameter, driven side by side into the ground, and strengthened above and below by cross beams. It is guarded outside by a forest of bamboo stakes about one foot long, fixed in the soil and projecting forwards at an acute angle, and unfortunate is he who runs unconsciously against these pricks. There are four gates, one at either end, and two on the eastern side, and all are closed immediately after sunset. A guard is stationed at each of the two extreme ones; and four or five outlooks in the form of thatched huts, perched at intervals on the top of the stockade, are called into requisition when an attack is expected from the dreaded Kakhyens. It contains about 500 houses, and allowing five persons to each, the population may be estimated at 2,500 persons, and it may be referred to two portions, one Chinese and the other Shan. The former quarter is in the middle of the town, and the houses number about 50 or 60. There are three principal streets, one running parallel to the river, the whole length of the town, another half a mile inwards from the two extremes of its middle third, and the last, starting from the centre of the latter, terminates at the most eastern gate. The majority of the houses lie along these three ways, but there are many other thickly wooded by-paths leading to scattered houses, dilapidated pagodas, zayâts, and monasteries. The street, following the course of the river bank, has a row of houses on either side of it, and is laid in its centre with a line of teak planks to afford a dry footing during the rains. The houses are all small one-storied cottages, in a continuous line, built of sun-dried bricks, with grey tiles of the same material, on concave roofs with deep projecting eaves. Those next the river have verandahs overlooking it, supported on high piles; and the street is approached from

---

[1] I am indebted to Captain Bowers for the position of Bhamô.

the river at intervals by high flights of steps; for the top of the steep bank, even in the height of the rains, is much above the river. The shops, as a rule, have a door and an open window facing the street, with a small counter inside, behind which the owner is usually seen smoking his long pipe. Manchester goods, long-cloth, Chinese yarns, ball tea, opium, spices, preserved oranges, jujubes, walnuts, chestnuts, raisins, apples, potatoes, beans, water-melon seeds, betel-nut, salt, flint, gypsum, yellow orpiment, vermilion from Talifoo, copper wire, lead, bees-wax, coarse sugar, sugar-candy, twine, catgut, and many articles of less importance are offered for sale by the enterprising Chinese who also regulate the cotton market of Bhamô. I was informed by a Shan that the cotton which is grown by the Kakhyens and Shans above the first defile, and brought to Bhamô during the rains, along with oil-seed (sesamum) and a kind of pitch, is more highly prized than that grown south of the town. Nearly all the cotton finds its way to the Shan states to the east and to the country beyond them, and the traffic in this valuable product is carried on even in the height of the rains, as is evinced by the fact that we passed a number of mule-loads on our return journey towards the end of July.

The Chinese have a neat little temple and theatre in one, consisting of an outer and an inner court terminating in the temple itself, which contains another court, their holy of holies. The entrance to the first was through what was a novelty to us, a circular doorway. The court is paved throughout, and lies at a lower level than the one immediately above it, which appears to be the orthodox fashion adopted in Chinese temples. The theatrical stage is over the entrance to the second court, and faces the religious part of the building, which, in its turn, is raised above the court immediately below it. The court of the sanctuary has a covered terrace round its three sides with recesses off two of them, containing seated figures nearly life-size, with rubicund, almost fiery faces, having black beards and moustaches of formidable cut and dimensions. They are all, in accordance with a Chinaman's just appreciation of the value of rupees, carefully protected from dust and injury by being placed in square boxes, which I ought to dignify with the name of shrines, closed in front with almost opaque, gauze netting. A few priests live in a court-yard at the side of the building which is built entirely of brick, and after the Chinese grotesque idea of architectural beauty. The head Chinaman is a person of considerable influence, not only among his own fellow-countrymen at Bhamô, but also with the Chinese between that town and Momien, and among the Burmese officials at Bhamô itself. He is the responsible head of the colony of his countrymen, and is appointed by the Burmese authorities to preserve order and settle disputes.

During the first fortnight of our sojourn, this man and the other leading Chinese evinced a deep interest in all our movements and in the objects of the Expedition, and used every argument in their power to dissuade us against attempting to enter China; and when we tried to reason them into the belief that we might possibly succeed, we were told that what princes had failed to accomplish, it was folly on our part to attempt. Under all this show of interest there was a strong current of vigorous opposition, and to hide it they professed great friendship, and even invited us to the theatricals in their temple, during which they feasted us in grand style on a variety of preserved fruits and delicious biscuits known only to celestials, on samshu and tea, followed by the inevitable pork, and samshu varied with tea, rice and pork, the changes again rung on pork, tea, samshu, and fowls. Failing to influence us through such media, and finding that we were still determined to go forward, they at once threw off the mask of friendship, and took active steps to prevent us accomplishing the end we had in view. We anticipated the opposition of the Chinese from the very first day we set foot in Bhamô, so were not at all surprised at its assuming the form which it did, when they found that they could not cajole us into a quiet abandonment of the mission. When we reflect that the monopoly of the trade has been held by them for centuries, and that they are far-sighted enough to perceive that if the market there, and in the country to the east, were thrown open, they would certainly be undersold by the wealthy merchants of Rangoon, and that their high profits would be irretrievably lost, we need not wonder at their raising the cry that their craft was in danger, and at their uniting to a man to ward off the impending change. Only one course now remained to them by which they could ruin our enterprise, and they unhesitatingly resorted to it. A Chinaman, named Leesetai, who had formerly held an important official position under the empire, before the Mahomedan rebellion in Yunan, and who still maintains his allegiance, had established himself as an independent chief along the line of march the mission was to traverse on its way to Momien. To this man, the Chinese, whenever they became aware of our unalterable resolve to go forward, addressed letters, imploring him on no account to allow us to proceed beyond his fortress, and to attack our party. I am not disposed to regard this as a very unjustifiable proceeding on their part, when we remember the deep stake they had in our failure, and also that we had an armed party of men with us, which doubtless led them to believe that we had come prepared to meet with opposition. The success which attended this endeavour of theirs to thwart our progress will appear as I proceed with this narrative.

The Chinese are, as a rule, unmarried, but a few have taken Shan wives. Their numbers are not great, and I should think that 200 would embrace more than the population.

The remainder of the inhabitants is exclusively Shan-Burmese, and the houses are all detached and built on low piles as is the custom universally over Burmah; the majority are very small, and not nearly so comfortable-looking or so well built as those at Katha. The Woon's house, which stands on a low promontory overlooking a swamp that runs through the centre of the town, behind the Chinese quarter, is enclosed by a high palisade covered with bamboo mats, an honour to which only princes are entitled, or officials occupying the position of governors of provinces. The house is a large, tumble-down, timber and bamboo structure, on high piles, with a double roof, which is another sign of rank. It is surrounded by a small plot of ground, in which I detected the remains of an old fish tank and rockery; but all such tastes have long since ceased to manifest themselves here, as well as in the dilapidated town, in which all the public works of former and later times have been allowed to fall into ruin and decay. A neglected brass cannon, mounted on a wooden carriage, stands on either side of the principal entrance under a low thatched roof, in keeping with the thorough disrepair of the big house inside. There is a large open space to the south of the Woon's residence on which the court-house stands. This building is a square wooden platform on piles, covered in by a high double roof. It is open all round, and the officials assemble in it every day for business, of which quiet repose seems to form an integral part, for I usually found them either reclining at full length on their sides, or squatted in circles, discussing the merits of pawn, betel-nut, and cheroots.

The inhabitants attribute the decay of the public buildings to the oft-repeated raids of the Kakhyens, to destructive fires, to the misrule and oppression of the governors and their officials, and to the decline of trade from the unsettled condition of the country to the east, ever since the Panthays raised the standard of rebellion. Evidence is not wanting in its numerous neglected pagodas and timber bridges, and in the shaky and, in some instances, charred remains of what must have been handsome zayâts, that Bhamô, in former days, must have been a place of considerable importance. Every Shan-Burmese house, as a rule, owns a loom, which is generally placed on the covered platform or front verandah. The time of the women is chiefly employed in weaving either silk or cotton putzos and tameins, in preparing and dyeing yarns, husking rice, tending the buffaloes before they go out in the morning to feed, caring for them on their return in the evening, and attending generally to the affairs of the household. The girls are taught to handle the loom at an early age, and are most useful helpmates to their industrious mothers. The men till the fields and attend to the crops, but are not nearly so industrious as the opposite sex. A few are employed in smelting lead, and others are goldsmiths, who prepare gold necklaces, chains and cups, and a few are the smelters of the silver used as the currency of the country. This last process is conducted as follows: six tickals of tolerably pure silver purchased from the Kakhyens who procure it from the Chinese are weighed out, and one tickal, eight annas, of copper-wire are added, and the two metals are melted together, the smelter adding a sufficient quantity of lead to bring the whole up to the weight of ten tickals. The addition of the lead is made entirely irrespective of scales, the operator trusting solely to his experience as a guide to the right quantity. The operation is conducted in little saucers of sun-dried clay which are placed in a bedding of paddy husk to make them lie evenly, and charcoal is heaped up over them, in hollow pyramids, which, being ignited, the bellows are vigorously applied, and as soon as the metals fuse, little pieces of lead are put in, according to the judgment of the smelter. When the mass is at a red heat, the charcoal is removed, and if a piece of wood, which is now held over the amalgam, freely ignites, a round, flat, brick button, about the size of a five-shilling piece, on which a smooth layer of moist clay has been spread, is then laid on the surface of the mass, two men previously blowing upon it through bamboo tubes. The brick disc does not cover the whole of the amalgam, and the surplus metal round the edge forms a thick ring round the centre, and lead is freely added to the ring to bring the mass up to the proper size and weight. As it solidifies, we have a white disc of silver surrounded by a thick dark brownish ring containing metal of the same purity as that of the disc, but covered with a coating of refuse and lead. The mass is then removed from the saucer before it is perfectly hard, and the brick disc falls off leaving the coating of moist clay adhering to the silver, which is then cleaned, and a number of round spots are dotted with cutch on the face of the amalgam. This, I was informed, was to make the mass look pretty. It is then weighed and ready for being cut up. The saucers in which the metal is melted are sold at Rs. 80 per 1,000 to the lead-smelters, who extract any silver and lead that may remain, and the refuse of this smelting is sold to the potters, who use it as a glaze for tiles. I have been also informed that it is employed as an enamel for silver ornaments. There are a good many Burmese shops scattered throughout the town that sell rice, various kinds of dried peas and beans, and different spices, also betel-nut and lime. A small fish and vegetable market is held every morning in the middle of the street in the Chinese quarter, but it is a miserable affair, consisting only of a few women who squat down before their baskets, each provided with weights and scales to weigh the silver, the produce of their custom. Among the other occupations of the women, it may be mentioned that they make capital chatties from a tenacious yellowish-grey clay which is found all over this portion of the Irawady valley, and that attains in some places a thickness of 40 feet. They are generally coloured red by an earthy ferruginous substance found imbedded in the clay in the form of nodules.

Outside the town, a number of Shan-Chinese, from the valleys of Hotha and Latha, manufacture excellent sun-dried bricks from the same clay. Another temporary colony of these people within the stockade make a large number of dâhs, and so industrious are they, and so great is the demand for these formidable weapons, that their anvils are heard going late in the night. These Shans visit Bhamô for only a few months in the year, arriving about October, and leaving again in March, when they return to their own homes to attend to their crops. In some cases their eyes are very oblique, and the majority present this Chinese feature in a marked degree. Their complexion, although fair, has a sallow hue, and their eyes are black. Their language is quite distinct from Burmese, and is a peculiar dialect of Shan with a strong intermixture of Chinese. They dress in blue jackets and with trousers which reach to the knee, and wear enormous blue turbans, and their bare shins are bound with long bands of blue cloth. They smoke metal tobacco pipes of the same form as those from Tibet and Eastern China. A number of Kakhyens are always to be seen in Bhamô. They come down from their hills, which are about 10 miles off, bringing rice, silver, pigs, goats, and opium. The goods are carried on ponies, mules, and oxen, and the pigs in baskets on the backs of the men, and when they encamp, they are tied up with pieces of wood on either side of the animal's neck behind the jaws, fastened by a cord above and below. They take back salt, dried fish, and ngapé, and occasionally a little grey shirting and red cloth; but their chief object in visiting the place is to procure salt. They are not permitted to encamp within the town, but are allowed to do so close to three of the gates. Their only shelter is a few branches of trees fixed in the ground and meeting in a cone. This primitive tent is covered with small twigs, and serves as a hut in which they cook during the day and sleep at night. While in camp they live on rice, pork, fish, and some roots. They have bamboo hookahs in which they smoke plantain leaves soaked in opium. The leaf is cut up into very fine shreds and dried at the side of the fire, and a little opium, dissolved into a thickish paste, is heated in a copper spoon, and the little pellet of plantain leaves is made to take it up. The pipe somewhat resembles the one in common use in India. One reason why they are excluded from the town is, that the Shan-Burmese have a thorough dread of their weakness for kidnapping children, and even men; and also because, as they assert, they can never be certain that a band may not be the precursors of a raid. On reaching Bhamô, we were told, but with what degree of truth it is doubtful to say, that 600 Kakhyens had collected about 10 miles off meditating an attack on the town, but that they dispersed whenever they heard of our arrival. After I had been only a few days in Bhamô, I saw four children who had been stolen by the Kakhyens and recovered, and one was brought to me by her mother with large round holes in the back of her ears bored by her captors, after the fashion in vogue among Kakhyen beauties, but one which does not meet with the approval of Burmese belles. I was fortunately able to remove the deformity, and was immediately installed to a high place in the esteem of the fair ones of Bhamô. The three others, all little, fat-faced, oblique-eyed Chinese girls of seven and eight years of age, were in the possession of the head Tsikkay, and as much cared for by him as if they had been his own daughters, whose place they supplied, as he was childless. One, a nice, lively, little girl of about seven, could not speak a word of Burmese. In connection with Kakhyen man-stealing, the following illustration came under my own observation. My Burmese interpreter informed me one day that he had met, outside the stockade, among a number of Kakhyens, a man who had told him privately that he was a *Kala* or foreigner who had been ten years in slavery among those wild hill people, and that having heard of our arrival, he wished to see some of us. I went by appointment to meet him, and immediately recognising in his features that he was a native of India, spoke to him in Hindoostanee, and finding that he could speak a few broken sentences of the language, I desired him to come to our residence. He appeared the following day, and gave me his history in a jumble of Kakhyen, Hindoostanee, and Burmese. Deen Mahomed, a petty trader, and a native of the zillah of Midnapore, went to Burmah about ten years ago along with nine of his countrymen, attracted by the glowing accounts he had heard of the money that was to be made by the sale of piece-goods and muslins. They first made their way up as far as Tongoo, on the frontier, where they were delayed for a year by severe sickness and the death of some of their number. From thence the survivors proceeded through Upper Burmah, first to the capital and then as far as Bhamô. One day, while in the neighbourhood of the latter town, they halted in the morning by the roadside to cook their food, and all had gone into the jungle to collect firewood, except Deen Mahomed and another man, who were in charge of the property. These two were suddenly attacked by a gang of Kakhyens, and made prisoners along with all their goods. The Kakhyens divided the booty, and one party retired with Deen Mahomed, while the other carried away the remaining captive. A log of wood was fastened to one of his legs above the ankle, and he was further secured by two ropes tied to the end of it, and passed over his shoulders. He was compelled to wear this for two months, but during that time he was not required to work, and a Kakhyen was placed over him as a guard. At the expiry of this period, he was asked if he were willing to remain, and on his promising not to attempt to escape, the log was removed. A few days after this, the village was attacked and plundered by some hostile Kakhyens, but he escaped along with his master, who fled to another village where he settled. Here he was exchanged to another Kakhyen for a buffalo. His new master treated him well, and after two or three years gave him a Kakhyen woman in marriage, by whom he has had three children, the eldest now about seven years old. The only restriction he was subjected to at first was, that he was not permitted to leave the hills, but in time that was remitted, and he was regularly in the habit of visiting Bhamô, but always in the company of other Kakhyens. Whenever he heard that the *Kalas* had arrived, he resolved to effect his escape. He had almost entirely forgotten his language, and only knew that he must have been about ten years in slavery, by the fact that his eldest daughter is about seven, and that he was not married for the first two or three years of his captivity. After communicating with Sladen, I promised him protection, and sent him among his fellow-countrymen in our guard, who acted the good Samaritan, and clothed him in decent raiment. We resolved to take him along with us, as he might prove useful as an interpreter, after he recovered the command of his native tongue. He was a man of extreme simplicity, and, as far as I could judge, had nothing of the rogue about him. After a few days, he was installed as Captain

Bowers' syce, which he continued to be till the return of the Expedition, when I brought him to Calcutta, and sent him to Midnapore.

The country behind Bhamô runs up to the base of the Kakhyen hills in a series of undulations so long that the general appearance is as if it were nearly a level slope. What I visited was covered almost exclusively with moderately sized *Eng* trees, with an undergrowth of tall, rather delicate grass. The forest has been cut down in the immediate neighbourhood of the town, and its place taken by a dense matted jungle of shrubs and grass. For about a mile outside the stockade, the surface is cut up by numerous deep jheels, evidently old offshoots of the Irawady, which once flowed in a long curve to the south-east of the town, as is evinced by an old river-bank, and by a broad expanse of low level land between it and the present channel. Bhamô has a kind of suburb in a few villages along the river-side beyond the north and south gates; one of these to the north is inhabited by the descendants of a number of Assamese who were brought over to Burmah about fifty years ago, on the occasion of the marriage of the king of Assam's daughter to the then reigning king of Ava. A few have intermarried with the Burmese, but the majority of their alliances are made among themselves. I at once detected that these people were not Burmese, although they have adopted their dress and language, and what led me to do so was their less pronounced Mongolian features, and the difference in the colour of the skin. The shape of the face, although to a certain extent Mongolian, has a strong affinity to the ordinary form met with in Eastern Bengal, and my first impression was that they were exclusively of Indian origin, but this was chiefly due to the strength of the contrast, when they were compared with the pronounced Mongolian features of the Shan-Burmese.

About one mile and a half to the north of Bhamô, I came unexpectedly in my wanderings in the jungle, in search of animal life and plants, upon the ruins of an ancient city, which, I was afterwards informed by the chief phoongyee of Bhamô, were those of the old town of Tsampenago, the capital of a once powerful Shan Tsawbwaship. They are buried under splendid trees and in dense thickets of bamboo and long elephant grass, which made it extremely difficult to gain any accurate idea of their extent. The wall, however, which was easily determined, commences about one mile and a half above Bhamô, it runs inwards from the river-bank, and appears again upon it about one mile further up, below the pagodas of Shuay-keenah. The sweep of the wall is now the distinctive feature of the ruins, and the one which first attracted my attention. It is composed almost entirely of bricks with an intermixture of shingle, hidden under a deep layer of soil supporting magnificent trees, which, from their elevation on the wall, tower high above the surrounding forest. Inside and outside the wall, there are a number of low flat plots of land on which paddy is cultivated, and rounded hillocks outside are cleared for cotton, groundnuts, and capsicums which thrive well in the rich loam.

The pagodas of Shuaykeenah which occur close to the ruins, in a dense cluster numbering about 300, and few of them exceeding 20 or 30 feet high, are much resorted to on religious festivals; and I was shown by a very intelligent Shan a grove of high trees on a slight eminence, commanding a fine view of the large golden pagoda, about 200 yards off, where the whole of Bhamô and the surrounding district assemble to worship once in every March.

As I had the good fortune to witness the laying of the foundation of a pagoda at Shuaykeenah, and as an account of the ceremony may prove of interest, I will describe it. A small, square plot of ground, the exact size of the proposed pagoda, was railed off by a prettily twisted bamboo fence about 2 feet high, decorated with flowers, and little flags of Chinese paper. The enclosure was smoothed and levelled with the greatest nicety, and a wooden pin, with its head covered with silver tinsel and bearing a yellow lighted taper, was driven into the centre of the square, and another into the ground about 2 feet from the south-east corner. A quadrangular trench was dug round the central taper, and a deep hole at the side of the other. Eight bricks about 1 foot long and 4 inches broad, the exact size of the sides of the trench, were now prepared. On four the name of Guadama was written in black paint; and on the others, a leaf of gold was placed in the centre of one, silver on the second, a square of green paint on the third, and red on the fourth, and round the margin of each was a narrow line of green. After the trench and the hole at the corner had been dug, both were sprinkled with water. A round earthen vase, containing little bits of gold and silver and some precious stones, besides rice and various sweetmeats, with its mouth closed with wax, in which a small lighted yellow taper of the same substance was inserted, was then deposited in the hole in the south-east corner by the builder of the pagoda, who repeated a long prayer while the vase and its taper were being buried in the earth sprinkled with water. On enquiry into the significance of this part of the ceremony, I was told that the south-east corner pointed in the direction of the abode of the great earth-serpent, and that offerings of gold, silver, and food were deposited in the vase as a propitiatory offering to him. This is an interesting relic of the snake-worship which was once so prevalent among the Shan race to the south, and holds the same position in its relation to Buddhism as nât worship, the last trace, as it were, of the primitive religion of the race, if the dread of evil and the propitiation of its power can be regarded as religion. A similar engrafting of the two systems in Western Yunan is evinced by the canopies over the heads of Buddha being represented by many-headed snakes, resembling what is seen in some of the Indian Hindoo architectural remains. In the next part of the ceremony, the depositing the bricks in the trench, the Shan was assisted by his grandmother, his wife, and daughter. They all knelt around it, the man to the north side, with his wife facing him, his grandmother on his left, and his daughter on his right hand. The silvered brick, with a lighted taper placed on it, was handed to the old woman who raised it over her head, and devoutly murmuring a long prayer, placed it in the trench which had been previously sprinkled with water. The wife did the same with the red centred brick and its taper, and the daughter followed with the green, and her father took the gold one. The girl, in raising her brick, burst into a fit of laughter, tickled at the idea, I was told, of not knowing her prayers. These bricks having been properly deposited, those bearing the name of Guadama were placed over them with the name downwards, and a layer of cloth was spread over all. Earth was then thrown in, sprinkled with water, and the hole having been filled up, the ceremony was completed.

While I was looking on at this interesting ceremonial, two old Shans, who were assisting at it, and whose child-like admiration of my watch had induced me to show them a few other nick-nacks, expressed a strong desire that they might be allowed to examine my hands, and read my fortune from them. I complied, and the two old fellows, carefully tracing out the folds on the palm and the lines on the finger-tips, shook their wise heads, and protested that they had never seen such a fine hand, one that had a better fate in store for it, and from the earnest way they acted and spoke, I verily believe they had faith in their divination.

The Shuaykeenah pagodas stand on a high bank at the angle formed by the Tapeng at its junction with the Irawady; and about 500 yards to the east of them, or nearly so, is the small village of the same name. Here the Tapeng, through which Klaproth carried the waters of the Sanpo, runs down from the Kakhyen hills to the east, through a rich alluvial plain, closed in to the north by the wooded hills which mark the termination of the first defile of the Irawady. The Tapeng, at its mouth, is about 200 yards broad during the dry weather, and from 2 to 12 feet deep, but obstructed by many sand-banks; the northern bank in the same locality is rather high and wooded, but the opposite one is low, and covered with patches of rice cultivation. All the rice on the Bhamô side is raised in swampy hollows which have once been river channels.

The second or third day after our arrival at Bhamô, large crowds from all quarters came to visit the steamer. One of some heavy logs of timber, lying on the bank, unfortunately rolled over on a little girl, and fractured her thigh; and happening to be present at the time, I had the girl, an interesting child of ten years of age, carried on board, and set the fracture, to the delight of her parents. My reputation as a doctor was established at once, and during a month's residence, I held regular levees from 10 A.M. to 1 and 2 P.M., and on these occasions was consulted by people of both sexes, and all ages and conditions. Some of them came long distances by water, especially old men and women with defective eyesight, who were seemingly firmly impressed with the belief that I had the power to restore sight, and such was their importunity, that even after explaining that I could not give them back their youth, they still begged that I would give them some medicine, alleging that if it did them no good, it could do them no harm. None would go away empty-handed, and many a poor creature that I refused as hopeless would so hang about and haunt my steps, that I was forced to give, out of sheer compassion, but without hope. My great difficulty was ignorance of the language, but Major Sladen with wonderful patience gave me his valuable assistance as interpreter, on almost every occasion. The diseases I had chiefly to treat were indolent and irritable ulcers on the legs, itch, eczema, psoriasis, and acute purulent ophthalmia in all its stages, to complete destruction of the cornea, as well as every form of opacity, resulting principally from that dire scourge, small-pox, which had been very prevalent a few months before among the children, many of whom it had blinded for life. Half-a-dozen cases of cataract presented themselves, chiefly among men of mature years. My deaf patients were numerous, and the afflictions, when enquired into, were usually found to date either from a severe fever, scarlatina, or small-pox. Some formidable whitlows were treated among the Chinese. I did not observe a single case of phthisis, and the only chest disease that came under my notice was one of asthma in a young woman. The most common form of sore was an intractable, spreading form of cuticular inflammation, going on to ulceration, confined chiefly to the ankles and shin, although it occurred sometimes on the hands, principally among men whose occupation led them into the jungles. The usual history was that the skin or the affected part had been torn against bushes, and that it had become very painful, and that the skin rose in watery blisters, which hardened into a yellow crust, covering a raw ulcerated surface most difficult to heal. I tried every possible treatment that my limited medicine chest would permit of, but with no very marked success, but rest, poulticing, and water-dressing did the most good. I was at first inclined to attribute it to the scratch of some poisonous plant, but was afterwards led to doubt this explanation, as two simple bruises on my own person followed the same course, and maimed me for a month. One on my thumb was very painful, and necessitated my arm being carried in a sling for some weeks, and as I lost the nail, I did not recover the full use of my right hand for two months. I had two cases of urinary calculus, but operated only on one unfortunate man; the operation was one of considerable difficulty: the man stood it heroically, and recovered rapidly. I had a number of phoongyees among my patients who came long distances to consult me about their ailments. During our sojourn I had not a single case of fever in our party, which numbered about one hundred strong, nor did any come under my observation among the natives, which speaks well for the healthiness of the locality in the cold weather. I was informed, however, that fever is rather prevalent during the rains.

We lived on board the steamer until the authorities had time to build a house for us in accordance with a royal order from Mandalay, which they were obliged to carry out, although they disliked it much, as they did not wish it to appear that they were in any way favouring the Expedition, and by reason of dissensions among themselves. Our residence was built entirely of bamboo on a clear space of ground close to the east of the Woon's house, and it was completed in five days after the first bamboo had been driven into the ground. It was a long house raised three feet above the soil, with a verandah at both ends, the one at the back serving for a bathing-place, and three bed-rooms in a line on either side with a little window in each, the suites of apartments being separated from each other by a broad hall in which we sat during the day. A small out-house was erected for our servants and baggage, and the guard was put up in a zayât close by, and others of our followers appropriated the out-houses in the governor's enclosure. We had a tent in the open space in front of our house, and in it we breakfasted and dined.

On the morning after we arrived, the two Tsikkays or magistrates, who are respectively designated north and south, according as they govern one or other of these divisions of the town, formally visited us on board the steamer. We had come with the impression that our stay at Bhamô would only extend over a few days, but this was quickly dispelled after a few minutes' conversation with these officials. Before our departure from Mandalay, Sladen had secured the despatch of a written order to the Woon at Bhamô, to have mules in readiness for our journey, but we were now informed that it had only reached the late Woon a few days before his death at Momeit, and that, in the absence of a governor, nothing had been done to give it effect. The next four weeks of our residence were spent by our able leader in a fruitless attempt to get the Tsikkays to give us their assistance in making the necessary arrangements for our departure; but although they promised to do everything that was required of them, they did not move a finger to assist us. When we started from Mandalay, we had the full expectation, and the assurance of the king, that the new Woon would follow us in a day or two, and that he would reach Bhamô about the same time as ourselves. This, however, he did not do, and as time was of great importance to us, Major Sladen was anxious that our departure from Bhamô should be delayed as little as possible, but in this he signally failed, as the Tsikkays declined to act on their own responsibility. But if simple inaction had been the only feature in the conduct of the Tsikkays we had to complain of, it would have merited little more than a passing remark; unfortunately it was not so. Their policy at first was to appear as if they were interested in the success of the Expedition, while at the same time they used every argument they could think of to induce us to abandon it. They told us that the principal routes were closed to all traffic, but the arrival of the large Shan caravans and the constant influx of small companies of trading Kakhyens were standing proofs that such was not the case, and they were obliged to confess that a small trade existed along the Tapeng and Ponline route. As no caravans had arrived by the other routes, and as we had no other means of ascertaining the real state of matters regarding them, or of disproving the assertion of the Tsikkays that they were closed, it was decided that we should go by the Tapeng road. We were denied all reliable information regarding the routes, the extent and character of the trade, whether the Kakhyens were at peace or war among themselves, and of the relations of the Shans to the Panthays; all of these being enquiries deeply affecting the Expedition. A poor but intelligent woman, the daughter of an old Assamese, in charge of the most eastern gate, knew "Kakhyen," which she had learned from the petty traders who weekly encamp outside the gate. She had been in the habit of supplying us with milk, and had acted as our interpreter on several occasions to these despised hill people, and had thus incurred the wrath of the Tsikkays, who had her beaten in the public streets. They had, however, trumped up a complaint against her, that she had burned a light at her home after hours. But the woman told us she understood well why she was so treated, and the rest of the inhabitants took the hint that was intended, and carefully abstained from giving us any assistance, and in fact avoided being seen near our residence when any official was expected to pass. Combined with this covert opposition, the Tsikkays openly circulated the most exaggerated accounts of the treachery of the Kakhyens, and, as events have proved, utterly false statements as to the determined opposition we were certain to experience from the Shans. The picture that was daily drawn for our edification, before we had become acquainted with the Kakhyens, was, that this people were hill savages, armed with spears and poisoned arrows, and that they lurked like wild beasts among jungle on the road-side, and shot their fell darts at every comer who was worth killing for his putzo, gun, or buffalo; but when the narrators found that we did not believe in this idle fable, and that we cultivated the acquaintance of the Kakhyens who found their way to Bhamô, they punished the unfortunate woman who acted as interpreter, and thus effectually deterred the towns-people from performing similar services to us, and thus closed what would have been a valuable and reliable source of information to the Expedition. The effect was not only to deprive us of Kakhyen but also of Shan interpreters as well, and when we left Bhamô, we were unprovided with either, if we except Deen Mahomed of Kakhyen experience.

The worst feature in the attitude of the Tsikkays towards the mission was the fact that they were aware that the Chinese residents of Bhamô were intriguing with Leesetai for our extermination, and had written to the Ponline Tsawbwa not to assist us, and that they concealed from us both of these treacherous attempts to defeat our intentions.

When this intrigue came to the ears of our leader, the turning point of our fortune had arrived, and I cannot speak in too high terms of the way in which Major Sladen met it, for the course of action which he pursued at this trying time proved the means of saving the Expedition from an ignominious, and, in all likelihood, disastrous retreat from Ponsee. With a promptness and decision worthy of the highest commendation, he, unknown to us, resolved to outwit these Chinese, and did so in a masterly way. All the information we had been able to gather at Bhamô, regarding the political state of the country beyond, was of no service to us. We were not aware that the Burmese had little or no authority in the Kakhyen hills, and were utterly ignorant of the political relations of the Shan states; and our knowledge of the Panthay government was simply this, that it extended as far east as Momien, which Major Sladen believed to be the residence of certain Mahomedan chiefs of importance. We were informed that the highway to Momien and Talifoo was commanded by the so-called robber-chief, Leesetai, who had undertaken to annihilate us if we attempted to proceed by it. Major Sladen's policy was to secure the good-will and assistance of these chiefs, and he was induced to believe that they would be inclined to favour the revival of the old trade that had existed between Western Yunan and Bhamô, because the large caravans which visited Mandalay once a year by the long and difficult Theinnee route were the evidence that a necessity existed for the interchange of the products of Yunan and Burmah. He accordingly wrote to the chiefs, explaining the advantage they would derive if the shorter and more practicable route, which had been recognized by many centuries of experience as the great highway to Yunan, were re-opened to trade; and fully explained to them the peaceful object of the mission, and that we had arrived at Bhamô in consequence of certain rights which had been conferred on the English Government by its treaty with Burmah, and with the full approbation and support of the Burmese Government, and sent copies of the treaty and proclamation. He informed them of the opposition we had met with at Bhamô, and requested their co-operation in counteracting the intrigues of the Chinese with Leesetai. The letter and documents were despatched with the utmost secrecy, on the 19th February, by three Kakhyens who had manifested a kindly interest in the Expedition.

The next character who merits our attention is the Kakhyen chief or Tsawbwa of Ponline who came to Bhamô on the urgent request of Major Sladen, after he had refused to comply with the order of the Tsikkays. He visited us, on board the steamer, dressed as a mandarin of the blue button, and attended by six to eight men armed with matchlocks and dâhs. He wore a chocolate-coloured long satin coat, richly decorated with gold dragons and other grotesque-looking figures, and the members of his staff were dressed in blue Shan jackets, and loose breeches of the same colour reaching to the knee, and their shins were bandaged in long rolls of dark blue cloth. He carried a gold umbrella, which he had received from the king of Burmah about seven or eight years ago, when he had the honorary title conferred on him of Papada-raza (Raja), a word of Pali extraction, signifying mountain-king. The Tsawbwa is a tall, thin man with a stoop, a contracted chest, long thin neck, very small retreating forehead, flat face with high cheek-bones, oblique eyes, with a deep depression instead of a bridge to his nose, which is represented by a small nodule in the centre of his oval and repulsive visage. Suspicion and deceit are written on his face, of which I had at first some difficulty in obtaining a glimpse, for during the interview he sat with his body bent over the arm of his chair, gazing restlessly on the floor, with his head bowed, as if he were conscious that his looks would betray him. He was accompanied on board the steamer by all the Burmese officials, and to let him, and the Bhamô Tsikkays as well, understand that we respected his position as an independent chief, we had the police escort drawn out under arms to receive him. The Tsikkays brought a Kakhyen interpreter along with them in the person of the *Tamone*, or petty magistrate, of a neighbouring village, whose loquacity was in strong contrast to the taciturnity of the chief, whose short and almost monosyllabic answers to Major Sladen's enquiries regarding the routes, were distorted and expanded into discursive but disheartening accounts of difficulties to be overcome, and dangers to life to be faced, if we attempted to proceed beyond Bhamô. It was evident that the chief's reserve was due, in great part, to the presence of the Burmese officials, and as he understood sufficient Burmese to appreciate the drift of the elaborate replies of the interpreter, it is no matter for wonder that he exercised caution in committing himself to our side. Major Sladen indignantly exposed the lying tricks of the *Tamone*, and requested the services of a man who would confine himself to correctly interpreting the conversation, and not take advantage of it for expressing his own views on the subject of the conference. The culprit retired discomfited, and his place was taken by another Burman, by whom we were informed that the Tsawbwa would guarantee us a safe passage through his territory, although he could not be answerable for the conduct of other Kakhyen chiefs. It was evident, however, that he was ill at ease in the presence of the Burmese officials, and Major Sladen wisely brought the interview to a close by offering him a friendly cup of *eau-de-vie*. But one did not satisfy the Kakhyen capacity for strong drink, and he repeated his demands for more till he and his retinue, aided by the Burmese Tsikkays, had exhausted one bottle, and now begged for another, which we promised to send after him. On leaving us, his last words were, "remember the brandy, and send it quickly."

We had another visit from this chief on the following day, when he undertook to procure one hundred mules, and to have them assembled in ten days, at the village of Tsitkaw, on the right bank of the Tapeng, 21 miles from Bhamô. Major Sladen had a private interview with him, as we had discovered that the Kakhyens, as a rule, are nearly as familiar with Chinese as with their own language, and that the presence, therefore, of the Burmese officials, or their creatures, could be dispensed with. The chief threw off all his former reserve, which, he said, had been forced upon him, as it was necessary for his own interests that he should not offend the prejudices of the Chinese at Bhamô who traded by the Tapeng route, and who had advised him not to countenance the Expedition. It was his own desire to afford every facility for our passage through his hills, but he could not shut his eyes to the strong opposition maintained by the Chinese both at Bhamô and beyond, who would be certain to accomplish his ruin if they thought that he alone had been instrumental in assisting us to enter Yunan. He, therefore, insisted on Burmese co-operation, to convince the Chinese that the Expedition had the permission and support of the Burmese government, and stipulated that we should be accompanied by a small Burmese guard. We shall find, however, that this suggestion was anything but palatable to those high in authority at Bhamô. He now undertook to convey us in safety as far as Manwyne, the first Shan town, and boasted that he was the most powerful chief along the route we were to follow, and that he was on friendly terms with all the other Tsawbwas. He left Bhamô on the following morning (2nd February) to make all the necessary arrangements for our departure in ten days.

The new governor of Bhamô arrived on the 20th February. We thought that all our difficulties would now disappear as he came fresh from the presence of the king, who had professed to favour the Expedition, and whose royal orders it would be a high crime in a governor to frustrate. He declined, however, to leave his boat for three days, notwithstanding the earnest entreaties of our leader that he would at once assume the duties of his Woonship, and make the necessary arrangements for our departure. The three days were declared to be unpropitious for so important an event, and as no protestations on our part would affect the decision of the fates, we had quietly to submit. Sladen, however, made full use of the delay by keeping up a vigorous conversation with the Woon by messengers, and the governor sent word to say that we might have boats at any moment to take our baggage to Tsitkaw, but advised us to wait until he had fired his guns, and had brought in the various Tsawbwas with whom he would arrange for our march through their territories, and to each of whom we were to make certain presents. Sladen urged in reply that every day was precious to us, and hoped that the Woon would see it to be his duty to call the Tsawbwas at once, and to this we received the answer that the guns would be fired on the 25th. He landed on the 23rd, and proceeded to his official residence, mounted on an elephant, and followed by two or three hundred villagers armed with old flint muskets, and with the dàh, the familiar weapon of the Burmese, Shans, and Kakhyens. Sladen visited him the same day, and arranged that the guns should be fired on the following evening, and that the Ponline Tsawbwa should be sent for at once to complete the arrangements. The Woon professed to be actuated by the very best motives, and to have the welfare of our project at heart; but on the following day, when Sladen visited him, along with the Ponline Tsawbwa, who had heard of his arrival, and had come into Bhamô of his own accord, and the latter asked for a Burmese guard to accompany the Expedition, for the reasons I have already given, the request was scorned by the Woon as quite uncalled for. The Tsawbwa, however, pressed the importance of our having some tangible recognition of the support of the Burmese government, and adduced as a precedent that a guard had been sent along with the king's cotton two or three years before. In answer, he was given to understand by the Woon that the two cases were entirely different, and that the Expedition was to be allowed to take care of itself, as the Burmese government had no immediate concern in its success. After such a declaration, it was difficult to reconcile his friendly professions with his deeds. The Tsawbwa then undertook to fulfil his part of the engagement independent of Burmese aid, but he informed the Woon that he had received letters from the Chinese at Bhamô, admonishing him not to allow us to pass through his territories. The Woon admitted that he was aware of the opposition of the Chinese, but stated that he had not been able to discover whether it had its seat at Mandalay, or at Bhamô, but promised at the same time, on Sladen's representation, to call up the head Chinaman, and warn him that he would be held responsible for our safety.

The Ponline Tsawbwa afterwards confessed to Major Sladen that the Chinese and Burmese were both against us, and urged that we should leave Bhamô as soon as possible, and ascribed their opposition solely to their determination to preserve, if possible, the monopoly of the trade in their own hands. Everything was now arranged with the Ponline Tsawbwa, and the mules were waiting for us at the village of Tsitkaw. On the morning after the Woon's arrival, the proclamation announcing his appointment was read at the court-house, to which he proceeded escorted by one hundred armed men, dressed in the ordinary peasant clothes, and ranged in single file on either side of him, in two long lines. He wore the fantastic dress of a Burmese prince; a short, tight-fitting, richly coloured coat, covered with gold tinsel, and with two enormous rigid epaulettes like the wings of a bird, and a tall gold-gilt hat, like a fireman's helmet, surmounted by a tapering, pagoda-like spire. The guns were fired at 7 P.M. on the same day, after fully an hour had been spent in driving home the powder and a novel cartridge of green plantain leaves, but they failed to call in any Tsawbwas.

Our baggage was despatched, on the 25th, by boats up the Tapeng to Tsitkaw, and we decided to start on the following morning. But two difficulties remained yet to be overcome. We had no interpreters, and our rupees had not been changed for the coin of the country. Sladen's representations to the Woon on the former head were barren of any result, and owing to some mysterious cause, silver had disappeared from Bhamô, and in this apparently helpless condition, we started on the morning of the 26th February. Mr. Burn, who had accompanied us thus far, returned to Rangoon, as Captain Bowers found that there was neither sufficient work nor funds for both of them.

I will dismiss Bhamô by narrating two incidents that came under my notice during the last few days of our sojourn there. While we were at dinner one evening, a cry was raised that a tiger was in the town, and we at once started with our rifles, and were met by a man who informed us that a woman had been killed. We hurried on, and in a hollow below a clump of bamboos came upon the body of the poor woman, over which her niece was crying bitterly. The back of the skull was completely smashed in, and a long rent ran from the base of the occiput to above the ear, and part of the scalp was torn off. The woman had been sitting in the low verandah of a ground hut, making thatch, and had evidently been whisked out by one fell swoop of the tiger's paw, for no marks of the teeth could be discovered. A number of people were seated close beside her talking loudly; but this only verifies what I have heard about man-eating tigers that they rather take advantage than otherwise of a noise to secure their prey, and this one, a tigress, had a decided partiality for human flesh, for she had carried off another woman a year before, and the towns-people asserted that she cleared the stockade, nine feet high, with the woman in her mouth. In the present instance, she had dragged her prey about fifty yards, but whenever the people discovered what had happened, they rushed from their houses with torches, and shouting drove her off. When we arrived, there were about fifty men, all armed with spears and guns, and many carried torches, and fires had been lit in every direction to frighten the brute away. The scene was a most exciting and effective picture. We had the body removed, and beat the thickets, but could discover no trace of the tigress. The woman was buried the same night in accordance with the Burmese custom followed in all cases of persons killed by tigers. On the following morning, we found the tracks of the animal clearly imprinted on fresh bricks laid out to dry, and its sex indicated by the footprints of her cub.

Proceeding for a stroll outside the stockade, I encountered a number of old Shan women seated round a large bowl of water, in which three small pieces of cotton wool were floating. They were ugly, wizened, and bowed, and as they sat smoking their long pipes, with their eyes rivetted on the bowl and its floats, they forcibly recalled the witch-scene in "Macbeth." The meaning of the curious spectacle was this: three men had gone to the Kakhyen hills, and a report having reached their families that one of them had died, the old hags were deciding upon the truth of the rumour, and determining which of the men it was who had passed into nâtland. To arrive at this, they had taken, for each of the men whose fates were to be determined, a small piece of cotton wool and strung it through the eye of a needle; and giving to each a special mark and the name of the man, they had let the needles gently into the water in which they were suspended by the cotton float. It takes some time before the cotton becomes so thoroughly wetted as to sink, but the needle which first drops to the bottom consigns the unfortunate, whose name it bears, to the land of forgetfulness. The proof is conclusive, more especially if the other two needles approach each other at the same time. The needles, however, seemed to be expected to comport themselves in such a way as to favour the chance of the result tallying with the rumoured fact: if not doing so, they are all taken out and placed on a tray, along with an offering of rice for the nâts, and one of the witches lifts the tray above her head, and mutters a low chant. They are again placed in the water, and their course and end carefully watched, so that if Mung-Thazaunoo has been reported dead, his needle does not belie his fate. Truly, in all things the Shans are too superstitious.

CHAPTER XI.

BHAMÔ TO PONSEE.

The Tapeng being navigable to the foot of the hills, at all seasons of the year, for moderately-sized boats, we sent all the baggage we did not require on our two days' march direct by water to Tsitkaw, and our lighter baggage preceded us on the morning of our departure to pick us up at the village of Tahmeylon. The distance between Bhamô and Tsitkaw is only about 21 miles, and might easily be got over in one day by a single pedestrian, but when a party of one hundred persons has to be ferried over the stream, in a limited number of canoes, the journey cannot be accomplished under two days.

We started on the morning of the 26th February, with no guide, and without an interpreter, a telling comment on the value to be attached to the professions of assistance vouchsafed to us by the Woon and his officials. We had the fortune, however, in passing through Bhamô to meet a good-natured and well-disposed Shan, who held the office of head jailor, and whom Major Sladen persuaded to show us the road, on the understanding that he would use his influence at head-quarters to clear him from any responsibility that might accrue from his having given us his services. Our way lay through the northern gate, and about half a mile beyond the town, we struck off to the right, passing the ruins of Tsampenago and the pagodas of Shuaykeenah, and a few hundred yards beyond the latter, we came to the Tapeng river about half a mile above its mouth. The road, so far, lies through a dense forest, and is broad enough to allow of two ponies walking abreast. We crossed the river, which is about 200 yards wide, in canoes, swimming the ponies alongside, and halted till our men came over. We then started and marched 2 miles, as far as the village of Tahmeylon, where it was arranged that we should remain the rest of the day, as there was no other halting-place till Tsitkaw is reached, and as the boats containing our provisions and bedding could not arrive before dusk, the current being against them the whole way from Bhamô. We put up in a small monastery, the phoongyee or priest of which had lately died, and here there was a profusion of small marble Buddhas seated in recesses in miniature pagodas, besides numerous boxes, decorated with little bits of mirror-glass and coloured filagree, containing the library of the deceased: also many manuscripts carefully rolled up in blue cloth were suspended from the roof by cord slings.

I went out in the afternoon to shoot, accompanied by the son of the headman of the village. He conducted me for some distance through dense grass jungle and occasional extensive rice clearings to a long *jheel*, where *Anas pœcilorhyncha*, *Casarca rutila*, and *Querquedula crecca* were rather plentiful, but very wary. I also observed *Ardea purpurea* and *Herodias egrettoides*, and a moderately-sized leopard came skulking along the side of the water evidently in pursuit of fish.[1] We watched each other attentively, but as I had only small shot in my gun I did not venture to disturb him. *Gallus ferrugineus* occurred in large coveys on the old rice clearings, but they were very shy, and flew off on the slightest noise to high trees in the centre of the jungle, where they nightly roosted in large numbers. As it was getting dark, I hurried back and found that the rest of the party had thought I had lost my way, and had been firing off their guns to attract my attention. The boats containing our light baggage had arrived, and we were comfortably quartered for the night.

27th February. We started at 7 A.M., skirting the banks of the Tapeng through tall grass, occasionally broken in upon by rice clearings, but bearing a very small proportion to the large tracts of uncultivated land in this fertile but thinly peopled valley. This grass, which averages 10 feet in height, is confined to a narrow belt along both sides of the river. Interspersed among it occur lofty cotton trees (*Bombax malabaricum*), sweet limes, and a profusion of rich orange-flowered *Zinziberaceæ*. The rice clearings are almost entirely confined to this land, which is annually washed by the unfailing floods of the Tapeng. A belt of higher ground beyond the influence of the river, and covered with fine forest, lies to the right, and in riding along, we speculated on the facilities it afforded for the construction of a road which might be travelled dry-shod at all seasons. At half past 9 A.M., we arrived at the narrow but deep Manloung river, which flows from a small lake of the same name behind the village of Tsitkaw. At the junction of this stream with the Tapeng, a number of ruined pagodas on the right bank mark the site of the second town of Tsampenago, which flourished centuries after the city of the same name near Bhamô was a heap of ruins.

---

[1] The natives of the Bengal Sunderbunds assert that the tiger also feeds on fish.

We swam the ponies across, and ferried ourselves over the Manloung in a small canoe. While waiting till all the men got over, I had the first sight of Mrs. Jemadar, in her marching costume, which consisted of silk trousers tucked up to the knee, a blue silk padded jacket, a bag and Burmese dâh slung over her shoulders, her shoes tied behind her back, and a red silk handkerchief over her head, and fastened under her chin; a dress which became her slim figure, and gave her a model *fille-du-regiment* air as she appeared by the side of her husband, at the head of his men.

A small village is situated on the banks of the Tapeng, about half a mile above the opening of the creek, and passing through it, our path lay over a large expanse of old rice land covered with the yellow-flowered strawberry (*Fragaria indica*, Andr.) now rapidly running to fruit. About 3 miles further on, we came to another narrow but rapid and deep stream which runs from the Tapeng to join the Manloung. It was crossed by a rickety bamboo bridge which entirely gave way in the middle after a few of us had got across, and we had to send to a village near at hand for a boat to bring the rest of our party over. We reached the village of Tsitkaw at noon, and were received inside the low stockade by the Burmese officials, and by a miserable guard armed with rusty flint muskets, and were conducted to a small barn-like zayât, which had been cleaned for our use, and railed in with a low bamboo fence. It was raised on piles, and the entrance was by a break-neck wooden ladder, guarded below by a rusty gingall. It was, as I have said, no better than a barn, and our only resting-place was the floor. Outside the village as we entered, we passed through a large enclosure filled with about 100 ungainly-looking Shans and Kakhyens, our mule-men to be, who jeered and laughed at us as we passed, a reception which did not give us a very favourable impression of their good breeding. The villagers are Shans and Chinese, but nearly all the officials are Burmanized Shans.

There is a collector of customs whose monthly receipts amount to the pittance of Rs. 190, and a small monastery behind the zayât, in which the village children may be heard *en masse* vociferating their tasks from day-break to near midnight.

Tsitkaw lies close to the bank of the river on a broad alluvial plain, and almost under the shadow of the Kakhyen mountains. The Tapeng is a quiet flowing stream about 100 yards broad, marked by a few sand-banks and islands. The plain is devoted to paddy cultivation, and stretches away to the north for many miles, and I am inclined to think that it communicates with the plain of the Irawady to the north of the first defile.

Soon after our arrival, our dwelling was besieged by inquisitive Shans and Kakhyens, who attempted to swarm in upon us, and were only kept at bay by a guard of armed police. This, however, did not prevent their scrambling up the walls of our dwelling, and from peering in with apparently as much curiosity as it would have been possible for them to exhibit, supposing we had been denizens of another planet. Great caution had to be exercised in keeping them back, as some of them were evidently disposed to be quarrelsome, and would have appealed to their dâhs on the slightest provocation. As darkness set in they retired, but we were requested to have a guard under arms all night for the protection of our property.

28th February. The Ponline Tsawbwa made his appearance this morning, accompanied by the Talone and Ponsee Tsawbwas, the latter a youth of 21 years, and the son of the Seray chief, and each had one or two Pawmines, or lieutenants, along with him. Their first request was for liquor, and before the day was far spent, they were all more or less intoxicated, with the exception of the Ponsee Tsawbwa. Before they were deep in their cups, they gave their assent to our passage through their respective territories, and the mules were sent to have their loads adjusted. The shouting, squabbling, disputing, and general confusion which ensued, as each man helped himself to whatever load he thought was most suited to his mules, baffles all description; but, in time, each managed to secure a load, and tolerable quiet reigned while they were busily engaged in lashing their packages to the cross-trees. But a surplus still remained, and the storm of voices and threatening gesticulations of our friends again broke forth, to quiet down, however, as each man had secured what he thought was his due. Then, all the packages were arranged in little groups, and each man, with a slip of bamboo in hand, passed from load to load and broke it across into joints, at regular intervals, corresponding to the number of mules that would be required, and carefully preserved his primitive tally against the day of reckoning. While we were congratulating ourselves that we would be able to start to-morrow, the Choungoke, a wretched Burmese official, who had done all in his power to discourage us by hinting that the chiefs were at variance with the mule-men, and that a rupture was certain sooner or later to occur, came, accompanied by some of the chiefs, and dissipated all our hopes by announcing that to-morrow was the 9th of a Kakhyen month, when to engage on any important business would be certain to incur the displeasure of the náts. As reasoning was out of the question, we had quietly to acquiesce in their arrangement that we should not start till the day after to-morrow. I went out in the evening, and shot a few birds, and on returning at twilight, accompanied by my Burmese servant, we sighted two men coming along the road; as they approached us, they both drew their dâhs, and began to flourish them in such a way as to indicate that they defied me to come on. I took no notice, and walked straight forwards, and when they saw that I did not return their bravado, and was well armed, their dâhs were soon sheathed. The explanation I received was that they had mistaken us for Kakhyens.

29th February. To-day I visited the Manloung lake, which lies almost one mile and a half behind the village, and went all round it in a small canoe which held three people with difficulty. The western bank is high and wooded, and the Manloung leaves the lake on that side by two channels which enclose a small island, on which the village of Manloung stands. The high bank is continued on the north, beyond the lake, as a prominent ridge covered with high trees, in a bold sweep to the foot of the Kakhyen mountains, and there can be little doubt that it is an old river bank, and that the lake marks what was once the channel of the Tapeng. The lake is about half a mile long and quarter of a mile in breadth, and the natives assert that it is of great depth, and it certainly appeared to contain a large body of water. On the east, it is surrounded by a succession of extensive swamps hidden in tall trees. I carefully examined its surroundings to ascertain from where it derived its supply of water, but could discover no streams running into it. As there is a constant but small outflow through the Manloung stream, I am led to believe that its supply is derived from springs. The great body of water, however, passing through the Manloung channel comes from the Tapeng itself through the stream we crossed on our way to Tsitkaw. During the rains the whole of the level plains about the lake and neighbourhood is frequently flooded to about two feet, for two or three days at a time, by the waters of the Tapeng, which rise very suddenly, and rapidly subside. There is said to be three months of rain in the plains, but the rainfall on the hills is very great, and lasts for five months. The village of Manloung contains 80 houses, and all the women were busily engaged in weaving. They procure their cotton from the Kakhyens, who grow it on the hills. The village boasts of a large monastery in a much more flourishing condition than any I observed at Bhamô, and with a large number of resident pupils. I was shown the dormitory by the chief phoongyee. The beds were arranged along one side of the room, and each boy had a nice clean mattress and coverlet, with superior mosquito curtains. The village is entirely Shan.

On the lake I observed *A. pœcilorhyncha*, *A. caryophyllacea*, *C. rutila*, *Sarcidiornis melanonotus*, *Branta rufina*, *Q. crecca*, *Podiceps phillippensis*, *Nycticorax griseus*, *H. egrettoides*, *H. alba*, *Porzana fusca*, *G. phœnicura*, *Rallus striatus*, *Graculus fuscicollis*, *G. carbo*, and *Plotus melanogaster*; and on the old paddy clearings to the east, large flocks of *Grus antigone*. On my return I found that the mule-men adhered to their agreement to start to-morrow morning.

1st March. Our hopes that we were to start this morning were doomed to disappointment, as the day was pronounced to be an unlucky one, and we are not to move till to-morrow. During the day all the packages were re-arranged, and the mule-loads, which yesterday only amounted to 78, have now been largely increased, with the sole object of screwing as much money out of us as they possibly can. Salt was demanded for distribution among the different villages which we are to pass through, but no sooner had the baskets containing it been brought in front of the house than the men helped themselves, and no more was heard of it. The mule-loads are bound on cross-trees which fit into transverse pieces of wood on the pack-saddles, and are thus kept firm in their places, and are secured to the mules by a band passed in front of the shoulders. We have had our patience sorely tried to-day, as the Tsawbwas, and our Chinese interpreter, Moungshuay-Yah, have all been drunk from morning to night, and have favoured us with more of their company than was pleasant. Sala, the Ponline Tsawbwa, is becoming every day more objectionable. We are now beginning to find that either samshu or opium has done its work on him before noon, and this was fully exemplified to-day in a manner anything but pleasant, when this mandarin of the blue button and *Papada raza* coolly relieved himself before us all in our only apartment! Our inclination was to kick the brute out, but as our success at present depends on the good-will of this disgusting savage, we have quietly to bear these offensive insults.

2nd March. Rose by daylight, expecting to start immediately after sunrise, but were delayed till 2 o'clock P.M. The first delay arose from the mule-men not having eaten their rice at 9 A.M., and afterwards by the Tsawbwas coming for an advance on the mule-hire, the distribution of which occupied an hour. The silver (Rs. 200) was laid out upon a mat on the floor, and the eagerness with which they all gathered round and handled it spoke volumes for their greed. One of the Tsawbwas had been anxiously watching Sladen's private cash-box during the morning, and asked in the most pressing manner to be allowed to take charge of it, but his over-anxiety indicated his intentions. Another fellow set his mind upon obtaining possession of Captain Bowers' fowling-piece which was in charge of his servant, and followed the man up and down, trying to coax him to give it up to his care, but the servant was too sharp for him, and suspected his proffered assistance.

The Talone Tsawbwa, the younger brother of Ponline, has an atrocious squint, and considers himself a man of importance, but he has sulked all the morning, because he has discovered that his brother received the present of a musket while at Bhamô. His distemper has infected the Ponsee chief, who also considers that his merits are on a par with those of the favoured, and the disappointed chiefs.

The phoongyee, who has been residing for some days in the adjoining khyoung, and who has daily visited us since our arrival, paid his farewell call this morning, and presented each of us with a little sweet-smelling powder, and with some small, hard, scented, seed-like pellets as a cure for headache and fever, caught by smelling culinary operations in which oil is used. He is a very intelligent man, and one of the best specimens of his cloth I have met in Burmah. He was free in communicating his information, and the only objectionable features in his character, and they are pardonable ones, were the persistence with which he favoured us with his company, and a habit he had of wandering about our apartments, after the conversation was at an end, prying into everything that came in his way.

All the mules were loaded about 1 P.M.; an hour after, we were mounted, and on our way to Kakhyen land. The mules went ahead preceded by the Tsawbwas, and our course lay in a north-easterly direction and along the river as far as the village of Hentha. The cash-box, an unwieldy load, carried on two bamboos over the shoulders of eight men, was placed in the charge of four sepoys, and accompanied the Tsawbwas at the front. We left the river on our right at Hentha, and struck across the plain from the hills; a march of half a mile brought us to the village of Old Bhamô, which we passed on our right. It is a long straggling place with a considerable population compared with the surrounding villages, and lies in a dense grove of bamboos and tall trees. A solitary and almost ruined pagoda, the last of those Burmese religious edifices, on this side of the Kakhyen hills, if we except two in the Hotha valley, is seen outside the village of Tsihêt, which lies on slightly undulating ground immediately below the hills. The road from Tsitkaw to this village runs through a succession of dry and swampy patches, cut up at intervals by deep long nullahs. We overtook the Tsawbwas just as they were approaching the village, and they seemed to be attracted to the cash-chest like needles to a magnet. When they saw us coming, the Ponline Tsawbwa ran up to Sladen, and pointing towards the hills said, "go on, don't be afraid," but the exhortation was thrown away on us, as we were at a loss to understand its meaning. The Talone Tsawbwa, however, spoke in plainer terms, asking in an aggrieved tone, as if he were only demanding what he was entitled to, "when are you going to give me the gun?" We proceeded, and immediately commenced an abrupt ascent to an elevation of about 500 feet, over a series of rounded hills which are quite distinct from the main mass of the Kakhyen mountains, although they are connected to it by its spurs, up one of which we next ascended to about 1,500 feet. When little more than half-way up this ascent, we heard a shot fired above us, followed quickly by others; on proceeding a few hundred yards, we were informed that a body of badly-disposed Kakhyens were in front to dispute our progress. A number of the mules had gone on, and many of their drivers gathered about us flourishing their dâhs, and yelling like fiends. As we advanced, a few more shots were fired, and we came upon two Kakhyens of our party who had gone on before us, standing in an open, by the road-side, where the shots were supposed to have come from. One fellow was armed with a cross-bow and poisoned arrows, and the other with a flint musket, and by signs they tried to make us believe that when they had fired into the spot from which the first firing had come, their evil-disposed brethren had bolted down the hill-side. My own impression is, that this alarm had been improvised to try our metal, and am inclined to attribute its commencement to some of our own half-intoxicated mule-men who were ahead of us. Immediately after this incident, Sladen and I had the ill-luck to be thrown into the company of a semi-intoxicated Shan mule-man. He kept rushing past us on his pony backwards and forwards on a bridle-path, in some places hardly sufficient for a single pony, firing off his musket at one time over Sladen who was in front of him, then, rapidly re-filling it, firing over his shoulder and over my head, without looking back.

From 1,500 feet, we made a steep descent into a narrow, level glen of rich alluvial land, watered by a small mountain stream, running over granite boulders. The descent was rough and slippery, as the path was nothing more than dried-up rocky water-courses. From this glen, which was in reality a valley separating two spurs, we again ascended and reached 2,000 feet above the sea level, afterwards making a slight descent to reach another long spur leading up to the village of Talone. On approaching Talone we were requested to dismount, as we were told that Kakhyen etiquette forbade that we should ride past a village. We walked through a small, grassy glade sacred to the nâts, and surrounded by fine trees; on one side of it, there were a number of bamboo posts split at the top into four pieces which were expanded to support a small platform or altar on which the offerings to the nâts, consisting of cooked rice and sheroo, were placed. Large bundles of a long grass were laid in front of these primitive altars devoted to the propitiation of the evil spirits who are known to interfere with the welfare of Kakhyens, and a few old men were kneeling before them muttering a low chant. After passing the village, we mounted our ponies and climbed a short, steep ascent through deep cuttings in low secondary spurs, then kept along a tolerably level pathway, and again made another short ascent to the village of Ponline, situated in a hollow on the eastern side of a saddle connecting two principal ridges, and about nine miles from Tsihet. It was dark when we reached the village, but the moon was shining brightly, and we were conducted by one of the Pawmines to a Kakhyen house which had been cleared for us.

The first news that met us on our arrival was that eight of the mules with their loads had been driven off by dacoits, and that only a few mules had arrived. We went down to the village, and found the latter part of the report true, but could obtain no reliable information about the first part of it. Williams, who had come on slowly to take the altitudes, turned up in about three-quarters of an hour with the news that a shot had been fired at the Ponline Tsawbwa, who was in front of him, after leaving Talone village. He had heard also of the dacoity of the mules. Sladen wandered round to the Tsawbwa's house, and found him seated comfortably with his wife and children round a fire. The chief's wife is a superior woman, and she treated him very kindly, providing a comfortable seat for him by the fire, and showed her hospitality by expecting him to drink bamboo buckets-ful of sheroo; but as there was no interpreter, the conversation could not have been brilliant. On a large open space in front of the Tsawbwa's temporary house (for he is building a large new one), we found a number of his girls pounding rice by moonlight, accompanying their work with a low, musical, suppressed cry, pleasantly mingling with the tinkle of their girdles of little metal bells. As neither Williams' nor Bowers' bedding had come up, we divided what we had, and turned in for the night, thoroughly tired, and not over-satisfied with our day's work, for none of our guard had come to the front, the cash-chest was behind, and eight of our mules were reported to be lost.

3rd March. Last night we were continually disturbed by loud shouts and yells from men who seemed to be posted on different heights about the village, and who, we concluded, were the village guard. In the morning Mrs. Ponline sent us a large capon and two bamboos of sheroo, and came herself after breakfast accompanied by seven women. She was in full dress, and wore the necklace distinctive of her rank, as well as two large silver hoops round her neck which Tsawbwas' families are only entitled to among Kakhyens. The necklace consisted of short cylinders of a hard, clayey-looking substance, with occasional amber beads and bits of ivory and bone. Her head-dress was most grotesque; it resembled a huge inverted pyramid of blue cloth, towering about one foot and a half above her head. Over her shoulders, she wore a black velvet jacket without sleeves, ornamented down the two sides in front with four circular, green, enamelled plates about three inches in diameter, and the same number down the back. A circle of large, embossed silver buttons ran round the neck, prolonged down the front of the jacket in two lines. Below this, she wore another tight-fitting jacket. Her petticoat of thick blue cotton cloth, with a broad red woollen border, reached a short way below the knee, and was fastened round her loins by being tucked in at the sides, and brought down in front, so as to expose a great part of the belly. It was supported by a profusion of ratan and other girdles; her legs immediately below the knee were encircled by many scores of fine, black ratan rings fitting tightly in a mass. She had two silver bracelets, one on each arm, one a hollow and the other a flat ring about three inches broad. Her earrings were two long cylinders of rolled silver, thrust through enormous holes in the lobes of the ears. She is a little, short woman, with high cheek-bones, and slightly Chinese eyes, with fair features and an intelligent face. She was accompanied by two of her daughters, one a child in arms, the other a little girl of twelve years. They wore the bells in addition to other broad girdles ornamented with three or four rows of cowries. The latter are in high estimation, and are worn by every Kakhyen woman of any position. The unmarried attendants had their hair cut short over the forehead in a straight line, but long behind, and were without head-dresses. She brought two bamboos of sheroo, and four goose eggs, and apologised for having so little to give, but said she must send us something every day to eat. We seated her and her women on a mat inside the front of our house, and Sladen presented her with some silk handkerchiefs and red cloth, and a splendidly coloured table-cloth, which took her breath away when she realized she was the happy owner of it.

The guard arrived at 1 P.M. without the cash-box, which has been kept by the Talone Tsawbwa at his village, along with the eight mules which were reported to have been stolen. The Jemadar states that the Tsawbwa and all his people, along with Moungshuay-Yah, are helplessly drunk, and the native doctor informs me that one sepoy died at Talone where the guard had put up for the night. The man had been drinking large quantities of water on the march, and when he reached the village, he took another draught, and was immediately seized with vomiting and purging, and died in two hours. The sepoys had nothing to eat yesterday, but before they started this morning, they managed to get a little rice. In the afternoon we were attracted to the village by the sound of a tom-tom; nearing the house in which it was being played, we found some men sitting outside cooking two chickens from which the entrails had not been removed. We asked permission to enter, which was willingly granted. On going in, a rather nice-looking Kakhyen girl brought two logs for us to sit on. The house was a small one, but constructed after the usual Kakhyen fashion, being a thatched structure, raised on bamboos about two feet above the ground, and divided longitudinally down the middle by a partition, on one side of which were the separate rooms of the household, and on the other an open passage common to all, in which the cooking operations are conducted. There are no windows nor chimneys, and the smoke disposes of itself as it best can. There is a door at either end of the house, but strangers are only allowed to enter and depart by the main entrance, for the other is sacred to the nâts, and only the occupants can go in and out by it. The principal entrance has a covered portico ornamented with buffalo and deer heads, and at night the pigs, cattle, and poultry are herded into it. A narrow log of wood, with deep notches cut in it at regular intervals, served as a flight of steps leading to the common hall or passage. Each room, which usually contains a family, has a square fire-place in its centre, sunk a little below the level of the base, and supported on shorter piles than the rest of the house, the bottom being made of split bamboos covered with a layer of earth. We found a number of men, women, and children dancing round the common hall, each carrying a small stick, which was waived up and down in unison with their pedal movements which consisted of a rapid shuffling gait, first with one leg and then with the other, intermixed with the vigorous beating of two tom-toms by a man and girl; the dancers burst out occasionally into bounds and yells, and rushed round the apartment with renewed energy and excitement. We were beckoned to join them, which we at once did, but when we had made two rounds, the whole party suddenly rushed to the door with a fiendish shout, the foremost man clearing the way with his stick which some of our party mistook for a dâh. We all followed, and the house was left, as we thought, empty. On going in again to discover the object of the dance, we found, to our horror, a dead child lying in a corner carefully screened off, and the poor mother standing by its side weeping bitterly. The dance was to drive the spirit of the infant from the house, which it was supposed to leave when the rush was made for the door, and we were informed that our presence had contributed in no small degree to hasten its temporary departure. We were now presented by one of the women with sheroo, which was handed to us in primitive cups extemporized out of plantain leaves, folded in such a way that not a drop of liquor escaped. On leaving, we discovered that the chickens were intended as an offering to the nâts. We had again occasion to pass the house, when we found the girls busily pounding rice, and laughing as if nothing had happened.

The Tsawbwa sent his son to the Talone chief to bring in the cash-chest and the eight mules, and all arrived this afternoon.

Bowers and Sladen have each lost a valuable box, containing knives, forks, &c., and all our boxes have been liberally looted by the mule-men, who have deliberately opened them, and appropriated whatever they fancied in the way of comestibles.

Ponline lies in a deep, thickly-wooded hollow, the houses being all at short distances from each other. A rounded bold summit of the main range rises immediately over the village to an elevation of about 2,000 feet. Above the village, and standing out prominently on an almost inaccessible spot half-way up the mountain, is a large conical Kakhyen grave, so much resembling a pagoda in form, that I am inclined to think they have borrowed the idea from the Burmese. The rocks we passed yesterday and those exposed here are all primitive, consisting of a bluish-grey, fine-grained gneiss and quartzose rocks, and the hill-sides are covered with huge boulders of the former rock. The hills are clothed with a dense tree forest, with a large intermixture of bamboos; and about Ponline I observed some very large oaks, and a few small palms belonging to the genus *Corypha*, and a number of very fine *Pandani*. One fallen palm stem was fully 60 feet in length, and with a diameter of 2½ feet a little above its base. Some superior plantains are cultivated in the village, and the sides of the spurs below it are extensively cleared for rice cultivation. All the villages are built on heights, and, on the opposite side of the Tapeng valley, of which a splendid view is obtained behind the Tsawbwa's house, many may be seen near the highest summits, at an elevation of about 6,000 feet above the sea.

4th March. I devoted the early part of the day to shooting in the neighbourhood of the village, and procured a new squirrel and a number of interesting birds. In the forenoon Sladen made presents of cloth and salt to all the chiefs and their Pawmines. The salt was highly prized, and also some yellow silk handkerchiefs which were given away at the same time. The Tsawbwa intimated to Sladen that he was doubtful whether the nâts were favourable to our advance, and that he intended to consult them in the evening, and asked our presence. We went up after dinner to the ceremony which was held in one end of the new house which he is building. His wife brought mats, and for some time we lay round a fire chatting with him and the other chiefs and their head men. When the Meetway or priest made his appearance, the ceremony began. He sat down on a footstool in one of the corners of the house which had been previously sprinkled with water, and no sooner was he seated than he blew through a small tube, and uttering a groan threw it from him, and began to shake from head to foot, making the whole floor vibrate. He then grasped the sides of his head, and quivering all over, uttered long-drawn yawns, shrieks, and groans, as if he were in great suffering. He also went through occasional chants, and the Tsawbwa and his Pawmines kept up short conversations with him in a coaxing tone, when he appeared to be suffering more than usual. The only way I can describe this remarkable scene is by comparing him to a maniac. After this had gone on for some time, Sladen was politely informed that the nâts required to be appeased by an offering of silver and cloth before it would be lucky for us to advance from Ponline; fifteen rupees and some pieces of cloth were offered. The rupees were placed in a small bamboo which had been previously sprinkled with water, but no sooner were they placed before the priest, along with the cloth, than he kicked them away, continuing his shrieks and groans even more vigorously than before. This was to indicate that the offering was not enough, and in the midst of shakings, groans, and yells, he signified through the Tsawbwa that nothing under Rs. 60 would suffice. Sladen added Rs. 5 to his offering, and told the man that no more would be forthcoming, but when it was laid before him, he again kicked it away, but this time no one took any notice of his rejection of it. He continued his unearthly sounds for another full quarter of an hour, when they began to be less frequent and violent. A dried leaf rolled into a cone and filled with rice was then handed to him by one of the Pawmines. He took it, and raised it to his forehead two or three times, uttering a low chant, and then threw it on the floor. He then took a dâh which had been carefully washed before the ceremony began, and treated it in the same way as the leaf-cone. This over, he gave expressions to his feelings in gentler groans and sighs which gradually died away, and the ceremony was over. He left his seat laughing, and directed our attention by signs to his legs and arms which he gave us to understand were very tired. We were informed that the nâts had taken a favourable view of affairs, and that we were to be allowed to proceed.

5th March. This morning the Tsawbwa sent down to say that he would neither talk nor stir from his house until he had received a present in money for having allowed us to pass through his territory; he would not mention any sum, for Sladen knew well what was the right thing to do, but he indicated that he would take Rs. 600, but he ultimately came down to Rs. 300.

The cash-chest has been a great mistake, and the Tsawbwa now demanded Rs. 300 to take it as far as Manwyne. We dispensed with the chest, and divided the money among the sepoys, who carried it round their waists. The mules started about 8 A.M., and Williams and I went with them, leaving Sladen, Stewart, and Bowers to follow with the guard. A descent to the bottom of the Tapeng valley is necessitated by a deep gorge to the east of Ponline, down which the Nampung, a narrow stream, precipitates itself. This hill stream was formerly the eastern boundary of the Chinese province of Yunan, and is only 9 miles from the plains of Burmah. The remains of the old Chinese fort are still in existence on the hill to the east of Ponline. The descent begins about a mile beyond the village and lasts for about 2 miles and a quarter, till we are on a level with the bed of the Tapeng, about 337 feet above Bhamô, and taking Ponline at 2,541 feet, we have a descent of 1,766 feet. The path is very precipitous in some places, and winds down as a zigzag line, with the turns sometimes so abrupt that it is difficult for the mules to get round the corners, especially when they occur in deep cuttings, which is often the case, as the track is in great part a water-course. It is also covered with formidable boulders, and with sharp pointed masses of quartzite, obstructing the way both of man and beast. In the largest water-course, before reaching the Nampung, I came upon a small section showing a mass of greyish micaceous schist through which ran large veins of quartz. It was tilted up nearly vertically, and there were distinct indications of the bedding running in a nearly northerly and southerly direction. The beds of the streams, too, are filled with fine granite boulders. The schist weathers to a light grey and becomes very friable, breaking readily under the hoofs of the mules.

We forded the Nampung on our ponies, but the current was so very strong that they had considerable difficulty in keeping their footing, and if any of us had fallen off, we should certainly have been carried into the Tapeng close at hand, which was rushing down to the plains as a mountain torrent of the grandest kind.

Leaving the Nampung, the path wound up the face of a bold precipice, beneath which the Tapeng rushes over its rocky bed with enormous velocity. As we ascended, we gradually lost the river, but caught occasional glimpses of it from the heights above. To reach these we had a most tedious and precipitous ascent, and we had frequently to dismount, and allow our ponies to scramble up the deep, narrow, rocky cuttings as they best could. There was considerable danger in rounding the abrupt turns which were usually found to occur over some giddy precipice, and to terminate in some very steep part of the road. Williams had a narrow escape in rounding one of them, over a precipice of about 1,000 feet. The ground on the edge of the road gave away under his pony's hind feet, and he was only saved by the animal recovering itself by a violent effort.

Our road after this lay over the long spurs that run down from the mountains defining the northern side of the valley, and was alternately up hill and down dale, over a bridle-path covered with pebbles, or through narrow cuttings which had begun as mule tracks, but had been deepened year after year by the torrents that rush down them during the rains. Some of the spurs are capped with tolerably level ground, and in such cases the road was comparatively smooth. The valleys too, between the spurs, have level patches of rich loamy soil. The principal spurs run nearly due south, but they give off secondary spurs nearly at right angles, connected to them by precipitous ridges, affording only bridle-paths on their summits, and so narrow that the pedestrian or equestrian can look into the gorges on either side.

We had a fine view of the range on the opposite side of the valley, varying from 5,000 to 6,000 feet above the sea, and cultivated to near its summit. The clearings we passed were devoted to paddy, and they occurred in the heads of the valleys, between the spurs and on their slopes. There was, on each clearing, a small thatched hut raised on piles as a watch-tower for guarding the crops. In the neighbourhood of the villages, we observed small patches of terrace cultivation, and in one instance a small stream had been turned aside for irrigation.

We passed numerous tree-ferns and magnificent screw-pines; and two species of *Jonesia* in full flower; one, apparently, *J. asoca*.

At 2 P.M., we encamped in a grove of bamboos under an enormous shoulder of the mountain, called Lakong, which towered to about 2,000 feet above our camp. We strung our lamps on the bamboos, and dined, and slept comfortably in the open air.

6th March. Before starting, the Ponline Tsawbwa informed us that the Meetway, consulted at the ceremony the day before yesterday, advised us always to fire a volley before starting, as it would be grateful to the nâts, and would frighten evil-disposed Kakhyens, and the former suggested that we should use a double charge of powder to make the report as loud as possible. He also volunteered that the Ponsee Tsawbwa was offended because he had not received a musket, and he recommended caution as to how we proceeded. We left our encampment at 9 A.M., and had a tolerably good and level road as compared with our yesterday's experience. This arises from the circumstance that we are now almost on a level with the origin of the main spurs, and high above where they divide into secondary offshoots. We reached Ponsee (3,185 feet) about 11-30 A.M., after an easy march, and as no accommodation had been provided for us, we took up a position under a clump of bamboos in a hollow below the village.

CHAPTER XII.

RESIDENCE AT PONSEE.

At two o'clock A.M., on the 7th March, a violent thunder-storm passed over our camp, but, luckily for us, there were only a few drops of rain. We were all sleeping in the open air, and when the rain threatened, one of our party, to be more luxurious than the others, drew his bed under a small thatched shed close at hand, where he was well protected. In the morning, however, he awoke to discover that he had spent the night in a Kakhyen grave. This reminds me that I visited yesterday afternoon some old burial-places on a rounded hill close to our camp, and it may be as well to describe them, as a traveller who had not examined the recent structures would be puzzled by their appearance. They are circular trenches, about 2 feet in depth, and 38 feet in diameter, containing low rounded mounds; and a few of the posts, which had formed the supports of the cone which had covered in the centre, were still standing. If these had been of stone instead of bamboo, we would have had structures, in their general form, in every way resembling the circular cromlechs in England, or the so-called *dolmens* of the French. There is this further similarity between them, that the Kakhyen graves contain only one body, and the still more striking one which I observed in the neighbourhood of Ponline, that the trenches are in some instances built round with slabs of stone. The latter were on the rounded summit of a spur overgrown with dense tree jungle.

The mule-men were very noisy last night, and early this morning, without the slightest warning to us, they began to unstrap their loads, and to walk off with their mules to Manwyne. We tried to remonstrate with them, but to no effect, and on enquiring into the cause of this extraordinary proceeding, we were told that it originated from their not having received their hire. Ponline, however, asserts that this is not the reason, and that they have left because they have received a warning from the Sanda and Muangla Tsawbwas that it will be at their peril if they assist us to enter the Shan states. He also informs us that there is an army of Shans commanded by many officers within one day's march a-head, determined to oppose any attempt we may make to get into their country. He hints, however, in a sly way, that they might be quieted with money, and suggests that 2,000 rupees would be a befitting bribe to offer them. We are perfectly helpless, and must be content to take events as they come. After the mule-men had left, we removed our camp to the place they had occupied, on the top of a very small spur projecting from one side of the hollow below the village. It has been cut into a number of terraces for rice cultivation, and we pitched our tents on the highest terrace on the back of the spur, and our men erected temporary huts to protect themselves from the threatening rain. Ponline came down in the afternoon grievously drunk, and dressed in a yellow silk cloth which he had stolen a few days ago from one of our Burmans. The first absurd demand he propounded was that Sladen should split a bamboo about forty yards off with a ball from his rifle, but on his hesitating to put his skill as a marksman to such a "William Tell" test, he was favoured with some select Kakhyen insolence and foul abuse, very trying to human nature.

The Tsawbwas of Nyuugen, Wacheoan, and Ponwah, petty chiefs who occupy the hill between this and Manwyne, came in to-day with presents of fowls and rice. The latter chief was dressed differently from any of the Kakhyens here, and appears to be in much better circumstances. He wore a coarse blue woollen kilt, with a broad blue and red border, and elaborately embroidered leggings of the same materials: add to this, a blue turban and a thickly padded jacket of the same colour, a cloth bag by his side, containing his metal pipe and his bamboo of samshu, and thick solid Shan shoes with blue woollen uppers, and the shoulder-belt of his well-tempered dâh ornamented with a tiger fang, and we have his costume complete. He is a little, wiry highlander, with strongly pronounced, almost Tartar features and oblique eyes, and with two sparse side-tufts for a moustache, and a beard restricted to the front of his chin, over which the samshu bamboo frequently finds its way to his droughty lips. In drinking, he first dipped his finger into the liquor, and then drew it across his forehead, pouring a few drops on the ground as a peace-offering to the nâts.

8th March. I awoke at 2 A.M. to find my blankets a pool of water, and the tent threatening every minute to collapse under the heavy gusts of wind and rain that were sweeping down from the enormous shoulder of the ridge above us. Williams and I stood manfully at our post, and averted the impending danger to our tent, although we were powerless to staunch the streams that poured in upon our beds.

Ponline came down in the forenoon, accompanied by a Burman who has arrived with orders from the Woon to take the Ponsee Tsawbwa to Bhamô to consult about the working of the Ponsee silver mines. The Burman says that he met, at Tsitkaw, Moungshuny-Yah, who deserted us at Ponline, on his way back to Bhamô. His history is this: he is half Burmese and Chinese, and said to be on good terms with the Panthays, and to have crossed the Kakhyen hills on several occasions, travelling in disguise, and hiding at night for fear of his life. He behaved very well on board the steamer, but whenever we reached Bhamô, we had reason to suspect that he was not wholly for us, and events since then have verified our suspicions. Ponline informs us he was advised by him, the night he arrived in his village, to murder Sladen and the head writer, and to seize the cash-chest. He was more or less intoxicated during the few days we were at Tsitkaw, and he remained behind when the cash-chest was detained by Talone, and its detention has been accounted for in this way, that he and Talone had been concocting some plan for stealing it, and that the device they had hit upon was the one he broached to Ponline.

To-day a demand has been made for Rs. 300, as compensation for five houses which are said to have been destroyed by a jungle fire which originated at our Lakong encampment. In the evening some women of the village brought a fowl, a bamboo of sheroo, and some cooked rice, rolled in plantain leaves, ostensibly as a present, knowing well, however, that they would receive something in return. We presented them with a few four-anna pieces, but they were not satisfied, and indicated by signs that they wanted five rupees. I gave the most importunate a charming little bottle of scent, and thinking that her feminine taste would fully approve it, I poured some on her hands, and signed to her to rub it on her face. This, however, will be my last experiment of the kind, for no sooner had she done so, than she abused me as if I had offered her some gross insult, and indicated her disgust by wry faces and vigorous spitting.

9th March. This morning we ascended to about 600 feet above our camp, and had a splendid view of the Burmese plain as far as Bhamô, and of the junction of the Tapeng with the Irawady. We passed a number of oaks, and through a grove of trees yielding a nut exactly like the hazel of Europe. At the highest point we found ourselves in the neighbourhood of a Kakhyen village, situated immediately above a small stream in a beautifully wooded cool dell, in which we passed three women going to draw water, which they carry in bamboos in a wicker basket on the back, suspended from a band of plaited ratans passing over the forehead. They were evidently astonished at our sudden appearance from above, and quickly retreated into a hollow by the road-side, turning their backs to us as we passed. At 3,000 feet we heard a troop of hoolocks (*H. hoolock*) howling at the pitch of their voices, in a deep ravine about 1,000 feet below us.

On our return we were favoured by a visit from the Ponline Tsawbwa, who again brought forward the affair of the burned village, and repeated his demand for Rs. 300. Sladen offered Rs. 50 and a musket to the two men of Lakong, but this was refused, and Rs. 100 were mentioned. We were told that we would not be allowed to leave Ponsee till we had settled this matter, and that it will be necessary to spend Rs. 600 in presents on the way to Manwyne to secure the opening of the road. The latter demand is only one out of many others by which Ponline hopes to fleece us of money for his own aggrandisement. While the discussion about the mule-hire was going on in Sladen's tent, the Meetway or priest who had officiated at Ponline's village brought in a splendid specimen of the bamboo rat, *Rhizomys pruinosus*, Blyth, which he said he had dug out of the ground. It was very fierce, and dashed violently at every object placed before it, seizing it with its powerful incisors, uttering a peculiar cry which I can only express by *chuck, chuck*. As this rat is highly esteemed by the Kakhyens as a choice article of diet, I had to pay a large sum for it. The arrival of this beast put an end for the time being to Sladen's conversation with Ponline; and it was further interrupted by the arrival of two men, accompanied by half-a-dozen others, the bearers of a letter from the Panthays at Momien. We were extremely puzzled at first to make out who they were, for they seemed to recognise us, and it was not till one began to strip off his finery, and exhibit his ragged Kakhyen clothes below, that it flashed upon us that they were the messengers Sladen had sent forward from Bhamô. The two men were got up most gorgeously in blue jackets and Mahomedan skull-caps, richly braided with silver and gold, and below the former they wore yellow silk coats reaching below the knee, and, suspended from the upper button-hole of their jackets, one had a pink and the other a blue, square piece of cloth, like a pocket handkerchief, with an embroidered square at the attached corner. They wore Chinese shoes and new broad cane hats over their other head-dresses, and the shoulder-belts of their dâhs had the half of the lower jaw of a leopard attached to them. They spoke very highly of the kindness they had experienced from the Panthays, and alluded with pride to their fine garments. The letter was carefully rolled up in paper with a large red stamp on one corner, and the envelope had a strip of red paper down the centre, on which the address was written in Arabic. The letter was also written in the same character. An examination of the outer wrapper revealed another letter carefully pasted into one end of it, and written in Chinese. The native doctor and the Jemadar attempted to read the Arabic epistle, but miserably failed, and as we were without an interpreter, the contents of the Chinese letter were unknown to us. We have, however, the distinct assurance of the messenger, that the Panthays are most anxious that we should visit them at Momien, and their explanation of the two letters was this, that the Chinese was to mislead regarding the Arabic letter, in case they should fall into the hands of their enemies. They had travelled with ease, experiencing no opposition, although they wore the Panthay uniform from Momien through the Shan states which are said to be opposed to our further advance. One of the men who accompanied the Kakhyens is a Panthay officer from Momien. He is a tall, well-built, fair-skinned man, dressed in blue, with a fine, intelligent face, and the quiet self-possession of a gentleman.

When Sala, the Ponline Tsawbwa, saw our friends arrive, and deliver the letters from Momien, his countenance, which at any time is anything but pleasant, became hideous, and he got up and left, accompanied by all the Kakhyens who continually hover about our tents, and hid himself for the remainder of the day. The relief of being rid of these inquisitive semi-barbarians, even for a few hours, was great. They have been constantly passing in and out about the tents, and have thought nothing of going inside and seating themselves on our beds, and of squatting for hours together at a time, smoking, and chewing tobacco and betel-nut. If they were opposed in anything, they immediately fumbled at their dâhs. The other day, when the mules were leaving, I went to look after my boxes, but was immediately waived off by a Kakhyen who got quite excited, and threw his dâh in such an unmistakable way that retreat on my part was the better part of valour. On another occasion, after I had been talking good-naturedly to some men, I gave one to understand that I wanted to measure how tall he was, but he shrunk back with an angry scowl, and in an instant his dâh was from its scabbard. Remonstrance was useless, and I contented myself by staring him out of countenance, and by following him up as he sneaked away. He has avoided me ever since. I experienced, too, the greatest difficulty in getting Kakhyen words, as some of the Ponsee Tsawbwa's people take the villagers away, whenever they see them giving me any assistance of this kind. The Shans and Kakhyens are much alike physically, and as many of the former are also daily in our camp, one is very apt in his ignorance of both languages to mistake

Kakhyen for Shan, and *vice versâ*. In the afternoon, the Ponsee Tsawbwa slunk into my tent, and carefully closing the fly after him, indicated by signs that he wished to say something of importance, and on the arrival of Deen Mahomed, we were informed that the villagers intended to attack us, and loot everything.

10th March. I had a ramble this morning over the hill-sides in search of land shells, but found only one (*H. huttonii*). On my way back over the rice terraces about our camp, I came on two species of violets, and a profusion of wild strawberries in flower and fruit, and many varieties of brambles.

About noon, I observed, at a great height overhead, large numbers of Sarus (*Grus antigone*) passing in the direction of the Burmese plains, flying in V-shaped flocks. My attention was first attracted to them by their loud call. When the advance flock was opposite the summit of the mountain, the birds flew round in a great circle, and waited till the nine other flocks which followed had come up. They then all united, and afterwards marshalled off into two great bands, which broke up again into V-shaped flocks which continued their flight to the plains. I counted 60 birds in one flock, and as all were nearly of uniform strength, there could not have been less than 600 birds.

We hear nothing now of the Chinese dacoits beyond, who were going to oppose our advance, and we are now informed that Leesetai has abandoned his fortress at Mawphoo, and the reason assigned is that he had heard that we were going to effect a junction with the Panthays. Ponline has not shown his face to-day.

11th March. Ponline came down before breakfast, and the burned village was again the burden of his song. He agreed to take Rs. 50, and a bottle of salt, and a muslin head-dress for each house. His Pawmines took the money and the salt away with them, carefully secreting the muslins under their jackets, which led us to believe that they intended to appropriate them. They returned, however, in half an hour with the articles and money, alleging that they did not compensate for the damage done, and that the villagers would not agree to the terms. During their absence, the subject of opening the road before us by money-presents had been again discussed, and Rs. 600 demanded. It was ultimately arranged, however, that each chief should receive a carpet, some red cloth and a head-muslin, and a small sum in rupees. The other things were all laid out and dispatched in the afternoon under the care of Sladen's Burmese writer, Ponline's Pawmines, and one of the Burmese officers, who brought the orders from the Woon for the return of the chiefs to Bhamô, and whose services as Kakhyen interpreter Sladen has succeeded in securing for the Expedition, by the promise of Rs. 100 when we shall return to Bhamô, and protection from the Woon. Ponline informed us that if he had followed the advice of the Tamone who left yesterday, he should have been now on his way to Bhamô, and we should have been consigned to the tender mercies of the Kakhyens, lost, to use his own words, in the hills never to be heard of more.

The Panthay letter has evidently made a great impression on him, for he asked Sladen this morning to say a good word for him to the Momien authorities.

12th March. I went out in the morning to shoot, but had to restrict my movements to the hills in the neighbourhood of our camp, as it is unsafe to venture any great distance, the Kakhyens being hostile to us at present. Shooting to any advantage is extremely difficult on account of the density of the jungle, and the steep character of the hill-sides and gorges in which the birds are principally found. When a bird drops, it most likely falls a long way down an almost precipitous hill-side covered either with impenetrable scrub, or with long grass and the re-vivified stumps of old trees, in which to search for a small bird would be to verify the proverb, "seeking for a needle in the hay-stack." In walking through a deep hollow on a hill-side, over well-cleared ground, I raised two partridges, male and female, belonging to the genus *Bambusicola*, and new to science.[1] An oriole is very common in the thickly wooded parts, but I have never been able to see it, although I have frequently followed up its cry. *Otocompsa jocosa, car, chinensis,* and *Pycnonotus intermedius* are the most common birds around our camp along with *Passer monticolus, Pica caudata,* and one or two small flocks of *Melolophus melanicterus.* We are daily visited by a few large crows, *C. culminatus,* and by a solitary kite which hovers over our tents in the early morning and evening. In a dense grove of trees, I shot *Pteruthius erythropterus,* and *Leucocerca albofrontata;* and in the hill-side clearings a *Hypsipetes,* intermediate between *H. nigerimus* and *H. psaroides.* Among lizards I procured *C. emma,* which is not uncommon here.

On our return, we found Ponline and his Pawmines with Sladen, once more at the vexed question of the burned village. They adhered to the Rs. 500, and threatened that if the sum were not paid, that the villagers all round were determined to murder us, and Ponline, by a sawing

---

[1] I have described this species, and figured it in the Proceedings of the Zool. Soc. of London, as *B. fytchii,* in honour of Major-General Fytche, the direct promoter of the Expedition.

movement with his hand across an imaginary neck, indicated the fate in store for us. We were informed that for every man well-disposed to us, there were one hundred anxious to kill us. Sladen firmly adhered to the Rs. 100 and presents which had been declined yesterday, and they again accepted those terms, on the distinct understanding that the subject was never again to be brought forward. In the afternoon, I bathed under a small waterfall on the stream immediately below our camp. The water leaps over a large boulder, in a splendid bower of bamboo (*B. gigantea*), ratans, elegant ferns, and oak trees, and no artificial douche could compete with it. I was unfortunate enough, however, at first unknown to myself, to have attracted the attention of some Kakhyens, who, when they found me "a forked straddling animal with bandy legs," all their awe of me was gone, and they amused themselves by pelting me from the hill-side with pebbles and small branches, so much so that I verily believe in Teufelsdröckh's proposition that "man's interests are all hooked and buttoned together and held by clothes."

13th March. In the evening I went up the hill behind our camp with Williams and Stewart, but remained half-way to shoot in a thickly wooded spot. After they were gone for some time, and I had fired a few shots, I heard four others above me, and concluded that they were from my companions. As night was closing in I began to descend, but before I had got half-way down I was met by my Burmese servant, the sergeant, and four sepoys, who had come out to seek me as they were alarmed for my safety. I mention this to show what the general feeling is, that we are liable to be attacked at any moment. On reaching the camp I found that the Seray Tsawbwa had arrived with a number of followers by the high road, and that the firing had been to announce his approach.

14th March. The Seray Tsawbwa, a short, stout man, about forty-five years of age, dressed in blue from his turban to his shoes, visited us this morning. According to his account we cannot go forward by the Manwyne and Sanda route, as the Tsawbwa of the latter place has emphatically declined to allow us to pass through his country, and that on account of this opposition, the three Tsawbwas returned the presents that had been sent to them under the care of Pouline's Pawmines. He offers, however, to take us through his own territory by the road over the mountains which again reaches the valley to the east of Sanda. The country beyond has declared for the Panthays, and the only difficulty we will have to encounter will be at Mawphoo on the other side of Muangla. The Manwyne people, although favourable to us, will not allow us to remain more than one night in their town, as they are afraid to let it appear that they are inclined to be friendly. They are in dread of the Manhleo Poogain, a notorious Shan official, whose head-quarters are on the opposite bank of the river from Manwyne, and who is at sworn enmity with all who profess friendship for the Panthay cause. He committed indiscriminate slaughter, a few years ago, on a Panthay caravan, a bloody deed which has made his name a terror to all peaceful Shans. In the afternoon, Deen Mahomed came and told Sladen in a confidential whisper that the men of the village were much dissatisfied because the question of the burned village had not been settled, and that they had collected in numbers, determined to attack us during the night. We have now, however, become accustomed to those threats, and attach little importance to them; we took precautions, however, to place additional sentries round the camp, and kept our fires burning.

15th March. We had a long interview with the Seray and Ponline chiefs which lasted to 6 P.M., and it was so far fruitful that the village question was settled. The Panthay officers and the Kakhyen messengers have been sent with friendly letters to the authorities at Momien, and to the Sanda Tsawbwa, and the Manhleo Poogain.

We were again warned this evening to be on our guard, Ponline sending down a messenger requesting us to keep our fires burning over night, and to take precautions against attack, as about 100 men had collected on the heights commanding our camp, determined to try their luck against us. Ponline had ordered them away, but telling them if they would fight, to go and do so, and he would look on and see them killed.

16th March. The night passed way quietly. I went out for three hours this morning over the hill-sides, but did not shoot a single bird; athough I heard a number of small birds chirping in the dense coppice, I could never get a glimpse of them. A small monkey belonging to the genus *Macacus* was brought to-day by a Kakhyen. It differed from any species I am acquainted with, in its short, stout body and limbs, its mere rudiment of a tail (one inch), its red face and dark-brown, thick, and rather long fur. It is said to be a common monkey on the hills. The Seray Tsawbwa came down to-day accompanied by a Chinaman who has been in his employment from his youth, and who now acts as his chief trader, taking down rice, opium, &c., to Bhamô, bringing back salt, dried fish, and a small quantity of piece-goods, long-cloth, needles, buttons, &c., suited to the Shan and Kakhyen taste. The village fire was again mooted, but finally quenched in a bottle of rum. The chances of our advance were again discussed without any practical result, and another demand for rupees was made by Ponline, who now informs us of his intention to return to his village. He claims the whole of the mule-hire, and demands the preposterous sum of Rs. 20 a mile, and when this barefaced attempt at extortion met with the derision it deserved, the semi-savage had again recourse to the sawing motion across an imaginary neck to intimidate our worthy leader into a surrender. When he found, however, that threats of the kind were unheeded, and he could not gain his point, he left the tent in a rage, and with an oath that he would return to his village, and leave us to our fate. The Wacheoan Tsawbwa arrived in the afternoon with a present of rice and sheroo to make the pertinent enquiry, why we were delayed at Ponsee.

17th March. Ponline, Ponsee, Seray, and two other Tsawbwas came down this morning, and remained for many hours discussing the hire of the mules from Tsitkaw to Manwyne. The mules were hired at Bhamô for Rs. 11-8 each, and of this, Rs. 600 have already been paid, with the addition of Rs. 300 to Ponline. We had 116 mules in all, and the latter chief was much disgusted to find that we had kept an accurate account of the number, and of the names of the owners. He disputed our figures, and his Pawmines brought what they alleged were the tallies they had taken at Tsitkaw, and which mounted the number of the mules up to 160, but we had evidence that these vouchers had been specially provided for the occasion. Sladen, by a happy thought, told the chiefs how much he had given that arch-robber Ponline, in presents and money, to distribute to the villages on the way, and in doing so, he threw a fire-brand among them that will be certain to rid us of the Ponline nest of importunates, for no sooner had Ponsee got an inkling that his neighbouring chief had been receiving money without giving him a share, than his ire and chagrin began to show themselves by unmistakable signs. Seray broached the mule-hire to his village, and had the unblushing effrontery to ask Rs. 25 a mile for a journey of a few hours; and that, too, only a few minutes after his own Chinaman had told Sladen that the charge of Rs. 11-8 from Tsitkaw to Manwyne, a distance of three marches, ought to have been only Rs. 2. While this subject was being discussed by the assembled chiefs and their Pawmines, whiz went a bullet through the tent, shortly followed by another. The Pawmines rushed out, and shouted to some men in the village, and the chiefs made a precipitate retreat, the Seray expressing his intention to retire at once to his home. During the day the Tsawbwas had asked us if we could fire the village, but we declined to enlighten them on this point, but after what has occurred, we have taken the precaution to exhibit the only two rockets we have.

18*th March.* The first news that greeted us in the morning was that Sala and Ponsee had quarrelled about the money the former had received, and that the latter had threatened to kill him, and that he was in a great fright, and intended to leave to-day for his own village. He has appropriated all the presents which were entrusted to his care for distribution to the Tsawbwas on the road to Manwyne, and refuses to give them up. He left during the course of the forenoon, carrying off the Kakhyen interpreter with him by force. News reached us to-day that the Sanda people are in a difficulty how to act in relation to us, as a Panthay official has been sent there to receive us, but they cannot well favour us without bringing on themselves the wrath of the Chinese chief, Leesetai, and they dare not refuse the Panthays.

19*th March.* I got on my pony accompanied by some of our men, and set out to ascend the mountain above our camp. A Kakhyen lad had agreed to accompany me as guide, and Deen Mahomed came as interpreter. My road lay through the village, but no sooner had I passed the Tsawbwa's house, than a hue and cry was raised by one of the Pawmines, and the boy was told he was not to show me the way. I passed on, however, along a narrow bridle-path for a short distance, and at a place where my pony backed and refused to go on, the little delay that ensued gave the villagers time to overtake me, and one Pawmine rushed in and carried off my guide by force. I returned in the hope of finding the Tsawbwa more reasonable, but all I could get out of him was, that there was a village above of very bad Kakhyens, and that he would not allow me to go up, and Deen Mahomed was warned that if he got any more guides for me, his throat would be subjected to the sawing process. There was nothing for it but to return, and explore in some other quarter. I visited a Kakhyen burial-ground on the top of a thickly wooded hill to the east of our camp. Two of the graves were quite recent, and beside each, there was a little tobacco and a small cylindrical box containing chillies, and outside the circle, some tobacco, and the skull of a pig that had been killed at the burial feast. The way to the burial-ground from the nearest village was sprinkled at intervals with ground rice as an offering to the nâts. The top ornament of the conical covering of bamboos and grass is cut out of wood into flag-like arms, painted with red and blue figures resembling rosettes.

20*th March.* I accompanied Stewart on a ramble, and followed a tolerably good path leading to the Tapeng, but did not see a single bird. After breakfast I ascended behind our camp, and after sitting in the shade of a clump of trees for nearly an hour, shot two birds, the only ones I saw. From this clump I skirted along the side of the mountain about a couple of miles, and descended through a dense patch of forest, but met with no better success. Indeed, the only chance one has of getting birds is to sit for hours at a time near an opening in the jungle, and pot them as they appear, but even this unsportsman-like plan does not yield much.

21st March. Last night we sent a message to the Ponsee Tsawbwa that we wished a guide to the Tapeng, and he promised that we should have one. The path lay along the tops of the long spurs running down to the river, and in its first part passed through a temperate area, in which I observed cherry, apple, peach trees, and oaks, but further down the trees become more tropical, and in the bottom of the valley they were essentially so, with a few intersprinklings of musæ, bamboos, ratans, gigantic cable-like creepers, orchids, and splendid ferns. We crossed one tolerably large stream, and on its other side ascended one of the numerous secondary spurs, and descending again, reached a sandy open on the banks of the roaring Tapeng shaded by a fine banian which was festooned with a large, fragrant, yellow-flowering orchid. I wandered a short way down the banks, scrambling over the enormous boulders, on the outlook for birds, or other living things that might present themselves, but observed only two water wagtails flitting from boulder to boulder, in the middle of the torrent. The rocks in position along the river bed are porphyritic gneiss, with veins of quartz, in addition to the large oblong pieces of the same mineral imbedded in them, and which, at first sight, give them the appearance of a conglomerate, from the circumstance that the matrix weathers first, leaving the quartz standing out in bold relief. The boulders, too, consist chiefly of this rock, with, however, a fair proportion of others of pure white crystalline marble. A very good section of the gneiss was obtained in the channel of a stream I crossed before reaching the Tapeng. It is about 50 feet high in the upper part of the stream, but at one spot there is a perpendicular cliff in the channel, over which the water falls, and standing below this, a clear section of 80 feet can be obtained. In this splendidly wooded glen, a large troop of monkeys (*Presbytis albocinereus*) was observed wandering leisurely among the highest trees. The Tapeng below Ponsee is about 40 yards broad, and rushes over a rocky bed in a succession of seething rapids, with occasional deep reaches. Its bed is about 1,000 feet above the plains at Tsitkaw, a distance of about 16 miles, which accounts for the suddenness of the inundations on the plain, and their rapid disappearance. The rise of the river in the rains, as indicated by the high-water mark, does not appear to exceed 12 feet.

A foot-path runs along the right bank for about three-quarters of a mile to a raft which is attached by a loop to a rope of *Sterculia* bark, stretched from bank to bank, in the comparatively smooth water above a rapid. The silver mines are on the opposite bank, and some years ago they were largely worked by Chinese, but they have been deserted, in all probability, from causes originating in the Mahomedan rebellion. My guide offered to take me to them if I paid him well, but declined to go to-day. In wandering over the boulders on which I was constantly slipping from the polished state of my soles, I had the ill-luck to fall backwards about ten feet into a shallow part of the river, but kept hold of my gun, which was indented against the rocks. The descent from Ponsee to the river was very difficult, as the narrow path was strewed with dead leaves, and the dried spathes of bamboos, over which we slipped at every step, and could only maintain our equilibrium by clutching hold of every passing twig. A false step on the part of any one in the rear would have been attended with serious results in those places where the path turned at an acute angle on the crests of the precipitous spurs, for he would certainly have tripped up the others in front of him, and instead of one, half-a-dozen would have rolled down the perpendicular slopes. If our difficulties in descending were great, they were all in the right direction, but in returning, the whole tendency was the very opposite of that for which we were struggling. On our return to our camp, we found that the Seray Tsawbwa had come back, having learnt of Ponline's departure.

22*nd March*. We have been informed to-day that the Panthays have sent one of their officers to meet us at Sanda, and that the country so far has declared in their favour. The Seray Tsawbwa brought a letter which he has received from Tasakone, the governor of Momien, who requests him to give us all the assistance in his power, and promises that the Panthays will repay him for any expenses he may incur on our account. About sunset my attention was attracted to a Kakhyen woman on the hill-side rolling about evidently in great pain; she was returning from wood-gathering, and had her little infant, about three days old, tied in a cloth by her side. She was noticed by a passing Kakhyen, who went to her assistance, and true to his race, out flashed the national weapon, his dâh, with which he made two or three cuts through the air over the woman, and then threw some earth over her head, concluding his good work by making one or two passes with his hand over the same part. He then ran up to the village, and had her carried home. His first instinct had been to defend the poor creature from the nât who had attacked her. We had a visit from Seray in the evening to inform us that he was going to start to-morrow morning in search of mules. He is evidently anxious to give us all the assistance he can, and he appears fully to appreciate the advantages that would accrue to his countrymen if trade were promoted by this route. He is a man of considerable intelligence, and takes a lively interest in everything in our camp, and is much taken up with our facility in writing, and is curious in everything relating to guns, iron bedsteads, lamps, and lanterns.

23rd March. Seray started this morning, and has very considerately left his Chinaman to act as our interpreter, giving as his reason for so doing, that he thought it was not right that we should be without one: conduct that contrasts strongly with that of the debauched Ponline.

24th March. Ponsee came down this afternoon, and asked for the presents that Sladen intended to give him, but he was informed he would receive none, until he had returned a box of silver-plated forks and knives, which had been entrusted to the care of one of his men at Ponline. He protested that they were carried off by a man from another village, but engaged to return them to us.

25th March. Yesterday the widow of a Tsawbwa on the way to Manwyne sent us a present of fowls, eggs, and an uninviting mixture of flour and chillies, with a message that when we left Ponsee, she would come out with her people, and meet us and accompany us as far as Manwyne. I record this incident, because it shows that the people are gradually beginning to realize that our mission is a peaceful one. A little opium, the white-flowered variety, is grown in the village for the use of the inhabitants, but it is also cultivated in small plots outside the village for the supply of the Shan population on the western side of the Irawady about Mogoung, and to the south of it. The opium from Tali and Yungchan finds its way to Mandalay in the caravans, where I saw it selling at Rs. 15 per vis.

26th March. A heavy thunder-shower during the night from the south-west. A month has passed to-day since we left Bhamô, and we are still virtually prisoners here.

27th March. The other day I opened a deep-seated abscess, below the groin, of one of our Kakhyen messengers. He started immediately after the operation on a visit to the nâts, and returned to me quite cured. His own account is, that he offered two pigs, and was immediately made whole. The cuckoo is now heard on the tree jungle to the east of our camp. This morning a number of Shans from Manwyne arrived with sugar-candy, salt, rice, and preserved milk for sale. The latter is in thin cakes like a dried film of cream, but I could get no information as to its preparation. When steeped in water for a night, it becomes exactly like milk. At night, the hill-sides on the opposite side of the valley are covered with great jungle fires, preparatory to cultivation.

28th March. In the afternoon, two Chinamen arrived in the village from Bhamô, with an armed escort of Burmese, for the professed object of making arrangements for working the Ponsee silver mines, on the other side of the Tapeng, on behalf of the Burmese Government. Two buffaloes have been stolen from the plains, as the Tsawbwa and some of the people he has about him are determined to appeal to the nâts regarding our fate. This theft must have been committed in some of the villages beyond Tsitkaw, as the Burmese close to the hills pay black-mail to the hill-men, and in return receive their protection.

29th March. Rain during the night. One of the buffaloes has been killed this morning as an offering to the nâts, who have been consulted, but we have not been informed in what light they regarded us. After it became known to the Shans at Mauwyne and to the peaceably-minded Kukhyens that there was a chance of our being detained some time here, they had arrived regularly every morning with rice, fowls, &c., for sale; in fact, we had quite a small bazaar to which all our men looked for their daily supplies of food. This morning, after the arrival of the Burmese, the Kukhyens from the village were early on the ground, and turned each trader away as soon as he came.

30th March. Sladen and I left our camp this morning at eight, on a visit to the silver mines. We were accompanied by two of Ponsee's Pawmines, and one of their sons. We reached the river by the next spur to the westward of the one by which I had descended on the former occasion, and arrived at our old encampment, and leaving our servants to prepare breakfast, we made for the raft. The main rope is fastened to a fallen tree above the river on the southern side, and to a large boulder on the opposite bank, where, to make it on a level with the other, it is raised on forked branches of trees driven into the ground. The raft was on the other side, and one of our Burmans pluckily caught hold of the rope, and by passing his hands one over the other dragged himself through the strong current to the opposite bank. A Pawmine followed, and from the ease and dexterity he evinced, it was evident that he was an old hand. The raft was now brought across, one man standing in front running the loop along the rope, and another sitting behind, paddling on sideways to the stream. It carries only six at a time, and simply consists of a number of bamboos tied side by side, the centre one being the longest in front, but all are of equal length behind. Those in front gradually decrease from the centre to the sides, so that a kind of prow is formed which is kept against the stream. Two bamboos overlie each other at the side, and split bamboos are laid across them as a seat, only a few inches above the water, and when laden, all the rest of the raft is one to two inches under water. I was struck by the very great prevalence of pure white marble, and by the extraordinary contorted folds of an abrupt cliff of blue crystalline quartzose rock, about 50 feet high, overlooking the ferry. We crossed over to the north-east of this cliff by a narrow foot-path, and next came upon white marble, weathering deep brown. It has the same crystalline structure of the marble of the Tsagain hills. It forms a small ridge running nearly parallel to the river, east-north-east and west-south-west. We walked along its comparatively level top for about a mile, and crossing to its eastern side, we reached a small pleasant valley, at the head of which there was some terrace cultivation, indicating the neighbourhood of a village. The ridge terminates to the north in a rounded low hill, covered with water-worn boulders of the same description as the rock on the opposite bank. This hill is separated from the ridge by a small water-course which marks the limit of the marble, which terminates so abruptly that the attention is at once attracted by the change. Whenever we reached this point, the Kakhyens abruptly stopped, saying that it was unnecessary to go any further, as there was no silver beyond. All the smelting is carried on, on the banks of the water-course and its immediate neighbourhood, and the ground was covered with heaps of slag that evidently contained a large percentage of metal. The ridge is about 600 feet above the level of the river, and is entirely free from trees. The mining is chiefly made in the slope facing the river and near the summit of the ridge, and consists of a series of low narrow tunnels run into the hill-side. They average about four feet high, and about the same in breadth or even less, and are directed inwards with a faint, downward slope, and run in from two to four hundred feet, giving off an occasional passage at right angles. The roofs are supported by bamboo props when the mines are being worked. I went a considerable way into one, preceded by a man carrying a lantern, and indeed until further progress was stopped by a portion of the roof having fallen in. The tunnel lay through red earth, with occasional small masses of marble and quartzite. The Kakhyens were resolved to show us all they could of the extent of the mines, and led us along the steep hill-side through long grass and shrub jungle so dense that each man had to cut a way for himself with a dâh. We saw about thirty borings in half an hour's scramble, and passed large masses of iron pyrites lying over the surface. The mines are on the Ponsee territory, which runs right across the valley from ridge to ridge of the two main ranges of mountains defining it. The clearings were extensive, and a good deal of cotton appeared to be cultivated.

On our return we had breakfast on the banks of the Tapeng, and treated the Kakhyens to some of our eatables, of which they indicated their approval by sundry shakings of their fists with the thumb extended, which is the Kakhyen's way of emphasizing that anything is very good. A good man is indicated by the first finger held straight, and one whose ways are dubious by its being held up crooked.

A white-flowered *Bauhinia*, with a voilet centre, was in full bloom on the southern side, along which it occurred in great profusion, but it was very scarce on the opposite hills.

The Seray Tsawbwa arrived in the evening, but had made no arrangements for mules, and the only explanation he could give was that the hire of the first batch had not been paid. The widow of a Tsawbwa sent us this evening the following curious present, two Kakhyen bags, and a tooth-brush and tongue-scraper combined in one.

31st March. We had a visit from Seray this morning to inform us that Ponsee will be content with eight maunds of silver, and that when he receives it, we will be allowed to depart out of his coasts. When Ponsee discovered that Seray was trying to procure mules for us, he sent out orders along the road that all intended for us were to be looted. This morning he came down to our camp with his drawn dâh, and in an imperative way ordered off all the Shans with provisions, and followed them up the hill, driving them before him, and has issued strict orders that no Shans for our camp are to be allowed to enter his district. The Seray's people have again promised to procure mules, and they left this afternoon for the purpose.

1st April. A Chinese boy, who came last night with some provisions for the Jemadar's wife, was looted on his way by some of the Ponsee's people, but the Tsawbwa, strange to say, went out this morning, and recovered the property.

A few Kakhyens came in the morning with rice and two or three fowls, but the contrast is a strong one to the thriving bazaar of the Shans, and the prices have gone up greatly, and an empty beer bottle does not bring twelve chittacks of rice as formerly, which reminds me to recommend travellers who may think of visiting these parts to value their bottles as they would do their rupees. We could frequently purchase with bottles what no amount of silver would have induced the owner to part with. A pint beer bottle was a handsome present.

One head Pawmine, "Death's Head," came down this afternoon, and in the course of conversation mentioned that two other Tsawbwas were with Ponsee, and that the three wished to attack us, but that the proposal has been discountenanced by the Pawmines. Sladen invited him to bring the two disaffected chiefs to the camp, and in about half an hour he returned with them. They are second-rate, petty Tsawbwas, and if their characters were to be judged of by their faces, I would pronounce them to be great blackguards. After a glass of Chinese spirit, an empty biscuit tin, and a bottle, they became our fast friends.

2nd April. Nothing of any note occurred till the afternoon, when two Shans came hurriedly and stealthily into the camp. One was the bearer of official letters in Chinese from the Panthays, but as there was no one with us who could read them, and as the man only spoke Chinese and Shan, we did not gain much information. We learned, however, that Leesetai has been defeated by the Panthays, and has retreated from Mawphoo hill.

3rd April. The Momien messenger came to Sladen this morning, and asked to be allowed to return, as he had only 16 days given him. He seemed anxious to get away, and was continually referring to the small bamboo tally on which he had marked off the days as they had passed. It was the same as in use among the Kakhyens, a thin strip of bamboo broken across at intervals.

4th April. The Pawmines and the Tsawbwa are still at variance, and the bone of contention is the Rs. 500 which are to be given when we reach Manwyne.

A half-caste who has, according to his own statement, a fair amount of Indian blood in his veins, and who professes to be one of the headmen of the Tsawbwa-gadaw of Manwyne, arrived at the camp this evening in an excited state, saying that he had succeeded in hiring 200 mules, but that they have been stopped by some ill-disposed Kakhyen Tsawbwas on the way, but that they would allow them to pass if we would pay Rs. 100; and on the chance that we would agree to this ransom, they had entrusted him with an amber chain valued at Rs. 100 as surety for their delivery. The amber when produced was valued at about 8 annas.

5th April. The breach between the Tsawbwa and his Pawmines is daily widening, and they visit us alternately. The latter stole a march on their chief, and were the first to promise to procure mules, which they affirm that the Tsawbwa is unable to do, as he dare not show himself at

Manwyne, having lately cut down a Shan. We agree to their proposals, and promise to pay Rs. 500 on reaching Manwyne, viz., Rs. 200 for the mules and Rs. 300 for the old hire. They have their eye on this last sum, which will never reach the mule-men if they are true to their present resolves. The Pawmines gone, Ponsee makes his appearance with his disreputable associates, mostly young men and boys, and advises us to have nothing to do with his officials, whose whole object, he says, is to loot us which would be a misfortune to him, as it would give him a bad name. He promises to get mules for us in a few days, and to accompany us as far as Manwyne. This is followed by Sladen's account of the promises we have just received from his Pawmines, and Sladen advises him to come to some arrangement with them, so that they may all be of one mind. This appeal, however, is of no use, and nothing has been settled after all.

The Seray's Pawmines have arrived without their chief, but accompained by 60 men and 6 mules. The numbers, however, are not sufficient for the baggage of 100 men, which is about the strength of our party; but they assert they will be able to carry it all, and facetiously recommend us to build houses if we do not intend availing ourselves of this opportunity to remove, for the Ponsee Tsawbwa will never be able to procure mules. Sladen sent a message to the chief, asking him to join the consultation, but he refused to attend; the Pawmines, however, were advised to go and arrange matters with him, as Sladen is unwilling to leave without his full concurrence.

The Kakhyens inform me that elephants occasionally visit the hills, and that one was killed near Seray, and another close to this village not many years ago. One species of *Manis* is common, but is difficult to procure. I obtained one specimen at Bhamô closely allied to *M. javanicus*. Porcupines are also not rare, and the quills of one which was lately killed near the summit of the hills were brought to me. Five species of monkey are said to occur in this neighbourhood; two of them are evidently *Hylobates*, two *Macacus*, and the other *Presbytis*. The latter I observed near the banks of the Tapeng, and regard as *P. albocinereus*, Blyth.

6th April. The Ponsee and Seray Pawmines came down early this morning, but they have not been able to come to any agreement with the Tsawbwa. The latter followed after they left, and used an argument that has a show of truth in it, that mules are better than light-handed Kakhyens, and advised us to wait, repeating the proffer he had made yesterday, but not till we promised to pay the Rs. 300 into his own hands at Manwyne if he succeeded, and to give him a present of Rs. 20 besides.

We had a visit to-day from the younger brother of the Tsawbwa of Sanda, one of the most powerful chiefs beyond. He came at the request of his brother to ascertain the real objects of the Expedition, and he appeared quite satisfied when they were fully explained to him.

The remainder of the Burmese have gone on to Manwyne, and it is arranged that we start to-morrow morning with 8 mules, and with the Seray's men and some others that have been hired in Ponsee.

7th April. We rose with the sun, packed all our things, and struck our tents, and were ready for a start a little after 7. The men came in in dribblets, and the last arrived about 9 A.M. They were all armed either with matchlocks or spears, and were the most ruffianly-looking set of human beings I ever came across.

I must here explain what I ought to have stated before, that the four Ponsee Pawmines are brothers, and that the youngest is regarded with jealous eyes by all the others. The eldest is a good-for-nothing Merry Andrew, in a chronic state of intoxication. The next in age is a quiet, sensible man, who seems fully to appreciate the advantages that would fall to the Kakhyens if the trade with China were revived across these hills, and has frequently told us that he is most anxious to lend us all the help he can. He is always to be seen with the third, who is by far the ablest of the brothers, but a man of quick, nervous temperament and violent temper, in very bad health, and with all the appearance as if he were suffering from phthisis. From his little spare frame, with sharp features, high cheek-bones, and deeply sunken eyes, he has been appropriately dubbed *Death's Head*. The youngest brother resembles him in many ways, and in point of excitability of temper they are almost one; but he has not the same influence and ability. The latter, who was among the first to arrive this morning, at once selected Sladen's baggage for his men to carry, but when Death's Head came up, he claimed it as his right. When his brother declined to give it up, he entirely lost command of himself in a fit of violent passion, and the first thing he bethought himself of was Sladen's gold-handled dâh which he had received from the king as a mark of authority, and seeing it in the hands of one of Sladen's servants, he tried to wrest it from him, and would have done so had not Williams gone to the rescue. Foiled in this, he caught hold of the Burmese clerk who was taking the names of the coolies and counting the loads, and threatened to cut him down if he listened to his brother's pretensions. This created a general hubbub, to the utter confusion of Sladen and the interpreter round whom they all crowded. He got still more excited, and, pointing his gun at the clerk and the interpreter, threatened to shoot them both. He then had recourse to his dâh, and after brandishing it about and vociferating like a fiend, a sudden thought seemed to strike him, and pulling out a long piece of cord he hurried off to one of the camp-fires, lighted it, and returned coolly, priming his matchlock, and when opposite to Sladen and Williams fired in the air. One of our surveyors, more brave than judicious, foolishly fired off his gun, on hearing which, the majority of the Kakhyens bolted towards the village, while the more intrepid rushed into the camp flourishing their spears. We treated the whole incident with the contempt it deserved, and in a few minutes the men were all again at their loads. Death's Head, however, walked to the other end of the camp, and sat down by himself loading his gun. I followed him, and asked him to return and explain his grievance, and all would be right, and, with a little coaxing, got him to come with me, and to send his gun up to the village. The Tsawbwa upbraided him, and told him he had lighted a fire in his village, and that we would kill them all by some spell.

After the loads were arranged, we found, as we had supposed, that we had not sufficient men; we were prepared to sacrifice some of the articles, but when we were ready to start, we were told that we could not possibly reach Manwyne to-day, and that we must postpone our departure till to-morrow.

8th April. The first news that greeted us this morning was that the men had returned to their villages, so that all our hopes of freeing ourselves from this life of inaction are doomed to disappointment. The Kakhyens, however, are now beginning gradually to realize that the object of the mission is a peaceful one, and that we do not wish to injure them, and I was much pleased this morning to find the Tsawbwa, who has hitherto kept aloof, waiting for me with a little sick boy, and that another Kakhyen came in during the day for treatment.

9th April. Williams and Stewart sent to the village where the Burmese are living to ascertain if they would take letters to Bhamô, and forward them to Mandalay, but they declined. In the evening two Kakhyens arrived with a letter from Moungshuay-Yah, who is said to have reached Momien by the hill road, but it gave us no information as to his whereabouts.

To-day I received a much-damaged skin of a *Hylobates*, which I believe to be *H. hoolock*, and I have now seen all the monkeys, with the exception of the light-coloured species of that genus which is said to inhabit those hills.

10th April. A Burman brought another letter to-day from Moungshuay-Yah, which he says he received from the writer at Tapeng.

In the course of the day, the youngest Pawmine came down to say that the nâts had decided against the Tsawbwa going to Manwyne to hire mules, and that he had now to propose that our baggage should be carried by men, and our tents and heavy things on ten mules. It was ultimately arranged that an attempt should be made to procure mules, and a man left in the afternoon ostensibly to try and get them.

While a very intelligent Shan was in our camp to-day, Williams suggested that he might be able to read the Momien letters which are in Chinese, and it turned out that he was. The contents of the last letter were to the effect that we were to wait here till the Panthays have defeated Leesetai, when they will come to meet us. The first was addressed to the Kakhyen chiefs, as a circular letter, requesting them to do all in their power to assist us, and that if we could not pay them in full, that they were not to allow that to stand in the way of our advance to Momien, and that the Panthays would repay them any expense they might be at on our account.

Moungshuay-Yah's letter was to the effect that he had deserted us at Ponline because he was in danger of his life from the Tsawbwa and his Pawmines, who had threatened to kill him. That he should have remained so long silent is difficult to conceive, and his retreat in the first instance to Tapeng, and his stay there, and his after-advance to Momien unknown to us, are equally puzzling.

11th April. We have ascertained to-day from a petty Burmese official that he met Leesetai's brother at Tsitkaw on his way to Bhamô where his mother resides. He has heard that the Shans are under the influence of Leesetai, and that they have determined to exterminate us if we attempt to advance without their permission, and he strongly advises us to wait until the Panthays have conquered Leesetai, and arrived at Manwyne. Leesetai has been surrounded by the Panthays at Mawphoo, and his supplies have been cut off, and the Mahomedans are now only waiting till he runs away, in accordance with the principles of Chinese warfare.

12th April. During the day, up to 4 P.M., the wind had been blowing in fitful, cool gusts from the south-west, but at that hour there was a sudden lull; thunder was heard in the distance, and deep black clouds came rolling up from the south-west. The barometer stood at 26°62' at the commencement of the storm, which was issued in by a few drops of rain, followed immediately by a heavy shower of hailstones, like lumps of ice. This was accompanied by heavy gusts of wind from the south-west, and in a few minutes the barometer rose to 26°63', and in a few more it went up to 26°65′. The storm lasted twenty minutes, and as it passed over, the aneroid rapidly fell to 26°63′, but rose again to 26°65′, where it remained. The attached thermometer registered 67°.

Thunder was rumbling over-head, but the lightning was very faint; the ice fell in circular disc-like pieces, convex on one side and flat on the other, about the size of a shilling. The centre of each was occupied by a white nucleus about one-eighth of an inch in diameter, surrounded by a pellucid zone encircled by an opaque one, which in its turn was encased in a large zone of clear ice. The external zone was filled in its inner margin with a dark substance resembling mud entangled in delicate ice crystals. The nucleus in many cases was surmounted on its convex surface by a prominent boss of clear ice. On fracturing the masses the nucleus separated as a small short cylinder, flattened at one end and rounded at the other. When perfect, the discs had all the appearance of artificial glass eyes.

13th April. A thunder-storm, accompanied by heavy rain at 5 P.M., which lasted for three hours with occasional intervals. The upper current travelled from the south-west, but the lower current was from the north-east.

14th April. A heavy storm set in at 5 A.M., and another still more severe at 9 A.M. The last was very impressive. In a few minutes a dense curtain of mist rolled up the valley in gigantic folds, obscuring everything from view, and darkening the air as in early dawn. The rain fell in torrents, the wind at first blowing from the south-west, but suddenly veering to the north-east, the barometer rising from 26°72′ to 26°82′, and, as the wind shifted to the south-west, falling again to 26°73′. We are informed that the mules are expected to-morrow.

15th April. Thunder-storm with heavy rain during the night. The Pawmine who went for the mules arrived this forenoon, but he has succeeded in getting only 30, so it is proposed to employ men to carry the rest of our baggage, and that we are to start to-morrow morning, if it does not rain heavily during the night.

A Chinaman from Momien, accompanied by our two Kakhyen messengers, arrived this afternoon. The former, who speaks Burmese fluently, has been sent by the Panthays to ascertain our real object in wishing to go to Momien. They acknowledge to have received Sladen's letters, but could not read them. They are anxious to receive us, but some ill-disposed persons are unfavourable to us. They have been informed that we have come with the intention, not of making friends, but to arrange with the Chinese with whom we have a treaty, for their destruction. Sladen fully explained to the Chinaman the object of our visit, and said if the Panthays had any doubts as to our intentions, he was willing to go alone to their city, and consult with the authorities, and if they did not agree to that, they might send some one to meet him at Manwyne, to whom he could fully state the object of our mission, and that if it did not meet with their approval, we would return. This appeared to give full satisfaction.

16th April. Thunder with heavy rain during the night. No signs of a start this morning. After all, the rain cannot be the cause of our not moving, for it has made very little impression on the road, and the hill-stream at the side of our camp is much as usual. Nearly all the women from the village came down this morning with presents of rice, sheroo, yams, tobacco, and eggs, expecting to receive in return beads and the much coveted anna-pieces. The small opaque green, red, and black beads are the kinds that are most highly prized, and a traveller with a fair stock of these, some red broad cloth, and his exchequer replete with new 8, 4, and 2-anna pieces would be almost certain of a good reception at every Kakhyen village. We bartered strings of black beads for the girdles of ratan and straw, which the women wear round their loins as a support to their short kilt-like petticoat, and a small bit of red cloth and two rupees procured for us a bell girdle which hitherto silver of itself had failed to purchase. The red cloth acted like magic, and I verily believe that if we had been more lavish with it, we could have bought one of these fair damsels and all her pertainings. As it was, they parted in the greatest glee with their girdles, seed necklaces, ear and finger rings, and many of them returned to their husbands and lovers shorn of all their ornaments, but rich in beads and seductive little bits of Her Majesty's coin. I have been struck on a number of occasions with the grey heads found among the young Kakhyen girls, some of them not over 11 years; and among our female visitors to-day, a girl of 14 or 15 had so many white hairs among her thick locks that they might have belonged to a person well up in years. I can only explain this by the hard work, insufficient nourishment, and want of rest they have to endure at an early age. The females of a family do all the hard work, and while the boys are left to amuse themselves as their inclination leads them, the little girls of even nine years of age go out twice every day in all weathers over the hill-sides, with their sisters and mothers, to cut and gather firewood, a work of considerable labour.

Sladen had a visit this afternoon from the Tsawbwa and Pawmines. It was a stormy interview, and "Death's Head" and the former drew their dâhs, and flourished them at each other. They had favoured us in the morning as well with their company, and on this occasion renewed their old demand that the Rs. 300 should be paid here before we leave, but nothing was said about our departure. A Shan arrived from Manwyne, and informed us that all the people along the road are favourable to us, even at Sanda, and wish us to go forward. Thunder and rain after sunset.

17th April. Violent storm of rain, accompanied by thunder and lightning, during the night. We rose this morning with a faint hope that we might make a start, but it did not last long, as the youngest Pawmine came down early, shouting at the pitch of his voice, demanding whether we intended to pay the Rs. 300 before we left, and as Sladen has justly resolved to withstand this imposition, we cannot hope to get away so long as the payment of this sum is made the condition on which we depart. In the forenoon the Tsawbwa came down, accompanied by all the Pawmines and our Shan acquaintance, to state that they had arranged among themselves about the division of the money, and that the Shan was to go to Manwyne for mules. The Tsawbwa brought me a fine monkey (*Macacus*) of a very deep blackish-brown, with a red face, and very short tail, not more than one inch in length. This form I have never before seen, and it is probably new.

Many women from the surrounding villages again visited us to-day with presents of sheroo, fowls, rice, tobacco, and huge yams, expecting to receive beads in return. Among them were a few who came to consult me about sores on their legs contracted in their jungle work, while some children were brought suffering almost from stone-blindness, resulting from the ravages of small-pox.

18th April. We were again importuned this morning for beads by women and young girls, who never, however, came empty-handed. No steps after all have been taken to procure mules. The Shan, Tsawbwa, and Pawmines were all present again to-day to demand the Rs. 300.

Lawloo, our staunch Kakhyen friend and messenger, arrived this afternoon. He confirms the defeat of Leesetai at Mawphoo, and states that he retreated to Shuemuelong mountain, on the opposite side of the valley from his old fortress.

19th April. The Tsawbwa has had the cool impudence to say to-day that all the past talk and promises about getting mules were false, but that he now faithfully undertakes to procure them, and, to indicate that what he said might be relied on, he locked his two forefingers together, and gave them a shake, as much as to say that his word was now binding.

Lawloo informs us that he met the Shan on his way to Manwyne to obtain the necessary number of mules.

20*th April*. Two Shans arrived to-day from Manwyne informing us that a circular letter had been sent by the Panthays to all the Shan Tsawbwas along the road to Momien, requesting them to give us all the assistance in their power in hastening our advance. They assure us that the road is now open, and that we have nothing to fear from Leesetai. They say that the Kakhyens have spread the report that we have been delayed here because we have not paid the mule-hire from Tsitkaw. Sladen, however, explained to them the whole facts, and they have promised to report them, and to get mules for us. The Kakhyens here, we have learned from those men, are friendly to Leesetai.

The oak trees are now in full blossom, and their prevalence becomes very apparent; they are chiefly confined to heights above 3,500 feet. On a visit to the village, I saw a Kakhyen woman at her loom, which is usually brought out to the open door, as the houses are too dark for work of this kind. In rain the weaving is conducted under the eaves of the house. In the evening one of our men brought us a damp log of wood, which he asserted gave off sparks in the dark, while he was breaking it with his axe. On removing it from the light of the fire where we were seated, we found it glowing with a wonderfully brilliant, phosphorescent light, along the newly-cut surface. More logs in the same state were brought to us by others of our men, who were greatly astonished at the remarkable phenomenon. Only the soft damp portions of the wood were phosphorescent, but they seemed, as it were, to be saturated with it, for even in thin layers, the light was quite brilliant. They were all from a low, damp hollow, and smelt strongly of fungi. The light was pale, bluish-green, and flickering.

21*st April*. A party of Burmans, said to be for the silver mines, passed through the village to-day on their way to Manwyne, accompanied by "Death's Head," who has deserted us since his younger brother undertook to get mules.

22*nd April*. A number of sick visited me to-day, and among my patients, I now reckon the Tsawbwa himself, who is suffering from inflammation of his gums, and while I was prescribing for him, he confessed that he had hitherto behaved like a fool, but he now intended to turn over a new leaf, and desired us to consider him as our friend. I believe this generous impulse was solely prompted by the kind treatment he was experiencing at the moment, and the credit of having awakened it redounds to medicine.

I ascended to-day the high summit above our camp, and met no one on the way. It is fully 2,000 feet above the village of Ponsee, and is the highest visible point on the northern side of the Tapeng, but some higher peaks appear to the south and to the north-east. The country to the north of this range is a sea of hills as far as the eye can reach, with the main chains running nearly north and south, with slight easting in their northerly course. The rocks on the summit consist exclusively of schistose gneiss. There is a village on the top of this ridge close to the highest peak, and its presence is announced, before it is seen, by the usual small bamboo platforms by the roadside, with offerings of rice, &c., to the nâts. There is a well-trodden bridle-path along the summit of the ridge, and I suppose this to be the route that the Seray Tsawbwa proposed we should follow to Sanda. The Kakhyens here say that the Chinese army went by this road. Looking to the north-east, I had a glimpse of the narrow flat of the Sanda valley lying far below me in the distance, defined by a noble ridge of mountains on either side, two colossal walls shutting in the peaceful valley from the world without. The summits of all the hills, except in the immediate neighbourhood of villages, are covered with a dense forest, in which there appears to be a remarkable absence of animal life, for I returned with only one bird, *Chleuasicus ruficeps*, Blyth, and I did not observe a single mammal.

After dark, our Kakhyen messenger, Lawloo, and his companion, with two Panthays, arrived with letters in Chinese, but we were unable to read them. The men left us after a few hours for another village, as they were afraid to remain here over the night.

23rd April. The Tsawbwa has been called to Manwyne, and it is reported that the Pawmine, who left this for the same town with the Burman, has been taken prisoner by the Shans, in retaliation for the Tsawbwas having cut down one of their people who came to sell provisions to our camp. This is the budget of news for the day.

24th April. A messenger arrived late last night with a letter from the Panthays in Arabic, telling us not to delay at Ponsee, but to advance as quickly as possible, and that they were anxiously awaiting our arrival. He received a few rupees, and a penknife which gratified him much more than the money.

We had a very severe thunder-storm about sunset yesterday, attended by torrents of rain. My tent, on this as on previous occasions of a like kind, proved no protection against rain, and my bed was a pool of water, and had it not been that I was protected by a water-proof blanket, sleep would have been out of the question.

In a ramble over the hill-sides to-day, I came upon an ingenious Kakhyen trap for jungle fowl and pheasants, in a dense clump of bamboos. A miniature fence of the stems of tall jungle grass extended down the hill-side for about 200 feet; there were a number of little open ways through it, and in these, a pliable bamboo was firmly fixed into the ground by one end, while the other was bent down and only sufficiently fixed to prevent its springing up of itself, and a cord with a running loop attached to it was fastened to this end. The game make for the openings, and coming in contact with the loosely fixed end of the bamboo it springs up drawing the noose tightly around the animal, and if the latter is light, swinging it into the air. I also met some boys snaring birds with the sticky juice of the root of some plant. They had a trident, made of wood, fixed into a long bamboo, and the prongs were smeared with the so-called lime, and had a cord stretched across them, and were baited with winged ants, so fastened that they had the free use of their wings, the constant flutter of which attracted the unwary birds to perch on the prongs, where they became easy captives. This snaring apparatus is usually laid against the side of some dense jungle by the road-side, with the stalk well hidden so as not to excite suspicion, and it proves a very effective snare.

25th April. We have had numerous visits to-day from women, old and young, all intent upon obtaining beads, the young ones for themselves, and the mothers for their children. They appeared in a new light, throwing off all the timidity and reserve that has hitherto characterized their interviews with us, and one young sprightly maiden hinted that if we would prepare fowls and rice, they would favour us with their company at the feast.

26th April. On the 18th of this month, Sladen had addressed a circular letter to the members of the Expedition, stating he considered that the Expedition had no longer any practical existence in the sense in which it originally started, and that the survey of the routes between Burmah and South-Western China was effectually put a stop to, for the present at least, by the setting-in of the south-west monsoon, and the advanced state of the season; but as he saw that political advantages of no slight importance might in all probability be secured if he could succeed in reaching Momien, he intended to remain here, or elsewhere, for at least two or even three months longer. He did not see why his stay should necessitate the detention of the whole party, and stated that a diminution in its numerical strength might be conducive to his own progress and success, when estimating the limited funds at his disposal, and the necessity for reducing our luggage and expenditure to the lowest possible limit. He stated that he had neither the power nor authority to order the withdrawal of any one in particular, but that any member who might be inclined to return to British territory would do so with his full concurrence and support. I have taken till now to consider, and to-day I wrote to Sladen to the effect, that the only argument in his letter for a reduction of our party at all applicable to me was the pecuniary one, and that I would not be justified in remaining longer with the Expedition unless I saw a reasonable probability that the funds would admit of carriage being provided for my specimens, as my services had been given to the Expedition by the Government of India solely on the strength of the advantages likely to accrue to the Indian Museum from the collections formed by me while in the field. In reply to this, Major Sladen has written to me that my expenses will not add so materially to his own as to interfere with the plans he has in view of prosecuting the object of our mission, and on the strength of this assurance, I have resolved to remain with him. Captain Williams and Mr. Stewart have decided with much reluctance to sever their connection with our party. The former was led to the decision he has arrived at, having formed the same opinion as Major Sladen, that little can now be done in the way of surveying, and towards acquiring the other information which he was desired to collect by the instructions he received from the Chief Commissioner. Moreover, as our leader has distinctly stated that the Expedition has no longer any practical existence in the sense in which it was constituted, and that a reduction in the numerical strength of our party may conduce to his progress and success in securing certain political advantages, Captain Williams' sacrifice of his own wishes for the future well-being of the Expedition is most laudable. The pecuniary argument does not apply to Captain Bowers, who has come provided with funds of his own, so that he has resolved to remain.

27th April. It has been finally arranged that Williams and Stewart start on the 29th, with a guard of six men, and that their luggage is to be carried by their own men, some of the guard, and Sladen's lascars.

29th April. Williams and Stewart left at 6 A.M., accompanied by Moungmo as Kakhyen interpreter. They go as far as Ponline, where they sleep for the night, and next morning proceed to Tsitkaw, which they ought to reach by noon, and if they succeed in getting boats there at once, they should arrive at Bhamô the same day.

30th April. The Tsawbwa has informed us to-day that the Panthays are as far as Sanda, and that in ten days more they will be to meet us here. They are consolidating their power at Muangla and Sanda, both of which Tsawbwaships are now under their protection, and pay them tribute.

1st May. To-day I have despatched five boxes of natural history specimens and plants to Williams' care, in company with his photographic and other boxes. I have had a number of successful cases within the last few days, and among my patients I had one of the Pawmines, who is very grateful for my having dispossessed him of an enormous *Tænia solium*, a parasite, which, as was to be expected, is very prevalent among these hill people, who live largely on pork derived from the most foul-feeding swine it has ever been my lot to witness. A Syme's bistoury, used to two well-set abscesses, electrified the bystanders, and gave instant relief to two Kakhyens, who seemed to doubt in their own minds whether I was a good nât or a devil. Their little offerings, however, of rice and sheroo, shortly afterwards brought to me and laid at my feet, were pleasing proofs that these untutored hill people are keenly alive to the feelings of gratitude.

2nd May. To-day we despatched two Kakhyen boys with letters to Williams, asking him to send us one or two books to read, as our present library is composed of two volumes of "Half Hours with Select Authors." These boys started from here in the morning, and were to reach Tsitkaw the same night, which, they said, they could do with ease, and the letters are to be delivered to Sladen's head lascar, who, we hope, will not have left that village before the arrival of the messengers. This incident shows that we are gaining on the good graces of the Kakhyens, and that they are now much more willing to assist us than at first. Of late the villagers have become very friendly with our men, and during the day they may be seen in numbers in the camp smoking and chatting, but an incident which happened two days ago shows that they are dangerous characters to deal with. One of our guard, who alleges he was only joking and chatting with a Kakhyen, was without any warning felled to the ground by him, receiving a cut over the forehead with a dâh, the savage decamping into the dense jungle on the hill-side. The gash was nearly four inches long and laid the bone bare, and the man had another cut across his arm from the downward sweep of the dâh. He recovered, however, in a few days.

3rd May. The only piece of news to record to-day is, that a Shan arrived this morning with a letter from Moungshuay-Yah, to the effect that Tusakone, the governor of Momien, has arrived at Sanda, and requests us to go forward as soon as possible with all our luggage.

4th May. The men who accompanied Williams and Stewart returned this afternoon. They tell us that no sooner had Moungmo arrived in

Bhamô than he was imprisoned for having conducted them back. Our men, however, behaved very well, going to the Woon, and informing him that he had no right to imprison Moungmo as he was now in the employment of the Expedition, and had been sent to Bhamô expressly on our business, demanding his liberation, and offering to let one of their members be confined in his stead. This had the desired effect, and the man was liberated, and he arrived at our camp this evening.

5th May. I had a long ramble to-day over some new rice clearings, and obtained a good view of the rock which forms the greater part of the hills. It is a pale blue schistose gneiss, very finely grained in some localities, and much coarser in others, as, for example, in the porphyritic bed near the Tapeng. The finer beds have frequently white quartz bands running through them, parallel to the line of cleavage, and many of the larger rounded boulders on the hill-sides, some of which are of enormous size, become prominent objects from the prevalence of those quartz layers, which are so regularly distributed that at a distance they look as if they had been carefully drawn by the hand of man. I have hitherto been puzzled in my walks over these hills with the numbers of old tracks overgrown with dense jungle that one sees, but I met with a full explanation to-day of their origin and use, on a hill-side that had been newly cleared. It is this, that when a portion of a hill-side is cleared for the first time, a road is regularly cut along it, and joined to the nearest path communicating with the village, and if there be a deficiency of water on any part of the new clearing, the new path is usually brought near some neighbouring stream which is diverted into a channel dug on the inside of the road. The stream is thus carried down precipitous hill-sides, and by secondary channels devoted to the terraces of cultivation. The roads and canals of irrigation in some cases extend one or two miles. The terraces of cultivation are carefully tilled with a wooden plough, in every respect resembling the one in use in Bengal, but the steep hill-sides have the ground only broken up with a hoe, and the rice and Indian corn are grown together in long lines. The people are now busily preparing the soil.

In the afternoon, Lawloo arrived with a Chinese letter from the Panthays, informing us that Tasakone was at Sanda, and that Moungshuay-Yah was with him. The former sent a message by Lawloo to the effect that the first account he had received of us was, that we were an armed party come with the intention of fighting against him; but as he was now satisfied that our mission was a peaceful one, he was most anxious to receive us, and had arranged with the Shan Tsawbwas that they should send representatives to meet us. Moungmo has received a letter from his wife to-day, telling him that she has been put in the stocks by the Burmese officials for his having joined us, and that she is to be kept in them until he is forthcoming. On the man's earnest entreaty, Sladen wrote to the Woon, informing him of what the Tsitkaw officials had done, and requesting him to order the woman's release, and desiring that he might be held responsible for the non-appearance of the man. As Moungmo informs us that he had privately heard at Bhamô that the Woon had received orders from Mandalay to advance any money to the Expedition that we may require, Sladen has resolved, in the present low state of our exchequer, to apply for the loan of Rs. 5,000, or any smaller sum they may be able to give us.

7th May. Nothing worthy of note has happened beyond Sladen's having despatched the Panthay Chinaman and Lawloo with a letter to Moungshuay-Yah at Sanda, informing him of the cause of our delay, and that we have little or no prospect of getting away from this unless he can arrange with the Shan Tsawbwas to send us some mules. As we have heard that Tasakone has so far arranged with the Shan Tsawbwas to assist us that they are now collected at Manwyne for the purpose, the messengers with the letters have been instructed to make enquiries there how matters stand, before they go further, and if they are favourable to us, to return and report progress.

8th May. This has been a most eventful day, as the Panthay Chinaman and Kakhyen returned, accompanied by the representatives of the Shan towns. The very appearance of the latter is a pleasure, as their persons are scrupulously clean, their faces intelligent, and their whole man in strong contrast to the ignorant and filthy Kakhyens. They are nearly as fair as Europeans, and the eyes of some of them are light brown. They are dressed in dark blue from head to foot, from their turbans to their shoes. After they had breakfasted in the village, they returned, accompanied by the young Pawmine, who wore a bright red turban, rose-cheeked trousers of the Shan cut, and a gorgeous red blanket over his shoulders. He was fully impressed with his own importance, and shouted at the pitch of his voice to impress us with it as well. The Shans remained in our camp for some hours, and are unanimous in inviting us to go forward, and in promising us all the assistance in their power, and they deny that they ever threatened to attack us in the event of our having gone forward to Manwyne. After a long consultation about the mule hire, in which the Pawmine took a vigorous part, they all agreed that the muleteers had no further claim, but Sladen being willing to adhere to his promise, it was arranged, with the Pawmine's approval, that the Rs. 300 are to be paid to the chief Shan at Manwyne, who will distribute them. Two men have been sent to Manwyne for mules, and we are to leave this the day after tomorrow. They take an enlightened interest in all that has been said to them about the Expedition, and appreciate the advantages that would accrue to the country if trade were revived. They are immensely taken with our guns, camp-table, bedding, knives, forks, &c., and it was a pleasure to observe that even the ignorant Kakhyen Pawmine had been impressed with our civilization, and acted as the cicerone of the party. The Manwyne representative has pressed Sladen to remain a few days at his town, as his daughter is sick.

9th May. The Shans spent the greater part of the day, strolling about, examining everything in the camp.

Now that I look back on the last two months, it is subject of wonder how we should ever have thought that we were to experience no delays, and that we were to march right on to Momien without opposition; for it must be remembered that the Shans and Panthays had no intimation of our visit, beyond the reports circulated by the Burmese, and the letters sent by Sladen; and that we had come, as it were, suddenly upon them as an armed party, among a people, too, who had never before seen an European. In such circumstances, the marvel is that they have so soon appreciated the real objects of the mission. If we had gone straight to Manwyne instead of remaining here, it is very probable that some serious complication might have arisen on account of the Burmese reports, but remaining quietly in the hills, and declining to go forward until we had received the full consent of the chiefs, the people had time to learn for themselves that our coming was a peaceable one; and it has been fraught with no little good to them, in having led to the ousting of Leesetai from Mawphoo on the high road to Momien.

We were told to-day by the Shans that the Ponline Tsawbwa is the greatest blackguard on this route, and that under Chinese influence, he had sent gunpowder to Leesetai for our destruction, and that he and Ponsee are both in league with the Chinese. The messengers returned this morning from Bhamô with a few books.

10th May. While I was out this morning trying to shoot some birds, not an easy undertaking in these hills, Sladen had a very satisfactory conversation with the Shans, who spend most of their time in our camp. All the Shan towns are represented, and the envoys are most desirous for the re-opening of this route, which they say is the direct one. They bitterly complain, however, of the unsettled state that the country has been in for the last fifteen years, and of the incessant fighting that has been going on, and of the raids for plunder to which their towns have been subjected by the Panthays. They allege that our coming among them has already produced good results, and that the defeat of Leesetai is entirely attributable to it; they also express a strong wish that we would not return until order has been restored among them, even if it should require two seasons to accomplish it. Another of their grievances is, that they cannot visit the annual fair at Bhamô on account of the extortion that is now the order of the day among the Woon and his officials. If they were to go with three buffalo skins, the Burmese officials would appropriate one, and if they were not very good, two would be taken, and, moreover, a heavy tax is levied on every coolie carrying rice. They give it as their sober opinion that if the Kakhyen hills did not intervene, there would be a large influx of population from Upper Burmah into the Shan states to escape the oppressive taxation of the Burmese. They pay at present a moderate tribute to the Panthays, and their own taxation is light.

The Pawmine, who has behaved so well within the last few days, came this morning to say that he had talked with the Tsawbwa, who is very glad to learn that everything has been arranged for our departure. We have lived so long in his village, he says, that there is neither a man, woman, nor child who does not possess some gift from us, and that our residence has been productive of great good to the community. The Pawmine himself is most anxious that this route should be opened, and says if we come back again, he will place himself at our disposal to make what use we like of him, and that he will kill buffaloes and pigs, and that the Tsawbwa and other Pawmines will drink the blood, and dip their dâhs and spears in it, and that whatever agreement we may then decide upon will be binding for ever.

An old respectable Kakhyen Tsawbwa has arrived within the last few days, on behalf of another hill chief who claims Deen Mahomed as his slave, to whom he had given a wife, buffaloes, and pigs. Sladen refuses to give him up, as he came at our request and under our protection, but agrees when we return to Bhamô that the matter will be settled in accordance with the usages of the country.

CHAPTER XIII.

PONSEE TO MOMIEN.

The Shans came down very early on the morning of 11th May to announce that sufficient mules had arrived for us to start. We packed up with right good will, and at 8 A.M., the mules came straggling down the hill-side from the village. Some time, however, elapsed before everything was arranged, and just before we had struck our tents, it seemed doubtful whether we would get away after all, for "Death's Head" Pawmine appeared on the scene, and attempted to create a disturbance about Williams having taken a photograph of his house in his absence. He alleged that his wife and child had been sick ever since, and that we had taken the picture of his house to bewitch him, in revenge for his having stolen our cow, which he wished now to return, on condition that we removed the spell under which he was suffering; and another Pawmine demanded that the Kakhyens should receive two rupees for each mule, threatening to attack us if we attempted to start before agreeing to this proposal. Sladen took the bull by the horns, and treating them like school-boys, mentally tucked up his sleeves, and told them to come on, and, suiting the action to the word, fumbled at his revolver. This acted like magic, and both sneaked away thoroughly crest-fallen.

We started at half-past eleven, but not having sufficient mules, we abandoned our tents, and now trust for shelter to the hospitality of the people beyond. The first mile and a half of the road is tolerably level as far as the village of Kingdoung, from whence we made a steep descent to a comparatively flat country, covered with many rice terraces, now flooded for cultivation, while here and there the ground was only being roughly broken up by men and boys who used a large hoe for the purpose. This steep descent could easily be avoided by the road skirting a spur to the east, which runs down nearly to the valley of the Tapeng in a long gradual slope. On the flat below Kingdoung, there are numerous small streams which drain into the Tapeng from the south and north. It is in reality a hollow closed in on all sides but one, and, receiving the drainage of the surrounding hills, it has a rich alluvial soil. The largest stream running through it is the Thame, which flows nearly due south, turning abruptly to the east to reach the Tapeng, which flows on the other side of the long spur from the Kingdoung village. At the northern extremity of this hollow, we obtain a fine view of the Tapeng valley stretching away to the east-north-east, shut in on both sides by ranges of mountains. Our distance from Ponsee was 4 miles, 5 furlongs and 140 yards, and beyond this point, which is the north-easterly water-shed of the hollow, we descended in a long gradual slope over inequalities, rounded grassy hills, and dried-up water-courses, to the valley of the Tapeng. After we had gone 2 miles of this part of the road, which is destitute, or nearly so, of trees, we were met by the old Tsawbwa-gadaw of Muang-gan, accompanied by a number of young women with presents of cooked rice, sheroo, and flowers. We dismounted, and after a refreshing drink of good, newly-brewed Kakhyen beer (sheroo), and a short, friendly talk with the old lady who had come out chiefly in the hope of getting beads, we proceeded on our way over a tolerably good road about six feet broad. Shortly after leaving the Tsawbwa-gadaw, we met two men who had taken up their position by the road-side to inform us that they knew of the whereabouts of some of our property that had been stolen on our way to Ponsee, and promising to bring it on to Manwyne. About 2 miles further on, we crossed another small stream running into the Tapeng, and from a mound over which the road lay, we had a view of the Tapeng entering the hills through a very narrow gorge; before doing so, it is a fine, broad stream with low, white, sandy banks; but at this season, it is fordable almost at every point. Whenever we reached this open valley, the indications of civilization were apparent in the well-cleared and richly cultivated fields, and in the numerous villages situated in isolated clumps of bamboos and fine trees, on the highest undulations. It runs nearly east-north-east and west-south-west, and is about 4 to 5 miles in breadth, and appears almost level. It is defined on either side by a range of mountains about 2,500 feet high, and of nearly equal height throughout. At its northern extremity the two ranges appear to approach each other, and another is seen in the far distance running nearly at right angles to them. The level ground approaches the hills in gentle slopes, and is cut up at intervals into deep hollows by the drainage of the hills, but these channels are nearly empty at present, as the water has been turned off for the irrigation of the rice-fields. Two crops are raised in a year, one of opium and another of rice. At present the whole low ground appears to be under the latter, but the slopes at the base of the hills and the lower hill-sides are covered with rich herbage supporting large herds of cattle and buffaloes. The Tapeng winds through the centre of the valley, and numerous villages occur on the high ground along its banks. From the long reaches of sand on either side of it, it is evident that it must flood a great part of the country during the rains. The superficial formations are seen to be, fine, granitic, and schistose river gravels, resting on tenacious, bluish and yellowish clays (used by the Shans in making bricks and coarse earthen-ware), generally capped by a rich soil of nearly the same colour.

After entering the valley, our road lay past several villages, about which large crowds of Shans and Chinese had collected, and had been anxiously waiting for hours to see us pass, and when we reached the first one of any importance, we found mats laid out for us under two fine trees, and as we approached we were challenged by the officials of Manwyne, who addressed Sladen somewhat to this effect: "you say you are a man of authority, therefore we allow you to pass." We were, however, not expected to take any notice of them, and passed on, they following in the rear mounted on ponies, with a crowd of boys behind them. On reaching Manwyne, we found the sandy bed of the river, in front of the town, covered by a dense crowd of men, women, and children, and that our mules had been unloaded on this arid waste, where we were expected to encamp; but as we had no tents, our first impression of Shan hospitality was not very flattering to that kind-hearted people. No sooner had we dismounted than the crowd closed in about us, so that we were almost suffocated by the intense heat. It was certainly the most inquisitive crowd I ever had the ill-luck to encounter, and our persons were made the subject of close scrutiny, and one fellow, more daring than his comrades, had the cool impudence to feel the texture of my beard. The Shan women are very fair and good-looking, and their dress peculiar but picturesque. The head-dress is a long, blue turban coiled with great precision and neatness, and so arranged over the forehead that each successive coil exposes a narrow crescentic margin of the one below it, stretching from ear to ear, and the effect of this is to throw the turban slightly backwards. It towers nearly a foot above the head, and the back hair is plaited with silk, and twisted over and incorporated with the last coil of the turban. The back of the head is exposed in the hollow of its blue inverted cone, and is ornamented with large silver buttons. The women wear neat, little, light or dark-blue coloured jackets, usually ornamented here and there with red trimming, and fastened with square, enamelled, silver brooches, and the sleeve is turned back so as to expose a plump, little arm with a large silver bracelet. The petticoat reaches to the ankles, but is usually tucked up a short way to nearly the knee, and is bound round the waist by a roll of blue cloth, and this, with a small apron, completes their attire. There was a good sprinkling of Chinese women among the crowd, in the usual costume of their country, and with dwarfed feet; but they were much more poorly clad than the Shans, and were evidently not in such good circumstances. The Shan and Chinese men were all dressed in dark blue; the Shan peasantry wore blue turbans with their long hair plaited with a pig-tail, which is wound up among the coils of the head-dress; while the townsmen, Tartar-like, had skull-caps with pendant pig-tails, and each carried a long-stemmed pipe either with a small clay or brass bowl.

After a mild remonstrance on our part at being expected to encamp out on this sandy flat without any covering, it was arranged that we should be accommodated in a Buddhist monastery or khyoung in the town.

Manwyne is situated on a slight rising ground on the right bank of the Tapeng, and is approached from the river by a rough way laid with rounded boulders. It is surrounded by a low wall, about six feet high, of sun-dried bricks, with a foundation of rough stones, about one foot high, to keep it dry. There are two entrances close to each other: the first leading into the bazaar, and the other into an open court-yard in which the khyoung stands. This building faces the river, and is a low square edifice, built partially of sun-dried bricks and of wood, the walls having a rubble foundation, and the floor being raised about three feet off the ground on piles. It is roofed with fired tiles; and a kind of closed verandah facing the river is built almost exclusively of wood, and has a door at either end. It has two roofs, a lower and upper, the latter in itself somewhat like a smaller khyoung perched on the top of the former. The curves of the roof, as in the case of all the houses, are as markedly concave as the eaves are convex, and the sides of the upper roof have each two small latticed windows. As there is no centre wall, the roof is supported on strong teak pillars. The floor of the main body of the building is slightly raised above the verandah, and two wooden partitions shut off a narrow strip, on both sides, as the dormitories of the priests and their pupils. A kitchen in one corner, with an outside door and one communicating with the khyoung, completes the domestic arrangements, if we include two or three coffins, and the materials for more, piled in one corner of the verandah, to be in readiness for the next death. A long table stands against the centre partition covered with models of pagodas, in which are seated figures of Guadama in marble and wood; one principal Buddh occupies the centre of the table, with an umbrella suspended over his head from the roof. During the evening prayers of the priests, two large candles were lit on this altar, strongly reminding one of the ceremonial of the Roman Catholic Church, a resemblance which is heightened by the ringing of bells and the intoned prayers of the priests. In the verandah, there are three square niches facing this altar, and one contains the model of a horse while the others are empty. We had no sooner arrived in this interesting religious house than it became filled with a dense but well-behaved crowd, who stared at us with astonishment, and favoured us with their presence till we retired for the night.

12th May. Sladen and I strolled through the village in the morning, first visiting the bazaar which is held every day for some hours, below the khyoung, outside the wall. Here the vendors were chiefly young women, and each sat in front of a small basket with a tray on the top of it containing her stock-in-trade. Among eatables, I observed a gelatinous substance resembling curds, said to be made from peas and beans, and in great request; peas in which germination had proceeded a considerable way seemed a staple vegetable, along with beans, onions, and a plant resembling a cabbage, with a long, succulent stem which is the only edible part. Among fruits, there was a profusion of luscious, wild brambles of two or three species, and wild plums and cherries. Numerous sweetmeats were also offered for sale, also a mixture of green leaves resembling Burmese ngapé, betel-nut, and all its necessary accompaniments, and various kinds of tobacco. Among grains, I noticed Indian corn, rice, and barley. One end of the bazaar was devoted to the sale of unbleached, cotton cloth of country manufacture, with a small sprinkling of English piece-goods, and red and green broad-cloth. The bazaar is resorted to by the peasantry of the surrounding villages, and many Kakhyens, principally young women, were present with loads of firewood and short deal planks for sale, and what struck us as in forcible contrast to our Bhamô experience, was the perfect freedom enjoyed by these people who are so oppressed whenever they visit Burmese territory. We re-entered the village through the narrow doorway close to the khyoung entrance, and found ourselves in a narrow, filthy street, with a deep, open gutter on each side, close under the shop windows, and alive with swine of all ages. The street is about nine feet in its broadest part, and paved with rounded, water-worn boulders. The houses are built of bricks, and, as a rule, have only the ground-floor, with one room to the street having a door and open window, the sill of the latter serving as the counter over which the goods are sold. Nearly all the shops were devoted to the sale of pork. Five minutes' walk through this piggery brought us to the southern exit, with the Shan quarter to the north of it. This part of the town is very clean, and all the houses are detached, each in a little court-yard of its own, in which the ponies, buffaloes, cattle and farm implements are kept under substantial sheds, along two sides of the enclosure. Each house seemed a miniature farmstead.

A few villages lie close outside the so-called town, each enclosed by a bamboo fence, and intersected by narrow paths railed in on either side, and marking off the plots of the villagers. None of the houses are raised on piles as in Burmah, and all of the better class are built of bricks and tiled, while the smaller cottages have mud walls. In one village we saw a man cutting tobacco for the use of the gentler sex, and on looking at the process, we were politely offered stools by some women, and invited to be seated while we were instructed by the tobacconist in the mystery of his art. The fresh leaves are rolled firmly together, and pushed through a circular hole in an upright piece of wood on a stand, and very thin slices are rapidly cut off from the other side, while the green mass is kept moving forwards through the circular aperture. The cut tobacco is only partially dried, and smoked while it is still green. Some was brought to us, and we filled our pipes, and sat chatting with these homely Shans for a full half-hour.

During the day, the khyoung was crowded with Shans, Chinese, and Kakhyens from the surrounding villages, and my time was fully occupied for hours in prescribing for the numerous patients who visited me. In the afternoon, I went out to shoot followed by a troop of boys and pigs, but as the latter soon discovered that I was not intent on contributing to their enjoyment, I was soon rid of them; but the boys followed me up pertinaciously, and when a bird fell, a pack of human retrievers dashed wildly forward, and scrambled for the birds. I had not fired many shots, however, when a Shan came out of one of the villages, and entreated me not to shoot, for I should certainly exasperate the great nât if I persisted, and he in his ire would deluge them with rain, and ruin their crops. Sladen and Bowers spent the whole day planning with the Kakhyens about the disposal of the Rs. 300, but the matter is still unsettled.

15th May. In the early morning I was awoke by the matin-bell, and by the rapid chant of the priests and their pupils at their morning prayers. On opening my eyes, I found our apartment thronged with precise old matrons and buxom Shan girls at their devotions. Each carried a neat little basket over her arm with an offering of rice, a portion of which was placed in front of one of the images, and the rest went to the priests. A few also brought offerings of flowers. On entering, they first knelt in front of the altar on which the chief figure of Guadama was seated, but they did not venture on the raised platform, which is forbidden to women. After muttering a short prayer, they turned to the niche in the verandah, in which there was the image of the horse, and here they repeated another prayer standing, and then deposited their little offering of cooked rice in front of this revered representation of the equine race. We next became the objects of their attention, but they were too timid to give us much of it on this first occasion. After the priests had finished their prayers, I found all the women arranged outside the khyoung in a long line waiting for the head-priest, a burly, jolly individual, with shaven head, draped in the yellow toga of his order. He soon appeared, and drawing a long face, with downcast eyes, walked with a large bowl in front of his female parishioners, each of whom placed a handful of rice in the capacious vessel, and this done, they all dispersed to their homes. This practice of the phoongyees' gathering their daily food from the women on their visits to the khyoung, instead of going about the town with the sacred patta, begging for it from house to house, is an instance, among others of a much more serious kind, of the laxity that prevails amongst them.

A final settlement of the Rs. 300 was arrived at this forenoon; and afterwards, Sladen distributed presents to the principal officials or head-men of the town, and to those of Sanda and Muangla, and all seemed well pleased with their gifts. In the afternoon we visited the Tsawbwa-gadaw accompanied by the officials. Her house is the largest in the town, which, however, is not saying much, for it is about the size of a small English cottage. To reach it, we had to pass through two court-yards, the sides of the outer one forming the stables, and those of the inner one the kitchen and servants' apartments, with the house filling up its other side. The entrance from the first to the second court is so constructed that it forms a waiting hall, and a bench covered with a silken coverlet had been placed for us. We had not many minutes to wait there, when we were invited to go through the court to the house, which we found raised about three feet above ground, with an open reception hall, corresponding to the one we had just passed through, apparently separating off another court, in which were the private apartments. The court in which we were received was laid out with flowers, with two dwarf yews as centre pieces, and a small vine trailing over a trellis. High-backed chairs with red cushions were set for us, and the Tsawbwa-gadaw soon appeared from her apartment, accompanied by some Buddhist nuns in white, and by three waiting-maids: her daughter, who has taken the veil, was one of the former. She wore an enormous blue turban that towered about one foot and half above her head, expanding upwards from the forehead, a white jacket fastened with large, square, enamelled silver clasps, and having a narrow, richly embroidered collar that stood erect round her neck, a blue petticoat with a beautifully ornamented silken border, and broad silken stripes from the knee downwards, in novel patterns and in a variety of soft, exquisitely grouped colours. Tight-fitting leggings of the same character as the petticoat, and Shan shoes covered with embroidery, completed her toilet. She came in smoking a long pipe with a handsome silver mouth-piece. Sladen had a long conversation with her on various subjects, but chiefly with reference to our mission. She expressed much pleasure at the prospect of the re-opening of trade with Burmah, and promised us her hearty support. She is a little, stout woman, with a round, fair face, and of a quiet and self-possessed manner. A waiting-man presented us with small cups of bitter tea, and little saucers with all the necessaries of a betel-nut eater, and after managing to swallow the first and chewing the latter to our intense discomfort, we retired having evidently won the esteem of the old lady. The nuns took a prominent part in the conversation, and impressed us as women of considerable intelligence.

To-day, the khyoung has again been crowded by people from all quarters, and I had numerous patients of both sexes and ages who were very grateful for any kindness shown them, and some of the old, almost blind men and women who came to me, appeared to think that I had only to touch them, and they would be made whole. In the evening we were warned to be on our guard during the night, as some evil-disposed Shans from the other side of the river have come over with the object of trying their fortune in our camp. The towns-people, however, have placed an armed guard round the khyoung for our protection.

14th May. The town was in an excited state this morning, and when we went down to our camp, we found that all the people had turned out on the bank of the river to see us depart. The young women had their head-dresses beautifully decorated with sweet-smelling flowers which were ungrudgingly given to us by many of them; when we were fairly off, the good-natured smiles and nods from the crowd were unmistakable evidence that our short stay had made a favourable impression.

Our course lay along the right bank of the river, over a tolerably good, but narrow, mule path, and slightly undulating ground. At a point about three or four miles from Manwyne, where the road runs along the top of a rather high bank overhanging the river, our attention was called to a number of men, on the opposite side, who rushed out of a village down to the river bank, as they saw us approaching. Although we could see that they were all armed, we did not suspect that they had any hostile intentions, especially after our friendly reception at Manwyne, and kept on our way thinking that they were only influenced by curiosity. However, when we were opposite to them, and ascending and descending some hollows, whiz went a shot over our heads, so startling Sladen's pony that his hat fell off. At this, they raised a yell, and bang went some more shots, while we observed some of them springing about, and brandishing their dâhs, which flashed in the bright sunshine. We took no notice, but they kept firing occasional shots at our men as they filed past. At first, they seemed inclined to follow us up, but our apparent indifference to their fire cooled their ardour, and as the road soon diverged from the river, we escaped further molestation. From the circumstance that small and well-armed Shan guards were stationed at intervals along the road, the officials had anticipated some hostile demonstration, although no such contingency had been hinted at to us. Beyond this, we passed village after village, and in every case the road was lined with eager crowds who welcomed us by "*Kara, Kara*," "you are welcome, you are welcome," and waved us on; indeed, our march, after the firing episode, was a continued ovation as far as Sanda.

Half-way between Manwyne and the latter town, we passed through Karahokah, the chief market of this thriving valley. As it was market-day and the crowd was great, we went round the outside of the village to escape it, but all the people streamed out as we passed and nearly closed the road. This village consists of two long, parallel lines of houses separated by a broad-way, down the centre of which the booths and stalls are placed during market-day, which happens once a week.

After Karahokah, our way lay chiefly along the embankments of the paddy-fields which are now all flooded from the small streams, and the Tapeng itself, which have been turned aside, at intervals, to irrigate them. The rice is raised in small nurseries, and the young plants are in many places about two inches above water. Tobacco is now being grown on the higher ground below the hills.

About half-way between Manwyne and Sanda, the low mountain spurs on either side have a very red soil, and are almost entirely destitute of trees, except at their extremity, where they jut out on to the valley. They are rounded and free from rocks, covered with short grass, and their strongly pronounced red and green give a richness of colouring to the landscape which I have seldom met with before.

We arrived at Sanda at 5 P.M., and were conducted to a small temporary Buddhist khyoung built of wood and bamboo, on the site of a building that had been destroyed by the Panthays five years ago. It is little better than a thatched hut, and the only floor is the bare ground. The soil at the back part is raised above the front, and on the former, there is a dais leading to a broad and deep recess, in which a small figure of Guadama is seated on an altar, surrounded by the usual tinsel ornaments, under a number of finely-coloured umbrellas suspended from the roof. On each side of this recess are the sleeping apartments of the phoongyees and resident scholars. The priests here, as at Manwyne, are very fond of the good things of this life, and have a marked failing for gay attire, and their persons are covered with a profusion of silver ornaments, buttons, rings, chatelains, and they all carry tobacco pipes with handsome silver mouth-pieces, a state of things at utter variance with some of the first principles that ought to regulate the conduct of a rahan, who declares that he puts on the habit of a priest, not for the sake of vanity, but to cover his nakedness, and indeed with the very spirit of Buddhism itself, which teaches that the vestment of a phoongyee should be of the very poorest kind. Their dress, therefore, is entirely different from what prevails in Burmah. They wear yellow skull-caps, round which a long, thick, yellow turban is coiled from the forehead, covering the greater part of the ears and back of the neck, till it stands out like a broad, solid glory behind the head. The jacket is usually white, and buttons on the right side, as is the case generally among the Shans, and their bright yellow trousers are bound round the waist with kummerbunds of the same colour. They allow themselves the luxury of shoes, although the religious, according to the tenets of Buddhism, ought to go bare-footed, unless suffering from some infirmity. Their legs below the knee are also bound with yellow cloth, and a broad, trimmed straw hat is usually carried over the back in a covering of green oiled skin to protect it from the rain, during which it acts as a kind of umbrella.

Sanda, a small town of the size of a moderately large English village, is situated at the end of a ridge in a northerly bend of the valley, about one mile and a half from the Tapeng, at the entrance of a short valley, that runs up to the north. The spurs behind the town are marked with numerous tracks to the Kakhyen villages, and as they are bright red, they become very prominent lines, and are seen a long way off. The town is surrounded by a thick loop-holed wall, about six feet high, now in a ruined state, since the raid made by the

Panthays a few years since. The inhabitants are only beginning to recover from these serious disasters which laid their town nearly in ruins, and reduced the majority of the inhabitants to great misery: very many of the houses are still in ruins, or only partially repaired. The streets are roughly paved in the middle with small water-rounded stones, and there is a broad deep ditch on each side of the principal street which runs in an almost straight line through the town, past the Tsawbwa's house, with numerous narrow lanes running off from it on either side. The houses, as a rule, are built of brick, but the Tsawbwa's and some of the better class are made of blue gneiss.

The bazaar is a village itself, about 400 yards from the north-east doorway to the town: like Karahokah, it consists of two parallel lines of houses, separated from each other by a broad open space with a paved way down the middle, and each end is closed by a wall with a narrow doorway in its centre. A Chinese joss-house, in ruins, but with enough of its walls still standing to indicate that it had once been a place of considerable importance, stands to the left of the town entrance, but all the other buildings are of uniform size, and like the cottages and shops one sees in a village at home. The population is exclusively Chinese. In addition to the shops, a row of temporary stalls during market-days is ranged along each side of the central path, and the sellers sit on stools behind them with their goods arranged on small platforms, about a foot above the ground. In these stalls, I observed pork, peas, pears, cucumbers, tea, salt, cutch, lime, pepper, coloured Chinese papers, pipe stems and bowls, tobacco, English needles, brass buttons, Chinese coloured yarns, and gypsum. In our afternoon wanderings through the bazaar, we met two women from the hills to the north of Sanda, of an entirely different race from either the Shans, Chinese, or Kakhyens. They called themselves Leesaws, and on taking down some of their numerals, we found that they had a remarkable affinity to the Burmese.

15th May. We visited the Tsawbwa to-day at his house, a handsome structure in its way, enclosed by a high wall, with a rather imposing stone gateway facing the principal street. We passed through three large, well-paved court-yards before we reached the reception hall, which is of the same construction as the one we were received in by the Tsawbwa-gadaw of Manwyne, but on a much larger scale. Chairs had been placed for us, and in a few minutes the Tsawbwa came to the front accompanied by his officials. He was dressed in sombre Shan blue, with a long coat reaching to the ankles, and a black satin, Tartar-like skull-cap. He is a tall man with a slouching gait, but very intelligent face, and has all the manners of a gentleman. He was evidently very nervous, and nearly all the talking was done by his officials, who are also men of education, considerable intelligence, and gentlemen in all their ways. They were unanimous in expressing the hope that our mission would be the means of settling the country, and re-establishing the trade. The little grandson of the Tsawbwa, a child in arms, was brought to be introduced to us. As the chief has no sons, he doats on the boy, and one of his most urgent requests was that Sladen would consider the child as his own, and when he learned that Sladen had already a little son, he exclaimed, "then let them be brothers." This is one Shan way of indicating friendship. Betel-nut and tea were handed round by respectably-dressed waiting-men, and after we had requested his acceptance of a handsome, coloured table-cloth, and some other small presents, we took our departure.

In the afternoon, I shot over the red spurs and got a few birds. Magpies and doves abound, and one large tree close to the town wall was literally white with two species of egret, *Herodias garzetta*, and *H. egrettoides*, and associated with these birds were *Buphus coromandus*, *Graculus javanicus*, *Acridotheres tristis*, and *Sturnopastor nigricollis*. We received a present in the evening from the Tsawbwa of rice, fowls, ducks, and firewood. It is arranged that we leave for Muangla to-morrow morning.

16th May. The Tsawbwa visited us this morning, accompanied by his grandson with a present to Sladen of a rich, silken bed-quilt, and hard, oblong pillows with embroidered, silken ends to Bowers and me; a richly enamelled silver pipe-stem, about a yard in length, was given to Sladen as a present from the child whom he was again requested to regard as his own son. It was arranged that on leaving the town we should pass in front of the Tsawbwa's house, and about an hour after he left us we started, and as we neared his so-called palace, two men who stood in front of the gateway with long brass trumpets faced us, and blew lusty blasts as we approached. He himself was standing on the steps with two large umbrellas over him, one in gold and the other in red, surrounded by his chief men, and with his grandson, in arms, by his side. We dismounted to shake hands, a proceeding which he did not seem to understand, and this done, we remounted our ponies, and on leaving, a salute of three guns was fired, and the trumpeters preceded us, bellowing like bulls through their instruments, till we were out of the town.

Quitting the town, the road follows the embankments along the paddy-fields, across the entrance to the short valley of the Sanda stream, which is forded, and it then strikes over a low red spur which nearly meets another from the opposite range, dividing the valley at this point into two basins, one of Sanda, and the other of Muangla. After crossing the spur we descended into the latter basin, and forded a small stream which was quite warm from its proximity to a hot spring. The Muangla division is a repetition of that of Sanda till the head of the basin is reached, where the main body of the Tapeng flows down from the north-east through a fine valley, which is shut off from the Muangla valley by an intervening grassy range of hills. Another large branch of the Tapeng, the Tahô, comes down from the east-north-east, between the high hills which appear to close in the head of the entire valley. The lower halves of the high ranges in this, as in the Sanda basin, have no trees, but are covered with good pasture, and the villages are very numerous, and gave us the same hearty welcome that we had met with on our way to Sanda. The two most striking features in animal life are the immense number of magpies and minas.

Near the head of the valley, the Tapeng, below where it enters, runs nearly across it from one side to the other, and we forded it at the village of Namon where a tolerably large bazaar was being held by the road-side. The Tapeng here, even at this season, is about 100 yards broad, and broken up by numerous sand-banks. Crossing it, we passed over a slightly elevated flat, very richly cultivated, and covered with charming villages embowered in high trees and splendid bamboo topes. It is a narrow tongue of land bounded on the east by the Tahô, and on the west by the united Tapeng and Tahô, and passing over it, we came to the banks of the latter river which has an old channel fully one mile in breadth, with high banks on either side of it. It is evident that the river has excavated the whole of this large surface, over which it now flows in narrow, broken streams, which are very much reduced in size, as they are diverted every here and there for the irrigation of the rice-fields, which cover the greater part of one-half of this level flat. A very neat pavilion of bamboo work had been erected for us on the high bank overlooking the Tahô, and here we rested for half an hour, and then crossed the channel to Muangla, which was seen on the high opposite bank below a range of low, red hills that almost blocks up the downward passage of the Tapeng. We reached the town about half-past three, ascending the steep, old river-bank, and entering it by the southern gateway which is screened outside by a brick traverse. The door is of wood, and there is a short covered passage in the portico with a bench on each side. We entered a short, but very broad street, terminated at the far end by a stone wall with a large, double, blind portal, and were conducted to a ruined Chinese khyoung off one side of this street. Our quarters were little better than an open shed, about 50 feet long, and 25 broad. There was a small yard in front of the khyoung enclosed by a narrow bamboo fence on one side, and by a brick wall about 4 feet high on the other, with a school for Chinese boys forming the third side of the court, and as it was merely a small open square about 20 feet broad, covered with a thatched roof, we were soon aware of the proximity of the school by the shouts of the pupils at their tasks, and by a line of eager, boyish faces peering over the wall. The roof of our dwelling was in that pleasant degree of uncertainty that it did not seem to have determined whether it was to stand or fall, and the rafters and their crevices being the roosting places of swallows by day, and of bats by night, we were almost blinded by the showers of dust they rained down upon us. No sooner had we arrived, than a great crowd besieged every available spot from whence they could obtain a glimpse of us, and as we were fully exposed to the public gaze, they had their hearts' content of staring. The police guard, surveyors, and native doctor were put up in a Buddhist khyoung in a back part of the town.

22nd May. I have spent the greater part of these few days in shooting round about, tracing out the course of the Tapeng, enquiring into the geology of the neighbouring hills, and visiting the ruins of old khyoungs outside the wall of this once thriving town.

Muangla, as I have said, is situated on a high slope overlooking the Tahô, and on the left bank of the Tapeng, which flows down from a valley to the north; it is enclosed by a wall, 9 feet high, with numerous loop-holes and guard-houses at intervals along it, and six strong gateways closed by wooden doors protected by traverses. The wall is of no strength, and to prevent the bricks from being gradually washed down by the rains, it is substantially tiled along the top. The houses are all built in cottage fashion, and none that I observed had more than the ground floor. All the more respectable ones are enclosed by walls of their own. The market is held in the broad street we entered by, and the same articles are sold as at Sanda. I observed many Leesaws, and also Poloungs, who appear to be closely allied to the Shans, although their language is distinct, and their dress more like Kakhyens. All the streets are laid with small water-worn boulders, and are rather narrow lanes than streets. There are a number of large villages close to the town, and nearly forming part of it, and in one there are the ruins of some very fine Chinese khyoungs that were destroyed by the Panthays five years ago. One of these is picturesquely built in a series of terraces, on a steep, beautifully wooded hill-side, and still retains evidences of its former grandeur in its elaborate carving and colouring, in the number of life-sized figures which occur along the sides of the different courts, and in a splendidly toned bell of no ordinary size on the highest terrace. In another khyoung below it, overlooking the Tahô, and shaded by fine trees, there is an interesting representation of what I was informed symbolized the passage of souls into the life hereafter. A bridge in miniature spans a watery, miry hollow in which human beings are being tortured, and are struggling with devils and monsters resembling serpents and dogs, while others are being hurled from the bridge into this hellish quagmire by two human-like forms who guard the far end of it, for which all are making. Some of the souls, however, are represented as having passed to the other side, on their way to *Neibban*. In another recess, on the opposite side of the same court-yard, there is a low, square, hollow pillar with an opening on one side, facing a structure on the opposite wall resembling a small brick stove with an opening on its top, over which a number of men and animals are delineated on the wall as issuing from the chimney-like orifice. This curious arrangement is intended to figure the transmigration to which the vital principle is subjected in the whirlpool of existences, from which it is the aim of every good Buddhist to escape, by reaching *Neibban* through a good life.

The Tsawbwa is a mere boy, and the affairs of this Raj are managed by his uncle, associated with three of the leading Shans of the town. He pays an annual tribute to the Panthays of 5,000 baskets of rice, and his estate is the largest of the three Tsawbwaships in the valley, and extends nearly as far as the town of Sanda, along both banks of the Tapeng, and on the other side of the river as far as Manwyne. The Chinese population is confined almost entirely to the market-place, and few, if any, occur in the neighbouring villages. The population of the town of Muangla does not exceed more than 1,500, if so much, and with the villages outside the walls, I do not think it can be computed over 3,500.

The hills to the back of Muangla, lying between the junction of the Tapeng and Tahô, are rounded and grassy, and quite free of trees and even bushes, except in the case of the hill immediately behind the town, which is densely covered on its western face with fine trees, and on the top by bamboos. About one mile from Muangla, on the summit of one of the heights, is the burial-ground of the Tsawbwas, out of sight of their ancestral halls, and overlooking a desolate sea of hills. Besides the handsome horse-shoe tombs, with their broad terraces and lofty portals of well-hewn gneiss, the resting-places of these old chiefs are marked by a few straggling pines *(Pinus khasianus)*; and this reminds me that on our march from Manwyne, we passed numerous grave-yards, and that the burial-ground for Muangla lies on the tongue of a high meadow-land that intervenes beetween the town and the junction of the Tapeng with the Tahô. The graves are all raised and rounded as in old church-yards at home, with a broad stone slab at the head, and they seem to lie towards all points of the compass. The burial-places, with the exception of those of the chiefs, appear to receive little or no care, as no means are taken for their protection; and in this the Shans are in marked contrast to the Chinese, who are kept in yearly remembrance of their dead by the festival of the tombs.

At Muangla, the range, forming the western side of the valley, culminates in a bold and precipitous mountain with the Tapeng at its foot, a mile to the west of the town, and is continued away to the north, along the right bank of the river. The hills, however, behind Muangla soon rise to a considerable height, and stretch to the east-north-east defining the left side of the valley of the Tahô, and the gap at Muangla between these two ranges is so small that, viewed in the distance, they appear to form a continuous line. Following the Tapeng from below Muangla through a narrow gorge, we arrive in a broad, level valley, flanked on the west by a range of the same character as that to the west of Muangla, while the hills, forming its eastern side, partake of the same character as those behind the town. The high mountain facing Muangla has a most picturesque, long, deep valley running up from the Tapeng along its eastern face to a considerable elevation, marked on both sides with numerous Poloung and Kakhyen villages, and with dark, green patches of fir forest. A stream which flows down this valley to the Tapeng is carried across the latter in its gorge by a wooden aqueduct for the irrigation of the fields on the left bank, to the west of Muangla, as the low, rounded, grassy hills have no streams of their own sufficiently large for irrigation purposes. The gorge, through which the Tapeng enters the Muangla valley, is about half a mile long, and the river is about 30 yards broad in its narrowest place, and rolls over large rocks; above this, it is a clear stream flowing over a broad, pebbly bed. At its exit, it is as quiet as a mill-pond and very deep, and at this point there is a boat-ferry which was in constant requisition during the hour I visited this beautiful spot, which recalled to me some of the finest mountain scenery of Scotland, but on a grander scale. As we were warned not to go any distance from the town, my collections give only a very imperfect idea of the zoology and botany of the country.

Moungshuay-Yah has arrived, accompanied by a small Panthay guard, and three officials from Momien, all fine-looking, well-made men. The latter speak Chinese, and on arriving, sent in their names on little bits of red paper. The Muangla officials, who had been raising difficulties about our advance, on account of the reported presence of dacoits along the road between this and Nantin, have consigned us to the care of the Panthays, and it has been arranged that we start to-morrow. We are to be accompanied by the Tsawbwa of Hotha, who comes from the other side of the range to the south of this valley. He visited us shortly after our arrival here, and is a man of education, great energy, and intelligence. He reads and writes both languages fluently, and is evidently much respected by all the Shan officials here, and also by our friends from Momien. He is to take advantage of our escort to proceed to Momien with one hundred of his mules laden with cotton. He is one of the largest traders between Bhamô and Momien, and a great part of the merchandize that changes hands at the former town is either purchased or sold by his agents; and as he is on intimate and friendly relations both with the Shans of the Tapeng valley and the Chinese traders at Momien, he has little or no difficulty in finding a market for his goods.

The nuns of Manwyne followed us up here, and as they have visited Rangoon on more than one occasion, and are fully alive to the power of the British Government, and appear to have been very favourably impressed with the toleration and mildness of the English rule, they have been the means of great good to us in explaining to their fellow-countrymen who we are, and from whence we have come, and in spreading good reports regarding us. They are held in high respect by the people both on account of their good works and experience gained by long travel, and by reason of their social position, as many of them are the near relatives of the very highest Shan families. Besides the daughter of the Tsawbwa-gadaw of Manwyne, the sister of the Hotha chief is also a Rahanee.

We have had occasional heavy showers of rain during the last few days, and everything betokens that the rains are about to set in.

23rd May. We started this morning at 8 A.M., accompanied by the Panthay officials, and the towns-people turned out in great numbers to see us depart. Our course lay across the muddy and sandy flat of the Tahô to the east of Muangla, to where the river issues from the upper part of the valley, which contracts at this, its lower end. We were met here by the Hotha Tsawbwa with his large caravan of well-laden mules, but he had no sooner joined us than a halt was called, as a report came in from the front that there were 300 Chinese ahead, determined to oppose our advance. Moungshuay-Yah proposed that we should remain for the night in a village close by, but on further consideration we resolved to advance. When we had reached the village of Nahlow, four miles and a quarter from Muangla, at half past ten A. M., the number of Chinese had become magnified to 500, and we were pressed to halt here, and fire a volley, in the hope that it might reach their ears, and make them re-consider their determination to risk their lives against such a brave army as ours. We again proceeded, and halted after another hour's march at the village of Kampton, where we were told that the Chinese had taken up their position on the side of a hill about one mile ahead, and the villagers pointed vaguely in the direction, but after thoroughly scanning the hill-sides from a tree, with a pair of good binoculars, we could detect no indications of a hostile force. We were told that two men had been killed in the morning, one shot through the heart, and the other cut down with a dâh. All the mules were collected under a large banyan, and the drivers took advantage of the halt to unload them, and allow them to nibble at the capital pasture. Some men were now observed about 1,000 yards ahead; and the Panthay officers and a Kakhyen Tsawbwa, who had been appointed by the Mahomedans to the charge of the Mawphoo district, since Leesetai's defeat, galloped forwards to ascertain the real state of affairs, and during the delay that ensued, the villagers collected, and women brought for sale buckets of pea curds, and fried beans run on to bamboo spales. The scouts returned, and reported that the road was open. We started a little after noon, following in the rear of the mules, and passing over undulating, boggy ground for one mile and a half, when we descended about 80 feet to the bed of the Tahô, which here forms a long, oval basin, covered with gravel and small, water-worn boulders, and closed in on three sides by high, grassy mountains. After we had gone a short way over this horribly rough path, where riding was out of the question, we came upon a man lying by the side of the stream, with a frightful gash across the head, and an open wound in his chest. He was a poor trader who had been attacked by some dastardly ruffians, and robbed of his little all. The two men who were now with him had made a bamboo chair on which they intended to carry him on to Mawphoo. I did what I could, and brought him on, but he died in a very short time.

At the head of the valley we commenced rapidly to ascend, by a slippery, zigzag path, the steep face of one of the great spurs of the

Mawphoo mountain, and attaining its summit we commanded a splendid prospect of the rich valley of the Tapeng, with its green mantle of young paddy, and of the wild, barren gorge below us. The sides of the two parallel ranges, which here approach each other to within a few hundred yards, are marked, in the course of the mountain streams, by large landslips, further indications of the vast disintegration which is going on in this wild mountain valley. Many of them are as white as snow, and our path lay along the top of one which formed a perpendicular precipice about 500 feet above the bed of the Tahô. The rocks examined were all quartzose and gneiss. The high mountain at the head of the valley, facing Mawphoo hill, is the Shuemuelong, a well-known name in the wars between China and Burmah. From the summit of the spur, we turned along a tolerably level path to the north-east for about one mile, when we arrived (2·55 P.M.) at the village of Mawphoo, 9¾ miles from Muangla. Mawphoo is situated at the extremity of a high, comparatively level basin marked by two terraces on the northern side, cut up, however, by deep water-courses from the hills above. The river flows along the hills defining the southern side, and is completely hidden from view in a deep, precipitous gorge. At first sight, one feels inclined to regard this as an old lake basin, for it is so closed in on every side by hills, that if a person were set down in the middle of it, he would little suspect the presence of the Tahô.

Mawphoo is a wretched, walled village in ruins, said to be the result of the recent attack of the Panthays, and is inhabited by a few ruffianly-looking soldiers, part of the disreputable Panthay garrison, armed with matchlocks, and spears with shafts about twelve feet long. It appears to have been in a ruined condition for a much longer period than six weeks, as they would have us believe, for it is overgrown with a dense jungle of weeds which never could have sprung up in two months, and, besides, the tumble-down walls are covered with vegetation which one rainy season would hardly account for. The plants that were formerly cultivated have now run wild, and are as rank as road-side weeds. Whenever I saw the ruins, my first remark was, this cannot be the Mawphoo that fell some weeks ago, and the question suggested itself, is it not possible that even the Panthays may have, at the first, been afraid of our intentions in wishing to visit their country, and that the report that Leesetai was still at Mawphoo may have been circulated by them to deter us from advancing, but that when they found our mission was a peaceful one, they gave us news of his defeat? I am forced to fall back on such a supposition, because there is nothing in Mawphoo itself, and in the villages about it, to favour the truth of the report of their recent destruction, for all have the appearance as if they had been in ruins for years. Rumours reached us at Ponsee of the great slaughter that had taken place on both sides, but the only indication we had of fighting was a dismembered skeleton lying in a paddy-field, so bleached that it might have been there for years. It is possible that Leesetai, when he learned from the Burmese of our proposed advance, may have attempted to take up a position on the road in some of the ruins of his former towns on the hill-sides, or it may be, even attempted to retake Mawphoo, but that he held it up to six weeks ago, I can never credit; and when we bear in mind that when the Panthays made their raids into the Shan states, five years ago, and exacted tribute, they must have gone by the Mawphoo road, and that the tribute must have reached Momien by the same way, we can hardly believe that they were so impolitic or short-sighted as to allow Leesetai to hold it. The conclusion, therefore, is forced upon us that Mawphoo did not fall six weeks ago, but that its destruction probably dates some years back.

After resting about half an hour at Mawphoo, in a ruined stable, we proceeded, accompanied by a strong guard of Panthays. The road skirts the north-eastern side of the hills, but although its course lies along the margin of the level flats of the valley, these are cut up by deep watercourses, so that it becomes very fatiguing, and the difficulties were increased in our case by the rain that had fallen within the last few days, and which rendered the path very slippery to man and beast. It bears evidence, however, in its occasional, substantial, arched bridges of durable gneiss and granite masonry, and the rounded stones with which it is laid, also in the numerous ruins of villages, that it must have been a considerable highway in former days. Everywhere, too, there are evidences of a once industrious agricultural population, but the country is now a desolate waste, and the lurking-place of daring bandits. For some miles to the east of Mawphoo, all the heights along the road were manned by strong Panthay and Kakhyen guards, who carried a profusion of yellow and white flags striped with white, black, yellow, green, and red, also banners and pennants emblazoned with Chinese characters. They were all armed with matchlocks which they fired off as we passed, and with spears, crescentic spear-guards, and formidable spear-tridents, all on shafts about twelve feet long. Each picquet, as we passed, followed in our rear, beating its clear-sounding gong.

At the end of this remarkable valley, which is about six miles long, we made a rapid and steep descent to the long, treeless valley of

Nantin, which now opened to view, sweeping round to the north-east as a level flat with the Tahô towards its western side, and shut in by high, grassy hills. At the foot of the descent, the river, which leaves the Nantin valley through a deep gorge, with precipitous, rocky banks, is spanned by an elegant, iron-chain, suspension bridge, with massive stone buttresses, and an arched gateway on either bank. The span is about 100 feet, and planks are laid crosswise over the chains, and covered with earth and straw, while one of the chains sweeps down from the top of the gateway in a graceful curve as a kind of protection or railing to the sides. Situated on a rounded hill above the bridge, there is a small, circular, Panthay fort, garrisoned by about half a dozen men who look after the bridge. About half a mile further on, we reached the valley which is surrounded on both sides by three well-marked river terraces. Our course for one mile lay along the right bank, which we forded at a place where the stream is very rapid and three feet deep; and from thence we continued our march for about two miles, when we reached the Shan walled town of Muangtee or Mynetee, the Tsawbwa of which is a relation of the Tsawbwa-gadaw of Manwyne. A small guard of Shans was stationed outside to receive us. The walls of this little, compact town were covered with crowds, and the short, narrow street through which we passed was densely thronged, chiefly by women and children, and the preponderance of the fair sex was due, we were told, to the numbers of men who had been killed in the incessant fighting which has been going on for the last few years.

Leaving Mynetee, we marched about one mile across a gravelly flat cut up by numerous water-courses to the small Panthay, originally Chinese, town of Nantin, situated on the bank of a small, rapid stream and about half a mile from the Tahô, which runs along the western side of the valley. Two officers on ponies came out to receive us, and we entered the town through the south-western gate or rather door.

Nantin is close to the base of the rounded, grassy hills defining the side of the valley, and is surrounded by a brick wall six feet high. It is an extremely dilapidated and filthy place. A few yards from the gate we were shown into a tumble-down Chinese khyoung which bears evidence of having been once a handsome structure, but its walls are now riddled with shot, its images defaced, and their breasts broken open for treasure. A present of firewood and rice was sent to us as soon as we arrived, shortly followed by a visit from the governor of the town, and a veritable Mahomedan *hadji*, who has an inordinate opinion of his own importance. The former is a little energetic man, with his head buried in an enormous white turban, that eclipses all we have yet seen. With the exception of a pair of long, black velvet over-boots, reaching to nearly the knee, and a fly switch made of horse's hair, which he kept continually twirling about, his dress was that of on ordinary Panthay. He has strongly pronounced oblique eyes, and the features rather of a Tartar than a Chinaman. The *hadji* comports himself in such a way that there is no mistaking his religion, to which he takes every possible opportunity to refer in his conversation. He was fair, and had an European-like face, but wears a long pig-tail similar to those of his co-religionists in this part of the world. The visit was one of ceremony, and nothing of importance occurred. Our residence is enclosed in a court-yard, and we have been cautioned to place guards as a protection against thieves.

24th May. Early this morning our friend of last night, whose official title is Tu-tu-du, came, accompanied by Tasakone's nephew, who has been sent here to meet us, and by the Chinese chief, Thongwetshein, who has lately given in his adherence to the Panthays, and by some officers of the guard that is to convey us to Momien. A lively conversation ensued on the subject of the presents intended for Momien, and we were requested either to furnish a list of them, or to allow our baggage to be examined, and they alleged as a reason for this outrageous request that they are only acting under instructions from Momien. Sladen stoutly refused to accede to it, and the subject has been again referred to Momien, and we must wait the answer. The governor sent us a present of a young bull, and supplies of rice and firewood, and seemed most anxious to treat us well. He was very polite and affable last night, but this morning his manner was dry and constrained, but the cause of this change became apparent when he let out, on another visit he paid us during the day, that he had heard all kinds of evil reports regarding us, such as that our boxes contained shells and explosive weapons, and that we carried about with us live dragons and serpents which we let loose on people: this fully explained the desire of the officials to satisfy themselves as to the contents of our boxes. To convince him of the absurdity of these rumours, I showed him the riches of my collecting boxes, producing a few snakes and frogs for his special benefit, which greatly astonished him. He seemed quite satisfied, and asked us to visit him on the morrow, as our so doing would greatly tend to give him a position among the people who are a most ruffianly set of thieves.

The Hotha Tsawbwa, who had remained behind at Muangtee, visited us to-day, accompanied by the young Tsawbwa and some Shan women, old and young, who came for medical advice, bringing presents of baskets of rice, fruits, ducks, and eggs. The Jemadar visited the *musjid* which is held in the house of the *hadji*, who knows a little Persian and Arabic. He describes it as a dirty, miserable place, with no water wherewith to wash, and the worship as exceedingly lax. The nearest trees visible from this are two large ones in the town of Muangtee, as the rest of the level flat of the valley and the neighbouring hill-sides have no trace of trees, nor even of shrubs; and the only birds to be seen are a few ducks *(Anas pœcilorhyncha)* on the flooded rice-fields about the town. I obtained, however, in great numbers, a large brown *Newt*, with a line of rounded bosses or nodes along its sides.[1]

25th May. After breakfast we made our official visit to the Tu-tu-du, and to please him went in state, with a guard of eight men, preceded by two gold umbrellas. We passed through the bazaar, a narrow, dirty street with small Chinese shops on either side, and a double row of stalls, each covered for shade by a tattered umbrella. Hoes and ploughs, a little cloth, thread, paper, and eatables of various kinds comprise the staple articles. Peaches almost ripe were in abundance. The street is not more than 100 yards long, and nearly represents the extent of the inhabited part of the town, the total breadth of which cannot be over 300 yards. The wretchedly poor and disreputable-looking inhabitants turned out of their filthy cottages to see us pass, and proceeding up a short, narrow lane, we arrived at the residence of the governor, where we were received by a salute of three guns fired in the first court-yard. Its construction is nearly similar, in every respect, to those I have described at Manwyne and Sanda. We dismounted at the gateway of the upper court but one, and passed from the latter into the centre apartment or reception hall. We were received by our friend and one of his officers, and were seated on a raised dais with a table in front of it, and mats were spread for us, and silken cushions placed for our feet. Our host sat in the lowest place, on a bench at the side of the room. After a few complimentary speeches on both sides, he suddenly took it into his head to retire, but soon re-appeared in the mandarin costume of his class and rank. The explanation of this was that when he saw Sladen in staff corps uniform, he thought the correct and polite proceeding on his part was also to appear in official robes. On his re-appearance we had two rounds of tea out of charming porcelain cups, followed by betel-nut. Before leaving, Sladen presented him with a musket and 100 rounds of ammunition, and on taking farewell he accompanied us down the steps of the reception hall, and dismissed us under a salute of three guns.

[1] This newt constitutes a new genus which I have named *Tulototriton*. I have described it in the Proc. Zool. Soc., Lond., 1871, as *Tulototriton verrucosus*.

On my return to the khyoung, I was besieged by a crowd of patients, chiefly Chinese women, and took the opportunity to make two of them show me their feet, which viewed from above seem to have only the great toe. Ophthalmia, skin diseases, and barrenness were the ailments I was expected to treat.

The messengers returned from Momien with letters to the effect that we were allowed to proceed without submitting a list of the presents, and it is arranged that we start to-morrow morning. The north gate, which looks along the road to Momien, has a regular traverse, and is loopholed, and its outside is indented with the shots fired by the Panthays when they took the town. The streets are all laid with rubble, but in some places the muddy dirt lies knee-deep. The population is entirely Chinese and Panthay, and I do not compute it over 300 at the utmost.

26th May. We started this morning at 7 A.M., and in passing through the town, the Panthay garrison lined part of the street, and when we crossed a neat stone bridge spanning a small burn that runs through the centre of the town, we were met by the governor and his chief officers, and the Chinese chief, Thongwetshein. We dismounted and shook hands with the former, and after bidding them adieu, the band struck up a rattling pleasing air on the gongs. A guard accompanied us, and of all the irregulars it has been my lot to witness, none eclipse these. The officers were intelligent men, of fine physique, cleanly, and well-clad, but the troops were dressed not much better than beggars, and without any attempt at an uniform, unless the little yellow flag carried by each man at the back of his waistband can be regarded as such. They were armed with dâhs, spears of various kinds, and matchlocks. They preceded us headed by their officers.

Our course lay along the eastern side of the valley, skirting the lowest river terrace. The road is most dreary and uninteresting. In a march of seven miles, we passed only one small walled village, in a ruined condition, and with about a dozen inhabitants: but on the top of the first river terrace, on the opposite side of the valley, we saw numerous large villages, which we are told are now all deserted and in ruins. A few miles beyond Nantin there is no cultivation, although there are plenty evidences of the agriculture of former days. The occasional glimpses we got of the hills to our right reminded us much of English scenery, in their long sweep, and in the dense clumps of wood near or on their summits, and with this change in the scenery, we observed that the rocks, brought down from them by the streams, were nearly all trappean.

About seven miles from Nantin, we arrived at the famous hot springs of the valley, and with the permission of the Panthays and Shans stopped to visit them. The small column of steam that is continually rising is visible at this season for nearly a mile, but during the cold weather, it is seen at a considerable distance off. They occur a short way up a grassy hill-side, 300 yards from the road, and the rather large stream that flows from them is so hot, even to the path below, that it gave a sudden shock to the men and ponies, and as we approached them, the atmosphere became sensibly hotter. The stream is of considerable size, and of sufficient depth below to afford a capital bath. The vapour gives off a strong alkaline smell; and the water has a similar taste. We had a vapour bath at the springs, and at 300 to 400 yards below them we attempted to bathe, but were driven further down on account of the water being much too warm, and even in the last locality, we could only remain in it for a second or two.

When we had gone about two miles and had rejoined the rear of our party, we heard four shots fired in front, but as the road only admitted of single file, and lay along a rather thickly wooded hill-side, with the ruins of many villages along it, we could not ascertain the cause of the firing. We soon learned, however, that dacoits were ahead, and news came to the rear, that the mules in front had been attacked, two mule-loads carried off, and that two of the Panthay officers who were in advance had been wounded. Proceeding onwards we discovered that the attack had proved a much more serious one than we anticipated, and that the two officers and another man had been killed. We soon came up to the bodies of the officers, wound in their ample turbans, and tied on to bamboos to be sent back to Nantin, and the other man lying in a rocky hollow, by the side of a clear mountain stream. The other officers and two of the female relatives of the deceased, who had taken advantage of our coming to proceed to Momien, were weeping bitterly over their friends thus cruelly killed. Both officers had been great favourites, and high in the esteem of the governor of Momien, for whom they had done good service in the field. They met their death in this wise: the two were riding at the head of the mules, when, in turning a corner in the narrow path, a body of Chinese rushed out from among the trees, shot down the first, and the second, on rushing forward to the rescue of his friend, was shot through the leg, and then cut down with a dâh. Eight mules in front had their loads thrown off, and ransacked on the spot, and were then driven up the hill-side.

A little further on, we came upon the nearly empty packages lying by the road-side, and among them my two boxes containing all my books and clothes. One had been cut open, and nearly all the articles carried off, but the other was unopened, although it was prodded with spears to discover its contents. I was forced to leave it behind, as I had no one to carry it, and left it in charge of a Panthay officer who promised to see it brought on. The other mule-loads were completely looted.

At the head of the valley, a mile further on, we halted on the top of the second terrace, below a steep hill-side which we had now to ascend. Here we waited until all the Panthays came up, and in the interval, the Hotha Tsawbwa informed us that we might expect another attack in a thickly wooded hollow above. At this point the terraces sweep round to form the head of the valley, but the Tahô has cut a deep gorge for itself through them. The second terrace is continued to the north in a long upward slope, a prolongation, as it were, of the Nantin valley at a higher elevation, for it is defined by a continuation of the same hills. It is thrown into rounded mounds, the sites of small villages, and is seen to terminate to the north in a broad, level plain, a still further continuation of the valley. The sides of these hills were covered with pines, and the road ran through a belt of dense forest between the shoulder of the spur and the main body of the mountains, and, as it was here that we were to expect the attack, we had to keep a vigilant eye on the jungle on either side of us. We passed the ruins of many villages buried in the dense vegetation, which consists largely of fruit trees and garden plants run wild. We went on unmolested, and making a short descent came upon the Tahô rushing down its steep rocky channel, spanned by a substantial, broad, parapeted bridge, built of gneiss and granite. The roadway across it corresponded to the curve of the arch, and as it is paved with flat, smooth, gneiss slabs, worn almost to a polish by the constant traffic of bye-gone days, our ponies had considerable difficulty in keeping their footing, and the only way was to take them over at a rush. Across the bridge, and up a small ascent overlooking the right bank of the Tahô, we were met by a guard of Panthays who informed us that they had given chase to a body of Chinese who had been lurking in the dreaded hollow. About a mile beyond, we were on a level with the plain I have described as the upward termination of the Nantin valley, and nearly skirting its eastern side, from which rises a long conical hill stretching nearly north and south, a black sterile mass of lava, with the exception of its round grassy top. This remarkable extinct volcano of Hawshuenshan is in strong contrast to the rounded grassy sea of hills, that cluster round it on all sides, except its western face, and it is rendered more marked from the circumstance that it rises abruptly from the plain. A few small plants have gained a footing between the interstices of the bare rocks, but they are so few and hidden, that in the distance they do not impart even a trace of verdure to its barren sides, which are thrown into long, rocky, rounded lines, evidently old lava flows, many of which have broad, flat summits. We rode over the eastern extremity of this volcano by a broad path laid with long granite and gneiss slabs, lying lengthwise, and again came upon the Tahô running as a narrow, rapid stream between it and the abrupt sides of the grassy hills to the east. We crossed the river over another handsome stone bridge, and passed the ruins of a rather large village lying in the level flat. The Tahô issues at this point from between a high spur and the volcano, through a very narrow gorge, and our road wound up the side of the spur, and was laid with a double line of stone flags to facilitate the ascent, as the soil is very slippery during wet weather.

On the top we gained a fine view of the small, circular valley from which the Tahô makes its exit below, and saw numerous villages encircling the dead level in its centre, which is covered with young rice. Continuing a slight ascent over the tops of the grassy hills, by a good, broad road, we again descended about 300 feet, with a rounded hill in front of us capped by a white Chinese pagoda, to the valley of Momien. Crossing the southern tail of the pagoda hill, the valley of Momien lay before us, about four miles long and two broad, shut in on all sides by rounded hills, with no trace of trees, but covered with rich pasture. It is surrounded by an almost unbroken line of towns and villages either in ruins or deserted.

The walled town of Momien lies immediately below the pagoda hill, and from its size almost merits the title of city. We were met by a Panthay officer, who informed us that the governor, Tasakone, had come out to meet us, and was waiting in state on the other side of a knoll in front. We were requested to dismount, and turning the knoll, a most gratifying sight met us. Both sides of the road were lined with troops carrying a profusion of flags and banners of all sizes and colours, and as we walked leisurely on between the double file, matchlocks were fired in rapid succession, and gongs beaten to welcome us. Tasakone was seated in a luxuriously-cushioned chair, at the end of this grand display, dressed as a mandarin, with two large red umbrellas held over him, and accompanied by his principal officers. He rose to receive us, and shaking hands with him, we passed on and remounted our ponies. A dense Chinese crowd lined both sides of the road and of the chief street of the extensive suburb that lies outside the western gate. We were conducted by one of the officers to a Chinese khyoung immediately below the wall, but outside the town, and close to the left bank of the Tahô. We arrived at 6 P.M., after a march of 21 miles. Fowls, rice, firewood, and water were freely supplied to us.

27th May. A message came from Tasakone in the morning that he would receive us and the presents to-morrow. We have had a succession of visitors all day, each more anxious than another to inspect our persons, goods, and chattels, and expressing astonishment at everything they saw.

My two boxes have not turned up, and the Panthay officer, to whom I entrusted them, now protests that they were both empty, which was certainly not the case. The loss is too serious to be thought of, as they contained my natural history note-books, extending over four years, my notes of the journey from Rangoon to Mandalay, and all my sketches from Rangoon to Ponsee, besides nearly all my private property.

28th May. It took us till two in the afternoon to arrange the presents, and when they were all ready, we entered the town, preceded by twenty men carrying them. They consisted of green and yellow broad-cloths, figured muslins, gauze muslins, carpet-rugs, richly coloured table-covers, long-cloth, American drill, two double-barrel guns, two revolvers, powder and shot flasks, two shot-moulds, two bags of shot, pistol cartridges, twenty-three tins of powder, a musical box, two four-bladed and six one-bladed penknives, six scissors, one binocular glass, one telescope, and a profusion of Bryant and May's matches and fusees. A great but well-behaved crowd had turned out to see us pass, and we were much struck with the extreme poverty that prevails among the Chinese, and even among the Panthays, and with the ruinous and filthy condition of the houses in the bazaar suburb. We entered by the north-western gate, which is protected in front by a strong crescentic traverse, with the entrance at one side. The main gateway within the traverse, through the wall, is more like a short tunnel than a gateway, and has ponderous folding-doors at its outer end, and is surmounted by a watch tower, with a concave roof supported on strong wooden pillars. A number of men and women were sitting in the gateway selling sweetmeats. We passed a short way along a narrow, dirty street, laid with rounded stones, and with small cottage shops on either side of it, and turning to the left down a narrow lane, we reached an open court-yard in front of the governor's house. It is surrounded by a low wall, and the gateway, about 15 feet high, consists of plain, erect, squared stone pillars, with others placed across them at right angles, like the wooden beams of a door. In a small, circular pavilion, at one side, there were a few musicians in rags who welcomed us with a lively air, and as we crossed the court to the house, three small cannon that were stuck in the ground by the breech-end, and pointed upwards, were fired as a salute. A rabble followed us into the last court but one. We found Tasakone seated in his reception hall at the end of the inner court. He rose to receive us, and motioned us to sit on his left hand at a long table in front of him, on which we deposited the presents. Behind where he sat, there was a raised recess covered with red cloth, and with a small chair of state in its centre. The sides of the apartment were hung with long narrow stripes of blue and red cloth, covered with Chinese characters in gold leaf. A number of his officers were seated on chairs, along each side of the room, and the minor officials had collected in a crowd at the entrance. Tasakone is a powerful man, fully 6 feet 3 inches high, with prominent cheek-bones, heavy, protuberant lips, slightly hooked nose, faintly oblique eyes, and is much browned by exposure. He has a deep indentation between his eyes from a spent bullet, and many other wounds. He had on, a grey felt hat, somewhat resembling a helmet placed sideways, the front half of the rim being turned up, and the back downwards. A gold rosette, set with large precious stones, formed a handsome ornament in front, and a blue silk top-knot fell down behind his back as a long tail. A richly figured, pale blue silk coat reaching to the ankles, and overlapping on the right side, completed his costume.

Sladen expressed our deep regret at the death of the two officers, and promised to inform our government of the circumstances, and to suggest that something should be done for their families. He replied, that we were not to distress ourselves, as they considered it an honour to die as those men had done. In speaking about the opening of trade, he said that any number of English merchants might visit Momien next November, and that he had made all the necessary arrangements with the Tsawbwas, and would easily manage the Kakhyens, and that caravans should pass in safety. He hinted, however, that as so many people were present, it would be better to discuss the subject on some other occasion. He expressed great pleasure in receiving the presents, and the musical box has been a most successful hit, and is the admiration of all. The fusees, too, and the matches astonish them, but the revolvers and guns are what most take their fancy. Tea, preserved oranges, jujubes, and sugar-candy were then served round to us, and in the course of the conversation, he stated that the king had learned with pleasure of our intended visit to Momien, but that the road to Tali is so infested with bands of Chinese, that it is out of the question to think of proceeding beyond this. His own brother is out fighting against them.

29th May. To-day, Tasakone paid us an official visit, accompanied by his officers and an armed guard. He was very affable, and strong in his professions of friendship and desire to open this route for trade, and promised to send an embassy to Rangoon next November with presents to the English governor.

I went out shooting in the afternoon, but saw very few birds; some of them, however, are new to me. The absence of trees is, in all probability, one of the principal causes of their scarcity.

The Tahô is about 20 yards broad from bank to bank, and about 3 feet deep, and runs along the northern end of the valley, flowing down from the Kananzan range of mountains, about 10 miles distant, to the north-east of the city, through a narrow, tortuous course between grassy hills, and leaving the Momien valley at its north-western extremity. The whole of the flat of the valley is devoted to rice cultivation, and is almost entirely under water, diverted from the Tahô and other streams for the irrigation of the land. The soil is a rich black loam. The lower slopes of the hills are covered with graves, which may be said to encircle the valley as a broad band, which, with the ruined and deserted towns and villages below them, are telling indications of the dense population that must have been supported in this sequestered vale during peaceful times. The evidences of the Panthay rebellion become very apparent at Mawphoo, and all the villages, with only a few exceptions, along the road from that hill to this valley, may be said, without exaggeration, to be deserted, and a heap of ruins.

Tasakone sent us a present to-day of a young bull, two sheep, 4,000 cash, vegetables, and two salted geese, two packets of caked tea, and a large supply of fancy cakes put up in white paper, and neatly folded in pink wrappers.

30th May. This morning we had another visit from Tasakone, accompanied by his relations and principal officials, to invite us to a feast and theatricals. We went shortly after they had left, and were received in the same room as yesterday, and were no sooner seated than we were served with tea, cakes, and sweetmeats, fresh relays of which kept coming in till we were all but surfeited. Shouts of laughter came from the women, who were amusing themselves in a neighbouring room with a magnetic battery that Tasakone received as a present this morning. One old lady, the Tsawbwa-gadaw of Muangtee, now on a visit to the governor, came in, attended by some other women, and joined our tea-fight and conversation, without any restraint. We were then shown over the private apartments by the governor himself. He led us through his bed-room, a snug little room with a large four-poster, a comfortable couch, and the walls decorated with Chinese pictures, and an English eight-day clock. There were no windows, and all the light came from two doors facing each other. Passing through the room we entered a small court, and in a verandah a number of tailors were busily at work making cushions. From this, we entered another small court surrounded by the apartments of the women, and ornamented with dwarfed fruit and pine trees, in large earthern vases, and small tanks filled with gold fish. On our way back we passed through a room the walls of which were hung with war-hats, decorated with the tails of the golden and Lady Amherst pheasants. We were now conducted to an open hall in another court in which the theatricals were held. Here we were followed by tea and cakes, of which we were expected again to partake. Large copper vases of incense burned close to our noses, and their heavy fumes produced a drowsy feeling in all. The stage is a small pavilion about 20 feet square, closed on three sides, and with two doors behind, through which the players pass in and out. The orchestra sits in the back of the stage, and the musical instruments were violins, a pair of brass clappers, gongs, and tom-toms. The only furnishings were a table like an inverted pyramid, and a chair on each side of it, and the scenery, a small panelled picture of birds and flowers. The chief character had his face painted red, and wore a long, black, Napoleonic beard and moustache, black satin boots, red trousers, and a gorgeous coat, richly embroidered with figures of dragons and flowers, and his hat with a fine bushy tail of *Ælurus fulgens* depending behind. The music was very monotonous, and resembled the clatter of crockery interspersed with an occasional thud from the tom-tom, and screech from the fiddle, and the movements of the actors were quite as *outré* in their own way, consisting principally of violent forward motions of the legs as if some imaginary person were being kicked, and of sudden bounds in the air, when the performer usually took the opportunity to kick himself with his heels. The stride across the stage is an exaggerated goose-step, and he of the red face bellowed and blustered, but whether he imitated Chinese humanity abominably or well, I do not pretend to judge. While the play was going on, we were expected to consume the contents of eight bowls, containing boiled fowl chopped up with small pieces of salted goose, fowl cooked in another way, dried prawns, vegetables, walnuts, mushrooms, and a number of other products of the chief's *cuisine* which my palate failed to recognize. Ahyèk, or samshu, was next served, and followed by small saucers with cooked rice, but as we had now been eating nearly for three hours, we apologized for the poverty of our appetites and retired. The play, however, lasted till late in the evening.

31st May. The Tahô, about one mile to the north-west of the town, precipitates itself over a cliff about 100 feet high, in an all but unbroken sheet of water, and, below the fall, runs with great force down a deep glen to the little, circular valley of Hawshuenshan which is closed in by high grassy hills. The river is spanned above the fall by a substantial, arched stone bridge, and there are the ruins of numerous monasteries and houses on the sides and flat summits of the small, isolated, conical hills that here close in the valley.

Six men were executed to-day on the road-side within sight of our residence. They were led out under a strong escort, with music and banners flying, to about a quarter of a mile from the city wall, with their arms pinioned behind their backs. They were made to kneel down by the road-side, and a gun-shot was the signal for the executioner to do his bloody work, and another announced its completion. The bodies were afterwards buried where they lay. We were told that the men had been found in the bazaar selling stolen goods, and that they had been identified by the owners, and led before Tasakone, who at once condemned them to instant death. Three guns from the city announced the sentence.

We visited the governor this afternoon at his request, and were again surfeited with tea, sweetmeats, and cakes, and entertained with two short plays of no special interest, and were afterwards accompanied to the bazaar by two officers, to keep the crowd in order. The bazaar is outside the town wall, and the principal street runs nearly straight east from the western gate, having considerable breadth, and a line of small shops along either side, with a row of stalls in front, each of which on sunny and rainy days is shaded by a large umbrella. There is a thoroughfare down the centre, and a narrow one between the shops and the stalls. The street is about half a mile long, and on market days it is thronged by a dense crowd of Chinese-Shans and Panthays, with a small sprinkling of Kakhyens and Leesaws. The shops are small cottages with only a ground-floor, and each is devoted to a special department of trade; some are occupied by drapers, others by booksellers, provision merchants, dealers in tobacco and nuts, hardware merchants, and druggists. A number of eating-houses were resorted to by the better class of Chinamen, while the poorer classes from the surrounding villages could get a cheap meal at some of the stalls, or from boys who hawked comestibles on the street. In the stalls, there was a rich display of vegetables and fruits; among the former were peas, beans green and dried, potatoes, celery, carrots, onions, garlic, yams, bamboo shoots, cabbage, spinach, and ginger; and among the latter were apples, pears, peaches, walnuts, chestnuts, brambles, rose-hips, and three other fruits new to me. A dried, almost black lichen is sold commonly as an article of food, and mushrooms are much run after. Black pepper, betel-nut, and poppy capsules are seen in almost every stall; salt is sold in compressed balls with the government stamp on it. In other departments may be noticed coloured Chinese cloths and yarns, a little English long and broad cloth, English needles, and brass buttons, Chinese buttons, and small daggers, Mahomedan skull-caps ornamented with Chinese figures in gold thread, amber and serpentine finger-rings, pipe mouth-pieces and brooches, opium pipes and brass Chinese hookahs. Running at right angles to the principal street is another devoted to the tailors and copper-smiths, in which clothes are sold ready-made, and where all the appliances for the kitchen can be found, and in which the large copper discs for cutting serpentine are manufactured. Along this street we came to the house of the principal Chinese merchant, where we were kindly received by him, and the Hotha Tsawbwa who is residing with him. Sladen talked about the advantages that would accrue to the inhabitants of Momien generally, were trade revived and confidence established between them and their present rulers; and the merchant's answer to this was that it did not matter to them whether they were governed by the Panthays or Chinese so long as they prospered; but as he had been complaining bitterly of the reverses of fortune he had experienced since they had been under Panthay rule, there could be no doubt as to the inference he expected us to draw as to the light in which he regards the present government, and from what we have already observed, it seems evident that the Chinese portion of the population would hail the return of their old rulers. Heavy rain and thunder at 4 P.M. Wind S. W.

1st June. Rain during greater part of the night. Nothing of any note to record, nor does there appear to be any prospect of my being able to do much here in the way of natural history, as I have been warned not to cross the river; in other words, I am not to venture 400 yards beyond the town wall, and as all around is either grass or paddy-fields, few, if any, birds are to be seen.

The wall of the town is built of a blackish-grey, lavaceous rock, cut into oblong pieces about two and a half feet long and one foot in thickness, laid together with mortar. The town appears to have been originally surrounded by a deep ditch about 20 yards from the wall, and it is still very perfect on the eastern and southern sides, but can be hardly traced to the west, next the bazaar, where it has degenerated into a dirty, stagnant puddle for pigs to wallow in. Where intact, its sides are seen to be built of the same materials as the wall, but without mortar, yet so accurately cut and laid together that the blade of a penknife can with difficulty be inserted between the stones.

The Tahô, immediately above its exit, flows for a short way between banks about 10 feet high, and the rice-fields on the higher elevation are irrigated from a large wheel, which raises the water in a number of long bamboos tied on at an angle to its broad circumference, and which, as they are brought up by the revolutions of the wheel, and begin to ascend, shoot their contents out into an open wooden pipe which communicates with the fields. There are a number of these wheels in the valley.

One of my collectors is down with the small-pox which is very prevalent here at present. Yesterday one of our Kakhyens had to be sent to other quarters, as he had been attacked by a very virulent form of the disease.

2nd June. We ascended the pagoda hill this morning, the summit of which is about 900 feet above the town. The pagoda is a white-washed, round brick tower with a stone base, and tapers slightly to the top, which is surrounded at regular intervals by six projecting rings. The hill and all the others about it for many miles are covered with fine grass, having occasional patches of bracken near their summits, affording capital cover for pheasants, hares, and foxes. On reaching the top, after a hard climb, we started a fine cock-pheasant with very long tail feathers, in great requisition among the Panthays as full-dress ornaments for their military hats.[1] We beat the bracken beds, and Sladen bagged the hen, but the cock bird could not be found. We started a hare, and also a fox with a golden yellow coat and a white tip to its tail, and, on returning, procured a youngish specimen of the latter, which is quite distinct from the Himalayan fox. We encountered a small Panthay guard protecting a large number of mules grazing on the fine pasture.

The hill commands a splendid view of the Momien valley, and of the surrounding hills on that side; and to the north-west, of the extinct volcano, which is seen lying at the eastern margin of a great plain surrounded by a lofty range to the west and north, and to the east by low

---

[1] I have described this species, and named it *Phasianus sladeni*. Elliot has since described it under the name of *P. elegans* from specimens in the garden of the Zoological Society of London, which I have seen, and which are identical with my specimens from Momien.

rounded hills. The volcano forms the western side of the Hawshuenshan valley, which appears to have been originally only an eastward prolongation of the plain in which the volcano stands. It rises gently from a barren, rocky slope to a grassy cone in the centre, which forms a remarkable contrast to the black lava mass encircling it. The horizon on every side, except to the south-east, is bounded by lofty mountains tending nearly north and south, with peaked and jagged outlines, differing entirely in their physical appearance from the intervening lower ranges which have the general direction of the mountains, although more broken and disturbed. On the sides of the former, there are seen dark patches which were pointed out to me as pine forests, and in the hollows of the latter, at some distance from the town, a few pine trees are still standing. These grassy hills, however, offer no evidence that they were ever entirely covered with forest.

At the foot of the hill, we passed fields of potatoes now in flower, grown in long rows as in England, with the earth thrown up about their roots. The leaf is smaller than that of the home plant, and the young tubers now in the bazaar have a thin and very red skin. The existence of celery here is almost quite as remarkable as that of the potato. Both plants have been in all likelihood introduced by the Chinese trading up the Irawady *viâ* Bhamô, but where and when they were obtained, and how the cultivation was learned, are subjects for conjecture, as the inhabitants could give me no information.

The Hotha Tsawbwa called to-day, along with the chief military officer, to inform us that it has been arranged by Tasakone and himself that we are to accompany him as far as Muangla, and then cross to his own valley. Tasakone objects to the Sawaddy route, as he imagines, and I dare say correctly, that if it were adopted, all the trade or nearly so would be taken direct to Yungchan instead of finding its way to Momien.

3rd June. We had a visit from Tasakone and the Hotha Tsawbwa just as we were sitting down to breakfast, and as they were accompanied by a number of their underlings who had never before seen Englishmen feed, we were surrounded by a crowd of anxious gazers, who watched our every movement with interest, criticising our dishes, way of eating, and appetites, in a manner known only to a Chinese, but as we are now accustomed to treatment of this kind, we were in no way disconcerted.

Bowers, in a characteristic outburst of generosity and kindly feeling, presented Tasakone with his rifle and its accompaniments, which prompted the chief to ask what things we would like to take back with us, and on Sladen mentioning daggers, among other things, he at once presented him with his own, a handsome, little dirk with a gold handle and scabbard, with a large massive gold chain attached to it, and followed it up by giving him his finger-rings as well, which included a centre ring of beautiful green jade, with two plain gold ones on either side of it.

Breakfast over, we accompanied him to see the garden of the chief military official, and were much pleased with the reception given us, but the garden was not of the kind we expected. It was contained in a small court, and the plants were all dwarfed trees and shrubs in large vases on pedestals. They were chiefly peach and apple trees, tea shrubs and boxwood, and the only flowering plants were some hollyhocks and passion-flowers, with indications of coming peonies. Two small tanks of solid stone, containing gold fish with remarkable doubly-divided tails, stood against the wall facing the house, with small vases grouped around them with great taste, and in one corner there was a model, in roughly cut stone, of a hill-side with pagoda and caves. A verandah with a handsome balustrade forms one side of the court, and leads into one of the rooms of the house, where we were feasted with tea and a profusion of cakes and preserved fruits, and our servants were also liberally supplied with these good things at tables in the verandah. The eaves of the house were peaked arches with handsome carvings, in relief, of bridges, birds, trees, and flowers. A few characteristic Chinese landscapes and pictures of birds in Indian ink and colours were hung about the walls, on rollers, like school maps. The youngest son of our host, a most energetic and intelligent looking boy of eight or nine years, said to be deaf and dumb, was brought to me to see if anything could be done for him, and on my repeating some sounds, and finding that he attempted to imitate them, I concluded that his hearing was not in fault, and on examining his mouth, I discovered that he was tongue-tied. I explained what I believed to be the cause of his dumbness to the great astonishment and delight of his father, who cherishes the boy more than any of his other children, and at once received his permission to operate.

The small tree-frog (*Hyla chinensis*) is very common in some bushes outside the city, and in a few minutes I collected about twenty, and also procured a handsome *Tropidonotus*. On the north-western side of the pagoda hill there is an old quarry cut out in the form of a splendid arched cavern, from which a great deal of good stone has been removed for building purposes. It is a trachytic rock; and a few hundred yards to the north of it, at a much lower level, there is a portion of the thick bed of basaltic trap over which the Tahô precipitates itself. The trachytic bed dips to the south.

We enquired pointedly of Tasakone to-day if it would be safe to visit the hills to the north, or indeed any of those surrounding the valley, but he laughed at the idea, and asserts that they are infested by dacoits, and that even the people from the town and the few remaining inhabitants of the villages cannot go any distance to cut grass, except under the protection of an armed guard. About 11 P.M., a message came from the governor, asking us to be on the alert, as we might be attacked by some dacoits who were in the neighbourhood. My impression, however, is that the Panthay officials are nearly as much in dread of their own rabble as of undisguised robbers.

4th June. Terrific thunder-storm with heavy rain at 2 P.M., and I verily believe that it drove all the mosquitoes within doors, for they buzzed and bit in a way never felt before.

5th June. We have all been suffering for the last few days from severe diarrhœa, and many of the men are affected in the same way, and the native doctor among them.

The Tsawbwa-gadaw of Nantin, along with two old Shan coolies, two young waiting-maids, and some male attendants, visited us this afternoon, and brought a present of fowls and ducks, and one pillow with embroidered ends. She was very well dressed, and wore an enormous head-dress, ornamented in front with the Panthay rosette of green, blue, and pink stones, set in gold, and at the sides, with small imitation flowers fastened to little silver rods, in the form of a triangle. Her skirt was nicely worked with coloured silks and gold thread; and her light-blue silk figured jacket was trimmed at the wrists with black satin which contrasted well with her massive gold bracelets, and amber and jade finger-rings, and a handsome silver chatelaine and richly embroidered fan-case by her side, completed her toilet. One of her waiting-maids carried her small Chinese hookah, and the other her embossed silver boxes containing betel-nut and lime. She received a carpet, coloured threads, brass buttons, and scissors; and, what most took the fancy of the young men and women, a number of circular looking-glasses, about the size of small plates, which they suspended as ornaments from their jackets.

In the afternoon I shot thirteen birds. They were all from the neighbourhood of a small pond, fed by a subterranean stream that issues from a rounded basaltic knoll at the base of one of the hill slopes, close to the northern side of the town. The birds occurring on the pond were *Podiceps philippensis, Porzana fusca, Gallinula chloropus*, a solitary *Herodias alba*, and an occasional couple of *Anas pœcilorhyncha*.

6th June. I visited the bazaar, and in a druggist's shop was shown the horn of an antelope that is ground down and used as a strengthening medicine, each tickal[1] weight costing one rupee. In the same shop, the shells of *Testudo platynotus*, Blyth, from Burmah, were treated in the same way, and offered for sale at a ransom, and the horn of the sambur was sold in the form of snuff, as a styptic in bleeding from the nose.

Late last night Moungshuay-Yah came in, and informed Sladen in a very confidential way that Lowquanfang, a Chinese official of high rank, who still remains true to the Imperial cause about Momien, had sent one of his officers with a message to the effect that he would guarantee our safe return by whatever route we wished, provided we were unaccompanied by the Panthays, and a pony as a token of his good faith. Sladen declined to see the messenger, or to receive the gift, and referred him to Tasakone, informing Moungshuay-Yah that we had not come to play two parts, one with the Panthays, and another with the Chinese.

7th June. The interpreter came in this morning to say that Lowquanfang's messenger had had a long conversation last night with the Hotha Tsawbwa, and that they had arranged it between them that the former is to give in his adherence to the Panthays;[2] the latter himself appeared shortly afterwards, and confirmed the news that the chief will guarantee not to attack us on our return journey, which he appears to have had thoughts of doing.[3]

Ever since our arrival here, the killing of sheep and cattle for food has been strictly prohibited, as rain is much wanted, the idea being that it will not fall so long as life is taken; now, however, that it has rained heavily for some days, the objection no longer exists, and plenty of butcher-meat is now exposed in the bazaar.

9th June. Heavy rain all night, and throughout the greater part of the day. We are all suffering so much from depression of spirits, diarrhœa, and dyspepsia, which we attribute to this dull residence in which we are now shut up from morning to night, on account of the heavy rains, with only a small patch of leaden sky visible over our

---

[1] One hundred tickals = 36,516 grains avoirdupois.

[2] By last accounts, February 1870, Lowquanfang was strongly entrenched in the valley of Hawshuenshan, close to Momien, and only waiting to attack it.

[3] I am convinced that the above incident was extemporized by the Hotha Tsawbwa and Moungshuay-Yah either as a test of our sincerity, or from a desire on their part to try and win us over to the side of the Chinese, with whom their whole sympathies lay. This was my opinion at the time, and after-events have fully verified its correctness.

head, that we proposed to Tasakone to remove into another khyoung, close at hand, but outside the bazaar wall. He would not listen to the proposal, as he says we might be attacked at any moment, and that he is even now most anxious about our safety, on account of the very many bands of robbers that are going about, who would not hesitate to attack us, if they saw that they had any chance of success. In our present quarters, however, we are comparatively safe, as we are immediately under the town wall, and protected on the other side by a strong guard-house, but the other khyoung has none of these advantages.

10th June. Tasakone was out late last night in our neighbourhood with a strong guard, as his suspicion of a meditated attack had been raised by some shots heard in the distance. He has appointed one of his officers to be permanently stationed with us on duty. The governor sent us a present of two sheep and a goat. The former are fine large animals with highly convex black faces, and the latter are usually long-limbed, dark brownish-red, with a black list down the back, and flat spiral horns somewhat like *Capra megaceros*, directed backwards and slightly outwards. In the evening the interpreter brought a message from Tasakone that we are to be on our alert to-night, as there are a number of suspicious characters going about, and requesting us to put on a strong guard. Constant and heavy rain from morning to night.

11th June. Incessant rain all night, and during the day. My collector died at 9 A.M., and the Kakhyen petty chief, who contracted the disease about the same time, died yesterday. Tasakone was informed of the sad event, and at once made the necessary arrangements for the burial, and sent 6,000 cash (Rs. 12) in charity. The body, first washed and then rolled in cloth, was laid in a Panthay grave-yard on a slope to the north-west of the town.

Every day, the front of our residence is besieged by beggars of both sexes and all ages, from little ragged urchins of four or five years of age to old, bowed and blind men and women of seventy. They are pictures of wretchedness and dirt, and are clad in rags of the filthiest description. The inhabitants of the bazaar appear to be very poor, and there can be little doubt regarding their dirt. The shopkeepers are the most respectable part of the community, but even among them, there are few, if any, evidences of wealth. In the whole of Momien, there is only one Chinaman entitled to be ranked as a merchant, the man in whose house we met the Hotha Tsawbwa the other day.

All the women, and the majority of the men, wear clogs in the rainy weather, and any of the former that appear in the streets, and there are not a few, are ugly and ill-clad. The majority wear pork-pie hats, and all, excepting slaves, and even the Mahomedan women, have their feet dwarfed: trousers drawn tight round the ankle, a long, loose, blue coat reaching to near the feet, with loose sleeves folded back, and a large, blue, double apron in front, is the prevailing costume. The small feet do not prevent the women coming three or four miles carrying heavy loads to market, and they think nothing of shouldering two buckets of water slung to the end of a bamboo. The women and men are very fair, and the children have chubby faces and red cheeks.

Goitre is very prevalent among the population at Momien, where it constantly obtrudes itself on the notice of the visitor, and some goitres are to be seen as large as the human head, and so heavy as to require special support. Men, women, and children alike are afflicted with this disease, which they assert is hereditary, and attributable to the water of the Tahô.

The peasantry are clad in uniform blue like the Shans, and all who come any distance, and those who are working in the fields, wear a flat covering like an apron over the back, as a protection from the rain. It is made of the dried brown spathes of a palm, and at first sight resembles the skin of some animal. It is also used as a covering for mule-loads that require to be kept dry.

12th June. Rain all last night up to the evening, when it faired about 9 P.M., but only for half an hour. Tasakone sent the Hotha Tsawbwa to-day to ask if we have everything necessary for our comfort, and get proper food; the latter also came to ask us to dine to-morrow at the principal merchant's. Yesterday each of us received from the governor a Panthay officer's white cotton jacket, with silver buttons down the front, and ornamented across the front with white braid.

14th June. Heavy rain continued up to half an hour before sunset, when there was a short fair interval during which I went out for a stroll below the city wall, keeping my eyes about me for land shells, which seem to be remarkably scarce here. While so engaged, I heard a female voice calling to me from the battlements, and looking up saw a pretty face peering down, and intent that I should give her something, and not catching very distinctly what she said, I imagined that she was asking for cheroots, and indicated by signs that if she would unwind her long head-dress, and let down one end of it, I would give her some. She disappeared for a few minutes and returned with a long cloth, and on her letting it down, I tied a few cheroots into it, congratulating myself that I had satisfied her demands; but no, no sooner had she drawn it back and examined the contents than she became as importunate as ever. At last catching the word *keenza* the mystery was explained; she was begging for round mirrors, and I recognised her as one of the Shan ladies attached to the suite of the Tsawbwa-gadaw of Nantin. I tried to make her understand that I did not carry *keenzas* about with me, but as she would take no denial, I jokingly offered to catch her in my arms if she would jump down, and come to the khyoung for them; but although this highly amused her, she was not to be diverted from her desire to possess the coveted mirrors, and waved me off for them; and I had to obey, and returning with one and a packet of needles, the cloth was again lowered, and great was her glee when she pulled it up, and found herself the happy possessor of the much-longed-for *keenza*.

15th June. Heavy rain all night and up to 4 P.M., when it faired for about an hour, after which it again commenced, and was still raining at 9 P.M. During the interval in the afternoon we walked as far as the water-fall which is now in splendid condition, and the body of water is so great that the bottom is shrouded in a dense cloud of spray that rises high above the fall, and can be seen at a distance of two miles. So dangerous is it to go even this distance from the city that on our return, we found ourselves joined by a Panthay officer, and a few men who had been sent out for our protection along with some of our own guard.

16th June. Rain from 3 A.M. to near sunset, and so heavy during the day that we did not venture out.

17th June. Still heavy rain, but there are faint indications of a coming change. Our Kakhyen friend, Lawloo, who has been away visiting his home, brought back news to-day that the Ponline Tsawbwa has been attacked, and driven from his village by the Tsawbwa-gadaw of the Khanlung Kakhyens, who is known as the long-haired woman, from the unnatural length of her hair on other parts of her body besides her head, which admits of her wearing it as a girdle.

Sladen procured to-day a history of Tali and another of Momien; the latter is now very scarce, as all the type blocks have been broken up by the Panthays for firewood.

18th June. Many heavy showers after mid-day, the morning being tolerably fair. I went to the bazaar, and saw the manufacture of the copper discs used in cutting jade. They are very thin, bend easily, and measure about one foot and a half in diameter. The centre is beaten out into a cup-shaped depression which receives the end of the cylinder on which the disc revolves. I afterwards visited the manufacture of the jade ornaments carried on by a number of men in their houses by hired labourers. In one establishment, two men were at work, one using the cutting disc, and the other a revolving cylinder tipped at the free end with a composition of quartz and little particles resembling ruby dust. Both were driven by the feet. The stone is held below the disc, under which there is a basin of water, and fine silicious mud, in which the stone is dipped at intervals, the operator filling his hands with as much of the mud as possible. The stones are cut into discs one-eighth of an inch in thickness, when they are intended for earrings, and are then made over to the man at the silicious-tipped cylinder, who bores a round hole in the centre of each. The same course is followed in the case of the larger and thicker rings. The most valuable jade is that of an intense bright-green colour, something like the emerald; but the red and pale pinkish kinds are also highly prized. In the extensive ruins outside the bazaar, there is ample evidence, in the rejected fragments of jade lying about, that the manufacture of ornaments from this valuable stone must have been carried on formerly on a much more extensive scale than now. A pair of bracelets of the finest jade costs about 100 Rupees at Momien.

In the bazaar there were many displays of the mineral wealth of this province, which is rich in gold, silver, lead, iron, copper, mercury, arsenic, gypsum, lime, flint, and chalk; and I obtained some small specimens of the lead, copper, and iron ores from a range of hills two days' journey to the north-west of Momien, and specimens of yellow orpiment said to be from the neighbourhood of Tali, and brought in considerable quantities every year to Yungchan and Momien for exportation to Burmah.

To-day, intelligence reached the governor of the capture, by the Mahomedan army, of Yunan city, the capital of the province.

Tasakone, who has on more than one occasion impressed on us the necessity of exercise to preserve our health in this climate, which he describes as injurious to strangers, and offered to give us a strong guard whenever we felt disposed to go out for an excursion in the neighbourhood, sent us to-day, of his own accord, 16 soldiers and 4 officers to chaperone us through the Hawshuenshan valley. Under this well-armed escort, strengthened at his request by six men of our own guard, we made the circuit of the pagoda hill returning by the Tahô water-fall, a short way to the south of Momien, and on the eastern slope of the hill we passed a solitary heap of lava, remarkable from the fact that not another rock is to be seen for miles around. It has all the appearance of a small volcanic vent, and this view of its origin is strengthened by the fact that it is composed of the same lavaceous rock that occurs at the extinct volcano to the west. Rounding the hills about two miles from Momien, and making a slight westerly descent, we reached a short, narrow gorge at the south-eastern angle of the little circular valley of Hawshuenshan. The village of Shuayduay lies at the head of the gorge, on an abrupt slope, in a series of terraces faced with dry stone walls of very porous lava, and protected by parapets of sun-dried bricks. The stones are laid together with the same nicety that characterizes the facings of the ditch around Momien. The village was once a place of great wealth. A small stream runs through the ravine, which is not more than a quarter of a mile in length and about fifty yards broad, and empties itself into a substantially-built tank, at the bottom of the glen, crossed by a broad stone platform, arched at one side to allow the surplus water of the tank to escape. Facing Hawshuenshan valley, this platform on the southern side expands into a handsome crescent-shaped terrace, enclosed by an elegant stone balustrade, and forming the entrance into a fine khyoung built on the southern side of the gorge, opposite to Shuayduay village.

This temple consists of a series of terraces on the steep hill-side, and forms a most pleasing picture against a back-ground of green hills. It is the only temple in the neighbourhood of Momien that has been spared by the Mahomedans, and I believe its beauty has been its sole protection. It is approached by two crescentic court-yards with handsome arched gateways, and at the head of the upper one, the temple buildings begin. The first court is an open square, with three sides built on the same level, but the other, with its back to the hill, is raised on a stone terrace about four feet above the rest. The lower side contains the apartments of the priests, and the higher platform some of the principal deities of the temple, fine-looking, life-sized, gilded figures, before whom incense is continually kept burning in small black stone vases; and on a table in front of them lay a large drum, and grotesque, hollow, wooden figures of fish, which are beaten with short sticks by the priests and the faithful. There is a neat little garden with dwarfed fruit trees on two sides of this square, the centre of which is occupied by a few stunted trees, covered with a profusion of yellow orchids in full flower, and a magnificent *hydrangea* in a colossal vase. A passage leads through either side of the court-yard to a stone staircase proceeding to the terrace above, and converging in its middle in an upper-chambered hexagonal tower, supported on stone pillars, about seven feet high, which form an arched way, from which a short flight of steps leads up, but divides to the right and left, to reach the third or highest terrace, nearly on a level with which is the chamber or little temple on the top of the hexagonal tower. The upper temple corresponds to the length of its terrace, and is a single line of building which, with the exception of the back and end walls, is built entirely of wood, and the front is panelled in its lower half with richly-covered lattice work. The eaves and all the ceiling decorations, as well as the altars on which the three figures are seated, are in imitation of coloured Chinese porcelain. The wooden screen in front of the figures is a richly-coloured carving of birds and flowers, and the gods are almost life-sized and are gold-gilt. The principal one is in marble, and represents a female holding a naked infant seated in one of her hands, and supported by the other in front. The child's sex is strongly marked, and his shrine is the frequent resort of barren women. The woman holding this prodigy of virility is seated on a lotus, and a flower of the lily is below her feet.[1] The attitude of this figure and its relation to the *padma* forcibly recalled to me some of the sacred figures of the Hindus, and this reminds me to mention that in the khyoung in which we are living, there is a four-armed male figure, *Paang-ku*, the creator, seated on a bed of leaves, having a strong general resemblance to a *padma*. This remarkable figure is about life-size, and is perfectly naked with the exception of a garland of leaves (*vanamálá*) around his neck and loins. He is seated cross-legged like Buddha, with the two uppermost arms stretched out nearly at a right angle to the body, the elbows being bent at a right angle to the humerus, and in the right hand he holds a white disc, and in the left a red one.[2] He is represented in the act of carving with his other arms, holding an iron mallet in the right, and a chisel in the left hand. But to return to the Shuayduay khyoung. The stone walls of the highest temple do not reach the roof, but are connected to it by wooden panelled walls, with large circular windows in wonderfully elegant designs, and so adjusted that the light falls directly on the figures. This terrace, like all the others, is built of stone, and a narrow

---

[1] I cannot avoid thinking that this figure has been borrowed from Hinduism, and that the woman is *Kamalé Kámini*, the lotus woman *(Durgá)*, and that the child is her son, *Ganesá*. In statues of *Ganesá*, the trunk is often brought well down the belly, and it appears to me probable that, through time, the trunk may have been metamorphosed into an entirely different organ, through ignorance of the legend, and a fancied resemblance of the parts.

[2] This figure also may have been borrowed from the Hindus, and may represent *Visva Karmá (Vishnu)*, the Mercury of the Hindu Pantheon, and the legendary builder of the temple of Jagannath.

staircase from its middle leads down to the apartment on the top of the hexagonal tower which contains a handsome seated Buddhistic figure with the head in white marble, tinted brown.

From the khyoung, a good bridle-path runs along the hill on the eastern side of the valley, which is abruptly closed in on three sides by rounded, flat-topped, grassy hills which suddenly terminate around the dead level of the centre, which is now almost entirely flooded for rice cultivation, and on the fourth side, to the south-west, it is shut in by the long, barren, rocky slope of the extinct volcano, which is lower than any of the surrounding hills. A white pagoda stands out in bold relief against its black desert of rock. A quarter of a mile brings us to the walled town of Hawshuenshan built on the slope of the hill, and a much larger place than Shuayduay, with a fine khyoung overlooking the small stream that runs down from the village, and forms a considerable pond, or little lake at this season, in front of the town, and on which some men were paddling about in small, rough rafts, collecting for firewood the dead branches of some large willows that overshaded it. Immediately below the khyoung, but outside the town, this lakelet is crossed by a handsome stone bridge, with picturesque arched gateways at either end. The town must have been formerly a place of considerable importance, and judging from its extent, I should think the population would not have been overstated at 3,000. Crossing the bridge, we followed a raised paved way leading up through the valley to its head, about one and a half mile distant, where there is a small village, and from whence we made a gradual ascent of 3 to 400 feet to reach the Momien valley, passing the Tahô waterfall on our left. The vale of Hawshuenshan, although not more than two miles long by one broad, has once been encircled with large villages, the ruins of which attest that they must have been places of no little wealth. The whole excursion did not exceed two and a half hours.

20th June. Nothing to record except that the chief military officer came to ask us to dine with him to-morrow, bringing for each of us an invitation on pink paper. It has rained almost incessantly during the day.

21st June. Strong wind all night, with heavy rain. At 1 P.M., a messenger came to inform us that the feast was ready, and as we had had no breakfast, we were not slow to respond to the invitation. The house was within the city walls, and was approached through an outer court in which were the stables. It formed a large square with a central court, and the principal building facing the entrance from the outer court was raised on a terrace about four feet high, with a flight of steps near either end, each leading into an apartment or audience hall open to the terrace, off which were two doors to the apartments of the women. The other three sides of the square somewhat resembled Swiss cottages in their deep eaves, and in the large, folding, latticed windows of the second floor. Their ground-floor was used for the kitchen and store-rooms, and the side facing the main building as a dove-cot. Passing through a room at one angle of the yard, we reached the garden, which was outside the main body of the house, surrounded by a high wall. We received a hearty, genial welcome from our host and his two young sons, and from the Hotha Tsawbwa who was residing with him, and the entertainment commenced whenever we arrived with tea and cakes, followed by delicious newly-ripened plums and nectarines, washed down by a beer made from rice, succeeded by a decoction of samshu seasoned with every imaginable kind of herb. Our host, a Mahomedan, evinced an insatiable appetite for this highly-seasoned cup, and first took a long draught at it before he passed it round; in order to approve of his taste, we were forced to circulate it till it was finished, and as it fell to my lot to drain the last dregs, the high repute of this rather pleasant drink was at once dissipated by the discovery of a large piece of bristly pork-skin lying among the aromatic herbs and spices of the heel-tap. At this stage, we were each presented with a jade ring, our worthy friend expressing his regret that they were not more valuable. Small bowls of lamb, goat, necks of fowls, rice, and vegetables were now served, but after the large quantities of fruit and cake we had been forced to devour, we did but poor justice to the more solid good things he had so liberally provided for us. While we were doing what we could to the latter part of the entertainment, the women kept peeping out at us from behind the curtains over the doors, and the female servants, who are not permitted to dwarf their feet, were passing out and in from the various apartments. I was consulted regarding five of the women of the household who were said to be barren, but on declining to give any opinion until I had seen them, three mustered courage to show themselves, young, buxom wenches, dressed in Chinese fashion, with dwarfed feet. After this episode we left him highly pleased with our visit.

In the afternoon I went out to shoot round the wall, but did not see a single bird new to me. I returned through the city, and visited a fine ruined khyoung of great size, with a large tank in the centre of it, and passed the *musjid*, a small Chinese building, in an extremely filthy enclosure.

Eight Chinese said to be thieves, and the ears of fourteen others, were brought in to-day to Tasakone, and the former were at once marched out, and had their heads cut off within a few yards of the principal entrance of the bazaar.

The Hotha Tsawbwa starts to-morrow for his own valley, and accompanies the Tsawbwa-gadaw of Muangtee as far as her town, but promises to return for us in a day or two to conduct us to Hotha, as we are to return to Bhamô by the old embassy route, which leaves the Nantin valley at the iron bridge crossing the range bounding its southern side.

22nd June. A strong south-west breeze during the night, with heavy rain from midnight to 9 A.M. The south-westerly wind continued all day, and the sky is now beginning to clear. To-morrow is a Chinese feast, and the governor has sent us a present of three fowls in recognition of it. The priests in this khyoung, whose only religious duty seems to be to light the incense in front of the various deities twice a day, have hitherto abstained from burning it in the portion we occupy, as we objected to the heavy, sickly smell; they came in this evening, however, to re-kindle it, excusing themselves on the ground of to-morrow's feast.

23rd June. Heavy rain during the night, and a strong breeze from south-west. One thunder-shower at 5 P.M.

The festival is in honour of the goddess of agriculture, but beyond the stem of an iris and a branch of the wild indigo plant hung up over every door, and a general holiday, there is nothing in the conduct of the people to distinguish the day from any other.

26th June. Our friend, the chief military officer, has called to say good-bye, as he starts to-morrow on an expedition against some Chinese who have attacked the Panthay village of Khyto, the site of the famous silver and copper mines, three days' march to the north-east of Momien. He was presented with an old double-barrelled rifle, which he said he valued more than gold, 4lbs. of powder, a flask, and a box of caps, with all which he seemed to be much gratified.

27th June. Heavy rain during the night with strong breeze from south-west. This morning our military friend sent Sladen a present of two porcelain tea-cups with brass saucers, some old Chinese coins, a small, black, long-bodied Chinese terrier, with short bandy legs, and a book of pictures of extremely doubtful propriety, which Sladen very properly returned. The troops, about 500 strong, collected at the guard-house outside the bazaar wall, close to our residence, and proceeded to the governor's where they were received by a salute of three guns. After they were inspected by Tasakone in person, they left the town under another salute, but their departure did not excite the slightest show of interest among the Chinese, who preserve sullen indifference to everything Mahomedan. Heavy showers during the day with a strong south-westerly breeze.

28th June. Heavy rain since day-light to 9 A.M. To-day, a number of woodcutters were attacked at some distance from the town by the Chinese, who attempted to seize their mules, but as the former were fully armed, the attacking party had the worst of it, and the head of one of their number was brought in, and hung up by the hair at the side of the town gate.

29th June. Strong south-west wind all night, with heavy rain. I have been again warned not to go beyond the river, and as there is nothing to be done towards any further investigation of the natural history of this valley, I now spend the days wandering in the bazaar, and among the ruined khyoungs. The latter are very numerous in the town and suburbs, but although by far the greater majority are complete ruins, a few have been only partially destroyed, and are still the residence of some devoted priests who keep the incense burning in front of the gods of their forefathers. The richly-carved roofs, and the elaborate decorations of the altars and deities in these temples afford ample evidence of their former importance, and of a high proficiency in art. The designs are largely drawn from combinations of plants and birds, and are produced either as well-executed carvings or richly-coloured paintings on the ceilings, or on the panels of the altars. In the carvings, dragons and other monsters are frequently substituted for natural objects, and all are generally coloured; but although red, blue, green, and yellow are the standard tints, the effect is pleasant without being gaudy; even the outsides of the principal walls are frequently decorated with medallion pictures of small animals and birds, in black, grey, and white, alternating with squares or circles of complex geometrical figures in similar colours, producing a very novel effect to an European eye, but pleasing withal. The gods are nearly all life-sized, and in each temple there is usually a principal one, or it may be three, seated in a pedestal in the centre of the chief hall, surrounded by the statues of renowned sages and distinguished scholars. In one khyoung in which the central images were undoubtedly Buddhistic, the walls of the outer court were surrounded by about 50 life-sized, all in a sitting posture, male and female figures, probably representing the company of the *Thagyameng*.

In another temple, the chief deity was a colossal seated image with a dragon at each knee, and the body of a snake-like dragon passing under the double girdle round the loins, with its anterior part breaking up on the breast of the figure into a number of heads, somewhat resembling the effect produced by the seven-headed cobras of Hindoo mythology. The head and neck of a serpent-like dragon issued, too, from underneath each armpit.

It appeared to me that these temples were a mixture of Buddhism, Tauism, and Confucianism, and it is worthy of note that four-armed figures are occasionally present, and that some of the female figures are seated on lions, while others have the heads of bulls and birds, which suggest that they are in some way affined to Hinduism. None of the numerous images, if we except those in the Shuayduay temple, are made of stone. They are constructed in this way. A frame of wood, representing the body, legs, arms, and head, is roughly put together, and afterwards filled out with straw wound tightly over it, so as to bring the parts nearly up to their proper size. A layer of clay completes the form, and when it dries, the flesh tints are laid on with marked truth and fulness, and the garments coloured after certain conventional rules. It is apparently the custom, as in Burmah, to deposit some valuable, either a piece of gold or a precious stone, in the breast of each figure of any importance, for almost all have had their chests broken open by the Mahomedan iconoclasts, in the hope of gain.

The priests at Momien are apparently all Tauists and Confucianists, for I did not observe a single Buddhist. They are very poor, and only a few are to be found living in the temples, where their chief occupation seems to be to keep them clean, and to renew the incense which is kept burning in stone vases before the figures. They have no distinctive costume, and they live, as a rule, in their own houses in the suburbs. I found only four khyoungs permanently inhabited by priests, and all of them were situated without the town, in out-of-the-way places, and had thus partially escaped the complete ruin that overtook their more prominent neighbours. One is a boys' school conducted by an intelligent priest. The pupils, as in Burmah and the Shan states, shout out their lessons all at once at the pitch of their voices, but even this babel, like the miller and his mill, does not prevent the dominie from taking many a quiet nap during the labours of the day.

Sladen visited Tasakone to-day, and a despatch, announcing the fall of Yunan to the Panthays, was read to him. It contained all the particulars about the generals engaged, and stated that the city had been taken, but that the merchants had not been interfered with. The city is described as being four times as large as Tali, and as having eight gates, while the latter has only four. Many of the Chinese officials are said to have given in their adherence to the Panthays. Sladen, in the interview, had suggested the possibility that the Cambodia might ultimately become a trading route to Southern Yunan; but Tasakone ridiculed the idea, as the river, he says, is a succession of shallows and rocky rapids above Kianghung-gyee, and utterly impracticable for boats of any kind. A letter has been received from the Hotha Tsawbwa from Nantin, announcing his intention to return to his own village as the Kakhyen disturbances have spread so far. The governor will not listen to any talk about our return, and says we cannot leave this until we receive further accounts of the doings of the Kakhyens. I believe his chief object in detaining us now is to give him time to prepare some suitable presents.

1st July. Rain during the greater part of the night. Spent the day in sketching.

4th July. The weather has decidedly improved; we have only had half-a-dozen showers the whole day, and these, too, very short, slight ones, but during one, I was driven to take refuge in the khyoung devoted to the school, and was politely invited by the master to take a seat at his table. This movement, however, on my part, was too much for the curiosity of his pupils, who immediately ceased their howlings, and crowded round us. I signed to them to be off to their seats and tasks, but although they declined to stir, they recommenced their lessons with great gusto, shouting at the pitch of their voices, in all keys, till their faces were almost blue. As talking was out of the question in the midst of this pandemonium of voices, I requested my friend to order them to their seats, and one word from him sufficed to disperse them. He was a quiet, intelligent looking man, and when I entered, was seated behind a low, black writing-desk busily engaged on a book. I gave him a cheroot which he appeared fully to appreciate, and he in his turn sent for tea, and we sat and smoked the calumet of peace for nearly an hour. Lying on his table was a flat piece of wood like a gigantic paper-cutter, and to explain its use he called up a little urchin, and taking one of his hands first rubbed the palm with the pseudo paper-knife in a mysterious way, but a rapid rise and descent of the grim instrument soon revealed its use. Tears started to the little fellow's eyes, but a kindly word from his master soon dried them. The boys evidently enjoy their lessons, and as far as my observations go, the school-hours are nearly double those of children of the same age at home. They commence at nine in the morning and last to five in the afternoon, with an interval of about an hour and a half during the day. Each boy goes supplied with a little cash to buy his lunch from an itinerant hawker of small bowls of Chinese dainties. The ages of the children vary from six to fifteen, and each learns his task by repeating it aloud. Every boy has his own books, and with these he is seated at a table, one of a long row, with the other scholars similarly engaged, and shouts out his own lesson until he thinks he knows it. He then summons courage, and approaches his master, to whom he hands his book, and turning his back, does his best to repeat his task. While at their books they are at liberty to leave their seats, and to become peripatetics for the time. They learn to write at the same time as they learn to read, for each boy first copies his lesson, and while so engaged gets the exact pronunciation of each letter and word from his master, and in this way whole books are committed to memory. On my taking leave of my host, he expressed his approval of the cheroot by asking for more.

6th July. Tasakone visited us this forenoon, and his first words were an apology for our having been detained so long; he hopes, however, that we will now be able to start in a few days. He has written for the Mynetee Tsawbwa to accompany us as far as his town, where we will be joined by the Hotha chief, who is most anxious that we should visit his valley. He also promises to send a guard of 300 men with us as far as Nantin.

The presents for us, which were sent from Tali, have been stopped at Sheedin, along with some baskets of silver for the government here, and twenty mule-loads of cotton, a present from the Burmese government to Tasakone, by reason of the fighting that is at present going on between the Chinese and Panthays betwixt this and Yungchan. One of the messengers with letters from Tali was killed on this side of Sheedin, but the other escaped. The presents will not reach this before we leave, but Tasakone promises to send a mission to Rangoon in November, along with them. He says that nearly all the government presents he received from us have been sent to Tali, but this is doubtful, for if the road is closed to the presents from Tali, it is difficult to understand why it should be open to those from Momien.

7th July. Thirty mules belonging to Tasakone's nephew, while grazing on the pagoda hill, under the protection of a strong armed guard, were carried off by a band of Chinese. This is the only incident of the day. Heavy rain from morning to night.

8th July. Still heavy rain, with strong wind from the south-west. Tasakone sent word this morning that we are to have our boxes in readiness for a start, and that they are to be carried by men, and the reason why men are preferred is that they are a cheaper mode of carriage than mules.

9th July. We dined with Tasakone this afternoon at 5 P.M., and as usual began with tea, which was followed by a profusion of admirably-cooked dishes. A short interval succeeded, and another course of red rice and crisp slices of eggs was served, and the feast was completed by another round of the indispensable tea, and of a liqueur that has the reputation of being an excellent diuretic. Before dinner, Sladen presented Tasakone with sealed copies of the treaty with Burmah, and with two of his own seals which had been specially asked for by the governor. A long letter in Chinese, stating their desire to enter into friendly relations with our government, and to encourage trade between the two countries, and promising, as soon as the country is restored to tranquillity, to despatch an envoy with letters to Rangoon, was handed to Sladen. Heavy showers all day up to sunset.

10th July. Heavy rain from midnight; calm to-day. I bought a number of stone implements in the bazaar for four and six annas each. They are worn as charms, and are carefully kept in small bags. The general opinion is that they are thunder-bolts, and they are alleged to be found, although rarely, all over the district, lying on the surface soil doubtless turned up by the plough.[1]

A man condemned to death for theft managed to escape from the town, but was not caught, although a hue and cry was raised as soon as it was discovered that he had fled. Showers up to noon, with occasional drizzle afterwards.

11th July. Paid our last visit to Tasakone this forenoon, when Sladen received a letter from him, stating that the duties to be levied on goods from Burmah were to be twelve annas a mile between Mawphoo and Nantin, a distance of about twelve miles, exclusive of Momien itself. It does not include the duties in the Kakhyen hills and the Shan states, which can only be settled by the chiefs of Ponline, Ponsee, Seray, Manwyne, Sanda, and Muangla. He assured Sladen that he would rather receive for his share of the duties only eight annas instead of a rupee, if the exaction of the larger sum would in any way discourage the full development of trade, and that he would see to it that goods which paid duties at Momien were entitled to a free pass to Yung-chan and Talifoo. He affixed his official seal to the document relating to the duties, and stamped it also with two fancy seals that Sladen had given him. We took leave of him after the business was settled, and a few hours afterwards, he made his appearance at our dwelling with his return

---

[1] Appendix C.

presents, consisting of a mandarin's full-dress, long, richly-embroidered satin coat, and hat, and boots; three pieces of figured silk, four figured silk jackets, a leather jacket, two pairs of long boots; seventy white jackets for the men, and as many large bamboo hats; three fine straw hats covered with oil-cloth, eight silver-mounted daggers, four silver-mounted spears, a gold and jade chatelaine, and four amber bead rosaries. The mandarin's coat was his own, and he gave it as it was the only valuable article he had to offer. The other presents were of little worth, if we except the silver spears, chatelaine, and rosaries, but I believe he has done his very best to make as good a show as possible, and that if it does not amount to much, the Panthays must be excused on account of their poverty, and not from any want of liberality. They have treated us with great hospitality, supplying us with oxen and sheep, firewood, rice, and vegetables enough for the wants of all our men during our residence.

The letter regarding the duties was again produced, and stamped with a large official seal which he has given Sladen, along with a silver vase containing red ink for stamping letters. His idea is that Sladen should use it in the event of his communicating with him by letter, and that by the impress of the seal being affixed, the letters will not be tampered with, and that they will be much more likely to reach him than if they were despatched without it.

We are to start to-morrow morning, and he advises us not to loiter on the road, and to remain only a single night at each stage. A body of men will precede us, and another will bring up the rear. Heavy showers during the day.

12*th July.* Rose very early, and had everything ready for a start. A few men arrived at 7 A.M., but only in twos and threes; and it soon became apparent that we should not get away to-day, as there was an evident difficulty in procuring the requisite number of porters, and as those who did come were unprovided with ropes and poles to carry their loads. Materials for the latter, in the shape of unwieldy rafters from old khyoungs, were brought and cut up on the spot, but as this was evidently going to be the labour of half a day, it was resolved to postpone our departure till to-morrow.

The reason why there has been such a difficulty in procuring men is, that they were not hired till the last moment, in order that the news of our departure should not reach the ill-disposed Chinese on the road, which it certainly would have done if the men had been engaged some days before. This fear of encountering the opposition of the Chinese is also the real reason why men were preferred to mules, for if the latter had been selected as the mode of carriage, it would have been absolutely necessary to have made the arrangements some days before our departure. Tasakone reprimanded his officers for the bungling way in which they had conducted the arrangements, and one of them, an old Chinaman, who had been stationed at our khyoung as Burmese interpreter, excused himself to Tasakone, on the ground that we were taking away an unnecessary number of boxes and that many of them were filled with such worthless rubbish as dried weeds and bird skins, stones and mud, and that we were carrying back a number of boxes of powder which could be of no possible use to us. Moungshuay-Yah, who reported this, says, Tasakone was annoyed that we had not given him all our gunpowder as it would be most useful to him here, but that he explained to him that we had only a box of cartridges for the men, and that he had received the whole of our stock. The arrangements for to-morrow are committed to four other officers, and on their arrival at the khyoung, Sladen thought it advisable to satisfy them regarding our supply of gunpowder.

CHAPTER XIV.

MOMIEN TO HOTHA.

ONCE more, our departure from Momien seemed rather doubtful, owing to the difficulty of finding men willing to carry our boxes, and latterly porters had to be impressed into the service. If they demurred to take a particular box, or complained of the weight of their loads, they were quieted by a torrent of abuse from the Panthays, or treated to severe blows, and none got the least consideration. However, we got started about 8 A.M., on the 13th July, and as we left the khyoung, we waved an adieu to Tasakone, who had come out on the town wall overlooking our residence to bid us farewell, and our guard gave a feeble cheer in Hindustanee, which they again repeated as we passed out of the bazaar gate. Two Panthay officials accompanied us for nearly a mile, and when we came to part with them, they burst into tears, and after we had gone a long way, and turned round to take our last look of Momien, we saw the two figures standing on the spot where we had left them, gazing wistfully after us. One of them had spent the last two days with our men, refusing to go to his own house, and, I believe, that his strong liking to the society of our guard arose from sympathy of feeling in matters of religion. There cannot be a doubt that a great part of the success of the Expedition is due to the presence of the Mahomedan element in our guard. The Panthays at once fraternized with them, and our khyoung from the first day we arrived in Momien was the constant resort of all the most respectable Mahomedans.

We had only proceeded a short distance when it began to rain in a way that is only known among those hills, and the result was that the roads became very slippery and difficult to travel on to men carrying heavy loads, and under these circumstances we were soon ahead of our porters. As we began the descent into the Nantin valley, the road was as if it had been well oiled, and pedestrians and ponies slid down the steep hill-path in wild confusion, many of our number coming to serious grief. A little Chinese girl, who has been presented to the jemadar and his wife by Tasakone, in recognition of his appreciated services at the musjid, accompanied us, mounted on a pony to which she was secured in a small bamboo chair, but as the beast was allowed to select his own course, the trepidation of our little

Mahomedan neophyte was beyond all measure, and reasonably so, for she was treated as if she were little better than a bale of cotton.

When we reached the scene of the attack made on us on our way up, we passed two men, evidently newly dead, pitched into a hedge by the road-side, and a little further on some of our looted boxes. We halted at the hot springs to allow the porters to come up, and I took the temperature, immersing the thermometer about one foot, and allowing it to remain for nearly five minutes. The temperature of the springs is 205°, which is the boiling point of water at Nantin, a few feet below them. We learned here that the Panthays had killed three Chinese robbers, who had been found lying in wait by the roadside with long spears, ready to prod the first mule that passed, and that the dead bodies we saw were two of them who had been thrown aside to be out of sight. As there were no signs of the porters we went on our way, and as we neared Nantin, we met many men and boys carrying rice to Momien for to-morrow's market. A few miles from the town we were requested by the Panthays to wait till the rest of their numbers, immediately behind us, came up, as we were given to understand that we had to pass a place frequented by robbers, whose plan of attack is to secret themselves in the long jungly grass that skirts the sides of the valley below the river terraces, fire at passers-by, and then rush out and cut their throats, seizing their property, and retreating with it to the hills. We formed into a line with a Panthay guard before and behind; and with a gong beating ahead, we marched in this way into Nantin which we reached at 6 P.M. During the next two hours our men and baggage came straggling in, but my bed did not appear, and my Burmese boy who had been placed over the porter carrying it, with strict injunctions that he was on no account to leave him, was the last to arrive with the unpleasant news that the porter had stoutly refused to go beyond a village some twelve miles from this. Many of our boxes have not come up, and the probability is that we shall never see them again.

We have put up in the same khyoung that we stayed in on our way to Momien, but when we arrived, we found it occupied by a Panthay guard and a number of ponies, and in a most filthy condition. We turned the ponies out, but could not eject the guard and a sick man who lay groaning in one corner, and as the place is alive with flies and mosquitoes, it is anything but pleasant. My attention was at once given to the sick man, not from any very compassionate feeling, I am afraid, but from a resolve, if possible, to have a quiet night by putting a stop to his moaning. I found him a Kakhyen Tsawbwa, who had been suffering from severe fever for some days, and mixing up a strong draught of sulphate of magnesia in two tumblers of water he swallowed it, and I followed it up with a good dose of quinine. The effect was marvellous, and in a few hours his groaning ceased as he fell into a profound sleep. Our old friend, the governor, made his appearance at 8 P.M., accompanied by his guard, one of whom carried an enormous, oval, gauze lantern, suspended from a stick which opened out as a tripod, and from which the lamp was suspended in the centre. He assured us that if he had known we were coming, he would have come out to meet us, and would have had the khyoung in readiness. He has had a great fight with Chinese dacoits (Imperialists) since we were here, and a Chinese chief and his villages have given in their adherence to the Panthay cause.

The most interesting piece of news that met us on our arrival was that 50 Burmese have reached Muangla to accompany us back. This display now, of good-will and interest in our welfare and success, is a typical illustration of Burmese diplomacy.

14th July. Showers during the morning. Many of our packages turned up after sunrise, and among them my bedding; but my iron bedstead, shot-box, and magazine-box have yet to appear. The Panthays, and especially Tasakone, took such a great fancy to the former, that it is doubtful whether it will ever reach me. They had the same feeling towards the shot-box which was carefully stowed away in a corner before we left in order that it might be overlooked; and the magazine-box, which contains all my stock of caps, powder, and wads, and a number of other valuable articles, seems to have been included in the list of baggage to be lost on the way. If the magazine-box is not recovered, there is an end to my shooting, as it contains all the materials for my gun, and as Bowers and Sladen have only a few caps between them.

The Momien officers, who accompanied us, seem to be much annoyed at our loss, and sent men this morning to enquire after the missing articles, but the messengers have not been able to find any trace of them. All the porters were examined after their return, and the plausible explanation was given that the men who had not come up were those who had been impressed for the occasion. The governor, it is stated, has also written to Tasakone informing him of the circumstances, but as there is little or no chance now of recovering our property, we start to-morrow morning for Muangla.

The Hotha Tsawbwa has not kept his agreement to meet us here, and it is reported that he is still in his own valley. The number of Burmans at Muangla has now risen to 150.

15th July. I was awoke this morning by one of our Hindustanees saying to Sladen, "Of the three ponies not one is left." During the night, thieves had made a hole in the wall of the court-yard, and carried them off under the noses of the sentries who were posted within twenty yards of where our steeds were tied. The hole was only large enough to admit of one pony passing out at a time, and it had been made within a few feet from where Sladen's pony was standing. On examining the spot, we found that the animals had been decoyed away by oats, and on following up the foot-prints, we discovered that another hole had been made in the town wall, and that the animals had been liberally supplied with grain *en route* between the two openings. On our previous visit we had been cautioned to take care of our ponies as they were liable to be carried off, but the warning had entirely escaped us. On one occasion, while Tasakone was staying in this same khyoung, a similar robbery was attempted, but the alarm was raised before the thieves had succeeded in purloining more than one gun and a dâh, and the latter was dropped and recovered. We got the loan of ponies to carry us as far as Muangla, and started at half-past ten. At the last moment, however, as has been usually the case, we experienced considerable difficulty in procuring the requisite carriage for our boxes, and in the present instance the dearth of porters was due to the fact that nearly all the ones from Momien had run away. As a sufficient number of men could not be procured, mules had to be sent for, and the proverbial character of these animals was fully verified by the Nantin ones, who for nearly an hour stubbornly refused to be caught. During this interlude, the Panthays were doing their best to impress men for the lighter loads, and if they refused, they were dragged along by soldiers with drawn dâhs. So opposed were the men generally to lend their services, that each had to be followed up by a spearman, who would have thought little of egging him on with his spear, if he had made any overt resistance to proceed. As we passed through Mynetee (Muangtee) the townspeople had turned out at their doors, and the Tsawbwa-gadaw and all her retainers were waiting for us, and waved a parting as we passed. Outside the town, a strong Shan guard was drawn up in our honour, and accompanied us as far as the chain-bridge across the Tahô, about 2 or 3 miles to the west of the town. During the rains, the river is unfordable at Mynetee, and the road lies along the left bank, as far as the bridge, between hedge-rows round paddy-fields.

Crossing the bridge, we commenced the ascent into the Mawphoo valley, which lies at a higher elevation than either the Nantin or Sanda ones, on both sides of it, with the Tahô flowing in a deep gorge along its southern boundary. The ascent at this season is a most arduous one, as the road becomes extremely slippery after rain. Both man and beast were constantly sliding and falling, and some of the former, as they made slight descents over the spurs, got very severe bumps, as their legs went from under them, and they came down with a thud. It was a great relief to all when we reached Mawphoo, and had a rest for nearly an hour previous to the descent into the head of the Muangla section of the Tapeng or Sanda valley. It rained incessantly up to Mawphoo, which we left at half-past 3 P.M. The descent is very precipitous, and the road consists of a series of zig-zags, some of them over frightful precipices, where a slip of the pony's foot would be certain destruction. At the beginning of the declivity, before the zig-zags are reached, the only possible mode of motion for the ponies was sliding, and while mine was so engaged he came down on his side, but recovered himself before he had slipped any great distance. I fortunately got my feet out of the stirrups, and clutching hold of a tuft of long grass stopped my downward progress. At this season the Tahô issues as a tremendous torrent from the Mawphoo hills, and in the distance the Tapeng appeared almost as large as the Irawady in the dry weather.

We reached Muangla at dusk, and on entering the town were astonished to meet an Englishman in company with some Shans. He rushed up to Sladen, and introduced himself as Mr. Gordon, Civil Engineer, from Prome. He had been sent by the Chief Commissioner of Burmah with funds for our use, and to act as Engineer to the Expedition. He received his instructions, by telegraph from Rangoon, to follow our party as quickly as possible, and he has evidently carried them out with laudable energy. He travelled under a guard of 50 Burmans, and the money he brought was in addition to a sum of £500 from the Chief Commissioner of Burmah, which had been forwarded from Bhamô at his request, under the protection of 100 men officered by the *Sayaydawgyee*. Gordon suggests that we should go back to Momien, and attempt to return either by the Yang-tse-kiang or by Canton, but it appears to us that such a proceeding would be highly injudicious, and almost certain to prove a failure. If an advance had been possible, we would not have returned over the same ground, and to go back now, after all the negotiations with the Panthays have been completed, would be certain to arouse suspicion, and lead them to doubt the integrity of our motives. Any attempt to pass through Panthay territory into imperial ground by an armed Expedition like ours would be a most hazardous procedure, and certain to fail, and the feeling against the Chinese government is so strong that the Panthays would never consent to our leaving their territory. They are not sufficiently enlightened to appreciate our wish to travel across the breadth of Yunan, out of a simple desire to promote zoological and geographical science; and they would immediately conclude that our object was to join the imperialists, and if we attempted to carry our point, certain discomfiture would be the result. The case, however, would perhaps be different if a party were unarmed, and if, instead of four Englishmen, only two, with a few followers, were to go with the professed object of acquiring a knowledge of the country, and for sport, furnished at the same time with letters from the imperial government to the mandarins, ordering that the travellers should be received, although they came from rebel territory. Yet it would be extremely doubtful, whether, in the present disturbed state of Yunan, these letters would meet with much respect from the mandarins bordering on Panthay ground, who act according to their own pleasure, or from the bands of robbers and armed bodies of Chinese who infest the province, and utterly disregard imperial authority.

We have put up in our old quarters. The lad who was carrying my thermometers, and whom I kept at my side as far as Mawphoo, where I lost sight of him, has not shown face, and the Panthay officers inform me that as all the other porters have arrived, there is little or no chance of seeing my instruments again. They are the only ones remaining, save a maximum and minimum thermometer, as the duplicate set was in my boxes that were lost on the way to Momien.

16th July. We are not to start till to-morrow, as the money has to be taken over to-day from the Burmese. I received £150, and spent the greater part of the day in purchasing Shan products and articles of dress. This is the first time, I may say, we have been able to spend any money in securing illustrations of the art and productions of the country, for the pittances available at Momien were utterly insufficient, and only permitted of shilling and sixpenny investments, so that any specimens of the art and manufactures of Western Yunan procured at Momien were very inferior, and of the most tawdry kind; now, however, we hope to secure many good illustrations of art among the Shans.

Gordon met the Hotha Tsawbaw at Manwyne, and was advised by him to wait for a day or two, but he rejected the advice, and came on here as fast as he could, passing Sanda, but not entering it. He says Hotha is a gambler, and spent the greater part of the day in the bazaar throwing dice, and playing other chance games.

17th July. Our departure is again delayed as the arrangements have not been completed. The Panthays left to-day, and were evidently very sorry to return, and one wished to go to Rangoon, saying if he once got there, he would never go back to his own country. The khyoung has been besieged by crowds of Shan and Chinese men, women, and children, offering articles for sale, chiefly cloth, clothes, and silver ornaments.

18th July. The arrangements for our departure are still incomplete, and we do not start till to-morrow. I have purchased a large number of articles, both Shan and Poloung, but only a few Leesaw and Kakhyen ornaments. This valley is a perfect babel, and besides the languages of the foregoing people, there is the Chinese, and also a Kakhyen dialect, with a remarkable affinity to Burmese, spoken by the Khungs.

A Kakhyen came to say that our ponies are in a village on a hill not very many miles off, and that they can be ransomed, and we have requested the authorities to enquire after them.

19th July. A very wet morning, and as only one mule came to the front, and there was little or no prospect of any more turning up for some time to come, we resolved to postpone our march for another day. A second message has come in about our ponies, and Rupees 320 are demanded for them, but as the authorities here will not assist us we are perfectly helpless, although we would willingly give the sum asked.

20th July. We experienced considerable difficulty even this morning in procuring porters for our baggage, and I had to leave my collecting boxes behind under charge of two of my men. We crossed the Tapeng above its junction with the Tahô in ferry boats, in which the boatmen at first refused to take us unless we paid them 5,000 cash beforehand. This we indignantly refused, and declined to pay them until we had crossed, but promised them their proper fare on the other side. They still held out and we had to take forcible possession of the boats, but when they found we were not to be imposed upon, they worked with wonderful good will, and quickly crossed and recrossed for the remainder of our party. On the other side we joined Sladen and Bowers who had preceded us, and then set out in a body for Sanda, the road at first lying along the top of some old river terraces which are cut up at intervals into deep narrow gullies, by small mountain streams which were crossed by two narrow planks laid side by side. Our ponies, however, went bravely at them, and all got over with ease except Gordon's which he had brought with him from the plains, and which was unaccustomed to the

Blondin exploits that the others thought nothing of; so it got nervous on one, over which it was being led, and disappeared head over heels into the deep gully below, to the consternation of all. Wonderful to say, the animal broke no limbs, and shortly re-appeared a little further down, on the river terrace below. About two miles beyond where we had forded the Tapeng on our upward journey, we descended towards the level centre of the valley, which during this season is more or less under water for the irrigation of the crops, and in consequence of the flooding of the river and the heavy rains, the road is carried along the top of a substantial bund that has been built to restrict the floods. The whole extent of the valley was clothed in a mantle of exquisitely fresh verdure, in beautiful contrast to the dark mountains that towered like a protecting wall around it. A day of alternate cloud and sunshine gave us all that could be desired for the full display of the scenery of this lovely vale. The deep shadows of giant clouds betimes flitted down the mountains and over the sunny plains, while occasional fleecy mists wrapt the highest peaks in their murky folds, and black storms rolled down the hills obscuring them as with a curtain "lashed at the base with slanting storm," the rest of the splendid landscape basking in the sunlight. I kept a good look-out for the warm streams which occur about five miles from Sanda, but they were so flooded that I could not detect them. Nearing Sanda, we had to cross a tolerable stream much swollen by the late heavy rains, so strong that our ponies had the greatest difficulty in stemming its current, and so deep that our saddles were under water. We reached the town about 5 P.M., and put up in our old quarters. Shortly after our arrival, the Tsawbwa's head man visited us with a present of rice, fowls, and firewood, sufficient for all our wants.

21st July. It rained all last night, and my boxes have not yet arrived. In the morning I missed my fishing-rod which had been tied up with a number of bamboo pipe stems, and placed at the head of my bed, and on mentioning my loss, I found that a packet had been likewise stolen from Sladen's bedside during the night. His, however, was a more valuable collection, for it contained the long, solid, silver pipe stem which was presented to him by the Tsawbwa of this place on our previous visit, also a riding cane, and some other presents. We informed the authorities of the theft, and the Tsawbwa has offered a reward of Rs. 200 for the recovery of the articles.

The Hotha, or Hosa Tsawbwa as the Shans pronounce it, is to meet us at a village on the borders of his district, and not at Manwyne as we were informed at Muangla. My boxes came in, in the afternoon.

22nd July. Heavy rain all night, and still raining. Crowds of men, women, and children, bringing every imaginable article of clothing and domestic economy for sale, filled the khyoung during the day. The priests, whenever articles of female attire were produced, seemed to be much shocked, and when I bought a pair of woman's leggings and threw them carelessly on my bed, I elicited a howl of astonishment at my introducing such dangerous objects among men enjoined to strict celibacy, and prohibited from even touching their own mothers.

23rd July. The phoongyees have complained to the Tsawbwa about the women selling articles of female attire in the khyoung, and an order has been issued forbidding it. No women showed face during the day, but plenty of men came as their substitutes.

24th July. Rain all night, and up to noon. The large market which is held every five days occurred to-day. The crowd was very great, and the long, broad street was lined with stalls on either side, and was a perfect sea of umbrella-like straw hats. There were a large number of Kakhyens present who had brought oil, bamboos, and firewood, and Leesaws were also numerous with well-laden baskets of the same materials. The men and women of the latter people dress so much alike, that it is sometimes difficult to make out the sexes of the young ones. Both shave a circle round the head, leaving only a large patch on the upper and back part, with a small, short pig-tail behind. I induced a man and two boys, for a rupee each, to come to the khyoung, and give me some of their words.

25th July. Thick, drizzling rain during the early part of the day. A respectable-looking Shan, who has been bringing articles for sale during the last few days, asked me to go to his house to look at some Leesaw clothing which he said he had. Gordon accompanied me, and seats were given us, and his daughter served us with some plums which we ate with salt, and mangoes cut into thin slices. It turned out that he had no Leesaw clothing after all, but a quantity of old coats and trousers of his own, which he thought I would be simpleton enough to take as examples of the Leesaw dress which I have hitherto failed to secure, as none of that people are found nearer than six or seven miles from Sanda, high up the hill-sides. His two wives were present, and some other women who had collected from the neighbouring cottages as the news of our presence spread. On enquiry whether it was usual for the Shans to have more than one wife, we were told that it was not, but that a man was allowed to please himself in such matters. The usual age for marriage is between 18 and 20, and the consent of the parents is all that is required to make a marriage binding. It is unattended by any ceremony, and the priests have no voice in such matters. This house, like Shan cottages generally, is enclosed in a small court-yard, and consists of three rooms; a central one, with a sleeping apartment on each side of it. Against the wall of the former, facing the door, stood the family altar, a small table having on it an incense vase and the tablet of some of his ancestors. A broad verandah ran along the front of the cottage, and a large indigo vat hollowed out of solid wood lay at one end of it. The hands of the female members of his household were blue with indigo, as is generally the case with Shan women, but it speaks well for their industrious habits.

From his house we visited the Shan and Chinese khyoungs. The former is a plain bamboo structure built on the site of a monastery which was destroyed some years ago by the Panthays, and contains only one figure of Guadama, but as there was nothing of any interest in it, and as the phoongyees were seated at breakfast round a low bamboo table, we retired to the Chinese khyoung next door. This is also built of bamboo with a similar history to the former. There is one principal figure of Buddha crowned with a circlet resembling ostrich plumes, but intended to represent a glory, and the body is enveloped in a yellow robe. A few other small figures of Guadama, recently gold-gilt, stood on the altar, on which lay a number of old pictures. At the side of the altar, on a small table, was the wooden fish which is of so frequent occurrence in the khyoungs at Momien. Tradition says regarding it, that Guadama was shipwrecked in one of his former existences, when a large fish swallowed him up, and carried him to land, and that he ever afterwards fed it till it died. The similarity of this legend to the Jewish story of Jonah is remarkable. The head phoongyee was very polite, and had seats brought for us covered with red rugs, and tea and fruit handed round by his waiting-man. He showed us a number of paintings representing the judgment, and tortures of the damned. One figure, evidently the judge, was seated at a table with a book before him, and with pens and ink at his side, and on either hand stood two figures, one a hideous-looking monster, and the other a being of more human and humane appearance. One was the good, and the other the bad recording angel. In front of the judge, the wicked and pious spirits, in the flesh however, were seen departing to their respective places. Some of the former were being dragged away by devils, while others in the foreground were being subjected to all imaginable forms of devilish torture that the fertile imagination of a tormenting fiend could contrive. The punishment of the unfortunate spirits had reference to their failings while on earth; he who had been troubled with an unruly tongue was now having it torn out of his head, while the slayer of animals was being hacked in two with his head downwards and legs stretched apart. Horrible as these scenes were, they had a touch of humour about them that extracted a smile even from the priest. Before the inroads of the Panthays, the Sanda khyoungs were institutions of considerable wealth and importance, and have been described to me as splendid structures.

26th July. Heavy rain from midnight to about sunrise. Gordon and I started at 1 P.M., with one of the chief men of the town, to visit the hill from whence the lime sold in the bazaar is said to be obtained. Our road lay along paddy-fields, and was either knee-deep in mud, or up to our ponies' girths in water. We crossed the Sanda river that flows down to the Tapeng from the north, through a short, narrow valley, on the other side of which is the limestone hill. The stream was so deep and strong that when I had reached the centre, and found my pony reeling under me, I had doubts whether he would be able to pull through without my getting a serious ducking. He held his ground, however, but on scrambling up the bank on the other side, he precipitated me into a ditch. The hill rises in a gentle declivity from the river, and the road lay through cotton-fields, now in full flower, and kept so clean that not a weed was to be seen. Shan girls, dressed in dark blue with short trousers, and petticoats with little aprons in front, and with their sleeves tucked up above the elbows, looked up at us from their work in the fields, with an air of mute astonishment depicted on their red-cheeked, round, chubby faces. Rice cultivation was once tried on the slopes, but had to be abandoned as it did not pay. About 400 feet up the grassy hill, which is entirely devoid of trees, we were conducted to a spot covered with long grass, in which the limestone is found lying in masses that have fallen down, year after year, from the rocks above. They are dug out of the ground, and carried to the villages where they are burned with grass, which, it is alleged, fires them better than wood. Some superstitious idea is attached to the occurrence of the limestone in this locality, and it was shown to us as something very remarkable. The limestone is bluish-grey, very crystalline and hard. An old kiln, which had been built by some Chinamen who had come from Talifoo to work it, was pointed out to us. On my return, the Tsawbwa wished to know whether the hill contained silver, because the Shans have an absurd idea that our field-glasses and telescopes confer on us the power of detecting the existence of precious metals and gems in the very inmost recesses of the mountains. We have only to direct them on a hill, and we have all its mineral wealth revealed to us at a glance. During our absence, the Tsawbwa informed Sladen that he could not undertake the responsibility of sending us to Hotha by the route which crosses from this to that valley, as he is afraid that we might be attacked by the Muangla villages on the opposite side of the Tapeng. He, therefore, recommends us to write to Muangla, and request the assistance and countenance of the officials of that town who are all-powerful throughout their own district. There is a strong objection among the officials here to our going to Hotha, owing, we are inclined to think, to the circumstance that the other route is the best, and that they do not wish us to have any practical knowledge of it, in case we should recommend it as the most feasible one.

27th July. I went out this forenoon to shoot over the hill behind the town, and first directed my attention to a dense grove of fine trees behind the Tsawbwa's house, marking the last resting-places of his ancestors. I selected this spot as it is the only cover for birds about Sanda, but no sooner had I fired one shot than a dozen men rushed out from the Tsawbwa's house, and implored me not to fire again, for if I did, I would certainly bring some great calamity upon their chief. There was nothing for it but to desist, and I moved off, followed, however, by them, and they did not leave me till they had seen me a long way beyond the trees. But even then, my steps were dogged by a Shan, and I gave myself a long, needless climb up the hill-side hoping to shake him off; but, no, he stuck to me like a leech, and tracked me wherever I went, and would not be driven away although I used every possible means to intimidate him. Birds are very scarce on these grassy hills, yet, notwithstanding the protestations of my Shan friend, I shot a few warblers, when the report of my gun would not reach the Tsawbwa's ears. The rocks composing the hill are, a pale blue splintery quartzose rock and a limestone resembling some of the masses found on the hill we visited yesterday. On my return to the khyoung, I ascertained that a request had already been made to Sladen that we should not fire on the hills behind the town, as a nât is believed to reside on them in an old cutting on the face of one of the ridges marking the spot where the Chinese army of 1767 was entrenched. The Shans believe that if a gun is fired on the hill it excites the displeasure of this cantankerous demon, who might vent his wrath by assuming the form of a tiger, and carry off children, or even proceed to the extremity of killing the Tsawbwa. The people live in constant dread of the evil spirit, and it is only the other day that the Tsawbwa sent to me complaining of headache and cough, and asking me to prescribe for him as he thought the nât had come down to claim him as his own. He was in terror of his life, but I exorcised the devil by a strong dose of that active remedy, sulphate of magnesia, which has proved to me of such service in trifling ailments, and which now forms the back-bone of my medicine chest.

28th July. While strolling in search of birds over these uninteresting lifeless hills, I met some very Kakhyen-looking boys and a man resting under the shade of a fine banyan, by the side of a pretty mountain stream, and sat down beside them to talk. They denied they were Kakhyens, and stood up manfully for their nationality which they said was Chinese, and which language they spoke fluently as well as Kakhyen. They assured me they were hill-Chinese, and that they lived in a Kakhyen village, along with others of their countrymen. The boys were in rags, and their chief protection against the weather was the thick layers of dirt which incrusted their hides in Kakhyen fashion. The man's clothes were a little more respectable, but the dirt was quite as rich, and evidently supported an extensive fauna which was constantly making him aware of its presence.

While we were sitting, numbers of Shan men and women passed down from the hills laden with the ashes of a plant which are used as a mordant in indigo-dyeing.

29th July. About 3 o'clock in the morning, I was awoke by Sladen springing out of his bed, and shouting at the pitch of his voice. I followed his example as did the others, and seized first a dâh and then a revolver, imagining in the darkness that we had been attacked, for no sooner had I sprung from my bed than bang went a shot close to where Sladen was. On feeling my way round to his bed, the small door at the head of it, which has always been kept closed, was open, and Sladen outside with some of the men. The explanation of all the hubbub was this, that a thief had opened the door, and carried off one of the silver-mounted Panthay spears, the jingle of which had awakened Sladen, who had rushed out and fired a shot into the darkness after the retreating robber. The theft could only have been effected by the cognizance and assistance of some one in the khyoung, and suspicion points strongly to one of the phoongyees, who sleeps in a small room close to the door through which the thief escaped. A sentry with a lamp was stationed not more than twelve feet from the door, and he says that the robbery happened in a minute while he turned his lamp in the opposite direction, and walked two yards to look at the hour on a watch that hung on a post close by. A few minutes before, he had heard the phoongyee moving about in his room, and his door being open, he had raised his lamp to see who was astir, but saw no one. A few hours after the robbery, and when we were in bed, a man came to the door through which it had been committed, and called the phoongyee away, and when this was brought forward against him in the morning, he explained it by saying that he had been called to see a sick man. There can be little doubt that he has been a party to the theft, and when the circumstances were repeated to the Tsawbwa, he was among the first to be suspected, as his private life is known to be a dissolute one.

At 7 A.M., Gordon and I started on a visit to the hot springs in the centre of the level ground of the little valley we had crossed to the limestone hill. They occur in the bed of a small stream in two groups, separated by an interval of about a quarter of a mile. In the most easterly set there is at present only one spring, which rises like all the others, in the almost dry channel of a rivulet. It is a shallow basin about six inches deep and one yard in diameter, and the water bubbles up through a gravelly bottom over which there is a deposit of a fine micaceous mud from below. In the cold weather when the water has had time to collect, and when the integrity of the basin has not been disturbed for some time by floods, it is said to be much warmer, and a number of small springs form round it. All about the basin lay the remains of animals that had been cooked in the spring. During the winter the villagers deepen the basin by piling stems about its margin, and mix the hot with cold water, and use it for bathing, in cases of disease. When a malady has resisted all other cures, the water is sometimes had recourse to as a drink.

The other group consists of five openings through which the water bubbles up in the bed of the stream which has been purposely diverted to expose them. All their basins, with one exception, had been obliterated by the floods and their temperature much reduced, but on inserting the bulb into the holes through which they issue, they were found to have the same temperature as the first spring. In approaching them a heavy smell is felt, but it cannot be detected in the vapour rising from the water. The atmosphere around the springs for some distance is very warm, and the ground in some places so hot that the natives with us could not stand on it with their bare feet. Our guide, an intelligent Shan, informed us, with a serious face, that hell was in the immediate vicinity, and that they owed their origin to Guadama having walked over the spot, when the flames of the lower regions burst forth, and endeavoured to devour him. We were told that one of his footprints was close at hand, and setting out to visit it were conducted to the western side of the valley into a short romantic glen through which the Chalktaw runs as a mountain torrent. This stream is bridged below where it enters the valley by a double-spanned bamboo structure, supported in the middle of the stream on a large boulder, and at either end by two bamboos driven into the ground, and bent over and connected to the pathway of the bridge, so that it is partly suspended and partly arched. Many Kakhyen and Leesaw men and women were coming down the hill on their way to the bazaar at Sanda, carrying great loads of vegetables, firewood, and planks of wood about 3 feet long, 15 inches broad, and one and a half inch in thickness. A basket of vegetables, and a plank of heavy wood, was a young woman's load down these steep hills. I tried the weight of one, and although it took me all my strength to lift it, a young woman shouldered it with ease. About a quarter of a mile up this wild glen, which is strewn with enormous, water-worn, granite boulders, which have been brought down by the Chalktaw in years long gone by, we came to the giant footprint on the end of one of them, in a spot surrounded by some fine, old, spreading banyan trees. The origin of this footprint was at once apparent. It was on the end of the boulder looking up the glen, and it was evident that the hollow corresponding to the heel had been produced by the constant friction of some other boulder which had lain above it. In time the river changed its course, and the boulder with this peculiar depression lay exposed. Some devout, but doubtless withal, cunning Buddhist, with a lively imagination, saw in it a similarity to the imprint of a human heel, and immediately bethought himself of carving out the lineaments of a human foot, and of passing it off as a wonderful discovery of his own. It is evidently of considerable antiquity, for, on the other face of the rock, there are the carved outlines of two tablets, but the inscriptions have been so erased by the hand of time, that it is impossible even to decipher the character in which they were written. The tradition is that the footprint and tables were miraculously produced by Guadama in commemoration of his visit to this favoured spot, which was much resorted to by devotees prior to the decay of Buddhism in the Shan states.

We bathed in the Chalktaw, and then breakfasted under the shade of a fine banyan. On our way back to Sanda we passed a Leesaw girl with a great display of beads, and succeeded in coaxing her to part with four strings and six hoops from her neck for two shillings, and a little further on we met some more of her tribe resting under a tree by the road-side, and they rose and offered us rice spirit out of bamboos. We drank, and in return gave them a little watered mountain dew, which their hill palates seemed to relish.

Sladen has failed to get permission for us to go by the Hotha route opposite to this, and we are now advised to proceed to Manwyne, from whence, it is said, there is a capital road across the hills, and that the Hotha Tsawbwa will meet us there, which he could not do here, as he has some dispute with the officials of this town. Sladen has written to him, and has received an answer to the effect that he is waiting for us at a village on the border of his territory. This afternoon, two Shans, head men of villages, came to Sladen, and told him confidentially that there is a route across the hills between Sanda and Manwyne to a river called the Mohay, which falls into the Irawady above the Tapeng, and that it can be reached in two days from this, and that boats can be obtained to take us to Bhamô, and they offer for a consideration to convey us by this route, if the Hotha one should prove a failure. The river is said to be navigated by large salt boats during the rains, and the road to be good and over moderately high hills.

30*th July.* This forenoon all the head men of the town collected in the khyoung to investigate the circumstances connected with the theft of the spear. The guilt was thrown on the phoongyee, and he was plainly informed that he had been guilty of a most disgraceful crime in stealing the present of one government to another, and that they would allow him a certain time to restore it, and that if it was not forthcoming, they would insist on his ejection from the priesthood.

A letter has arrived from the Hotha Tsawbwa to the effect that he will meet us at Manwyne in a few days. There is an unruly district opposite Manwyne, and we are to be conducted through it by the Manhleo Poogain, the very man who is said to have threatened to attack us if we entered the Shan states, and who discomfited and slew about 400 Panthays a few years ago. His son arrived here yesterday to accompany us to Manwyne. His father has become religious in his old age, and devoutly counts his beads.

31*st July.* Heavy rain all night. The head men proposed that we should start to-morrow, and Sladen agreed to do so, provided all the arrangements are completed to-night. They returned, however, in the afternoon to say that the Tsawbwa does not wish us to leave until he has had a little more time to try and recover the spear, of which some trace has been discovered.

Gordon's Burman assistant, who had gone yesterday to make a survey of the Tapeng opposite Sanda, was prevented from doing so by the villagers, who said that the nât would be offended if he took any measurements. Sladen sent to the Tsawbwa, requesting that one of the officials would explain to the villagers the object we had in view. The Tsawbwa, however, also adopted the nât view of the question, and in addition closely cross-questioned the interpreter if we had an evil object in visiting his country, and if it were not our intention to return next year with a strong force to wrest it from him. Rain during the greater part of the day, but fair in the afternoon and evening.

1st August. Very heavy rain during the night, accompanied by thunder; continued to fall in torrents till 3 P.M., when it faired with a clouded sky.

In the early morning, an old woman came crying to the khyoung, and as she entered, threw down her pipe, and went up to Sladen with clasped hands and tears streaming down her wrinkled cheeks. We were at a loss to understand the cause of this outburst of violent grief, but the interpreter soon explained it. She was the mother of the suspected phoongyee, and had come to intercede for him. She was soon followed by another of her sons, but Sladen explained to them that he had no power in the matter, and advised them to go to the Tsawbwa. The phoongyee came in while she was being shown the door through which the spear had been stolen, and no sooner did she detect his presence than she went up to him, and, in her deep grief and anger, struck him several blows with her closed fist, driving him from the khyoung. In the afternoon it was reported that the spear had been found in a Chinaman's house in the bazaar, but on further enquiry it turned out to be without foundation. The Tsawbwa has resolved to excommunicate the phoongyee to-morrow, and to proceed against him afterwards for theft. The head men seem to have no doubt of his guilt.

2nd August. The excommunication of the phoongyee took place this morning, and was a very brief ceremony, lasting only five minutes. He was brought by all the head men, and was accompanied by his mother and brother, and the latter carried the clothes of an ordinary Shan which the culprit was to put on after having been divested of his priestly robes. All sat down, and his mother, who was greatly affected, was most earnest in her appeals to him to confess if he were guilty; he, however, preserved a dogged silence, and the poor woman retired as he commenced to take off his turban in front of the altar. She left exclaiming with her clasped hands above her head, as if in the act of prayer. Having removed his turban, he took a water-lily from an offering of flowers in front of the figure of Guadama, and placing it on a tripod, deposited it in front of the image. The chief priest now appeared on the dais, and the culprit knelt behind his lily muttering a few sentences, occasionally rising from his knees, and bending his body in worship before the figure, and gradually retreating a little before every prostration until at last he found himself beyond the pale of the dais on which the priests worship. He then knelt before the head phoongyee, and repeated a few words after him, and then retired to his room, where he removed his priestly garments, and came out as a plain Shan. He was then taken away by the head men, and brought back some hours afterwards led by a chain secured to an iron collar round his neck. In the evening he was again marched down to the khyoung, led by his chain and accompanied by all the head men, who informed us that they had not been able to find any trace of the missing spear, and that they had failed to establish his guilt. During the conversation that ensued regarding our departure on the day after to-morrow, he was chained to one of the pillars of the khyoung, and guarded by a lictor on either side.

3rd August. The khyoung has been crowded all day with Shans, Chinese, and Leesaws, drawn either by curiosity, or from a desire to obtain two and four anna bits or rupees in exchange for cloth, clothing, and jewellery. I purchased a pony, not very old, for Rs. 50, and a quantity of capital Shan tobacco at one Rupee for 3½ pounds.

4th August. The mule-loads were nearly all arranged last night, and just as we were about to start, the Tsawbwa came to bid us good-bye, accompanied by his grandchild, and a present of cloth. Sladen presented the child with a silver hunting watch which greatly delighted the old man. He requested us not to mount our ponies until we had passed his house as he intended to give us a salute. He then left, and we followed shortly afterwards. As we approached his residence, three men stationed in front of it blew a lusty blast on their long brass trumpets, and three guns were fired as we ascended the steps leading to the gateway of his so-called palace, under which he was waiting to receive us with his grandchild, and surrounded by his head men. Shaking hands with him and mounting our ponies, we rode away under another salute of three guns, escorted by the trumpeters until we had left the town. The road at this season is more towards the base of the hills than during the dry weather, and lies chiefly along the low bunds marking the paddy-fields. We crossed many streams from the mountains, but of no great depth; their courses, however, were the scenes of great devastation caused by the unprecedented floods during the last week. They had broken over their banks, and carried away whole rice-fields, and their waters had been so charged with sediment that the other fields they had flooded were hopelessly buried in silt. Their courses were strewn with the roots and stems of fallen trees which the villagers were now busily cutting up for firewood. The sides of the mountains, especially on the left, were red with landslips, some of them of enormous size, and one had buried a village of 40 houses, only nine of the villagers who happened to be away at the time having escaped.

We reached Manwyne about 5 P.M., the distance being about 19 miles. We went to our old residence, and at once placed sentries at the door to keep out the crowd, a task of no easy accomplishment. One of the sentries trying to eliminate some unruly Chinese who had forced their way in, was kicked and struck by them, which so roused the wrath of one of our party that he rushed to his assistance, and using his fists freely, soon cleared the door-way. The phoongyees seem to have become more religious of late, and no sooner had the sun gone down, than the bell for prayers was rung and a huge candle lit in front of the altar, all the priests kneeling down on the highest dais, backed by the boys on the one below it, chanting the evening prayer.

5th August. Bell-ringing and prayers ushered in the day, and many women with rice and offerings of flowers were early at their devotions.

The Ponsee Pawmine "Death's-head" has appeared, under the impression that we intend to entrust ourselves once more to his tender mercy, and was chagrined when he heard that we were to return by Hotha.

The Hotha Tsawbwa has not yet arrived on account of the difficulty of crossing the mud on the other side of the river, deposited by the late floods, and which is so deep that it takes a pony above its girth, and will be impassable for a few days. In the evening we had an interesting conversation with the phoongyees and two of the Sanda head men about telegraphs, railways, and other wonders of modern civilization, and one of the Sanda men said that they were highly privileged to hear such things, and that we must have met in some previous existence, and that we would doubtless meet again in others yet to come. We showed them the moon through a good telescope, and so great was their simplicity that they seemed to believe that each of us could exercise some special power over the luminary, and when they were told of the coming eclipse of the sun, we rose in their estimation to the acme of greatness as astrologers. The chief phoongyee was concerned at the news of the eclipse, and eager to know whether it was the precursor of war or famine.

6th August. The Hotha Tsawbwa arrived late yesterday afternoon, and came to the khyoung this morning apparently chokeful of objections to our going by his valley, but the only ones as yet advanced are the difficulty of crossing the mud with laden mules, and the circumstance that the opposite bank of the river is in the Muangla district.

I succeeded to-day in procuring one of the necklaces worn by the Kakhyen chiefs. The Hotha Tsawbwa says they are brought from the neighbourhood of Mogoung, and that the beads are procured by delving with a bamboo, when they are said to be brought up, out of the ground, shaped, bored, and ready for use. If they were sought for in any other way, the nât would take great offence.

Hotha, finding that we are determined to return by his route, now laughs at the difficulties, and leaves to-day in order that he may be at his house to receive us, and promises to entertain us in his own residence. One of our men brought an old woman to us who had come to the town to-day with some Kakhyens, as he found that she knew a little Bengalee. A number of Kakhyen girls accompanied her, and she stated that she was a Munipooree by birth, and had been stolen by Kakhyens when quite a young girl, and sold from Kakhyen village to village, till at last, many years ago, she reached the village in which she now resides. She remembered a few Bengalee words, but could only speak in Kakhyen and Shan.

7th August. We dined at the Tsawbwa-gadaw's this afternoon, and were received by the Hotha Tsawbwa, by our hostess's daughter who has taken the veil, and by the nun-sister of Hotha, a number of waiting-maids, and male retainers. We were at once requested to be seated at the table, and tea was served, followed by dinner, which consisted of well-cooked roast and boiled fowls, stewed pork, pork balls, with small plates of onions, peas, and sliced mangoes. Then came sauce and rice, followed up with another service of tea. All the dishes were served on fine Chinese porcelain, and the samshu from a Birmingham tea-pot in tiny cups of solid jade. Our hostess came in for a minute or two as the dinner was placed on the table, and apologized that she had nothing better to give, and after it was over, again joined us. We were waited on by men, but the maids and the two nuns favoured us with their presence, prompted by curiosity to see the lions feed. Being attracted by the red-dyed nails of the young women, I asked one, a lively young lass with rosy cheeks, and teeth of ivory whiteness, to show me the dye. She offered to give me a practical illustration of the process on my own person, and soon produced from the inner apartment a pulpy mass of the petals and leaves of a red balsam beaten up with cutch. She selected my little finger to operate on, but declined to begin until I had given her my ring which she wished to retain as a remembrance of our visit. She encased the tip in a quantity of the mass, and covered it with a green leaf tied on with thread. After dinner Hotha entertained us with airs on the Shan guitar. The instrument has only three strings, and the sounding-board is made of a stretched snake skin. It has a sweet, pleasant tinkle, and the airs, though simple, were full of music and well played. This chief is a man of great ability and taste, and a perfect gentleman in his manners. On our return to our khyoung, the two young nuns and the waiting-maids brought us a few small presents from the Tsawbwa-gadaw, and remained with us for nearly two hours, asking questions about our country and religion, in a way that evinced they were possessed of more than ordinary intelligence, and that they had a real pleasure in adding to their stock of knowledge.

The Hotha Tsawbwa left in the afternoon for his valley, and has entrusted all the arrangements about the carriage of our baggage to the Manhleo Poogain, and it is finally agreed that we will start the day after to-morrow. The hire of each mule is to be Rs. 4, and this high price is asked on account of the extremely bad roads on the other side.

8th August. All the arrangements for our start have been completed. The most difficult point to settle was the carriage across the Tapeng, but it has been at last decided that we are to be taken over for Rs. 30.

Yesterday we had promised to visit the nuns at their khyoung, and in the afternoon, when we had almost forgotten the engagement, a message came to say that they were waiting for us. Gordon and I went, and were received by them and by two lay matronly attendants. Their khyoung consists of two bamboo houses, side by side, enclosed by a fence, one for religious purposes, and the other their residence. The latter, like the generality of respectable Shan houses, consisted of three apartments, the centre one being the sitting-room. The religious house is a pavilion, about 24 feet square, raised on piles 4 feet above the ground, and closed in with mats on all sides, except that facing the dwelling-house, to which it is so close that the two roofs touched. Its only decorations were a few strips of white paper cut into ornamental figures, and suspended as banners from the roof, and a few small images of Guadama. When we arrived, the Hotha nun was engaged in weaving, and I mention this because Manwyne is the first place in which I have observed the religious of the Buddhists put their hands to any useful occupation. We were invited into the dwelling-house, and were helped to mangoes and woman's tobacco, and were requested to light our pipes. In the course of conversation the Manwyne young lady asked if we were Buddhists, and if we had come to worship at their shrines, and was astonished when she heard we were not, and more so when we expounded the doctrines of Christianity. We soon became great friends, and she asked us to consider her as a sister. We now accompanied her on a visit to her mother, and the old lady received us in the reception room of the inner court. Tea was served, and we were soon fully established in the good graces of all. The Tsawbwa-gadaw expressed a great desire to obtain a portrait of the Queen, and Gordon promised to send her one from Rangoon, but as a temporary substitute, I asked her to accept four new rupees which greatly pleased her.

9th August. We were all ready for an early start, but were much delayed by the difficulty of procuring a sufficient number of porters to carry our baggage to the river. Just before we started, the Tsawbwa-gadaw sent us a dish of rice and spirit to strengthen us by the way, and the head Phoongyee gave us each a piece of cloth, and very heartily expressed his good wishes for our welfare. We left the khyoung at about half-past eight, passing through the town, and were very well received by the people, many of them waving us an adieu, and hoping that we would soon return, whilst others called out " *Kara, kara,*" and wished us a prosperous journey.

Arrived at the river, we were detained about two hours in crossing, as it was no easy matter to get the ponies over, on account of its breadth, which was certainly not less than 600 yards. The mule-loads went a long way down to escape the mud on the opposite side. We were all on the other side by noon, and for nearly two miles the road lay over a mud flat that in some places was a veritable *Slough of Despond*, out of which we only extricated ourselves after the greatest difficulty and fatigue. It engulphed the ponies half-way up the saddles, and at one spot, worse than all the others, they so floundered about and stumbled from the difficulty of drawing their legs out of the tenacious mud, that we were reluctantly forced to dismount at the very worst point. I shall never forget the twenty minutes that ensued, when with the reins of my pony in one hand and my dog by the cuff of the neck in the other, I plunged and struggled through this slimy ooze, dragging my legs only by main force from the firm grasp of the sucking mire. At one place, my pony made a sudden lounge forward, and for the time was completely under the mud, and the strain on the reins set me rolling forwards, and I had to be helped to regain my footing by a man behind me without encumbrances. The stoutest of our party had to be dragged along by two men, and his pony had become so hopelessly stuck in the mud that two

Shans had to be employed to dig it out. This mud had been freshly deposited by the recent floods of the Tapeng, and the enormous amount of silt held in suspension by the river may be guessed at from the circumstance that this tract extended over three or four square miles, and had an average depth of about four feet. Following the bunds around the paddy-fields for about two miles, we halted for breakfast on a grassy slope at the foot of the hills, under the shade of wide-spreading banyan trees, and were eagerly stared at by crowds of villagers. We started about 2 P.M., and at once commenced to ascend the hills, which from Manwyne did not appear to be more than one thousand feet high. The road was a rough bridle-path right up their steep sides, and the ascent coming so soon after the muscular exertion in the quagmire, was most trying to man and beast, and was intensified by the blazing heat of an unclouded sun. The mules were ahead, but our men soon began to lag, although we went as slowly as was compatible with the prospect of reaching the village of Manloi on the other side before night-fall, for we had already abandoned our intention of reaching Hotha in one march. A short way up the hill, we, passed fine, white, crystalline marble standing out in bold cliffs, and weathering to a dull brown: further on we came upon quartzose, and still higher, crossed a bluish gneissose rock forming the upper mass of the hills. We passed through a number of Kakhyen villages, and had to pay toll at two, giving a few rupees to the head men who were sitting by the road-side waiting for us. Approaching the summit, we had a splendid view of the course of the Tapeng through its narrow valley to the Burmese plain. A high curtain of clouds to the westward hung over the entrance of the river into the hills, and below and beyond it, in the far distance, the immense plain of the Irawady was distinctly seen backed by high hills, and the great river, swollen by the summer floods, winding through it like a silver band. To the right, we commanded a magnificent view of the valley below us, as far as the spur above Sanda, and I can recall no landscape to rival the placid grandeur of this lovely vale, walled in by its splendid mountains, and rich in every variety of effect produced by the grouping, in light and shade, of flood, fell, and verdant field. After crossing the ridge we came upon some Leesaws with a newly-killed deer in a basket, and offered them Rs. 10 for it, but they would not be induced to part with it. A little further on we passed through one of their villages on the face of a steep spur: its situation was very picturesque among fine forest trees, and enormous grey boulders standing out in bold relief among the houses which some of them equalled in size. We entered through a wooden gate-way, and the path or street had huts on either side of it. These differ entirely from those built by the Kakhyens, and are small square structures, the ground forming the floor, which is kept dry by a deep trench enclosing the mud walls, and that allows the water to drain off. We passed out under a long, covered passage thickly clad with handsome climbing plants. The inhabitants were chiefly Leesaws, with an intermixture of Chinese-Shans, and I had considerable difficulty in detecting the men from the women, as their dress is so much alike, and both wear trousers. The view, looking down upon Hotha valley, was a miniature picture of the valley we had just left, and beyond its south-eastern side, we saw two other hill ranges in the distance, which led us to imagine a series of parallel valleys still further to the south, in all probability, resembling, in their broad features, the one now lying before us. The Sanda aspect of the ridge was much cleared for cultivation by the Kakhyens and Leesaws, but the remains of dense patches of fine forest indicated that it had had at one time a uniform covering of trees. Near the summit there were extensive tracts of a peculiar, short, thin-stemmed bamboo which I had never before seen, and many temperate forest trees, such as oaks and birches. The sun had set shortly after we had commenced the descent, and when we were about half-way down it was nearly dark.

Sladen and I, accompanied by the Manhleo Poogain, the Shan interpreter, and three Burmese policemen and two or three mules, had become detached from the rest of our party, and in passing through a strip of forest we came to a division of the road. The Poogain wished to take the track to the left, but a mule-man a-head, with a stubbornness characteristic of the dumb animal before him, persisted that the other was the right one, which was undoubtedly the case in one sense, but not in the sense we wished. We followed it, but had not gone any distance when it became apparent that we were on the wrong track. We pressed the muleteers to return, but they would not, as they assured us that it led into the road we had left. It was now quite dark, and as the path was only a rough bridle-track covered with loose stones, cut up here and there by dry water-courses, and lay along the precipitous hill-sides, our ride was anything but pleasant. The men shouted at the pitch of their voices to attract the attention of our party, but were only answered by the echoes from the hills. It soon became evident that the road was leading us to the wrong end of the valley, but as we had now gone too far to return, we continued on, and when nearing the base of the hills our men again began to shout to attract the notice of any villagers that might be near; as good luck would have it, we met some men at a point where another hill road came down, and were told that we were close to a village called Mentone, and that we could not reach Hotha till cock-crow. Now we consulted whether we would go dinnerless and supperless to bed, or proceed to Hotha, but preferring the former alternative we made for the village khyoung, which we reached at half-past 8 P.M. We could get nothing to eat, and thoroughly tired, we unsaddled our hungry and exhausted ponies, and taking their saddles for our pillows, fell asleep on the floor, in front of the altar. Our slumbers, however, were soon disturbed by the phoongyees squatting down close to our heads, irreverently yelling out their evening prayers, and with an utter disregard for the sacredness of sleep. The chief phoongyee, a shrivelled old man, was seated cross-legged, with a small stool in front of him on which the lesson-book lay, and a little boy sat by his side with a wooden pointer in his hands, running along the lines to keep the eyes of the priest from wandering. Six lads sat before him yelling at the pitch of their voice in all imaginable keys. To attempt to sleep in this tumult of voices was out of the question, and we began to discuss whether it would not be better to start at once, whenever the moon rose. While the phoongyee was in the middle of his devotions, our Shan interpreter shouted out to him that he wanted to buy four annas worth of rice, and the priest at once stopped his prayers to bargain how much he was to give for the coin which was new to him. This piece of business settled, he went again to his devotions, which were once more interrupted as he had not sent any one to give out the rice. Prayers ended, we asked for something to eat, and were told that there were some pears on a tree outside which we might help ourselves to, an offer which we politely declined. He gave us, however, quilts to lie on, and we again fell asleep, but waking before dawn, we were well on our way to Hotha by the time the sun rose. The khyoung was a substantially-built stone structure, and evidently well supported by the people. It was too dark, however, to make out whether it differed from the ruins of those in the Sanda valley.

The Hotha vale is so narrow that there is no level ground in its centre, so the road lies along the end of the spurs. It is kept in admirable condition, and in many places is cut out along the slopes, and is paved nearly throughout the distance we travelled, about four miles. The bridges are substantial arched structures, built of granite and in excellent taste, and at intervals there are charming springs or wells of drinking water, carefully protected from all impurities by being built over, and incased in stone, each usually with a white marble frieze along the top. In one place there were as many as five of them in a line, close to a village. Opposite

Manloi, which is situated in a picturesquely wooded hollow surrounded by grassy knolls, there is a handsome gold-gilt pagoda on the summit of one of the hillocks. This is the first pagoda of the Burmese type we have met since crossing the Kakhyen hills. We passed many villages embowered among fine trees, and on the opposite side of the valley each spur had a village at its base. Nearing Hotha, the Poogain set off to announce to the Tsawbwa that we were close at hand. We arrived at 8 A.M., and were received by the Tsawbwa and his son in their robes, the former being dressed as a mandarin of the blue button, in a purple and figured satin long coat. A salute of four guns was fired in our honour, and after the Tsawbwa had doffed his robes we were shown to our quarters on the upper floor of one of the side buildings in the court, in front of his residence, in which an apartment was set aside for Gordon and Bowers. All our party came in, in the course of the day, and everything was received in perfect order. This march has been better managed in every way, as far as carriage goes, than any other, owing entirely to the arrangements having been entrusted to two such energetic men as Poogain and Kingain. Gordon and Bowers and the majority of our men put up at Manloi for the night, but a few did not get beyond the Leesaw village on the hill, where they had to pay two rupees a-head for their night's lodging. All kinds of evil reports have been spread by the Muangla people, who have been far from favourable to the Expedition, and the people at the khyoung last night asked us in an aggrieved tone why we had come to their valley to bring flying dragons and other evils upon them. It is stated that eleven villages have been destroyed by landslips in the Sanda valley, and that nearly all the villagers have been buried in the ruins: these sad catastrophes are ascribed to some evil power possessed by us, and we are told that a person has died in every village we have visited. Hotha is a small, dilapidated village, and its ruined condition is due to its having been attacked last year by the Tsawbwa's own subjects, who rose in rebellion against him, on account of some new tax that he had imposed. The houses are of the same type as those in Sanda, but the better class are raised on a platform about two feet high. There are two Tsawbwaships, *viz.*, Hotha and Latha, the former owning the eastern half, and the latter the western half of the valley. The Shan name for the latter is Hansa, and the former is called Mynesu or Mynetha by the Shans, Hotha or Haesa by the Chinese. There are no shops, properly so called, in the valley, but bazaars are held weekly at different villages in the two districts, and the people make all their purchases on these occasions.

We spent the day in the house, and many people came to stare at us. The Tsawbwa has commenced to learn Burmese, and asked to-day for a note-book to take down sentences and words. He went on very steadily all the afternoon cross-questioning our Shan interpreter who understands Burmese, and when he came to us after dinner he had his note-book with him, and was still busy at work.

11th August. Heavy rain during the night. Sladen settled with the mule-men yesterday, and this morning gave the Poogain and Kingain a present, and they promised of their own accord to give every assistance to future travellers and traders who may wish to cross from Manwyne to Hotha, and the best proof of their sincerity was their request that Sladen would give each of them a certificate that they had been very successful in the arrangements for our march.

The Tsawbwa came up to our quarters in the evening, and had a long talk about various modern inventions he had heard of from Chinese who had visited Rangoon. Some of the accounts he had received were gross exaggerations, for he talked of flying machines, of telescopes that enabled people to see through mountains, and of others that divested people of their clothes. He had some vague ideas about gas, railways, and steam-ships, and it was most refreshing to find with what anxiety he desired to learn more about these wonders of western civilization. We urged him to visit Rangoon and Calcutta, but he is afraid to leave his valley in the present disturbed state of the surroundin gcountry; he speaks, however, of sending his son, a youth of thirteen, to visit Rangoon, the only British town known to him by name. He has a number of wives, and two of these reside in his house, but he keeps up establishments for two or three others in separate villages. He has a son, and two grown-up daughters, one fourteen and the other about twenty years of age. They are about as fair as Europeans, and with rosy cheeks, and both are tall, handsome girls, full of life and fun. They have the high cheek-bones and slightly oblique eye of the Chinese. In the evening, Gordon and I walked down to the river, a distance of about one mile, and found it a much smaller stream than we had supposed. Here it is only about 12 to 15 feet broad, and about 4 feet deep, flowing in a deep channel which it has cut out for itself. While we were out, the Namboke Tsawbwa arrived accompanied by his Pawmines, and a strong guard armed with spears and matchlocks, the Tsawbwa and his officers being mounted on ponies. He is a little, good-natured, intelligent man with a remarkably Tartar cast of countenance, which is heightened by his Tartar-like skull-cap. He has come in at the request of Hotha, and as he entered, he noticed

Sladen sitting in his quarters, and went down on one knee before him according to the Shan fashion of greeting between an inferior and any officer of importance. He informed Sladen that he had visited us at Bhamô, and had received a head-dress as a present. He greeted Hotha also with a genuflexion, who did the same to him in return. After dinner he visited us along with Hotha, and the latter treated him to an eloquent discourse on the advantages which they would derive were trade revived by this route. He says that if he had known that we had ever contemplated returning by any other, he would have gone over to Sanda to press this one on our attention, which claims to be the central or embassy route. Hotha is entertaining us very liberally, and has supplied rice to all the men, and presented us yesterday with fowls and a goose.

12th August. Heavy rain during the night. Hotha has written a letter addressed to all the Tsawbwas along the route, requesting them to come in and arrange about our return, and the Pawmines of Namboke have started to deliver it.

The bazaar which is held here every fifth day took place to-day. It partakes more of a fair than an ordinary market, and is held on a grassy slope about half a mile from the village. There are no permanent stalls, and the sellers sit down in long lines with their goods before them. One section was devoted to the sale of dâhs, which are largely manufactured by the peasantry of this valley, and another to the sale of the handles and scabbards. The inhabitants of the Sanda valley and the Kakhyen hills generally get their dâhs from hence, and during the cold months, as I had occasion to notice in speaking of Bhamô, numbers of Hotha and Latha Shans club together, and go down to that town for some months to carry on the manufacture for the use of the Shans, Burmese, and Kakhyens who trade with Bhamô. I purchased two fine blades for Rs. 2 each, but was afterwards told that I had given a third more than their value. Another section of the fair is given up to the sale of samshu, and close to it is the feeding quarter, where a hungry Shan, Chinaman, Kakhyen, or Leesaw may feast to his fill on hot pork, vermicelli or an article strongly resembling it, a variety of cooked vegetables, and peas, all hot, and nicely served in white bowls. A brisk trade in bamboo shoots is carried on in another place, and a long line of Kakhyen women offer for sale joss sticks, pears, apples, plums, peaches, the leaves of the mustard plant, and a variety of hill vegetables, along with basket-loads of nettles for the swine which form an important element in Shan household economy. In a double row of stalls occupying the centre of the bazaar, we find various kinds of cloth of Shan manufacture, Shan caps, coloured Chinese papers, rice, cutch, flint, lime, white arsenic, yellow orpiment, and a variety of trifling articles; while in still another quarter we come across superior kinds of cloth, such as English green and blue broad-cloth, along with red flannel for which the Kakhyens have a special failing, while the former fabrics have the patronage of the Shans and Chinese. The broad-cloth was being sold at the exorbitant sum of Rs. 10 per yard, but it seems to me that a few pieces would surfeit the market. This enumeration of the goods displayed at this interesting and thriving fair would be incomplete were I not to mention that one section was devoted to the sale of pork and butcher meat, and another to indigo, the staple dye of the Shans, Kakhyens, and Chinese of Western Yunan. What interested me most, however, were the peculiarly picturesque and varied costumes one met with in this novel assemblage; especially striking were the Shan-Chinese and Hotha-Shan women's dress, for the men, with the exception of an occasional red turban, are dressed in blue like their near kinsmen of the Sanda valley. The costume of the women of the latter tribe can be dismissed in a few words, for its chief peculiarities, as compared with that of their Sanda sisters, are the number of large silver hoops which are worn round the neck, and the prevalence of dark-green jackets. The dress of the Shan-Chinese women is a mixture of Shan and Chinese, but I have fully described it elsewhere.

The fair was attended by many people, old and young, the former intent on making purchases, while the latter had come to gossip with their friends, and to stroll about in want of any better employment. They were generally very clean and tidy, and had an air of respectability about them, which spoke well for their worldly circumstances. The women, as a rule, were little, and rather squat, with round, flat, high cheek-boned faces, and slightly oblique eyes; their skins very fair, and their cheeks rosy. The better class among them dye their teeth black, a hideous custom which is thought to add greatly to their beauty.

13th August. This is the fire-festival of the Shans, and about 20 bullocks and cows were killed in the early morning on the site of the market, but when we arrived nearly all the flesh had been disposed of, all that remained being the clean-scraped skeletons, for the bones are not sold. Immediately after sunset, the Tsawbwa's retainers began to beat gongs and to blow loud but uncertain blasts from long brass trumpets, and when night set in, torches were lit, and a party, preceded by the gongs and trumpets, searched the central court-yard for the fire nât, who is supposed to be lurking about at this season with evil intent. After satisfying themselves that he was not there, they rushed into our apartments with their flaming flambeaux, and not finding him, next directed their attention to the Tsawbwa's house, and to all the outs and ins about and around it, carefully scrutinizing a small garden behind our quarters, throwing light into every dark corner that might serve as a hiding-place for the evil spirit. One strange part of this ceremony remains still to be noticed. Part of the flesh purchased in the morning is cooked and eaten, while a portion of it is fired out of guns at sunset, and those pieces which alight in water are supposed to become leeches, and those that fall on land, mosquitoes, but what connection this had with the fire nât my informants failed to explain. Four such festivals are kept during the year, one devoted to each of the nâts of rain, wind, cold, and fire.

The people are now beginning to bring in articles to us for sale, and we were inundated to-day with cloth, clothing, and jewellery, and the prices were much more moderate than in the Sanda valley. The infection has spread to the Tsawbwa's family, and Gordon and Bowers, whose apartment is only separated by a wooden partition, with a door in it, from the courtyard of the Tsawbwa's apartments, have frequent visits from his pretty daughters and his youngest wife, who offer their surplus clothing and ornaments for sale through the small door, but beat a precipitate retreat whenever they hear the Tsawbwa approaching. Their business transactions are made the excuse for a great deal of fortune-telling, pretty speeches, and harmless flirtation on the part of the two gay Lotharios, who are high in the good graces of these Shan ladies.

14th August. We went this morning on a visit to the Tsawbwa's house at Tsaycow where another of his wives resides. He left early to have everything in readiness, and we started about noon. The road lay over a succession of grassy spurs devoid of trees except around the villages. The majority of the smaller trees are pear, apple, peach, chesnut, and sweet lime. No paddy is cultivated on the slopes, which are chiefly devoted to tobacco which is now being planted out. The road is laid with stones throughout its length. In the neighbourhood of villages they are cut into long dressed slabs, but in parts remote from them they are simply water-worn boulders laid close together. The numerous rivulets from the mountains are crossed by bridges of two kinds; those over the smaller streams are only long slabs of granite or gneiss supported on blocks of the same rocks, while those over the larger ones are elegantly arched stone structures, some of them with a span of 25 feet.

The valley is very beautiful, and the glimpses of mountain and vale scenery that it affords are perhaps unequalled. The approach to each village is usually a long narrow lane arched by trees and feathery bamboos, terminating in a picturesque gateway. The majority of the streams run over rocky channels broken up by large boulders, grey with lichen, or green with moss; and when the sparkling waters of one of them are spanned by a rural bridge, while perhaps a small pagoda is perched on a grassy knoll on its bank, and a many-roofed monastery is seen in the middle distance peering over the deep green trees with occasional glimpses of cottages clustered round it, and a back-ground of long green slopes stretches up to the giant mist-wrapt mountains behind, we have a picture that fully satisfies the eye, and we revel in its beauty. On our ride we passed the small pagoda of Comootomay picturesquely situated on the summit of a long grassy knoll devoid of trees. It is about 50 feet high, and is peculiar in its shape, and in having a long attenuated spire, and so differs considerably from the generality of pagodas in Burmah, although, I dare say, some resembling it could be found at Bhamô. The village of Tsaycow is about five miles from Hotha, and is embowered in thick wood on the extremity of a spur, at the termination of a little dale, through which runs a fine mountain stream. It is much larger than Hotha, and was formerly the Tsawbwa's head-quarters, and is known as Old Hotha. Although his house here is smaller than the one we are residing in, it is a much more pleasant residence, by reason of its situation, and from its being in much better condition than the other. The Tsawbwa received us in the reception hall of the minor court, and as we entered, all the women were waiting around him, but rushed off as we approached; chairs covered with red cloth were set for us, and after we had partaken of tea, the Tsawbwa took us to visit a Shan and a Chinese temple, built after his own design, on the hill-side behind the village. They stand one above the other, the Shan being the lower, and separated from the Chinese khyoung, which is enclosed by a high wall, and consists of a court-yard with two covered ways on two sides, and a raised pavilion-like building on the third, facing the temple, which forms the fourth side of the enclosure, and towers above all the lower portions of the building, on the highest of two granite-faced terraces. Covered staircases lead from the two sides of the court to the upper terrace on which the khyoung stands, and each terminates in a little rounded tower containing a large bell. The temple is the breadth of the terrace, and has a covered verandah in front and behind, paved with stone, and a little stream passes underneath the floor, and bubbles up into a small stone basin in the front verandah, and then precipitates itself from terrace to terrace to the court below. The entrances to the temple are at either end of the verandah, in the middle of which there is a large window facing the richly carved altar-piece within. On a table in front of the window there are a number of boxes containing the library, and some vases with incense and flowers. The altar-piece is about 20 feet high, and resembles the front of a large cabinet with a centre and two wings, and is an admirable example of open wood carving. It is enclosed by a simple wood railing of about four feet in height, and before it stands a small table on which incense is burnt, and another at each of the sides with a wooden model of a fish and a stick to beat it. The recesses in the altar are about ten feet above the ground, and each contains a life-sized figure with a gauze curtain in front of it. At the same elevation, a beam runs out from each side of the altar to the front wall, supporting two life-sized figures. A row of eighteen small figures on a long platform, with a vase and joss-sticks before each, is arranged along either side-wall. The central deity in the altar is called *Chowlainglon*, and the Tsawbwa informed me that he was the king of the nâts, and had existed before Guadama, but he could not say whether he was eternal. The figures in the recess on either side of him are called *Coonsang*, and are regarded as his agents for carrying his commands into effect, and the two standing figures on either side of the beams are the four rulers of the four great islands that compose the world, and who keep a record of all the actions of their subjects. At death, the latter are presented to the deity, and made over to the *Coonsang*, who give them, according to their merits, to one or other of the 36 nâts who are represented on the sides of the temple, and are regarded as the army of the *Thagyameng*. It is interesting to observe that one of these nâts is represented with six arms, holding a bell, bow, arrow, club, and dagger, while one hand is empty. All the others are represented in different attitudes, each with an instrument of some kind in his hand, and a long robe-like band around his neck and shoulders reaching to the ground, and by which he is supposed to be enabled to fly. The Shan khyoung, situated below, is composed of two oblong buildings facing each other, with an interval of twenty feet between them. The uppermost has a long verandah in front, guarded at either side by a grim-looking nât seated close to the door leading to the hall or temple in which there are three colossal Buddhas, the past, present, and future, seated together in the centre, with a guardian figure on either side of them. The one on the right hand of the Buddhas is mounted on a pigmy elephant, and the one on the left on a mongrel monster, half-lion and half-tiger. There is also a well-executed figure of a tortoise, and on a table in front of the Buddhas, there are vases of curious devices in which joss-sticks are kept constantly burning while others are filled with variously coloured flowers. Life-sized figures are seated in a row on a long pedestal at each side of the building, and the majority of them are cleverly executed and evince no little knowledge of art. One shrivelled old man, with his chin resting on his knee, and with the flesh tints of his naked body admirably given, would take a high place even in European art. The other section below this is open in front, and the middle of the central wall is occupied by a figure of *Quanyin* holding the virile child. The story given me of this deity is, that she was the daughter of an emperor of China, and took the white robes, and became a Rahanee, and spent her days in seclusion in the forest. She is surrounded by a number of small figures, represented in relief on the wall in the act of adoration, and a parrot, perched on a twig above her head, carries a rosary in its bill. Back to back with this figure, which has little of Buddhism in it, on the opposite side of the wall, in the other half of the khyoung, there is a colossal figure of Guadama and two gigantic figures at either end, one of which holds a rat. The Tsawbwa asserted that all of these temples were Buddhistic, and there can be no doubt that they have a dash of it, but in a remarkably corrupt form.

On our return to the house, we found a capital dinner prepared for us.

17th August. Nothing of any note to record during the last three days, except that a case of fever, successfully treated, has given me wonderful power in the eyes of this simple people, and that our residence has been besieged by the halt, deaf, and blind.

18th August. The eclipse of the sun commenced to-day at 9, 5', 14", A. M., and lasted till 12, 30', 29', P. M. The Tsawbwa showed his intelligence by being able to see through the telescope, and to understand what he saw, a feat which very few Shans can accomplish, for their usual procedure is to look over the instrument, and picture unseen wonders to their imagination. No sooner had he satisfied himself that there was an eclipse than he ordered his guns to be fired, and the long trumpets to be blown, and we had to fire two volleys to satisfy him. The chief and all the Shans who had collected round our telescope agreed, after the maximum of the eclipse, that they would have known nothing about it but for us, as there was little or no visible diminution of the light.

19th August. Gordon and I set out at 7 A.M., accompanied by the Tsawbwa's factotum, on a visit to the head of the valley which is completely closed in by a transverse ridge connecting the two ranges. We reached our destination about 10 A.M., and had a good road the whole way up, but there is only a narrow track across the ridge, the highest point of which does not exceed 400 feet. From the top there is a steep declivity into another valley, most probably connected with that of Muangwan; and looking across to the east-north-east, another valley is seen running off in that direction, and I imagine that the road to Nantin lies along it. The rain was too heavy to let us see any distance, but occasional glimpses through the mist revealed high hills on every side, and enough to convince us that the route by Hotha, if it is ever used, presents a greater extent of hilly and undulating country than the one by Sanda. This also becomes apparent if the relative elevations and dimensions of the two valleys are borne in mind. The latter is the course of a large river, while the former is traversed by a mere mountain stream, one of the numerous affluents of the Tapeng. But apart from physical characters, the greater population and productiveness of the Sanda district would be greatly in its favour when the two valleys came to strive for the trade between Bhamô and Momien.

20th August. Yesterday afternoon, the Burmese surveyor left to survey the Muangwan route, accompanied by one of the Tsawbwa's men as Shan interpreter, and a Burmese sepoy as servant. He travels as a Shan, and has an aneroid for the heights and a compass to take the bearings. The Tsawbwa dined with us this evening, and got on wonderfully well with fork and knife, though not with the dinner itself. He had prepared a dinner for us as well, and insisted that his soup should be substituted for ours. It was made from fowls' intestines, but excellent in a way. The intestines are slit open, and thoroughly washed, and every Burman and Shan highly esteems these parts not only of fowls but of other animals.

21st August. Very heavy rain during the night, and until noon, when it cleared. We pressed the Tsawbwa to give us a guide to the opposite hills, but he stoutly refused on the plea that the bridge over the stream has been washed away, and that the road would take us up to the eyes in mud; but we are aware that these difficulties do not exist, and that there must, therefore, be some other reason for his opposition.

A number of Kakhyens arrived last night, and two Tsawbwas have come in to-day. All the mules are in readiness, and our departure has been arranged for the day after to-morrow.

After dinner, the Tsawbwa introduced the subject of religion, and was astonished to find that we did not believe in the previous and future existence of individuals in different phases of life, and put the remarkable question whether we knew in what country Guadama at present lived. It is curious to note that in speaking of Guadama, he mentioned him as distinct from and above Buddha. The majority of the Buddhists I have conversed with have also spoken in the same way, so that whatever may be the abstract teaching of their religion, the belief of the common people is in a God and Buddha. I remember a most intelligent phoongyee and learned Buddhist, who spoke English admirably, and had an intimate knowledge of the leading doctrines of Christianity, saying to me, "Why, Sir, our Guadama is your Christ; the two systems have had but one origin."

22nd August. Incessant rain during the day. In a fair interval before sunset, Gordon and I visited a small, dilapidated khyoung close to the village. It is dedicated to the worship of certain nâts, and is under the charge of a beggarly priest who lives in a wretched hut in the enclosure. The entrance to this little temple is guarded by two horsemen each stationed at the head of his steed. We gave the priest a rupee, and he offered us tobacco in return.

23rd August. Heavy rain all night and during the day. In the afternoon Gordon and I mounted our ponies, and, accompanied by Hotha, visited the principal Buddhist khyoung of this valley, in the pretty little village of Tsendong which lies at the extremity of one of the wooded spurs behind Hotha, enclosed by a low wall. The khyoung is the finest in the district, and boasts of some skilfully carved altar-pieces, and richly gilt book-cabinets. It is built on a low stone platform, and surrounded by a narrow terraced verandah, and the whole of the outside is well but roughly carved: its internal arrangements are those of the khyoungs of Burmah. The remains of an old and venerated phoongyee, who had died two months before, lay in state under a double-roofed temporary pavilion close to the khyoung. The sarcophagus, supported on two dragons, was a handsome structure surmounted by a richly carved miniature pagoda, and the whole was carefully railed off, and the ground nicely levelled and kept scrupulously clean. Close to the khyoung, there is an octagonal building on a terrace enclosing a small pagoda in its centre. It consists almost entirely of wood and has five roofs which diminish in size from below upwards, and are capped by a gold-gilt *tee*. The wall is about six feet high, and a series of open windows of carved wood-work runs round the building, each having two beautifully carved panels above it representing some simple object, as a plant, bird, bat, or deer, thrown into an attitude adapted to the form of the panel. Each roof is slightly raised above the one below it by three lines of beams, the ends of which project outwards to different lengths, and terminate in grotesque carvings of the heads of griffins. The enclosed pagoda is a square-shaped structure with its delicately tapered spire reaching to the highest roof. On one of its sides there are two figures of Guadama, one being seated in front of the other, the one furthest back being ensconced at the end of a small covered cave, with the other in front of the entrance and almost hiding it. The pagoda and its enclosing *zayát* were repaired about thirty years ago, but I could obtain no definite information regarding their ages, or that of the khyoung. They are reported to be very old, and the latter is said to have existed long before the village. The phoongyees spread carpets for us, and produced walnuts, cucumbers, plantains, pine-apples, and tea. The Tsawbwa sat on a chair in a recess beside a blazing fire and chatted to the chief-priest, and to the villagers, who had collected whenever our arrival was noised abroad. We gave the priest Rupees four, which he accepted with great glee, and apparently with a full appreciation, Buddhist priest though he was, of the value of the precious metal. On our way back we visited two other khyoungs at the village of Kateow, close to Hotha. They were both Chinese, and the first was in two sections, an outer and inner. In the former, the red-faced evil nát *Quanshihyen*, and *Showfoo*, the *Prah* or god of the Chinese of Yunan, and *Quanyin* were worshipped; while in the inner, *Támo*, nát, once a famous teacher, reigned in undisputed possession.

In the other temple there were a number of náts, such as *Tsiongouag, Yengouag, Cheng-ghin, Yansooyangin, Woonjhan, Teejin, Quanyin, Sigh-Shan*, to the entire exclusion of any trace of Buddhistic worship.

26th August. Again heavy rain over-night, but it cleared up during the day, and we shall start to-morrow if it continues fair.

The Mantai Tsawbwa has arrived as a messenger from the Bhamô Woon, to find out where we are, and to accompany us back. There was a keen discussion this evening with Hotha whether we should visit his near relative, the Latha chief, a frail old man who is afraid that he will be bewitched if we go near him, and who is in great dread that we will take his likeness, and measure his house. Hotha is decidedly against our going, and compares his father-in-law, Latha, to a buffalo, which he says always goes in the opposite direction from that in which it is driven. The old chief believes that our residence at each town and village has been marked by the death of some one, and Hotha naturally declines to take us, as he says that if any evil happened in his father-in-law's family he would be sure to get the blame of it.

CHAPTER XV.

HOTHA TO BHAMÔ.

The daughters of the Tsawbwa and his young wife came out to bid us good-bye, as we bade farewell to Hotha, on the 27th August, and their tears were an eloquent testimony to the kindliness of their hearts. We offered to shake hands with them, but the eldest daughter, a model of propriety, declined, as it was contrary to the custom of Shan women; the young wife, however, mustered courage to defy public opinion. A large concourse of people had collected to see us depart, and as we left the Tsawbwa's house, a salute of four guns was fired. The villagers along the road turned out to see us as we passed, and nothing could be more gratifying than the good-will manifested by all. The Tsawbwa accompanied us about six miles, parting with us as we reached the boundary of his estate. Here we were made over to the care of the Kakhyen Tsawbwa of Namboke.

The Latha portion of the valley is even more picturesque than the one we have just left, as it is more thickly wooded and the hills are nearer each other. The town of that name lies on the right bank, and is a much larger place than any of the villages in Hotha, and might almost be ranked as a town. Some very picturesque pagodas cap the rounded hills and thickly-wooded knolls, and many-roofed khyoungs lift their heads above the deep-green trees among which the villages lie hid. The road to Namboke crosses to the other side of the valley about a mile above Latha, and the stream, Namsa, is spanned by a planked bridge. It then takes a bend to escape the muddy rice-fields, and afterwards enters a perfect maze of little, conical, grassy hills which block up this end of the valley. Rounding a few of them, the road emerges, and follows the bank of the Namsa to where again they close in upon it, restricting its course to a narrow glen. From amongst the hills, the path turns to the left, and follows the course of the Namboke stream, a mountain rivulet now much swollen by the heavy rains. We commenced a gentle ascent which, after a few miles, became more abrupt, as a number of small hills were crossed, and reached the summit of the first spur of the easterly range of the Hotha and Latha valley at half past 4 P. M. Hitherto, the water-shed had been to the east-north-east, but on descending the spur through a dense forest with little or no under-growth, the streams were running to the north and the west of north. From thence to Namboke the road lay over a succession of spurs from the westerly continuation of the Hotha and Latha hills, and from the great ridge that forms the left side of the Tapeng valley in the Kakhyen hills, of which the Hotha is only a secondary valley. Namboke may be said to lie among a sea of little, peaked, and rounded, thickly-wooded hills formed by the junction of the spurs of the ranges just mentioned, which are here connected to each other by a narrow isthmus. We arrived at the village at 5 P.M. in a downpour of rain, and were first conducted to a roofless shed in which it which it was intended we should pass the night, but we politely declined to avail ourselves of it. The Tsawbwa then took us up to his house where we were received with a salute of three guns, and he gave us the stranger's hall to put up in, and provided accommodation for our men in another house close by. The strangers' hall is the front-door extremity of the house, from the rest of which it is partially shut off, but as there was not room for all of us inside, Gordon and I put up in the portico, in which all the cattle and pigs are huddled at night. As I had no bed, and it was desirable under these circumstances to be off the ground, the Kakhyens brought me two planks for a bedstead.

28th August. Spent a miserable night from the constant sensation of creeping things passing over me, and suspect that my troubles arose from the fauna of my temporary bed. It was not at all certain when we rose this morning whether we were to start, because neither of Sladen's boxes had arrived. They, however, came in at 7 A.M., and the mules followed soon after, but when we were ready to move, the Tsawbwa brought forward so many reasons why we should not go to-day, that we had at last to succumb, and honour him with our presence till to-morrow.

The Latha Tsawbwa accepted the presents we forwarded by the interpreter, and sent a piece of cloth in return, with a message that he was very poor, and had nothing better to give; that he himself would have been very glad if we had visited him, had not he had some old men about him who were afraid of us from the reports that had reached them, regarding the dire consequences that had befallen the Sanda valley from our visit. It rained in torrents the greater part of the day, and everything was enshrouded in thick mist. In the portico we were surrounded by inquisitive Kakhyens and a few Leesaws from some villages close at hand, all eager for *compraw* or silver.

29th August. It was only by dint of dogged determination and resolve on the part of our leader to listen to no excuses, however plausible, for a further sojourn in this village, that we got away at 12, 35 p.m. Some of the Hotha men had made off with their mules, and we experienced great difficulty in procuring Kakyhens to carry the loads. My spirit collecting-boxes were left behind, but Hotha's man, who had charge of the arrangements across the hills, promised to bring them; however, when we arrived at the end of our march he appeared without them.

Leaving Namboke, the road winds down the western face of the spur on which the village stands into a deep hollow, and then commences the ascent of the eastern side of the main range forming the left side of the Tapeng valley in the Kakhyen hills, and in doing so crosses a spur till it reaches the summit of the range. It then lay along the ridge of the hills till we reached the village of Ashan where we halted for the night, putting up in Kakhyen houses. The road was a mere footpath, and had been so little frequented of late years that it had had to be opened specially for us by the Kakhyens, who had sent a party of men a few days before to cut a way through the parts that had become impassable for mules, and the work of their dâhs was everywhere visible throughout the march. From Namboke to the summit of the main range, the path lay through splendid virgin forest, and some of the glimpses down the precipitous hill-faces were magnificent. Reaching the top we looked to the right into the deep valley of the Tapeng, the village of Ponsee lying as a small speck on the slopes of the parallel range on the other side, half-way between the bed of the Tapeng and the summit of the highest peak, Chittie-doung, on the northern side of the valley. Beneath us to our left were two little, deep valleys running nearly east and west, separated from each other by a low ridge, the termination of the line of hills that forms the left side of the Hotha valley, and which loses itself in the maze which results from the division, sub-division, and commingling of the great spurs of the main lines of upheaval of these mountains. There is a sea of hills in every direction, as far as the eye can reach, and some of the great waves rise as enormous dome-shaped masses, 6,000 feet above the sea, clothed with dense forest to their summits, where man has not interfered with their economy. The greater number, however, of the lesser hills have been cleared for the cultivation of rice and Indian corn, and in looking down their abrupt slopes, we saw them marked, as it were, with broad flights of steps, the terraces of cultivation, and in turning our field-glass towards these, we could usually detect little villages lying among them. The village of Ashan belongs to the Ponsee Tsawbwa whose territory extends from summit to summit of the two parallel ranges. It is literally situated on the ridge of this side, but considerably below the highest peaks, and looks down upon Ponsee through a deep, steep valley, formed by two spurs that run to the Tapeng, the most westerly one of which has the silver mines at its lower end. The village contains about a dozen houses; we passed no villages between Namboke and Ashan, and although we observed a fair sprinkling on the Tapeng side of the ridge, we did not see a single one to our left.

30th August. Left Ashan at 11, 10 A.M. and immediately commenced to descend the crest of a long spur running down to one of two villages on the southern side of the left main ridge of the Tapeng. The descent was extremely difficult, and as the ground was wet and slippery, our pace never exceeded one mile and a half an hour. The ponies and mules were continually sliding down on their hind-quarters, and as there were steep declivities on either side, our progress was not unattended by danger. It was quite as difficult for pedestrians, and the only chance of keeping one's footing lay in catching hold at every step of the long grass, and thus gradually letting oneself down. We reached the bottom at 12, 5 P.M.

The Namkong, a usually small stream, but now a mountain torrent, had to be crossed, and it took our ponies up to their saddles, and all their strength was needed to keep their footing in the impetuous flood, and the men had to dig a staff into its bed at each step to prevent themselves being carried away. We were joined here by Lawloo, our Kakhyen messenger, and a number of his men.

Across the Namkong, the path lay over a narrow alluvial flat covered with tall grass, and knee-deep in mud in the hollows. Rounding a spur we entered another valley, and had to cross another mountain torrent to reach the opposite slope, along which we gradually ascended for a short distance, and then commenced a very steep ascent up a mountain-side. Here we passed a village on our left, perched on the summit of a rounded peak, a considerable height above us, and we had a splendid view of the ranges to the south, all running nearly parallel to each other, east-north-east and west-south-west, with valleys between, much broken up by the commingling of their spurs. The valley we had just quitted was seen to communicate with another small vale to the south of it, with narrow, level patches in its middle devoted to cultivation. We descended a few hundred feet, and reached the village of Muangwye at 2, 30 P.M., lying on the side of a peak covered with trees and enormous granite boulders. We were conducted to the Tsawbwa's house, and when we began to think of dinner, we discovered that our commissariat had been taken on to the village of Lonylone which is to be our next march. The Tsawbwa's house is about 150 feet in length, and the number of buffalo and pig skulls in his portico attests to his wealth. He was most hospitable and liberal in his supplies of sheroo and samshu, two Kakhyen luxuries for which he has a special failing.

31st August. The Tsawbwa and I did a brisk trade in land shells before we started, as he had found out my weakness for such objects the night before.

The morning was very wet, and in descending into the Muangkah valley we had a repetition of the mishaps of yesterday, but fortunately the descent was neither very abrupt nor long. The valley, or rather glen, is about 400 feet in its greatest breadth, and the soil is a rich black loam, and apparently very fertile, judging from the appearance of the small rice-fields. The Muangkah is a deep stream about fifteen feet broad, and flows in an alluvial channel which it has cut out for itself to a considerable depth, so much so that it is entirely hidden at a distance. Swimming the mules and ponies across, we managed to scramble over on the trunk of a tree, not more than six inches broad, steadying ourselves as we best could by a ricketty bamboo that had been tied on to one side as a railing.

The valley is about one mile long, and we crossed it obliquely to the south-east, where we ascended, and going over a ridge, descended 100 feet to the village of Loaylone, situated on a steep slope which stretches out on either side of it like an amphitheatre. This village or town is the largest and most thriving we have seen in these hills, and the Tsawbwa's house was enclosed by a high bamboo fence. Our party was put up in two old granaries raised on piles, about five feet above the ground, and our men were lodged in the porticoes of some of the houses. The Tsawbwa, one of the most influential chiefs in these hills, visited us shortly after our arrival, and sent presents of sheroo and fowls. The Mutthin Tsawbwa arrived in the evening with a number of mules. He is the younger brother of the Loaylone chief, and a man of great intelligence and self-possession, quiet in his demeanour and with manners quite as polished as any Burman or Shan gentleman. He wears his hair in Burmese fashion, but his dress is a mixture of Shan and Chinese, a costume which accords with his perfect familiarity with the two languages, in addition to his native tongue, Kakhyen. After dinner he came up to our quarters, and had a most frank and intelligent conversation with Sladen on the advantages that would accrue to the Kakhyens were the trade to Western Yunan revived, and expressed his willingness to do everything in his power to facilitate its re-establishment and development, and naturally extolled this route as the best.

1st September. Heavy rain all last night and up to noon, when the clouds rose from the hills giving us the prospect of fine weather.

The Muangwye Tsawbwa, who is going to accompany us to Bhamô, with the Namboke man and all the others through whose territories this route passes, brought a kid as a present yesterday afternoon, and the Loaylone chief killed a fatted calf this morning, and sent us a liberal portion. We could not be on better terms with the Kakhyens than we are at present, and the probability is that if we had had the Burmese with us at the beginning, our progress through the hills would have been then quite as successful and easy as it is now, and that what has taken nearly eight months to accomplish might have been achieved in half the time. There can be little doubt that if we had followed this route to Momien, or gone by the Sawaddy one to the south of it, we should have been beyond reach of that bugbear, Leesetai. As this place has been recognized for very many years as one of the principal stages on the embassy route, and one at which the porters and muleteers are invariably changed, we have had to discharge all our Hotha men, and hire fresh coolies and mules. It was once a Chinese garrison, and the remains of the old fort are said still to exist on the heights above the village, from which a view can be obtained of the Muangwan valley. The usual route from this to Momien is said to be by Muangwan, and from thence to Nantin avoiding the Hotha valley.

2nd September. Very heavy rain during the night with strong gusts of wind from the south-west. At the very last moment before we took our departure from Loaylone, two of the Namboke Pawmines refused to allow a mule-load containing Captain Bowers' baggage to start, as they asserted they had not received payment for a load of rice, which was paid for yesterday. This is Kakhyen tactics to the life. Leaving Loaylone the road descends a gentle slope into a small glen, in which we met a number of mules from Bhamô laden with cotton and salt.

We passed the direct road to Hoetone shortly after leaving Loaylone, as the Mutthin Tsawbwa wished us to go through his village. We afterwards found that in order to oblige him, we had made a detour of ten miles, while the direct road between Loaylone and Hoetone is not more than five miles, and that the latter was a comparatively level one along the paddy-fields, while the former necessitated us going right over the summit of one of the highest ranges.

From the glen we made steep ascents over a succession of spurs and descents into shallow, intervening valleys till we reached the summit of the main ridge at an elevation of 5,000 feet. Close to our left was a prominent dome-shaped hill which we had seen on our way to Ashan, and from the top of the ridge it appeared to be only 400 or 500 feet above us. There were a few higher peaks still further to the south-east and south, but it is doubtful whether any of them exceed the point we reached, by more than 500 or 600 feet.

On this high level, which was covered with fine turf and a few trees, and was strewn with enormous boulders, we passed a village, the houses of which were picturesquely built under the shelter of these granite boulders. The descent of the main mass of the Kakhyen hills begins in earnest after leaving this village, and the path winds along the spurs, and is a continuous declivity to Mutthin, situated on the ridge of one of these. We were received with the beating of gongs and cymbals, and by a salute of three guns. This is, next to Loaylone, the most thriving Kakhyen village we have yet seen, and the Tsawbwa's house, although built after the plan prevalent in these hills, is enclosed by a substantial stone and brick wall with a very Chinese-looking gateway, and is approached by a paved path which leads through the court-yard. We accompanied the Tsawbwa into his house for a minute or two, and were then conducted into the upper room of a small pavilion or watch-tower close on the wall, and there we ate our lunch and were regaled with sheroo and samshu. Leaving Mutthin, we continued the descent to Hoetone on the same spur, but about half an hour's march further down. It stands on a flattened depression of the crest, strewn with great granite and gneiss boulders. We put up in the portico of the Tsawbwa's house, in front of which there are three flat blocks of stone, about three feet high, stuck into the ground in a line, and said to be the altar on which the buffaloes are offered to the nâts. I observed some others in a grove outside the village, which had evidently been the scene of numerous offerings, as the quantity of skulls lying about was very great. In this place there was also a circular stone wall about three feet high, with one of the standing stones built into it, and the ground was covered with the decaying skulls of buffaloes that had been killed to the nâts. The hill-sides generally, when not cleared for cultivation, are covered with dense forest, and in some neighbouring hollows we found capital rice crops, and above and below the village were large clearings for a mixed crop of Indian corn and rice grown together in long lines.

3rd September. Heavy rain all night with thunder. Lawloo and some of his associates attempted to delay us by asking compensation for the death of the petty chief, who died of small-pox at Momien. The mules came in in dribblets, and as we could do nothing to expedite matters, we started when a fair number had got off. A few hundred yards from the village we came upon a division in the road, and a discussion took place with the Mantai Tsawbwa, who was acting as our guide, about which of the two paths we were to take. We wanted to go by the road which appeared to be the straight one, as it lay along the spur we had come down, while the other turned off to the left, down a deep hollow, on to another spur to the south. The Tsawbwa's object was to take us through his village without regard to the distance we had to travel, so he insisted that the one to the left was quite as short as the other and a better road, and we had to give in, and follow him. We made a steep descent and then ascended the other spur to his village, which is situated on the northern slope, commanding a splendid view of the plains of Burmah and their noble river. On entering it we were glad we had given in to him, as all the people had been on the tip-toe of expectation to receive us, and saluted us with five guns as we approached. We dismounted and went into his house which was enclosed by a bamboo palisade, and found mats spread and a liberal supply of sheroo and samshu awaiting us under the care of his wife and daughters, strapping Kakhyen maidens. We gave them a few small silver pieces which greatly delighted them, and mounting our ponies made a very steep and slippery descent through bamboo jungle in which we were in imminent danger of being empaled against the fallen stems, as our ponies slid down for yards together on their haunches, and it mattered not what danger was in front for they were helpless to change their course. At the bottom we came to a roaring mountain torrent over which a small bridge had been constructed for us to cross, as fording the stream was out of the question. A large boulder lay in the middle of the channel, and two large bamboos were placed from it to the banks on either side, with smaller ones between them, crossed at intervals of about a foot with transverse pieces to keep the others together. This primitive bridge was 18 inches broad, and as one division ran up at a considerable incline to reach the boulder and the other bank, and the other sloped down with equal abruptness from it, the passage across was accomplished with fear and trembling, lest we should lose our footing and be carried by the irresistible force of the current into the Tapeng, where death was certain to the most expert swimmer.

On either side of the stream there is a considerable extent of level land covered by tall grass, but closed in on every side by high hills. The latter echoed with the roar of the Tapeng, which was evidently close at hand but hidden from us by the long grass. Crossing the alluvial flat and a low hill spur, we found ourselves on the banks of this river, which was wildly rushing to the plains in incomparable grandeur. The road lay along its banks for about two miles over tolerably level ground, and at one point where it left the river and divided, we followed the wrong path for about a mile before we discovered our mistake, and in returning found that the Kakhyens who had passed along after us had thrown a branch across it to direct others who were following, to the right path. Crossing a low spur, to the south-west, we left the Tapeng to our right, and came upon a moderately-sized, deep-flowing stream, the Namthabet. There is a low range of undulating hills at the entrance to the Tapeng valley running nearly north and south: the Tapeng as it issues from the hills flows round its northern extremity, and the Namthabet comes down between it and the main mass of the Kakhyen hills, and flows into the Tapeng just where the latter begins to bend round it. Continuing along its bank for about three-quarters of a mile we encamped for the night, as the raft which was being prepared to carry us over was unfinished. The work had been entrusted to two Kakhyens who had started last night from Hoetone for the purpose. Having no tents we each set to work to construct some shelter, and there being plenty of bamboos we soon erected a number of small huts which we roofed with long grass. The sand-flies were intolerable, and mosquito curtains were little or no protection against these persistent pests.

4th September. We breakfasted at 6 A.M., and afterwards set to work to complete the raft as the Kakhyens were doing nothing. After it was finished we put a number of Burmans on it along with the jemadar, his wife, and adopted child, with bamboos about 20 feet long to pole it across, but the current was too strong, and it was carried a long way down the stream, and only brought ashore by some of the men jumping into the water and guiding it to the bank, where all held on by the branches of the overhanging trees. They had a narrow escape from being capsized and carried down to the Tapeng. As poling was out of the question, we tried the Kakhyen method of stretching a rope from bank to bank across the stream, and made one from long strips of the external layer of the bamboo and connected it to the raft by a loop. In crossing with this arrangement, the art lies in keeping the raft sideways on to the current by a paddle behind. This attempt was not more successful than the poling one, for the rope snapped in two when the raft was in the centre of the stream. The men, however, kept a firm hold of the half of the rope from the opposite bank, to which they managed to pull themselves. We now resolved to adopt a different plan, and to have a rope attached to the raft from each bank, and make the men pull it across from side to side. This plan succeeded, and after we had sent all our men and baggage across, we went over on the raft up to our knees in water, and in a torrent of rain that had been falling all the morning.

Immediately after leaving the left bank, we were met by the *Choungsa* of Sit-nga mounted on a pony, and accompanied by a number of men sent to conduct us to Nampung. The road lay over the small outlying range of hills above-mentioned, whose highest point cannot be more than 600 feet above the Namthabet. They are rounded hills with tolerably open hollows, and on the western side they fade gradually into the Terai land in long undulations, covered by thick tree jungle. Their eastern side, overlooking the Namthabet, is covered almost exclusively with bamboos. In the Terai, the trees are chiefly *Eng* with a thick undergrowth of long delicate grass. There was little or no cultivation. Reaching the Tapeng after a march of five miles, we found two large boats in readiness, and one of them nicely carpeted and a number of men sitting in the stern beating gongs and tomtoms. We were towed across the now quietly-flowing river by two war-boats manned by about 30 men each, and on reaching the other side, were conducted by the Woon's private secretary to a small pavilion which had been carefully prepared for our reception, and in wonderful contrast to the place provided for us on our upward journey. The name of the village is Sit-nga, and immediately adjoins Tsihot. The officials who received us were the same men who could not let us have a couple of fowls, on our former visit, for less than Rs. 18; they now, however, gratuitously overburdened us with rice, plantains, pork, ngapé, and other eatables, more than sufficient for the wants of all, and in addition, fed the despised Kakhyens who accompanied us.

5th September. The hire of the mules and porters was settled to-day without a dissentient voice, and not a single article has been lost between this and Hotha, and even my spirit-boxes and the mule-load that had been detained at Leaylone came up all right. The latter was brought by two porters who had opened it and divided it into two bundles, but although it contained many things that would take the Kakhyen fancy, and among them an open bottle of brandy, not one had been tampered with.

We left Sit-nga in boats for Bhamô, and on our way down had a splendid view of the two peaked mountains that mark the opposite sides of the Tapeng in its course to the plains, the one overlooking Ponsee, the Chittie-doung, and the other facing it on the left bank, the Kad-doung. This latter is the hill over which we have lately come and which we made to be over 5,000 feet, which may be taken as a fair average of the height of the hills seen from the Irawady valley, but there are others, such as those facing Muangla and to the south of Mawphoo, which must be 6,000 above the level of the sea.

As we neared the mouth of the Tapeng we were met by the *Sayay-dawggee* accompanied by two war-boats that took us in tow, and we reached Bhamô at 2, 30 P.M., having left Sit-nga at 9 A.M. The Tapeng is at this season 1,500 feet broad, and so deep that an ordinary river steamer would experience no difficulty in going up it as far as its exit from the hills.

We went to our old quarters which have been thoroughly repaired. The boxes, however, which we left behind, have been liberally looted during our absence. A supply of rice and plantains was sent us as a present from the Woon. We were accompanied by all the Tsawbwas of the route we had come by, and the Burmese provided accommodation for them outside the town, and supplied them with food.

I remained in Bhamô till the morning of the 13th, to witness the Kakhyen ceremony of swearing eternal friendship to us, and their engagement to afford protection in future to British merchants and travellers through their hills. The ceremony, which I have described elsewhere, consisted of the sacrifice of two buffaloes to the nâts, and the blood of the animals had to be drunk, after the dâhs and spears were dipped in it. This is considered by these people an oath of the most sacred and binding character which nothing can annul, as all the nâts are believed to be present when it is taken; a Kakhyen would dread breaking it, for his so doing would subject him to the wrath of the nâts, of whose displeasure he lives in constant fear.

The phoongyees at first objected to the ceremony on the ground that it was opposed to religion (Buddhist) to take life, but this objection was met by the indisputable fact adduced by Major Sladen, that the nâts are propitiated every day in the palace at Mandalay,[1] and that during the last rebellion a special prayer was issued by the Government imploring them to lend their aid in re-establishing order and the authority of the king.

After the ceremony was ended, and the flesh of the slain buffaloes was distributed among the respective clans that accompanied us, the chiefs collected in our verandah, and some of the blood of the buffaloes was poured into a large wash-hand basin which was filled up with samshu. Two of our spears and dâhs were then dipped in the fluid, of which each chief drank a good bumper till it was finished. On the second day, after a repetition of all the incidents of the previous one, presents were given to all the

[1] In the Burmese documents giving an account of the Embassy to Bhamô from China in 1833, it is recorded that the Governor of Bhamô ordered sacrifices to be made to the guarding nâts of the town.

chiefs, and the heads of the buffaloes were then fixed on poles in front of the altars, the Tsawbwas with their retainers retiring to the hills.

Gordon and I devoted a day to explore the exit of the Molay river which enters the Irawady about four miles above the Tapeng, and which we had first heard of at Sanda. The Irawady at Bhamô, at this season, has more the appearance of an immense lake than a river, and those portions of the country that during the dry weather seemed to be old river-banks, had the water now many feet up their sides, and the long grass-fields over which I used to roam were submerged from 12 to 15 feet. We sailed along under the banks the whole way to avoid the current, and when opposite the Tapeng, we passed a large herd of round-headed dolphins, disporting themselves in the deep water. There were many of all ages, but they are extremely difficult to shoot as they expose little of the body in rising to breathe, and are no sooner visible than they disappear. Opposite the lower mouth of the Molay stream which flows out between two low ranges of hills, there were large flocks of pelicans (*R. philippensis*) with a large percentage of immature birds, and some trees on the delta-like strip of land between the two mouths of the river were covered with them as with a white blossom. Here, the Irawady is divided into two branches by a large island some miles in length, and supporting a number of villages. The Molay is an inconsiderable river, not nearly so large as the Tapeng; at this season boats can proceed up it a considerable distance, but during the dry weather it can only be navigated by very small boats. The boatmen informed us that it leads right into China, and that a small trade finds its way along it to the country to the north of Sanda. The Burmese do not venture on it as they allege that the Kakhyens along its banks bear a very bad name, and are always fighting among themselves. The hills, on either side, average about 600 feet high and run in an east-north-east course, becoming lower as they recede from the Irawady. Gordon and I arranged to go down the river together, and we went on board our boats on the evening of the 13th of September, bidding farewell to Bhamô on the morning of the 14th, and reached Mandalay on the 23rd of the month, after visiting many of the places of interest along the river.

APPENDICES.

APPENDIX A.

ROUTES TO CHINA.

ROUTES FROM BHAMÔ AND MANDALAY (AMARAPURA) TO PEKIN AND YUNAN CITY; AND FOUR ROUTES FROM BHAMÔ TO THE EASTWARD.

Route from Bhamô to Pekin travelled by a mission deputed by the King of Ava to the Emperor of China in the year 1833, taken from Burmese documents by Lieutenant Colonel Burney, Resident in Ava, in 1837.[*]

1833.		Miles.
11th August	Bhamô to Momauk	12
12th „	Ta-da-gyee	8
13th „	Village of Kakhyen Chief Tein	12
14th „	Matheng	12
16th „	Foot of Muangkhah mountain	12
17th „	Loaylone Fort (Chinese)	14
18th „	Muangwan	16
22nd „	Kendat Fort (Chinese) Shuemuolone mountain (distance not given).	
23rd „	Mantoun	16
24th „	Nantin	14
26th „	Tengyechew or Momien	20
7th September	Kanlantshan	16
8th „	Pá-weng after crossing iron suspension bridge over Shuaylee	16
9th „	Phupyauk after crossing Salween by boat	14
10th „	Yung-chang-fú	12
12th „	Kuonbó	8
13th „	Shya-maho after crossing iron suspension bridge over Mekong	16
14th „	Youn-pyeu-hien	18
15th „	Khuon-leng-phú	18
16th „	Yan-pyin-hien, between this and the previous halt crossed a river 10 miles from Khuon-leng-phú by an iron suspension bridge (distance not given).	
17th „	Hokyanpo, crossing at Yan-pyin-hien an iron suspension bridge over the Hokyan river	12
18th „	Tsauk-chow	18
19th „	Khoun-haik	16
20th „	Yit-nan-yi	18
21st „	Phu-poun	12

[*] Journ. Asiatic Soc., vol. VI, p. 546.

APPENDIX A.

			Miles.
1833.			
22nd September	...	Shya-khyauk ...	16
		Kyen-nan-chow, a walled city with a governor and commander of cavalry ...	6
23rd "	...	Li-hô ...	6
24th "	...	Tshu-shyoun or Tschou-hiung, a large walled city with six gates, with a governor and garrison	12
25th "	...	Kueng-toun-hien ...	14
26th "	...	Shyê-tsho ...	12
27th "	...	Lu-thoun-hien, a large walled city with a governor	16
28th "	...	Lo-ya-kuon ...	12
29th "	...	An-leng-chow, a large city almost in ruins	16
30th "	...	Yunan-fu or Muangtshi, a large walled city with seven gates, with a civil and a military governor, a collector of customs, judge, and military examiner	12
21st October	...	Wun-khyauk ...	10
22nd "	...	Yan-loit ...	14
23rd "	...	Yi-loun-tsan ...	18
24th "	...	Ma-loun-chow, a city with a governor. It is about the same size as Yunan city ...	14
25th "	...	Shya-yi-chow, a walled city with a governor	10
26th "	...	Pô-shue ...	14
27th "	...	Pyeng-yeng-hien, a large walled city with a governor	12
28th "	...	Yi-za-khoun ...	14
29th "	...	Yo-kuon-teng-tsan ...	14
30th "	...	Shyan-tsain ...	14
31st "	...	Pe-shya-ti ...	8
1st November	...	A-tu-teng ...	12
2nd "	...	La-taing, a small walled city with a governor	12
3rd "	...	Bo-koun ...	12
4th "	...	Tsein-leng-chow, a large walled city with a governor	12
5th "	...	Au-shue-fu, a large walled city with a governor	12
6th "	...	Ngan-pyeng-hien, a large walled city with a governor	16
7th "	...	Tsheng-tsein-hien, a small walled city with a governor	12
8th "	...	Kue-chow (Yue-chow?), a very large city of the second class with a military officer and four governors	16
10th "	...	Loun-li-hien, a small city of the third class	12
12th "	...	Kue-tsiu-hien, a large city of the third class	14
13th "	...	Lhyo-yan-tsan ...	12
14th "	...	Yeng-pyeng-hien, a very large city of the third class	16
15th "	...	Khan-pyeng-chow, a city of the second class	14
16th "	...	Tsi-pyeng-hien, a large city of the third class	
17th "	...	Tsein-ynon-fu, a city of the first class, but not so large as Kue-chow. It appears to be the Tong-chwen-fu of Du Halde situated on a navigable branch of the Yang-tse-kiang. Here the mission embarked in boats and dropped down to ...	14

ROUTES TO CHINA. 393

1833.			Miles.
20th November	...	Tshi-tshein-hien, a walled city of the third class	12
21st "	...	Tá-yi-tan, a fort on the Yang-tse-kiang	18
22nd "	...	Pyan-shue	20
23rd "	...	Yi-pyen-hien, a walled city	14
" "		Yuón-tso-fu, a walled city of the first class, surrounded by numerous villages, and from thence in the same day to...	6
24th "	...	Kyin-leng-dan	6
25th "	...	Khyay-ya-hien, a walled town of the third class	20
26th "	...	Tshi-tshi	18
27th "	...	Shyeng-yi-wun	32
28th "	...	Tseng-kyl-hein, a walled city of third class	26
29th "	...	Lú-kyi-hien, a walled city of third class	15
30th "	...	Shyeng-tso-fu (Tching-tcheou), a large walled city of the first class	12
1st December	...	Kaing-shyo	34
2nd "		Tsoun-seh	30
3rd "	...	Tshan-tek-fu. Here the mission left the Yang-tse-kiang and proceeded by land to	12
5th "	...	Ta-loun-tsan	12
6th "		Tsi-khun-ye	12
7th "	...	Li-chow, a large walled city with five gates	12
10th "	...	Shue-leng-yeng	12
12th "	...	Koun-gan-hien, a large walled city	12
14th "	...	Tshuon-léng-ye	10
15th "	...	Kyeng-tso-fu (Kin-tcheou), a very large city with very handsome walls surrounded by a ditch on which the mission saw a great many boats plying	12
17th "	...	Kyeng-yeng-ye	18
20th "	...	Kyeng-mein-chow (Kinmen), a large walled city of the second class	18
22nd "	...	Shi-Khyauk	12
23rd "	...	Leng-yan-yé	12
24th "	...	Yi-tshein-hein, a walled city	18
25th "	...	Tbuon-tcheng (Syang-yang), the mission state that the whole of the country between this city and Tshan-tek-fu, where they left the Yang-tse-kiang, had been destroyed by an inundation in 1829, and that the effects of it were still everywhere visible, and that on account of the damage it had done, they experienced great difficulty in procuring post-horses and porters, and had taken 22 days to travel a distance, that prior to the inundation had never occupied more than 12 days. From this city they proceeded in covered chairs in order	

394   APPENDIX A.

1834.			Miles.
		to facilitate the journey; the chairs were drawn by mules harnessed before and behind	18
1st January	...	Lhyó-yeng-yi	12
2nd "	...	Yi or Ri-hien, a walled city of third class	12
3rd "	...	Wa-teng	6
4th "	...	Nan-yan-fu (Nanyang), a large walled city	12
5th "	...	Tseng-teng	6
6th "	...	Tsó-hô	12
7th "	...	Yi-chow, a walled city, stopped by a fall of snow	8
8th "	...	Kyo-sheng	18
9th "	...	Yui-hien, a walled city	6
10th "	...	Shan-hien, a large walled city of third class	12
11th "	...	Tshan-ko-hien, a walled city of third class	22
12th "	...	Sheng-tseng-khyeng, a large walled city	12
13th "	...	Tseng-chow (Tchingow) a large walled city. Beyond which they reached the Ho-ang-ho, which was frozen, so that they were unable to proceed by the route followed by the governor of Bhamô in 1823, and deviated to the north-west to	20
14th "	...	Youn-yan-hien, a walled city	14
15th "	...	Hú-ló-kuon, a large walled city	8
		Koun-hien, a large walled city	8
16th "	...	Yan-tse-hien, a large walled city	12
17th "	...	Moun-hien, a large walled city	12
18th "	...	Hunik-kyeng-fu (Hoaiking?), a large walled city	12
		Tsan-fu, a large walled city	8
19th "	...	Tsheng-hua-yi, a small walled city	6
		Tit-su-hien, the largest city met with between Bhamô and Pekin	12
		Hô-ya-hien, a very large walled city	4
20th "	...	Shyeng-nan-hien, a large walled city	4
		We-kue-fu (Oue-kiun), a large walled city, where they joined the road travelled by the governor of Bhamô in 1823	10
21st "	...	Khyi-hieng, a large city with mud walls, with brick parapets	
		passed through	
		Tsan-tek-fu (Tchang-te), a large walled city	
		to	
		Yi-koan	12
		passed through	
22nd "	...	Tsan-chow, a large walled city	
		to	
		Oun-lo-kyeng	11
23rd "	...	Han-tan-hien, a walled city	20

ROUTES TO CHINA.

1834.			Miles.
24th January	...	Younn-leng-hien, a walled city	10
		Shya-hòk-hien, a walled city	6
		Yuon-tek-fú (Chun-ti), a large walled city	10
25th „	...	Nue-shyu-hien, a walled city	12
		Po-shya-hien, a walled city	12
26th „	...	Tsauk-chow (Tcha), a walled city	12
		Luon-tshoun-hien, a large walled city	12
27th „	...	Tseng-tcin-fu, a large walled city	12
28th „	...	Teng-chow (Ting), a large walled city	6
		Wun-tu-hien, a very large walled city	12
		Myeng-yi-teng	6
29th „	...	Puon-tsheit-khyo	12
30th „	...	Pauk-teng-fu (Pao-ting), a large walled city	12
31st „	...	Ngan-shyu-hien (Ngan ?)	10
		Pe-kho	12
1st February	...	Teng-tsi-hien, a large walled city	2
		Tsue-chow (Tso-tcheou), large walled city	14
2nd „	...	Leng-yan-hien, large walled city	14
3rd „	...	Pe-kyin (Pekin), the capital of China	20
			1,745

From the foregoing itinerary, it appears that the Yang-tse-kiang is 60 marches from Bhamô, or 794 miles. The mission proceeded for 14 days down this river, and accomplished 270 miles in that time, and from the point they disembarked on the banks of the Yang-tse-kiang to the Ho-ang-ho, was a distance of 326 miles, which they overtook in 26 marches of about 12½ miles each. From the Ho-ang-ho they were 21 marches in reaching Pekin, a distance of 359 miles, making marches of 17 miles a day in Sedan chairs drawn by ponies, the entire distance 1,745 miles was overtaken in 121 days, giving an average of 14¼ miles per diem.

Route, from Amarapura to Pekin, vid Theinnee and Yunan city, travelled by a mission deputed by the King of Ava to the Emperor of China in the year 1787, taken from Burmese documents published by Colonel Burney, Resident in Ava, in 1837.*

1787.			Miles.
24th June	...	Amarapura to Phra-gyih	2
25th „	...	Kangyih, a city	12
26th „	...	Oun-lhut	16
27th „	...	Thoun-zay	20

* Journ. Asiatic Soc., vol. VII, p. 424.

APPENDIX A.

1787.			Miles.
28th June	...	Nan-mo	12
29th „	...	Ban-gyi or Ban-kyi	18
30th „	...	Kywe-goun	8
1st July	...	Bò-gyò	12
2nd „	...	Thi-bô, a city	6
3rd „	...	Thi-det, after crossing the Moday river	14
4th „	...	A té erected specially for them on the bank of the Naung-bô river	12
5th „	...	Lashio	12
6th „	...	Theinní (Theinnee) city, and remain 10 days	20
16th „	...	Teng-gan	8
17th „	...	Maing-puon	6
18th „	...	Na-ti	14
19th „	...	Nan-laiu	12
20th „	...	Peng-gno	10
22nd „	...	Kuon-loun, after crossing the Salu-een (Salween) river	10
25th „	...	Pan-theng	12
26th „	...	Peng-hin	8
27th „	...	Crossed the Nan-phoung or Nam-baung river, the boundary of Theinní. (Nam is water, in Shan language)	4
		Peng-ma-khô on the Nan-Tein river	2
28th „	...	Tsin-het	8
30th „	...	Khout-loh	6
31st „	...	Maing-Kaing	6
1st August	...	At the monastery of Bodnen-gyih (great silver mine)	8
3rd „	...	Man-bú, on the little hill of Luay-wun-bú (Luay or Lói is the Shan for a mountain)	8
4th „	...	Kaing-mah, a city with a governor. (Here the ambassadors appear to have remained for 5 months)	2
1788.			
12th January	...	Wein-youk	8
13th „	...	Maing-Tha	10
14th „	...	Maing-Yaung, in the province of Yunan and under the city of Shuen-li	16
18th „	...	Maing-Lá	16
19th „	...	Toun-dauk-shue	14
20th „	...	Yuin-chow (Maing-Yú)	12
23rd „	...	Shuen-li a city (Maing-Chan). (Here again they appear to have stayed 5 months)	18
25th June	...	Tsinkay	12
27th „	...	Nyo-kay, after crossing the iron-bridge over the Mekhaung (Mekkong) or great Cambodia river (Chinese, Lout-san-Kyang)	20

ROUTES TO CHINA.

1788.			MILES.
28th June	Tshu-kay		20
29th „	Moun-khna, a city		12
30th „	Than-shyen-ban		12
1st July	Ta-thí or Ta-yi (city of Tali)		14
23rd „	Tso-chow		12
24th „	Yuinan-ngay (city of little Yunan)		24
25th „	Keyen-nan-chow, a city		28
26th „	Tshu-shyoun (Tchon-hiung)		12
27th „	Kueng-toun-kien, a city		12
28th „	Lu-thoun-hien		26
29th „	An; lin-chow		30
	Yui nan-gyih (great) called by the Shans		14
	Maing-Tshi (Yunan)		620

After Yunan city, the route pursued by this embassy to Pekin is similar to that tabulated in the previous route.

As the distance from Yunan to Pekin is about 1,293 miles by road, the sum total of miles to be travelled between Amarapura (Mandalay) and Pekin is 1,913 miles.

ROUTES FROM BHAMÔ TO THE EASTWARD.

The following routes have been kindly placed at my disposal by Mr. Gordon, who joined the Expedition at Muangla on its return from Momien.

The routes from Bhamô to the Muangwan valley are each called by the name of the gate from which the person starts on his road. The first three were supplied to Mr. Gordon by a Shan trader of Muangwan brought to him by the king's interpreter.

First Route.—Bhamô from east gate to Leyin 6 miles; Manbong 1½ mile, near the Namsagyee-choung to the north of it; Momauk (S) at the foot of hills 1½ mile; on hills is Momauk, a Kakhyen village, 1½ miles off; going up to the head of a stream Pongwa, not the same as the Pongwa village near Matin. There is still another village of the same name on the opposite side of the stream, 3 miles from Momauk; Pin-ma-yiu (Kakhyen) 1 mile, crossing the Namsagyee-choung 18 feet broad; Pin-koh 1½ miles; near this place is the highest point of the ridge line which divides the territory. Crossing this the Namtha-choung flows towards Mowun; Namtha (Kakhyen) 2¼ miles; about 2 miles from this a Shan village called Manen; Leytha 1½ mile; Noung-num ½ mile, crossing the Mowun-choung or Nomwan by a bridge. Hwan-seng 1 mile; Sin-houng a bazaar village (every five days)

1 mile; Toon-hein ½ mile; Ley-kham ½ mile; Homoung ½ mile; Noung-swan (Shan) and Wing-koot on each side of road ½ mile. Tawkhoung 1 mile; Kawtin 1½ mile; Ma-wyne north-east from Kawtin with a small stream intervening, ½ mile; here is a large pagoda near Wynemow which is to the south of the road, while Kat-tin-kam is to the north of it. A large bazaar is held at the latter place, 2½ miles; Nam-toh 2 miles; Muangwan 1½ mile.

Second Route.—Bhamô from Nyey-noo gate, south gate, to Kotyen 3 miles, crossing the Namsagyee-choung. This debouches about one mile south of Bhamô. Then crossing a small stream, Namsanling, which flows into the Namsagyee, about 1½ mile, reach the foot of the hills, and ascending arrive at Wa-loung (Kakhyen) 2 miles from foot of hills; Lamadoung 2 miles; Muangwye 1 mile; Meroo 1 mile; this hill is the highest near Bhamô; Maing-pie or Pa-kowan about 9 miles; one night is passed in the jungle between Meroo and these places; Seedoung 2 miles, and near this two roads diverge, the one to the north going to Manen 2 miles, and the south road leading to a Panthay hill 1 mile; Noungen 1 mile; Leytha 1½ mile.

Third Route.—Bhamô from south gate, Pankon ½ mile; Myoungbin-tha close to the Namsagyee stream, after crossing which reach Kanjie 2½ miles. Here another stream the Theing-min is met with, and following it reach Theing-min village ½ mile; Manyuat ½ mile; Mankin 1 mile; at foot of hills opposite this Nanma-pwey village; Theingpwat (Kakhyen) 2½ miles; Letka south of road ½ mile; north of the latter village is Peh-toh; and still further is Pa-la; Pong-seing 3 miles; Nau-say 2 miles; Nam-koh 2½ (Kakhyen); descending reach Noungen 2 miles; on keeping to the south from Nam-kal reach Nam-toh in 2 miles; Ling-houng 3 miles.

Fourth Route.—From north gate of Bhamô, Nampawa stream and village 2 miles; Mobeing 2 miles; Leemin 4 miles; Nam-thabet river 5 miles to about 4 miles above where the Expedition crossed it; then Namtha-boke rivulet 2 miles; Mantai 2 miles; Hoetone 2 miles; Mutthin 2 miles; Loaylone, Muangkah; 2 miles to Katsan having a large bazaar, and also called Muangwan. There is in reality no town of Muangwan, which is the name of the district.

ROUTE FROM KAUNGTOUNG TO MUANGWAN.

A road to the south of Kaungtoung leads to Mansey 6 miles; this leads in a straight line along the Moh-yew river to the north of Kaungtoung; Shnay to Manthy 3 miles; Kwey-gyee, Kongteing 1 mile; to Mankai 1½ mile; Mausey near Mansy to Nankin, and arrive at foot of hills;

ascending reach Looaysoon (Kakhyen) 2½ miles; Pongkan 2 miles; here there is a stiff hill, but no further difficulty as the road is good. The road follows a pass, and on the south of it Pakwan 2½ miles; north, Nausey 3 miles; Manseing 2 miles north; Kastan 2 miles south; Namtoh (Shan) 2 miles off after crossing Namwan.

ROUTE FROM MUANGWAN TO SEHFAN.

From Namtoh (last village on preceding route) to Leikpoo 2 miles; Main-peik 1 mile ascending a Poloung hill, and going east reach Holam, 1½ mile; Mammok ½ mile; Pinhok 1½ mile; Luaylone ½ mile; Manpin 2 miles; Luayleik (iron hill) 2½ miles; Moeyleik (iron mine), this is about the base of the hills from which the road descends, 1½ mile; Hokoung (bazaar) one mile; Noungkan 2 miles; Mansan ½ mile; cross the Namyin river which flows into the Nammow; Natcheen 2¼ miles; Sehfan (town) 4 miles.

ROUTE FROM MUANGWAN TO MUANGMOW.

From Mausey to Petah 3 miles; Leamut 5 miles; Nankhai 4 miles; Kutlung 1½ mile, after crossing the Namwan at the base of the hills; Noungwan 1 mile; in the Muangmow district, Katlung-low (bazaar) 1 mile; Low-peike 2 miles; Hokhai 1 mile; Muangwing, 1½ mile; Fweyhoi 2 miles; Muangmow ½ mile.

ROUTE FROM MUANGWAN TO MUANGTEE.

From Muangwan to Paulin 2 miles; Howan ½ mile; San-pah ½ mile; Payey on hills 1 mile; Shuemuelong 2 miles; Panchan 1 mile; Wanen 2 miles; Hintan 1 mile; Mantong 1 mile; Chouk-toh near the iron bridge in the Nantin valley, on the main road near the Tahô 4 miles; Muangtee 2 miles.

FROM SANDA VALLEY TO SEHFAN.

After crossing the hills to the south of Sanda, Hotha or Muangsa is reached, about 12 miles from Manwyne. Crossing another ridge on the south side of the Hotha valley and going to the south-west for about 17 or 18 miles, Muangwan is reached. South and east from Muangwan is Muangmow, 2 days' journey, each belonging to separate chiefs and in distinct valleys; a ridge of hills having to be crossed to reach the latter. One day's journey east of Muangmow is Sehfan, and north from Sehfan is Muangkwan. Sehfan is a Shan town close to Theinnee and is in possession of the Chinese; one day's journey north of Muangkwan is Languin, a Chinese town in possession of the Panthays; east of this is Kaingma (Shan) under the Panthays; and 7 days to the east of it is Muangmun, a Shan town under the Chinese.

APPENDIX B.

VOCABULARY.

Upwards of two hundred words in five languages.

English.	Kakhyen.	Shan.
One	Langai	Loong
Two	Lakong	Song
Three	Masoum	Sam
Four	Malee	Si
Five	Mangah	Ha
Six	Kroo	Hoak
Seven	Sanet	Saet
Eight	Matsat	Pyet
Nine	Tsikoo	Kow
Ten	Shi	Sheep
Eleven	Shi langai	Sheepate
Twenty	Koon	Sow
Twenty-one	Koonlangai	Sowate
One hundred	Latsa	Packlaing
One thousand	Hainglangai	Hainglaing
I	Ngai	Kow
We	Antaing	Mowshoo
You	Nongtaing	How
He	Torawah	Mung
Of me	Ngaihome	Kowlai
Of us	Antainglo	Howhalai
Of you	Nangtainglo	Mowsoo
Of him	Keyraich	Hongmyoon
Of them	Kangtengraich	Myonhowlai
Above	Lata	Kaneh
Below	Lawoo	Kantow
Far	Nowtsanai	Kaiyow
Near	Aneesharengai	Cowalai
Alone	Nanaisha	Yonlai
Inside	....	....
Behind	....	....
Before	....	....
North	....	Kanen
South	....	Kantow
East	....	Wanoak
West	....	Wantoak
Best	Kajai	Leesabinah
Bad	Inkajah	Yunglee
Worse	....	....
Worst	Toomsa inkajah	Moataykhew
High	Tsawah	Ansoong
Higher	....	Aykhera soongsa
Highest	Lata	....

APPENDIX B.

401

VOCABULARY.

Upwards of two hundred words in five languages.

Hotha Shan.	Leesaw.	Poloung.
Ta	Ti	Lay.
Seuk	Hunit	Eh.
Soom	Sa	Ooay.
Mee	Li	Pone.
Ngwa	Ngaw	Pohn.
Ho	Chaw	Taw.
Huit	Tshe	Ta.
Het	Hay	Poo.
Kaow	Koo	Teen.
Takkhay	Tsi	Kew.
Khayta	Tsili	Kewlay.
Sow	Meetzee	Ehkew.
Sowta	Meetzeeti	Ehkewlay.
Tabae	Teengha	Oobooyaw.
Tahaing	Titoo	Oohaing.
Ngaw	Nga	Ow.
Ngawtookay	Ngaeuh	Nuibey.
Kewtakah	....	Eo.
Mong	....	Peh.
....	....	....
....	....	....
....	....	....
....	....	....
....	....	....
Attaw	Khanashee	Kiggo.
Loongbaw	Meekhya	Kirrei.
Vaylai	Oorah	Loong.
Neenay	Tialah	Puloang.
Notah	Nwaday	Mowloutsay.
Ahhow	Nagwah	Kaffan.
Noongbah	Kanashee	Howlaybonow.
Numram	Jagushee	Howlaiow.
Hobah	Meetloakhew	Keyko.
Oobah	Meegoakhew	Keyroi.
Meetope	Wadashee	Keygo.
Neekconm	Godashee	Makkayroi.
Soobudaykhaybaw	Leosoometsighaw	Tsika.
Makhay	Magee	Putzee.
Highmakhay	....	....
Highmakhayaw	Oumamagee	Putzee.
Mahanglai	Moodah	Ko.
Soobudaymahanglai	Akkeymo	Kokakai.
Soobudayma-hanglaibaw	....	Hoakmureemurra.

APPENDIX B.

VOCABULARY.

English.	Kakhyen.	Shan.
Low	Nemai	Tumalai
False	Nanginasonai	Monlonlai
Fine	Tsomai	Sanay
True	Raiai	Lonlai
Thin	Kasherai	Yongmai
Fat	Kubai	Peach
Thick	Tatday	Lalai
Oily	Toesa	Hackaylai
Pretty	Tsomai	Hanglilai
Ugly	....	....
Beautiful	Tsomai	Hanglilai
Clean	Tsomai	Senshitnai
Dirty	Shoeshakai	Hangwheylai
Dusty	....	....
Cheap	....	Mouwai
Dear	Matzanneh	Paneh
Rich	Soneh	Me-eh
Poor	Matzaneh	Panyou
Old	Toonglasa	Tonalai
Young	Kacheeai	Onyou
Tall	Sawai	Soongai
Little	Indehkacheeai	Onzalai
Small	Kacheecheeai	Onzeesee
Big	Kubai	Yansdai
Tight	Teetai	Kapai
Wide	Koccabai	Quangai
Close	Meesa	Kowai
Painful	Matzeeai	Sipai
Pleasant	....	....
Red	Khrenai	Aneng
Yellow	Somai	Amaing
Green	Chitai	Anhew
Blue	Chitai	Anpyah
Orange	....	....
Black	Changai	Anam
White	Prongai	Angpuck
Hand	Lata	Mew
Foot	Lagong kheytai	Tang
Nose	Indee	Hunglan
Eye	Me	Waydah
Mouth	Incoop	Soap
Tooth	Wa	Shew
Ear	Na	Maylobo
Hair	Karah	Hoonhow
Head	Pong	Ho
Tongue	Shinglet	Lin
Belly	Khan	Tong

APPENDIX B.

VOCABULARY.

Hotha Shan.	Leenaw.	Polonng.
Mahlawhoonlai	Kula	Quoikaroi.
Manbay	Mungaw	Ownow.
Tomelai	Byeedah	Tseah.
Poybaw	Ghoolecaw	Hawhoi.
Hyamlai	Battah	Mangah.
Powlai	Tsuddah	Kalana.
Kanlai	Guadah	Nakakoi.
Kokklai	Khuddah	Kaiaw.
Tomelai	Bheda	Tsi.
....	Mabyee	Putzee.
Tomebaw	Bheda	Tsikaw.
Penbaw	Phaw	Lweehaw.
Tseetbaw	Neemughoondah	Highai.
Soodah	Shenggew	Peevunay.
Polai	Noodah	....
Kolai	Kaddah	Gnaw.
Chodo	Tsobo	....
Panlai	Saddah	Anpan.
Mangah	Tsomaw	Takkaw.
Thoay	Lanew	Taheelay.
Mangbaw	Monkkaw	Onyou-haw.
Asaw	Wablaneu	Konou.
Moonmoonsaw	Rumurraw	Koulay-lay.
Khuybaw	Woodaw	Langhaw.
Shinglai	Tsodah	Pakkaw.
Quanglabaw	Haydaw	Loouhaw.
Naygawabaw	Thyeedaw	Chambaw.
Atoohenlai	Goodoonnuddah	Tocowsayowlow.
Kneelawkaybaw	Tseanaw	Khysnhaw.
Ouaah	Yeenee	Yow.
Aloom	Yeeshee	Eela.
Akkew	Yeneetshee	Eeveng.
Amyauh	Lasay	Lenay.
Aloongasaw	Attew	Quonlaylay.
Annaw	Yeenah	Eewong.
Appew	Yeepoo	Eelooee.
Taw	Lapah	Tai.
Hkay	Khaypah	Ronaw.
Nayhong	Nalibay	Koerookmoo.
Knoydzee	Myetzoo	Nigh.
Myoot	Malay	Moay.
Khowny	Tsitshee	Shang.
Neeshaw	Nahaw	Choak.
Oo	Oochay	Henckhyn.
Owgong	Oolew	Khyn.
Whaw	Latehay	Latah.
Oondow	Hickhay	Vot.

APPENDIX B.

VOCABULARY.

English.	Kakhyen.	Shan.
Rock	Shemah	Lung
Iron	Phee	Lĕh
Gold	Tsa	Hum
Silver	Comprong	Goom
Copper	Makree	Tong
Lead	Masoo	Chun
Tin	Pheyprong	Laypuck
Brass	Makree	Tonglung
Earth	Kah	Lunglean
Father	Kowah	Paw
Mother	Gnoo	Ma
Brother	Apoo	Tsailoong
Sister	Mongsow	Nongsow
Man	Chingpaw	Khoom
Woman	Noom	Pahying
Wife	Mashanoom	Meh
Child	Mang	Laon
Son	Kashah	Look
Daughter	Mawhonkashah	Looksow
Slave	Kashahpyeelai	Loogyonow
Cultivator	Toangnaiai	Toangla
Shepherd	Peinamremai	Sowpalingpeh
Hunter	Mounwhomai	Sowmonso
God	Shingrawah	Sowpara
Devil	Nateabai	Peahighloong
Sun	San	Wan
Moon	Ladah	Lhun
Star	Lagree	Laow
Fire	Wan	Phai
Water	Intzin	Nam
House	Indah	Huln
Horse	Comerang	Mäh
Cow	Toomsoo	Bow
Dog	Quhay	Mah
Cat	Ningyoueh	Myew
Cock	Oorang	Kiephoo
Duck	Oopyaet	Pyet
Ass	......	....
Bird	Nhoopyen	Leak
Mule	Latsayla	Mälaw
Bamboo	Kawah	Myĕh
Stone	Loong	Heen
Elephant	Maguay	Tsang
Buffalo	Ngä	Why
Flea	Wahkaree	Mat
Louse (body)	Sakhep	Mien
Louse (head)	Chee	How

APPENDIX B.
VOCABULARY.

Hotha Shan.	Leesaw.	Poloung.
Wholoong	Kamah	Yahow.
Shan	Hhew	Tsigh.
Say	Keypah	Yoang.
Noway	Poo	Reun.
Toangwah	Gishshee	....
Keway	Tsew	Pachat.
Shanphew	Hoepew	Leckleway.
Tungpur	Yeguw	....
Me	Naybew	Katai.
Apaw	Baba	Koon.
Aggah	Mama	Ma.
Among	Aiyee	Peeow.
Ham	Mala	Peenangow.
Chow	Latehoe	Taee.
Inggnaw	Lamurah	Yeban.
Aymaw	Lameuh	Peeow.
Tsoee	Lanay	Yebanay.
Tanlooalisa	Tsobahla	Eemeilay.
Eengnawsa	Lameangha	Eebanay.
Khyun	Chebah	Myeh.
....	....	....
....	....	....
Muso	....	....
Oorah	Whöo	Chuprah.
Tam	Gnay	Canom.
Poee	Neemee	Lata.
Pulaw	Habackhee	Takkew.
Khew	Coosah	Law.
Pose	Attaw	Nigh.
Tea	Yeghaw	Em.
Een	Ghnee	Krep.
Mang	Amho	Myong.
Nocheanatsaing	Anyemah	Muckamah.
Quhoee	Annah	Sow.
Kollaw	Urrah	Yewh.
Capaw	Urupah	Yeherow.
Pay	Ah	Pyet.
Mahlee	Khyamyeh	Myonglee.
Ghnaw	Nga	Ngow.
Mulaw	Teemee	Tolelaw.
Chewgen	Wahmah	Khyang.
Leekaw	Takhee	Maou.
Khyang	Hamāh	Chang.
Noloway	Annaga	Kha.
Ghlu	Catteuh	Khang.
....	Chinutah	Oo.
....	....	....

APPENDIX B.
VOCABULARY.

English.	Kakhyen.	Shan.
Deer	Po	Pangdai
Goat	Painam	Pay-yah
Sulphur	Khan	Khan
Salt	Tsoom	Khu
Sugar	Tsantang	Khuwan
Milk	Tsoo	Loam
Sheep	....	Toe
Turban	Poonkaw	Khynhoe
Jacket	Polong	Seu
Trousers	Teboo	Pa
Woman's Jacket	Polong	Sou
Woman's Turban	....	Klynhoe
Petticoat	Soomboo	Shin
Shoes	....	Whyepteen
Earring	Lakan	Pehwho
Rice	Shat	How
Opium	Yeepyen	Phey
Serpent	Laboo	Moo
Frog	Sboo	Koap
Grass	Nam	Yah
Tree	Poonsaw	Tonemai
Leaf	Poonlap	Mowmai
Wood	Poon	Mytsing
Fish	Nga	Pa
Cold	Kachee	Kat
Warm	Katetai	Oonai
Ice	Tsin	Ghoulam
Snow	Khen	Lie
Rain	Marangto	Phoontoak
Wind	Umboong	Loom
Thunder	Mahmoomooai	Phasowai
Lightning	Meeprap	Phamypai
Sky	Moo	Bhă
Day	Sheenee	Khangwan
Night	Shenah	Khanghŭm
Light	Shenee	Phalaing
Darkness	Insin	Lapsing
Cloud	Soomoay	Moay
River	Mereeha	Lamkew
Hill	Boom	Loiloo
Insect	....	Pieta
Heart	Mashin	Hosow
Go	Samo	....
Eat	Shamo	....
Sit	Domo	Langda
Come	Wamo	Mada
Beat	Tookmo	Tainda

APPENDIX B.

VOCABULARY.

Hotha Shan.	Leesaw.	Poloung.
Twing	Myloo	Ahjaw.
Pa	Utchee	Meh.
Khanteuk	Khang	Khan.
Khaw	Tsabow	Seh.
Saow	Shantah	Mahmollooay.
Nonow	Atchee	Emboo.
....	Atchunew	Atchaw.
Wootoop	Wootew	Kameh.
Tsay	Bucheu	Kayeup.
Ghiaw	Meckee	....
Eenawtsay	Samen buchee	Kayeup yebaw.
Eenaw ootoop	Samen wootew	Kameh yebaw.
Eenaw tungaw	Meekyee	Kalang yebaw.
Khypteen	Khynee	Khypteen.
Kneechaw	Knockaw	Paywhoo.
Tsen	Dthapoo	Lakow.
Yappingyen	Yappay	Yapping.
Mowee	Who	Hhau.
Paw	Oopah	....
Sieaw	Shi	Mat.
Tsidsaing	Shidzee	Hoi.
Skihow	Tsibeeyah	Phooan.
Shake	Taidzee	Hoi.
Mushaw	Ngwa	Ka.
Kaulai	Gyaddah	Kaw.
Poolai	Tsaddah	Myahcaeeai.
....	....	....
....	....	....
Mowrowbaw	Mahā	Qnoi.
Ghli	Mayhee	Koo.
Mowrow	Mooggoo	Polong.
Shapmyng	Bhyyeh	....
Aunyow	Kneemeetchee	La.
Knee	Myeemalaw	Tsungai.
Tmoot	Yeetah	Keisin.
Mowbowbaw	Kneeowmah	Qneh.
Mowehootbaw	Nayaw	Tsaymawchoak.
Hangeen	Mookoo	Mok.
Kaw	Yeegyah	Emhongfie.
Boom	Kneekee	Panang.
....	Biddee	....
....	See	Hogiow.
....	....	....
Kawda	....	....
Kneeah	....	....
....	La	....
Tayda	....	....

APPENDIX B.
VOCABULARY.

English.	Kakhyen.	Shan.
Stand	Rotmo	Lookda
Lie	Karengmo	Einlengda
Die	Seesa	....
Call	Shegah	Ma
Throw	Shedeng	Tim
Drop	Hatsa	Toak
Place	Sherah	Teayou
Lift	Ta	Yong
Pull	Kung	Teat
Smoke	Loo	Lüt
Love	Nheyrai	Hachlai
Hate	Neimcome	Hhanhan
What is your name?	Nung meing ganging sagaieh.	....
How old is this horse?	Daiee comerang kadeh tinglaeh goon.	....
I do not know	Ngai inchengai	Cow mhahow shay
How far is it to Sanda?	Sanda mying kadeh sanai.	Muang Sanda kai halow.
It is a journey of one day	Intwey langai toosa	Lam wan qua tenglai

APPENDIX B.   409
VOCABULARY.

Hotha Shan.	Leesaw.	Poloung.
Yapda	Hatesa	....
Ayda	Yeeta	Ee.
....	....	....
Lawah	Kooyay	Tayau.
Koondah	Law	Vuneh.
Tahyoudah	Tsayloho yeuk	Oonsayau.
Anhedah	Takyah	....
Koobawdah	Qmw	Tayan.
Shaybawdah	Gho	Tutanlaybeneen.
Gnawshenbawdah	Yehbeckshe	Owkynowkuloak.
Nawnoilawdah	Nguanah	Owingau.
Cachencachaw	Kneemahandau	Owchungkakai.
Nong day pay cainay	....	....
Myang honehyay mang laybounay.	....	....
Ngaw mosa	....	....
Chanda quhonhay wenenay.	....	....
Tanyen samhet tah	....	....

APPENDIX C.

The Stone Implements of Yunan, with a notice of a bronze, axe-like weapon, from the Sanda Valley.

Noticing a stone implement exposed for sale on a stall in the Momien bazar, I purchased it for the equivalent of a few pence. No sooner was my liking for such objects known than I was besieged by needy persons who willingly parted with them for sums varying in value from four to eighteen pence each. After my first investment, specimens to the number of about one hundred and fifty were procured by different members of the Expedition; but all were purchased, none being discovered by any of us. Most were obtained at Momien, and a few in the Sanda valley.

I was informed at Momien that stone implements were not unfrequently turned up in ploughing the fields, and that they occasionally were found lying exposed on the surface soil. The belief prevails that they and also bronze implements are thunderbolts, which after they fall and penetrate the earth take nine years again to find or work their way up to the surface. The man who sold me the bronze weapon stated that it had been a valued possession of his family for some generations, who held the tradition, that it had killed one of three men who happened to be in a field where it fell, and that it was picked up nine years after the event, on the very spot where the man had been struck dead.

The Burmese and the Shans of Burmah also regard stone implements as thunderbolts or *miogyos*, and have the same superstition about their finding their way to the surface of the soil in after years, but consider that in order to ensure it an earthen vessel should be inverted over the spot where the lightning was seen to strike, and the belief that they are thunderbolts is remarkably similar to the idea which prevails among the ignorant peasantry of Europe.

The wonderful resemblance of stone implements to each other from all parts of the world, apparently indicates that such productions of human skill originate in a designing faculty of mind, little if at all removed from instinct, and common to untutored man at some period of his history.

Burmese, Shans, and Chinese alike attribute great medicinal virtues to stone and bronze implements, and some of the latter are so highly prized in Yunan that their weight in gold can alone purchase them. The fresh fractures result from small pieces having been chipped off to be ground down and sold as medicine which commands fabulous prices. Both kinds of implements are also carried about the person as charms, to ward off the evil influences of badly-disposed spirits or *nâts*.

The high estimation in which they are held, both in Yunan and Burmah, suggests the suspicion that the Chinese in former days did not neglect to take advantage of the desire to possess those implements or charms and made a profitable traffic in their manufacture. A consideration of the character of some of the Yunan implements has led me to this conclusion. A considerable percentage of them are small, beautifully-cut forms with few or none of the signs of use that distinguish the large implements from the same localities, and, moreover, all of them are of some variety of jade. These facts taken in conjunction with their elaborate finish, and the circumstance that jade was formerly largely manufactured at Momien into a variety of personal ornaments, are the reasons which have made me doubt the authenticity of many of the small forms, and to regard them only as miniature models of the large and authentic implements, manufactured in recent times as charms to be worn without inconvenience.

Although the implements I now figure and describe represent no more than twenty-three out of the hundred and fifty collected by Major Sladen, Captain Bowers, and myself, still they may be regarded as a typical series, for my two friends considerately allowed me to select from their sets of implements any types not already in my possession.

All the specimens are polished and belong to the neolithic group; but although none of palæolithic age were obtained, it may be that the river gravels which yielded the elephant's molar, of which I had a sight at Manwyne, will yet be found to yield implements of that period. The materials before me, however, establish the Neolithic period and an Age of Bronze.

The implements have been fashioned from the following rocks, *viz.*, quartz, Lydian stone, chert or hornstone, jade, agalmatolite, basalt, greenstone, sandstone, schist, micaceous schist, clayslate, and a brown calcareous shale-like rock.

Plate I, figures 1, 1*a** drawn in half-size, represent the second largest hatchet in the collection, which is distinguished from all the others by

---

* All the figures are of natural size, with the exception of the first 3 on Plate I.

its long, narrow, tapering form and by the convexity of its four surfaces, which make it almost cylindrical. The blunt end is also carefully rounded. Forms closely resembling it have been figured by various authors from Ireland,* the north of Dauphiny† and from Denmark. It appears besides to be a type not uncommon throughout Europe and India. It has been well polished, as can be seen in places where the gloss has not been effaced by the weathering of the compact greenstone of which it is made. Figures 2, 2 a give a half-size view of a flat celt 6' 6'" long, the lateral margins nearly parallel, but converging very slightly to the blunt end, and ground to a flat surface. It is broadest across its hatchet-shaped extremity and is of a nearly uniform thickness, in no place exceeding one inch. It has a very close resemblance to some of the flat-shaped implements of Europe, and weapons of the same type have been found in Burmah, but not so highly finished. Figures 3, 3a represent a weapon of the same type as the former, only it is shorter, broader, and more triangular and has its cutting edge angular at the corners. This implement and the previous one are compact schists, and the latter contains faint traces of mica. They are much more highly finished than the majority of schist implements in Europe, which it is curious to observe are usually of the flattened type with a hatchet edge. Figures 5, 5a illustrate an axe-edged tool, with parallel, faintly bulging, smooth sides, and a rounded, blunt end, flat on one face, but convex on the other. The cutting edge is worn away obliquely on one side. This implement bears the marks of having been well polished.

Plate II, figures 6, 6 a, is a flattened broad axe of Lydian stone, with ground divergent sides, continuous with the cutting edge and blunt end into the latter of which they are rounded off. The next implement, figures 7, 7a, is a small weapon of greyish, black, speckled, weathered jade, of a slightly broader type than figure 2, but only half its size and not exceeding 9'" in thickness. Its cutting edge is worn away on one side. The chisel (figures 8, 8 a) is flat on one face and convex on the other. Its sides are ground flat and are nearly straight and parallel. It is made of a dark slate-coloured greenstone weathered to pale yellowish. It is much chipped and has a fresh fracture at the blunt end, due in all probability to a portion having been broken off for medicinal purposes. Figure 9 of clayslate is a peculiar implement, slightly convex on one aspect and concave on the other, with its edge abruptly bevelled off as a chisel on the latter face. The sides are ground to a flat surface.

---

* Cat of Ant. Royal Irish Acad., p. 41, figure 37.
† Études Palæonthologiques, Chantre, Plate VII, figure 2.

Plate III, figure 10, is one of the most typical chisels in the collection. It is of black basalt, faintly convex on both aspects (10a) and is bevelled off to a cutting edge, with the sides partially flattened. The axe, figures 11, 11a, is a well-formed broadish flattened implement of Lydian stone, and is slightly convex on one side and more so on the other, which is more bevelled than the former, with its sides bulging and nearly equilateral. Figures 12, 12a, represent the most symmetrical of the series and may be described as elongately unguiculate. The two faces are equally convex and the sides are very narrow but blunt, while from the angle of the inferior extremity the cutting edge is carried on to the lower fourth of the sides which taper inwards to the narrow, rounded head of the tool. This beautiful implement is made of grey mottled jade. The next is of dark reddish-brown jade (figures 13, 13a), and is perfectly flat on one side, with its cutting edge ground off like a chisel on the convex side. The chisel (figures 14, 14a) is slightly convex on one side, more so on the other, which is more bevelled than the former. Figures 15, 15a represent a greenish speckled jade short and broad implement, weathered into reddish spots; one aspect is more convex than the other and is abruptly ground to a cutting edge from about its middle. The other side rounds continuously towards the chisel sharpened edge.

Plate IV, figures 16, 16a depict a very rough and seemingly unfinished implement of a highly calcareous, soft, shaly-like rock, of so little consistence that it is difficult to conceive to what practical use it could have been put. One side is slightly convex, but nearly straight, while the other is much divergent, forming an acute angle with the cutting edge. It is convex on one face and flat on the other above the sharpened edge, and the sides are more or less flattened. The small hatchet, figures 17, 17a, is also made of a soft mineral, agalmatolite, and is flat on one face, convex on the other, with rounded sides, divergent at different angles from the head or blunt end. A beautifully formed small jade chisel is represented in figure 18. It has divergent, slightly convex, flattened, ground edges, and an exceedingly narrow flat head. It is the only specimen of its kind, and has a strong resemblance to a chisel figured by Nilsson from Scania.* Figure 19 is a small, slightly elongated, hatchet-edged implement, with much divergent, almost sharp sides, and is fashioned of a dark-bluish jade. The next implement is of a very different type from the preceding one and is allied to figures 16, 16a. It is almost square and only a little longer than broad. Its sides are

* Prim. Inhab. of Scandinavia, Pl. XII. Fig. 161.

unequal, one diverging more than the other and both are ground to a flat surface. One face is not so convex as its fellow and is prolonged to the cutting edge, while the opposite one is more convex and broadly ground off to it. This face also shows, besides the bevelled area, three distinct facets, the result of grinding probably of the stone against another. Figure 21, (21a,) is a small, almost square chisel, but differing from the former in being broader than long. Its sides are symmetrical, ground smooth and divergent more on one side than the other. One face is considerably convex and abruptly bevelled, while the other aspect of the cutting edge is simply continuous with the slight convexity of the face. A very perfect little implement of greenish-tinted jade, the use of which it is difficult to conjecture, if it be authentic, is figured at 22, 22a. Its sides are blunt and unequal, one being more divergent than the other, whilst its chisel edge is well defined. Figured at 23, 23a, is a pure quartz chisel 1" 8''' in length, 7''' in its greatest breadth, and of almost uniform width throughout, its upper end being a little less broad than the cutting edge. The rounded sides are very slightly convex and faintly convergent towards either extremity. Chisels of this form have been found in Europe, but none, so far as I am aware, of so small a size. The remarkable shaped implement of rich green jade, figured at 24, 24a, is flat on one face and convex on the other, with rounded edges which are bulging in the lower two-thirds and concave in the upper third. It seems to have been formed from a jade pebble, and the shape probably follows the original form of the stone.

I have figured at Plate I, figures 4, 4a, an implement from the Mishmi Hills to the north-east of Suddyah, Assam. It was picked up in that locality by Captain Gregory. In type it approaches figure 10, differing however from that specimen in the greater convexity of one of its faces, which is continuous with the cutting edge, whereas its other face is almost flat and bevelled at its extremity. Its sides are divergent, almost sharp, but more or less rounded. It is figured of the natural size and is a hard, greenish-grey, schistose rock.

Bronze weapon from the Sanda Valley, Yunan.

The bronze implement, Plate V, that I was fortunate enough to secure at Manwyne for the equivalent of £2-10, and of which three other specimens—its exact fellows—were shown me, but for which as much as £5 each was asked, belongs to the socketed type of celt without wings. In its greatest length it is 4½ inches, and the curve of its cutting edge is 4 inches. The thin flattened cutting surface or body of the celt is set on at an acute angle to the socket. The latter portion contracts towards the blade, and then expands to meet it. Its greatest external thickness is not more than 8''', but where it joins the blade it is only 5''' thick. The length and outline of the socket into which in all probability a curved wooden handle was lodged, is shown by the dotted lines in the figure, extending to within 1" 2''' of the cutting edge. At the base of the socket, the blade is 3''' in thickness, but half-way between this and the cutting edge it is only 2'''. The socket at its orifice is 1" 7''' in length and its walls are little more than 1''' in thickness, and the cavity first contracts and then expands towards its base. The most striking feature of this instrument is the forked process on its upper side, half-way between the cutting edge and the orifice of the socket. The two points diverge, the one backwards and the other forwards, and are separated by a curved notch; the one nearer the socket is the more sharply pointed of the two. This appendage projects about 10''' beyond its origin from the body of the weapon. The notch of the inferior end of the cutting edge is another feature peculiar to this bronze weapon, which appears to belong to a type unrepresented in the bronzes of Europe. The forked process and the shallow notch terminating the cutting edge below seem to have been more for ornament than use.

It is certainly remarkable that the composition of this bronze is the same as that which characterises the bronze implements found throughout Northern Europe, the percentage being copper 90, tin 10 = 100.*

There are considerable copper and tin mines in Yunan at the present day, as is shown by the quantities of these metals that are brought by the Chinese caravans to Mandalay.

---

* I am indebted to Dr. Oldham for this analysis.

APPENDIX D.

Bhamô, Tamalone and Tsitkaw, February 1868.

			THERMOMETERS.					
			Dry Bulb.			Wet Bulb.		
Feb.	Maximum.	Minimum.	7 A.M.	4 P.M.	9 P.M.	7 A.M.	4 P.M.	9 P.M.
	Bhamô	Bhamô	Bhamô	Bhamô	Bhamô	Bhamô	Bhamô	Bhamô
1	76·°	51·4	56·4	76·°	58·	56·3	68·3	58·7
2	...	49·	52·5	......	......	51·	......	......
3	82·6	40·	......	74·	64·	......	69·6	65·6
4	84·6	58·	58·	77·	62·	59·	70·	60·
5	74·5	52·	53·	69·	56·	52·5	64·5	56·5
6	78·5	45·	48·	74·	56·	48·	71·5	56·5
7	77·	44·5	46·	76·	56·	45·5	72·3	58·
8	81·	44·5	48·	71·3	60·	48·	70·	59·
9	D 81·4 W 73·5	D 50· W 49·	52·	69·1	63·	52·	65·	61·
10	D 80· W 74·7	D 50·5 W 49·5	57·	71·	66·5	56·5	66·	65·5
11	D 74· W 81·7	D 51· W 50·6	52·5	73·	59·	51·5	63·5	57·5
12	D 81·2 W 74·5	D 47· W 46·5	48·	77·	61·	48·5	69·9	59·5
13	D 82·7 W 76·1	D 48· W 47·	53·5	79·5	66	62·	71·5	63·5
14	D 83·7 W 76·1	D 56·7 W 54·0	58·4	76·	62·	57·	69·3	60·3
15	D 85·7 W 77·5	D 53·8 W 53·2	56·1	74·5	63·3	54·9	69·5	61·5
16	D 84·8 W 77·3	D 55·2 W 54·7	57·	77·9	63·	56·	72·	61·3
17	D 85· W 78·	D 51·6 W 49·8	53·	78·4	62·	52·	69·7	60·
18	D 84·8 W 78·	D 52· W 51·5	57·3	78·3	60·8	55·8	66·7	59·8
19	D 87·3 W 79·3	D 51·2 W 50·	53·2	77·	66·	52·5	72·	63·7
20	D 88·7 W 82·	D 58· W 57·4	60·	81·	67·	59·4	70·	66·
21	D 70·4 W 68·3	D 60·3 W 59·5	63·3	65·8	65·3	62·5	65·5	63·5
22	D 70·4 W 68·4	D 60· W 59·	62·5	75·	66·7	60·9	71·9	65·5
23	D 81·2 W 73·4	D 58·5 W 57·5	61·	78·0	69·	60·	71·6	66·
24	D 73·4 W 68·4	D 58· W 57·4	63·	71·3	66·1	61·5	68·1	65·8
25	D 81· W 75·4	D 6·5 W 60·	62·3	81·	69·7	62·1	74·6	67·9
	Tamalone	Tamalone	Tamalone	Tamalone	Tamalone	Tamalone	Tamalone	Tamalone
26	D 82·8 W 74·4	D 61·7 W 61·	65·	78·2	62·8	64·	70·6	60·9
	Tsitkaw	Tsitkaw	Tsitkaw	Tsitkaw	Tsitkaw	Tsitkaw	Tsitkaw	Tsitkaw
27	D 81· W 71·	D 50·3 W 49·8	53·	78·6	64·6	51·5	67·4	61·5
28	D 79·8 W 71·2	D 50· W 49·	53·5	79·6	65·	52·	69·6	62·
29	D 89·7 W 71·5	D 55· W 53·7	57·	......	65·5	56·	......	63·4

APPENDIX D. 417

Bhamô, Tamatone and Tsitkaw, February 1868.

Feb.	Aneroid Barometer with attached Thermometer.			Wind.					
				7 A.M.		4 P.M.		9 P.M.	
	7 A.M.	4 P.M.	9 P.M.	Lower.	Upper.	Lower.	Upper.	Lower.	Upper.
	Bhamô	Bhamô	Bhamô	Bhamô	Bhamô	Bhamô	Bhamô	Bhamô	Bhamô
1	Th. 51 B. 29·62	89 29·65	55 29·63	S.W.	O.*	S.W.	O.	S.W.	O.
2	Th. 50 B. 29·66	... ...	... ...	S.W.	.....	S.W.	.....	S.W.	.....
3	Th. ... B. ...	70 29·64	61 29·68	.....	O.	Calm.	S.W.	Calm.	O.
4	Th. 55 B. 29·60	71 29·58	59 29·60	S.W.	S.W.	S.W.	O.	N.W.	S.W.
5	Th. 50 B. 29·62	67 29·66	54 29·66	Calm.	O.	Calm.	O.	Calm.	.....
6	Th. 46 B. 29·62	69 29·62	51 29·64	Calm.	O.	N.W.	O.	Calm.	O.
7	Th. 43 B. 29·67	71 29·70	52 29·68	S.W.	S.W.	S.W.	S.W.	S.W.	S.W.
8	Th. 45 B. 29·72	47 29·70	57 29·73	Calm.	O.	Calm.	O.	Calm.	O.
9	Th. 49 B. 29·71	63 29·70	59 29·74	Calm.	O.	N.N.W.	.....	N.N.W.	.....
10	Th. 53 B. 29·72	67 29·70	63 29·72	Calm.	O.	Calm.	O.	Calm.	O.
11	Th. 49 B. 29·70	69 29·70	55 29·67	Calm.	O.	Calm.	O.	Calm.	O.
12	Th. 44 B. 29·65	73 29·67	58 29·69	S.S.W.	O.	Calm.	O.	Calm.	O.
13	Th. 59 B. 29·65	75 29·64	64 29·71	N.W.	S.S.W.	Calm.	S.W.	Calm.	O.
14	Th. 56 B. 29·77	72 29·75	58 29·78	Calm.	N.N.W.	N.N.W.	N.W.	Calm.	O.
15	Th. 53 B. 29·79	70 29·76	61 29·78	N.E.	S.W.	N.N.E.	N.N.E.	N.N.E.	O.
16	Th. 54 B. 29·78	73 29·73	59 29·72	Calm.	S.W.	N.N.E.	O.	N.E.	O.
17	Th. 51 B. 29·70	75 29·64	59 29·67	N.E.	S.S.W.	N.N.E.	O.	N.N.E.	O.
18	Th. 53 B. 29·67	74 29·64	57 29·67	N.E.	S.W.	N.E.	O.	N.E.	O.
19	Th. 50 B. 29·66	73 29·59	62 29·66	N.E.	W.	S.W.	S.W.	S.W.	S.W.
20	Th. 57 B. 29·60	77 29·57	64 29·67	N.E.	S.W.	N.W.	S.W.	N.W.	S.W.
21	Th. 59 B. 29·69	61 29·67	61 29·70	N.E.	S.W.	N.E.	S.W.	N.E.	S.W.
22	Th. 59 B. 29·73	71 29·71	62 29·72	N.E.	S.W.	N.E.	O.	Calm.	O.
23	Th. 58 B. 29·65	74 29·60	64 29·61						
24	Th. 60 B. 29·53	68 29·47	62 29·53	N.E.	W.	N.E.	.....	N.E.	.....
25	Th. 58 B. 29·50	78 29·49	64 29·52	Calm.	W.	Calm.	W.	Calm.	.....
	Tamatone	Tamatone	Tamatone	Tamatone	Tamatone	Tamatone	Tamatone	Tamatone	Tamatone
26	Th. 60 B. 29·55	74 29·52	59 29·62	N.	.....	N.	O.	N.	O.
	Tsitkaw	Tsitkaw	Tsitkaw	Tsitkaw	Tsitkaw	Tsitkaw	Tsitkaw	Tsitkaw	Tsitkaw
27	Th. 50 B. 29·62	74 29·52	61 29·62	N.	O.	N.	O.	N.	W.
28	Th. 50 B. 29·62	74 29·51	61 29·53	N.	O.	N.	N.N.	N.W.	
29	Th. 53 B. 29·52	62 ...	62 29·53	N.W.	N.W.				

* O. signifies that no upper current was observable.

418   APPENDIX D.

Tsitkaw, Ponline, Lakong and Ponsee, Kakhyen mountains, March 1868.

March	\multicolumn{2}{c}{}	THERMOMETERS.					
	Minimum.	Maximum.	Dry Bulb.			Wet Bulb.		
			7 A.M.	4 P.M.	9 P.M.	7 A.M.	4 P.M.	9 P.M.
	Tsitkaw	Tsitkaw	Tsitkaw	Tsitkaw	Tsitkaw	Tsitkaw	Tsitkaw	Tsitkaw
1	D 79·7 W 73·7	D 58 W 57	60·5	79·5 on the march.		60·5	73·4	65·
2	D W	D 60·5 W 59·8	64·3			63·		
	Ponline	Ponline	Ponline	Ponline	Ponline	Ponline	Ponline	Ponline
3	D 81·8 W 71	D 58 W 53	64·8	71·7	67·	59·	69·3	64·
4	D 79·6 W 72	D 57·8 W 55·4	63·	77·4	68·	59·5	70·5	64·
	Lakong	Lakong	Lakong	Lakong	Lakong	Lakong	Lakong	Lakong
5	D 83·4 W 75	D 60 W 57	62·	78·6	68·	58·5	71·8	63·8
	Ponsee	Ponsee	Ponsee	Ponsee	Ponsee	Ponsee	Ponsee	Ponsee
6	D 80·6 W 72·3	D 56·3 W 54·4	59·	72·3	64·	56·	68·2	56·3
7	D 69· W 64·5	D 57·5 W 53·	56·	69·	60·	59·8	64·4	57·
8	D 63·2 W 59·8	D 52·5 W 52·5	53·2	59·8	53·	53·2	58·3	52·3
9	D 66·2 W 64·	D 47· W 46·5	58·	61·3	50·2	55·5	59·	49·
10	D 77·4 W 69·3	D 45·4 W 44·	53·	67·3	51·2	51·	62·	52·
11	D 77·4 W 69·4	D 48·5 W 46·2	57·7	71·3	58·7	53·2	64·9	57·
12	D 73·8 W 81·4	D 49·5 W 50·	55·8	71·	53·	53·8	64·1	51·2
13	D 71·3 W 80·3	D 47·2 W 48·3	53·	70·	55·	50·	64·	53·2
14	D 76·3 W 83·	D 48·5 W 49·	55·8	67·	55·	53·	65·	54·
15	D 75·3 W 81·8	D 48·4 W 49·6	57·7	66·	58·	54·8	66·8	55·7
16	D 78·4 W 87·8	D 51·4 W 52·8	62·	70·	58·	57·8	69·3	56·5
17	D 78· W 87·4	D 54· W 52·5	59·7	76·	59·	56·8	70·	57·
18	D 78· W 88·	D 55· W 50·3	60·	70·3	58·	54·3	68·7	56·
19	D 78·2 W 87·8	D 53·5 W 51·7	62·	74·1	58·	59·3	68·2	57·
20	D 77· W 86·3	D 53· W 51·4	62·4	71·8	55·6	59·8	65·2	54·
21	D 77· W 82	D 51·5 W 49·8	57·	78·5	57·3	53·5	71·5	57·
22	D 75· W 86·4	D 51·3 W 49·5	53·2	78·	65·	52·	71·	53·
23	D 79·3 W 88·2	D 52· W 49·3	60·	72·	59·	55·5	70·	56·1
24	D 85· W 87·	D 54·8 W 52·5	62·5	73·4	59·	60·	69·4	57·
25	D 85· W 87·	D 56·3 W 52·4	65·	80·3	57·	58·	73·	55·
26	D 68· W 80·	D 53·4 W 50·	63·	88·	60·	56·	77·8	56·4
27	D 71· W 79·	D 56·3 W 53·	72·	76·3	60·8	62·	67·8	58·
28	D 79·3 W 79·	D 58·5 W 54·5	63·	72·	59·	59·5	67·	56·
29	D 75·4 W 87·4	D 54· W 53·	60·5	76·4	57·	62·8	68·	55·
30	D 84· W 85·	D 53·9 W 51·	65·2	73·4	60·8	60·	69·4	59·
31	D 74·3 W 84·8	D 56· W 54·4	71·2	75·3	69.	66·5	69·	62·8

APPENDIX D.   419

Tsitkaw, Ponline, Lakong and Ponsee, Kakhyen mountains, March 1868.

March	ANEROID BAROMETER WITH ATTACHED THERMOMETER.			WIND.					
				7 A.M.		4 P.M.		9 P.M.	
	7 A.M.	4 P.M.	9 P.M.	Lower.	Upper.	Lower.	Upper.	Lower.	Upper.
	Tsitkaw	Tsitkaw	Tsitkaw	Tsitkaw	Tsitkaw	Tsitkaw	Tsitkaw	Tsitkaw	Tsitkaw
1	Th. 58 B. 29·53	66 29·50	68 ...	N.W.	S.W.	S.W. on the march	West	Calm	O.
2	Th. 58 B. 29·62	on the "	march "	S.W.	S.W.				
	Ponline	Ponline	Ponline	Ponline	Ponline	Ponline	Ponline	Ponline	Ponline
3	Th. 59 B. 27·42	65 27·41	58 27·42	S.S.E.	S.E.	S.S.E.	Clear	S.S.E.	O.
4	Th. 59 B. 27·39	66 27·38	60 27·39	S.S.E.	O.	S.S.W.	S.S.W.	S.S.W.	O.
	Lakong	Lakong	Lakong	Lakong	Lakong	Lakong	Lakong	Lakong	Lakong
5	Th. 58 B. 27·32	67 27·46	60 27·46	E.N.E.	S.W.	S.S.E.	S.W.	Calm	O.
	Ponsee	Ponsee	Ponsee	Ponsee	Ponsee	Ponsee	Ponsee	Ponsee	Ponsee
6	Th. 55 B. 27·46	66 26·74	60 26·77	E.S.E.	O.	S.W.	S.W.	S.W.	S.W.
7	Th. 54 B. 26·72	67 26·63	58 26·64	S.W.	S.W.	S.S.W.	S.S.W.	S.S.W.	S.S.W.
8	Th. 50 B. 26·68	58·2 6·65	50 26·70	S.S.W.	O.	S.S.W.	S.S.W.	N.	O.
9	Th. 56 B. 26·78	59 26·76	49 26·79	S.W.	O.	S.W.	Clear	N.	O.
10	Th. 50 B. 26·81	64 26·76	59 26·74	S.E.	O.	S.E.	S.W.	N.	S.W.
11	Th. 55 B. 26·74	68 26·70	55 26·71	N.W.	S.W.	W.	S.W.	N.W.	S.W.
12	Th. 53 B. 26·79	67 26·77	50 26·78	N.	O.	S.W.	S.S.W.	N.	O.
13	Th. 59 B. 26·70	68 26·73	53 26·75	N.	O.	W.S.W.	W.S.W.	N.	O.
14	Th. 53 B. 26·73	65 26·72	52 26·73	S.E.	O.	S.W.	Clear	N.	O.
15	Th. 55 B. 26·75	65 26·74	54 26·76	E.	O.	S.W.	Clear	N.	O.
16	Th. 60 B. 26·79	69 26·77	56 26·79	E.	S.W.	E.	W.	N.	O.
17	Th. 55 B. 26·80	66 29·78	54 26·78	E.	S.W.	N.W.	W.	N.W.	O.
18	Th. 55 B. 26·76	65 26·74	54 26·72	N.	N.W.	W.S.W.	W.S.W.	N.	O.
19	Th. 57 B. 26·69	68 26·66	53 26·68	W.S.W.	O.	S.W.	S.W.	N.	O.
20	Th. 57 B. 26·71	66 26·73	50 26·74	E.	O.	S.E.	N.N.W.	N.	O.
21	Th. 53 B. 26·76	69 26·76	54 26·80	N.E.	O.	E.	O.	N.W.	O.
22	Th. 59 B. 26·79	68 26·74	60 26·74	E.	S.W.	S.W.	S.W.	N.	O.
23	Th. 55 B. 26·73	64 26·70	54 26·70	E.	O.	S.W.	O.	N.	O.
24	Th. 57 B. 26·72	69 26·70	55 26·71	E.	O.	S.W.	S.W.	N.	O.
25	Th. 57 B. 26·77	70 26·74	53 26·75	N.E.	O.	S.	O.	N.	O.
26	Th. 56 B. 26·75	69 26·72	55 26·73	E.	O.	S.W.	S.W.	N.	O.
27	Th. 57 B. 26·73	68 26·69	56 26·70	N.E.	S.W.	S.W.	S.W.	N.	O.
28	Th. 58 B. 26·70	67 26·68	53 26·70	S.W.	S.W.	S.W.	S.W.	N.	O.
29	Th. 56 B. 26·74	66 26·73	54 26·75	N.	O.	S.W.	S.W.	N.	O.
30	Th. 55·2 B. 26·75	66 26·71	60·6 26·73	N.E.	S.W.	S.W.	S.W.	S.W.	O.
31	Th. 59 B. 26·75	68 26·74	61·4 26·76	...	...	...	...	N.E.	

420   APPENDIX D.

Ponsee, April, 1868.

April	Maximum	Minimum	Dry Bulb 7 A.M.	Dry Bulb 4 P.M.	Dry Bulb 9 P.M.	Wet Bulb 7 A.M.	Wet Bulb 4 P.M.	Wet Bulb 9 P.M.
1	D 78· D 57·5	W 69·4 W 55·	59·	72·	61·	57·5	67·	59·
2	D 81·2 D 73·2	W 70·5 W 66·	73·2	71·	62·5	66·	65·	59·6
3	D 84· D 57·	W 73· W 54·	66·	81·	61·	61·2	70·	58·5
4	D 86· D 57·	W 73·8 W 54·	68·	81·	60·	65·	69·5	57·
5	D 88·4 D 57·	W 75·5 W 53·3	62·3	75·4	63·	57·5	69·5	60·5
6	D 80· D 55·1	W 71· W 54·5	59·	68·5	60·5	58·	69·	58·
7	D 79·7 D 52·4	W 71·5 W 51·5	60·	74·	55·3	58·5	67·5	54·5
8	D 83·8 D 52·7	W 73· W 51·	56·	81·	61·5	53·5	69·	60·
9	D 80· D 50·	W 80· W 54·	61·	84·	63·	59·	74·	61·
10	D 91· D 57·8	W 79·7 W 57·	67·	75·	66·	62·8	71·	64·
11	D 79· D 61·	W 69·8 W 59·5	65·3	67·5	62·	63·	65·	60·
12	D 84·7 D 77·	W 58· W 57·5	63·	78·8	64·	60·8	73·	61·
13	D 76· D 59·5	W 69·8 W 58·5	61·	73·	61·	60·	66·	58·5
14	D 75·5 D 57·5	W 72· W 56·4	62·	71·	66·	58·5	66·	61·
15	D 73· D 56·4	W 68·8 W 54·	64·	66·4	58·	59·4	64·5	58·
16	D 81· D 53·	W 78· W 53·4	61·3	73·	60·8	59·4	69·	60·
17	D 86· D 58·4	W 78·7 W 57·8	69·	78·7	62·8	64·4	73·4	62·
18	D 82·4 D 58·	W 75·6 W 57·5	65·8	76·	63·	63·	72·4	61·
19	D 84·8 D 60·	W 75·8 W 58·8	68·4	77·2	63·	64·4	71·3	62·
20	D 85·5 D 61·3	W 72·5 W 60·	69·5	78·7	64·	65·4	72·5	62·8
21	D 88· D 60·5	W 76· W 60·	68·	84·8	69·	64·5	74·8	66·
22	D 82·5 D 60·3	W 79·5 W 57·5	73·8	82·5	67·2	70·4	79·5	64·
23	D 87·8 D 59·2	W 87·8 W 59·	65·5	78·8	59·	64·	72·4	59·
24	D 84·3 D 55·	W 77· W 57·5	61·	78·	60·	60·5	75·	59·
25	D 80·4 D 56·	W 72·3 W 51·5	64·5	67·4	58·	63·	62·	57·
26	D 78·4 D 54·2	W 72·3 W 54·4	66·	67·	60·	76·3	64·5	59·
27	D 82·3 D 55·	W 71·4 W 54·5	62·	73·7	59·5	60·5	73·	58·
28	D 84·3 D 57·3	W 76· W 56·5	65·	71·2	63·5	61·8	71·5	62·
29	D 84·5 D 59·	W 77·2 W 58·	63·5	74·5	64·	63·	71·	62·7
30	D 87·2 D 62·5	W 79·5 W 61·5	69·	80·	64·	66·6	72·	63·5

APPENDIX D.

Ponsee, April, 1868.

April	Aneroid Barometer with attached thermometer.			Wind.					
				7 A.M.		4 P.M.		9 P.M.	
	7 A.M.	4 P.M.	9 P.M.	Lower.	Upper.	Lower.	Upper.	Lower.	Upper.
1	Th. 58° B. 26·78	64° 26·77	58° 26·79	N. E.	S. W.	S. W.	S. W.	North.	S. W.
2	Th. 58° B. 26·80	68° 26·71	60° 26·75	N. E.	O.	S.	S. W.	N. W.	S. W.
3	Th. 59° B. 26·74	68° 26·70	68° 26·72	S. W.	O.	S. W.	O.	N.	O.
4	Th. 59° B. 26·74	67° 26·73	58° 26·74	N. W.	S. W.	S.S.W.	S. W.	N.	O.
5	Th. 57° B. 26·78	65° 26·74	60·4 26·76	E.	S. W.	Calm.	S. W.	N. W	S. W.
6	Th. 57° B. 26·80	62° 26·75	58° 26·78	N. E.	S. W.	S. W.	S. W.	N. W.	N. W.
7	Th. 55° B. 26·74	66° 26·70	54° 26·74	N.N.E.	S. W.	S.	S. W.	N.	O.
8	Th. 54° B. 26·70	68° 26·69	60° 26·72	N. E.	S. W.	S. W.	S. W.	Calm.	S. W.
9	Th. 57° B. 26·69	66° 26·66	60° 26·68	N. E.	S. W.	S. W.	S. W.	N.	S W
10	Th. 58° B. 26·69	68° 26·66	61° 26·71	N. E.	S W.	N. E.	S. W.	Calm.	O.
11	Th. 61° B. 26·72	62° 26·68	58° 26·70	N. E.	S. W.	N. E.	S. W.	N.	O.
12	Th. 58° B. 26·67	74° 26·62	60° 26·64	N. E.	S. W.	S. W.	S. W.	N.	O.
13	Th. 57° B. 26·68	62° 26·66	58° 26·70	N. E.	S. W.	S. W.	S W	N.	O.
14	Th. 56° B. 26·71	65° 26·69	60° 26·70	N. E.	S. W.	N. E.	S. W.	N.	S. W.
15	Th. 57° B. 26·75	60° 26·71	56° 26·73	N E	S. W.	S. W.	S. W.	N.	S. W.
16	Th. 58° B. 26·72	68·4 26·68	57° 26·68	N. E.	O.	S. W.	S. W.	Calm	O.
17	Th. 59·4 B. 26·71	68° 26·68	60° 26·70	N. E.	S. W.	S. W.	S. W.	N.	S. W
18	Th. 61° B. 26·70	66° 26·65	61° 26·67	N. E	S. W.	S. W.	S. W.	N.	O.
19	Th. 58° B. 26·70	66° 26·65	60° 26·67	N. E.	S. W.	S. W.	S. W.	N.	S. W.
20	Th. 60° B. 26·65	69° 26·62	61° 26·63	N. E.	S. W.	S. W.	S. W.	Calm.	O.
21	Th. 61·4 B. 26·63	70° 26·58	64° 26·59	W.	S. W.	S. W.	S. W.	N.	O.
22	Th. 62° B. 26·61	70° 26·60	62° 26·60	Calm.	S. W.	S. W.	S. W.	N.	S. W.
23	Th. 68° B. 26·72	68° 26·64	57·4 26·70	N. E.	S. W.	N. E.	S. W.	N	O.
24	Th. 57° B. 26·70	66° 26·70	57° 26·68	N. E.	S. W.	S. E.	S. W.	N.	O.
25	Th. 58° B. 26·69	60° 26·68	57° 26·69	N. E.	S. W.	N. E.	S. W.	N. E.	O.
26	Th. 58° B. 26·68	62° 26·63	60° 26·66	S. W.	S. W.	S. W.	S. W.	N.	S. W.
27	Th. 58° B. 26·68	74° 26·62	58° 26·64	N. E.	S. W.	S. W.	S. W.	N.	S. W.
28	Th. 59° B. 26·64	65° 26·58	61° 26·61	N. E.	S. W.	S. W.	S. W.	N.	S. W.
29	Th. 60° B. 26·63	66° 26·62	62° 26·64	N. E.	S. W.	E.	S. W.	N.	S. W.
30	Th. 62° B. 26·66	72° 26·65	63° 26·67	Calm.	S. W.	S. W.	S. W.	N. E.	O

APPENDIX D.

Ponsee, Sanda, Muangla, Nantin and Momien, May, 1868.

May.	\multicolumn{7}{c	}{THERMOMETERS.}
	Maximum.	Minimum.	Dry Bulb.			Wet Bulb.		
			7 A.M.	4 P.M.	9 P.M.	7 A.M.	4 P.M.	9 P.M.
1	D 87·5 / W 84·8	D 61·8 / W 61·	67·	87·5	64·5	65·	71·	62·
2	D 88·3 / W 84·4	D 62·4 / W 60·8	70·	86·5	64·5	67·	73·	64·
3	D 85·8 / W 81·5	D 62·5 / W 56·3	67·3	86·7	66·	61·3	74·	63·
4	D 84· / W 81·	D 62·5 / W 57·4	72·	85·5	64·	63·5	72·5	61·
5	D 85·2 / W 80·	D 62· / W 57·	66·1	81·7	64·9	60·1	73·5	63.
6	D 84· / W 79·	D 61·5 / W 58·	68·	82·5	60·3	61·5	73·5	59·5
7	D 80·4 / W 73·7	D 60·5 / W 59·	64·5	80·	65·5	62·7	74·	64·
8	D 81·7 / W 76·	D 55·5 / W 55·	60·5	81·3	60·	60·	70·	58·3
9	D 86· / W 76·8	D 59·5 / W 57·5	65·3	64·	62·	61·4	63·	61·
	Sanda	Sanda	Sanda	Sanda	Sanda	Sanda	Sanda	Sanda
15	D 80·5 / W 79·	D 59·5 / W 57·5	69·	70·	66·	63.	70·	63·
	Muangla	Muangla	Muangla	Muangla	Muangla 71·3	Muangla	Muangla	Muangla 65·5
17	D 94· / W 83·	D 63·5 / W 57·8	68·9	......	72·5	60·4	......	66·5
18	D 83· / W 75·2	D 68·5 / W 62·8	73·	70·5	68·	65·2	68·	64·
19	D 81·8 / W 75·	D 64·5 / W 63·8	67·2	77·6	71·	66·	70·	63·
20	D 81·5 / W 78·5	D 66·5 / W 64·2	69·5	78·7	70·	66·6	69·5	66·5
21	D 89·5 / W 80·5	D 63·7 / W 62·	67·5	82·5	71·	64·5	71·5	66·5
22	D 78· / W 75·3	D 65·6 / W 63·1	69·	74·	70·5	65·5	70·5	68·
	Nantin	Nantin	Nantin	Nantin	Nantin	Nantin	Nantin	Nantin
23	D / W	D 65·8 / W 64·5	66·8	0·	73·	64·9	......	69·
24	D 80·2 / W 66·7	D 63·6 / W 61·8	67·	79·7	69·5	64·	71·7	65·7
25	D 88·7 / W 78·7	D 64·5 / W 63·	70·	81·5	73·	66·4	73·	61·2
26	D / W	D 63· / W 63·	64·8	......	......	62·	......	......
	Momien	Momien	Momien	Momien	Momien	Momien	Momien	Momien
27	D 80· / W 71·4	·....	72·5	60·3	......	66·5	64·	......
28	D 87· / W 76·4	61·5 / 69·	68·	79·5	66·4	64·	69·	63·5
29	D 67· / W 61·2	D 61·4 / W 59·5	62·	61·5	58·5	61·5	57·	55·
30	D 76· / W 71·	D 55·5 / W 53·	58·7	74·	65·	57·	60·9	62·
31	D 79· / W 70·6	D 59·7 / W 58·2	61·5	out	64·4	60·	out	63·5

APPENDIX D.

Ponsee, Sanda, Muangla, Nantin and Momien, May 1868.

May	Aneroid Barometer with Attached Thermometer.			WIND.					
				7 A.M.		4 P.M.		9 P.M.	
	7 A.M.	4 P.M.	9 P.M.	Lower.	Upper.	Lower.	Upper.	Lower.	Upper.
1	Th. 62 B. 26·68	79 26·70	63 26·69	N.E.	S.W.	S.W.	S.W.	N.	O.
2	Th. 62 B. 26·72	78 26·72	63 26·71	S.W.	S.W.	S.W.	S.W.	N.	O.
3	Th. 60 B. 26·74	... 26·73	... 26·70	N.E.	O.	S.W.	O.	N.	O.
4	Th. 63 B. 26·76	78 26·72	61 26·71	N.E.	O.	S.W.	O.	N.	O.
5	Th. 61 B. 26·72	67 26·68	63 26·67	E.	O.	S.W.	O.	N.	O.
6	Th. 61 B. 26·68	70 26·63	61 26·68	E.	S.W.	S.W.	S.W.	N.	O.
7	Th. 60·5 B. 26·67	70 26·62	62 26·60	N.W.	S.W.	N.W.	S.W.	N.W.	S.W.
8	Th. 60 B. 26·72	74 26·70	60 26·68	S.W.	S.W.	S.W.	S.W.	N.	S.W.
9	Th. 60 B. 26·74	62 26·71	60 26·70	N.E.	S.W.	S.W.	S.W.	N.	S.W.
	Sanda	Sanda	Sanda	Sanda	Sanda	Sanda	Sanda	Sanda	Sanda
14	....	... ...	69 27·32	......	......	......	N.E.	S.W.	
15	Th. 62·4 B. 27·34	70 27·35	67· 27·36	S.W.	S.W.	S.W.	S.W.	Calm	O.
	Muangla	Muangla	Muangla	Muangla	Muangla	Muangla	Muangla	Muangla	Muangla
17	Th. 64 B. 27·38	... ...	73 27·31	S.W.	S.W.	S.W.	O.	O.	O.
18	Th. 67 B. 27·38	71 27·32	67 27·34	N.E.	S.W.	N.E.	S.W.	N.E.	S.W.
19	Th. 64 B. 27·32	76·7 27·27	68 27·31	N.E.	S.W.	S.S.W.	S.W.	O.	S.W.
20	Th. 64 B. 27·28	71 27·23	68 27·26	Calm	S.W.	S.W.	S.W.	O.	O.
21	Th. 64 B. 27·26	72 27·19	68 27·22	Calm	S.W.	S.W.	S.W.	Calm	O.
22	Th. 65 B. 27·24	70 27·20	70 27·25	Calm	S.W.	N.W.	S.W.	N.	O.
	Nantin	Nantin	Nantin	Nantin	Nantin	Nantin	Nantin	Nantin	Nantin
23	Th. 64 B. 27·22	... ...	71 26·64	Calm	O.	......	......	......	O.
24	Th. 69 B. 26·75	74 26·67	70 26·62	Calm	O.	S.W.	S.W.	N.	O.
25	Th. 66 B. 26·65	70 26·56	72 26·64	S.W.	S.W.	S.W.	S.W.	S.W.	O.
26	Th. 64 B. 26·66	... ...	... ...	S.W.	O.	......	......	......	O.
	Momien	Momien	Momien	Momien	Momien	Momien	Momien	Momien	Momien
27	B. Th.	78 25·12	64 25·15	......	S.W.	S.W.	S.W.	S.W.	S.W.
28	Th. 63 B. 25·16	78 25·12	65 25·15	Calm	O.	S.E.	S.W.	S.W.	O.
29	Th. 62 B. 25·13	62 25·09	60 25·08	S.W.	S.W.	S.W.	O.	S.W.	S.W.
30	Th. 59 B. 25·05	66 25·08	64 25·04	Calm	O.	S.W.	S.W.	O.	O.
31	Th. 61 B. 25·07	... ...	64 25·12	S.W.	S.W.	......	......	S.W.	S.W.

APPENDIX D.

Momien, June, 1868.

June	THERMOMETERS.							
	Maximum.	Minimum.	Dry Bulb.			Wet Bulb.		
			7 A.M.	4 P.M.	9 P.M.	7 A.M.	4 P.M.	9 P.M.
1	D W	D 55·3 W 54·	59·5	...	...	54·7	...	...
2	D 76 W 70	D 51 W 51·4	52·4	73	63·	52·4	63·6	60·5
3	D 80·3 W 73·3	D 50·5 W 58	62·2	76·5	69	60·5	71·3	65·5
4	D 73·8 W 70·3	D 58 W 58	62·	68·3	...	68·3	65·5	...
5	D 80·2 W 74·	...	...	73·5	65·4	...	68	63·8
6	D 78· W 71·8	D 58·3 W 57·5	63	72·5	63	61·5	68	61
7	D 72· W 66·	D 61·3 W 60	65·5	69·5	64·6	63·5	66	64
8	D 73· W 60·8	D 62·7 W 62·4	62·8	64·7	64·5	62·5	62·5	64·5
9	D 73·8 W 71·2	D 62·5 W 62·5	63·1	70·8	66	63·1	68·	64·5
10	D 72 W 70	D 63·5 W 63·	64·5	67·2	63·5	64	66	63
11	D 70·8 W 69·	D 62·5 W 62·5	64	69·3	65	64	68	64
12	D 71·4 W 69·5	D 63·5 W 63	65·2	68	65·5	64·5	66·7	64·8
13	D 70 W 68	D 64 W 63·8	65	68	65·5	64·3	66·7	64·5
14	D 70 W 68·8	D 63·7 W 63·2	65	67·2	65	64·5	66·6	64·5
15	D 71·3 W 69·3	D 63·5 W 63·	65·5	67·4	65·7	65·2	66	65
16	D 71·3 W 69·2	D 64·7 W 64·3	65	69	65·5	64·8	68	64·7
17	D 73·0 W 71·	D 64·5 W 64·5	64·8	70	67·5	63·7	68·6	66·9
18	D 76 W 73	D 65·6 W 65	66·3	76·5	68·5	65·7	70·7	67·3
19	D 76·2 W 73·	D 66·5 W 65·6	68	73·3	68·3	67·5	70·7	67·5
20	D 77·5 W 73·3	D 66 W 65·5	67·5	72·5	68	66·8	69·7	67
21	D 76 W 72·3	D 64·5 W 64·5	67·4	72·5	67	66	69·7	66
22	D 77 W 73·3	D 65 W 64·5	68	74·5	68	66·5	71	66·5
23	D 79 W 74	D 65 W 64·	65	71·7	68·5	64	68·7	66·8
24	D 81 W 76·5	D 65 W 62·8	66	76·5	69·8	65	72·5	68
25	D 77·6 W 74·	D 67·5 W 66·3	69	75	69·4	67·4	71·5	67·5
26	D 76·7 W 72·8	D 66·5 W 65·4	68·4	75·8	69·2	67·4	71·8	68
27	D 78·7 W 74·7	D 66·5 W 65·5	67·5	74·7	69·5	66·5	70·2	68
28	D 75 W 72·3	D 66·4 W 65·5	67·9	72	66·8	66·8	69	65·5
29	D 75·4 W 72	D 66 W 65	66	67·4	67	65	66	65·5
30	D 72·3 W 69·2	D 61·5 W 61·	62·5	68	66·5	61	65·5	61·

APPENDIX D.

Momien, June, 1868.

June	Aneroid Barometer with attached Thermometer.			WIND.					
	7 A.M.	4 P.M.	9 P.M.	7 A.M.		4 P.M.		9 P.M.	
				Lower.	Upper.	Lower.	Upper.	Lower.	Upper.
1	Th. 58 B. 25·15	... ...	61 25·10	S.W.	S.W.	......	......	......	......
2	Th. 55 B. 25·10	66 24·99	64 25·95	Calm.	O.	S.W.	O.	S.W.	O.
3	Th. 61 B. 25·07	69·5 25·02	68 25·06	S.W.	O.	S.W.	N.E.	S.W.	S.W.
4	Th. 63 B. 25·11	64 25·09	....	Calm.	O.	S.W.	N.N.W.	......	......
5	Th. ... B. ...	68 25·04	68 25·07	......	......	S.W.	N.E.	S.W.	O.
6	Th. 61 B. 25·09	66 25·04	66 25·09	S.W.	O.	S.W.	S.W.	S.W.	O.
7	Th. 62 B. 25·11	66 25·06	65 25·09	S.W.	S.W.	S.W.	S.W.	N.E.	S.W.
8	Th. 63 B. 25·10	64 25·05	64 25·08	S.W.	O.	S.W.	S.W.	S.W.	S.W.
9	Th. 62 B. 25·07	66 25·00	65 25·07	S.W.	S.W.	S.W.	S.W.	S.W.	S.W.
10	Th. 63 B. 25·06	64 25·02	64 25·08	S.W.	S.W.	S.W.	S.W.	S.W.	S.W.
11	Th. 62 B. 25·08	64 25·01	63 25·04	S.W.	S.W.	S.W.	S.W.	S.W.	S.W.
12	Th. 62 B. 25·01	64 24·96	64 24·98	S.W.	S.W.	S.W.	S.W.	S.W.	S.W.
13	Th. 65 B. 24·98	63 24·95	63 25·05	S.W.	S.W.	S.W.	S.W.	S.W.	S.W.
14	Th. 63 B. 25·04	64 25·11	60 25·05	S.W.	S.W.	S.W.	S.W.	S.W.	S.W.
15	Th. 63 B. 25·03	63 24·96	64 25·00	S.W.	S.W.	S.W.	S.W.	S.W.	S.W.
16	Th. 64 B. 24·98	64 24·93	64 24·96	S.W.	S.W.	S.W.	S.W.	S.W.	S.W.
17	Th. 62 B. 24·95	65 24·91	66 24·95	S.W.	S.W.	S.W.	S.W.	S.W.	S.W.
18	Th. 64 B. 24·94	69 24·88	67 24·94	S.W.	S.W.	S.W.	S.W.	S.W.	S.W.
19	Th. 65 B. 24·94	66 24·95	67 24·95	S.W.	S.W.	S.W.	S.W.	S.W.	S.W.
20	Th. 65 B. 24·96	68 24·90	67 24·94	S.W.	S.W.	S.W.	S.W.	S.W.	S.W.
21	Th. 66 B. 24·93	67 24·89	66 24·90	S.W.	S.W.	S.W.	S.W.	S.W.	S.W.
22	Th. 65 B. 24·93	68 24·89	68 24·93	S.W.	S.W.	S.W.	S.W.	S.W.	S.W.
23	Th. 64 B. 24·95	68 24·92	67 24·95	S.W.	S.W.	S.W.	S.W.	S.W.	S.W.
24	Th. 64 B. 24·99	70 24·92	68 24·98	S.W.	S.W.	S.W.	S.W.	S.W.	S.W.
25	Th. 66 B. 25·00	68 24·91	66 24·96	S.W.	S.W.	S.W.	S.W.	S.W.	S.W.
26	Th. 65 B. 24·98	68 24·93	68 24·93	S.W.	S.W.	S.W.	S.W.	S.W.	S.W.
27	Th. 66 B. 24·97	69 24·89	67 24·93	S.W.	S.W.	S.W.	S.W.	Calm.	O.
28	Th. 65 B. 24·97	68 24·91	67 24·89	S.W.	S.W.	S.W.	S.W.	S.W.	S.W.
29	Th. 64 B. 24·99	66 24·99	66 25·30	S.W.	S.W.	S.W.	S.W.	S.W.	S.W.
30	Th. 62 B. 25·20	66 24·93	65 25·20	S.W.	S.W.	S.E.	N.E.	S.W.	S.W.

APPENDIX D.

Momien, Nantin, Muangla and Sanda, July, 1868.

July.	THERMOMETERS.							
	Maximum.	Minimum.	Dry Bulb.			Wet Bulb.		
			7 A.M.	4 P.M.	9 P.M.	7 A.M.	4 P.M.	9 P.M.
1	D 72 W 69·3	D 63 W 62	64·6	69·5	66·5	64	67·5	65·8
2	D 71·6 W 69	D 65 W 64·4	65·6	69	66	64·9	67·5	66·5
3	D 77 W 73	D 64·2 W 64	65·3	71·4	67·5	64·8	69·7	66·5
4	D 74·8 W 71·7	D 65·5 W 64·6	66	71·1	66	65	69·5	66·7
5	D 75·6 W 72	D 65·5 W 64·6	67	70·5	67	66	68·2	61·6
6	D 76·7 W 72·3	D 65 W 64	62·5	74·1	67·5	61·1	70·7	62
7	D 71·2 W 68·9	D 65 W 64·5	66	67·5	65·5	65·6	66	64·5
8	D 70 W 68	D 64·5 W 64	65·5	66·5	65·5	64·8	64·9	63·5
9	D 71·8 W 69·3	D 64 W 62·5	65	68·5	65·5	63·5	66·2	64
10	D 71·8 W 69·8	D 64 W 63·5	65	69·5	65·5	64·6	68	64·8
11	D 71·8 W 69·3	D 65 W 64	66·5	68·5	65·5	65·7	66·8	64
12	D 74·9 W 74·9	D 64·3 W 63·5	65·8	70·5	66·5	65	68	64·8
13	D W Nantin.	D 65·3 W 64· Nantin.	65·5 Nantin.	... Nantin.	... Nantin.	64·3 Nantin.	... Nantin.	... Nantin.
14	D 74·4 W 71·8	......	...	71·8	69·7	...	70	69·2
15	......	D 68·1 W 59·9	68·4	...	...	68	...	...

Between Nantin and Muangla all the thermometers with which the previous observations were made were stolen: the observations which follow are on minimum and maximum dry bulbs.

	Sanda.	Sanda.	Sanda.	Sanda.	Sanda.	Sanda.	Sanda.	Sanda.
21	90	......	...	78·4	73·5	...	...	...
22	83·8	70·8	73·8	70	78·7	...	...	...
23	86	71	71	79·8	74·7	...	...	...
24	87·2	71	74	...	75·2	...	...	...
25	84·5	72·5	74·5	80	74·7	...	...	...
26	90	71·2	72·7	86	76	...	...	...
27	91	72·6	76	...	73	...	...	...
28	90·3	71	78	...	77·5	...	...	...
29	91·5	73	81	86	77	...	...	...
30	91	73	76	81	76·5	...	...	...
31	86	73	76	80·7	74·5	...	...	...

APPENDIX D.   427

Momien, Nantin, Muangla and Sanda, July, 1868.

July.	Aneroid Barometer with attached Thermometer.			Wind.					
				7 A.M.		2 P.M.		9 P.M.	
	7 A.M.	4 P.M.	9 P.M.	Lower.	Upper.	Lower.	Upper.	Lower.	Upper.
1	Th. 63 B. 25·00	65 24·95	64 24·99	S.W.	S.W.	S.W.	S.W.	S.W.	S.W.
2	Th. 64 B. 24·99	64 24·95	65 25·00	S.W.	S.W.	S.W.	S.W.		
3	Th. 63 B. 24·99	67 24·93	66 24·98	S.W.	S.W.	S.W.	S.W.	S.W.	S.W.
4	Th. 64 B. 24·97	68 24·92	66 24·96	S.W.	S.W.	S.W.	S.W.		
5	Th. 65 B. 25·00	67 24·95	66 25·10	S.W.	S.W.	S.W.	S.W.		
6	Th. 64 B. 25·10	63 24·90	66 25·30	S.W.	S.W.	S.W.	S.W.	S.W.	S.W.
7	Th. 64 B. 25·10	65 25·00	65 25·20	S.W.	W.S.	S.W.	S.W.		
8	Th. 64 B. 24·99	64 24·90	64 24·99	S.W.	S.W.	S.W.	S.W.		
9	Th. 63 B. 24·40	64 24·90	64 24·95	S.W.	S.W.	S.W.	S.W.		
10	Th. 64 B. 24·95	66 24·90	66 24·98	...	...	S.W.	S.W.	Calm	Calm
11	Th. 64 B. 25·10	64 24·93	64 24·95	...	...	S.W.	S.W.	Calm	Calm
12	Th. 64 B. 25·20	67 24·98	65 25·30	...	S.W.	S.W.	S.W.	Calm	S.W.
13	Th. 64 B. 25·10	...	...	S.W.	S.W.				
14	Nantin. Th. B.	Nantin. 67 26·44	Nantin. 69 26·40	Nantin. ...	Nantin. ...	Nantin. S.W.	Nantin. S.W.	Nantin. S.W.	Nantin. S.W.
15	Th. 66 B. 26·46	...	...	S.W.	S.W.				
	Sanda.	Sanda.	Sanda.	Sanda.	Sanda.	Sanda.	Sanda.	Sanda.	Sanda.
20	Th. 66 B. 26·95	71 26·87	69 26·94	S.W.	S.W.	S.W.	S.W.	S.W.	S.W.
21	Th. 71 B. 27·03	70 27·05	70 27·11						
22	Th. 66 B. 27·13	70 27·08	69 27·11	S.W.	S.W.	S.W.	S.W.		
23	Th. 66 B. 27·14	68 27·06	69 27·12	S.W.	S.W.	...			
24	Th. 66 B. 27·19	... ...	70 27·13	S.W.	S.W.	S.W.	S.W.	S.W.	S.W.
25	Th. 67 B. 27·12	69 27·05	70 27·12	S.W.	S.W.	S.W.	S.W.	S.W.	S.W.
26	Th. 66 B. 27·11	71 27·04	70 27·11						
27	Th. 68 B. 27·15	... ...	72 27·11	S.W.	S.W.	...	S.W.	W.N.W.	S.W.
28	Th. 67 B. 27·14	... ...	72 27·11	S.W.	S.W.	...	...	S.	S.E.
29	Th. 68 B. 27·15	74 27·07	72 27·11	S.W.	S.	S.N.	S.E.	S.N.	S.N.
30	Th. 68 B. 27·15	72 27·04	70 27·09	S.W.	S.W.	S.W.	S.W.	S.W.	
31	Th. 68 B. 27·06	70 27·00	68 27·05	...	S.W.	S.W.	N.W.	N.W.	N.W.

APPENDIX D.

Hotha and Bhamô, August and September 1868.

August.	THERMOMETERS.				
	Maximum.	Minimum.	Dry Bulb.		
			7 A.M.	4 P.M.	9 P.M.
...	......	......	...	...	...
	Hotha	Hotha	Hotha	Hotha	Hotha
10	82·5	78	...	...	72·5
11	......	68	72	...	72
12	80	67·6	...	...	72
13	......	69	71	...	69·5
14	......	67·8	70·5	70	...
15	......	68	68·7	...	70
16	78·8	62	72	73·3	69
17	78·2	67·5	69·7	74	71·2
18	78·9	69	73	72	79·5
19	81	69·5	71	77	72·5
20	82	68·5	74·3	75·6	72
21	76	68·4	70	72·2	68·5
22	68·8	67·5	69·5	73	70
23	72·7	68	68·9	73·4	75·2
24	75·8	67	68·5	69	67·5
25	77	66·5	67	69	67·4
26	74·9	65·8	69·8	72·8	68·5
September	Bhamô	Bhamô	Bhamô	Bhamô	Bhamô
10	91·5	75	78	...	80
11	85·2	75·4	78	84·5	80
12	91	78	79·5	91	80
13	91·7	75·4	80	89	...

APPENDIX D.

Hotha and Bhamô, August and September 1868.

August	ANEROID BAROMETER WITH ATTACHED THERMOMETER.			WIND.					
				7 A.M.		4 P.M.		9 P.M.	
	7 A.M.	4 P.M.	9 P.M.	Lower.	Upper.	Lower.	Upper.	Lower.	Upper.
8	Th. ... B. 29·29	... ...	72 29·25	S. W. Calm.	......	Calm. N. W.	...... O.	Calm.	
9	Th. 69 B. 29·32	... ...	... ...						
10	Th. ... B. ...	72 25·46	68 25·47	......	......	S. W.	S. W.		
11	Th. 64 B. 25·44	... ...	68 25·44	......	E.	...	......	S. W.	S. W.
12	Th. 64 B. 25·45	71 25·42	69 25·46	S. W.	S. W.	S. W.	S. W.	Calm.	O.
13	Th. 64 B. 25·45	67 25·39	64 25·44	S. W.	S. W.	S. W.	S. W.		
14	Th. 63 B. 25·44	66 25·46	... ...	S. W.	S. W.	Calm.	S. W.		
15	Th. 63 B. 25·44	... ...	65 25·46	S. W.	S. W.	...	......	S. W.	S. W.
16	Th. ... B. 25·43	67 25·39	65 25·44	Calm.	O.	S. W.	S. W.	S. W.	S. W.
17	Th. 63 B. 25·47	68 25·45	66 25·49	S. W.	S. W.	S. W.	S. W.	S. W.	S. W.
18	Th. 65 B. 25·51	60 25·48	65 27·52	S. W.	S. W.	S. W.	S. W.	Calm.	
19	Th. 64 B. 25·56	74 25·45	65 25·45	Calm.	S. W.	S. W.	S. W.	Calm.	Calm.
20	Th. 64 B. 25·42	69 25·38	... ...	S. W.	S. W.	S. W.	S. W.		
21	Th. 64 B. 25·43	66 25·47	67 25·42	S. W.	S. W.	S. W.	S. W.	Calm.	
22	Th. 62 B. 25·43	66 25·41	64 25·47	S. W.	S. W.	S. W.	S. W.	Calm.	
23	Th. 62 B. 25·44	63 25·40	62 25·45	S. W.	S. W.	S. W.	S. W.	S. W.	
24	Th. 62 B. 25·46	63 25·44	62 25·49	S. W.	S. W.	S. W.	S. W.	Calm.	S. W.
25	Th. 61 B. 25·49	63 25·46	61 25·51	S. W.	S. W.	S. W.	E.	S. W.	
26	Th. 60 B. 25·53	66 25·48	62 25·54	S. W.	S. W.	S. W.	S. W.	S. W.	S. W.
Sept.	Bhamô	Bhamô	Bhamô	Bhamô	Bhamô	Bhamô	Bhamô	Bhamô	Bhamô
10	Th. 72 B. 29·27	81 29·17	76 29·28	Calm.	N. E.	Calm.	N.	S. W.	S. W.
11	Th. 73 B. 29·35	78 29·20	76 29·36	N. E.	N. E.	N. E.	N. E.	S. W.	O.
12	Th. 74 B. 29·21	81 29·16	76 29·23	Calm.	O.	S. W.	S. W.	S. W.	S. W.
13	Th. 74 B. 29·24	84 29·17	... ...	Calm.	O.	N.	O.		

NOTE ON THE MAPS.

Of the two maps which accompany this Report, the first delineates the country to the eastward of Bhamô over which the Expedition travelled, and the second illustrates the views expressed in the Report, and which are the result of many enquiries regarding the sources of the Irawady and the probable distribution of the Salween and Cambodia rivers.

The materials for the construction of the former were derived from Captain Bowers' observations from Bhamô to Momien, and from his and Mr. Gordon's joint labours from Manwyne to Bhamô, combined with my own notes on the general direction of the mountain ranges and valleys, and sketches of the physical features of the area which it was our good fortune to explore.

In addition to the district traversed by the Expedition, I have incorporated that part of Dr. Bayfield's map of the route from Ava to the Assam frontier which exhibits the course of the Irawady from Bhamô to Tsenbô, and the country from the latter locality onwards to the north of Meinkhoom, having made, however, a few alterations on information derived from Dr. Griffith's Report, as that traveller visited both the Amber and the Jade mines to the north of Mogoung.

I have endeavoured to add to its value by showing how much those remarkable and indefatigable men, the Roman Catholic Missionaries of China, have achieved, and I have taken advantage of the positions which they determined on the western limits of Yunan province, where it touches the Shan States dependent on Burmah. As already stated in the body of the Report, that reliance justly may be placed on the accuracy of their observations, seeing that they triangulated as they went along, I have adopted their position of Momien, because they resided a considerable time in that town during the period they were engaged in the survey of Western China which had been entrusted to them by the Emperor.

As the instruments which were left with those Members of the Expedition who proceeded onwards from Ponsee were of the most limited and imperfect description, unquestionable exactitude cannot be claimed for Captain Bowers' and Mr. Gordon's observations.

The heights given in the Report were made under the same disadvantages as attended the determining of the longitudes and latitudes.

I have indicated in colours the two leading geological features of the country, viz., a platform of metamorphic rocks overflowed in the Nantin and Momien districts by an outburst of trap.

With regard to the second map, as any opinion expressed on the probable sources of the Irawady, the Salween, and the Cambodia must be purely hypothetical until they have been fully explored, this map has been put forth chiefly with the object of drawing attention to the interesting geographical questions which have yet to be settled respecting these great rivers. No doubt exists in my own mind that Wilcox had too little ground to justify his theory that the western branch of the Irawady was the main stream, as he had no experience whatever of the magnitude of the river below where he stood, or of the great size of its eastern branch which the natives who reside on it regard as the main stream of the Irawady.

I believe, it would be a very simple matter indeed to determine the question regarding the relative importance of these two branches, and that there would be no difficulty in obtaining boats at Bhamô which could reach the mouths of the two streams in a journey of a few days, as Mogul merchants are in the habit of doing every year. Now that steamers run pretty frequently from Rangoon to Bhamô, the problem could be solved in little more than three months by an explorer from Calcutta, without any fear of opposition from the villagers on the banks of the river who, in my experience, were very friendly.

GENERAL INDEX.

Abasside Kaliph, 138.
Abhirája, founder of Tagoung, 205.
Abu Jafar al Mansur, founder of Bagdad, 138.
Abu Zaid "Ancient Accounts," 139.
Aconitum, arrow-poison, 42, 134.
Acridotheres tristis, 298.
Ælurus fulgens, 317.
Agriculture near Bhamô, 63, 64.
    ,, capabilities of Nantin valley for, 90.
    ,, among Shans, 83, 110.
    ,, ,, Kakhyens, 63, 70, 83, 132.
Ahoms, 2.
Alékyoung, island of, 197.
    ,, town of, 197.
Alsus nipalensis, 70.
Alompra, Burmese Emperor, 11.
Amarapura, Chinese embassies to, 33, 34.
Amavan, Chinese Regent, 18, 19, 21.
Amber, 49, 63, 107, 108.
    ,, mines or *Payendwen*, 54, 65, 66.
    ,, colour and uses of, at Momien, 66.
Amherst, Lady, pheasants, 317.
Amusements of Shans, 113.
    ,, Kakhyens, 135.
Analyses of hot-springs by Dr. Macnamara, 81, 89.
Anas caryophyllacea, 242.
    ,, *poecilorhyncha*, 211, 238, 242, 309, 323.
Animals, domestic, of Kakhyen hills, 73.
    ,, ,, in Sanda valley, 84.
    ,, ,, at Nantin, 90.
    ,, ,, at Momien, 93, 94, 325.
Anôratha-mengzo, king of New Pagan, 12.
    ,, covets tooth of Gaudama, 12.
Arah, Chinese minister of Suance, 140.
Arabs, introduction of, into China, 138 *et seq.*
Arabia, 144.
Arabic, use of, in China, 143.
    ,, in Yunan, 152.
    ,, letters, 257, 279.
    ,, MSS., 138, 143.
Ardea numatrana, 196.
Arracan, 59, 205.
Arrow-poisons of Kakhyens, 42, 134.
Arsenic, 92, 328.
Art, character of Shan, 111, 112, 113, 346.
    ,, among Kakhyens, 134.
Ashan, 156, 379, 380.

Assam, 1, 7, 42, 191.
    ,, conquests of, 2, 164.
    ,, Wilcox's memoir on, 50.
    ,, Kakhyen slaves from, 132.
    ,, Griffith's route to Mogoung from, 161.
    ,, Jenkin's description of country between Hukong and, 165.
    ,, trade between Upper Burmah and, 166.
    ,, ,, ,, Tibet and, 175, 176.
    ,, tea cultivation in, 176.
    ,, present commercial position of, 177.
Assamese at Bhamô, 224, 229.
Assays of galena ore by Professor Oldham, 69, 93.
Ascamedha, 116.
Ataces, Kakhyen clan of, 118.
Augbenglé, irrigation reservoir of king, 196.
Augwa (Ava), 15.
Ava, 1, 3, 29, 35, 49, 52, 180.
    ,, Soonampha's flight to, 8.
    ,, invaded by Pong and capital destroyed, 10.
    ,, emperors nominate Pong kings, 11.
    ,, Marco Polo on Tartar invasion of, 14.
    ,, said to be tributary to China, 14.
    ,, new capital founded, 15.
    ,, Maha Yazwen or great history of, 16.
    ,, Chinese missions to, 16, 34.
    ,, ,, invasions of, 16, 17.
    ,, ,, princesses sent to king of, 33.
    ,, ,, travellers to, 23.
    ,, ,, generals propose peace with, 29.
    ,, conquered by Pegu, 18.
    ,, restoration of, 18.
    ,, demands surrender of Bhamô chief, 18.
    ,, threatens to invade Yunan, 18.
    ,, Yunle forwarded to, 19.
    ,, Mithari Katan, 20.
    ,, Loli sent as a prisoner to, 24.
    ,, army defeats Chinese at Kaungtoung, 25.
    ,, and Shan States, 27.
    ,, concludes peace with China, 1769, 31.
    ,, embassies to Pekin, 32, 33.
    ,, Mien or Ava proper, 14, 43.
    ,, factories at, 45.
    ,, Dod's mission to, 46.
    ,, Symes and Hamilton Buchanan's mission to, 47.
    ,, Crawford's embassy to, 50.

GENERAL INDEX.

AVA, Colonel Burney appointed Resident at the Court of, 53.
„ Pemberton on trade of, 53.
„ Hannay on trade between China and, 54.
„ Bayfield's mission from, 54.
„ proposed route to Yunan by, 56.
„ capabilities of Irawady to Bhamô from, 167.
„ tributaries of Irawady between Mogoung and, 183.
„ Burmese itineraries on route to Pekin from, 189.
Avaloketeswara, 116.

Bagdad, founder of, 138.
Bhaloo, 175.
Balamenden, governor of Kaungtoung, 28.
Bamboo fenced villages, 110, 209, 213, 214, 216, 292.
„ girdles, 121, 146.
„ rafts, 265, 267, 385.
Bambusa gigantea, 260.
Bambusicola fytchii, 259.
Banshoa, rebellion of, 139.
Barley, 93, 201.
Basalt, 88, 91, 92.
Bass' Beer, 12, 200.
Bathang, 175, 192, 193.
Bauhinia, 269.
Bayfield, Dr., 54, 57, 178.
„ „ on Old Bhamô, 45.
„ „ journal of, 55.
„ „ on depth of Irawady, 183.
Bazaar of Manwyne, 291.
„ „ Karahokah, 295.
„ „ Sanda, 297.
„ „ Momien, 93, 173, 318, 328.
„ „ Muangla, 346.
„ „ Hotha, 368, 369.
Beal, Mr., on Buddhist relics, 13.
Becsa, 165.
Behar, analysis of opium of, 72.
Beikkarota or Bhikshurashtra, 3.
Benares, analysis of opium of, 72.
Bengal, 52, 176.
„ analysis of opium of, 72.
„ and Mien, king of, 14.
Berghaus, 193.
Bhagavati, 116.
BHAMÔ, 4, 52, 75, 90, 97, 136, 154, 157, 174, 184, 262, 267, 282.
„ one of the Shan States or Koshanpyi, 4, 33, 48.
„ Chinese name of, 4.
„ annexed to Ava, 18.
„ arrival of Yunlie at, 19.
„ Yunan governor at, 19.
„ trade of, Pemberton on, 53.
„ „ with China, 23, 24.
„ „ „ Western Yunan, 51, 172, 173.
„ „ in jade at, 67.
„ „ gold at, 69.

BHAMÔ, trade in opium at, 110.
„ Loli's quarrel with officials of, 24.
„ Chinese army advances on, 25, 27, 28.
„ Burmese army advances to, 26, 29.
„ „ defeat Chinese at, 26, 29.
„ general restores the allegiance of Shan States to Ava, 8, 27.
„ memorable peace of, 31, 32.
„ treaty of, 1769, 31; Sir A. Phayre on, 32.
„ Burmese mission to Pekin by, 33, 34.
„ country between Mandalay and, 43, 194.
„ different spellings of the name, 46, 52.
„ position of, 47, 59, 60, 216.
„ Hannay and Griffith on population of, 54.
„ Baron Otto des Granges on political importance of, 55.
„ Bishop Bigandet at, 56.
„ character of population of, 55, 60, 96, 216.
„ character of country about, 60, 224.
„ neighbouring inhabitants, 60.
„ „ towns, 60, 61.
„ Irawady at, 61, 62; Colonel Hannay on, 182, 215.
„ soil and cultivation at, 64.
„ temperature and climate at, 64, 65.
„ earthquakes felt at, 91, 110.
„ Burmese language and customs have superseded Shan at, 96.
„ Kakhyens to the east and west of, 118.
„ fortified, and reason why, 119.
„ distance from Yunan city of, 160.
„ as a starting-point to China, advantages of, 167.
„ practicability of a railway considered, 168.
„ residence at, 216.
„ description of, 216, 217.
„ market at, 217.
„ Chinese temple at, 217.
„ „ opposition to Expedition at, 218.
„ Shan-Burmese at, 219.
„ decay of, and causes of, 219.
„ manufactures at, 221.
„ Shan-Chinese at, 221.
„ Kakhyens at, 221, 222.
„ Assamese at, 224.
„ chief Phoongyee of, 224.
„ medical practice at, 227.
„ Teikkays or magistrates of, 228; their conduct, 229.
„ arrival of new governor at, 233.
„ incidents at, 235.
„ to Ponsee, 237.
„ return to, 389.
„ sacrifice to the náts at, 387.
„ Chief or Tsawbwa,—
„ „ independence of, 11.
„ „ receives seal from China, 14, 15.
„ „ escapes to Yunan, 18.

GENERAL INDEX.

BHAMÔ Chief or Tsawbwa,—*contd.*
"   "   surrender demanded by Ava, 18.
"   "   death of, family transmitted to Ava, 18.
"   "   receives overtures from Yunlie, 19.
"   "   Balamauden, 28.
"   "   blamed for war of 1769, 29.
"   "   sent on embassy to Pekin, 33.
"   "   Buchanan Hamilton and, 47.
"   Woon, 208, 210, 283, 284.
"   "   house of, 219.
"   "   arrival of new, 233.
"   Route from Burmah to China, 23, 32, 52, 53, 56, 77.
"   "   capabilities of, 167.
"   "   embassy, to China, 35.
"   "   golden road, 32.
"   "   importance of, 35.
"   "   to Moungwan, 33.
"   "   by Molay river, 356.
"   "   General Fytche's proposal for exploration of, 1867, 58.
"   "   advantages over Theinnee route, 35, 160.
"   Routes to Momien, 153.
"   "   general character of, 153.
"   "   confluence in Nantin valley, 155.
"   Old, 43, 243.
"   "   mart of, 43.
"   "   probable cause of desertion of, 44.
"   "   Hayfield on, 45.
"   "   position of, 61.
Bigandet Bishop, at Bhamô, 56, 57.
Birth-ceremonies among Kakhyens, 129.
Bier-Gaum, Singphò chief, 53.
Blacksmiths, Shan-Chinese, 111.
Bodwan, silver-mines, 30, 49.
Bokhara traders, 151.
Bombax malabaricum, 238.
Bonjour, Père, survey of Yunan, 46, 188.
Boorce Dehing, 161, 166.
Borkamipti, 183.
Bouillon, Lord Cardinal de, 140.
Boundary of Burmah, 9; of Pegu, 17; of Yunan, 250.
"   between Ava and China, views on, 30.
"   British, the Kamyoem or Kammairon, 162.
Boundaries of Pong, 7, 10.
Bowers, Captain, 194, 243, 248, 292, 321.
Bracelets, 197, 328.
Brahmakund range, 179.
"   river, 179, 191, 192.
"   route by valley of, 174.
Brahmaputra, 58, 174, 179, 181, 183, 192, 193.
"   on routes between Mogoung river and, 161, 164.
"   on proposed route to Talifoo from, 174.
"   on trade with Tibet *vid*, 176.
Branfa rufina, 242.
Bricks, manufacture of, 64, 92, 122.

Bricks, impressions on, 206.
"   at laying foundation of pagoda, 225.
Bridge of gold and silver, 32.
"   over Tapeng proposed by Loli, 24, 167.
"   iron-suspension, over Shuaylee, 159, 188.
"   "   "   Cambodia, 159, 190.
"   "   "   Tapeng, 167, 188.
"   "   "   Tahô, 311, 344.
Bridges, stone, in Shan States, 306, 310, 307, 312, 331, 365, 370.
Britons, early, similarity of Shan ornaments to those of, 106.
Brica Pani, tables of, 121.
Bronze implements, Shans' belief in restorative power of, 114 (see Appendix C.)
Buchanan, Dr., Francis Hamilton, 4, 23.
"   "   on origin of Shans, 5.
"   "   on Tsampenago, 7, 47.
"   "   on Burmo-Chinese war of 1769, 30.
"   "   on Ponsee (Bodwan) silver-mines, 30, 48, 49.
"   "   on Burmese mission to Pekin, 33, 47.
"   "   on Geography of Upper Burmah, 47.
"   "   on Bhamô, 47, 49.
"   "   route between Assam and Tibet, 175.
"   "   on Irawady river, 181.
Buddha, finger of, in Shooshi, 13.
"   images of, 206, 237.
"   canopies over the heads of, in Western Yunan, 236.
Buddhism among Shans, 38, 99, 111, 375.
"   peculiarities of, in Sanda valley, 99, 114, 296.
"   Onigours abjure, 139.
"   at Momien, 354.
Buddhist relics, 13.
"   pagodas, 30.
"   phoongyees, 111.
"   monasteries (see khyoungs), 127.
Buffaloes sacrificed to *nâts*, 57, 127, 337.
Bupaua coromandus, 298.
Burial-places, Shan, 114, 302.
"   "   Kakhyen, 253, 263.
"   "   Chinese, 202.
Burial-rites, Kakhyen, 131, 248.
Burlton, Captain, 178.
"   on source of the Irawady, 179.
BURMAH—
"   Chinese name of, 9.
"   wars with China, 12, 24, 26, 27.
"   relations with China, 15.
"   peace with China, 22, 32.
"   Marco Polo on country between, Kardandan and, 42.
"   trade between China and, 40.
"   British treaty with, 56, 23, 38.
"   Expedition, result of treaty with, 58.

BURMAH, Kakhyen States between Namboke and, 135.
" plains of, 153.
Burmah Upper, 58, 98, 99.
" " trade of, 49, 56, 166.
" " Buchanan Hamilton on geography of, 47.
" " Col. Burney on geography of, 52.
" " " on wars of, 53.
" " Dr. Williams on, 57.
" " information about Irawady obtained in, 62.
" " trade-routes of, 153 et seq.
Burmese chronicles, 7, 10, 14, 16, 19, 34, 53.
" annexation of Koshanpyi, 9.
" first invasion of Pong, 10.
" refusal of tribute to China, 14.
" army, champion of, 16.
" " advances to the Cambodia, 25.
" " advances of, 26, 27.
" " defeats Chinese, 28, 29.
" " relieves Kaungtoung, 26, 29.
" officers treat with Chinese about peace, 31.
" embassies to Pekin, 32, 33.
" influence in Kakhyen hills, 30.
" work silver-mines, 30, 40, 69, 267.
" frontier with China, 52.
" plain, 44, 68, 158, 363.
" influence and customs among Shan's, 96.
" nât worship among, 37, 116.
" estimate of Kakhyens, 119, 222.
" affinity of Leesaw language to, 136.
" surveyor on Sawaddy route, 153, 156, 158.
" " on Muangwan route, 44, 374.
" police guard, 194.
" court-official, 194, 203.
" steamer and crew, 194.
" present to Tasakone, 337.
" arrival of, at Poasee, 267; at Muangla, 343.
Burmese-Shans, Shan-Burmese, 55, 96, 219, 222, 224.
Burn, Mr. 194, 235.
Burnett, Captain, route across the Patkoi range, 164, 165.
Burney, Colonel, on Burmese claims to territory, 10.
" " translations of Burmese chronicles, 12, 25, &c.
" " on Chinese embassies, 33.
" " on geography of Upper Burmah, 52.
" " on opium from Medoo, 72.
" " on Mahomedan traders, 148.

Cabul, route from, to Tibet, 36.
Cachar, Pong invades, 2.
Cachuries, 120.
Cajat, nât, 125.

Calcutta, 151, 176, 224; Kakhyen tobacco tested at, 83.
Calotes emma, 259.
Cambodia, 3, 6, 28, 78, 149, 170, 193.
" Shan principalities, 4.
" Burmese army advances to, 25.
" Kyaing-young Tsawbwaship on the, 29.
" routes to, viâ Momien, viâ Theinnee, 35.
" Kakhyen hills, country between, 76.
" and Irawady, relations between, 77, 192.
" iron-suspension bridge over, 159, 190.
" Hokyan river, branch of, 159, 190.
" from China, great water-highway, 171.
" and Rangoon, tramway between, 172.
" delineation of, in Jesuits' map, 189.
" Burmese itineraries on, 189, 190.
" no connection with Tibetan rivers, 190.
" D'Anville on, 192.
" Tasakone on trading-route by, 336.
Camein, 16.
Camellia thea, 64, 70.
Canal, Chinese, in Burmah, 15.
Canals, 283.
Canton, Yunlie proclaimed king at, 19.
" king of, joins U-san-ghey, 22.
" value of jade-rings at, 67.
" proposed railway to, from Rangoon, 170.
" river, 171.
Capra bubalina, horn of, 109.
" *megaceros*, 94, 325.
Caravans, trading, 118, 143, 160, 173, 175, 229, 261, 366.
Casarca rutila, 196, 211, 242.
Castanea vesca, 70.
Cathay, Yule's work on, 145.
Celery, 93, 321.
Celts, similarity of Shan ornaments to those of, 106.
Cetacea, 203.
Ceylon, 33, 115.
Chagie, nât, 125.
Chaktaw, 355.
Chambroo, nât, 125.
Chamienchou, robber chief, 20.
Chan, nât, 125.
Chang-gnan, palace of, looted, 145.
Character of Shans, 117; of Kakhyens, 119, 120, 222; of Panthays, 151.
Charadrius longipes, 196.
Charlton, Captain, on communication between Saddyah and Yunan, 164.
Chatelaines, 108, 323.
Chekiang, Mahomedans in, 142.
Cheng-ghin, nât, 376.
Chengiz-Khan, conquests of, 139.
Children, purchase of, by Mahomedans, in China, 141.

Children, purchase of, in Yunan, 142.
„ kidnapping of, by Kakhyens, 222.
„ education of, by Phoongyees, 115, 239, 241, 292, 296, 300, 336.
CHINA, 1, 2, 6, 8, 30, 69, 176, 180, 272.
„ wars between Burmah and, 7, 12, 13, 24.
„ Koshanpyi tributary to, 9.
„ demands tribute from kings of Pagan, 13.
„ relations of, to Burmah, A. D. 1300, 15.
„ U-san-ghey introduced Tartars into, 21.
„ highways to Bhamô from, 23.
„ peace with Burmah after treaty of Bhamô, 32.
„ embassies to Burmah from, 33, 34.
„ Burmese mission to, 34.
„ embassy route to, 35.
„ emperor of, orders a map of Yunan, 46.
„ Symes on trade of, with Burmah, 49; Crawford on ditto, 51; Hannay on, 54.
„ Burney, on routes to, 55.
„ routes to, viâ Bhamô, 56, 57, 169.
„ opium cultivation in, 71, 72.
„ annexation of States in western Yunan to, 98.
„ proximity of Bhamô to borders of, 136.
„ Arabs in, 138.
„ embassy from the Kaliph to,
„ Abu Zaid's account of, 139.
„ Marco Polo's residence in, 139.
„ Gutzlaff's, 142.
„ probable origin of Mahomedans in, 145.
„ practicability of railway to, considered, 169, 170, 172.
„ three great water-highways of, 170.
„ English goods, market for, in, 174.
„ Central, 171, 174.
„ Eastern, 18, 221.
„ Western, 56, 57, 153, 171, 184, 186, 280.
„ South-Western, 24, 52, 280.
Chinese at war with Pong, 7, 17.
„ capture Pong capital, 8.
„ chronicle, discrepancy of, 8.
„ invade valley of Irawady, 12, 26.
„ defeated by Burmese, 12, 26.
„ Canal, 15.
„ army invades Burmah, 16, 17, 20, 25, 27.
„ missions to Ava, 17, 33, 34, 35.
„ attempt the conquest of Mogoung, 17.
„ kings and provinces, estimate of, 22.
„ travellers to Ava, Buchanan Hamilton on, 23.
„ traders cause of war with Burmah, 24.
„ army stockaded at Bhamô, 26.
„ „ besieges Kaungtoung, 26, 28.
„ „ route of, 279.

Chinese army, entrenchment of, in Sanda valley, 352.
„ generals sue for peace, 29.
„ letter proposing peace, 29.
„ desire Ponsee silver-mines, 30; once worked by Chinese, 265.
„ princesses for king of Ava by Chinese embassy, 33.
„ ambassadors, Colonel Symes on, 34.
„ garrisons in Kakhyen hills, 23, 34, 382.
„ merchants, 49, 51, 217, 309.
„ population in Kakhyen valleys, 75.
„ among the Shans, 84, 86, 99.
„ in Sanda valley, 86, 136.
„ relation of, to Shan language, 97.
„ language spoken by Kakhyens and Shans, 100.
„ population at Manwyne, 136; at Nantin, 137; at Momien, 150; at Bhamô 216; at Muangla 301.
„ physical characters of, in Yunan, 137.
„ slave girls, 142, 341.
„ sympathies with, of Shans and Kakhyens during Panthay rebellion in Yunan, 148.
„ interpreter, 194, 212.
„ opposition of, to Expedition at Bhamô, 217.
„ temple at Bhamô, 217.
„ province of Yunan, western boundary of, 250.
„ fort, remains of, near Ponline, 250.
„ letters, 257, 270, 279, 283.
„ medicines, 324.
„ attack Khyto valley, 333.
„ dacoits, 258, 334, 337, 343.
„ messengers from Momien, 275.
„ joss-house at Sanda, 297.
„ school at Muangla, 301; at Momien, 335, 336.
„ khyoungs at Nantin, 307; at Momien, 313, 334; at Sanda, 350; at Hotha, 371.
„ pagoda in Momien valley, 313.
„ theatricals at Bhamô, 217, 218; at Momien, 317.
„ Imperialist chief Lesuetai, 25, 148, 218, 230, 263, 270, 274, 278, 285.
„ Repository, on Mahomedan rebellions in Yunan, 142.
Chinese-Shans, or Shan-Chinese, 86.
„ „ in Hotha valley, 100.
„ „ physical characters of, 101.
„ „ women, costume of, 103, 369.
„ „ ornaments of, 103, 104, 105.
„ „ blacksmiths, 111; silversmiths, 111.
„ „ colony of, at Bhamô, 221.
„ „ in a Leesaw village, 364.
Tartar army march against Pagan, 13.
„ „ destroy Pagan, 15.
„ kings, conquests of, 98.
„ Yunanese traders at Bhamô, 209.

GENERAL INDEX.

Chinese-Yunanese, language of, 137.
Chingpaws (Singphos or Kakhyens), 96, 118, 119.
Chingtufoo, capital of Sechuen, 174.
Chinoo, nât, 125.
Chitans or Khanlungs, 119.
Chitkaing (Tsagain), 16.
Chitong, nât, 125, 126.
Chittie-doung, 76, 279, 379, 386.
Chloracious ruficeps, 279.
Chowlainglen, king of the nâts, 372.
Chowkyoung, island of, 208.
Chowkalkhum invaded Ava, 11.
      " defeated and slain by Chinese, 11.
Chowkhoolseng, last king of Pong, 11.
Chownakhum, Pong founder of Assam dynasty, 2.
Chouna, 175.
    " trade between Lassa and, 176.
Choungoke, a Burmese official, 240.
Christian massacre in China, 139.
Christianity at Yunlie's court, 19.
Christians in China, official position of, 140.
    " native, at siege of Ava, 20.
    "   of Madeya, 20.
    " Nestorian, 140.
Chronicles, Shan M. S.S., 1, 5, 8, 10.
    " Burmese, 7, 8, 10, 11, 16, 17, 19.
    "   Colonel Burney's translations of, 15, 16, 18, 20, 23, 25, 29, 31, 34.
    " Chinese, 8.
    "   and Shan, discrepancy between, 8.
    " Munipore, 10.
Chun-chi, Chinese emperor, 18, 21.
    " makes U-sang-gluy king of Yunan, 21.
    " policy with Mahomedans, 141.
Chungking, great commercial city of Central China, 174.
Cinnamomum cassia, 70.
    " *casdateum*, 70.
Cis-Cambodia Shan States, Chinese conquest of, 4.
Cis-Irawadian Shan States, 5.
    " provinces of Pong, 17.
Clays, 59, 64, 66, 81, 88, 91, 209, 221.
Climate of Momien, 40, 94, 95, 324, 328.
    " Kakhyen hills, 73; of Sanda valley, 85; of Yunan, L'Amiot on, 52, 53.
Coal, 65, 66.
    " on Mogoung river, 63; in Hukong valley, 65; supposed in Shuemuelong Mountain, 81.
Coal-mines on Irawady, 59, 198, 199.
Coal-depôt, Thingadaw, 202.
Coffer Father, at Yunlie's court, 19.
Coins, custom of burying, under skin, 118.
Conglomerates, 59, 207.
Conoozouay pagoda, 18, 371.
Compte, Louis Le, on Mahomedans in China, 140.
Confucius, 143; Confucianists, priests at Momien, 335.

Coonsang, nât, 372.
Cooper, Mr., "Leisus" of, 135.
    "   on "Quayze" and "Houize", 147.
    "   " Panthay rebellion, 149.
    "   " the Sanpo, 193.
Copper near Khyto, 92, 333.
    " at Momien, 173, 327.
Copsychus, 202.
Coracias affinis, 111.
Corvus culminatus, 259.
Corypha, 248.
Cotton, 63, 70, 110, 124, 133, 173, 209, 217, 303, 351.
Cow-worship of Hindoos, 116.
Cowries, 119, 122.
Crawford's "Ava," 15.
Crawford, Colonel, on embassy to Ava, 50; and Irawady, 75.
Cringwan, nât, 125.
Cross-bows of Kakhyens, 134.
Culleyang, 143.
Cultivation at Bhamô, 64; in Kakhyen hills, 70, 75, 110, 133, 283.
    " of Sanda and Hotha valleys, 83.
    " " Nantin valley, 89, 95.
    " " Momien valley, 93, 316.
    " " at Ponsee, 266.
    " " in the Tapeng valley, 110, 288.
Custom-house, on borders of Yunan, 23.
    " in Kakhyen hills, 23.
Custom of concealing coins under skin, 118.
Customs of Burmese, 5; of Karlandan, (Polo,) 9, 36, 37, 40; of Shans 9, 36, 37, 113, 114.
    " Kakhyens, 36, 123, 128.

D

Dacca, 10, 14.
Dâh, Shan weapon, 108.
    " made by Shan-Chinese, 111, 221, 368.
Dalrymple on aquatic land-carriage between Ava and China, 28.
    " factories at Bhamô, 45.
    " map of, 193.
D'Anville, map of, 190.
Darjeeling, cart-road to Terai, 153.
Daroo river, 161.
Davis, Sir J. F., on the country to the east of Bhamô, 52.
Daza Yâzâ, 206.
Death ceremonies of Kakhyens, 129, 247, 248.
Debong, 191, 192.
Deen Mahomed, history of, 222.
Defile, first or upper, of Irawady, 61; 63; Bowers' survey of, 61; Hannay's, 182; Bayfield's, 183; visit to, 184.
Defiles, lower, 60, 65, 186, 213, 214.
Dendrocitta, 202.
Denudations by Tahô, at Mawphoo, 86.
    " in Nantin valley, 86.
Deposits, superficial, 66, 80, 81, 83, 92, 289.
Devanagri, inscription in, 206.
Dewatuka, 205.
Dhena, goddess of wealth, 116.

Dibing, 179.
Dibong, capabilities of the, 175.
" route by, into Tibet, 175.
Dípankara (Buddha), 206.
Diseases among Shans, 114, 277; at Bhamô, 227, 228; at Nantin, 310; at Momien, 326.
Dod at Ava, 46.
Dolphins, round-headed, 203, 208, 388.
Dolmens, 253.
D'Orleans, Father Pierre Joseph, 20, 21.
" on U-san-ghey, 21.
Dress of Shans, 101, 289.
" " Shan-Chinese, 103, 369.
" " Kakhyens, 121, 246.
" " Kakoos, 122.
" " Leesaws, 136, 340.
" " Phoongyees in Sanda valley, 109, 114, 296.
" " peasantry at Momien, 326.
" " Panthays, 151, 256.
Du Chatz enters Burmah from Yunan, 46.
Du Halde, 19, 21.
" " "Empire of China" by, 138.
" " on Tung dynasty, 144.
" " on Ngan-loshan, 145.
Dupha Gaum, 53.
Durgá, Hindoo deity, 330.
Durrung, 176.
Dutch factories, 45, 61.
Dye, indigo, 84, 111, 173, 353, 360, 369.
Dzungaria, rebellion in, 149.

Ear-rings, Shan, Shan-Chinese, Poloung, 105.
" Kakhyen, 122.
Earth necklace (*Komooa*), Kakhyen, 122, 360.
Earthquakes at Momien, 91.
" felt in Burmah, 91.
Earth-serpent, offerings to, 225.
Earth-snake, offerings to, 116.
Earthenware, 66, 173.
Eclipse, solar, 373.
Edinburgh Review, 138.
Edi river, salt springs in, 67.
Education in Shan States, 115.
" at Momien, 336.
Elephants, 25, 43, 271.
Elephant's molar, 81.
Elephants' route from Suddya to Mogoung, 161.
Elephants sent to Pekin, 34.
Elevation of Shan valleys, 76, 78, 82.
" " Bhamô routes, 154 *et seq.*
Embassy route, course of, 153.
Embroidery among Shans, 111, 112.
" " Kakhyens, 133.
English factories, 45, 61.
" galena, 68, 91.
" goods, market for, 174, 319.
" treaty with Burmah, 56, 58, 231.
Eng tree, 207.
E-tsung and bone of Buddha, 13.
Excommunication of Phoongyee, 357.

Factories, Dutch, in Burmah, 45; at Old Bhamô, 61.
" English, 45, 61.
Fahian, Buddhist pilgrim, 18.
Feasts among Kakhyens, 128, 129, 130.
Ferry over Salween, 188.
" " Tapeng, 347.
Festivals, Buddhist, 213.
" Shan, 369, 370.
" Chinese, 333.
Finger-rings, 66, 67, 106.
Fire, method of striking, among Kakhyens, 134.
Fish, 'ngapé' or dried, 64, 124, 207.
" tame, at Theebadaw island, 201.
Fitch, English merchant, 58.
Flannels, coloured, market for, 173.
Food of Kakhyens, 135, 256.
" " Shans, 109.
Fokien, king of, 22.
Forests, 60, 70, 83, 198, 211, 215, 225, 248, 279, 321, 383.
Fort St George documents on factories in Burmah, 46.
Fossilized wood, 199, 202.
Fragaria Indica, 64, 70, 239.
Fridelli, survey of Yunan, 46; map, 188.
Fruits, 64, 70, 84, 93, 264, 291, 368, 370.
Funtchung, siege of Mahomedan general at, 140.
Fytche, Major-General, and treaty with Burmah, 58.
" " on Mahomedans of Yunan, 143.

Galena ore, in Kakhyen hills, at Ponsee, 68; assay of, 69.
" at Khyto, Yunan, 92; assay of, 93.
" in Knenapa range, assay of, 69.
Gallus ferrugineus, 238.
Gallinula chloropus, 323.
Ganesa, 360.
Ganges, 59.
" and Irawady contrasted, 183.
Garrison, Chinese, 23, 34, 382.
Gaudama, 225, 293, 296, 350, 351, 372, 374, 376.
" tooth of, in China, 113.
" figures of, 205, 357, 361.
" impressions of, 206.
" footprint of, in Sanda valley, 355.
Gauls, similarity of Shan ornaments to those of the, 106.
Gaya, 206.
Gazettes, Pekin, 142.
Geegunshur, 175.
Gems, custom of burying, under skin, 118.
Geree, silver neck-hoop, 122.
Ghosts, belief in, 117, 126.
Girdles, of Kakoo women, 121; of Kakhyens, 246.
" " Tsawbwa daughters, 122, 246.
Glass-ware, market for, in Shan valleys, 173.
Gneiss, 68, 80, 81, 83, 264.

GENERAL INDEX.

Goitre, prevalence of, at Momien, 41, 326.
Gold, 65, 67, 173, 328.
  ,, vessels of, demanded as tribute, 13, 17.
  ,, letters on, 14.
  ,, and silver road, 32.
  ,,   ,, bridge, 32.
  ,, plates, a present to Chinese Emperor, 33.
  ,, value of, in Kardandan, Polo, 39.
  ,,   ,, in Shan States, 39.
  ,, Kampti Shan, on, 40, 65.
  ,, covering of teeth with, 36, 40.
  ,, on Mogoung river, 63.
  ,, in the Kapdup, 67.
  ,, bartered for salt, 40, 67.
  ,, in Kakhyen hills, 69.
  ,, at Momien, 93.
  ,, washing, 200.
  ,,   ,, in Pon-nah creek, 201.
  ,,   ,, at Shuaygyeen, 201.
Goldsmiths, 220.
Gordon Mr., arrival at Muangla, 345.
  ,,   ,, on Hotha Tsawbwa, 345.
Goulangsigong mountains, 184.
Government, in Shan States 117.
  ,, Kakhyen, 131, 132.
  ,, Panthay, 149, 150.
Governor of Momien, Tasakone, 150. 313.
  ,,   ,, presents to, 314, 337.
  ,,   ,, visits to, 315, 316, 318, 335, 338.
  ,,   ,, presents from, 339.
  ,, of Nantin (Tu-ta-dui, 307, 308, 343.
Graculus carbo, 242.
  ,, *fuscicollis*, 242.
  ,, *javanicus*, 298.
Gradients from Bhamô to Momien, 167, 168, 169.
Granges, Baron Otto des, 57.
  ,, survey between Bengal and China, 55.
  ,, proposed route to Yunan, 56.
Granite, 68, 76, 80, 81, 83, 86, 88, 91, 383.
Graves, Shan, 114, 302.
  ,, Kakhyen, 130, 248, 253, 263.
Griffith, Dr., 57; from Suddyah to Bhamô, 54.
  ,, route to Mogoung, 161.
  ,, on Irawady, 178.
  ,, probable source of Irawady, 183.
Grosier, Abbé, on Mahomedans in China, 141.
Grus antigone, 242.
Gureeb Nuwaz, Rajah of Manipore, 11.
Gutzlaff, on Buddhist relics, 13.
  ,, on Yunlio, 19, 21.
  ,, History of China by, 19.
  ,, on U-san-ghay, 21.
  ,, Burmo-Chinese war of 1765, 24.
  ,, Mahomedans in China, 142.

H*adji*, appointed by emperor of China, 139.
  ,, at Momien, 144.
  ,, king of Talifoo, 149.
  ,, of Nantin, 151, 308.

Haesa (Hotha), 366.
Hailstones, remarkable shower of, 74, 274, 275.
Hair-dressing among Kakhyens, 121.
Hair, tying of, 5.
Hair-pins, Shan-Chinese, 103, 104.
  ,, ornaments, Shan, 111.
Haliastur indus, 211.
Hannay, 175.
Hamilton, Dr. Francis Buchanan, see Dr. Francis Hamilton Buchanan.
Hang-chew, 139, 141.
Hannay, Captain (Col.), on old boundary line between Pong and Ava, 7.
  ,,   ,, on Native Christians in Madoya, 20.
  ,,   ,, of, mission to Mogoung, 54.
  ,,   ,, journal, 55.
  ,,   ,, on term Kakoo, 119.
  ,,   ,, Irawady above Bhamô, 182.
  ,,   ,, Sůhmaī-Khā, 183.
  ,,   ,, figure of Dipenkara (Gnadama), 206.
Hansa (Latha), 366.
Harts, galena of, 69, 93.
Hawshuensban, extinct volcano of, 87, 90, 312, 320.
  ,, valley of, 87, 91, 318, 331; cultivation in, 93, population of, 94, visit to, 328.
Hawshuenshan, walled town of, 331.
Head-dress of Shan women, 101.
  ,, Shan-Chinese women, 103, 104.
Heen-tsung, and Buddhist relic, 13.
Helix battonii, 258.
Hentha, 243.
Henza or Brahminical goose, 113.
Herodius alba, 242, 323.
  ,, *egrettoides*, 237, 242, 298.
  ,, *garzetta*, 211, 298.
Hien-kiong, opium importation legalized by, 71.
Hill-Chinese at Sanda, 353.
Hill-ranges, rocks of, 59, 68, 77, 80, 81, 88, 268, 305.
Hills, character of, 76, 78, 79, 92; at Sanda, 79, 80, 302; at Mawphoo, 86; at Nantin 87; at Hawshuenshan, 90; at Momien 91.
  ,, Kakhyen, 68, 76, 167, 169, 214, 244.
Hindoo rite of *rasta-yaga*, 116.
Hindoos, cow-worship among, 116.
Hitsung, of Tang dynasty, 139; flight of, to Tibet, 139.
Hiuntsung, of Tang dynasty, 138.
Hiun-tsong or Haou-tsong, 145.
Hoetong, 44, 90, 155, 382.
  ,, Kakhyen chief, 135; house of, 383.
Hokyan river, 78, 159, 189.
  ,, Burmese itineraries on, 190.
Houan, barbarities of Channiuchon in, 20.
Hong-klang river, 170.
Hoochungtang, chief minister of China, 33.
Hookah (opium-pipe), Kakhyen, 134.

GENERAL INDEX. 441

Hoolock, 256, 273.
Horse, figures of, at Manwyne, 115; at Muangla, 116.
  ,, tails, Shan custom of tying, 41; Persian custom of tying, 41.
  ,, worship among Shans, 116, 293.
Hosong, 135.
Hotha Tsawbwa, 85, 135, 303, 308, 321, 333, 336, 343, 345, 348, 356, 359, 361.
  ,, family of, 367, 377.
  ,, valley of, 25, 78, 361, 365, 377.
  ,, ,, relations of, to Sanda, 76.
  ,, ,, description of, 82.
  ,, ,, rocks in, 83.
  ,, ,, rice and tobacco in, 83.
  ,, ,, formation of, 83.
  ,, ,, wild indigo in, 83.
  ,, ,, domestic animals in, 84.
  ,, ,, climate of, 85.
  ,, ,, priests of, 109.
  ,, ,, Shans in, 99, 101.
  ,, ,, Kakhyens in, 119.
  ,, ,, Leesaws in, 135.
  ,, ,, Burmese surveyor on,
  ,, ,, Sawaddy route to, 186.
  ,, ,, arrival of Expedition at, 365.
  ,, ,, visit to head of, 373.
  ,, ,, and Lassa, Lenylone route by, 155, 156.
  ,, bazaar, description of, 368.
  ,, dâks, 111, 368.
  ,, departure from, 377.
Hotha, Shan State, 4, 18.
  ,, ,, pagodas in, 10, 30, 99, 371.
  ,, ,, Burmese claim to, 10, 18, 30.
  ,, ,, Peguan army advance into, 18, 31.
  ,, ,, Buddhism introduced, 18, 99.
  ,, ,, monasteries built in, 18, 99.
  ,, ,, Burmese conquest of, 27.
  ,, ,, number of villages in, 85.
  ,, ,, population of, 86.
Hotha Old, or Tsaycow, visit to, 371.
Hot springs at Sanda, 81, 354.
  ,, ,, ,, analysis of water of, 81.
  ,, ,, ,, temperature of, 82.
  ,, ,, in Nantin valley, 88, 311, 312.
  ,, ,, ,, description of, 89.
  ,, ,, ,, temperature and analysis of, 89.
"Hasi-hasi," Chinese term for Mohamedans, 147.
"Howze", meaning of, 147.
Houses, Chinese, 110, 216.
  ,, Shan, 110, 292, 297.
  ,, Shan-Burmese, 219.
  ,, Kakhyen, 122, 247, 384.
  ,, of Tsawbwas, 293, 297, 309, 315, 317, 371, 378, 383, 384.
Htseszeh, village of, 197.
Hukong valley, 53, 54, 162.
Hullee, 175.
Hwasttsung, 18.
Hwaog-chou, rebellion of, 139.

Hyla chinensis, 322.
Hylobates, 256, 271, 273.
Hypsipetes, 259.

Ibn Batuta on Mahomedans in China, 140.
Indian corn grown by Kakhyens, 70, 83, 124, 283, 291, 379, 383.
Indigo-dye, 84, 111, 173, 353, 360, 369.
  ,, wild, 84, 333.
Indo-Chinese, nât-worship among, 115.
Inheritance, laws of, among Shans, 117.
  ,, ,, among Kakhyens, 131.
Interpreter, Burmese, 340.
  ,, Chinese, 242.
  ,, Kakhyen, 229, 232, 263.
IRAWADY, 4, 5, 8, 16, 25, 56, 173, 195.
  ,, never crossed by Chinese armies, 17.
  ,, Burmese army advances up the, 26, 29.
  ,, Chinese construct boats on, 28.
  ,, attempts to bridge, 29, 32.
  ,, Bhamô routes shortest and best between Yunan (China) and, 35, 57, 160.
  ,, Marco Polo, on the mart on, 39.
  ,, position of Kaungtoung on, 44.
  ,, Tsampenago highest Burmese town on, 47.
  ,, Crawford's estimate of, 50, 175.
  ,, Dr. William's opinion of, 57, 184.
  ,, character and resources of the, 59, et seq.
  ,, valley described.
  ,, descriptions of first or upper defile of, 61, 184.
  ,, floods in, 62.
  ,, branches of, 62.
  ,, coal mines along upper, 59, 65, 167.
  ,, distances between Cambodia and, 77.
  ,, capabilities of, for traffic from Ava to Bhamô, 167, 175.
  ,, prospects for trade on, 174.
  ,, two defiles on, between Bhamô and Mandalay, 186, 213, 214.
  ,, sources of, 178, et seq.
  ,, ,, Klaproth's hypothesis regarding Sanpo and, considered, 178.
  ,, ,, opinions of Wilcox, Burlton, and Neufville on, 179.
  ,, ,, opinion of Buchanan Hamilton on, 181.
  ,, ,, opinions of Hannay, Bayfield, and Griffith about, 182, et seq.
  ,, ,, opinion of a Kampti Shan, 186.
  ,, ,, claim of Wilcox to have discovered the, considered, 187.
  ,, ,, information gathered at Momien regarding, 188.

Irawady, sources of, probable accuracy of Jesuits map on, 189.
" " D'Anville's theory, 192.
" Mr. Cooper on upper waters of, 193.
" character of river-banks of, 196, 204, 207, 212, 213.
" channels in, 197, 203, 208, 211, 215.
" dolphin (new species) in, 203, 208.
" character of, at Bhamô, 215, 216, 388.
Irish ornaments, similarity of Shan to, 106.
Iron at Momien, 111, 173, 328.
" mines, 67, 173.
" suspension-bridges, 159, 188, 190, 311, 344.
Irrigation among Shans, 80, 89, 91, 251, 283, 288, 110, 295, 348.
" reservoir, 196.
Itineraries, Burmese, 34, 188, 189.
" Colonel Burney's, of Theinnee and Bhamô routes to China, 53, App. A.

Jade, 63, 65, 106.
" mines, 66, 67.
" trade in, 61.
" manufacture of, at Momien, 67, 327.
" bracelets, value of, at Momien, 328.
" rings, 107, 322, 323.
" rings, value of, at Bhamô and Canton, 67.
Jagannath, 330.
'Jámiut Tawáríkh' on Zardandan, 36.
Jasper, 66.
Jenkins, Mr., on country between Assam and Hukong, 165.
" " on Patkoi route to Burmah, 165.
Jesuit Fathers, on Mahomedans in China, 140.
" map (Yunan), 46, 52, 188, 190.
" " Sir J. F. Davis on, 52.
Jewish population in China, massacre of, 139.
Jonesia, 252.
Juglans regia, 70.
Jyepore, 166.

Kabynet, 198.
Kad-doung, view of, 386.
Kaingma, 4, 27, 159.
" Buddhist pagodas in, 30.
" Silver-mines near, 39, 49.
Kakhyens (Singphos or Chingpaws), 96, 118, 187, 219, 240, 257, 271, 318, 368, 369, 374, 381, 382, 385.
" nât-worship, 37, 125, 245, 249.
" Toomsah and Meetway, 37, 126.
" offerings and sacrifices to nâts, 37, 38, 127, 383.
" arrow-poison of, 42, 134.
" resemblance to Shans of, 99.

Kakhyens, language of, spoken by Chinese and Shans, 100.
" sepulchral urns of, 106.
" distribution of, 118, 122.
" term applied by Burmese, 118.
" clans, names of, 118, 119.
" Burmese estimate of, 119, 230.
" " oppression of, 119.
" in Hotha valley, 120.
" methods of warfare, 120.
" hospitality of, 120, 381.
" physical character of, 121.
" dress of, 121, 231, 246, 254.
" ornaments of, 121, 246, 275, 360.
" ornaments of chiefs' wives, and daughters, 182, 246.
" habits of, 122, 245, 257, 269.
" houses and domestic habits of, 122, 123, 247, 379, 383.
" industry of the women, 124, 276, 278.
" language and religion, 124.
" names of nâts, 125.
" religious feasts of, 127.
" customs of, 127, 245, 254, 265.
" marriage ceremonies of, 127, 128.
" birth ceremonies, 129.
" death and burial ceremonies, 129, 130, 247, 248.
" form of government amongst, 131.
" laws of inheritance, 131.
" offices of Tsawbwa and Pawmine, 132.
" slavery among, 132, 222, 286, 360.
" manufactures, 133.
" weapons, 134.
" art among, 134.
" amusements, 135.
" food of, 135, 256.
" chiefs or Tsawbwas of, 131, 135, 231, 233, 240, 254.
" relations of Leesaws to, 135.
" " to rebel Mahomedans in Yunan, 148.
" resemblance to eastern Karens, 212.
" at Bhamô 221.
" trade of, at Bhamô, 221.
" child-stealing by, 212, 222.
" Hindoo slave among, 222, 286.
" ceremony of consulting the wishes of the nâts, 249.
" graves of, 130, 248, 253, 263.
" villages of, 79, 255, 266, 277, 363, 379, 383.
" game-trap, 280.
" roads and canals of irrigation, 283, 288.
" at Momien, 318.
" trade with Sanda, 355.
" ceremony of swearing eternal friendship, 387.
" hills, Ponsee silver-mines in, 30, 48; visit to, 267, 268.

GENERAL INDEX.   443

Kakhyen hills, Burmese influence in, 30.
  „   „   Chinese garrison in, 34.
  „   „   height and position of, to Burmese plains, 60, 68.
  „   „   composition of, 68, 283.
  „   „   gold in, 69.
  „   „   crops of, 70, 133, 241, 283, 288.
  „   „   opium cultivation in, 71, 221, 266.
  „   „   domestic animals in, 73.
  „   „   climate of, 73.
  „   „   and Cambodia, country between, 76.
  „   „   analysis of silver in galena of, 93.
  „   „   character of roads over, 153.
  „   „   trade routes across, considered, 153, 158.
  „   „   practicability of a railway over, considered, 167, 168, 169.
  „   „   imposts in, 173, 338, 363.
  „   „   Expedition party crosses, 243, et seq.
  „   „   return from, 385.
  „   priests, 37, 126, 243.
  „   „   Toomsah and Meetway, 37, 126.
  „   lamshaus or altars, 125, 127, 129, 29, 61, 67, 186.
Kakhyo, advance of Chinese armies by, 17, 160.
  „   march of Burmese army, 25, 26.
  „   on route from Momien and Sanda to Mogoung, 160.
Kakoos, Kakhyen clan of, 119.
  „   Colonel Hannay on name of, 119.
  „   in valley of Upper Irawady, 119.
  „   dress of, 121, 122.
Kala Woon, 195.
Kala Shan, 6, 186.
Kaliph, Abasside, 138, 139.
  „   Abu Jafar al Mansur, 138.
Kamal Kamini, 330.
Kamptis, 8, 179, 180, 191.
Kampti-Shans, 40, 63, 191.
  „   plain, 118, 181, 191.
Kampti mountains, 178, 187, 190.
Kampton, village of, 304.
Kampyet river, 163.
Kamteechick river, 161.
Kamyoom or Kammairoam river, 162.
  „   „   „   British boundary, 166.
Kananzan village in mountains, 159.
  „   mountains, 9, 41, 63, 77, 78.
  „   „   appearance and composition of, 92.
  „   „   source of Tapeng in, 188.
Kanlantsan or Kananzan village, 159.
Kanzee, 139, 140, 145.
  „   Mahomedan rebellion in, 141.
  „   Yunan-Mahomedans claim to have come from, 146.
Kapdup stream, gold in, 67.

Kappilawot, 205.
Karahs, Kakhyen clan of, 118.
Karahokah, trading village of, 137, 295, 297.
Karainau or Yunan, 43.
Karam river, 161.
Karazan of Marco Polo, 6, 9, 41, 140.
Kardandan, 9.
  „   identity of, with Shan States, considered, 9, 39, 40.
  „   Marco Polo, on climate of, 40.
  „   „   on country between Burmah and, 42.
Karens, 97; Kakhyens' resemblance to, 212.
Kateow, khyoungs at, 376.
Katha, 4, 7.
  „   description of, 209.
  „   Woon of, visit to, 209, 210.
Kauliya, 205.
Kaung-toung, 25, 44, 61, 119.
  „   Tsawbwa of, 25.
  „   Chinese besiege, 25, 28.
  „   Balamanden, governor of, 26, 28.
  „   Burmese relief of, 26, 29.
  „   peace concluded at, 31.
  „   once famous mart of, 93, 214.
  „   or Sawaddy route, 154.
Kauthala or Kosala, 205.
Kazes or K'hazee, Mahomedan king, 144.
Keen lung, Chinese emperor, 1736, 24.
Keeuzar, appreciation of, 327.
Kethung, hill of, 197.
  „   village of, 197.
Ket-zu-bin, coal-mine, 199, 200.
Ken-king, Chinese emperor, 24.
Kewhom, eastern continuation of Irawady, 188.
Khaus-Delass, country of, 181.
Khanfa or Kang-chew-foo, 139.
Khangs, 119.
Khanlungs, or Chitans, 60, 119, 327.
Khamyen, Buddhist pagodas in, 24.
Khanti, pagodas in, 24.
Khansi, relations of, to Yunan, 72.
Khasse river, 162, 164.
Khasya hills, 74.
Khaytsong, Du Halde, 18.
Khathing river, 162.
Khotan, 66.
Khyoukdwen, Burmese name of 1st defile of Irawady, 48, 185.
  „   character of, 185.
Khyoungs or monasteries, 115, 117, 241, 243, 294, 325, 331, 334, 342, 349, 356, 358.
  „   schools in, 99, 300, 336.
  „   horse-worship in, 115, 116, 291, 293.
  „   Buddhistic figures in, 29, 117, 297, 334, 350, 372.
  „   at Manwyne, 115, 290, 361; worship in, 292.
  „   visit to nuns, at Manwyne, 361.
  „   at Sanda, 296; Shan and Chinese, 350, excommunication of Phoongyee, 357.
  „   at Muangla, Chinese, 300.

Khyoungs at Nantin, Chinese, 307.
,, at Momien, Chinese, 314.
,, at Shuayduay, 329; description of, 330.
,, at Hawshuenshan, 331.
,, at Mentone, 365.
,, at Old Hotha, 371; description of, 372.
,, at Tsendong, 375.
Khyto, copper at, 92, 333; silver at, 93, 333; analysis of the ore, 93.
,, salt at, 173.
,, Chinese attack on, 148, 333.
Kianghung, on the Cambodia, 149.
Kianghung-gyee, Leesaws at, 135.
,, ,, proposed railway by, 170.
,, ,, Cambodia navigable to, 171.
,, ,, tramway proposed to, 172.
Kidding, 161, 163.
Kienhung, 141.
Kincaid, Mr., at Bhamô, 55, 57.
Kinchi, Martini on, 5.
Kingdoung village, 287.
Klaproth, 66, 190.
,, map of, 56, 193.
,, hypothesis of, Sanpo and Irawady, 178, 181, 188.
Komoang or earth-necklace, 122.
Koran, in Chinese at Momien, 152.
Koshanpyi, or Shan States, 1. 4.
,, country of Tay-yays or Great Shans, 3; included in Pong kingdom, 4.
,, conquest of, and become tributary to China, 9.
,, Burmese claim to annexation of, 9.
,, Bhamô, one of, 3, 33.
Kotsui, Chinese general, 139, 145.
Kublai Khan, Mahomedanism in China in reign of, 140.
Kubo valley, south limit of Pong, 7.
Kudgin, 175.
Kuenapa hills, galena ore in, 69.
Kule, 205.
Kullack Boom, 162.
Kumday, 175.
Kunkur, 199.
Kwei-chew, 21.
Kyaing-young on Cambodia, 29.
Kyangnan, 20.
Kyangsi, 20.
Kyau-Nhyat, 203, 204.
Kyendwen river, 10, 205.
Kyouk-padoung, 205.
Kyô-zuá, king of Pagan, 15.
,, betrayed and deposed, 15.
,, Chinese attempt restoration of, 15.
Kyundo, island, 29.

Lackquee, 175.
Lahones, 119, 122.
,, guardian nât of, 126.
Lakones, 119.
Lakong, 256.
,, mountain, 252.
,, reported burnt village at, 255.
Laloon, 175.
Lama country, Captain Wilcox on, 178.
,, slave, 181.
L'Amiot, on the climate of Yunan, 52.
Lamoon, river, 163.
Lamshan or village altars, 125, 127, 129, 245, 383.
Land tenure in Shan States, 117.
,, ,, among Kakhyens, 131.
Language of Kakhyens, 124.
,, ,, Shans, 97.
,, ,, Chinese-Yunanese, 137.
,, ,, Leesaws, 136.
Laphais, 119.
Lasangs, 119.
Lassa and Assam, trade between, Captain Pemberton on, 176.
,, ,, Chouna, characters of trade between, 176.
,, Dalrymple on river through, 28.
,, and Hotha, Loaylone route by, 156.
,, outlets of drainage from, 193.
Latha, Shan State, 4, 31, 366, 377.
,, Peguan arms extended to, 18.
,, Burmese claim to, 10, 30.
,, Buddhism introduced into, 18, 30.
,, captured by Burmese, 1767 A. D., 27.
,, villages in, 84.
,, population of, 86.
,, and Hotha, priest in, dress of, 109.
,, Tsawbwa, 378.
Latong, 135.
Lava, 88, 90, 91, 328.
Lawloo, Kakhyen messenger, 277, 279, 283, 284, 327, 383, 388.
Laykan, Shan ear-ring, 122.
Lead, 173, 217, 220, 328.
Leesaws, 83, 118, 358, 363, 378.
,, distribution of, 135, 136.
,, physical appearance of, 136.
,, dress of, 136.
,, language, affinities of, 136.
,, at Sanda, 297, 355.
,, ,, Muangla, 300.
,, ,, Momien, 318.
,, village of, 363.
Leesetai, Chinese Imperialist, 25, 148, 218, 230, 258, 263, 274, 278, 285; defeat of, 279.
Leisus, Mr. Cooper on, 135.
Lek-ope-bin coal-mine, 198.
Lepchas, 42, 97, 127.
Letters on gold, 14, 34.
Leucocerca, 259.
Lewang, 20.
Licon, Chinese usurper, 21.
Limestone, 63, 66, 68, 80, 81, 92, 201, 214.
,, cliff of, below Bhamô, 59, 213.
Lizo mountain, advance of Chinese to, 25, 27.
Loakyung, Captain Wilcox on, 50.
Loaylone, Kakhyen chief, 124, 135, 382.

LOAYLONE, Chinese garrison station at, 34.
,, route to Momien, 153.
,, ,, description of, 155.
,, ,, embassy, viâ Muangwan, 155.
,, ,, viâ Lassa and Hotha, 155, 156.
,, ,, compared with Ponline route, 157, 158.
,, village of, visit to, 381.
Loglai river, 165.
Loli, Chinese trader, 24.
,, proposes to bridge Tapeng, 24, 167.
,, cause of war between Burmah and China, 24.
Long-chuen (Muangmo), 52.
Loom, Kakhyen, 133, 278.
,, Shan, 220.
Lowquangfang, Chinese Imperialist near Momien, 148; overtures to Expedition, from, 324.
Lu Khyang (Salween river), 6, 23.
,, Captain Wilcox on, 50.
Lû-ta-tshay-nhit-pana route, advance of Burmese army by, 27.
Lycopersicum esculentum, 70.

Macacus, 214, 261, 271, 277.
Macartney, Lord, mission to Pekin, 14, 33.
Mac'Cosh, on origin of Assamese, 3.
Mac'Leod, on Maingleng-gyee, 3.
Macnamara, analysis of Sanda hot-springs, 81.
,, ,, ,, Nantin ,, ,, 39.
Madeya, 20.
Magistrates or Tsitkays, of Bhamô, 228.
Maha Yazwen or great history of Ava, 16.
Mahomedan rebellions, 23, 24.
,, ,, in Yunan, 141, 142, 147; Chinese repository on, 142; Pekin gazettes on, 142.
,, raids, on Shan States, 94, 117.
,, purchase of children for converts, 141, 142.
,, traders, Colonel Barney on, 143.
,, king, Kazee or Khazee, 144.
,, present rebellion in Shan States, and Yunan, 148.
,, ,, ,, ,, and Yunan, Cooper on, 149.
,, king at Talifoo, 150.
,, ,, constitution of government, 150.
,, mandarins, 152.
,, hadji at Momien, 144; at Nantin, 151, 308.
,, general at Momien, visit to, 331.
,, neophyte, 341.
,, jemadar, 194, 247, 341.
,, police-guard, 194.
Mahomedans, at Muangtee, 94.
,, Shan tribute to, 117.

Mahomedans, in Yunan, 138 *et seq*; Marco Polo on, 140, 145; Rashid-ood-deen on, 140 145.
,, in China, General Fytche on 143; Major Sladen on 143.
,, ,, ,, Marco Polo on, 139, 140.
,, ,, ,, Ibn Batata on, 140.
,, ,, ,, Jesuit Fathers on, 140.
,, ,, ,, Louis le Compte on, 140.
,, ,, ,, Abbé Grosier on, 141.
,, ,, ,, Gutzlaff on, 142.
,, Chinese, pilgrims to Mecca, 143.
,, Yunanese, probable origin and history of, 146.
,, ,, probable future of, 146.
,, called Panthays by Burmese, 147.
,, Chinese terms for, 147; Mr. Cooper on, 147.
,, at Momien, possessions of, 148; dress of, 151; character of, 152.
Mahomed, Deen, 132, 142, 261, 263.
,, ,, history of, 222, 223.
,, ,, claimed by Kakhyen Tsawbwa, 286.
Maingla, 17, 188.
Maingleng-gyee, 3, 4.
Maingmah, 4.
Maingsee, Yunan city, Burmese name of, 6.
Mainla, 40.
Maintsoung, 188.
Makouk, 198.
Malé, Mali or Manlay, 29, 167, 203.
,, river, 205, 206.
Malong, Chinese princesses from, 33.
Manchester goods, market for, among Shans, 173; market for, in China, 174; in Sechuen and Tibet, 176.
,, ,, at Bhamô, 217.
Mandalay, 92, 118, 167, 184, 273, 284.
,, and Bhamô, country between, 43.
,, galena ore in hills near, 69.
,, Yunan opium at, 72.
,, Shan opium at, 111.
,, Talifoo iron at, 111.
,, Mahomedan caravans at, 143, 266.
,, to Bhamo, 194 *et seq*.
,, view of, from Mengoon, 195.
,, hairy woman of, 126.
Mandeiytoung, 195.
Manhleo Poogain, 261, 356, 361, 364.
Manis, 271.
Manlay or Malé, 48.
Manloi, 363, 366; Burmese pagoda at, 366.
Manloug (Muanlong), ancient capital of Pong, 4.
Manloung village, 241; monastery at, 241.
Manloung river, 238, 239, 241.

GENERAL INDEX.

Manloung lake, 241.
Manshi or Manji, king of, 6.
Mantai, visit to village of, 384.
"   Kakhyen Tsawbwa, 135, 378, 384.
Manroya or Mweyen, 7.
Mantchoo Tartars, 18.
Manufactures, Shan, 111, 112, 133, 173, 291, 369.
"   Kakhyen, 133, 134.
"   Chinese, 133.
"   of amber and jade ornaments at Momien, 66, 67, 327.
"   " bricks, 64, 93, 221.
"   " silver currency, 220.
Manuscripts, Shan, 1.
"   Arabian, 143.
MANWYNE, Shan-Chinese town of, 24, 42, 83, 135, 154, 233, 250, 253, 254, 260, 262, 266, 267, 272, 284, 285, 356.
"   basin or division of Sanda valley, 80.
"   rocks at, 80.
"   Rahance religious houses in, 115.
"   Chinese population at, 136.
"   distance of, to Nantin, 157.
"   route to, by Molay river, 160.
"   reception of Expedition at, 289.
"   Buddhist monastery at, 290; description of, 290.
"   bazaar at, 291.
"   Tsawbwaship, villages in, 85, 292; population of, 86.
"   Tsawbwa-gadaw of, 293; dinner with, 360.
"   nuns of, 293, 303.
"   priests at, 293, 359.
"   departure from, 295, 362.
"   attack on Expedition near, 295.
"   return to, 359.
"   visit to convent at, 361.
Maps of boundaries of Pong and Ava, 3, 7.
"   "   "   "   Burmah and Western China, 52, 186.
"   " Hamilton Buchanan, 7, 49.
"   " Jesuits (Yunan), 46, 52, 188, 190.
"   " Klaproth, Dalrymple, and Berghaus, 193.
Marai (bell, Shan), 125.
Marble, 68, 261, 264.
"   Buddhas, 237.
MARCO POLO, 6, 24, 118.
"   on Karazan, 9, 41.
"   " Tartar invasion of Ava, 14.
"   Marsden's, 5, 24, 39.
"   on South-West China, 24.
"   " Kardandan, 36; on customs in, 9, 36, 37, 38, 40; on climate of, 40.
"   " country between Kardandan and Burmah, 42.
"   " Mahomedans in China, 139.
"   "   "   " Yunan, 145
Marriages of Shans with Burmese, 96, 98.
"   "   "   " Poloungs, 100.
"   "   " devoid of religious ceremony, 113.

Marriage-ceremonies among Kakhyens, 127.
Marsden's "Marco Polo" 5, 24, 39.
"   on Karazan, 6.
"   " king of Mien and Bengal, 14.
"   " Kardandan, 40.
"   " Karainan, 43.
"   " spelling of Bhamô, 46.
Martini on town of Yunchan, 5.
Masa, nât, 125.
Masoo, nât, 125.
Matze, 147.
Mawphoo, 90, 260, 304, 345.
"   Leesetai's fortress at, 148, 258.
"   arrival of Expedition at, 305.
"   description of, 305, 306.
"   proposed duties on goods at, 338.
"   hill, 25, 78, 154, 157, 168, 305.
"   gorge, physical characters of, 80, 86.
"   " rocks and deposits at, 81.
"   " difficulty of, for road or railway, 168.
"   valley, 344.
Ma Yussu, *hadji*, king at Talifoo, 149.
Mecca, pilgrimage of Chinese Mahomedans to, 143.
Mechis, 97.
Medical practice at Bhamô, 227.
Medoo, 72.
Meetway, Kakhyen priest, 37, 252.
Meeya or Meeyatoung hills, 10.
Meinkhoom, 65, 66, 162.
Mekhaung or Mekhong (Cambodia), 25, 170.
Mekley, 43.
Melanopelargus episcopus, 196.
Melolophus melanicterus, 259.
Mengoon, 195.
"   pagoda at, 195.
Mentone village, 365.
Meteorological observations in Kakhyen hills, 73, 95, App. D.
Miautze, 118, 147.
"   raid of, into Sechuen, 149.
Midnapore, 132, 223.
Mien or Ava proper, 43.
"   Chinese fort of, 9.
Milvus govinda? 196.
Mimsahs, Kakhyen clan of, 119.
Mines amber or *Payendwen*, 54, 65.
"   jade, 66.
"   silver, or *Bodwan-gyee*, 30, 39, 49, 69, 93, 265, 267, 333.
"   coal, 59, 198, 199.
"   iron, 67, 173.
"   ruby, 208.
"   copper, 92, 333.
Mirbel, on Griffith, 183.
Mogoung, 6, 8, 26, 179, 180, 187, 191.
"   conquest attempted by Chinese, 17, 28.
"   chief, surrender demanded by Chinese, 17.
"   Tsawbwa, 29.
"   division of Burmese army, 29, 32.
"   district, independence of Shans in, 98.
Mogoung to Assam, Dr. Griffith, 161.

GENERAL INDEX.

Mogoung Captain Burnett's attempt to reach, 164.
" Beesa to, Captain Pemberton on 165.
" tributaries of Irawady between Ava and, 183.
" river or Namkong, 8, 186.
" " branch of Irawady, 62.
" " route between Brahmaputra and, 161.
" " breadth of Irawady at mouth of, 63, 182, 183.
" town of, 54, 60, 61.
" " Shan opium at, 111, 266.
" trade between Momien and, 160.
" coal at, 167.
Mohung Koshanpyi, 4.
Mohungleng, 3.
" silver-mines near, 49.
Molay river, 28, 59, 62, 76, 160.
" description of, 63.
" to Sanda, 160, 356.
" visit to, 388.
Momeit, 29, 208.
" route, 12, 19, 27.
MOMIEN, 9, 23, 24, 30, 35, 39, 147, 257, 285.
" antiquity of, 6.
" Fort of Mien (Burmah), 9.
" (Theng-ye-chow), 19, 52.
" to Yungchan, 23, 158.
" to Kakhyen hills, distance of, 24.
" name of Tapeng river at, 25.
" Burmese mission to China, vid, 34.
" silver-mine, north-east of, 40.
" climate of, 40, 94, 324, 328.
" amber and its value at, 66.
" jade and its manufacture at, 67, 327.
" mountain ranges east of, 77.
" to Irawady, distance from, 77.
" centre of Mahomedanism in West Yunan, 90.
" bazaar, 92, 318.
" " minerals sold at, 92, 111, 173, 328.
" gold at, 39, 93, 173.
" galena silver at, 93, 173.
" salt at, 173.
" Mahomedan rebellion at, 148.
" Panthays at, description of, 150, 152.
" trade between Mogoung and, 160.
" railway between Bhamô and Yunan vid, considered, 170.
" probable trade, 173.
" and Tapeng, 188.
" messengers from, 270, 274, 310.
" reception at, 313.
" Chinese khyoung in, 314.
" description of, 319.
" pagoda hill at, 320.
" potatoes and celery at, 321.
" priests at, 335.
" khyoung, school in, 336.
" farewell to, 341.
" district of Yunan, 17, 69.

Momien, governor of, 24.
" " description of office of, 150.
" " " Tasakone, 151.
" " entertainments by, 316, 338.
" " duties proposed by, 328.
" military governor of, 150, 333.
" " visits to, 322, 331.
" valley, 90, 155, 320.
" " height of, 78.
" " description of, 91.
" " physical features of, 91.
" " volcanic centre of, 91.
" " vegetable products of, 93.
" " fruits, 93.
" " domestic animals in, 94, 325.
" " population of, 94.
" " unhealthiness of, 95, 326.
" " Chinese pagodas in, 313.
" " routes to Bhamô, 153 et seq, 382.
Monasteries, 18, &c., see Khyoungs.
Mongmaorong, capital of Pong, 6.
Mongsan, Tartar Lamas, 22.
Mongsee, 6.
Monkeys, 198, 261, 264, 271, 277.
" colony of, 213.
Montgomery, Captain, on Irawady, 178.
Moo river, 10.
Moodootseitta, 205.
Moulas, 119.
Moulmein, 189, 214.
Moungshuay-Yah, 194, 242, 247, 273, 282, 303, 324.
Moungmo, Kakhyen interpreter, 281.
" imprisonment of, at Bhamô, 283.
" wife in stocks at Bhamô, 284.
Mowlain, ndt, 125.
Mowun or Muangwan route, 214.
Mrelap Shans or Shannas, 33.
Muangchan or Shuenli, 159.
Muang-gan, Tsawbwa-gadaw of, 288.
Muangkah river, 381.
Muangkhong, 54.
Muangkung, 2, 8.
MUANGLA, Shan State, 4, 67.
" captured by Burmese, 27.
" pagodas built in, 30.
" basin in Sanda valley, 80, 299.
" villages in, 85.
" population of, 86.
" town of, 76, 79, 154, 343.
" rocks at, 81.
" horse-worship at, 116.
" arrival at, 299.
" description of, 300.
" khyoungs in, 303.
" Tsawbwa of, 253, 301.
" return to, 345.
" Mr. Gordon at, 345.
" purchase of Shan products at, 346.
" Burmese at, 365.
Muanglan country, mines in, 67.

448 GENERAL INDEX.

Muanglam, 3.
Muangleng or Mohungleng, 3.
Muanglong (Manlong), 4, 8, 10.
Muangma, Shan State, 4.
Muangmo, 23, 52.
,, captured by Burmese, 27.
,, (Shuaylee) chief, 8.
,, chief, king of Pong, 15.
,, silver-mine at, 69.
Muangphee or *Tsojah*, (Shan) heaven, 125.
Muangsee, Shan name of Yunan city, 6, 8, 159.
MUANGTEE (Mynetee), Shan State, 4, 50, 89, 344.
,, Momien routes converge at, 90.
,, population at, character of, 94, 136.
,, arrival at, 307.
Muangting, 49.
Muangwan, 17, 49, 50, 382.
,, route, 25, 33, 34, 214.
,, ,, Burmese surveyor on, 42, 373.
,, Embassy route *viâ*, 155.
Muangwye, 135, 380.
,, Tsawbwa, 382.
Mamuts, 119.
Munipore, 2, 59, 133.
,, Rajah of, assists Pong kings, 10, 11.
,, proposed route to China, *viâ*, 56.
Muron, *nât*, 125.
Murrows, 118.
Mutthin, 44, 135.
,, Kakhyen chief, 124, 381, 382.
,, visit to village of, 383.
Museum, Indian, 281.
Musjid at Momien, 332.
Mweyen, capital of Shakya kings, 7.
Myadoung, village of, 208.
,, district of, 208.
Mya-leit-toung mountains, 195.
Myedu, 16.
Myenzain, 15.
Myitnge river, 27, 77, 195.
Mynesa or Mynetha, Shan name for Hotha, 366.

Naga hills, 161.
Nagas of Assam, 122.
Nagazein, 205, 206.
Nahlow, 304.
Namanoo, 175.
Namba, village on Tapeng, 24.
Namboke, Kakhyen chief, 124, 135, 368, 377.
,, village, arrival at, 378.
,, ,, departure from, 379.
,, to Hotha, 156.
,, river, 377, 380.
Namkho, Tahô or Tapeng, 50.
,, Captain Wilcox on, 50.
Namkin or Irawady, 180.
Namkong river, Pong capital on, 2.

Namkong or Mogoung river, 8.
Namkwún, 67, 135.
Namlong, 179.
Naulunai or Kyendwen, 162.
Nampean, 163.
Nampung hamlet, 155, 386.
,, river, 154.
,, ,, Chinese garrisons at, 24, 34.
,, ,, rocks at, 68.
,, ,, western boundary of Yunan, 250.
Nampyoka river, 163.
Namroop river, 161, 164, 165.
Namsa river, 76, 83, 377.
Namsan, 166.
Nam Sanda or Sanda river, 79.
Namsang, branch of Irawady, 186, 187.
Namthabet river, 125, 186, 385, 386.
Namthuga, 162.
Nam Tunail, 163.
Namturoon, 163.
Namtuseek, 163.
Namtuwa, 162.
Namtwonkok river, 67.
Nanken, Kakhyen chief, 135.
NANTIN, town of, 25, 52; description of, 307, 309.
,, Chinese advance by, 25, 29.
,, Burmese mission by, 34.
,, Mahomedan rebellion at, 147.
,, Hadji of, 151, 308.
,, iron suspension-bridge below, 188, 307.
,, arrival at, 307.
,, Chinese khyoung at, 307.
,, Tu-tu-du of, 309.
,, departure from, 310.
,, visit from Tsawbwa-gadaw of, 323.
,, return to, 342.
,, visit from governor, 343.
,, theft of ponies at, 344.
,, final departure from, 344.
,, valley, height of, 78, 168.
,, ,, river-terraces in, 86, 310, 312.
,, ,, description of, 86, 307, 341, 382.
,, ,, denudation at, 87.
,, ,, hills at, 87, 88, 307, 312.
,, ,, hot springs in, 88.
,, ,, ,, analysis of water, 89.
,, ,, ,, visits to, 311 342.
,, ,, cultivation in, 89, 90, 93, 310.
,, ,, population of, 94.
,, ,, inhabited by Shans, 99.
,, ,, relation to Bhamô routes, 154, 156, 157.
,, ,, capabilities of, for road-making, 156.
,, ,, and Sanda, difference of altitude, 168.
,, ,, and Hawshuenshan, 90, 169, 312.

GENERAL INDEX. 449

Nantin valley, difficult descent from Momien to, 341.
  ,, ,, ,, ascent to Mawphoo from, 345.
Nara-thù-padé, 15.
Nât, great, dread of, 292.
  ,, evil, ,, 352.
  ,, -worship among Kakhyens, 37.
  ,, ,, ,, Burmese, 37, 116.
  ,, ,, ,, of Indo-Chinese tribes, 116.
Nâts, Kakhyen, names of, 125.
  ,, household, 126, 128, 129, 130.
  ,, sacrifices to, 37, 127, 130, 131.
  ,, ,, ,, at Bhamô described, 38, 387.
  ,, offerings to, 73, 126, 127, 129, 263.
  ,, consultation of, at Pouline, 249; at Ponsee, 267.
Nattoung hills, 197.
Naungtalô island, 29.
  ,, Chinese propose a bridge across Irawady at, 29.
Necklace, earth, of Kakhyens, 122, 360.
Neck rings or *torques* of Shans, 106.
Nepaul, 42, 176.
Nestardin, Chinese Mahomedan General, 14, 15.
Nestorian Christians in Shensi, 146.
Neufville, Captain, 178.
  ,, ,, on sources of Brahmaputra and Irawady, 179.
Ngan-loshan, Chinese rebel, 138, 144.
Ngapé or Gnapé, 64, 198, 207, 210, 221.
Noa Dehing, 161, 165.
Nonjeeree hills, 10.
Nocian, 39.
Nongyang lake, 165.
Nuayliet, 25.
Numenius phæophus, 196.
Nunnun river, 164, 165.
Nuns of Manwyne, 294, 303.
  ,, ,, visit to, 361.
Nurans, 118.
Nycticorax griseus, 242.
Nyungen, Tsawbwa, 254.

Oaks on Kakhyen hills, 248, 255, 278, 364.
Official, Burmese Court, 194.
Old Bhamô, see Bhamô Old.
Oldham, Dr., on coal mines on the Irawady, 59.
  ,, ,, assays of Ponsee galena, 69.
  ,, ,, assay of Khyto galena, 93.
  ,, ,, geological features of Irawady, 59, 69.
Old Hotha, 371.
  ,, Pagan, history of, 7, 12.
  ,, ,, visit to ruins of, 12, 204.
Onono, 175.
Opium of Yunan, 70, 71, 266.
  ,, Shan, 72, 83.
  ,, price of, 93, 266.

Opium, Kakhyen, 124, 134, 221, 266.
  ,, comparative table of Yunan and Bengal, 72.
Opthalmia among Shans, 114, 310.
Orcella fluminalis, 203.
Oriental Repository, 28.
Otocompsa, 259.
Oudh (Kosala), 205.
Ouîgours, 138, 139.
Oung-loshan, 144, 145.

Padma, 330.
Pagan, Chinese invasions of, 12, 13.
  ,, kings of, 12, 13.
  ,, destroyed by Chinese-Tartars, 15.
  ,, capital of Mien, 43.
  ,, Upper, 206.
  ,, new, 13.
  ,, old, Burmese capital, 7, 12.
  ,, ruins of, described, 12, 204.
  ,, pagoda at, 12, 206.
Pagodas, 204, 206, 213, 243.
  ,, in Hotha and Latha, 10, 18, 31.
  ,, at Pagan, 12, 13, 206.
  ,, ceremony at laying foundations of, 116, 225.
  ,, at Mengoon, 195.
  ,, of Theebadaw, 198.
  ,, of Shuaybaw, 212.
  ,, of Shuaykeenah, 224, 225, 226.
  ,, Chinese, at Momien, 313.
  ,, of Comootanay, 18, 371.
Pahan, *nât*, 125.
Palæorni, 202.
Pali, inscription in, 206.
Pallas, mart of Selin, 139.
Pandani, 248.
Panglai river, 162.
Panmô or Bhamô, 46, 52.
Panthay, meaning of term, 147.
  ,, rebellion, 148, 149, 316.
  ,, king at Talifoo, 150.
  ,, form of government, 150.
  ,, messengers from Momien, 270.
  ,, officials, 303, 313, 341.
Panthays, 67, 137, 142, 255, 260, 300, 336, 345.
  ,, in Yunan, 148, 335.
  ,, at Momien, 149, 150, 339.
  ,, appearance and dress of, 151.
  ,, character of, 152, 339.
  ,, letters from, 159, 283.
  ,, tribute paid to, 286, 301.
Papada-raza (Raja), 231, 242.
Parsees, massacred in China, 139.
Partridge, (new species,) 259.
Passer monticolus, 259.
Patkoi pass, 53.
  ,, range, 54.
  ,, ,, Assam to Mogoung across, 164, 165.
Pawmines, 131, 245, 271, 358.
  ,, office and duties of, 132.

Payæ (Tay-yay), 47.
Payendwen or amber-mines, 54, 56.
Peat, 81, 91.
Pegu, 16, 33, 205.
  ,, tributary to China, 14.
  ,, army of, advances to borders of China, 17.
  ,, erects pillar at Khanti, 17.
  ,, conquers Ava, 18.
  ,, introduces Buddhism into Shan States, 18.
  ,, river of, 170.
Peguan king, conquest of Shan States by, 9,
  ,, empire, downfall of, 18.
Pekin, 33, 90, 139.
  ,, Lord Macartney's mission to, 14.
  ,, relations of Yunan to, 21.
  ,, Burmese embassies to, 32, 33, 34.
  ,, embassies to Burmah from, 33, 36.
  ,, elephants sent to, 34.
  ,, routes to Ava from, 53, 189.
  ,, gazettes, 142.
Pemberton, Captain, 57, 165, 176.
  ,, ,, "Eastern Frontier of British India", 1 *et seq.*
  ,, ,, on kingdom of Pong, 1, 6.
  ,, ,, on origin of Siamese, 2.
  ,, ,, on country between Burmah and Talifoo, 6.
  ,, ,, on position of Bhamô, 43.
  ,, ,, on trade of Bhamô, 53.
  ,, ,, on Hannay's mission to Bhamô, 54.
Penya, 16.
Persia, Malcolm's, 41.
Persica vulgaris, 70.
Pharmacopœia of Shans, 114.
Phasianus sladeni, 320.
  ,, *elegans,* 320.
Phayre, Sir Arthur, 115.
  ,, ,, on Bhamô treaty of 1769, 32.
  ,, ,, on treaty with Burmah, 1862, 56.
Pheasant, new species, 320.
Phee, *nât,* 125.
Phongan Tsawbwaship, 156.
Phoongyees or Shan priests, 116, 202, 224, 237, 241, 293, 296, 349, 353, 359.
  ,, dress of, 109, 296.
  ,, silversmiths, 111.
  ,, excommunication of, 357.
Phosphorescent wood, 278.
Phupyauk, 159.
Phwons, 60 63, 184.
Phylloscopus, 202.
Pica caudata, 259.
Picbile, Mahomedans at, 142.
Pingshan, 149.
Pinus khasianus, 302.
Plotus melanogaster, 196, 211, 242.
Podiceps philippensis, 242, 323.
Polo Marco, see Marco Polo.
Poloungs, distribution of, 5, 40.

Poloungs, tea grown by, 75.
  ,, relations of, to Shans, 100, 101.
  ,, women, ornaments of, 105, 107.
  ,, at Muangla, 300.
  ,, villages of, 302.
Pong, kingdom of, 1 *et seq.*
  ,, extent of, in 14th century 1, 6, 7.
  ,, in 777 A. D., 2.
  ,, Kings invade Siam, 2, 7, 11.
  ,, king, Muangmo chief, 4, 15.
  ,, reaches to the Cambodia, 4.
  ,, boundaries of, 4, 6, 7, 10.
  ,, wars with China and Burmah, 7, 8, 10.
  ,, Chinese conquest of, 9, 15.
  ,, Burmese invade, 10.
  ,, becomes a Burmese province, 11.
  ,, relations to Marco Polo's trading mart, 43.
  ,, and West Yunan, 99.
Pongmai-Kha, eastern branch of Irawady, 180.
Pongwah, 135.
Ponline, 24.
  ,, gold from, 69.
  ,, arrival at, 245.
  ,, death-dance at, 247, 248.
  ,, village, description of, 248.
  ,, consultation of nâts at, 249.
  ,, route, 44.
  ,, ,, to Momien, 153.
  ,, ,, direction and description of, 154.
  ,, ,, compared with Loaylone route, 157.
  ,, ,, recommendations in favour of, 158.
  ,, Tsawbwa, 69, 135, 230, 234, 240, 242, 256, 258, 261, 262.
  ,, ,, description of, 231.
  ,, ,, house of, 245.
  ,, ,, wife of, visit, and dress of, 246.
  ,, ,, Shan opinion of, 285.
  ,, ,, attack on, and defeat of, 327.
Pon-nah creek, gold-washing at, 200, 201.
Ponsee, 24, 27, 68, 379.
  ,, meteorological observations at, 73.
  ,, height of, 154, 157.
  ,, Bhamô to, 237 *et seq.*
  ,, residence at, 253 *et seq.*
  ,, detention at, 272.
  ,, return of some members of Expedition, 281.
  ,, arrival of Shan representatives at 284.
  ,, start from, 286.
  ,, to Momien, 286, *et seq.*
  ,, Tsawbwa, 69, 135, 240, 243, 262, 266, 269, 271, 285.
  ,, ,, extent of territory of, 379.
  ,, Pawmines, description of, 272.
  ,, silver-mines, 30, 48, 68, 255, 265 380.
  ,, ,, richness of ore, 69.
  ,, ,, comparative analysis of, 69.
  ,, ,, visit to, 267.

Ponwah Tsawbwa, 254.
Porzana fusca, 242.
Potatoes at Momien, 93, 217, 321.
Prah, of Yunanese-Chinese, 376.
Prammoo or Bhamô, 46.
Presbytes, 198, 264, 271.
Priests, Shan, *see* Phoongyees.
,, Kakhyen, *see* Meetway and Toomsah.
,, at Momien, 335.
Prinsep, James, 66, 206.
Prome, 14.
,, prince of, founded old Pagan, 12.
,, factories at, 45.
Prongproug-kha, 163.
Prunus puddum, 70.
Psidium guava, 70.
Pteruthius erythropterus, 259.
Puang-ku, 330.
Punica granatum, 70.
Pungaus, 118.
Pycnonotus, 202, 259.
Pyrus pashia, 70.
,, *Indica*, 70.

Quangtong, province of, famine in, 142.
,, Mahomedan purchase of children in, 142.
Quanshihyen, nát, 376.
Quanyin, Chinese deity, 376.
,, tradition regarding, 372.
Quayzay, Chinese term for Mahomedans, 147.
Quercus fenestrata, 70.
,, *spicata*, 70.
Querquedula crecca, 196, 238, 242.
Queychew, province of, 19, 21.

Rahanees, in Sanda valley, 115.
,, religious houses of, 115, 361.
Railway between China and Burmah considered, 160, 168, 169, 170, 172.
,, through Kakhyen hills considered, 167, 169.
,, capability of Tapeng valley for, 168, 169.
,, from Rangoon to Canton proposed, 169, 171.
,, advantages of, to trade considered, 169, 172.
Rallus striatus, 242.
Rangoon, 66, 115, 169, 362.
,, earthquakes felt at, 91.
,, proposed railway to Canton from, 169, 171.
,, to Cambodia, tramway proposed, 172.
,, visits of Shan nuns to, 115, 303.
Rasheemah, 175.
Rashid-ood-den, on Mahomedans in Yunan, 140, 145.
,, ,, on Zardandan, 36.
Ratan hoops and girdles of Kakhyens, 121, 246.

Rebellions, Mahomedan, in Yunan, 141, 142, 148, 172.
,, ,, causes of, 147.
Regis, Père, survey of Yunan, 46, 189.
Religion of Shans, 114.
,, Kakhyens, 124.
Repository, Chinese, 142.
,, oriental, 28.
Reservoir of king Augbenglé, 196.
Review, Edinburgh, 138, 140, 143.
Rheeshah, 175.
Rhizomys pruinosus, 256.
Rhynchops albicollis, 196.
Rice cultivation at Bhamô, 64, 227.
,, ,, in Kakhyen hills, 70, 124, 254, 283, 379, 383.
,, ,, in Shan valleys, 80, 83, 89, 91, 93, 295.
River-terraces, 86, 301, 347.
,, of Nantin valley, 86, 87, 169.
Rock-barrier in Irawady, 61, 185.
Rocks, metamorphic, 59, 68, 76, 86, 91, 92, 248.
,, crystalline, 59, 68.
,, trap, 59, 77, 86, 91, 182.
,, quartzose, 80, 81, 88, 248.
,, fossiliferous, 92.
Roman ornaments, similarity of Shan and, 106.
Routes, trade, between China and Bhamô, 23, 153, *et seq*.
,, Theinnee and Bhamô to China, 53.
,, from Upper Assam to Yunan, 161.
,, between Assam and Tibet, Buchanan on, 175.
Roads, on practicability of making, between Burmah and Shan States, 153, 158.
,, on practicability of making, through Kakhyen hills, 167.
,, to Yunan, probable trade advantages of, 171, 172.

Sacken, Dr. E. F. von, 105, 107.
Sacrificial rites in Kardandan, Marco Polo on, 37.
,, ,, of Kakhyens, 37.
Sagyen hills, 197.
,, ,, marble from, 197.
Sala, Ponline Tsawbwa, 257, 263.
Salt, 65, 125, 173, 176, 217, 221, 242.
,, gold bartered for, 67.
,, springs, 67.
,, Government monopoly in Khyto, 173.
Salween river or Lu Khyoung, 6, 23, 25, 170, 189.
,, ,, Captain Wilcox on, 50.
,, ,, direction of, 76.
,, ,, distances between Irawady, Cambodia, and, 77.
,, ,, ferry over, 159, 188.
,, ,, Jesuits on, 189.
,, ,, relations to Tibetan rivers, 190.

Salween river, relations to source of Irawady, 192.
Samlongpha, 2.
Samshu, Shan beverage, 109.
Sanda, Shan State, 4, 17, 27.
,, Buddhism in, 99, 114, 115, 350, 355.
,, pays tribute to Mahomedans, 117.
,, town of, 27, 51, 80, 154, 263, 265, 277, 293, 388.
,, position of, in Jesuits' map, 46, 189.
,, situation of, 79, 80.
,, basin, 80, 299.
,, Shans at, 99, 105, 107, 289, 358.
,, Kakhyens at, 99, 355.
,, Leesaws at, 355, 358.
,, Chinese at, 136, 297, 353, 358.
,, Panthays at, 281.
,, Tasakone at, 282.
,, our arrival at, 296.
,, Khyoungs at, 296, 349, 350.
,, phoongyees of, 109, 115, 296, 358.
,, description of, 296, 297.
,, bazaar at, 297, 349.
,, departure from, 298.
,, return to, 348.
,, robberies at, 348, 353.
,, limestone-hill at, 351.
,, nât at, 352, 356.
,, visit to hot-springs, 354.
,, foot-print of Guadama near, 355.
,, farewell to, 358.
,, Tsawbwa of, 253, 272, 297.
,, ,, house of, 297.
,, ,, grandson of, 298.
,, ,, presents from, 298.
,, ,, presents to, 358.
Sanda-foo (Sanda), 76.
,, size of, 76.
Sanda river or Nam-Sanda, 79, 351.
,, route, between Burmah and China, 26, 42, 90, 154, 260.
,, ,, viâ Kakhyo, 160.
,, ,, viâ Molay river, 160, 356, 388.
,, valley, 25, 27, 39, 63, 75, 94, 153, 157, 279.
,, ,, Tapeng in, 62, 63.
,, ,, elevation and length of, 78.
,, ,, relation to Nantin valley, 78, 168.
,, ,, description of, 79, 154.
,, ,, Tahó in, 80, 87.
,, ,, three divisions of, 80, 299.
,, ,, rocks of, 81.
,, ,, hot-springs in (see hot-springs).
,, ,, relation of, to Hotha valley, 82.
,, ,, crops of, 83.
,, ,, climate of, 85.
,, ,, population of, 85, 86, 99.
,, ,, phoongyees in, 109, 111, 115.
,, ,, rahanees in, 115.
,, ,, Kakhyens in, 119.
,, ,, Leesaws at, 135.
,, ,, borders of China in, 136.
,, ,, trade between Momien and, 160.

Sanda valley, proposal to bridge the Tapeng in, 167.
,, ,, arrival in, 289.
,, ,, landslips in, 366.
Sandstone, 59, 199, 201, 202, 207.
Sanpo, relations to Irawady, hypotheses regarding, 56, 178, 179, 181, 188, 192.
,, Mr. Cooper on, 193.
Santa (Sanda), 189.
Saracens, 140.
Saranath, 206.
Sarcidiornis melanotus, 242.
Sarel, Colonel, in Sechuen, 146.
Sawaddy, town of, 60, 215.
,, ,, position and size of, 60, 61.
,, route, 153, 154, 156, 158.
,, ,, relation to Hoctone and Sanda routes, 90.
,, ,, relation to Loaylone and Ponline routes, 153.
,, and Muangwan route, 42.
Sayaydawgyee, Burmese official, 345, 387.
Saxai river, 163.
Scotch galena, 69, 93.
Sechuen, province of, 20, 145, 175.
,, opium cultivation in, 71, 72.
,, probability of becoming part of a Mahomedan monarchy, 72, 146.
,, Colonel Sarel's visit to, 146.
,, present rebellion in, 149.
,, tea and mineral wealth of, 174.
,, trade with, prospects of, 174.
,, exports from, 176.
,, importance of, to Assam, 176, 177.
Selin or Singui, 139.
Seray, Kakhyen chief, 124, 240, 260, 261, 262, 266, 269, 271.
Serpent-worship, 225.
Sessoungan, pagoda of, 213.
Sginmac stream, 187.
Shakhya, 99.
Shakya race of kings, 7, 205, 206.
Shan chronicles or M.S.S., see chronicles.
,, kingdom of Pong, 1 et seq.
,, kings reign in Ava, 10, 16.
,, kings at Tsagain, 98.
,, chief, 16, 17, 117.
,, population, distribution of, 5, 60, 75, 86, 94, 96.
,, principality of Bhamô, 33, 48, 96.
,, customs, 5, 36, 40, 41, 116, 117.
,, weapons, 42, 109.
,, dâh, 55, 108, 212, 221.
,, ornaments, 66, 104, 106, 107.
,, industries, 55, 66, 212, 368.
,, agriculture, 62, 75, 110.
,, opium, 71, 72, 110.
,, market for tea, 75.
,, cotton, 110.
,, tobacco, 83, 110, 358.
,, indigo-dye, 84, 111, 350, 353.
,, domestic animals, 84.
,, language, 96, 97, 100.
,, dress, 101, 102, 231, 289.
,, women's head-dress, 101, 102.
,, ,, industry, 111, 220, 350.
,, diet, 109.

GENERAL INDEX. 453

Shan towns, 110, 136, 203, 208.
  ,, houses, 110, 291, 297, 350, 361.
  ,, arts, 111, 112, 113.
  ,, marriages, 113.
  ,, diseases and medicines, 113.
  ,, burial-places, 114, 302, 353.
  ,, education, 115, 335.
  ,, religion, see phoongyees and khyoungs.
  ,, horse-worship, 116.
  ,, snake or serpent-worship, 116, 225.
  ,, nât-worship, 126.
  ,, government, land-tenure, inheritance, 117.
  ,, traders, 160, 165, 209, 215.
  ,, iron-suspension bridges, 167.
  ,, loom, 220, 278, 361.
  ,, mulemen, 239, 244.
  ,, messengers, 270, 277, 278.
  ,, representatives arrive at Ponsee, 284.
  ,, products, purchase of, 346, 370.
  ,, temples in Hotha valley, 371, 373.
Shans, on the Irawady, Hamilton Buchanan on, 5.
  ,, Buddhists, 38, 99, 114, 226, 355.
  ,, relations of, to Burmese, 97.
  ,, introduction from Yunan into Upper Burmah, 98.
  ,, physical characters of, 100.
  ,, likeness to Kakhyens and Chinese, 99, 257.
  ,, of Sanda valley, 99, 100, 289.
  ,, character of, 117, 210.
  ,, superstition of, 236, 292, 351, 352, 366.
  ,, at Bhamô, 60, 96.
  ,, at Tsitkaw, 239, 240.
  ,, at Ponsee, 257.
  ,, at Manwyne, 285, 292.
  ,, at Muangla, 301, 303.
  ,, at Hotha, 366, 368.
  ,, fire-festival of, 369.
  ,, relations to Panthays, 117, 148, 229, 274, 285, 306.
  ,, relations of, to Leesetai, 274.
Shan Tsawbwa of Tumkhun, 6.
  ,, ,, of Bhamô, chief ambassador to China, 33.
  ,, ,, of Hotha, 100, 367.
  ,, Tsawbwas, 278, 283, 284.
  ,, mountains, 197, 207, 211.
  ,, States, Koshanpyi, 1, 3, 4, 16.
  ,, ,, extent of, 4.
  ,, ,, bordering on Irawady, 5, 7, 59.
  ,, ,, tributary to China, 9.
  ,, ,, conquest of Burmah by, 10.
  ,, ,, become tributary to Ava, 16, 53.
  ,, ,, Burmese capture of eight, 27.
  ,, ,, and Kardandan, 39.
  ,, ,, relative value of gold and silver in, 39.
  ,, ,, roads between Burmah and, 153, 158, 164.
  ,, ,, probable trade with, 173.
  ,, ,, Expedition dissuaded from entering, 230, 253, 257, 274, 356.
  ,, valleys, 58, 61, 71.
  ,, ,, trade of, with Burmah, 53, 110, 173.

Shan valleys, highways through, 158.
Shanking, capital of Queychew, 19.
Shanmas or Mrelap Shans, 33, 47.
Shanghai, interests of merchants at, 174.
Shanse, 142.
Sheedin, 337.
Sheffield goods, market for, in China, 174.
Shelling-khet, 163.
Shensi, province of, 20, 21, 142.
  ,, finger of Buddha in, 13.
  ,, opium cultivation in, 71, 72.
  ,, relations to Sechuen and Yunan, 72, 146.
  ,, Mahomedans in, 139, 140.
  ,, Nestorian Christians in, 146.
Sheroo, Kakhyen beer, 248, 288.
Sherzwan, gold from, 93.
Shienpagah, trade of, 173, 196, 209.
Shingrawah, nât, 125.
Shitah, nât, 125, 126.
Shoomaee, Shuaymai, or Namsang river, 187.
Showfoo, Chinese deity, 376.
Shnaybaw, island of, pagodas on, 212.
Shnayduay, khyoung at, 329, 335.
Shuay-goo-myo, 211, 212, 213, 214.
Shuaygyeen, proposed railway by, 170, 171.
  ,, village, gold washing at, 201.
Shuaykeenah, pagodas of, 225, 226, 237.
Shuaylee river, 12, 35, 49, 52, 92, 188, 190.
  ,, ,, Pong capital on, 1, 4, 98.
  ,, ,, probable southern limit of Pong, 7.
  ,, ,, advance of Chinese by, 14, 16.
  ,, ,, Pegu advances by, 18.
  ,, ,, navigable to Muangmo, 23.
  ,, ,, description of, 62, 63, 78.
  ,, ,, ranges defining, 76, 159.
  ,, ,, relations to Salween and Cambodia, 77.
  ,, ,, iron-suspension bridge over, 159, 188.
  ,, route, estimate of, 160.
  ,, ,, adaptation of, for railway, 160.
  ,, valley, trade by, 208, 214.
Shuaymai river, 63, 187.
Shuay-mein-loung hills, 207.
Shuay-nyaungbeng, Chinese stockade at, 28, 29.
Shuay or Sine Shan mountains, 188.
Shuay-toung-gyee, source of Kyendwen, 164.
Shnaytoung, 203.
Shuay-zeegong pagoda, 13.
Shuemuelong or Shuay-mue-loun mountain, 81, 90, 156.
  ,, advance of Chinese army by, 2 5.
  ,, head-quarters of Leesetai, 25.
  ,, height of, 99.
  ,, old choki of, 157.
Shuenli or Muangchan, 159.
Siam, 3, 99.
  ,, invaded by Pong, 7, 11.
Siamese, probable origin of, 2, 98.
Sighshan, nât, 376.
Sikkim, Lepchas of, 97, 121.
Silling, 176.
Silver-smiths, phoongyees, 111.

454 GENERAL INDEX.

Silver, 67, 176, 201, 221, 32.
,, and gold vessels, 13.
,, value of, in Shan States, 39, 40.
,, mines (see mines).
,, in galena ore of Kakhyen hills, 69.
,, from Khyto, 93.
,, ornaments, 104, 105, 106, 107, 108, 109, 121.
,, article of export from Momien, 173, 328.
,, coinage, manufacture of, at Bhamô, 220.
Sinan, fort of Mien included in, 9.
Singan, Marco Polo on, 140.
Singgaitswu, Chinese name for Bhamô, 4.
Singpho chiefs, 53.
Singphos, Chingpaws or Kakhyens, 60, 96, 111, 180, 187, 191.
Singui, mart of, 139.
Sinlah, *nât*, 125.
Sinmaï-kha, 180.
Siri Sirhit or Irawady, 179.
Sit-nga, 155, 386.
Situng, 184.
Sladen, Major, 194, 298, 308, 324, 353, 387.
,, ,, on Mahomedans of Yunan, 143.
,, ,, policy at Bhamô, 230.
,, ,, resolution to proceed, 280.
,, ,, abridgment of Expedition, 280.
,, ,, business interviews with governor of Momien, 336, 338, 339.
Slavery among Kakhyens, 132, 222.
Snake-worship, 225.
Snow on Kakhyen hills, 74.
,, at Momien, 95.
Soognampha, king of Pong, 8, 10, 17.
Soohoongkhum, Pong king, 10.
Sookampha, Pong king, 2, 7.
Sookopha invades Siam, 11.
Sooleyman, Mahomedan name of king at Talifoo, 150.
Soo-oopha destroys Tsagain, 15.
Soopengpha defeats Burmese, 10.
Staunton, Sir George, on Macartney's mission to China, 14, 33.
Steamer, king of Burmah's, 194.
Stewart, Mr., 194, 273.
,, ,, return of, 281.
Sterculia, 66, 265.
Stone implements, Shan faith in restorative powers of, 114.
Stufas or boiling-springs, 91.
Sturnopastor nigricollis, 298.
Suddyah, 59, 96, 111, 179, 190.
,, to Mogoung, Dr. Griffith, 54, 161.
,, and Yunan, Captain Charlton on, 164.
,, route to Burmah, along the Noa Dehing, 166.
,, ,, to Tibet, 175.
Súhmaï-kha, or eastern branch of Irawady, 180.

Súhmaï-kha, Wilcox on, 180.
,, Griffith on, 183.
,, Hannay on, 183.
Sumloy, 175.
Sung-yun, Buddhist pilgrim, 13.
Suspension-bridges, see iron-bridges.
Sutsung, emperor, 138, 145.
Sylhet, proposed route by, 56.
Symes, Colonel, on Burmese embassy, 33.
,, ,, on spelling of Bhamô, 46.
,, ,, on trade between Burmah and Yunan, 49.
Syriam, factories at, 45.

Tace-lon or Great Shans, 2.
Tænia solium, 282.
Tagazgaz, king of, 139.
Tagoung, 7, 29.
,, kings of, 7.
,, first recorded capital of Burmah, 12.
,, visit to ruins of, 12, 204.
,, probable destruction of, by Shans, 98.
,, ancient history of, 205.
,, modern village of, 206.
Tagoung-toung-daw (range of hills), 207, 208.
Tahmeylon, route by, 237.
Tahô river, 50, 79, 91, 168, 299, 301, 303, 305, 307, 312, 316, 320, 347.
,, ,, Tapeng called, at Momien, 25.
,, ,, Chinese earth-works on, 25.
,, ,, water, a cause of goitre, 41, 326.
,, ,, character of, at Mawphoo gorge, 80, 345.
,, ,, denudation by, 80, 92.
,, ,, waterfall at Momien, 91, 318.
,, ,, bridges over, 307, 313, 344.
,, ,, at Momien, 316.
Tahzyungyee, military officer at Momien, 151.
,, feast with, 151, 331.
Tai, or Shan nation, 98.
Tailungs, Buchanan Hamilton on, 5.
Taimin princes, 19.
Talain general, Thamein-puran, 17.
Talains in Pegu, 16.
Tali lake, 77, 78, 159, 189.
,, affluents of Cambodia from, 190.
Talifoo, 6, 9, 52, 78, 335.
,, distances from Ava, *viâ* Bhamô and *viâ* Theinnee, 35.
,, opium cultivation at, 71, 266.
,, minerals from, 92, 111.
,, crops and forest at, 93.
,, caravans to Mandalay, 111, 118, 266.
,, king of Panthays at, 150.
,, from Yungchan, 159, 170.
,, to Yunan city, 159, 170.
,, railway to, considered, 170, 171.
,, history of, 327.
,, presents from, 337.
,, letters from, 337.
,, trade duties, 338.
Tallies, Marco Polo on use of, 936.

GENERAL INDEX.

Tallies, in Yunan, 36, 270.
Talone, Kakhyen chief, 135, 240, 243, 248, 255.
Tâmo, *nât*, 376.
Tamone, 232.
Tapeng river, 23, 52, 80, 136, 184, 191, 263, 299, 301, 347, 384, 386, 388.
,, ,, proposal to bridge, 24, 167.
,, ,, known as Tahô or Talô, 25.
,, ,, Chinese army on, 27.
,, ,, (Nankho), Captain Wilcox on, 50.
,, ,, villages on, 60, 233, 239.
,, ,, branch of Irawady, extent of, 62.
,, ,, silver on banks of, 69.
,, ,, relation to Namsa, 76.
,, ,, main stream, course of, 79.
,, ,, Kakhyens on, 122.
,, ,, at Momien, 188.
,, ,, its sources, 188.
,, ,, iron-bridge over, 188.
,, ,, Jesuits on, 189.
,, ,, route, 237, 238.
,, ,, old channel of, 241.
,, ,, views of, 255, 288, 289, 299, 301, 302.
,, ,, breadth of, in rains, 387.
,, valley, 34, 345, 379, 385.
,, ,, character of, 69, 70, 76, 78.
,, ,, Ponline and Laoylone routes by, 153 *et seq*.
,, ,, capabilities of, for road-making, 158, 169.
,, ,, railway by, considered, 168, 170.
Tapo village, duty on jade at, 67.
Taroupuyo, 10, 14.
Tartar-Chinese (see Chinese-Tartars.)
,, invasions of Burmah, 14.
,, conquests of China, 18, 19, 20, 21, 138, 141.
,, oppression of Mahomedans, 141.
,, Lamas join the rebel king of Yunan, U-san-ghey, 22.
Tartars, introduction of, into China, 21, 139.
Tartary, 33.
Tasakone, governor of Momien, 150.
,, on origin of Mahomedans in China, 144.
,, description of, 151.
,, letter from, 265.
,, at Sanda, 282.
,, arrangements of, with Shan Tsawbwas, 284.
,, reception of Expedition by, 313.
,, presents to, 314.
,, house of, visits to, 315, 316, 318, 335.
,, visits from, 316, 337.
,, presents from, 316, 322, 325, 326, 333, 339.
,, on Sawaddy route, 321.
,, on trading route by Cambodia, 336.
,, present to, from Burmese Government, 337.
,, dinner with, 338.

Tasakone, Major Sladen gives copies of treaty with Burmah to, 338.
,, official letter from, on duties to be levied on goods, 338, 339.
,, adieu to, 341.
Tatze, independent Tartars, 147.
Tauism at Momien, 335.
Tayeow, visit to, 370, 371.
Tayshan or Kananzan mountains, 92.
Tay-yays, country of, 3, 92.
,, Payæ of Chinese, 47.
Tea, 64, 75, 100, 174, 217.
,, of Poloungs, 75.
,, Assam, 75, 176.
,, from Trans-Yang-tse-kiang provinces, 75.
,, tax on, in China, 138.
Teejin, nât, 376.
Teeth covering with gold in Zardandan, 36, 40.
,, blackening of, 9, 40.
Temperature at Bhamô, 64.
,, of Kakhyen hills, &c., see Appendix D.
Temple deities, construction of, 335.
Testudo platynotus, 324.
Tetsung, condition of China in reign of, 138.
Thagyameng, 334.
Thakyi kings, 205.
Thausein-puran, champion of Burmese army, 16, 17, 18.
Thamo river, 287.
Theehadaw, island of, 201.
,, stone pagoda of, 201.
,, tame fish, 201.
Theinnee, 26, 27, 49, 159.
,, Shan State, 16.
,, became tributary to Ava, 16.
,, route, 14, 15, 16, 19, 27, 53.
,, ,, missions from Ava to Pekin by, 32, 33.
,, ,, compared with Bhamô routes, 35, 51.
,, ,, distance of Yunan city from Mandalay, *viâ*, 159.
Thengat-tha-ratha or Thengat-tha-nago, 205.
,, Tsawbwa and war with Ava, 29.
,, ex-Tsawbwa of, refuge in Yunan, 25.
Theng-ye-chow or Tengye-chew (Momien), 19, 50, 52.
Theng-dué-myaung canal, 15.
Theta, 140.
Thigyain, 208.
Thingadaw, coal depôt at, 202.
Thinza-nuaylein mountain, 26, 27, 28.
Thongwetshein, Chinese chief, 308, 310.
Thubye hills, 197.
Tibet, 56, 108, 139, 193.
,, part of, ceded to Tartars, 22.
,, route from Cabul to, 36.
,, vicar-apostolic of, 56.
,, course of trade to, 174.
,, Suddyah to, 175.
,, route between Assam and, 175.
,, Turner's mission to, 176.

Tibet, importance of, to Assam, 176, 177.
Tibetans, *avaloketesvara* of, 116.
" Matze, 147.
Tibetan rivers, relations to Shuaylee, Salween or Cambodia, 190, 192.
Tiger-incident at Bhamô, 235.
Tisien river, 170.
Tobacco, 63, 70, 81, 195, 209, 292, 295, 361, 370.
" Shan, 83, 110, 358.
" pipe, Shan, 108.
" " Kakhyen, 133.
Tongoo, 210, 223.
Tontook hill, 165.
Toomsah, Kakhyen priest, 37, 126, 128, 129.
Toongances, 139, 146.
Toorkistan, rebels of, 143.
Toorks in North-Western China, 139, 146.
Torques or neck-rings of Shans, 106.
Torque-like bracelet, 107.
Trade between Burmah and China, 32, 51, 56.
" " " " Colonel Symes on, 149.
" " " " Crawford on, 50.
" " " " British treaty regarding, 56.
" " " " present prospects of, 171, 172, 173, 174.
" " Bhamô and Yunan, 23, 51.
Trade of Bhamô, 67, 173, 217.
" " Momien, 92, 93, 173.
" between Assam and Tibet, 175, 176, 177.
Trade-duties proposed by Tasakone to Major Sladen, 338.
Trade-routes of Upper Burmah, 153 *et seq*.
Trans-Irawadian Shan or Pong States, 5, 14.
Trans-Yang-tse-kiang provinces, tea from, 75.
Trappean rocks, see rocks.
Treaty with Burmah, 56.
" of Bhamô, 32.
Tropidonotus, 322.
Tsagain, 7.
" attacked by Pong, 10.
" history of, 15, 16.
" Yunlie at, 19, 20.
" and Shan kings, 98.
" hills, 195.
Tsakhyet, king's gunners at, 20.
Tsampenago, south limit of Pong, 7.
" Captain Hannay on, 7.
" Buchanan Hamilton on, 7, 47.
" ancient, ruins of, 47, 224, 237.
" second town, ruins of, 48, 237, 238.
" pagodas of, 203, 238.
Tsanntú, governor of Yunan city, 25.
Tsawbwas, Shan, government of, 117.
" Kakhyen, duties of, 131.

Tsawbwas, wives and daughters, ornaments of, 122.
Tseegooshan, 149.
Tseejanfoo, 149.
Tseeyoog, 144.
Tseitha, 198.
Tsenbo, Griffith on size of, 61.
" Irawady at, 182.
Tsendong, khyoung at, 375.
Tsiguen, 4.
Tsihet, village of, 124, 243, 245, 386.
Tsikkays, of Bhamô, 210, 228.
Tsilone village, 163.
Tsinggai (Chinese name of Bhamô), 4.
Tsiongoung, *nât*, 376.
Tsingmahs, Kakhyen clan, 118.
Tsinuhat, 204.
Tsitkaw, 155, 234, 237, 238, 239, 241, 262, 274, 281, 284.
" and Manwyne, Kakhyen chiefs between, 135.
" distance from borders of China, 136.
" phoongyees at, 243.
Tsiwaran, robe of Buddhist priest, 114.
Tsojah, Shan, for heaven, 125.
Tsong-ching, 18.
Tukkaka river, 161.
Tulototrition verrucosus, 309.
Tumkhan Tsawbwaship, 6.
Tung dynasty, kings or emperors of, 13, 14, 138.
" Du Halde on, 144.
Tung-huon-tsong, 144, 145.
Turner, on trade in English and Indian goods in Tibet, 176.
" on Sanpo, 178.
Tuscany galena, 69, 93.
Tu-tu-du of Nantin, 308.
" " visit to, 309.
Tuwintsen, Chinese title for Mahomedan king at Talifoo, 150.

Uuchian or Yungchan, 39.
Unciun, Marsden on, 39.
Universal History on Tay-yays, 3.
" " on Yunlie and Yunan, 19, 20.
" " on U-san-ghey, 21, 22.
" " on Mohungleng silver-mines, 49.
" " on Mahomedans in China, 138.
U-san-ghey, Chinese general, 21.
" king of Yunan, 21.
" D'Orleans on, 21, 22.
" Du Halde on, 21.
" proclamation of, 22.
" and Tartars, 21, 22.
" names his grandson emperor, 22.
" defeat of grandson and death, 23.

Valentyn on Dutch trade in Burmah, 45.
Vanamálá, 330.

GENERAL INDEX. 457

Vasta-yaga, Hindu rite of, 116.
Vegetable products of Kakhyen hills, 70.
Vegetables at Momien, 93, 319.
Village altars, see *lamshan*.
Villages in Shan States, 85.
" population of, 86.
Vishnu, 330.
Visva Karmá, 330.
Vochang, 6, 9, 14.
Volcano, Hawshuenshan, extinct, 87, 90, 312.

W

Wainmô, 25, 61, 188.
" Burmese army crosses Irawady at, 26.
" route, jade trade by, 67.
Wampama river, 164.
Waterfalls of Tahô, see Tahô.
Weesee, Mr. Cooper on Mahomedan rebellion at, 149.
Whantsyaw, rebellion of, 139.
Wheat grown at Talifoo, 93.
Widow-marriage among Kakhyens, 128.
Wilcox, Captain, 'Memoir on Assam,' 50.
" " on route to Momien, 50.
" " at Brahmakund, 62.
" " on sources of Irawady, 178, 179, 180, 190, 192.
" " estimate of Irawady, 181, 191, 192.
" " comparison of Brahmaputra and Irawady, 181.
" " on name of eastern branch of Irawady, 187.
Williams, Captain, 245, 273, 274.
" " return of, 281, 282.
Williams, Dr., on route through Burmah, 57.
" " proceeds to Bhamô, 57.
" " on Bhamô routes, 57.
" " on navigation of Irawady, 184.
Wooden horse at Manwyne, 115, 291, 293.
" fish, tradition regarding, 350.
Woon of Bhamô, 208, 283, 284, 386.
" " murder of, 208.
Woonjhan, nât, 376.
Woosankwei (U-san-ghey), 21.
Wullaboom river, 163.
Wyesoam, village on Irawady, 186.

Y

Yachi (Talifoo), 9.
Yamitheng, 17.
Yaupyinhein, 78.
Yang-tse-kiang, 34, 59.
" embarkation of Chinese army on, Gutzlaff, 28.
" and distribution of Tais or Shans, 98.
" to Canton river, suggested railway by, 170.
" importance of, 171.
" Irawady and Brahmaputra, commercial relations of, 174.
" and relations to source of Irawady, 192.

Yansooyangin nât, 376.
Yarlong river, Mr. Cooper on, 193.
Yaynan-Sekia, Burmese steamer, 194.
Year, divisions of, by Kakhyens, 132.
Yellow River, Mahomedans north of, 141.
Yenangyoung, 200.
Yengoung, nât, 376.
Yethaycoo pagoda, 213.
Yonephin, gold from, 93.
Yôyi mountain, 28.
Yoyins, Kakhyen clan of, 119.
Yu or *Yueesh*, Chinese jasper or phrase, 66.
Yuena dynasty, 9.
Yule, Colonel, 4.
" "Ava," 3, 69.
" on ruins at old Bhamô, 45.
" "Cathay," 138, 145.
" on Mengoon pagoda, 195.
Yunan, 1, 6, 28, 35, 59, 137.
" invasion of, Polo on, 8.
" viceroy of, conference with Pong king, 8.
" Bhamô chief escapes to, 18.
" escape of Yunlie to, 19.
" governor accompanies Yunlie to Bhamô, 19.
" flight of Chemienchou to, 20.
" state of, in 1651, 21.
" U-san-ghey king of, 21.
" close of war of independence in, 23.
" custom-house on borders of, 23.
" Shan ex-Tsawbwas refugees in, 25.
" Chinese army retreats to, 28.
" Malong, in, 33.
" Chinese missions by, Colonel Burney on, 34.
" Burmese missions to Pekin by, 34.
" Colonel Symes on embassies through, 34.
" or Karainan, 43.
" Du Chatz enters Burmah from, 46.
" map of, Fridelli and Bonjour, 46, 188.
" trade with Bhamô, 51.
" climate of, 53.
" opium cultivation in, 71; analysis of, 72.
" relations of, to Shensi and Sechuen, 72.
" cultivation in, 93.
" annexation to China, 98.
" Shans and Siamese from, 98, 99.
" Leisus or Leesaws in, 135, 136.
" Mahomedans in, 138, *et seq.*
" cause of rebellions in, 141, 147.
" Chinese Repository on, 142.
" routes from Upper Assam to, 161.
" trade prospects of, 172, 174.
" Nampung, western boundary of, 250.
Yunanese-Chinese traders at Katha, 209.
" Mahomedans, General Fytche on, 143.
" " probable history of, 146, 147.
Yunan city, 34, 52.
" " Muangsee, Shan name of, 6, 159.

Yunan city, capital of U-san-ghey, 22.
„ „ to Yunchan, 23.
„ „ Loli's complaint to governor of, 25.
„ „ capture of, in present rebellion, 148, 328, 335.
„ „ distance from Mandalay, 159.
„ „ „ „ Bhamô, 160.
„ „ railway suggested by, 170.
„ „ trade advantages of railway condered, 171, 174.
„ „ size of, 335.
Yungchan or Yunchan, 5, 6, 34, 51, 148, 160, 266, 328, 337.
„ Martini on, 5.
„ governor of, builds Momien, 6.
„ from Yunan city, 23, 159, 174.
„ to Momien, 24, 159.
„ and Kardandan, 39.
„ railway suggested by, 170.

Yungchan, salt from, 173.
Yung-peng-long, 20.
Yunlie proclaimed king of Canton, 19.
„ attacked by Tartars, 19.
„ escapes to Yunan.
„ makes overtures to Tsawbwa of Bhamô, 19.
„ residence at Tsagain, 19.
„ D'Orleans' opinion of, 19.
„ Du Halde on, 19.
„ Gutzlaff on, 19, 21.
„ surrender demanded by Tartars, 20 23, 44.
„ strangled at Pekin, 21.

Zaid Abu, account of China, 139.
Zinziberaceæ, 238.
Ziumae (Shuaymai) river, 187.
Zonchi, Chinese emperor, 18.

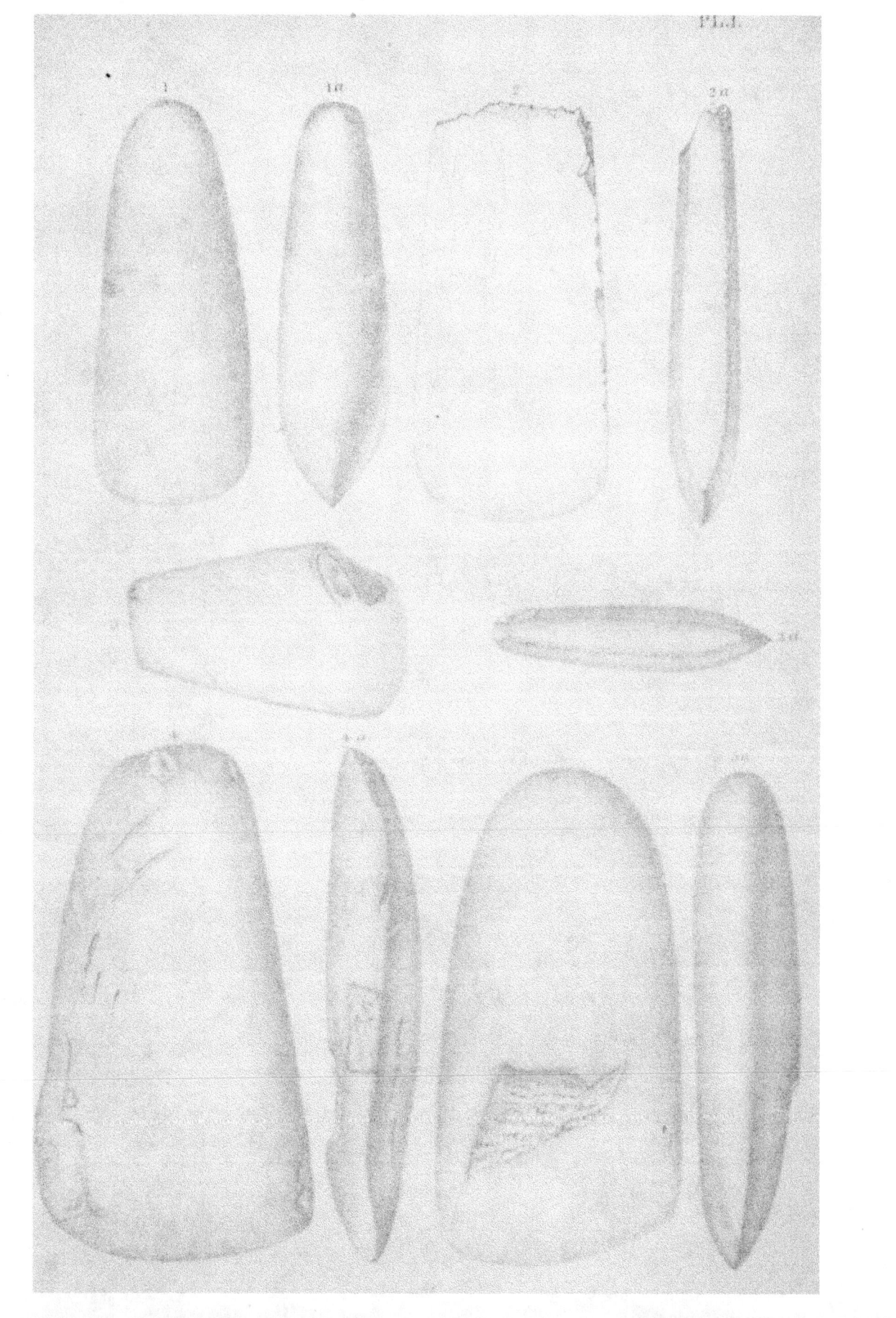

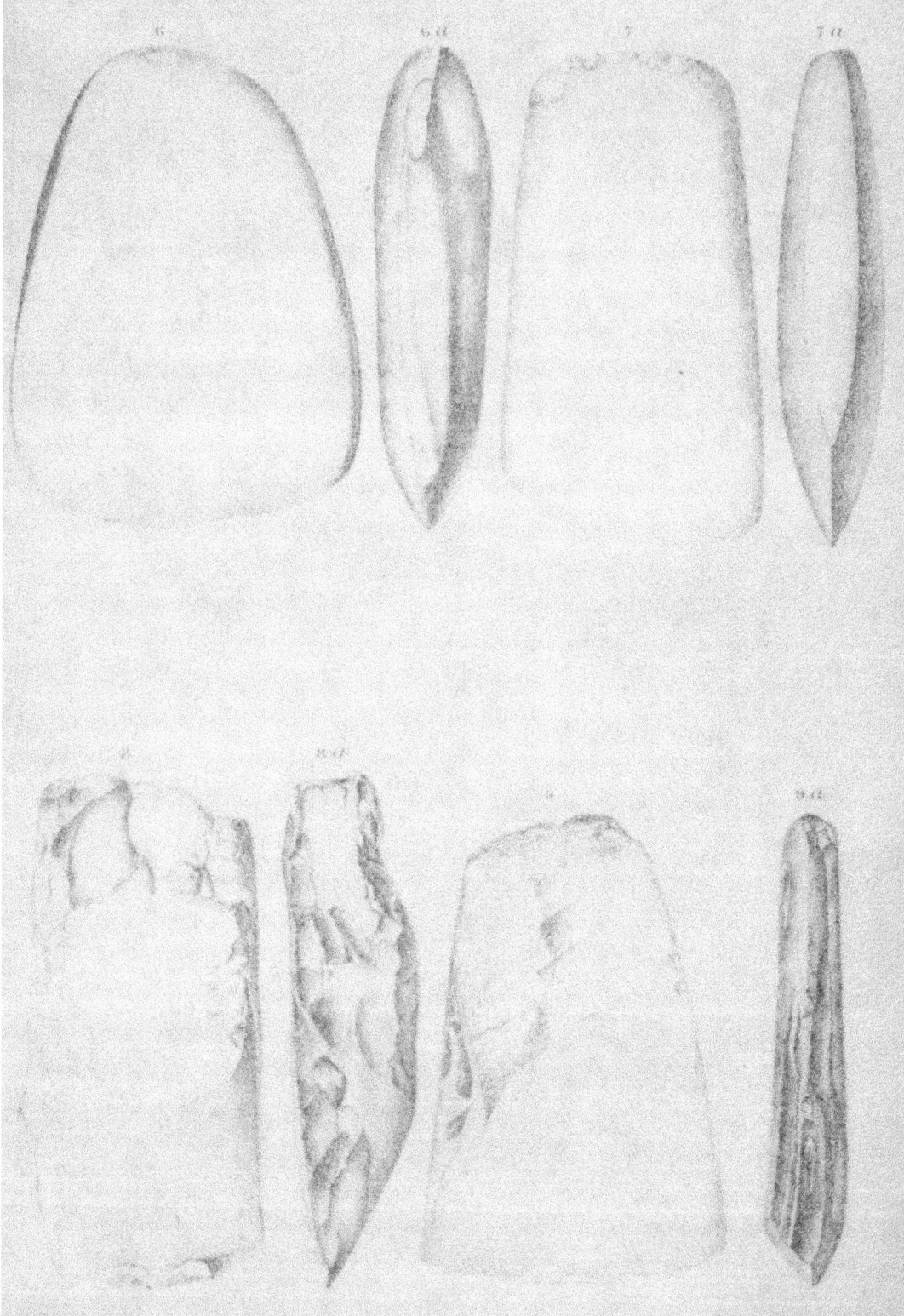

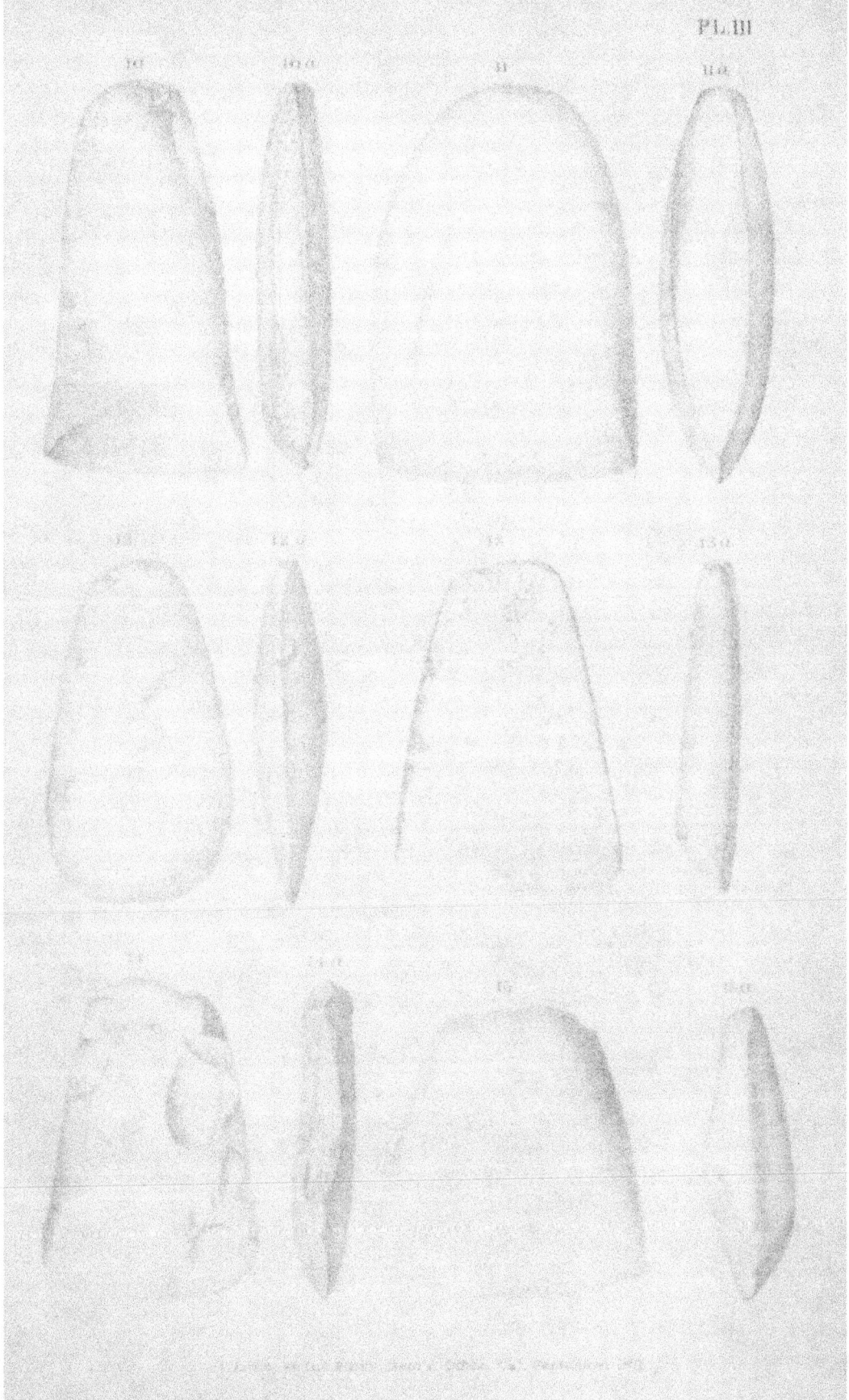

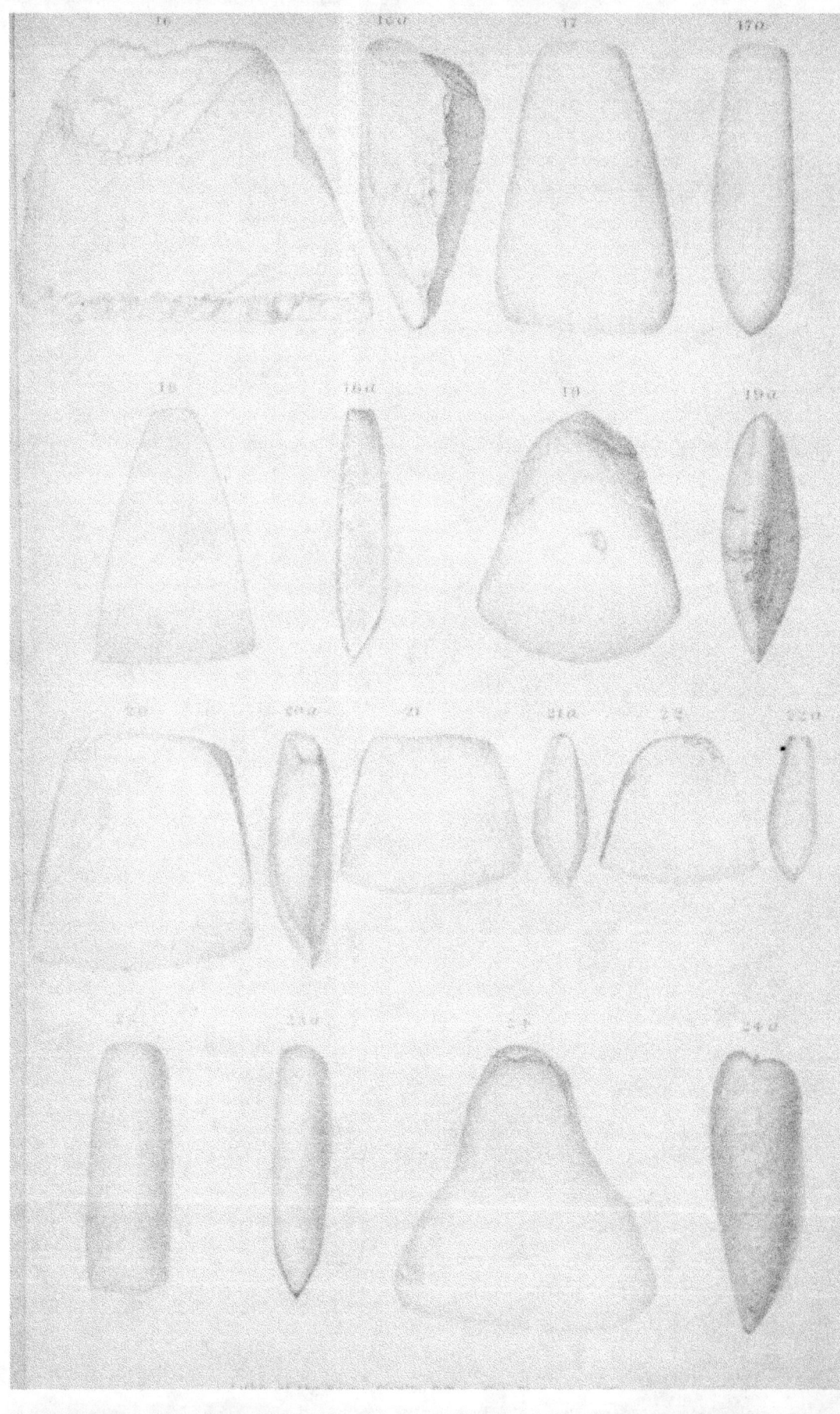

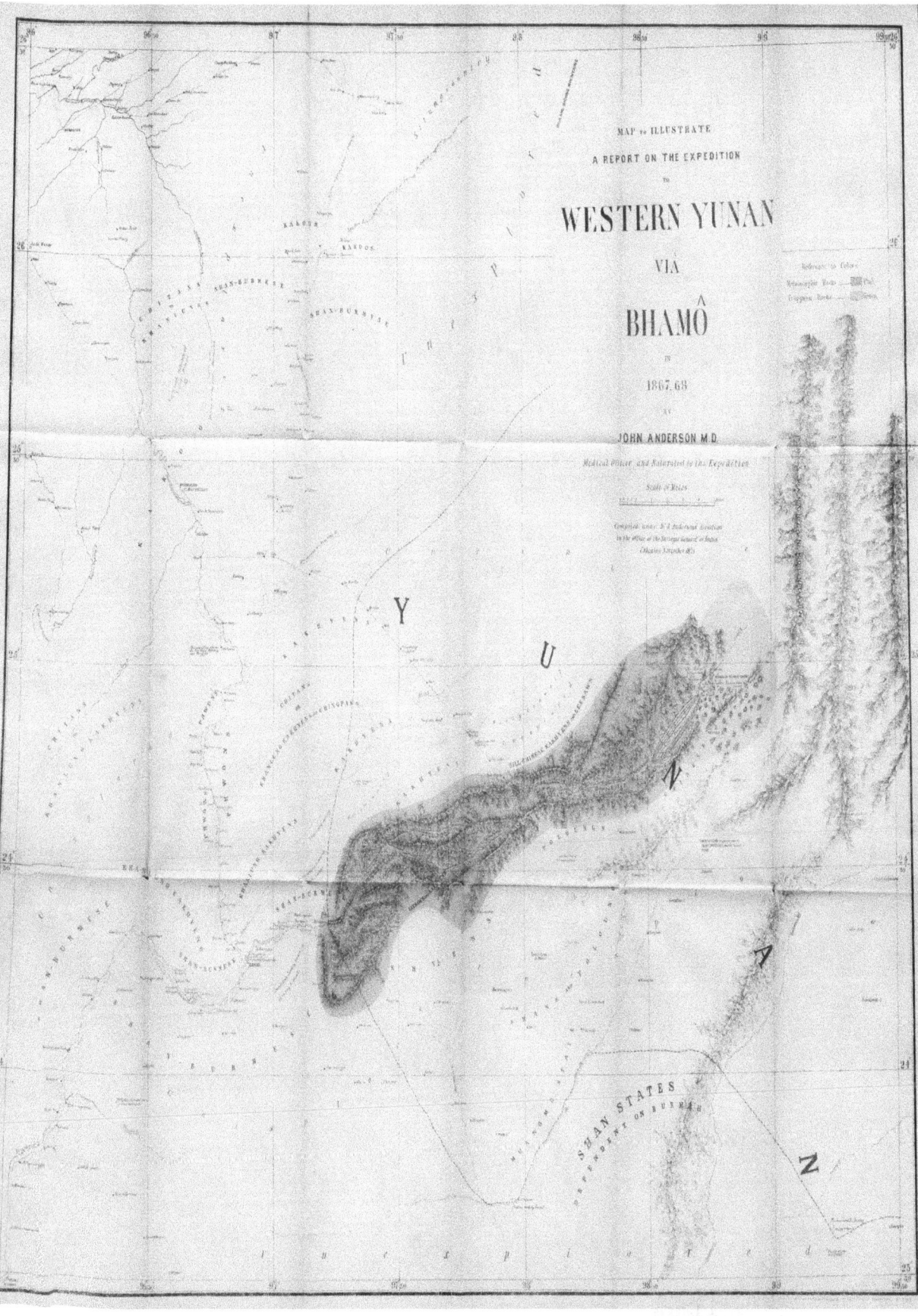

www.ingramcontent.com/pod-product-compliance
Lightning Source LLC
Chambersburg PA
CBHW080234170426
43192CB00014BA/2458